Sebastian Mock, Kristian Csach, Bohumil Havel (Eds.)
**International Handbook on Shareholders' agreements**
De Gruyter Handbook

# International Handbook on Shareholders' Agreements

Regulation, Practice and Comparative Analysis

Edited by
Sebastian Mock, Kristian Csach, Bohumil Havel

DE GRUYTER

PD Dr. *Sebastian Mock*, LL.M. (NYU), University of Hamburg; Doc. JUDr. *Kristián* Csach, PhD., LL.M., Pavol Jozef Šafárik University in Košice; Doc. Dr. *Bohumil Havel* PhD., Institut of Law, Czech Academy of Science, Prague

ISBN 978-3-11-050156-8
e-ISBN (PDF) 978-3-11-051702-6
e-ISBN (EPUB) 978-3-11-051524-4

**Library of Congress Control Number: 2018934505**

**Bibliographic information published by the Deutsche Nationalbibliothek**
The Deutsche Nationalbibliothek lists this publication in the Deutsche Nationalbibliografie; detailed bibliographic data are available in the Internet at http://dnb.dnb.de


Cover image: shironosov/iStock/thinkstock

www.degruyter.com

# Foreword

Shareholders' agreements are an integral part of company law and especially of its legal practice. However, the historical law makers mostly ignored this phenomenon of company law and limited the legislation to what is understood today as the constitution of the company and the (statutory) rights (and duties) of its shareholders. As the consequence shareholders' agreements are traditionally dominated by contract law and not by company law although the traditional contract law hardly provides the necessary tools. However, the influence of shareholders' agreements on the company, its management, its shareholders and – mostly in the case of corporations listed on a stock exchange – the market for corporate control established a dynamic interaction between these two worlds of company law and contract law. In contrast, the modern company laws often explicitly address shareholders' agreements and try to limit their influence on the company since they are mostly driven by a corporate understanding of shareholders' agreements. This contradiction of the general understanding of shareholders' agreements becomes even more complex in the case of cross-border shareholders' agreements including shareholders from several jurisdictions.

This book has its origin at a conference on shareholders' agreements which took place in March 2016 at the castle of *Smolenice* in Slovakia and rounds up the research on the modernization of Slovak corporate law including the introduction of basic regulation on shareholders' agreements (APVV-0809 – 12). By discussing various related topics with lawyers from several jurisdictions we realized that a broader and more complex discussion on shareholders' agreements is needed and welcome. We hope that this book will be the basis for such a worldwide dialogue of law makers, judges, practitioners and legal scholars regarding shareholders' agreements. By including general remarks on specific topics related to shareholders' agreement on the one hand and numerous country reports on the other we believe that this book provides the reader with a broad and fundamental understanding of shareholders' agreements.

Sebastian Mock/Kristian Csach/Bohumil Havel Hamburg/Košice/Prague

https://doi.org/10.1515/9783110517026-001

# Table of Contents

# Contributors


Dr. ***Marie-Agnes Arlt***, LL.M. (NYU), arlt.solutions, Vienna, Austria

***Anna Babych***, AEQUO, Kiev, Ukraine

Prof. Dr. ***Josef Bejček***, CSc. Masaryk University in Brno,Czech Republic

***Ive Binestock*** LL.B (Tel Aviv), AYR – Amar Reiter Jeanne Shochatovitch & Co., Isreal

Prof. Dr. ***Radu Catana***, Universitatea Babeş-Bolyai – Facultatea de Drept, Romania

Prof. JUDr. ***Stanislava Černá***, CSc., Charles University Prague, Czech Republic

Doc. JUDr. ***Kristián Csach***, PhD., LL.M., Pavol Jozef Šafárik University in Košice, Slovakia

Prof. Dr. ***Rolf Dotevall***, University of Gothenburg, Sweden

***Lukasz Gasinski***, LL.M. (Columbia), Weil Gotshal & Manges LLP, Warsaw, Poland

***JUDr. Barbora Grambličková***, LL.M., Comenius University Bratislava, Slovakia

***Achiad Harel***, LL.B (Tel Aviv), MBA (Northwestern), AYR – Amar Reiter Jeanne Shochatovich & Co, Isreal

Doc. Dr. ***Bohumil Havel*** PhD., Institut of Law, Czech Academy of Science, Prague, Czech Republic

Dr. ***Ivens Henrique Hübert***, Andersen Ballão Advocacia – German Desk, Brazil

Prof. ***Wulf A. Kaal***, University of St. Thomas, United States of America.

Prof. Dr. ***Omer Kimhi***, University of Haifa, Faculty of Law, Isreal

Prof. ***Nuria Latorre***, Universidad de Valencia – Facultad de Derecho, Spain

Prof. ***Corrado Malberti***, LL.M. (Chicago), Università degli Studi di Trento, Italy

***Tom Matthijs***, White & Case LLP, Belgium

Dr. ***Michael A. Meer***, LL.M. (NYU), Sirius Legal, Bern, Switzerland

***Prof. David Pérez Millán***, Universidad de Valencia – Facultad de Derecho, Spain

PD Dr. ***Sebastian Mock***, LL.M.(NYU), Universität Hamburg, Germany

Prof. ***Mette Neville***, Aarhus University – Department of Law, Denmark

Prof. JUDr. ***Mária Patakyová***, PhD., Comenius University Bratislava, Slovakia

Ass. Prof. Dr. ***Georgios Psaroudakis***, Aristotle University of Thessaloniki, Greece

JUDr. ***Žofia Šulekova***, PhD., Pavol Jozef Šafárik University in Košice,
University of Cambridge, Slovakia

***Ioan Şumandea-Simionescu***, Universitatea Babeş-Bolyai – Facultatea de Drept, Romania

Prof. ***Tibor Tajti***, Central European University, Budapest, Hungary

Prof. ***Wino van Veen***, Vrije Universiteit Amsterdam, Netherlands

***Willem van de Wiele***, A&O Antwerp, Belgium

Dr. ***Rafal Zakrzewski***, Clifford Chance, University of Cambridge, England

# General Remarks

Sebastian Mock, Kristián Csach and Bohumil Havel

# Shareholders' Agreements between Corporate and Contract Law

## Table of Content



---

**Doc. Dr. Bohumil Havel,** Institut of Law, Czech Academy of Science, Prague
**PD Dr. Sebastian Mock** LL.M.(NYU), Universität Hamburg
**Doc. JUDr. Kristián Csach** LL.M., Trnava University in Trnava.

https://doi.org/10.1515/9783110517026-002

## A. Shareholders' agreements and their status in the relation to corporate documents

Articles of association[1] represent the *constitution* of a corporation, regulating its existence, operation, structure, organization and relations among its shareholders, their relations toward the company and the powers of the corporation's bodies. Beside corporate documents, shareholders use to enter into special contractual agreements regulating their mutual relations. In practise, they are usually denominated as *bylaws* or *shareholders' agreements*.[2] A shareholders' agreement is an agreement of at least two shareholders establishing a contractual link in regard to their position as shareholder. The mere fact of *acting in concert* or the existence of joint interest between shareholders does not suffice as a shareholders' agreement but can nevertheless have the same consequences as a shareholders' agreement in e.g. capital markets law.[3] First of all it is necessary to define shareholders' agreements in a way that allows the distinction from articles of association. The distinction between the articles of association and a

1 For the purposes of this analysis and unless stated otherwise the terms articles of association shall cover all types of deeds of establishment, memorandum of association and all internal corporate documents, i.e. *Satzung*, charter, bylaws.

2 In German *Nebenabreden* or *schuldrechtliche Gesellschaftervereinbarungen*, in Italian *sindicati azionari*.

3 This e.g. the case in German law (see Germany D.II).

shareholders' agreement is sometimes hard to draw. According to a formal distinction, the articles of association and shareholders' agreements are distinguished based on the formalization of a particular provision in a formal document regulated by corporate law adopted by a defined body. In such sense, the articles of association cover all arrangements incorporated into the formal document they are. Thereby, a shareholders' agreement is any other arrangement between shareholders that is – formally – not included in the articles of association. On the other hand, shareholders' agreements and articles of association might be distinguished regarding their actual content. Articles of association cover any arrangement that governs the corporation and/or has an effect on all shareholders. Any other contractual arrangement must be considered as shareholders' agreements. However, such simplistic criteria have their limitations as articles of association and shareholders' agreements may deal with similar aspect and therefore overlap.

Articles of association do not have to regulate only aspects of corporate law that are dealt with by the law as their possible content. The articles of association may thus include: a) the mandatory rules of corporate law, b) alterations form the non-mandatory corporate regulation, c) the non-mandatory rules, and last, but not least, also d) regulation of other issues that are not foreseen by corporate law regulation, but are formally included into the articles of association (for example various contractual arrangements, arbitration clause for disputes related to the share in a company). It shall not be ruled out that articles of association may also deal with issues that are very loosely connected with the participation of the shareholders in the corporation (for example, an obligation of shareholders to provide each other loans, authority and conditions for the use of company's services, etc.). Hence, the scope of the articles of association may be extended by the shareholders, even beyond the limits laid down by the law. Articles of association will thus establish an obligation containing not only the rules of a corporate constitutive nature, i.e. those that are inevitable or foreseen for the existence of a company, but also other rules that are not inevitable and that express the intended will of its shareholders. However, this applies *vice versa*, i.e. the shareholders may decide that they will not incorporate into the articles of association all the issues that are foreseen for this instrument. The corporation might have articles of association complying with the law but still its shareholders might have wished to execute an ancillary shareholders' agreement containing arrangements that should be contained in the articles of association (limitations on the transferability of shares, rules for appointing members of the company's bodies, profit sharing etc.). This approach is usually employed due to the fact that the articles of association are publicly accessible, while the shareholders' agreements are not available to the public.[4] Although the form does not predetermine the content, the selection of a particular form, or placement of a particular arrangement in the articles of association or in a shareholders' agreement may have consequences. Unless provided otherwise the placement of a particular arrangement into a certain formalized document is in general irrelevant for the validity of a particular arrangement. The particular arrangement of non-corporate issues which is contained in the articles of association is not void only because it is contained in the articles of association and not in a separate agreement.[5]

## B. Regulation of shareholders' agreements

Although the execution of shareholders' agreements has become a commonplace corporate practise, usually, they are not subject to a specific legislation.[6] Although the concept of shareholders' agreements itself is basically left undefined in many jurisdictions, the frameworks or various specific consequences of such agreements are defined.[7] National legislators usually regulate only the limits and possible consequences of shareholders' agreements, for example, in the area of fiduciary obligations of the company's authorised representatives, or in the area of the law of corporate groups, while the rest is subject to the general rules of the law of contract.

However, some legislators enacted specific regulations on shareholders' agreements and their approaches vary between generalization and *casuistry (Kasuistik)*. In the United States, for example, Section 7.32 MBCA applies a general negative model:

4 See C. for further details.

5 Constitutive elements of a company will obviously not qualify for being a subject of shareholders agreements. It will be, for example, useless if a business name, registered office or amount of registered capital or the line of business are contained in the shareholders' agreement. This will not void the document but it will rather make such provision of the shareholders' agreement obsolete, since in order to accomplish their intended effect, such questions must be contained (also formally) in the articles of association.

6 This e.g. the case in German law (see Part B – Germany B.I.), shareholders agreements are delimited "in legislation", for example, in Article 36 of the draft model law UNCITRAL on a simplified business entity of 2015. (*UNCITRAL Draft model law on a simplified business entity.* A/CN. 9/WG. I/WP. 89).

7 See e.g. the Irish Companies Act of 2014.

Section 7.32 MBCA states:

*An agreement among the shareholders of a corporation that complies with this section is effective among the shareholders and the corporation even though it is inconsistent with one or more other provisions of this Act in that it:*

*(1) eliminates the board of directors or restricts the discretion or powers of the board of directors;*
*(2) governs the authorization or making of distributions whether or not in proportion to ownership of shares, subject to the limitations in section 6.40;*
*(3) establishes who shall be directors or officers of the corporation, or their terms of office or manner of selection or removal;*
*(4) governs, in general or in regard to specific matters, the exercise or division of voting power by or between the shareholders and directors or by or among any of them, including use of weighted voting rights or director proxies;*
*(5) establishes the terms and conditions of any agreement for the transfer or use of property or the provision of services between the corporation and any shareholder, director, officer or employee of the corporation or among any of them;*
*(6) transfers to one or more shareholders or other persons all or part of the authority to exercise the corporate powers or to manage the business and affairs of the corporation, including the resolution of any issue about which there exists a deadlock among directors or shareholders;*
*(7) requires dissolution of the corporation at the request of one or more of the shareholders or upon the occurrence of a specified event or contingency; or*
*(8) otherwise governs the exercise of the corporate powers or the management of the business and affairs of the corporation or the relationship among the shareholders, the directors and the corporation, or among any of them, and is not contrary to public policy.*

For example, an example of a positive approach existing since 2017 is the Slovak law.

Section 66c Slovak Commercial Code (*Shareholders' agreements*) states:

*(1) Parties may, by a written shareholders' agreement, agree mutual rights and duties resulting from their share in the company, in particular mode and conditions of the exercise of the rights related to the share in the company,*
*b) mode of the exercise of the rights related to the company governance,*
*c) conditions and extent of the involvement in the changes of the share/registered capital, and*
*d) ancillary arrangements related to the transfer of the share in the company.*
*(2) The conflict between a decision of the company's body and the shareholders' agreement shall not make such a decision void.*

Besides this example, which might be interpreted as determined by the local culture and legislative technique and thus superfluous,[8] other national legal system show a lack of positive regulation expressly allowing shareholders agreements.[9]

## C. Advantages and disadvantages of shareholders' agreements

Shareholders' agreements have become quite common in the current corporate practise. The reasons for concluding shareholders' agreements vary. The confidentiality or absence of publicity, of shareholders' agreements is considered as one of their major advantages. Contrary to the articles of association, they need not to be filed with the public register and thus are not available to the public or third parties. Shareholders' agreements show a certain degree of flexibility since their amendment is not subject to any special formal procedure as it is required for the amendment of other corporate documents. Another advantage is also a wide availability of contractual instruments of securing and enforcing rights and duties resulting from the shareholders' agreements. Last, but not least, the reason for entering into shareholders' agreements may also be the need to determine the relationship between some of the shareholders differently from the relations towards other shareholders. Shareholders' agreements also frequently involve other persons that are not bound by the articles of association.

The major disadvantages are the contractual nature of shareholders' agreements and consequently their limited effect upon third parties (especially upon assignees and share purchasers). Moreover, shareholders' agreements require a quite complicated amendment mechanism compared to the majority principle for the amendments of articles of association. Also, it is usually impossible to derive corporate consequences from a breach of obligations imposed by the shareholders' agreement (e.g. the exclusion of shareholders). As the national reports show, the absence of domestic case law might also be considered disadvantageous, to a certain extent, although the fact itself does not seem to limit the use of shareholders' agreements.

When searching for the reasons why shareholders' agreements are concluded, we have to consider wider structural links between the purpose of a company itself and the interests of those who have made up, manage or control it. It is

8 See also Denmark B.II.; Slovakia C.

9 This e.g. the case in Austrian, Belgian or German law.

well-known that especially registered companies basically serve as a tool to produce a benefit defined by their shareholders, i.e. profit, but it is also known that there is a kind of a wall standing between the company, its assets and its shareholders, known as "asset locking". In other words: the shareholders, on the one hand, define the purpose of the whole organization, but afterwards the organization lives its own autonomous life and the shareholders may only influence its activities indirectly. This concept of division of the company's assets from its shareholders is a more general justification of the necessity to make shareholders' agreements whereby the shareholders are trying to compensate their future limited influence on the company's management to a certain extent *ex ante*, at least, on a contractual basis. Law and economics analyses indicate that such contracts may *ex ante* decrease not only the risk of future disputes, but they may also provide the space for a later re-negotiation and application of the principles of contract law within the less flexible corporate law.[10]

## D. Shareholders' agreements and their impact on the company

A problem of representation that has been described many times (i.e. agency problem)[11] points out that despite of the unifying purpose of the whole organization there will always be a structural difference, at least, between the interests of the shareholders, the company, the members of its bodies, the creditors, and the like. Regardless of the extent to which it is possible to interpret the concept of the company's interest functionally and to let it cover also wider social interests, and even without considering what the interests of all shareholders and the company itself are and how they can get into conflict with the interests mentioned above, the statutory concept of dichotomy of interests of the shareholders and those of the company must be respected. Considering the fact that they are clearly differentiated, the analysis admits that these interests are kept distinct.

---

**10** See e.g. *Chemla/Ljungqvist* An Analysis of Shareholder Agreements. 5 Journal of the Economic Association 93 (2007).

**11** See e.g. *Armour/Hansmann/Kraakman* in Kraakman/Armour/Davies/Enriques/Hansmann/Hertig/Kanda/ Pargendler/Ringe/Rock, The Anatomy of Corporate law. 3rd edition, OUP 2017, Chapter 2; also see *Sjåfjell* Towards a Sustainable European Company Law, Kluwer 2009, p. 37 ff.; see also (from a German context) *Bachmann/Eidenmüller/Engert/Fleischer/Schön* Regulating the Closed Corporations, Berlin, 2014, p. 28 ff. (conflicts of shareholders in closed corporations); or *Roth/Kindler* The Spirit of Corporate Law, Munich 2013, p. 71 ff.; in Czech see, *inter alia*, *Havel* Obchodní korporace ve světle proměn, Praha 2010, and the literature quoted therein.

On the other hand, the interest of the company is supposed to prevail over the interests of all shareholders in order that the company could accomplish its purpose to protect third persons (creditors, employees, etc.). Further, it is obvious that members of the company's bodies are bound by the purpose and goal of the company itself, hence, they must take into account the will of the shareholders expressed by the company's purpose. Where the influence of a shareholder is to be strengthened, typically in various kinds of corporate groups, the loyalty of members of the company's bodies shifts toward the corporate interest. It should also be pointed out that a certain degree of loyalty binds also the shareholders themselves, not only because of the fact that they are parties to the articles of association, but also due to the fact that it is prescribed by the standard of fair conduct toward the company. Moreover, diverse interests may also arise, inter alia, among the shareholders toward one another.

Already in the 1930s, economic academia started to pose a rhetoric question as to whom the company management does actually serve. The problem became a topic during a period of so called managerial capitalism, i.e. at the time when the company basically served as a tool of profit maximization controlled by the management massively exploiting (scarce) resources. This concept then served not only to understand the functionalities of the company as such, but mainly to gradually re-define the standards of fiduciary duties of members of the company's bodies. To simplify, experts try to find out whose interests should be pursued/protected by the company's bodies. If we realize that the process was accompanied with a gradual change of the concept of responsibility of members of the company's bodies, i.e. from subjective to absolute liability, hence, the objectivised and identifiable standard was becoming the more important, it is no surprise that the attention of experts focused on whether the management is to pursue:

- only and only the interest of the company,
- the interest of shareholders or their majority (so called *shareholder model*),
- the interest of stakeholders in a more general sense, or such stakeholders as creditors, employees, etc. (so called *stakeholder model*), or
- various forms of enlightened models (*enlightened shareholder model*)[12], or later even wider models established on the basis of corporate social responsibility (*CSR model*) [13] and the like (e.g. *productive coalition model*)[14].

---

**12** See e.g. *Sjåfjell* (supra note 11), p. 88 ff.

**13** See the comparative study in *Güler/Crowther* in: Güler/Crowther, Global Perspectives on Corporate Governance and CSR, 2009, p. 1 ff.; *Sacconi/Blair/Freeman/Verceli* (eds.) Corporate Social Responsibility and Corporate, 2011.

**14** *Johnston* EC Regulation of Corporate Governance, CUP, 2009, p. 59 ff.

It is needless to say that the further development gradually oscillated between various approaches and/or their combinations and the model which prevailed finally was the one combining all of the above models also in relation to their socially sustainable development (similarly a coalition/cooperation model). Such a solution is pragmatic and foresees various nuances depending on the purpose selected for a particular company, for example, whether a public interest exists in respect of its activities, etc. Especially so if we realize that even today the management of companies is vested with non-corporate organizations, such as trusts that also enter in the shareholders' agreements.

Substantially, the company is therefore an arranged structure which becomes the (meeting) place for various unarranged interests. If we connect such a concept of the company with the contractual aspects arising out of shareholders' agreements, the question of a conflict of interests or complicacy of identification of such conflicts may grow significant. It is then disputable if the existence of contractual covenants outside corporate documents represents only the establishment of a parallel world of contractual obligation outside the company or even of a distinct category of a third kind. Obviously, the discussions about models of corporate governance are closely connected with shareholders' agreements since the external strengthening of the shareholders' positions may shift the company more toward the shareholders model, i.e. it may result in the strengthening of a utilitarian perception of the benefit of the owners of the company. At the same time, however, it cannot be expected that the resulting corporate structure would pursue or show only a single interest, because there would still be a rule that although the statutory grounds of the company established by the articles of association are wrapped up by the contractual net of shareholders' agreements. The company's bodies must nevertheless perform their statutory duties and must pursue wider interests than just those that would be pursued by the shareholders. In other words, the complicated and intertwingled relations among partial components of the company's governance would not result in creating a single uniform interest and in eliminating the agency problem.

The dichotomy of interests of all the shareholders and the company is not – conceptually – interfered with by the shareholders' agreement. The shareholders' agreement does not result in the change of the interest, nor does it create any common collective corporate interest that would prevail over the interests of the shareholders and that would automatically by itself define or interfere with the interests of the company for the purposes of determining the liability of members of the company's bodies. Even the agreement among all shareholders does not have any relevance for the articles of association.[15] The existence of the shareholders' agreement, however, will facilitate the identification of the shareholder's interest, or the interest of several or of all shareholders. Where the company's body proceeds in accordance with the shareholders' agreement it could be expected not to prefer any of the shareholders who are parties to the agreement. That still does not mean that it proceeds in compliance with the interest of the company.

## E. Differences between the articles of association and shareholders' agreements

Both shareholders' agreements and articles of association have a contractual basis. They are established by consent of shareholders, and they are dependent on that will. Their operation is, however, completely different. To put it simply, these are two parallel worlds each having their own rules that are not directly related, although they might cross each other. As mentioned before, besides a formal distinction between the articles of association and shareholders' agreements (the articles of association being a formalized contract meeting some requirements as to its form and content, whose amendment and operation are subject to a separate regulation) a substantive distinction might be proposed between corporate and non-corporate issues. Corporate issues cover the structure and functioning of the company and involve provisions which are considered as a possible or inevitable content of the articles of association as set by corporate law. In contrast, non-corporate (contractual) provisions regulate other issues of an obligatory nature regardless of where such provisions are contained in the articles of association or in the shareholders' agreements. From such a perspective, a corporate issue may be regulated in a shareholders' agreement, but also *vice versa*, a contractual (non-corporate) issue may be contained in the articles of association. Distinguishing according to a material criterion will play a role in considering particulars necessary for the validity of a given legal act, its effect, possibility of changes and legal consequences of defects or remedies available. It will also be important for the evaluation of the relation be-

15 From a point of view of German or Czech law, however, it should be pointed out that case law has repeatedly admitted a direct influence of shareholders' agreements on the articles of association (see e.g. arrangements of all shareholders contained in the shareholders' agreement regime may result in an *ad hoc* piercing the rule contained in the memorandum of association – Czech Republic IV.1.). See also Germany D.I.

tween the resolution of a general meeting and the articles of association. The fundamental distinctions between the articles of association and the shareholders' agreement may be outlined as follows.

## I. Different content and formal requirements for corporate and non-corporate provisions

The formation of a shareholders' agreement is subject to regulations governing legal conduct and its restrictions. Beside general prohibitions and limitations which are imposed by the law in relation to the content of contracts, other restrictions that respond to a stricter nature of some sections of the corporate law are to be taken into account. The law often regulates the content of the articles of association by its mandatory rules (the concept of *Satzungsstrenge*[16] and its more or less persuasive derivatives). The mandatory or cogent nature of a particular provision (rule) of corporate law, however, does not automatically make the provision of the shareholders' agreement contravening such a regulation void.[17] It is always necessary to examine the reasons why a particular arrangement in the articles of association is prohibited, or why it is prohibited to deviate from a particular rule by an arrangement in the articles of association. Where a statutory prohibition is aimed to prevent a particular result (constitutive elements or *status* of the company), but also aims at basic construction elements of individual forms of companies (for example, a prohibition to split a share, rules of maintaining the capital or the basic division of functions of the company's bodies), then an arrangement leading to such an undesired result is void even if it is part of a shareholders' agreement.

It may be concluded that it is not possible to agree, within a shareholders' agreement, on any arrangements that would interfere with the mandatory rules of the company, i.e. the rules that are considered so significant by the law that they are forming the very substance of a company. At the same time, however, even if such rules are agreed, they will not be void automatically, but they might be considered as having no effect externally and leading to specific consequences *inter partes*. The same might be said about those rules contained in the articles of association that could possibly contravene the non-mandatory rules. Even these rules may remain valid, but only in the contractual regime without having any influence upon third persons. These considerations

16 See also Part B – Austria A. for further details.

17 See e.g. in German law (Germany note A.).

may be important when discussing sanction schemes pertaining to such rules, or resulting from their violation.

Arrangements when shareholders' agreement threatens the company's interest not available to the shareholders themselves should be viewed critically. For example, a shareholders' agreement, whereby shareholders obligate themselves not to initiate an *actio pro socio* or derivative suit should be void (especially if the breach of such a duty would be sanctioned by a contractual fine). Regardless of whether such an arrangement would amount to an *ex ante* waiver of rights (which might be – in some jurisdictions – prohibited) or a limited *pactum de non petendo*, the arrangement in question should be void since it interferes with the interests of the company and the creditors. Its execution interferes with the company's interest which is not available to the shareholders and not even to the company itself. Nevertheless, in many jurisdictions the discussion is pending on a possibility to waive the rights related to a share in the registered company, i.e. on a possibility to agree, for example, a share without a profit-sharing right, without a voting right, etc. Even such discussions usually result in a conclusion that it is not possible to waive those rights which basically consist in the protection of minority shareholders, or in the retaining of control in the company.

Also, the application of general corporate substantive-law mechanisms among shareholders might be an option. For example, the content of corporate documents will be subject to a prohibition to abuse rights, and especially in some jurisdictions there might be a ban on abusive disadvantaging of some of the shareholders. The shareholders' agreement is of a contractual nature allowing contractual modifications of the legal regime and it represents a voluntary, rather than a mandatory, assumption of obligations (except for the arrangements that would vest the right to determine the content of this covenant with the majority). It is therefore limited by contractual mechanisms (good morals, fair business practices, ban on the abuse of a right, and the like).

In other cases, however, there is no reason why the mere fact that an arrangement in shareholders' agreements contravening the rules of the corporate law or the law regulating legal entities should inevitably result in its nullity. Nevertheless, it remains disputable if an inclusion of a particular provision in the shareholders' agreement which, if contained in the articles of association, must comply with the requirements of the prescribed written form (for example, in form of a notarial deed). In general, it may be stated that private law does not require that an act related to another act which is subject to a stricter statutory requirement of a written form would also have to comply with the same statutory requirement of a stricter written form. The fact that the articles of association require a stricter written form would still not imply that a similar contractual regulation must comply with the same formal requirements.[18]

## II. (Limited) Binding effect of shareholders' agreements and articles of association

A difference between the articles of association and shareholders' agreements is also the different extent to which the company, the shareholders and other persons are bound by them. Articles of association bind all shareholders as well as the company itself. They are also binding upon the shareholders who did not vote for the amendment to the articles of association if the quorum necessary for the change of the articles of association has been achieved, and all these entities are also entitled to derive their rights from the articles of association. The binding effect of the articles of association is inseparably connected with the share in the company *(causa societatis)*, and it therefore binds every person acquiring a share in the company. The articles of association also bind members of the company's bodies since they are bound to proceed in compliance with the given corporate documents. On the contrary, shareholders agreements bind only the persons that expressed their consent with them, and they do not bind those who did not express their consent thereto. It is not inevitable that all shareholders were also parties to the shareholders' agreement. On the other hand, it is not excluded that the shareholders' agreement can also bind third persons. The boundaries of the binding effect of shareholders' agreements might be illustrated on three entities, the corporation itself and the members of its bodies, the purchasers of shares and third parties.

### 1. Effect on the corporation and its bodies

First of all, shareholders' agreements do not automatically bind the corporation, unless the company (and other parties) agreed thereto.[19] The conclusion of a shareholders' agreement is not subject to the consent of a general meeting. However, the company may still derive its rights from such an agreement in accord-

**18** See e.g. in German law (Germany B.II.).

**19** On the contrary, a UNCITRAL Model Law on a simplified business entity of 2015 provides in its Article 36 that the shareholder's agreement will bind the company if the company was notified of their existence. UNCITRAL Draft model law on a simplified business entity. A/CN. 9/WG. I/WP. 89.

ance with the regulation on contracts for the benefit of third parties on the condition that the shareholders intended to grant the company such a benefit. Similar rules will also apply in cases where a member of the company's body is a party to such a shareholders' agreement. The contractual position is personally determined and does not extend to all members of the body. It will always be a specifically designated person who agreed to the shareholders' agreement, rather than any person who is holding an office of a member of the company's body. As it was already mentioned, the involvement of the corporation and its bodies in the shareholders' agreements is possible, but they must not exceed so called *statutory powers*, i.e. the core mandatory rules of general delimination of the powers of the company's bodies, including a ban on interference of third parties in the company's management. In other words, the structure of obligations built within the shareholders' agreement may not result in contravening the core mandatory rules on corporate governance which guarantee that governance and ownership of shares will be distinguished and which also guarantee the obligation of due performance of the company's bodies members' duties.

## 2. Effect on purchasers of shares

Secondly, even the share purchaser will not automatically become a party to the shareholders' agreement. The share purchaser could acquire the position of a party to the shareholders' agreement only under the rules of the law of contract which basically requires consent of other shareholders to the change of the entities who are parties to the agreement. On the contrary, the rights and duties agreed in the articles of association are "rooted" in the share, because the articles are published and everyone ought to know what properties are bought when acquiring the shares. Where the share is being sold only in the regime of articles of association, it is being sold under the conditions defined in the articles of association and in the law. The rights and duties defined in the shareholders' agreement bind only the parties to that agreement, which obviously also determines the public perception of the status of the share and the company. The legal provisions on how a shareholder may become a party to the agreement vary in different jurisdictions. For example, in the Italian[20] and Czech law[21] a cession of the shareholders' agreement is possible. Based on a share transfer agreement between the transferor and the transferee, it will be possible to assign also the

20 See Italy D.I.
21 See Czech Republic IV.2.

claims resulting from the shareholders' agreement if the rights and duties resulting from the agreement are assignable. For the transfer of other rights and duties it will be necessary to execute an agreement whose parties will also include other stakeholders (debtor). On the contrary, the articles of association will usually also bind the assignees. The question of the assignee being bound by the articles of association should be distinguished from the meritorious or contractual nature of a covenant contained in the articles of association. Special rules applying to the binding status of the assignee may be identified with the registered ancillary covenants in the shareholders' agreement within the joint stock company in relation to the shares which may be effective also toward third persons.

### 3. Effect on third parties

Finally, third parties can be parties of shareholders' agreements (e.g. creditors). The covenants agreed with third parties are always of non-corporate nature. However, the participation of a third party standing outside the shareholders' structure and its influence on the company may lead to the specific legal consequences or restrictions, for example, in respect of the question of a possible factual influence on the company governance. Hence, these cases of shareholders' agreements are usually joint ventures or other forms of consortial structures, basically in a regime of a civil partnership. Similar structures may also be created within arrangement proceedings (restructuring) of a company in crisis, while such models may serve to prevent the threat of bankruptcy etc. (within a more general concept or *standstill lock-up* agreements).[22]

## III. Different mechanisms for the change of corporate and non-corporate arrangements

Company law generally lays down the minimum quorum necessary to execute an amendment to the articles of association. The change of corporate documents is not necessarily subject to unanimous vote, in common, majority vote or qualified majority vote will suffice. Articles of association may be changed by a formal voting process by the general meeting of shareholders, or by passing a resolution outside the general meeting. The shareholders' agreement may be changed by

22 See Shareholders' Agreement Arrangement in Pre-insolvency and Insolvency Law.

a consent of all of the persons concerned. However, a possibility to agree the majority decision-making on the common matters is not excluded. The shareholders' agreement, by itself, does not effect a majority decision-making concerning its change. This difference, however, exceeds the framework of formalities distinguishing between the articles of association and the shareholders' agreement, and it is also manifested in different conditions of the amendments to corporate and non-corporate arrangements included in the articles of association. Even if contractual (non-corporate) arrangements are included in the articles of association, this will not change its nature, and majority voting thereon will not automatically suffice. However, a more complex position is to be taken when a corporate matter (for example, an establishment of the right of pre-emption or another restriction of transferability of shares) may be located either in the articles of association or in the shareholder agreement and thus the matter might appear both contractual and corporate. From the shareholders' decision to include a particular corporate arrangement within the articles of association, we should derive the intent of shareholders to attain not only a contractual nature of that arrangement but especially the corporate nature thereof. The worlds of the shareholders' agreement and of a corporate document are not fully separated. As will be explained later[23], a change or an attempt to change the articles of association may eventually effect a shareholders' agreement, and *vice versa.*

## IV. Different mechanisms for the enforcement and the consequences of the breach of a shareholders' agreement

The consequences of a breach of the shareholders' duties resulting from the articles of association or articles are defined by the law for each of the types of corporations (for example, a duty to pay late-payment interest, to refrain from competitive activities, a possibility of excluding a shareholder). However, the law usually does not provide for the specific consequences of a breach of shareholders' agreements. Common contractual tools will therefore be used. The injured party should basically have at its disposal the whole range of contractual remedies (damages, withdrawal from the contract, objections of default, liability for delay, etc.). In practice, shareholders' agreements are often enforced by a representative of a shareholder authorised by a power of attorney who will exercise the shareholder's rights instead of the shareholder (or several shareholders) and who is bound by the instructions resulting from the shareholders' agreement.

23 See F.II.

Nevertheless, in the above differentiation it is also necessary to take into account the content of the arrangement, or the nature of the obligation breached, and not only its location either in the articles of association or in the shareholders' agreement.

As stated before[24], an inclusion of a non-corporate arrangement in the articles of association will not affect the contractual nature of such an arrangement. It will remain a contractual covenant that is enforced as a contractual arrangement and binds the parties to such a covenant. If the shareholders opted for a contractual remedy for the breach of a certain obligation resulting from the articles of association and directed at the remaining shareholders, it would amount to a contractual covenant regardless of where it would be placed. And similarly, a provision of articles of association which would bind the shareholders to provide each other loans or which would impose subsidiary obligations upon the shareholders toward each other, unrelated to their corporate shares, would not become a corporate arrangement but remains contractual. A corporate arrangement operates in the world of corporate law and it allows a corporate enforcement instruments only if it is included in the articles of association. The corporate effect (i. e. an exclusion of a shareholder) is not only bound to formal requirements (provision in the articles of association or articles of association), but also to material prerequisites (a corporate issue). For example, a duty to pay an extra contribution provided for only in the shareholders' agreement will not allow of initiating the process of exclusion against the shareholder in breach of such a duty.

The possibility of enforcing duties or claims resulting from the shareholders' agreement or from the articles of association is associated also with a question of possible protective measures to be employed by the entities affected. Shareholders are protected against changes of the articles of association by an action to declare a resolution of the general meeting passing it as void, and they are protected against the shareholders' agreement or its changes by an action to determine a legal act void. Both of these actions have different condition (for example, varying term of time for bringing an action) and they are addressed against different entities.

---

**24** See E.I.

## V. Termination

A significant difference between the articles of association and shareholders' agreement also rests in the possibility and the mechanisms of their termination. Shareholders' agreements may be terminated regardless of the duration of the company or a share in the company, by an agreement of shareholders or even unilaterally. It is, however, necessary to take into account a connectedness of the shareholders' agreement with the status of a shareholder of a company. It is, *inter alia*, disputable if a particular party may withdraw from the shareholders' agreement in full, for example, in the case of a substantial breach of its duties by another shareholder. In our opinion, it is necessary to examine if the parties, when entering into the shareholders' agreement, might have intended, even in an implied manner, to bind the shareholders' agreement with the status of a company's shareholder, and not to allow him/her to terminate the agreement unilaterally, without terminating his/her share in the company. On the contrary, the status of a shareholder is firmly bound to the articles of association. Shareholders are allowed to withdraw from the articles of association only exceptionally, and exclusively along with the transfer of their share in the company or their exit in other way. It is impossible neither to agree, nor to unilaterally effect the termination of the articles of association during the life of the company.

## VI. Interpretation

Another difference between the articles of association and shareholders agreements might be a varying approach to their interpretation. Although it may be generally stated that the world of the articles of association and the world of shareholders' agreements are quite varying worlds, or varying animals,[25] their common contractual basis and their mutual interconnection cannot be omitted. Articles of association basically contain not only provisions pre-defined by the law, but they also contain covenants that exceed the statutory requirements and they include also rules which have been agreed by the shareholders in a regime of autonomous will, but which they intend to maintain only in a regime of external agreement. Such rules are the rules that, although resulting from contractual arrangement of shareholders, acquire as if "meritorious" effect by their being included in the articles of association, which has an impact upon their interpretation. Ancillary shareholders' agreements standing outside statu-

25 *Cadman* Shareholders' Agreements, London 2004, p. 2.

tory rules are sometimes called *sideletters.*[26] A statutory default regulation of the content of the articles of association[27] is supposed to offer such a normative solution on which the parties would agree if they had time and funds for detailed negotiations, and which, at the same time, guarantees a certain degree of protection of the minority and the creditors (in a more general sense, also other categories of good morals and public order). On the contrary, shareholders' agreements are foreseen to result from negotiation and from searching for a precise solution not relying on the protective network of dispositive rules of the law. While the articles of association are a manifestation and an embodiment of statutory rules with an increased occurrence of cogent rules, shareholders' agreements are a manifestation of an autonomous will.[28] It is obvious that the rules which the shareholders have agreed in excess to the statutory delimitation of the articles of association, but which, in spite of that, have been included in the articles of association, are the rules that are more like corporate (statutory) rules, although it is not always so, and so an overlap of corporate (statutory) rules and shareholders' agreement may occur in the articles of association. The above note on the substance of the articles of association, or shareholders' agreement is important for their *ex post* interpretation. It is logical that although the shareholders are trying, through these agreements, to settle the problems *ex ante*, their concrete application will take place thereafter, hence at the time when there will already be no harmony between the parties to the agreement. It is generally assumed that the interpretation of the two of the instruments must be distinct. This is because the articles of association inevitably require an interpretation where objectiveness is of a higher degree due to the very nature of the instrument, which distinguishes it from a more subjective interpretation of the shareholders' agreement. Similarly, it is necessary to distinguish registered companies from personal or closed companies. For example, the interpretation of articles of association of public companies/joint stock companies is less dependent on the will of the founders compared to the closed companies where no change of shareholders' structure has occurred, or to the shareholders' agree-

---

**26** Here the concept of *sideletters* is understood as the concept of the law of contract, which is the concept that is superordinate to possible shareholders' agreements as well as ancillary provisions of the articles of association.

**27** We assume that the silence of the articles of association themselves implicitly attracts into to their content a range of statutory rules, the "content of articles of association" should therefore be viewed more generally.

**28** It is also possible to find a different, or more complicated constructions, for example, when a statutory framework of such agreements exists, see above, for example Section § 7. 32 MBCA.

ment,[29] which are basically bound with their founders. Nevertheless, it is necessary to say at the same time that although making difference between the two of the ruling systems, they still result from the will and intentions of the same persons, and they therefore cannot be separated. Both structures thus make up a single, more general set of rules, the individual layers of which are related to one another and should be perceived in a more holistic way. Under certain circumstances it may be quite artificial to view the articles of association as separate from the shareholders' agreement and from its background, which should enable the courts, when interpreting the articles, to take shareholders' agreements into consideration.[30] The German case law permits – in certain occasions[31] – that the circumstances which are outside the scope of the articles of association, including the shareholders' agreements, should be taken into consideration when it is generally possible to expect that the members of the company's bodies were aware of them. However, when interpreting the articles of association, it is necessary to focus more on the fact that they regulate statutory (corporate) issues and by being published their effect is *erga omnes*. Nevertheless, it is not possible to omit their contractual background manifested not only in the possible ancillary provisions contained in the articles of association, but also, for example, in the shareholders' agreement (especially so if the company itself is a party to such an agreement).

## VII. Shareholders' Agreements in the case of structural changes

The consequences of structural changes of a company (change of legal form, merger, consolidation, splitting up, etc.) have a disputable impact on the validity and duration of shareholders' agreements. It is possible to start from the fact that if a particular provision is included in the articles of association, then if, as a result of the change, the original articles of association are replaced by new ones, the previous one terminates. The validity and duration of shareholders' agreements will be examined on a case by case basis according to contractual mechanisms (i. e. impossibility of performance). However, an automatic termination of this agreement is not inevitable.

---

**29** See for example German (D.I.), Danish (Denmark D.I.) and Austrian law (Austria D.I.).
**30** See for example English law (IV.1.).
**31** See Germany D.I.; for limitations toward third parties see also greek law (D.I.).

## VIII. Shareholders' Agreements in the bankruptcy of the company

It is possible to assume that the shareholders' agreements may change their function in the situation where the company or any of the parties enters bankruptcy proceedings. The foremost rule is that the bankruptcy of a company not being a party to such an agreement has no direct effect because such an agreement only binds the parties. Nevertheless, it will change the reasons and mechanisms of the agreement among the parties. It is quite common practice, especially in the life of bigger or economically interesting companies, that before the filing for the company management, with the support of its owners and major creditors, tries to find an informal solution of the whole situation. If, for example, the company which is funded by banks falls in a state of economic insufficiency or is threatened by bankruptcy, the bank will identify such a condition based on the agreed contractual instruments and will subsequently initiate an internal process within which it will seek for a possible solution that will generally presuppose not only the engagement of the company but also its shareholder or parent companies. Since the reason of the problem often rests in the current lack of income it is not necessary that the company should end up in bankruptcy. It is therefore the company itself which initiates various internal restructuring measures (sale of unnecessary assets, closure of unprofitable establishments, decrease of personnel costs, sale of a part of a business, etc.). Shareholders agreements are therefore often modified for such purposes and amended by new schemes, or other new covenants are added, now already with the engagement of creditors. So-called *standstill agreements* are a common instrument, i.e. agreements between the company, shareholders and major creditors, to the effect that the current increase of the amount of debt by interests is frozen, in other words the current amount of debts is fixed for a defined period of time (e.g. for six to twelve months). Similarly, in order to ensure the continuity of such agreements, various *lock-up agreements* are arranged, i.e. agreements restricting a possible transfer of the *position of a bank*, especially the assignment of its claims to third persons. The subsequent fate of these agreements will depend mainly on their economic success.

In some jurisdictions, within bankruptcy proceedings, the claims of shareholders become subordinate and they may be satisfied only after the satisfaction of claims that are not subordinate. Only those claims of the shareholder towards the company may be subordinate which are related to the position of the shareholder, but also any others to which the shareholder is entitled. If such a situation occurred it may result in that also other claims against the company resulting from shareholders' agreements will qualify as subordinate. Subordination shall mean a subordinate order of sequence of satisfying such claims in respect of other claims. If the company that is bankrupt were a party to the shareholders' agreement, the nature of the agreement may change in course of insolvency proceedings. First of all, its nature will basically amount to an agreement that has not been mutually (executory contract) performed (executory contract), yet, and its fate will be in the hands of the official receiver, or a person authorised to dispose of the debtor's assets. This option is used in many European jurisdictions, entitling the official receiver to terminate agreements which would unreasonably burden the debtor and would prevent a sound economic solution – the agreement may, of course, provide for such a solution, and it will either terminate automatically or it provides for its own survival, even without the company as its party. The official receiver may, of course, resist the shareholders' agreement, or its part in a regime of relative ineffectiveness, *actio pauliana*, should the company put some entity in advantage in relation to the bankruptcy, or, on the contrary, if the company disadvantaged anyone in relation thereto.

## F. Collisions between shareholders' agreements and articles of association

The articles of association and shareholders' agreements represent two worlds that are to a great extent, however not fully, linked to each other. Their collision or intersection is not excluded, and they may supplement and replace each other, but they may also change each other or influence each other in another way.

### I. Contradiction between the articles of association and shareholders' agreements

On an abstract level, a contradiction between the wording of the articles of association and shareholders' agreements might occur. This conflict may already reside in the fact that the corporate document regulates a particular question in a particular way and the shareholders' agreement does so differently. The contradiction itself between the articles of association and the shareholders' agreement will not automatically make any of these documents void. Regarding the parallel nature of their impact, these documents may be contradictory or colliding otherwise. Although legal regulations do not deal with a collision, it is possible to derive certain conclusions. For example, shareholders can agree in a shareholders' agreement to a different extent of the competition clause compared to that which results from the articles of association. Such an agreement could be concluded by only some of the shareholders among each other or just toward one of the shareholders. A competition ban agreed on a contractual basis should only have *inter partes* effect and its breach should basically not result in the rights of the company itself, unless such an agreement complied with the requirement of a contract in favour of a third party. It is even possible that the parties to a shareholders' agreement would intend to provide exactly for an issue that cannot be agreed in the articles of association. For example, in many jurisdiction articles of association cannot exclude the transferability of certain types of shares. Nevertheless, this will not prevent the shareholders from agreeing a limitation or exclusion of transferability with contractual effect *inter partes.* The contradiction between the articles of association and shareholders' agreements will not result in the invalidity of the articles of association. As it has been already stated the fact that a certain arrangement may not be included in the articles of association (or it contravenes another mandatory rule) does not cause the invalidity of the colliding part of the shareholders' agreement.[32] It is always necessary to examine why the regulation of a particular question in the articles of association is inadmissible.

## II. Impact of shareholders' agreements on the change of the articles of association

Although, in general a conflict between shareholders' agreements and the articles of association will not make any of these documents void, such a collision may affect their content. The articles of association will be amended by a formal procedure intended for that purpose, by adopting a decision of the general meeting on their change for the future. The shareholders may also adopt such a valid decision that contravenes the provision of the articles of association. The conflict itself between the resolution and the articles of association does not always result in an invalidity of the resolution as the resolution might be an *ad hoc* deviation of the articles of association or a general pro future amendment thereof.

A resolution of the general meeting may qualify as an amendment to the articles of association, either in general and for the future, or just for a particular case. The content as well as formal requirements applicable to the amendment to the articles of association must be met, however, and the shareholders must in-

**32** See D.

tend either to deviate from the articles of association *ad hoc* and to establish a rule exactly for a particular case without changing the content of the articles of association (so called piercing of the articles of association, *Satzungsdurchbrechung*[33]), or to manifest an intention to change the articles of association for the future and in general. In this respect a discussion whether an *ad hoc* decision of all shareholders whereby the shareholders would not intend to change the articles of association for the future, but only to establish a particular condition deviating from the articles of association, must meet all formal, procedure and content requirements, as if it was an amendment to the articles of association. The German[34] case law, in particular, but also the Czech case law admit the piercing of the articles of association as a special shareholders' agreement deviating in a particular case from the articles of association without meeting the requirements necessary for the amendment to the articles of association, those are supposed to be required only when the shareholders intend to establish a new legal status, i. e. to change the articles of association for the future (so-called *Satzungsduchbrechung*).[35] The Slovak case law, for example, has not been fully es-

---

**33** See Germany D.I.

**34** See Germany D.I.

**35** According to the Judgment of the Supreme Court of the Czech Republic of 22 April 2009, case ref. 29 Cdo 2254/2007: "*The Supreme Court does not find the reason why the shareholders should be able to word out a part of the content of the right to a settlement share (maturity, in particular) in the agreement to terminate a share, pursuant to Section 61 of the Commercial Code in the wording effective in the relevant period, whereas their intent concerning the remain elements of such a content (especially, defining the mode of determination of the amount of the share and the mode of its payment) would have to be determined by the shareholders in the memorandum of association or articles of association. Especially so, if their will – as in the case pending – was not aimed at the determination of a general regime of such a deviation (for an unspecified range of future cases), but rather at the enforcement of a single-case solution related to a single, concrete shareholder. An amendment to the memorandum of association or articles of association would not be suitable for such a purpose, if it was subsequently – after approving an agreement pursuant to Section 149a of the Commercial Code – necessary to review it again. Instead of the interpretation of the provision of Section 61 subsection 2 of the Commercial Code in the relevant wording proposed by the appellant, the Supreme Court therefore concludes that the said provision should be interpreted so as the memorandum of association or articles of association may , in advance, determine the mode of determination of the settlement share differently from the statutory provisions and thereby secure the shareholders in respect of how their settlement share is to be determined in the case of termination of their share in the company. That provision, however, does not prevent all the shareholders from agreeing in a particular case on the mode of determination of a settlement share of a shareholder whose share in the company is to terminate, of course, on condition that such a an agreement will not contravene the law, nor will it evade it (i-e- it will not damage the company's creditors, for example), and it will not be contrary to good morals or fair trading practices. It must be noted, however, that the said decision may also be interpreted so that the shareholders' agreement*

tablished, yet. After certain flexible hints,[36] however, it seems to be of a more rigid position.[37] It is, however, beyond any doubt that in order to change the articles of association – including their *ad hoc* piercing or general factual change – it is not enough if the shareholders' intent to adopt a regulation parallel to the

---

*creates a covenant, beside the memorandum of association (articles of association), which determines a reference rule to consider the compliance of the settlement share with good morals or fair trading practises.*" See also See Czech Republic IV.1. for further details.

**36** According to a decision of the Supreme Court of the Slovak Republic in the case referenced as Obdo V 79/2003, an assignment of a business share to a third person is valid, although the memorandum of association has not provided for such a possibility, but the assignment occurred with a consent of all shareholders. Quoted as: "*The memorandum of association is a manifestation of the common will of shareholders and all the shareholders jointly have the right to amend it also in way that they will proceed in a particular case differently from its wording.*" In this case it is a fusion of law-making amendment to the memorandum of association and *ad hoc* piercing of the articles of association. The Supreme Court of the Slovak Republic retained the general level of admissibility, and did not examine if that would also cause an amendment of the memorandum of association for the future, or only an adoption of an *ad hoc* solution contravening the memorandum of association. See Slovakia D.I. for further details.

**37** It might be sometimes demanding to consider and decide if a particular decision of the general meeting represents an amendment to the memorandum of association (articles of association), a decision within the existing memorandum of association (articles of association), or whether it is such a decision that will alter the wording of the memorandum of association (articles of association) only for the purposes of this single case. Professional public has been attracted by the case where a resolution of the general meeting on the removal of one from several members of an authorised body without appointed a new member in its stead, the Supreme Court of the Slovak Republic considered it as a decision on the amendment to the memorandum of association – a decrease of the number of members of an authorised representative body which requires a higher quorum to be valid (judgment of the Supreme Court of the Slovak Republic, case reference 1 Obo 95/2002, ZSP 9/2004, also see the note annexed in the particular journal). Such a procedure is incorrect (a contrary approach was taken, for example, the Supreme Court of the Czech Republic in its judgment of 30 October 2002, case ref. 29 Odo 269/2002). It is not possible to derive the intention to amend the memorandum of association from the very fact that the shareholders have decided to remove a director. The said decision was specific as to the facts in that the subject of the resolution of the general meeting designated as "the amendment to the memorandum of association" in the part where the memorandum of association specified the names of the company's directors. Even that, however, does not allow of concluding that the shareholders intended to amend the memorandum of association since the specification of the names of directors could be only a formal expression or could result from an incorrect interpretation of an obligation to state the names of first directors in the memorandum of association (and the shareholders could think that the memorandum of association should reflect the change of the person of the company's director, from the first to the last). It should therefore be examined if, by specifying the names of directors in the memorandum, the shareholders really intended to increase the quorum necessary to remove a member of a statutory body. See Slovakia D.I. for further details.

existing contractual sphere, but it is rather required that the will of the shareholders was aimed at the adoption of such regulation that would amend the articles of association. It remains unclear if a conclusion of or an amendment to the shareholders' agreement which establishes a rule deviating from the one foreseen by the articles of association may be considered as a decision that would pierce or factually amended the articles of association. In our opinion, the shareholders' agreement does not have a character of a decision of the shareholders that is necessary in order to pierce or change the articles of association. It may be assumed that in the case where a particular question deviating from the articles of association is provided for in the shareholders' agreement, its parties might not have intended to amend the articles of association, not even in form of an ad hoc piercing, but only to establish a contractual regulation standing beside the corporate document. With regard to the parallel existence and scope of the articles of association and the shareholders' agreement a subsequent shareholders' agreement basically does not amend earlier articles of association and neither does it *vice versa*.

It is also unclear if we could consider shareholders' agreements as agreements on the future amendment of the articles of association (*pactum de contrahendo*). The agreement imposing upon the shareholders an obligation to amend the articles of association should be basically considered as an agreement on the exercise of the voting right at the general meeting. But in the situation where it is possible to amend the articles of association also otherwise, for example in a contractual form by an agreement of all shareholders on the amendment to the articles of association, it should be also possible to conclude an agreement on the future amendment to the articles of association. Such arrangements shall render the doubts about the enforceability of voting rights agreements obsolete.[38] Of course, one condition is that the formal and content requirements of a *pactum de contrahendo* have been met.

## III. Conflicts between resolutions of the general meeting and shareholders' agreements

On the level of particular cases, a conflict between the corporate and contractual acts may arise in the case where the shareholders have voted at the general meeting differently from what has been agreed in a shareholders' agreement. Accord-

---

38 See I.1.

ing to (often criticised) German[39] or even Austrian[40] case law the conflict of a decision of the general meeting with the agreement of all of the company's shareholders is a reason to render such a decision void as if the articles of association have been violated. On the contrary, for example, the Slovak law provides explicitly for such cases that a conflict of a decision of the company's body with the shareholders' agreement will not make such a decision void.[41] This means that even an agreement made by all shareholders does not have the effect of a corporate act. The Slovak law, however, is intentionally silent about the consequences that may result from such a conflict. The consequences of a breach of the shareholders' agreement will remain contractual (for example, damages, contractually agreed legal consequences, and the like).

The shareholders' agreement may exceptionally have some consequences also outside its contractual framework. Shareholders' agreements could be considered as a (voluntary) restriction of shareholders' right. However, this will obviously be an extraordinarily rare case occurring, for example, when deciding on the payment of a dividend in the situation where the shareholder concerned would grant his consent in the shareholders' agreement to restrict his right. It would qualify as a manifestation of a contractual type of agreement, but its consequence would appear on the level of corporate law and through the mechanisms of corporate law. The reason why such a resolution should not be considered as restricting the rights of a shareholder should therefore not be such that the given result derives from the shareholders' agreement, but rather that the shareholders has granted his prior consent with such a restriction. The interference would obviously have to be such which allows of a consent having been granted in advance, regardless of the technicalities of the voting process, taking into account that the question itself could be decided upon only after some time has passed after the granting of such consent.

## IV. Invalid decision of the general meeting (shareholders) as a valid shareholders' agreement?

A consenting manifestation of the intent of the shareholders which does not meet the prerequisites of a valid resolution may be considered as a shareholders'

39 See Germany D.IV. for further details.

40 See Austria D.III. for further details.

41 See Slovakia E.II. for further details; see also Denmark F.V.

agreement.[42] In general, however, it is not possible to state that any invalid resolution of the general meeting should be automatically considered as the shareholders' agreement. We must start from the fact that the members of the general meeting, through their voting, have expressed their will to vote at the general meeting and to pass a resolution rather than to enter into an agreement defining their mutual rights and duties. For example, a resolution on such a change of the articles of association whereby the shareholders would introduce the pre-emption right to their shares would be declared void because the voting would impair the rights of the shareholders injured. It would obviously not be possible to assume that the voters intended to establish the pre-emption right also among the other shareholders, unless such an intention could be derived from the circumstances of a particular case. The unlawful and therefore void resolution of the general meeting should be never considered as a shareholders' agreement because the reasons of nullity should not admit a possibility of transformation of a corporate act into a contractual act.

## G. Content of shareholders' agreements

The content of shareholders' agreements may focus on various detailed issued among shareholders (a narrow definition) or they may deal with issues among shareholders as well as toward third persons or the company itself (a wider definition), which means that various *joint venture/consortium, etc.* are also ranked with such agreements.

What is generally agreed by shareholders in terms of a narrow definition of the shareholders' agreement?

1. A more detailed and extensive definition of rights and duties of shareholders:

a) a more detailed specification of the types of shares even without defining the kind of the share that must be contained in the articles of association,

b) introduction of specific rights and duties of shareholders not ranked with specific kinds of rights, or

---

42 See, e.g., the judgment of the German Federal Court of Justice as of 15.3.2010 – II ZR 4/09, NZG 2010, 988 stating that shareholders can agree on the amount of an appraisal right for the membership in a closed corporation (GmbH) in a shareholder agreement or in the articles of association. Also see *Ulmer* Schuldrechtliche Gesellschafterabrede zugunsten der GmbH – Geeignetes Ersatzgeschäft für formnichtige Satzungsdurchbrechung? in: liber amicorum Winter, Cologne 2011, p. 687 ff.

c) rules for voting at the general meeting (for example, *pooling* – agreements on the exercise of a voting right, or *voting trust* – an arrangement on the separation of the right to vote from the ownership right to a share whereas the title to a share is transferred under fiduciary rules upon a trustee under the trust who will then exercise the voting right with the effect that the right to a profit is retained by the original beneficiary – owner);[43]

2. Rules of company governance:

a) for example, the rules of structuring and appointment of members of corporate bodies, the right of deployment (*Entsendungsrecht*), the right of appointment, the rules of cooperation, the rules concerning determination of a reward (e.g. option schemes, etc.), of course, on condition that they have been approved by the articles of association,

b) rules for dealing with so called *deadlock*, i.e. the situation where, due to an internal conflict among shareholders or bodies, the functioning of bodies or the company itself is being blocked (e.g. Russian roulette, *Texas shoot-out*, freezing of certain rules, etc.), even in the situation where such a condition has been foreseen by introducing so called the right to veto;

3. Rules for the termination of a shareholders' share in the company – *call options, put options, tag along, drag along*, price fixation, various forms of the right of pre-emption, etc.;
4. Protection of minorities, typically by increasing the rights of a minority shareholder in terms of the right to be informed or the right to deploy its own member of a statutory body, and
5. Rules for dispute settlement (out-of-court-settlement, conciliation proceedings, mediation, arbitration, etc.).

Any shareholders' agreement must be further considered according to particular legal regulations, and the limitations and restrictions of the given legal concepts will be drawn mainly from the rules of that particular jurisdiction. Therefore, if the parties agree on the right of pre-emption to the business shares it may be necessary to examine the compliance of such an arrangement with the rights re-

---

43 We are aware that this solution employed, for example, in the U.S. law clashes with the continental law mainly in terms of non-existence of the legal concept of trust or discussion of whether it is possible to separate the voting right and ownership right in this manner. We believe, however, that the concept of trust, including a fiduciary transfer, are solutions that do not interfere with the principle of unity of share because through them the owner is deprived of ownership for a certain period of time, but s/he does so on a fiduciary basis, and not otherwise. This conclusion is also supported by the existence of the concept of fiduciary transfer of a right, etc.

lated to the pre-emption arrangement. In the case of an obligation to provide additional funds to the company the prerequisites required by the law for such financing (extra contribution, gift, loan) should be examined, in the case of an obligation to pay a contractual fine it is necessary to examine the requirements for a particular arrangement to be valid, etc. From a point of view of its purpose, the content of the shareholders' agreement will therefore often depend on the parties. The law does not require that all the company's shareholders should be parties to the shareholders' agreement. It is possible that only some of the shareholders will enter into shareholders' agreements. It is even not excluded that a party to a shareholders' agreement could be the company itself, members of its bodies or prospective shareholders, or any third persons (in general, funding creditors). Regardless of the wording of the law, the parties may use their shareholders' agreements for varying purposes that will appear in the content and wording of the provisions of the agreement. The general content of shareholders' agreements could be systematized according to a function which they fulfil, or according to partial goals which they pursue. In this perspective, the above survey of usual particulars of shareholders' agreements may be classified as follows.

## I. Shareholders' agreements as a tool of company governance

By entering into a shareholders' agreement its parties arrange for their mutual rights and duties, but the shareholders may not only agree on the mutual rights in the shareholders' agreement, but also the mode of exercise of their rights toward the company. The law outlines general rules for the manner and conditions of the exercise of rights related to their share in the company whether of a proprietary or non-proprietary nature. Hence, the shareholders' agreement may become another manner of company governance.

### 1. Arrangements on a specific exercise of voting rights

Shareholders' agreements often include agreements on the exercise of voting rights in various forms. Shareholders' agreements may agree, in advance, on a general voting procedure for voting or on a particular voting. It is possible to establish a voting consortium in which some of the shareholders will agree that before the voting at the general meeting itself they will meet separately and will decide by a majority vote on how they will vote at the general meeting (or some of the members of a consortium will be granted the right of veto). Even the shareholders who did not make up the majority are then under a duty to vote at the general meeting as it was decided by the majority of the consortium. Voting arrangements where shareholders undertake to vote in accordance with the instruction of another shareholder, or in compliance with the majority vote of the consortium of shareholders are usually admissible.

The validity of agreements on the exercise of voting rights whereby the shareholder undertakes to observe a voting instruction of a third person is not admitted without reservations. The validity of agreements on the exercise of voting rights concluded with third persons should not be excluded *a priori*. Even the uniformity principle, or a prohibition to split the share or a general impossibility to transfer to a third person the voting rights should not prevent a contractual agreement under which a shareholder is bound to abide by a third person's voting instruction.[44] Sometimes, such an agreement has reasonable grounds (for example, an undertaking not to remove a person, without a due reason, who is a member of a supervisory body delegated by the funding creditor). However, agreements whereby the exercise of the voting rights would be decided upon by a person that is precluded from their exercise (the company itself, members of its bodies), or that would be excluded from the exercise of the voting rights if such a person were a shareholder will obviously not be admissible. An agreement to fulfil the third person's instructions could collide in certain cases with a duty of corporate loyalty of the shareholder that should prevail over his contractual obligation *inter partes*. In such cases it is necessary to realize that the Czech law[45], taking the German law for its model, contains a ban on binding instructions interfering with the governance of registered companies. Hence, if another shareholder or a third person would attempt at giving binding instructions to the company's bodies, through various contractual structures, concerning the company's governance, it should be treated only as a recommendation that may be rejected by a member of the statutory body within the framework of a due care concept. At the same time, however, the person issuing such instructions exposes itself to the company law, including a possible conclusion that it may

44 Other way round, for example, the decision of the Appellate Court in Warsaw as of 5.1.2006 – I ACa 630/05, under which the binding of a shareholder's a voting by instructions of another person is contrary to the prohibition to split the business share, and is therefore void. This conclusion of the Court is, however, criticised in the Polish doctrine (see Part B – Poland note C.I.1. for further details). Even the Austrian practice arrived at a similar conclusion in relation to a partial assignment of the voting rights from one business share to another person, see the judgment OGH of 13 October 2011, case ref. 6Ob202/10i. See Austria B.II. for further details.
45 See Czech Republic III.1. for further details.

be harmful effect that may result in a duty to compensate damages or to assume liability. However, if such instructions are issued within the existing concern, they are basically binding and the statutory body of the controlled entity may reject them only if the harm caused by them was not supposed to be remedied in terms of the company law.

Agreements on the exercise of the voting rights are also connected with the problem of vote buying. It remains unclear if an agreement on the exercise of the voting rights should be valid if the shareholder was supposed to obtain a special reward (consideration) for a particular way of voting. Some assume that such an agreement should be invalid on the ground of a prohibition to split the business share, or a ban on the "assignment" of voting rights. In the German doctrine, the invalidity of agreements on the exercise of voting rights in a private limited liability company is derived from the contravention with good morals in the case where the shareholder undertakes to vote for a specific reward.[46] This is motivated not only by the effort to remove a corruptive aspect but especially by the protection of a duty of the shareholder's loyalty toward the company. If the shareholder votes on the ground of special advantaged rendered, he is doing so by preferring his own benefit to the benefit of the company and his exercise of the voting right is considered as being unfair. The general rule should be that the shareholder must always prefer the benefit of the company to its own benefit. It would be unfair, however, for the shareholder to prefer its own benefit at the expense of the other shareholders and the company itself. Similar, the agreement on the exercise of the voting rights for a reward may not result in avoiding the voting rights assignment ban, especially in the case of long-term agreements. However, the invalidity of the shareholders' agreement itself need not inevitably make a decision of the company's body void for this particular reason, but an unfair voting should not be taken into account.

The legal consequences of the breach of agreements on the exercise will always be limited to the contractual level. In our opinion, an agreement on the exercise of the voting rights is not an agreement on the future voting at the general meeting and it should not be governed by the rules on the agreement to enter into a future contract. In particular, it should not be possible to achieve, by bringing an action before the court, to replace or manifest the will of a shareholder during the voting at the general meeting. The reason for that is a breach of an agreement to exercise the voting rights is accomplished by voting contrary

46 In the area of the law of public limited liability companies/joint stock companies the situation is simpler since the sale of the votes of shareholders is a public law transgression/administrative offence (pursuant to Section 405 AktG), and hence is void due to its contravention of the law. See Germany B.III. for further details.

thereto, or by not voting where voting should be effected. A decision of the court replacing the manifestation of the will as a result of the breach of an agreement to enter into a future contract will be operative for the future where by its becoming effective it will replace a legal act which was not executed (in the case of an agreement to enter into a future contract, such an act is the conclusion of the agreement itself). As a result of such a decision, a backward change of one manifestation of will (voting contrary to the agreement) to another manifestation of will (voting in accordance with the agreement) may not occur. On the contrary, the claimant will only be able to seek the performance of the obligation to vote in a certain way. If the procedural law admits the approach according to which a judgment imposing a duty to perform a particular act will always replace such an act/manifestation of will even regardless of a possible substantive-law absence of an option to replace such an act/manifestation of will so that such a final judgment should be taken into account at the later voting at the general meeting as an act of voting of the obligated shareholder.

## 2. Agreements on the appointment of members of corporate bodies (*appointment agreements*)

Shareholders take part in the company governance especially by the exercise of their rights at the general meeting, but also outside the general meeting. This will include, in particular, agreements on the ways of submission of proposals, procedures for deciding on certain question, for example, in form of a preliminary negotiation in a particular body, but also in deciding on the staffing company's bodies. Shareholders may, for example, agree that the company's bodies will be composed of a particular number of persons appointed by particular parties. In contrast to a common agreement on the exercise of the voting rights in this case it will not be an agreement on the election of a particular person to an office, but also an undertaking to agree with such a person as will be proposed by a particular party to a shareholders' agreement. A potential candidate need not be (and neither will it actually be) specified. That candidate does not have a position of third party (beneficiary) and cannot by himself invoke the performance of such an agreement, or claims resulting from their breach. We may derive from the fact that the parties perceive the candidacy of a particular person as subject of their legal relationship, rather than taking a candidate as the subject of that legal relationship. The rules applicable to the agreement in favour of a third person will not apply.

### 3. Agreements on profit-sharing or other benefits in favour of shareholders

Shareholders may also agree on rules whereby they will govern the company's performance in their own favour. This includes, basically, dividends, settlement shares or other admissible performance in favour of shareholders. Such agreements will become effective only after all the shareholders agree. This will not be a disposition with the right to a share in profit (by assigning the right to pay the dividend), which is sometimes restricted by the law but it is a non-corporate agreement on the changes of the shares of profit or other performance. Such an agreement could also be a part of the articles of association. However, even the shareholders' agreement cannot exclude or amend the rules restricting the performance of the company in favour of the shareholders (a prohibition to return a contribution, prohibition or restriction to pay a dividend or other equity capital of the company), that are laid down in order to protect the company its shareholders or its creditors. If decision-making on the performance in favour of shareholders is in competence of a general meeting (profit sharing/dividend), this part of the shareholders' agreement will basically qualify as an agreement on the exercise of voting rights.[47] In other cases, where the performance is considerably independent of decisions of a general meeting (for example, conclusion of agreements with shareholders, agreements to decrease the right to a settlement share or functionally equivalent performance related to termination of a share in a company), such agreements will be different from classic agreements on the exercise of the voting rights because they may also be considered as a certain waiver of rights, even toward the company itself.

### 4. Shareholders' agreements on the funding of the company

In shareholders' agreements parties may also agree on how they will participate in the (further) funding of the company (e.g., conditions of additional contributions in excess of the contributions to the registered/share capital, granting donations or loans to the company as well as the mode and extent by which they will take part in the changes of the registered/share capital). As it has been suggested, such arrangements are often connected with the agreements concluded within the process of handling a threatening bankruptcy of a company[48], although they sometimes also take the form of an "unenforceable" *comfort letter*.

**47** See note J.I.1.
**48** See note E.VIII.

For example, it may be an agreement on the nominal increase of the registered/share capital from the sources of the company and on the mode of division of proportions of their share after a possible increase of the share/registered capital. The shareholders could consent that they will agree providing the company with other funds, for example, by efficiently increasing the share/registered capital in the case where the company is in the crisis. The parties are not excluded from agreeing on a division of the extent of liabilities among themselves to pay the contribution. The obligation to pay the funds may also be an obligation to provide the funds either in form of internal, as well as external resources. A legal approach to these arrangements may be complicated and it will obviously depend on the kind of pooling up of the share capital to which the shareholders commit themselves and the degree of legally binding force or legal consequences of such an arrangement. We may take into consideration an agreement to enter into a future contract (an undertaking to conclude a loan contract, but also an undertaking to amend the articles of association), but also a contract containing a condition precedent (a loan whose effect is conditioned by a certain critical financial position of the company). In the above cases the company should itself be a party to the shareholders' agreement. In the case where the shareholders undertake to fund the company we could also consider an agreement in favour of a third party where the company would be such a third party beneficiary. In that case the company itself would not be a party to the shareholders' agreement. It is also possible that the company, already as a party to the shareholders' agreement would be directly entitled as beneficiary under such an agreement. A complicate nature of the forced implementation of a funding obligation will depend on the character of the obligation assumed. The company as beneficiary could be entitled toward the shareholders bound to render the company funds from a loan or to conclude with the company a loan contract. In such a case, it will be a classic contractual relationship. A more complicated situation will occur if the shareholders undertake in the shareholders' agreement to pay up new contributions. A consent to the shareholders' agreement itself will not amount to the assumption of the obligation to pay up a new contribution, not even a conditional one because the new contribution will mean a change of the amount of the registered/share capital which must be first decided by a general meeting. Thus, the shareholders' agreement itself does not establish the company's entitlement to be paid a contribution that it would be able to enforce by an action in court. The agreement on the conditions and the extent of the participation in the changes of the registered capital binds the shareholders involved to vote in a particular way on the issue in question at the general meeting. Such an undertaking, however, has only a contractual nature. It is a contractual undertaking aimed to effect certain corporate conduct. A third person may also become a party to the agreement that may afterward request from the shareholders to issue a decision to increase the registered capital under the conditions of the agreement and to enable such a third person to become a shareholder of the company.

## II. Shareholders' agreements related to the transfer of shares

Shareholders' agreements will very often involve arrangements related to various restrictions of the sale or another kind of a transfer of the share in the company (business share, shares of stock), especially in form of various pre-emptive rights, options, restrictions or determinations of potential transfers.

### 1. Arrangements related to the transfers of shares provided in the articles of association

When determining the issues related to the transfer of the share in the company, discussions are focused on whether such an arrangement has corporate or contractual consequences. The conceptual distinguishing between corporate and contractual consequences, however, is not quite precise and it is obscuring the problem in the corporate context rather than clearing it up. Contractual consequences of a breach of the arrangement on the restriction of transfer will traditionally mean the *inter partes* consequences without binding or otherwise relating the third person, assignee of an object or a right thereto while being in breach of a given restriction. The corporate law consequences of the arrangement will mean two different things. First, the binding force or effect of such an arrangement also toward a third person is not involved in the arrangement, for example, toward the assignee of a share. Second, the invalidity of the act done in breach of an obligation. It is generally assumed that if a particular arrangement has only contractual consequences, it is related only to the contractual parties and its breach does not result in nullity. Nullity is not associated with the substantive (factual) nature of an arrangement, most probably, because it is a sanction or legal consequence which is also affecting the person not involved in the arrangement. In company law, however, we should not get lured by the simplification of the law of contract, and not only because the articles of association or the articles of association bind *per se* each assignee of a share, i. e. it is not possible to talk about a third person not involved in the articles of association at all. Moreover, the different consequences of the agreement to restrict the right of assignment of a share in the company need not result from a different understanding of the qualities of that agreement or the consequences of its breach (corporate or contractual), but they may be associated with different qualities of the given object of the assignment (assignability as a property of the object). For example, the agreement to prohibit further transfer of ownership (of a thing) has completely different consequences of its breach than the agreement on the prohibition of further assignment of a claim. The reason is not the substantive or contractual nature of these agreements but modification of the content of the given legal position (right of ownership, claim). Although ownership may not be changed by agreement of subjects, the content (properties) of a claim may be changed in such a way. It is possible to create such a claim which will extinguish upon the assignment. A contractual prohibition of the assignment could represent just that type of agreement. Even that, however, should not become grounds for the nullity of the assignment of a claim, but only for the liability for defects (non-existence of the object of the assignment). This should be taken into account also in the relation to the share in the company. The corporate or contractual consequences are thus more of a description of the functioning and effect rather than the reason of such consequences. A change of perspective is therefore necessary. The point is not whether a breach of such an agreement has corporate or contractual consequence, but rather if it is possible to change, in the articles of association, the properties of the share in the company (shares of stock, business shares). The admissibility of such an arrangement should be measured by the fact if the law allows to "close" the company and its shareholders' structure (closed company), or to determine the conditions of the assignability of its shares. The limit would be a ban on the closing of the company (public limited liability companies). If it is possible to exclude or restrict the assignability of a share in the company it is also possible to determine in the articles of association a special mechanism related to the assignment of that share. Such a mechanism would qualify as the exclusion or restriction of the assignability of a business share or a share of stock.

More correct is therefore the approach of the Czech Supreme Court,[49] also adopted by a part of the Slovak case law,[50] under which the right of pre-emption to a business share determined in the articles of association is treated as a restriction of the assignability of a business share. An offer made to the other shareholders to purchase that share is therefore considered as the objective pre-

**49** Judgment of the Supreme Court of the Czech Republic of 4 April 2000, case ref. 29 Cdo 2811/99; See Czech Republic III.3. for further details.

**50** Judgment of the Regional Court in Bratislava of 1 October 2013, case ref. 2 Cob /238/2012; See Slovakia D.II. for further details; see also Belgium note 30.

requisite of the assignability. This approach seems to be more persuasive compared to the approach of the Slovak Supreme Court according to which a reach of the right of pre-emption to shares of stock has only contractual consequences.[51] The distinctions made by the Slovak Supreme Court between the *substantive* and contractual consequence of a particular arrangement obviously resulted from the application of the concept whose consequences – in the non-corporate world – are usually distinguished on such grounds (pre-emptive right). Such distinctions will not help us if the shareholders would include in the articles of association a concept that is typical in the private law, for example, an obligation to inform others about the intended assignment, time specification of a possibility to transfer the shares of stock (open or closed period of a year), various options, etc. However, this shall not mean that the parties would not be allowed to determine, even in the articles of association, such rules to dispose of their shares in the company whose breach would only have contractual consequences.

With each particular provision of the articles of association related to the transfer of the share in the company we have to decide if it amounts to corporate restriction of the assignment of a share or an arrangement of parallel contractual (or even substantive or *substantivized*) regime. We should expect that by placing a particular arrangement related to the transfer of the share into a corporate document the parties intended to achieve its corporate effect, hence (in the extent admissible for a particular company) to condition or restrict the transfer of the share in the company, and not only to attain such consequences with which this institute is – in non-corporate world – commonly associated. Hence, they changed the properties of the share in the company. And therefore, if nothing else results from a particular arrangement in the articles of association it will be a condition of assignability a breach of which should make the assignment ineffective. Moreover, not every arrangement related to the assignment of the share should be considered as corporate restriction of the assignment – i.e. as corporate agreement on the change of the properties of the share. Shareholders are free to incorporate in the articles of association such a rule that will not be considered as restriction of the assignability of the share in the company, but only as a specific duty of a shareholder having contractual consequences. Nevertheless, that should not be presumed, but should be specifically proved. In other words, from the fact that the shareholders included in the articles of association a particularly named concept related to the assignment of the share in the company (for example, pre-emptive right), we should not automatically assume that

51 See Slovakia D.III. for further details.

we should apply the legal regulation of the consequences of its breach. That also means that if shareholders included an atypical concept in the articles of association admissible on the ground of their contractual freedom (for example, duties to inform connected with the intended assignment), but it should be determined if it qualifies as corporate restriction of the assignment or only as additional contractual regime.

## 2. Shareholders' agreements on the transfers of shares

The regulation of the rights and duties related to the assignment of the share in the company contained in the articles of association should be distinguished from the regulation of such rights and duties contained in the shareholders' agreement. Corporate practise knows a lot of such covenants, such as pre-emptive rights, rights of re-purchase (specified mechanisms for assignments of others), mandatory assignments and various agreements to enter into future contracts, options, drag-along or tag-along arrangements, regularly connected with various supportive mechanisms of price determination (shoot-out etc.). Subsidiary arrangements related to the assignment would have corporate effect and could be considered as restrictions or conditions of the assignment of the share only if they met a condition of formal corporate document, i.e. if they were contained in the articles of association. However, the cases where the articles of association have been "pierced" in an admissible extent will also be considered as covenants included in articles of association. As has resulted from the above mentioned, the arrangement standing outside a corporate instrument may not change the properties of the share in the company. We therefore have to consider their consequences according to general rules of the law of contract distinguishing between the traditional categories of corporate and contractual consequences. Such arrangements have always only contractual consequences in the shareholders' agreement and they will not bind third parties unless those became parties to the shareholders' agreement. Consequences of a breach of the contractual obligation related to the assignment of the share in the company will manifest itself only in the contractual sphere (as a rule, by a duty to pay damages or a contractual fine) and only exceptionally also in form of absolute nullity in the case of a breach of the right to re-purchase.

## 3. Collisions between shareholders' agreements and articles of association related to the assignment of shares

It may happen that a particular contractual provision for the assignment of a share in the company contained in the shareholders' agreement will collide with the statutory provisions related to the assignment of such a share or with the articles of association. A situation may occur where the shareholders will agree in the shareholder's agreement a certain limitation of the right to dispose of the share in the company, although they may not take into consideration any such limitation in the articles of association or the articles of association, or they will explicitly determine in these documents that no limitation of the assignment exists. Collision of these provisions will result in the nullity of the shareholders' agreement and the rules agreed therein regulating the right of disposition of the share in the company. Consequences of violation of one or another will become manifest in their separated worlds. It will therefore be possible that the assignment of the share will become effective; however, a breach of the shareholders' agreement establishing the right to damages will occur. Shareholders' agreements may also serve to agree the rules that would be inadmissible in the articles of association. Such practise is manifested in the arrangements relating to the assignment of the share in the company. In relation to this we refer to the interpretation of the relationship between the shareholders' agreement and the articles of association. A short excursion in this respect should be made to the German case law where a decision of the Federal Court of Justice was passed,[52] which laid down that an agreement between the shareholder and the joint stock company will be void if the shareholder is imposed a duty to transfer its shares to the joint stock company free of charge although the shareholder itself acquired them for a financial consideration.[53] It seems, however, that the reason of such a prohibition is just a coincidence of circumstances and the transaction context (a duty to transfer the shares in the company free of charge if those were acquired of a financial consideration), rather than a conceptual prohibition of an "ancillary" agreement on a mandatory duty to transfer the share in the company in favour of the company that is subject to strict conditions within the meaning of the German law on the joint stock companies (public limited liability companies).

52 Federal Court of Justice as of 22.1.2013 – II ZR 80/10, NZG 2013, 220.

53 German law on the joint stock companies allows that a joint stock company should be forced to receive/take over the shares *(Zwangseinziehung)* – § 237 German Stock Corporation Act (AktG).

## H. Shareholders' agreements regulating to the enforcement of rights and duties; dispute resolution

Shareholders' agreements also contain provisions related to dispute resolution and enforcement (execution) of rights and duties of shareholders. In such cases shareholders basically try to minimalize the risks of a violation of duties resulting from the shareholders' agreements, either by exerting factual and economic pressure to perform them or by ensuring various legal simplifications during their implementation. The aim is to achieve that the exercise of the rights and execution of duties should not be decided in ordinary proceedings before a court, but rather that an *ex ante* solution should be offered that will exclude a possibility to bring an action in a particular case or will diminish the motivation of the persons concerned to initiate such a dispute, because a lengthy court proceedings may cause long-term damage to the operation of the company. The parties to the shareholders' agreement have a wide range of tools available to reach that goal. These include arrangements on self-executory mechanisms of enforcement of shareholders' agreements (power of attorney to perform the rights of the shareholders, including an authorisation to transfer the share in the company while some them being already contained in the statutory law).

Arbitration clauses are common practice in shareholders' agreement. Disputes between shareholders, companies and its directors are generally arbitrable.[54] The inclusion of an arbitration clause into the shareholders' agreement underlines its contractual nature. However, some specific types of corporate disputes are either non-arbitrable are only arbitrable subject to specific limitations and conditions (declaration of nullity of a shareholder meeting resolution, disqualification of directors or disputes about liquidation or winding up of the company).[55] Parties to a shareholders' agreement might seek arbitration in order to enforce voting rights agreements. A possibility to declare the resolution of a shareholders meeting in breach of a voting right agreement null by an arbitral award might be an important step towards the enforceability of such covenants. However, the arbitrability of such claims is controversial. First of all, the declaration on the nullity of a shareholders meeting resolution has *erga omnes* effects while arbitration produces *inter partes* effects only. Unlike a stat-

54 *Born* International Commercial Arbitration, 2nd 2014, p. 1029 and the case law and literature cited therein.

55 *Born* (supra note 55), p. 1029.

utory court, an arbitral tribunal can have no powers vis-à-vis persons that are not bound by the arbitration agreement. Nonetheless, such limitation does not render the arbitrability of such matter impossible. Since shareholders can revoke or amend the resolutions of their meeting, there is no compelling reason for such disputes to be non-arbitrable *per se*. The conditions under which such disputes are arbitrable have been well developed by German[56] and Austrian[57] case law and legal literature.[58]

Austrian courts and literature adopted a more streamlined positive attitude towards the arbitrability of such disputes already in 1950.[59] In Germany, two landmark cases are to be brought into attention. In 1996, the Federal Supreme Court affirmed the general arbitrability of disputes for declaratory relief on the nullity of shareholder meeting resolutions.[60] The particular conditions necessary for the arbitrability of such disputes have been elaborated in a Federal Supreme Court ruling from 2009[61] and were confirmed in 2017[62]. These conditions ought to provide enough arguments for an *erga omnes*-like effect of an arbitral award. The most relevant ones might be helpful reflected by other jurisdictions as well. According to the conditions set by the German Federal Supreme court:

- All shareholders must be parties to the arbitral proceeding. All shareholders must be informed of the proceeding and must have the right and the possibility to participate in the proceeding.
- The appointment of the tribunal must be left to an independent appointing authority or the shareholders must have the right to participate in the appointment of the tribunal.

---

**56** German Federal Supreme Court as of 6.4.2017 – I ZB 23/16 (*Schiedsfähigkeit III*), NJW 2017, 657; German Federal Supreme Court as of 6.4.2009 – II ZR 255/08 (*Schiedsfähigkeit II*), BGHZ 180, 221 = NJW 2009, 1962; German Federal Supreme Court as of 29.3.1996 – II ZR 124/95 (*Schiedsfähigkeit I*), BGHZ 132, 278 = NJW 1996, 1753.

**57** Austrian Supreme Court as of 16.12.2013 – 6 Ob 43/13 m, Zak 2014/148 S 78 – Zak 2014, 78; Austrian Supreme Court as of 13.6.1990 – 7 Ob 548/93; Austrian Supreme Court as of 29.6.2006 – 6 Ob 145/06a.

**58** See e.g. *Duve* Arbitration of Corporate Law Disputes in Germany, in: Böckstiegel/Kröll/Nacimiento (eds.), Arbitration in Germany – The Model Law in Practice 2007, p. 1006; *Pitkowitz* The Arbitrability of Corporate Disputes under Austrian Law – Still Open Questions? In: Austrian Yearbook on International Arbitration 2014, Vienna 2014, p. 33.

**59** Ruling of the Austrian Supreme Court, file No 2Ob276/50. repeatedly confirmed afterwards. See rulings of the Austrian Supreme Court, file No 7Ob221/98w; file No 6Ob145/06a and decisions cited above.

**60** German Federal Supreme Court, supra note 57 (*Schiedsfähigkeit I*).

**61** German Federal Supreme Court, supra note 57 (*Schiedsfähigkeit II*).

**62** German Federal Supreme Court, supra note 57 (*Schiedsfähigkeit III*).

- The setup of the arbitral proceeding must prevent parallel proceedings and irreconcilable rulings on the same subject. It is thus required that all potential disputes concerning one particular resolution are concentrated in the same proceedings.
- It is advisable that all shareholders and the company itself including its bodies are parties to the arbitration agreement and thus bound by it.

In Germany, these conditions were incorporated into the model arbitration clause and the rules prepared by the German Institute for Arbitration and its Arbitral Rules.[63] Similarly, arbitration clauses are strengthening the enforcement possibilities of contractual arrangements concerning the rights and obligations of parties related to the sale of their shares (rights of first refusal, pre-emption rights, piggy-back clauses, put or call options and other arrangements).

63 Deutsche Institution für Schiedsgerichtsbarkeit (DIS-Ergänzende Regeln fur gesellschaftsrechtliche Streitigkeiten 2009) available under www.disarb.org.

Stanislava Černá

# Relationship of Shareholders' Agreements to the Management of a Company

**Table of Content**



## A. Introduction

Shareholders' agreements (*pacte d'actionaires, Aktionärbindungsverträge, Gesellschaftervereinbarungen)* are an important phenomenon affecting the operation of joint-stock companies. They have emerged from the practice, where a vast array of options are available under the law of contract to define the mutual relationships between shareholders or, taking a wider approach, the relationships of shareholders to the joint-stock company, under both heteronomous law provided for by statutes and autonomous law set out in the articles of association. Shareholders' agreements make it possible to "detail" the mutual relationships between shareholders to an extent that corporate law as such does not allow. Shareholders' agreements deal with various aspects of a shareholder's participation in a company, thus establishing the various criteria for their classification. From the perspective of the underlying legal regulation, one of the basic criteria centres on the issue of whether shares are treated as things or as relative rights which pertain to a shareholder relationship and are incorporated into a share. The former group comprises such agreements under which a shareholder undertakes to dispose, in future, of the shares in a specific agreed manner, for example, by complying with a pre-emption or redemption clause, by following the

**Prof. JUDr. Stanislava Černá,** CSc. The Faculty of Law, Charles University

https://doi.org/10.1515/9783110517026-003

steps taken by a majority shareholder who decides to transfer the shares (a drag along clause) or, conversely, by ensuring that an investor buys, in addition to the majority stake, also the shares of minority shareholders (a tag along clause), by accepting a takeover bid or by undertaking to reject a takeover bid, or to not make a takeover bid to the other shareholders (a standstill agreement), or to not put a charge on the shares, etc. From a general perspective, this group of agreements restricts the freedom of shareholders to dispose of their assets in future. This is reflected in the applicable legal rules. Essentially, it suffices to apply solely the law of contract, with a relatively broad contractual autonomy reflecting the freedom of general contract law. A similar approach was adopted by the Swiss Parliament which refused to include Article 695a on shareholders' agreements in stock corporation law (as part of the Obligations Act), arguing that the provision did not belong there as shareholders' agreements were governed purely by contract law.[1] A far greater complexity can be observed in the legal rules governing the latter group of shareholders' agreements, covering the rights attached to shares, i.e., the relative proprietary or non-proprietary rights of shareholders with respect to the joint-stock company. The underlying legal rules are based not only on contract law, but also on stock corporation law which puts limits on the freedom to exercise shareholder rights (for example, prohibiting the transfer of the voting right), as well as on the so-called autonomous law contained in the articles of association (for example, the rules governing a qualified majority or unanimity for the adoption of certain decisions). The freedom of contract in concluding such agreements is intrinsically more limited.

Both groups of agreements can be combined, which is used in practice when a strong investor joins the joint-stock company, when a company is being transformed, when a holding joint-stock company is being formed in a controlling or dominant position, as well as for other purposes. The following text will concentrate on the latter group of shareholders' agreements, in particular those that affect the manner in which a joint-stock company is managed.

## B. Pre-incorporation Shareholders' Agreements

Shareholders' agreements governing the rights attached to shares are primarily concluded in order to establish, strengthen, or alter the influence of contracting parties on the management of a (multi-person) company. Of particular relevance in this respect are the so-called **pre-incorporation agreements** (*metastatutární*

1 *Böckli* Schweitzer Aktienrecht, $4^{th}$ edition, Schulthess 2009, p. 1536.

*dohody*) which are concluded before the registration (more specifically, before the foundation) of a multi-person joint-stock company and which anticipate the provisions of articles of associations, particularly those dealing with filling (elected) management posts. Such agreements are more effective if stock corporation law makes it possible to remove a member of an elected body without giving any reason (*ad nutum*). Such rules are rather rare in Europe. For example, in Germany it is possible to remove in this way only the members of the supervisory board, whereas the members of the board of directors enjoy a more stable position as they are removable during their term of office only for important reasons. Such important reasons can include a gross breach of duties, incompetence to carry out management responsibilities, and loss of trust at the general meeting, unless this results from clearly unobjective reasons (s. 84 (3) AktG). In France it is possible to remove, without giving any reasons, members of the administrative board elected by the general meeting (Article 225–18 of the Commercial Code). Likewise, the administrative board can remove the general manager and, on the general manager's motion, the acting general managers. However, where the removal is not supported by reasonable grounds (*juste motif*), typically involving a breach of duties or organisational reasons, such persons are entitled to damages (Article 225-55 of the Commercial Code). If the French company has a dualistic structure, even the members of the board of directors can be removed without giving any reasons, by the general meeting or (if stipulated in the articles of association) by the supervisory board. They are also entitled to damages if they were removed without reasonable grounds (Article 225–61 of the Commercial Code).[2] Under English law, members of the board of directors can be removed without giving any reasons as well. The Companies Act (s. 169) sets out rules concerning a protest by a board member against such removal. Most American states also allow removal of a board member *ad nutum*, by making it possible to detail the conditions of removal in the articles of association. With a certain degree of simplification we may note that where members of elected bodies are removable without giving any reasons, shareholders may only be delayed by the mandatory time limits for convening a general meeting if they wish to replace the members of such bodies.

In order to regulate the influence of shareholders on the composition of management bodies within a joint-stock company, corporate law of certain countries offers the option to issue shares with multiple voting rights. Such shares are common primarily in corporate law of American states which regulate classes

2 *Charveriat/Couret/Zabala* Groupes de sociétés. Mémento pratique. 2015–2016, Editions Francis Lefebvre 2015, pp. 93, 94.

and sub-classes of shares rather flexibly.[3] In accordance with MBCA (1969) and RMBCA (1984), legislation of most American states, as well as the Delaware General Corporation Act, follow the basic rule of "one share (with no par value), one vote", expressly allowing derogations for companies in their articles of association. The option to differentiate shares according to the voting rights attached is taken up primarily by private joint-stock companies. By contrast, quoted companies usually respect the rule of proportionality of votes. This stems from the long-respected opinion of the New York Stock Exchange, and in particular the Securities Exchange Commission ("SEC"), which frowned upon any imbalance between voting rights and the capital share in a company from the 1920s to ca. 1980s (see SEC rule 19c-4, containing the principle of "one share, one vote"). In the 1980s, as defence against hostile takeover bids, shares were issued to give voting advantage primarily to company managers. The proportionality rule became significantly eroded[4] under the pressure of competitor stock markets (Nasdaq, AMEX), and in particular the Court of Appeal decision[5] which stated that the SEC lacked the power to ban quoting companies in the US with shares excluding, restricting or differentiating voting rights, because it was up to the individual states to regulate voting rights, rather than up to the federal bodies.

Compared to American stock corporation law, European continental law has been rather cautious as regards shares with multiple voting rights, owing to some negative experience acquired while using them. French regulation currently allows shares with double voting rights (*action à droit de vote double*), on the condition that the share has been fully paid-up and the shareholder has had an interest in the company for at least two years as evidenced in the shareholder register, unless a longer period was stipulated in the articles of association or in the decision of the general meeting (Article 225–123 of the Commercial Code). In addition, the Commercial Code contains provisions about preference shares (Article 228–11) stipulating that such shares, unlike their name suggests, may be issued with or without voting rights. In Switzerland, the articles of association may stipulate that one vote will be attached to each share, regardless of its par value. The shares with a lower par value than others, while having the same number of votes attached to them, must be registered shares made out

3 *Merkt/Gothel* US-Amerikanisches Gesellschaftsrecht, 2nd edition. Recht und Wirtschaft GmbH, Frankfurt am Main 2006, p. 277.

4 *von de Crone* Stimmrechtsaktien: Eine juristische und ökonomische Analyse, SZW/RSDA No.2 from 2010, p. 105 et seq.

5 US Court of Appeals for the District of Columbia Circuit. Business Roundtable v. SEC, 905 F2d 406, 407 (D.C.Cir 1990).

to the owner's name and be fully paid-up. The total par value of the other shares must not exceed ten times the par value of the "privileged shares" (*action à droit de vote privilegié),* which creates a limit to the advantages offered by these shares (Article 693 of the Code of Obligations). In Germany, it is not permitted to issue shares with multiple voting rights or shares with limited voting rights (s. 12 (2) of the AktG). Likewise, Austrian stock corporation law does not permit shares with multiple voting rights either (s. 12 (3) of the AktG).

In their traditional form, shares with multiple voting rights allow considerable flexibility. They can namely be construed both "generally", i.e., for all decisions of a general meeting, or they may be differentiated based on the subject matter of the decision at the general meeting. Taking the differentiation even further, the voting advantage can be applied depending on whether the shareholders are voting at a general meeting on a nominee for the first, second, third, or another post in the board of directors, the supervisory board, or the administrative board. Stock corporation law does not preclude a temporal limitation on multiple voting rights. The advantage of this corporate solution is that it prevents difficulties which often arise from non-compliance with shareholders' agreements. By contrast, the disadvantage consists in the rather "static" arrangement which fixes a particular distribution of powers that can be modified only by amending the articles of association. Therefore, it is possible to combine this option with a shareholders' agreement stipulating that a shareholder will use the multiple voting rights or, depending on the circumstances, will refrain from using such rights during the election or removal of members of bodies.

Potentially, shareholders may exercise their influence on the composition of elected bodies through shares with the so-called designation rights (*Entsendungsrecht*). In countries where this option is possible (primarily in the American and English legal systems), a particular post in an elected body of a joint stock company is filled with no involvement of the general meeting, in accordance with the nomination rights attached to a share. Germany and Austria have specific provisions governing designation rights (*Entsendungsrecht*) for the supervisory board of a joint-stock company. The original purpose was to enshrine a special position of the state or another public corporation in a joint-stock company. The first alternative as set out under the German regulation of the designation rights is of a purely obligational nature: the right to designate nominees for the supervisory board is vested in a specific shareholder and is not transferable. The second German option is of a (limited) corporate nature: the designation right can only be attached to registered shares whose transfer must be approved by a body of the company (s. 101 (2) of the AktG). German law does not allow the possibility of filling the posts in the supervisory board without any involvement of the general meeting because the number of designated nominees may not exceed one third of the members of the supervisory board.

Generally speaking, legal regulation need not expressly provide for shares with designation rights. The possibility to allow this type of shares in the articles of association depends on whether stock corporation law explicitly or implicitly restricts the manner in which members of elected bodies may be appointed; in other words, whether the posts in elected bodies may be filled otherwise than by being elected at a general meeting. A very liberal approach can be seen in the UK's Companies Act 2006 which lacks a competence provision that most European continental systems have. The UK's provisions about the competence of the general meeting are rather modest. The Companies Act 2006 does not regulate the appointment of the board members. Under the Model Articles for Public Companies[6] which apply to the internal structure unless the company's own articles of association provide otherwise, a board member is appointed by the general meeting (the so-called direct authorisation) or by the board itself. It is noteworthy that these rules allow election of a board member by a group of shareholders or the attachment of a designation right to a share.

## C. Voting agreements

As an alternative to the above-mentioned corporate solution, or in combination therewith, it is possible to use the law of obligations as a foundation in which the influence on the company, and specifically, on the election and removal of members of bodies (and thus indirectly on its management) will be rooted. This solution is based on voting agreements. Such agreements may be concluded *ad hoc*, designed to exert influence on the decision of the supreme body only on a single occasion. But as a legal tool enabling the joint influence on company management to be exercised on a regular basis, they can also be used for securing continuous influence. These agreements generally stipulate the rules under which the "joint" shareholders will reach agreement (*agreement to agree)* about voting on specific topics at the general meeting.[7] The specific content of such agreements is broad, as the contractual terms may be quite varied, including individual voting as well as common proxies, relatively free contractual relations as well as formalised voting trusts, etc. In general terms, all these arrange-

6 Model Articles for Public Companies, s. 20. Available at: www.legislation.gov.uk.

7 *Merkt/Goethel* US-amerikanisches Gesellschaftsrecht, 2[nd] revised edition, Verlag Recht und Wirtschaft GmbH, Frankfurt am Main, 2006, p. 356.

ments share an associative character. In other words, where shareholders become associated in order to exert joint influence, by exercising their voting right at the general meeting, on the composition of elected bodies in a company (and thus on the management thereof), such agreement essentially takes the form of an association. This applies even more so if the shareholders undertake, for a specific purpose, not only to pool their activities, i.e., the exercise of their voting rights, and to provide synergy in drawing up the draft resolutions of the general meeting and in analysing the consequences of the proposed decision, but also if they undertake to provide property (for example, equipment for the organisation of common meetings). This gives rise to a so-called inside (undisclosed) partnership (*Innengesellschaft*),[8] to use the terminology of German or Swiss law. Such partnership sets up an internal (shadow) structure which is clearly not reflected in the organisational structure of the joint-stock company; consequently, it cannot be regarded as its body or as a shareholder body. Yet its influence on the management of the joint-stock company is significant, sometimes even crucial. In practice, major shareholders in large joint-stock companies in particular set out their mutual rights and obligations in great detail in shareholders' agreements. The ensuing corporate (and logical) consequence of such (purely obligational) agreement is that a rebuttable legal presumption of acting in concert applies.

It is unclear to what extent corporate law is reflected in the purely obligational area, and to what extent the statutory and constitutional rules on the votes necessary for the adoption of a decision at the general meeting have an impact on the decision-making of shareholders in the inside partnership. Specifically, will the partners of an inside partnership be bound by their decision on the manner in which their voting right should be exercised at the general meeting if this decision was adopted (merely) by a simple majority of votes, although the law requires a qualified majority or unanimity for this decision to be adopted at the general meeting? And has a partner breached an obligation under the agreement on inside partnership if he or she voted at the general meeting on a draft resolution for which a qualified majority is required inconsistently with the decision that had been adopted in the inside partnership by a simple majority? The solution to this issue has both a theoretical and a practical significance, in particular where a contractual fine may be imposed for the breach of an obligation to vote consistently with the "inside" agreement.

This can be illustrated by the decision of the German Federal Court of Justice (BGH of 24 November 2008 – II ZR 116/08) in a case adjudicated by the Oberlan-

---

8 *Böckli* Schweitzer Aktienrecht, 4th edition, Schulthess 2009, p. 1226 et seq., p. 1298.

desgericht (OLG) in Karlsruhe. The case centred on a family joint-stock company which had been transformed from a limited liability company. Its shareholders concluded an agreement on a protective partnership which was designed to ensure a common procedure for exercising rights in the family joint-stock company. They undertook to vote at the general meeting according to a prior decision of the inside partnership adopted by a simple majority of votes. At the general meeting where the decision was to be made about the restructuring of the joint-stock company, a part of the shareholders voted against the decision, inconsistently with the prior decision adopted by the protective partnership by a simple majority of votes. They voted in a similar way at the general meeting – against approving a control agreement and a profit transfer agreement – arguing that, when voting on these decisions at the general meeting, they are not bound by the agreement adopted by the inside partnership. It should be noted that under German law there is a default provision (s. § 119 of the HGB) that decisions in an ordinary partnership are taken unanimously. In this case, the partners used the non-mandatory character of the provision and enshrined in the inside partnership agreement a majority rule which they subsequently applied in their decision on the manner of voting at the general meeting.

According to the German Federal Court of Justice, a voting rights agreement adopted by a simple majority of the partners in an (inside) partnership "operating" within a joint-stock company is valid under contract law and does not violate the stock corporation rules which require for certain decisions of the supreme body a (higher) qualified majority or unanimity. The voting rights agreement aims to pool votes in order to strengthen the influence on the company. The majority clause provided for in the voting rights agreement is designed to achieve a qualified majority in the decision-making process of the supreme body in a joint-stock company. The establishment of an inside partnership resulted from the autonomy of shareholders who could under German law replace, by contract, the default unanimity with a majority rule. It can also be argued that if a person can undertake to vote in accordance with another shareholder's directions, he or she can also undertake to vote in accordance with the decision adopted by a simple majority by the partners in an inside partnership. An agreement is a way of establishing a common procedure – and ultimately also a common will – which is subsequently presented as uniform at the general meeting by means of concerted voting. Such decisions adopted by interest groups of *shareholders are not subject to the corporate law provisions dealing with the requirements for adopting decisions by the supreme body.* In this case, the separation of contract law from corporate law cannot be regarded as conflicting with the principle of unity of the legal system. Thus if a shareholder who is a party to such agreement failed to vote at the general meeting in accordance with the decision adopted by a majority of votes, he or she has breached an obligation under the inside partnership agreement, and where a fine has been stipulated for such breach, he or she will be liable to pay it.

Yet the conclusion about the binding nature of a voting rights agreement adopted by the majority of shareholders joined through a voting rights agreement is not universally applicable. The majority clause is neutral because it does not address the content of the decision of the general meeting which has been put to the vote to shareholders, i.e., the contracting parties to the agreement. The majority clause is a *de facto* procedural provision designed to set up a voting system (covering such issues as whether or not to vote on a draft decision of the general meeting, how many votes should be used, etc.). However, the decision adopted by the inside partnership may be defective if it breaches the general private law rules on the validity of juridical acts (particularly where the shareholders were deceived as the content of the decision and its consequences were not properly explained to the partners of the inside partnership). Another legal defect of the adopted voting rights decision may involve a breach of corporate law. This may arise where the agreement which binds shareholders to vote for the decision of the general meeting clearly conflicts with the interests of the company, binding them thus to be very disloyal. Furthermore, unlawfulness may arise where shareholders are bound to vote for a decision clearly involving a breach of good morals (for example, for a resolution attaching extreme weight to particular shares, without proper justification by circumstances or conditions in the company). Shareholders' agreements, in particular where a breach thereof gives rise to contractual penalties, raise the following problematic issue: the shareholders themselves must determine whether an agreement adopted by a majority of votes binds them to undertake a lawful or unlawful act. Consequently, they must carry out their own, albeit informal, test to determine whether or not the agreement concerned is binding. Even if the decision of the general meeting is not challenged for violating the law, the articles of association, or good morals, when deciding about any liability to a contractual penalty for breach of a voting rights agreement, the court will determine whether or not such violation occurred – regardless of whether or not the decision of the general meeting was challenged by an action for annulment.

## D. A reinforced liberal approach to Shareholders' Agreements

Liberalising trends which have been continuously apparent in corporate law have, to a certain extent, influenced the approach to shareholders' agreements as well. It seems that under the influence of the practice, both the legislature and courts have adopted a more tolerant approach to shareholders' agreements. This also applies to determinations about the invalidity of voting agreements.

This trend can be illustrated by the approach of the American courts to the so-called *vote buying agreements*. Under vote buying agreements a shareholder undertakes to vote in a particular manner or to abstain, in exchange for certain consideration. Such shareholders' agreements were originally perceived as interference in the essence of shareholders' will and the courts drew a comparison with a public ban on buying votes in "political" elections to public bodies. Even the rather tolerant Delaware courts considered the vote buying agreements as invalid due to a breach of good morals. Traditionally, the key decision cited in this respect has been the Delaware case *Schreiber v. Carney*;[9] while dating from 1982, it is still seen as showing a modern approach to a shareholders voting rights agreement for pecuniary interest.[10] The court found that such agreements could be valid under certain conditions, arguing that if, during the negotiations about voting, one party is not interested in concluding a voting rights agreement, the other parties will provide a bonus as consideration for voting in a particular way. Such an agreement thus reconciles the interests of all contracting parties and is permissible and enforceable, unless it was concluded for unlawful purposes. Current commentaries agree that vote buying agreements cannot be regarded as impermissible *per se*, but only where they aim to defraud or otherwise harm other shareholders. Vote buying agreements are regarded as problematic if they are designed to secure re-election for a board member, unless this is in the best interest of the company.[11] Coming back to Europe, in France it is a crime (under the stock corporation provisions contained in the Commercial Code[12]) to have advantages accorded, guaranteed, or promised in exchange for voting in a particular manner or for abstaining at the general meeting of a joint-stock

9 Schreiber v. Carney, 447 A.2d 17 (Del. Ch. 1982).

10 *Pavelich* The Shareholder Judgment Rule: Delaware's Permissive Response to Corporate Vote-Buying, The Journal of Corporation Law 2005, p. 247 et seq.

11 *Welch/Saunders/Allison/Voss/Turezyn* Folk on the Delaware general corporation law 2016: fundamentals, Wolters Kluwer. New York 2015, p. 154 et seq.

12 Section III. Des infractions relatives aux assemblées d'actionnaires (CC).

company. Likewise, it is a crime to accord, guarantee, or promise such advantages (Article 242–9 of the Commercial Code). Clearly, these rules have a rather wide scope. It is significant that these provisions are hardly ever applied. In a wider context, the different approach to shareholders' agreements in France can be demonstrated by examining the so-called pure holding companies and the underlying agreements. In this case, the issue does not turn on examining the pecuniary interest offered for voting, but rather the point is that voting rights are in this way effectively (indirectly) transferred by establishing a pure holding company and contributing shares to this company. While in 1960 such companies designed to ensure that voting rights are exercised collectively were found to be invalid by the French Cour de cassation (Cass. Com. 10 June 1960 Bull. Cas. 1960, 2, n 277), designated as front companies (*société de façade)*, in 1980 the Parisian court (Cour de Paris, 2 October 1980) held that the formation of a legal entity whose object is to acquire and manage the assets of another company is not unlawful. Likewise, other decisions of the French Cour de cassation also accepted the formation of legal entities intended to define the economic policy of their members, if the latter possess the voting rights corresponding to their share of the registered capital in the holding company. In addition, reinforced liberalism in modern French case law is also emphasised by the French jurisprudence.[13]

# E. Agreement on another manner of influencing the company

Shareholders' voting agreements enable shareholders to exert a direct influence on the composition of elected (management) bodies. An agreement stipulating that a shareholder will make an effort or ensure that a member of an elected body takes a specific managerial decision is not a voting agreement, but rather an agreement about a different type of influence on the company. In practice, this obligation tends to be subject to penalties. It is therefore very important how the obligations of parties under such agreement are worded. If a shareholder undertakes to make efforts to influence members of an elected body to make a specific juridical act on behalf of the company; for example, if he or she undertakes to make efforts to influence members of a body to conclude a contract for the sale of shares to a subsidiary, the shareholder assumes (only) the obligation to carry out certain activities *towards* achieving a specific result, in this case towards a specific decision adopted by the members of the board of directors, the

13 *Germain* Les sociétés commerciales, 19th edition, LG .D .J. 2009, p. 413 et seq.

supervisory board, or the administrative board (*means obligation, obligation de moyens)*. The obligor then owes only this activity. In order to avoid legal penalties (in the form of damages for breach of obligations or a contractual penalty), the party to the shareholders' agreement will have to prove that he or she made efforts, undertook (lawful) juridical acts, or took effective steps towards ensuring that a member of an elected body behaved in a particular way. A different situation arises where a shareholder undertakes in a shareholders' agreement to *ensure* that a member (members) of an elected body acts in a specific way, for example that he or she concludes a specific contract on behalf of the company. In that case, the shareholders' agreement imposes an obligation to deliver a particular result (*absolute obligation, obligation de résultat*). The shareholder then owes this result to the other parties. Although the shareholder's obligation involves a performance by another person (the performance is not or cannot be provided by the obligor), it does not mean that such agreement must necessarily be invalid. It can be argued that where a person undertakes to deliver a specific result, which can be regarded as feasible in regular (usual) circumstances, this performance is not impossible, although it is dependent on another person's action. The general rules of the law of obligations usually provide for a situation where a person undertakes to ensure that a third party discharges an obligation agreed between the contracting parties, imposing liability to damages on the obligor if the third party fails to discharge the obligation.

The validity of a shareholder's obligation may be contested in the following situation. If a shareholder undertakes to induce a member of a body to act unlawfully or apparently contrary to the interests of the company, the member of the board may essentially not accept such influence. The undertaking to induce someone to commit unlawful acts should not have been made; consequently, the failure to discharge this obligation does not give rise to private law penalties.

It is noteworthy that certain countries have adopted legislation (in particular Germany[14] and the new legislation in the Czech Republic[15]) and developed case law (in particular the French legal concept based on the decision of the Cour de cassation in *Rozenblum*[16]) which make it possible to act in the interests of a corporate group and to the detriment of a company which is part of such group. A

14 Section 308 II AktG.

15 See *Čech* Neues tschechisches Recht für faktische Konzerne – vom deutschen Konzernrecht zu Rozenblum oder ein dritter Weg? in Hommelhoff,/Lutter/Teichmann (Hrsg.): Corporate governance im grenzüberschreitenden Konzern, Zeitschrift für Unternehmens- und Gesellschaftsrecht, Sonderheft 20, de Gruyter, Berlin, 2017, p. 65 *et seq.*

16 Bull. Crim. n. 54, JCP 1986 II, 20585 (before that, see the decision of the Parisian Tribunal correctionnel in Agache-Willot from 1974).

person at the top of a "compact" corporate group may give directions to bodies of a controlled (dependant) company concerning business management where such directions are in the interests of the group and provided that compensation will be subsequently made; however, compensation is not understood everywhere in the same way. An influential shareholder or shareholders of the company at the top of the group may undertake to ensure that a member of a body in the controlled company makes a managerial decision to the detriment of the controlled company, but in the interest of the (corporate) group. Such a liberal approach to corporate groups is not widespread throughout united Europe, and in its Action Plan[17] the European Commission has set the task to harmonise the approach of member states as regards the possibility to give directions concerning business management in controlled companies where it is in the interest of the corporate group.[18]

However, shareholders' agreements which impose an obligation on the contracting parties to influence the decisions made by the members of elected bodies in a joint-stock company may also have other consequences. If such agreements are fully honoured, they can give rise to the so-called shadow directors or even *de facto* directors with the risk that such directors may (in justified circumstances) face similar penalties as *de jure* directors.[19]

## F. Conclusion

One of the objectives of shareholders' agreements is to reach agreement or at least consensus for filling the posts in the administrative board (if the company has a monistic structure), or in the board of directors and the supervisory board (if the company has a dualistic structure). The influence of shareholders on the

---

**17** Communication from the Commission to the European Parliament, the Council, the European Economic and Social Committee and the Committee of the Regions: Action Plan: European company law and corporate governance – a modern legal framework for more engaged shareholders and sustainable companies [COM (2012) 740 final]. The same objective is being pursued in proposals drawn up by private groups of experts on company law, such as Forum Europaeum on Company Groups – FECG (see the proposals on the facilitation of cross-border management of corporate groups in Europe, published in German journals – ZGR 4/2015).

**18** *Habersack* Konzernrecht – Bestandsaufnahme und Perspektiven. Aktienkonzernrecht 19/2016, p. 695.

**19** The concepts of de facto director and shadow director have been examined particularly in English case law, for example in Re Hydrodan (Corby) Ltd, [1994] BCC 161; Revenue and Customs Commissioners v Holland and another [2010] UKSC 55, Re Mumtaz Properties Ltd [2011] EWCA Civ 610, Secretary of State for Trade and Industry v Deverell [2000] 2 WLR 907.

composition of such bodies can be strictly corporate-based, using multiple voting rights or shares with designation rights (*Entsendungsrecht*). In addition, the influence can be of a (purely) obligational character, where shareholders' agreements, in particular those concerning the exercise of shareholders' voting rights at the general meeting, can create an internal (shadow) structure which is not reflected in the "official" organisational set-up of a joint-stock company, but it can have a major impact on the decision-making. The shareholders' influence on the company may also subsist in the combination of these techniques. Compared to a voting agreement, a shareholder's undertaking to influence a member of a board (the administrative board, the board of directors) to make a particular decision has a different subject-matter. With regard to potential contractual penalties imposed for non-performance of such an undertaking, the exact wording is crucial: i.e., whether the shareholder undertakes to make efforts towards a decision (*means obligation, obligation de moyens*) or whether he or she undertakes to ensure that a particular decision is taken (*absolute obligation, obligation de résultat*). There is a vast array of shareholders' agreements. When considering whether or not they are lawful, in particular if they concern buying votes, it can be observed that liberal tendencies have been gaining ground.

Mária Patakyová and Barbora Grambličková

# *Ratio legis* behind the regulation of shareholders' agreements in the model acts: elimination of the application problems or over-regulation?

## Table of Content



---

**Prof. JUDr. Mária Patakyová**, and **PhD., JUDr. Barbora Grambličková**, LL.M.

https://doi.org/10.1515/9783110517026-004

# A. Introduction

A shareholders' agreement regulates the relationship between shareholders and possibly other entities within a company (or the company itself). It may serve as a tool for mitigation of agency problems which occur among different entities in the company.[1] A shareholders' agreement represents a set of various arrangements which establish, modify and amend corporate governance and control

1 *Armour/Hansmann/Kraakman* Agency Problems and Legal Strategies, The Anatomy of Corporate Law. A Comparative and Functional Approach. in R. Kraakman, J. Armour, J. Davies, L.Enriques, H. Hansmann, G. Hertig, K. Hopt, H. Kanda, E. Rock (Eds.) Second edition. Oxford: Oxford University Press, 2009.

in the company, and it enables the shareholders to regulate their rights and obligations if the statutory regulation does not provide sufficient solutions or the regulatory framework is not suitable for the company.[2]

Serving as a tool for the regulation of the fate of a company, it strives to eliminate harmful behaviour of shareholders and other entities, and it is more frequent in companies which have shareholders that are actively interested in the running of the company (shareholder activism). It is possible to identify different types of shareholders' agreements, for example, shareholders' agreements connected to the statutory body of the company – specifically, these may regulate:

- nomination, election and removal of the statutory body of the company,
- fulfilment of the vacant positions in the statutory body of the company,
- number of persons in the statutory body,
- quorum needed for the decisions of the statutory body,
- voting procedures in the statutory body,
- limitations of rights of the statutory body.

Moreover, shareholders' agreements may determine the creation of different committees within the statutory body, and outside the statutory body as well, and the procedure for election into these committees.

Additionally, shareholders' agreements may regulate the position of shareholders in the company, their information rights being traditionally strengthened by such arrangements. However, shareholders' agreements may impose new obligations on shareholders, such as an obligation to be present at the general meeting and vote in favour or against some of the proposals that shall be decided.[3]

Furthermore, shareholders' agreements may cover questions on limitation of transferability of a business share[4] or shares in the company. Especially, shareholders' agreements may regulate:

- right of the first refusal,
- pre-emption rights,
- tag-along rights,
- drag-along rights,
- shoot-out rights,

**2** *Chemla/Habib/Ljungqvist* An Analysis of Shareholder Agreements, LSE working Paper 006, 2004 (published as well in Journal of the Economic Association, vol. 5, No. 1, 2007).

**3** Such structures may pose a question whether a right might be turned into an obligation.

**4** A business share represents a shareholder's right and obligation and their corresponding participation in the company. The business share may or may not be in a form of a security, in Slovakia the business share cannot have a form of a security and is present in the private limited liability company.

- exclusion of the transferability.

Additionally, shareholders' agreements may also govern:
- corporate opportunities,
- election and removal of managers,
- extraordinary voting rights,
- solution for dead-lock situations in the company,
- pre-emption rights and preference rights,
- termination, amendments and changes of shareholders' agreements,
- questions regulating the applicable law, dispute resolutions.[5]

A shareholders' agreement represents bilateral or multi-lateral legal arrangement which is made (usually) between the shareholders of the company. However, it may happen that other entities, such as the company itself or the members of the company's bodies, may become a contractual party to a shareholders' agreement. From the above stated, it can be concluded that shareholders' agreements in the companies are based on the principle of private autonomy and contractual freedom. It is not common that shareholders' agreements are excessively regulated by national or international law and soft law regulation, however, some of the model acts or their proposals regulate them in a more detailed way.

The aim of this article is to analyse the following model acts:
- UNCITRAL – Draft model law on a simplified business entity (UNCITRAL – SBA),[6]
- Revised Model Business Corporation Act (RMBCA),[7]
- Proposed OAS Model Act on Simplified Stock Corporations (Model Act on SSC)[8] a
- European Model Companies Act (EMCA),[9]

5 Corporate Law Committee of the Association of the Bar of the City of New York, The Enforceability and Effectiveness of Typical Shareholders Agreement Provisions, The Business Lawyer, vol. 65, No. 4, 2010.

6 United Nations Commission on International Trade Law Working Group I (MSMEs), Twenty-fourth session: Micro, small and medium-sized enterprises Draft model law on a simplified business entity, Vienna, 29 June – 16 July, 2015.

7 Committee on Corporate Laws of the Section of Business Law of the American Bar Association: Revised Model Business Corporation Act (https://apps.americanbar.org/dch/committee.cfm?com=cl270000).

8 Project for a Model Act on Simplified Stock Corporation, CJI/RES. 188 (LXXX-O/12) (http://www.oas.org/en/sla/iajc/docs/ijc_current_agenda_simplified_stock_corporation.pdf).

9 European Model Companies Act (http://law.au.dk/fileadmin/Jura/dokumenter/forskning/projekter/EMCA/EMCA_Introduktion.pdf).

in order to determine **ratio legis** behind the regulation of shareholders' agreements in these model acts and whether these model acts serve as an *ex ante* tool of elimination of problematic issues that may arise from shareholders' agreements, or whether it is possible to draw a conclusion that the model acts over-regulate the contractual freedom what may eventually hinder the purpose of shareholders' agreements in companies.

Based on the above stated, we will analyse in the stipulated model acts the following issues:

## I. Contractual parties to a shareholders' agreement

- The analysis will deal with an issue whether the model acts specify contractual parties to a shareholders' agreement. Generally, contractual parties to a shareholders' agreement will be the shareholders of the company, however, it may happen that other entities (the company itself or the members of the company's bodies) will be contractual parties to a shareholders' agreement if they presented their free will to be its part.

## II. Entities bound by a shareholders' agreement

- The analysis will deal with the question which entities are bound by a shareholders' agreement. It is common that the shareholders who are parties to a shareholders' agreement will be bound by it. However, a specific situation might occur when the company itself or the company's bodies will be bound by a shareholders' agreement.

## III. Scope of a shareholders' agreement

- The analysis will focus on the scope of the matters that can be, possibly, covered by a shareholders' agreement, and especially, we will focus on whether the model acts provide contractual freedom or limit this principle in relation to a shareholders' agreement. Furthermore, we will analyse if the model acts exclude some of the issues that can be regulated or modified by a shareholders' agreement. Moreover, the analysis will deal with the possibility of whether a shareholders' agreement may cover issues in conflict with the mandatory requirements of the model act or the articles of association.

## IV. Registration of a shareholders' agreement

- The analysis will deal with whether shareholders' agreements must/shall be registered/filed with the company and/or archived in the company, what effect such a registration/filing with the company and/or archiving has towards the internal stakeholders of the company, who can access shareholders' agreements and whether such a registration/filing with the company and/or archiving has an impact on enforceability of the shareholders' agreements (internal registration).
- Moreover, the analysis will focus on whether a shareholders' agreement must/shall be registered by an external body, such as a company register, commercial register, business register or the registry of securities, and what effect this type of registration (external registration) has on the enforceability and effect on the third parties of the shareholders' agreement.

## V. Time aspects of a shareholders' agreement

- The analysis will deal with whether there is a time limit for which a shareholders' agreement may be made and whether this time limit can be prolonged.

## VI. Changes, amendments and termination of a shareholders' agreement

- The analysis will focus on the possibilities and requirements to change and amend a shareholders' agreement and whether it may be terminated.

## VII. Enforcement of a shareholders' agreement

- The analysis will focus on whether the enforcement issues of a shareholders' agreement are regulated by the model acts.

## VIII. Conflict between the decisions of the company's body and the content of a shareholders' agreement

- The analysis will deal whether such a conflict between the decision of the company's body and the content of shareholders' agreement may result into the invalidation of such a decision.

## IX. Formal requirements on a shareholders' agreement

- The analysis will deal with whether the model acts require any formalities regarding a shareholders' agreement, for example, the written form.

We will analyse, within the four described model acts, whether and to what extent the above-mentioned issues are covered.

# B. UNCITRAL – Draft model law on a simplified business entity (UNCITRAL – SBA)

The proposal for the model act UNCITRAL – SBA is a result of the 24th gathering of the Working group I, Commission for the International Trade Law of the United Nations in New York, which took place from 13 to 17 April 2015.

The proposal of this model act is aimed at the support and development of micro, small and medium-sized enterprises. The objective of this model act was to simplify the presence, functioning and activities of the micro, small and medium-sized enterprises, which are the cornerstones of developed as well as underdeveloped economies.[10] The introduction to this model act declares that based on the globalization it is crucial to structure the legislation and regulation of these entities in such a way that these entities will be able to grow.[11] This model act regulates shareholders' agreements in Article 36.

> *Art. 36. Shareholders' agreements*
>
> *Agreements entered into among shareholders concerning the acquisition or sale of shares, pre-emptive rights or rights of first refusal, the exercise of voting rights, voting by proxy, or any other valid matter, shall be binding upon the simplified business entity, provided that such agreements have been filed with the simplified business entity. Shareholders' agreements shall be valid for any period of time determined in the relevant agreement.*

---

**10** United Nations Commission on International Trade Law Working Group I (MSMEs), Twenty-fourth session: Micro, small and medium-sized enterprises Draft model law on a simplified business entity, Vienna, 29 June – 16 July, 2015, p. 2.

**11** United Nations Commission on International Trade Law Working Group I (MSMEs), Twenty-fourth session: Micro, small and medium-sized enterprises Draft model law on a simplified business entity, Vienna, 29 June – 16 July, 2015, pp. 2–3.

## I. Contractual parties of a shareholders' agreement

Shareholders' agreements are regulated in the proposal for the model act UNCITRAL – SBA in a general way. The UNCITRAL – SBA describes that the parties to the shareholders' agreement are the shareholders, however, it is possible to open a discussion whether other entities as the members of the company's body or the company itself would be able to be a valid contractual party to the shareholders' agreement under the UNCITRAL – SBA.

## II. Entities bound by a shareholders' agreement

When reading Article 36, it is possible to conclude that the entities bound by a shareholders' agreement under the UNCITRAL – SBA would be shareholders. However, this Article states that if the shareholders' agreement is filed with the simplified business entity, it will be binding upon the simplified business entity as well.

## III. Scope of a shareholders' agreement

The UNCITRAL – SBA in Article 36 specifies the scope of issues that can be covered by a shareholders' agreement, it is an open enumeration of the issues, for example, sale of shares, pre-emptive rights or rights of first refusal, the exercise of voting rights, voting by proxy. At the same time, Article 36 states that a shareholders' agreement may cover any valid matter.

## IV. Registration of a shareholders' agreement

Article 36 touches the issue of the internal registration of the shareholders' agreements within the company. If a shareholders' agreement is filed with the simplified business entity, this shareholders' agreement will be binding upon the simplified business entity. However, there are no particular details about the process of filing shareholders' agreements with the simplified business entity.

## V. Time aspects of a shareholders' agreement

The proposal for the model act UNCITRAL – SBA states that shareholders' agreements are valid for the time stipulated within them, thus, this proposal of the model act does not limit the time validity and effectiveness of shareholders' agreements.

## VI. Changes, amendments and termination of a shareholders' agreement

The proposal for the model act UNCITRAL – SBA does not deal with the issues of the changes, amendments and termination of a shareholders' agreement.

## VII. Enforcement of a shareholders' agreement

The proposal for the model act UNCITRAL – SBA does not deal with the issues of enforcement of a shareholders' agreement, except for the requirement to file a shareholders' agreement with the simplified business in order to be binding upon this entity.

## VIII. Conflict between the decisions of company's body and the content of a shareholders' agreement

The proposal for the model act UNCITRAL – SBA does not deal with the issue of the conflict between the decisions of the company's body and the content of a shareholders' agreement.

## IX. Formal requirements on a shareholders' agreement

The proposal for the model act UNCITRAL – SBA does not specify any formal requirements for a shareholders' agreement.

## C. Revised Model Business Corporation Act (RMBCA)

The RMBCA was prepared by the Committee on Corporate Laws of the Section of Business Law of the American Bar Association. This model act is followed by 24 states within the United States. The varieties of the corporation's definition in the United States led the Committee on Corporate Laws of the Section of Business Law of the American Bar Association to draft a model act that will harmonize the corporate law. The adoption of the model act resulted in the elimination of ambiguity and varieties of corporate regulation among states. Subsequently, this model act was revised and most of the countries that initially adopted the model act now follow its revised version. The revision of the model act lasted almost 5 years and brought about a complex revision of the model act after 30 years.[12] The revision of the RMBCA took into account especially the changes in the commercial and company interests within the corporations. The RMBCA was created both for private as well as public companies, and it takes into consideration rights and duties of shareholders, investors and board members.[13]

The RMBCA stipulates the shareholders' agreements in Section 7.32.

§ 7.32. SHAREHOLDER AGREEMENTS

(a) *An agreement among the shareholders of a corporation that complies with this section is effective among the shareholders and the corporation even though it is inconsistent with one or more other provisions of this Act in that it:*
   (1) *eliminates the board of directors or restricts the discretion or powers of the board of directors;*
   (2) *governs the authorization or making of distributions whether or not in proportion to ownership of shares, subject to the limitations in section 6.40;*
   (3) *establishes who shall be directors or officers of the corporation, or their terms of office or manner of selection or removal;*
   (4) *governs, in general or in regard to specific matters, the exercise or division of voting power by or between the shareholders and directors or by or among any of them, including use of weighted voting rights or director proxies;*

12 *W.H. Holmes* The Revised Model Business Corporation Act and Corporate Law Reform in Mississippi: Part One, Mississippi Law Journal, vol. 56, 1986.

13 *W.H. Holmes* The Revised Model Business Corporation Act and Corporate Law Reform in Mississippi: Part One, Mississippi Law Journal, vol. 56, 1986.

*(5) establishes the terms and conditions of any agreement for the transfer or use of property or the provision of services between the corporation and any shareholder, director, officer or employee of the corporation or among any of them;*

*(6) transfers to one or more shareholders or other persons all or part of the authority to exercise the corporate powers or to manage the business and affairs of the corporation, including the resolution of any issue about which there exists a deadlock among directors or shareholders;*

*(7) requires dissolution of the corporation at the request of one or more of the shareholders or upon the occurrence of a specified event or contingency; or*

*(8) otherwise governs the exercise of the corporate powers or the management of the business and affairs of the corporation or the relationship among the shareholders, the directors and the corporation, or among any of them, and is not contrary to public policy.*

*(b) An agreement authorized by this section shall be:*

*(1) as set forth (A) in the articles of incorporation or bylaws and approved by all persons who are shareholders at the time of the agreement or (B) in a written agreement that is signed by all persons who are shareholders at the time of the agreement and is made known to the corporation;*

*(2) subject to amendment only by all persons who are shareholders at the time of the amendment, unless the agreement provides otherwise; and*

*(3) valid for 10 years, unless the agreement provides otherwise.*

*(c) The existence of an agreement authorized by this section shall be noted conspicuously on the front or back of each certificate for outstanding shares or on the information statement required by section 6.26(b). If at the time of the agreement the corporation has shares outstanding represented by certificates, the corporation shall recall the outstanding certificates and issue substitute certificates that comply with this subsection. The failure to note the existence of the agreement on the certificate or information statement shall not affect the validity of the agreement or any action taken pursuant to it. Any purchaser of shares who, at the time of purchase, did not have knowledge of the existence of the agreement shall be entitled to rescission of the purchase. A purchaser shall be deemed to have knowledge of the existence of the agreement if its existence is noted on the certificate or information statement for the shares in compliance with this subsection and, if the shares are not represented by a certificate, the information statement is delivered to the purchaser at or prior to the time of purchase of the shares. An action to enforce the right of rescission authorized by this subsection must be commenced within the earlier*

*of 90 days after discovery of the existence of the agreement or two years after the time of purchase of the shares.*

(d) *An agreement authorized by this section shall cease to be effective when the corporation becomes a public corporation. If the agreement ceases to be effective for any reason, the board of directors may, if the agreement is contained or referred to in the corporation's articles of incorporation or bylaws, adopt an amendment to the articles of incorporation or bylaws, without shareholder action, to delete the agreement and any references to it.*

(e) *An agreement authorized by this section that limits the discretion or powers of the board of directors shall relieve the directors of, and impose upon the person or persons in whom such discretion or powers are vested, liability for acts or omissions imposed by law on directors to the extent that the discretion or powers of the directors are limited by the agreement.*

(f) *The existence or performance of an agreement authorized by this section shall not be a ground for imposing personal liability on any shareholder for the acts or debts of the corporation even if the agreement or its performance treats the corporation as if it were a partnership or results in failure to observe the corporate formalities otherwise applicable to the matters governed by the agreement.*

(g) *Incorporators or subscribers for shares may act as shareholders with respect to an agreement authorized by this section if no shares have been issued when the agreement is made.*

## I. Contractual parties to a shareholders' agreement

The RMBCA states that the contractual parties to the shareholders' agreements are the shareholders. As we have already mentioned in relation to the proposal for the model act UNCITRAL – SBA, it is possible to open a discussion whether other entities, such as the members of the company's body or the company itself, could be a valid contractual party to a shareholders' agreement under the RMBCA.

## II. Entities bound by a shareholders' agreement

A shareholders' agreement is, according to Section 7.32 of the RMBCA, effective upon the shareholders and the company itself.

## III. Scope of a shareholders' agreement

The RMBCA enumerates the scope of the issues that can be covered in a shareholders' agreement in an open way. In particular, shareholders' agreements may cover issues dealing with the board of directors, distribution of assets, voting powers in the company, related party transactions, transfer of the corporate powers, or matters that otherwise govern the exercise of corporate powers or the management of the business and affairs of the corporation or the relationship among the shareholders, the directors and the corporation, or among any of them, and is not contrary to public policy. Thus, the scope of shareholders' agreements is regulated in the RMBCA as an open enumeration and the contractual freedom of parties to a shareholders' agreement is protected. Moreover, Section 7.32 of the RMBCA states that shareholders' agreements may be inconsistent with provisions of the RMBCA and still be effective upon the shareholders and the company, however, shareholders' agreements must be in line with the section of the RMBCA regulating shareholders' agreements.

## IV. Registration of a shareholders' agreement

The RMBCA regulates in Section 7.32 a specific procedure under which the existence of an agreement authorized by this section shall be noted conspicuously on the front or back of each certificate for outstanding shares or on the information statement required by the RMBCA. Moreover, the RMBCA states in the respective section that the shareholders' agreement shall be made known to the company.

## V. Time aspects of a shareholders' agreement

The RMBCA states that the shareholders' agreement may be valid for 10 years, unless the agreement provides otherwise, which supports the contractual freedom within a shareholders' agreement.

## VI. Changes, amendments and termination of a shareholders' agreement

The RMBCA states that a shareholders' agreement authorized by Section 7.32 of the RMBCA shall cease to be effective when the corporation becomes a public corporation.

## VII. Enforcement of a shareholders' agreement

The RMBCA does not regulate separately the enforcement matters of shareholders' agreements.

## VIII. Conflict between the decision of the company's body and the content of a shareholders' agreement

The RMBCA does not deal with the issue of the conflict between the decisions of the body of the company and the content of a shareholders' agreement.

## IX. Formal requirements on a shareholders' agreement

The RMBCA states that shareholders' agreements are set forth either in the Articles of Incorporation or bylaws of the company and approved by all persons who are shareholders at the time of the agreement or in a written agreement that is signed by all persons who are shareholders at the time of the agreement and is made known to the company. Thus, under the RMBCA a shareholders' agreement may be in a form of a separate legal document or be part of the constitutional documents of the company.

# D. Proposed OAS Model Act on Simplified Stock Corporation[14]

The proposed OAS Model Act on Simplified Stock Corporation is a project which was created due to the need of development of company law in Latin America. This proposed model act stems from the Colombian company law. The aim of the model act was not to revise the existing regulation of the company law, but to prepare a new complex regulation of the company law.

Moreover, another goal of the regulation was to adopt a new type of a simplified limited liability company which was based on mixing the benefits of the partnership and companies with limited liability while the contractual freedom of the entities is protected.[15]

The shareholders' agreements are covered in the proposed OAS Model Act on Simplified Stock Corporation in Section 24.

Art. 24. Shareholders' Agreements
*Agreements entered into between shareholders concerning the acquisition or sale of shares, preemptive rights or rights of first refusal, the exercise of voting rights, voting by proxy, or any other valid matter, shall be binding upon the simplified stock corporation, provided that such agreements have been filed with the corporation's legal representative. Shareholders' agreements shall be valid for any period of time determined in the agreement, not exceeding 10 years, upon the terms and conditions stated therein. Such 10 year term may only be extended by unanimous consent.*

*Shareholders that have executed an agreement shall appoint a person who will represent them for the purposes of receiving information and providing it whenever it is requested. The simplified stock corporation's legal representative may request, in writing, to such representative, clarification as regards any provision set forth in the agreement. The response shall be provided also in writing within the five days following the request.*

---

**14** Project for a Model Act on Simplified Stock Corporation, CJI/RES. 188 (LXXX-O/12) (http://www.oas.org/en/sla/iajc/docs/ijc_current_agenda_simplified_stock_corporation.pdf).
**15** *F.R. Villamizar* The Proposed OAS Model Act on Simplified Stock Corporations.

**SubArticle 1.**
The President of the shareholders' assembly, or of the concerned corporate organs, shall exclude any votes cast in a manner inconsistent with the terms set forth under a duly filed shareholders' agreement.

**SubArticle 2.**
Pursuant to the conditions set forth in the agreement, any shareholder shall be entitled to demand, before a court with jurisdiction over the corporation, the specific performance of any obligation arising under such agreement.

## I. Contractual parties of a shareholders' agreement

Shareholders' agreements are regulated in the proposed OAS Model Act on Simplified Stock Corporation in a general way and the regulation shares many similarities with the UNCITRAL – SBA. The proposed OAS Model Act on Simplified Stock Corporation describes that the parties to a shareholders' agreement are the shareholders, however, it is possible to open a discussion whether other entities as the members of the company's body or the company itself would be able to be a valid contractual party to a shareholders' agreement under the proposed OAS Model Act on Simplified Stock Corporation.

## II. Entities bound by a shareholders' agreement

When reading Article 24, it is possible to conclude that the entities bound by a shareholders' agreement under the proposed OAS Model Act on Simplified Stock Corporation would be the shareholders. However, this Article states that if the shareholders' agreement is filed with the simplified stock corporation (to its legal representative) it will be binding upon this entity as well. This regulation, one more time, resembles the UNCITRAL – SBA model act.

## III. Scope of a shareholders' agreement

The proposed OAS Model Act on Simplified Stock Corporation in Article 24 specifies the scope of issues that can be covered by the shareholders' agreement, it is an open enumeration of the issues, for example, sale of shares, pre-emptive rights or rights of first refusal, the exercise of voting rights, voting by proxy. At the same time, Article 24 states that a shareholders' agreement may cover any valid matter.

## IV. Registration of a shareholders' agreement

Article 24 of the shareholders' agreement touches the issue of the internal registration of the shareholders' agreements within the company. If the shareholders' agreement is filed with the simplified stock corporation, it will be binding upon the simplified stock corporation. Moreover, the proposed OAS Model Act on Simplified Stock Corporation states that shareholders' agreement must be filed with the legal representative of the company.

## V. Time aspects of a shareholders' agreement

The proposed OAS Model Act on Simplified Stock Corporation states that a shareholders' agreement shall be valid for any period of time determined in the agreement, not exceeding 10 years, upon the terms and conditions stated therein. Such 10-year term may only be extended by unanimous consent.

## VI. Changes, amendments and termination of a shareholders' agreement

The proposed OAS Model Act on Simplified Stock Corporation does not deal with the issues of the changes, amendments and termination of a shareholders' agreement.

## VII. Enforcement of a shareholders' agreement

The proposed OAS Model Act on Simplified Stock Corporation states that pursuant to the conditions set forth in shareholders' agreement, any shareholder shall be entitled to demand, before a court with jurisdiction over the corporation, the specific performance of any obligation arising under such agreement. This provision may be considered as strengthening the enforcement of a shareholders' agreement.

### VIII. Conflict between the decisions of the company's body and the content of a shareholders' agreement

The proposed OAS Model Act on Simplified Stock Corporation states that the President of the shareholders' assembly, or of the concerned corporate organs, shall exclude any votes cast in a manner inconsistent with the terms set forth under a duly filed shareholders' agreement.

### IX. Formal requirements on a shareholders' agreement

The proposed OAS Model Act on Simplified Stock Corporation does not specify any formal requirements on a shareholders' agreement.

## E. European Model Companies Act (EMCA)

The EMCA project was officially introduced to the public in March 2017 in Rome. The proposal of this model act stems from the project which started in 2007 under the leadership of professor *Andersen* and professor *Baums* at the Aarhus University in Denmark.[16] This model act proposal shall bring a more flexible harmonisation tool of the company law in the European Union.

The EMCA does not regulate shareholders' agreements, however, within the official commentary we were able to find some traces of shareholders' agreements. The official commentary to the EMCA states that shareholders' agreements are acknowledged in all Member States of the European Union and that the general approach regarding shareholders' agreements in Member States of the European Union is that they are binding upon the shareholders who were involved as contracting parties in the shareholders' agreements, and this shareholders' agreements will not be binding upon the company or parties acquiring the shares in good faith in the company in which shareholders entered into a shareholders' agreement. Additionally, the official commentary to the EMCA states that the EMCA does not include specific provisions on shareholders' agreements but certainly would not want to prohibit them.[17]

---

**16** European Model Companies Act (http://law.au.dk/fileadmin/Jura/dokumenter/forskning/projekter/EMCA/EMCA_Introduktion.pdf).

**17** Official commentary to EMCA (http://law.au.dk/fileadmin/Jura/dokumenter/forskning/projekter/EMCA/EMCA_Introduktion.pdf).

Despite the fact that the EMCA is silent about shareholders' agreements in its body, it is possible to identify parts of the model act relevant in relation to shareholders' agreements. That would be especially Chapter 5 regulating the shares and Chapter 15 regulating the Group of companies. Section 13 of the Chapter 5 of the EMCA states that the shares are freely transferable unless otherwise stipulated in the bylaws, which is in line with Section 15 Chapter 5 of the EMCA which declares that the bylaws may limit or even exclude the transferability of the shares. The commentary to these sections of the EMCA states that the reference in this Section to the Articles of Association is not a ban on shareholders' agreements outside the Articles.

Moreover, the shareholders' agreements are reflected in the EMCA through the regulation of the Group of companies. The EMCA states that if the member of the body of the company was elected to their function based on shareholders' agreements, he/she will not be bound by the directions of the mother company.

## F. *Ratio legis* behind the regulation of shareholders' agreements in the model acts: elimination of the application problems or over-regulation?

The aim of this article was to analyse the selected model acts in order to determine *ratio legis* behind the regulation of shareholders' agreements therein and whether these model acts serve as an ex ante tool of elimination of the problematic issues that may arise from shareholders' agreements, or whether it is possible to draw a conclusion that the model acts over-regulate the contractual freedom what hinders the purpose of the shareholders' agreements in companies.

Based on the conducted research we could draw a conclusion that *ratio legis* behind the regulation of shareholders' agreements is the establishment of the general frame for the shareholders' agreements with an aim to eliminate the problems connected with shareholders' agreements and preservation of the contractual freedom. The above stated conclusion is based upon these partial outcomes:

## I. Contractual parties of a shareholders' agreement

Most of the model acts state that the contractual parties to a shareholders' agreement are the shareholders, however, none of the model acts explicitly excluded other entities, such as the members of the company's body or the company itself, to be a contracting party to a shareholders' agreement.

## II. Entities bound by a shareholders' agreement

It is possible to draw a conclusion from the analysed model acts that the entities bound by a shareholders' agreement are the shareholders who entered into the shareholders' agreement and the company provided the shareholders' agreement was filed with the company. The only model act going against this statement was the EMCA in its official commentary stating that only the shareholders are bound by the shareholders' agreement.

## III. Scope of a shareholders' agreement

Most of the model acts stipulate the scope of the matters that can be covered by shareholders' agreements in a general way, the enumeration is open, thus leaving a room for other matters to be covered, not only those explicitly mentioned within the respective section of the model act.

## IV. Registration of a shareholders' agreement

Generally, if a registration/filing with the company and/or archiving of a shareholders' agreement was requested by the regulation of the model act, it was an internal registration. The closest requirement of an external registration may be found in the RMBCA, which in Section 7.32 regulates a specific procedure under which the existence of an agreement authorized by this section shall be noted conspicuously on the front or back of each certificate for outstanding shares or on the information statement required by the RMBCA.

## V. Time aspects of a shareholders' agreement

It is possible to conclude that even though some of the model acts limited the validity of a shareholders' agreement, this time limit could be prolonged.

## VI. Changes, amendments and termination of a shareholders' agreement

There were not many regulations within the model acts dealing with changes, amendments and termination of a shareholders' agreement.

## VII. Enforcement of a shareholders' agreement

The enforcement of a shareholders' agreement was in most detail covered in the proposed OAS Model Act on Simplified Stock Corporation which states that pursuant to the conditions set forth in the agreement, any shareholder shall be entitled to demand, before a court with jurisdiction over the corporation, the specific performance of any obligation arising under such an agreement. This provision may be considered as strengthening the external enforcement of a shareholders' agreement. Otherwise, the model acts covered only the internal enforcement of a shareholders' agreement.

## VIII. Conflict between the decisions of the company's body and the content of a shareholders' agreement

Conflict between the decisions of the company's body and the content of shareholders' agreements was regulated only in the proposed OAS Model Act on Simplified Stock Corporation, this model act covered the problem of conflict in favour of shareholders' agreements.

## IX. Formal requirements on a shareholders' agreement

The formal requirements on a shareholders' agreement were in most detail covered by the RMBCA which states that the shareholders' agreements are set forth either in the Articles of Incorporation or bylaws of the company and approved by all persons who are shareholders at the time of the agreement or in a written agreement that is signed by all persons who are shareholders at the time of the agreement and is made known to the corporation. Thus, under the RMBCA, a shareholders' agreement may be in a form of a separate legal document or be part of the constitutional document of the company.

Kristián Csach

# Cross-border Shareholders' Agreements and Private International Law

**Table of Content**



## A. Introduction: Cross-border activities and private international law

Cross-border operation has become a prerequisite for corporations' success in a globalized market. The rise of cross-border interactions has led to the increase in the number of foreign shareholders participating in a corporation. Shareholders' agreements may represent a particularly effective tool of corporate governance and regulation of the shareholders' relations, and control the risk of conflict of laws posed by the uncertainty of applicable governing law.

Various states promote cross-border operation by using the regulatory competition which includes offering better tax and corporate legislation to attract in-

**Doc. JUDr. Kristián Csach**, PhD., LL.M., Trnava university in Trnava

https://doi.org/10.1515/9783110517026-005

vestors to set up a corporation in their state.[1] The mere fact that a corporation does not conduct any business in the state in which it has its registered office and pursues its activities solely or principally in the state where its branch is established[2] shall not be deemed *per se* as an artificial foreign element, a simulation of a foreign element, abusive nor fraudulent conduct.[3]

Cross-border operation raises questions concerning applicable governing law and jurisdiction regulated by private international and procedural law, namely conflict of laws' rules and rules on jurisdiction. Private international law requires the existence of a significant foreign element in the legal relation. Not any foreign connection constitutes a sufficiently significant foreign element for a dispute arising out of a cross-border legal relationship which would call for addressing the problem from the perspective of private international law.

A typical relevant or significant foreign element is, for example, a corporation's centre of interest located in a state different from the state of incorporation or its longer-lasting activities in other states. With regard to shareholders' agreements, the relevant foreign element is deemed to be particularly the personality of a shareholder (their habitual residence or nationality) which need not be a significant foreign element for other issues. The law applicable to corporations *(lex societatis)* is not dependant on the nationality of a corporation's shareholders. *Locus acti,* i.e. the place where the contract has been made, is not in general a significant foreign element within issues falling under the law applicable to corporations, but it might be of importance to the contractual arrangements in shareholders' agreements. Thus, a foreign element is to be determined on a case by case basis.

---

1 For various factors influencing the behaviour of stakeholders in corporate regulatory competition see *Lucian A Bebchuck* Federalism and the Corporation: the Desirable Limits on State Competition in Corporate Law, (1992) 105 Harv LR 1435, 1444 and following.

2 Within EU, the principle of freedom of establishment of companies set out in Articles 49 and 54 of the Treaty on the Functioning of the European Union (TFEU) allows free cross-border establishing of companies and subsidiaries (primary and secondary establishment) across the EU internal market, granting exception to the Member States only if there is a violation of the general principle of national public interest (public order), such exceptions include the prevention of abusive or fraudulent conduct, or protection of the interests of creditors, minority shareholders, employees or the tax authorities.

3 See Case C-167/01 *Kamer van Koophandel en Fabrieken voor Amsterdam v Inspire Art Ltd* [2003] ECR I-10155 [*Inspire Art*], paras 105, 136–139, 143, operative part 2.

# B. Contractual paradigm of a corporation and its impact on conflict of laws in corporate law

A corporation may have contractual foundations, since it is a bundle of rights and obligations or a nexus of contracts, yet its contractual nature does not fully fall under the ambit of private international law. From a conflict of laws point of view, a corporation is not a contract and specific rules apply on the existence, legal personality and internal structure of the corporation. The reasons are multiple.

The intervention of the state as a *sine qua non* for the corporation formation is not a relevant factor which could exclude the application of contractual conflict of laws' rules on corporations, as there are forms of companies that do not need a formal public act of registration to operate. It is the longevity of the contractual relation, the *erga omnes* existence of a distinct legal subject and the requirements of the third parties protection that do limit the choice of law applicable to corporations. The substitutability of the parties to the corporate contract (shareholders) creates also a bond of trust in an extent not known to other contractual relations, and therefore further adjustments of the contractual perspective have to be reflected also in private international law. The contractual principle is thereby not applicable to the governing law for a corporation, its internal organisation, the statutory bodies, and rights and duties of shareholders. Nevertheless, the corporation's contractual nature is still to some extent part of conflict of laws' regulation on corporations.[4]

# C. In search of the connecting factor for conflict of laws in corporate law

The concepts of conflict of laws handling of corporate law issues differ and are not unified, either worldwide or on regional levels.[5] In Europe, the theoretical

---

4 Case C-214/89 Powell Duffryn plc v Wolfgang Petereit. [1992] ECR I- 01745 [*Powell Duffryn*], according to which a "*clause contained in the Articles and adopted in accordance with the provisions of the applicable national law and those Articles themselves conferring jurisdiction on a particular court to settle disputes between that company and its shareholders constitutes an agreement conferring jurisdiction.*"

5 The Hague Convention of 1 June 1956 concerning the recognition of the legal personality of foreign companies, associations and institutions was not ratified by the required number of states and thus not come into force. Published in American Journal of Comparative Law, Vol.

concept of a *lex societatis* (the law governing a bundle of corporate issues) provides for the ascertainability of the law applicable to corporations,[6] whereas common law systems, predominantly the U.S., favour the Internal Affairs Doctrine.[7] Both share the same foundations – the internal organisation, the structure and the existence of the corporation is subject to the regulation by a particular (single) state, i.e. the state in which the corporation has been incorporated.[8] A particular legal order creates a legal entity (a corporation), and thus it is entitled to determine the rules and conditions of its existence and functioning.

Determining the connecting factor in relation to *lex societatis* is inconsistent and varies between individual states. This connecting factor is crucial as it specifies how the fact that a company originates from another jurisdiction is to be determined and when a state classifies a company as "foreign". Two contrasting theories regarding a 'foreign' legal personality have emerged overtime – Real Seat Theory and Incorporation Theory.

Real Seat Theory, originated in France and Germany in the 19th century,[9] holds that legal issues relating to a legal personality are determined by the law of the state where the head office of real seat (*siège réel, Realsitz)* is located.[10] It is a protective theory with the purpose of facilitating the relationship between a legal person and legal order of the state in which the real seat is located. Should a corporation set up in a particular state have its real seat in another state following Real Seat Theory, the corporation must conform to the requirements of the real seat state. This usually entails the incorporation of a new corporation in the form recognized by national law, even though its legal capacity under domestic law is retained.[11] This means that its internal affairs and organ-

I, 1952, p. 277. The Convention covers only the recognition of the legal personality and does not include any particular rule on the organisational structure, internal affairs or shareholders' agreements.

**6** See generally *Stephan Rammelloo* Corporations in Private International Law: A European Perspective. Oxford University Press, Oxford, 2001.

**7** Restatement (Second) of Conflict of Laws § 304. See also *Richard M. Buxbaum* The Origins of *the American "Internal Affairs" Doctrine Rule in the Corporate Conflict of Laws' in HJ* Musielak and K Schurig (eds), Festschrift für Gerhard Kegel. Berlin, Kohlhammer, 1987.

**8** For more details see *Christian Kersting* Corporate Choice of Law – A Comparison of the United States and European Systems and a Proposal for a European Directive, 28 Brook. J. Int'l L. (2002). Available at: http://brooklynworks.brooklaw.edu/bjil/vol28/iss1/1.

**9** *Guenther C Schwarz* Europäisches Gesellschaftsrecht, Nomos, BadenBaden, 2000, p. 179.

**10** See generally *Werner F. Ebke* The "Real Seat" Doctrine in the Conflict of Corporate Laws, 36 INT'L LAW, 1015 (2002).

**11** See for example the point of departure and factual background of the case in CJEU judgement in Case C-208/00 *Überseering BV v Nordic Construction Company Baumanagement GmbH* [2002] ECR I-9919 [*Überseering*].

izational structure may conform to the law of the state in which the management centre is located. The real seat theory is protective as it limits the incentives for creation of mere letterbox or pseudo-foreign companies without being subject to proper government control regulation in the state of their real seat.

On the contrary, Incorporation Theory is based on the principle that legal issues relating to a legal person should be governed by the law of the state of incorporation.[12] The theory has its roots in the 18th century English law. Incorporation Theory prevails, for example, in the United Kingdom, Ireland, Finland, Sweden, the United States and Switzerland. Founders of a corporation are therefore able to choose the law that shall regulate the corporate statute. The state which follows Incorporation Theory allows for a corporations' operation on its territory in the form they were originally incorporated, without specific obligations that would assimilate them to the domestic companies. Should the principal place of business transfer from one state to another, the corporation remains a legal person and may pursue its activities and the change of legal environment shall not affect its internal affairs (legal capacity, legal intent, etc.).

Incorporation Theory, reflected also in the Internal Affairs Doctrine, is currently on the rise, within EU it is also under the influence of CJEU case law.[13] Incorporation Theory encourages cross-border mobility of corporations and promotes the freedom of choice of law by corporations and thus serves the regulatory competition well.[14] In addition to conflict of laws' rules on ascertaining *lex societatis* applicable during the sound functioning of the corporation, other conflict of laws' rules may apply within the cross-border insolvency of a corporation (*lex concursus*) when a more factual approach is followed (Centre of Main Interest – COMI in Europe).

Conflict of laws regulations thus restrict the existence, internal structure and relationships within a corporation to the legal order of a single state. At first glance, it appears that shareholders' agreements, taking into account their contractual nature, should not be subject to such restrictions and that the choice of

---

**12** I.e. *Brian R Cheffins*, Company Law – Theory, Structure and Operation. Clarendon Press, Oxford, 1997, p. 427.

**13** For example, Case C-81/87 *The Queen v H M Treasury and Commissioners of Inland Revenue, ex parte Daily Mail and General Trust Plc* [1988] ECR I-5483 [*Daily Mail*]; Case C-212/97 *Centros Ltd v Erhvervsog Selskabsstyrelsen* [1999] ECR I-1459 [*Centros*]; Case C-167/01 *Kamer van Koophandel en Fabrieken voor Amsterdam v Inspire Art Ltd* [2003] ECR I-10155 [*Inspire Art*]; Case C-208/00 *Überseering BV v Nordic Construction Company Baumanagement GmbH* [2002] ECR I-9919 [*Überseering*]; Case C-210/06 *CARTESIO Oktató és Szolgáltató bt.* [2008] ECR I-09641 [*Cartesio*].

**14** *Jens C. Dammann* Freedom of Choice in European Corporate Law, 29 YALE J. INT'L L. 477, 479 (2004).

law pertaining to conflict of laws' rules on contracts would apply. However, appearances can be deceiving. It is necessary to first determine the scope of the issues that shall be governed by *lex societatis*, then to ascertain whether the legislation pertaining to shareholders' agreements falls under the governing law thus determined.

## D. *Lex societatis*/Internal Affairs Doctrine and the law governing corporations

Prior to making the final decision on what legal order governs shareholders' agreements, the scope of applicable *lex societatis* must be determined, i.e. the scope of issues pertaining to *internal affairs* of a corporation. As was mentioned before, it is important that matters involving a corporation's internal affairs be all governed by a single legal order. According to a famous quote: "*The essential incidents of the activities of any legal entity are controlled by one municipal law, a single ubiquitous personal law, parallel to the statute personal of individuals. (...) This law governs existence, capacity, internal structure, external legal relations, modifications of the charter and dissolution of the legal entity.*"[15] However, not all the issues regarding the corporation's internal affairs are governed by *lex societatis* or by the Internal Affairs Doctrine. The scope of issues that are governed by a corporate status is not clear and might cause further difficulties when considering the issues falling under both company and corporate law, such as shareholders' agreements. Although there is a general agreement, the devil is often in the detail.

In general, questions involving the internal affairs include the rights and liabilities of shareholders, directors and officers to the corporation, shareholders' and directors' meetings, the election of directors, and the validity of decisions of the corporate bodies, etc.[16] The state that has created the corporation shall be the only state whose law controls the relationships among the corporate entity, directors, officers and shareholders.[17] It is also stated that the applicable law of the corporation's internal organization governs all the interventions into *the*

15 *Ernst Rabel* The Conflict of Laws A Comparative Study, 2nd. ed. 1960, Vol II p. 3.

16 According to the comments to § 313 of the Restatement (Second) of Conflict of Laws corporation's internal affairs are involved whenever the issue concerns the relations *inter se* of the corporation, its shareholders, directors, officers or agents.

17 *Rosenmiller v. Bordes*, 607 A2d 465 (Del Ch 1991), *Ringling v. Ringling Bros.-Barnum & Bailey Combined Shows, Inc.*, Del.Ch., 49 A.2d 603, 607 (1946).

*legal status of shareholders* by granting of special rights or obligations to the shareholder.[18] Such an interpretation is too broad, since any additional shareholders' right or obligation, including the ones agreed *inter partes* only, falls thereby under the personal status of a corporation. However, the relevance of the impact of a contractual arrangement upon the shareholders or upon the structure of the corporation is determined by the applicable law itself and it is not really helpful for assessing whether the arrangement falls under *lex societatis* or *lex contractus*. Thus, questions pertaining to internal affairs should only include such arrangements concerning shareholders' rights and obligations which impact the corporation's structure, division of powers of corporate bodies, the position of shareholders *vis a vis* the corporation or among each other, if such an arrangement influences the will making process of the corporation. The personal status of a corporation is always affected by the intervention into the corporation's internal organization, i.e. all the interventions into the structure of corporate bodies, division of their powers and the fundamental division of rights and obligations among shareholders, supervisory and management bodies and the corporation itself.

The applicable rules of *lex societatis* govern also the formal requirements of legal conduct. For example, the amendment of Articles must meet certain formal requirements of the state of incorporation which must be met even if the annual general meeting is held in another state. It cannot be ruled out that the corporate bodies, including shareholders' meetings, will be convened abroad. The admissibility of general meeting held abroad is governed by law applicable to corporations. A foreign local notary is permitted to carry out or attest such actions, and the requirement of the notary's presence on such a legal action does not exclude the possibility of the action made abroad. Again, the *lex societatis* rules shall be essential for the assessment of whether the formal requirements of notary registration made by a foreign notary have been sufficiently met. The purpose of the formal requirements is much-discussed. If the purpose of the norm is only to ensure the certification of the course of action, the fact that it was done so by an official *functionally equivalent* to a notary from the state of incorporation should suffice. The principle of functional equivalence means that a foreign notary fulfils the same function as their counterpart in the state where a corporation is based and follows similar procedural rules on the notarisation.[19] However, should a notary also ensure the said legal action's compli-

**18** *Stephan R. Göthel* in Merkt, H., Göthel, S., R. (eds.) Internationaler Unternehmenskauf. 3. Ed. Köln : RWS Verlag, 2011, p. 554.

**19** German Federal Court of Justic as of 16.2.1981 – II ZB 8/80, BGHZ 80, 76, 78 and as of 17.12. 2013 – II ZB 6/13, NZG 2014, 219.

ance with the law (under *lex societatis*), [20] a foreign notary will fail to do so, thus the requirement of the notarisation could be regarded as the material condition of the action's validity.

## I. Mixed worlds: non-corporate elements of the Articles and corporate elements of Shareholders' Agreements

It could be tempting to state that all the issues referred to in the Articles fall under *lex societatis* (internal affairs). That is not necessarily the case. Should the Articles also include non-corporate issues, it is debatable whether they are governed by *lex societatis* or *lex contractus*. A differentiated view with regard to the substance of the arrangement in the Articles is to be followed.[21] In the author's opinion, it is necessary to proceed from the fact that *lex societatis* sets clear limits on the content of the Articles, thus there is a possibility to include contractual arrangements into the Articles as well as to execute shareholders' agreements besides the Articles. It follows that it is actually *lex societatis* which determines whether corporate documents can be open to contractual additions. Therefore, this law should also govern the determining of conflict of laws' rules regarding such an arrangement. The protective or regulatory nature of substantive *lex societatis* should transpire into conflict of laws' regulation.

Moreover, as was previously mentioned,[22] including contractual arrangements into the Articles does not change their contractual nature from a substantive point of view. The same shall apply to the conflict of laws' perspective. If an arrangement included in the Articles is of a contractual and non-corporate nature, the contractual conflict of laws' rules shall apply. The Articles might therefore include a choice of law clause for contractual arrangements (side letters) despite the fact that the corporate issues will be governed by the law of the state of incorporation.

The same should apply *vice versa* for the purposes of conflict of laws. Should shareholders' agreements contain corporate issues, *lex societatis* should again determine whether and to what extent contractual arrangements of corporate issues outside the Articles are permitted. Prohibition to contractually negotiate a

---

**20** Actually, a stricter form of recording the course of and decisions made during the general meeting does not ensure the compliance with the law, since it is generally the chairman of the shareholders' meeting, not a notary, who is responsible for ensuring the compliance. See i.e. the German Supreme court decision dated 21.10.2014 (II ZR 330/13, para 21).

**21** *Spahlinger/Wegen* Internationales Gesellschaftsrecht in der Praxis. C. H. Beck, 2005, p. 87.

**22** See *Mock/Csach/Havel* in General remarks, under A. and E.

certain corporate issue under *lex societatis* could also find its way into the conflict of laws perspective. The decisive factor is once again the reason for restrictive or prohibiting regulation of *lex societatis*. If the purpose of such prohibition is to prevent certain regulation also in shareholders' agreements, it will not be possible to avoid that reason by simply claiming to choose different applicable law. The contractual arrangement outside the Articles might not be a safe harbour from the perils of the corporate sea.

On the other hand, should a dispute under the contract law be held in the court different from the state of incorporation or the arbitral tribunal, conflict of laws' rules of that *lex fori* will be applicable, and the question is whether and how they allow for the interpretation of limitations set by *lex societatis* to the contractual arrangements (either as international mandatory rules or as a limitation of the scope of the applicable *lex contractus*).

## II. The EU approach: the corporate law exemption from private international law rules on contractual obligations

Within the EU some of the issues relating to the corporation's internal affairs are excluded from conflict of laws' rules on contractual obligations as defined in Rome I Regulation.[23] Under Article 1 (2)(f) of the Rome I Regulation the following is excluded from the scope of the regulation: "*questions governed by the law of companies and other bodies, corporate or unincorporated, such as the creation, by registration or otherwise, legal capacity, internal organisation or winding-up of companies and other bodies, corporate or unincorporated, and the personal liability of officers and members as such for the obligations of the company or body.*" A similar exemption might be found in Article 1(2)(d) of Rome II Regulation.[24] Due to the focus on shareholders' agreements, we shall further concentrate on contractual obligations only. The further said shall apply *mutatis mutandis* to the exemption for non-contractual obligations in Rome II.

However, even in the EU the differentiating between a personal and contractual set of conflict of laws' rules is not the question of the interpretation of the said exemption. Even if the issue is outside the scope of Rome I Regulation, it does not necessarily fall under *lex societatis*. There may be other national rules or doctrines that classify certain arrangements falling within the scope of

---

**23** Regulation (EC) No 593/2008 of the European Parliament and of the Council of 17 June 2008 on the law applicable to contractual obligations (Rome I). *OJ L 177, 4.7.2008, p. 6–16.*
**24** Regulation (EC) No 864/2007 of the European Parliament and of the Council of 11 July 2007 on the law applicable to non-contractual obligations (Rome II). *OJ L 199, 31.7.2007, p. 40–49.*

Article 1(2)(f) of Rome I Regulation as contractual arrangements governed by *lex contractus* and not as corporate *lex societatis*. Article 1(2)(f) Rome I exemption is thus no boundary between *lex contractus* and *lex societatis*. But what is actually excluded from the scope of Rome I Regulation?

According to the *Giuliano-Lagarde Report* serving as an explanatory report on the Rome Convention,[25] a predecessor of Rome I Regulation,

> *the exemption shall cover all the complex acts (contractual, administrative, registration) which are necessary to the creation of a company or firm and to the regulation of its internal organization and winding-up, i. e. acts which fall within the scope of company law. On the other hand, acts or preliminary contracts whose sole purpose is to create obligations between interested parties (promoters) with a view to forming a company or firm are not covered by the exclusion. Examples of "internal organization" are the calling of meetings, the right to vote, the necessary quorum, the appointment of officers of the company or firm, etc. "Winding-up" would cover either the termination of the company or firm as provided by its constitution or by operation of law, or its disappearance by merger or other similar process.*[26]

That shall be decisive also when ascertaining the conflict of laws nature of a shareholders' agreement. The shareholders' agreement falls outside the exemption if it creates obligations between interested parties only. Although, as will be discussed later, some contractual arrangements (e.g. the agreement on voting rights) are considered as part of the internal organization even if they appear to create only an *inter partes* obligation.

On a side note, the EU conflict of laws' regulation on contractual obligations do not fully mirror the rules on jurisdiction. The European Court of Justice in *Peters*[27] took the view that the relationship between an association with legal capacity (a corporation) and one of its members (a shareholder) concerning the recovery of sums payable by the latter constitutes for the purposes of interpretation of Brussels Convention (the predecessor of Brussels I Regulation) a contractual issue. However, the participants to the proceedings including the Commission jointly agreed that despite it being a contractual matter for the Brussels regime, the issue still falls under the scope of the corporate exemption in Rome I.[28]

---

**25** Convention on the law applicable to contractual obligations opened for signature in Rome 19 July 1980 (OJ 1980, L 266, 9.10.1980, p. 1–19).

**26** *Giuliano/Lagarde* Report on the Convention on the law applicable to contractual obligations, 1980 OJ C 282, 31.10.1989, p. 1–50 [*Giuliano-Lagarde Report*].

**27** In Case 34/82, *Peters v. Zuid Nederlandse Aannemers vereniging* [1983] ECR 00987 [*Peters*].

**28** Opinion of Advocate General Mancini in Case 34/82, *Peters v. Zuid Nederlandse Aannemers vereniging* [1983] ECR 00987 [*Peters*], para 7.

# E. A multi-layered approach to corporate law issues within conflict of laws rules

Although there is a wide-spread agreement on the need to harmonize the laws governing the issues concerning corporations, it is not possible and appropriate to have only one law to regulate all corporate matters at all costs. A contractual relationship related to corporate law may be multi-layered with various conflict of laws' implications and not every legal relationship concerning a corporation falls under *lex societatis* or the internal affairs. For example, a share transfer gives rise to interactions between various sets of conflict of laws' rules.

The law applicable to corporations (*lex societatis*) decides on the issue, whether the share is transferable or not, on the limitations and conditions of the transfer, the possibility of a partial transfer and division of shares, and the time when the transfer is effective (i.e. notice to the corporation). *Lex societatis* might also be decisive on the question of what actions are necessary for the transfer (delivery, notification of the corporation, registration in the Commercial Register), i.e. which of the three basic principles – "*Abstraktionsprinzip*" (Germany, Greece), causal approach (Austria, Switzerland) or consensus principle (France, Italy, Poland) – shall apply.

The law applicable to contractual obligations (*lex contractus*) defines the rights and duties of the parties with the formal requirements being subject to special conflict of law' rules.[29] In respect of the EU regional unification of conflict of laws' rules on contractual obligations, the *Giuliano-Lagarde Report* mentions that the exclusion of the applicability of the Rome Convention (now Rome I Regulation) on negotiable instruments only applies with regard to obligations arising out of their negotiable character.[30] Neither the contracts pursuant to which such instruments are issued nor contracts for the purchase and sale of such instruments are excluded.[31] It might be said that, therefore, a share transfer is also not excluded from the scope of Rome I Regulation, but the rights and obligations arising from the shares are excluded.

A wide choice of law is admissible within cross-border contractual relations. The application of law applicable to contractual obligations and not *lex societatis* can prove more efficient if national legislation of certain states reduces the

29 See the German Supreme court decision BGH NZG 2005, 41 (42).

30 Exemption according to Article 1(2)(d) Rome I Regulation.

31 *Giuliano-Lagarde Report* p. 11.

formal requirements on the transfer of shares.[32] However, if a regulation governing the formal requirements is aimed to protect other interests – i.e. the limitation of the free transferability of the shares – it entails the risk of not being considered as a standard formal requirement only, albeit a substantive condition, and thus *lex societatis* shall apply.[33]

The law applicable to property rights and to the ownership to movables determines the issues of the actual transfer of the title to the share, especially in case the share is incorporated and thus a movable. The question whether a share might be incorporated is nonetheless a question defined by the law applicable to corporations. The law applicable to succession to the estates of deceased persons can be also addressed, since it determines the rules governing the transfer of the shares belonging to the estate of the deceased person (a deceased shareholder). Whether succession regarding a share is allowed at all is defined by the law applicable to corporations. Similar questions need to be addressed from the point of view of shareholders' agreements.

# F. Shareholders' Agreements in cross-border interactions

A foreign element in shareholders' agreements raises the questions posed by conflict of laws. It is questionable what is the law applicable to shareholders' agreements or part thereof and whether it is possible to choose different governing law for shareholders' agreements than for the corporation's internal affairs (*lex societatis*). A sufficient foreign element is the fact that a shareholder is domiciled in another state. The relevance of the mere fact that a shareholders' agreement has been executed in another state than the state of incorporation is discussed, but shall also be sufficient. The determination of a foreign element shall be performed at the time of shareholders' agreement made, i.e. at the time of its creation. From a viewpoint of private international law, shareholders' agreement is not a defined type of a contract. Moreover, there is no uniform concept of a shareholders' agreement to characterise. The identification of the appli-

32 See Swiss Art. 785 (1) OR for a written form requirement. The parties, especially of a high volume transaction, might choose to execute the contract in a country with lower notary fees and less stringent formal requirements.

33 I.e. the requirement of notarisation subject to Section 15 paragraph 3 of the German GmbHG should therefore be considered as a material norm and therefore as part of the scope of the personal status of a corporation (*lex societatis*).

cable governing law therefore requires more than just one connecting factor. Thus, it is necessary to consider the content of a shareholders' agreement differentiating between the issues of statutory and contractual nature. There are several possible points of departure when addressing the issue.

Firstly, shareholders' agreements may fall under the personal status of the particular corporation (the scope of application of *lex societatis*). Therefore, no separate connecting factor needs to be found and the governing law of the state of incorporation (or a factual seat for those states adhering to the Real Seat Theory) applies. We do not recommend following this reasoning because shareholders' agreements may include various purely contractual covenants that need not be subject to *lex societatis.*

Secondly, it is important to characterise shareholders' agreements separately (not as part of the *lex societatis* of the corporation) from three additional different points of view.

A shareholders' agreement might be defined as a societal cooperation (*societa*, civil partnership, Innengesellschaft). If some organizational structure does not limit its activities to internal *inter partes* relation but also steps into operation in public, the societal connecting factors are applicable. If the shareholders' agreement is to be considered as such external societal organisation, *lex societatis* (but ascertained separately from the *lex societatis* of the corporation itself) shall apply. If the shareholders' agreement is operating internally only it shall fall under *lex contracts.*[34]

Should there be any arrangements included in the shareholders' agreement which interfere with corporate issues (i.e. the scope of the corporation's personal status), the law which governs also the corporation's internal affairs (*lex societatis*) shall apply. The same should apply in relation to voting rights agreements and agreements on voting proxies,[35] as such arrangements have impact on the core of the internal organisation of the corporation (its structure) and the essence of will making.[36] For example, it is said that nothing is more central to the internal management of a corporation than a shareholder's right to vote in the election of directors.[37] According to the U.S. Supreme Court: "*No principle*

34 *Stephan R. Göthel* in Merkt, H., Göthel, S., R. (eds.) Internationaler Unternehmenskauf. 3. Ed. Köln : RWS Verlag, 2011, p. 553.

35 We will not consider the problem of representation itself, which has its own connecting factors.

36 Followed also under the Internal Affairs Doctrine: "*Delaware . . . has a greater interest than does New Jersey in regulating stockholder voting rights in Delaware corporations.*" *Rosenmiller v. Bordes*, 607 A2d 465 (Del Ch 1991).

37 *Bagdon v. Bridgestone/Firestone, Inc.*, 916 F.2d 379, 383 (7th Cir.1990).

*of corporation law and practice is more firmly established than a State's authority to regulate domestic corporations, including the authority to define the voting rights of share-holders."*[38] Therefore, *lex societatis* (mostly *lex incorporationis*) applies. The same holds true in case ancillary bodies not foreseen by the Articles are being created (shareholders' committees). This means that it is prohibited to choose the governing law as the *lex societatis* does not allow for the contractual choice of law.

Otherwise, the traditional rules for determining the law applicable to contracts (*lex contractus*) shall apply to the remaining scope with the possibility of the choice of law applicable to the contractual relation. Such shareholders' agreements covenants should remain outside the scope of the corporate exemption subject to Rome I Regulation, and thus, the said Regulation shall apply. A contractual covenant may include i.e. mutual relations between shareholders that do not affect the will making process or division of powers of bodies not having impact on the will making during the annual general meeting,[39] and also various *inter partes* rules for the transfer of shares, piggy back clauses, drag or tag along, call or put options, etc. The extent of free choice of law is however limited by the other conflict of laws rules, as was previously mentioned with regard to the transfer of shares.

The choice of law is similarly limited in relation to the property law issues, i.e. in relation to the substantive law effects of the limitations to transfer, conditions for acquiring the title to a share. However, the determination of the scope of rights and obligations arising from a share (voting rights, their multiplication) shall be subject to *lex societatis*. Likewise, the issues of the pledge on shares are divided into substantial law issues (creation and existence) and personal status issues (the possibility and extent of rights arising from the pledge).

*Lex societatis* governs the admissibility and formal requirements (if aimed to protect corporate or similar interests) of the transfer of shares, including the rules for potential admissibility of a contractual limitation of transferability of shares. Exceptionally, such covenants might be governed by *lex societatis*, provided the corporation itself is bound by shareholders' agreements (preemption, first refusal, etc.) and thus the statutory body would be bound to adhere to the agreement.

---

**38** *CTS Corp. v. Dynamics Corp. of America*, 481 U.S. 69, 89, 107 S.Ct. 1637, 1649, 95 L.Ed.2d 67 (1987).

**39** I.e. already *Jürgen Dohm* Les accords sur l'exercice du droit de vote de l'actionnaire : Étude de droit suisse et allemand 1971, p. 150; *Hartmut Lübbert* Abstimmungsvereinbarungen in den Aktien- und GmbH-Rechten der EWG-Staaten, der Schweiz und Großbritannien, Baden-Baden, 1971, p. 469.

The applicable law to corporate issues defines the conditions under which the Articles can be amended as well as the impact of shareholders' decisions within or outside the bodies on the Articles. Hence, *lex societatis* shall determine whether shareholders' agreements have an impact on the Articles as well as the extent to which a shareholders' agreement result in the nullity of the decisions of the corporation's bodies. *Lex societatis* also determines whether the votes cast during the corporation's body vote comply with the law, i.e. whether the vote is valid or not, even if shareholders' agreement was violated.

Such a conclusion is not so evident *vice versa*, i.e. whether the Articles have an impact on the validity of shareholders' agreements. Should a shareholders' agreement be considered as an ordinary contract (distinct form its corporate structure), it would be possible to assess the limits of mandatory requirements under the law applicable to the contract (*lex contractus*) with international mandatory (imperative) norms and *ordre public* taken into account. This would lead to the situation that each case would be assessed on the grounds of whether a violated *lex societatis* rule is so important as to cause the nullity of the shareholders' agreement under *lex contractus*.

Dispute settlement and enforcement clauses are also a common part of shareholders' agreements. The alternative dispute resolution covenants may substantially influence the applicable law since the arbiters may tend to be more liberal in relation to the usage of *lex electa*.

# G. Change of the law applicable to corporations and Shareholders' Agreements (change of *lex societatis*)

In case of the change of applicable *lex societatis* (i.e. the transfer of a seat), it must be decided whether it impacts the law applicable to shareholders' agreements as such or only the shareholders' agreement's corporate or non-corporate part. The reasoning is identical to the one regarding the changes of contractual arrangements included in the Articles (and of corporate nature in shareholders' agreements *vice versa*) – once a contractual regime is established, whether by the Articles or by shareholders' agreements, the contractual regime of the choice of law shall apply. The change of governing law for a contractual shareholders' agreement shall thus require an agreement of the parties involved and not just a voting of a corporate majority. The mere transfer of a seat does not change the connecting factor of the contractual arrangement. However, if *lex societatis* is *"the closest connection"* factor of the conflict of laws' rule for contractual shareholders' agreement arrangements, the transfer of a seat shall imply also a change in the connecting factor for the closest connected shareholders' agreement.

"The mixed nature of shareholders' agreements transpires also into the private international law perspective. In general, l*ex societatis* defines the impact of shareholders' agreement onto corporate documents. The content of the Shareholders' agreement is relevant for ascertaining their contractual, corporate or *in rem* classification from the conflict of laws perspective. It is thus possible, that parts of a shareholders' agreement will be open for choice of law, others will be governed by laws different from *lex societatis*."[40]

**40** The chapter is part of the research project APVV-0809-12.

Bohumil Havel

# Shareholders' Agreement Arrangement in Pre-insolvency and Insolvency Law

**Table of Content**



**Abstract.** This article is concerned with the usability of shareholder'' agreements (SHA) and SHA-like arrangements in the period when a corporation is in distress, outlining also the forms of such distress. It further examines how the increased pressure of both national as well as EU legislators to settle the corporation's distress informally renders contractual arrangements (stabilization agreements) more significant ex ante as well as ex post. The importance of stabilization agreements (in particular standstill agreements) for the settlement of distress of a corporation tends to increase also due to the fact that with more complicated cor-

---

**Doc. JUDr. Bohumil Havel PhD.** is a researcher of the Institute of State and Law of the Academy of Sciences of the Czech Republic (www.ilaw.cas.cz), a member of the Scientific Board of the Centre for Restructuring and Insolvency of Harry Pollak of the University of Economics in Prague (http://iem.vse.cz/cri/english/), and a lecturer in Bankruptcy Corporate Governance at the Law Faculty of the Charles University in Prague; he also works as counsel in the law office of PRK Partners Praha. The work was supported (partly) by the grant project APVV-0809-12.

https://doi.org/10.1515/9783110517026-006

porate and financial structures formal solutions for a corporation in distress need not be necessarily suitable and beneficial, which, however, puts higher demands on the preciseness and content of such informal arrangements. This article also deals with formal insolvency rescue processes that might possibly be activated as well as proposals of preventive restructuring suggested by the European Union. The last section of this article is focused on the role of shareholder' agreements and stabilization agreements in the distress rescue process, including possible application of the rules for executory contracts.

**Key words:** shareholder agreement, corporation, insolvency, balance sheet test, going concern, liquidity test, standstill agreement, lock-up agreement, European Union, executory contracts, firm, obligations, nexus of obligations, contractualization, side-letters, Konzernrecht, group of companies, veil of ignorance, action Pauliana, insolvency law, London approach, companies rescue, prepack, reorganization

*Private law is a pervasive phenomenon of our social life, a silent but ubiquitous participant in our most common transaction.*
*Ernest J. Weinrib*

# A. Contractualization of corporation and its ex ante consequences

Nowadays, it is a widely known fact that the world of private corporations is not a world of statutory (mandatory) law, but rather a world where autonomy of will is quite a viable phenomenon which completes and determines the function of a corporation[1]. Despite of its diverse stages of development, a corporation is still a private law instrument with all of its land of variability. Moreover, a corporation is more than just a static object that is to be provided with some characterization, as was argued by legal normativists, it is variable phenomenon as was pointed out especially by *Coase*[2], and later by his followers *Williamson*[3] and *Jen-*

1 Similar focus on the selection of the rules is present, for example, in the work of *Easterbrook/ Fischel* The Economic Structure of Corporate Law, Cambridge: Harvard University Press, 1996, p. 2 an.

2 The Nature of the Firm in The Firm, the Market and the Law, Chicago: CHUP, 1988 (1990), p. 33 an.

*sen* with *Meckling*[4] who developed the *theory of the firm*. A corporation (firm) was understood as a social fact resulting from negotiations and efforts to decrease the business-related costs which got manifested during the negotiations, as well as efforts to maximize the benefit (not necessarily the profit). In this context some authors would also mention a function of "nexus of obligations (for example, on a contract basis)"[5], which is understood as an incomplete "*black box*",[6] which derives from the original incorporation documents, but which, on the other hand, varies according to an instantaneous condition of the business[7] and the environment. The incomplete nature of the contractual content of a corporation presumes that this union also involves externalities, i.e. side effects of a corporation (not) acting toward third persons and the environment. Various jurisdictions therefore contain some rules to internalize them or provide for other suitable solutions (accountability, public sanctions, public rescue, etc.).

A degree of the autonomy of will and thereby the role of the contractual law will always depend on the national regulation of statutory corporate law. As is known from history, the use of statutory regulation or contractual regulation underwent gradual development from autonomy to regulation, or from liberalism to a need of regulatory interventions, and later partly back to contractualization of the world of corporations. The conclusion that the role of contracts after the increased influence of mandatory regulation in the 19th century intensified again[8] is therefore quite tenable, although today it is exposed to a renewed interest in the relevant regulation often under the rule *comply or explain*. Although in some jurisdictions the efforts to have a restricting regulation still prevail – compare,

---

**3** Transaction Cost Economics: The Governance of Contractual Relations, Journal of Law and Economics, 1979 (cited according to *Sjåfjell* Towards a Sustainable European Company Law, New York: Wolters Kluwer, 2009, p. 24), or The Theory of the Firm as Governance Structure: From Choice to Contract, Journal of Economic Perspectives, 2002 (http://www.nicolaifoss.com).

**4** Theory of the Firm: Managerial Behavior, Agency Costs, and Ownership Structure, Journal of Financial Economics, 1976, cited according to *Jensen* A Theory of the Firm, Cambridge: HUP, 2000.

**5** *Jensen/ Meckling* Theory of the Firm: Managerial Behavior, Agency Costs, and Ownership Structure, l.c., p. 89.

**6** *Jensen/* Theory of the Firm: Managerial Behavior, Agency Costs, and Ownership Structure, l.c., p. 84.

**7** *Jensen* and *Meckling* also rendered a definition of private corporation as "*a form of legal fiction serving as nexus of contractual relations which is also characterised by the existence of divisible residual rights toward the corporation's equity. Such a nexus may be sold without a consent of other contracting persons*". (l.c., p. 88).

**8** Cf., for example, *Hansmann/Kraakman* The Contractualization of Organizational Law in *Grundmann/Haar/Merkt et al.* Festschrift für Klaus J. Hopt zum 70. Geburtstag, De Gruyter, Berlin-New York, 2010, p. 747 an.

for example, – the concept of *Satzungsstrenge* still maintained, although often challenged, in German[9] and Austrian[10] corporate law – it is well admitted across jurisdictions that the world of corporations is made up not only of the source statutory law, but also, an often prevailingly/especially, by the related autonomous regulations contained in the articles (in particular, in the *sideletters*), or outside them, in shareholders' agreements (SHA). Such a "nexus of obligations" concept of corporation, i. e. a firm in the meaning explained above, will certainly determine not only the content of the relationship among the corporation, shareholders or its management, but it will also (co)determine the rules of interpretation and application of respective rules. While we might incline to interpret the statutory rules in a more objective manner, the related contractual rules will be interpreted in a more subjective tone and from a perspective of their intended purpose.

The creation of such a wide set of rules to regulate the life of a corporation whose source would not be limited only to statutory corporate law is obviously not done only to set the rules for which there is no "room" in the articles, but it is also an expression of reasonable planning in case of future disputes or project failures. It is legitimate to expect that during the time of distress of a corporation it will be either positive or negative heuristics that will dominate the decision-making of the management and owners, and the selection of any of them will be influenced by the fatal lack of time, negotiation stress and restrictions imposed by insolvency law. Quite tenable is therefore the concept which has been repeated many times that if the parties of a future corporation have a chance and space to negotiate they should be foreseeing such a future possibility *ex ante*, in other words, they should set out foreseeable solutions. The *Rawls*'

---

**9** Some authors refer to it as "the highest degree of legal paternalism", see, for example, *Wiedemann* in Lutter/Wiedemann (eds.) Gestaltungsfreiheit Im Gesellschaftsrecht: Deutschland, Europa Und USA. 11. Zgr-Symposion "25 Jahre Zgr" (Zeitschrift F R Unternehmens- Und Gesellschaftsrecht/Zgr-Son), Berlin, De Gruyter, 1998, p. 10. This concept was subject to criticism also at page 67. Juristen Tagen in Erfurt 2008, in lecture of prof. *W. Bayer*, see http://www.beck-shop.de/fachbuch/inhaltsverzeichnis/Bayer-Empfehlen-Regelungen-Gesellschaften-9783406574559_0305201206152968_ihv.pdf, citation of 1/12/2015.

**10** However, compare a decision of the Austrian OGH 6Ob28/13f z 8.5. 2013 which concludes that *"Since AktG (in contrast to the German AktG) does not contain an explicit provision of "Satzungsstrenge", AktG may not always be interpreted so that a particular provision of articles is admissible only if it is explicitly foreseen in AktG or when a deviation provision is explicitly permitted in the AktG. In the case of a joint-stock company which is not listed on the stock exchange a shareholder's pre-emption right provision is admissible to be included in the articles for the share transfer cases, at least, for the transfer of shares blocked pursuant to Section 62 subsection 2 of the AktG".*

concept of the "*veil of ignorance*"[11], which is frequently pointed out in the theory of insolvency law[12], offers a possible solution, nevertheless, in the absence of agreement it will still not guarantee that a particular national regulation will offer a reasonable and enforceable solution. It therefore makes sense, and it is the very nature of the contractual law itself, to foresee a possible future critical situation (*failure*) and to prepare possible procedures that will be activated during the time of threatening economic insufficiency or threatening bankruptcy. The significance of such arrangements cannot be seen only in the setting of the rules that could subsequently influence the process of remedying the critical situation of a corporation, but also, and especially, the process of setting the standard of care to be pursued in such cases by the management or the owners themselves. Such rules may provide security not only to the corporation itself, but also to its management and the owners. It will be shown later on that not all such rules will survive the management when the corporation is in distress and its critical situation is to be managed.

## B. SHA as a tool in foreseeing a distress of a corporation

As was already described in the first chapter, the parties to a shareholders' agreement may also include third persons standing outside a corporation, which indicates that partial projects of such corporation agreements may manifest themselves also in the pre-insolvency and insolvency period, in form of so called stabilization agreements (in particular, *standstill agreements*). If we are able to negotiate concrete rules to remedy a distress which will draw on the concept of shareholders' agreements, it should also be possible to set the rules already in the shareholders' agreements or articles of association that would prevent or restrict the necessity of stabilization agreements to occur. In other words, the law of contract offers some alternatives which allow of *ex ante* foreseeability of a distress of a corporation and has several solutions to settle such cases. For example, it might be possible to arrange for a duty to pay extra contributions to the corporation's equity/share capital as is known in the German or Czech jurisdiction, or it might be possible to agree a duty to provide a private or commercial

11 Mentioned in his book "Theory of Justice", cited according to the Czech translation of 1994, p. 92.

12 *Jackson* The Logic and Limits of Bankruptcy Law, Washington: BeardBooks, 1986 (2001), p. 17 or *Finch* Corporate Insolvency Law, Cambridge: CUP, 2002, p. 33

loan, or other similar payments substituting the share/equity capital, as is known, for example, from the Austrian or Slovak law, another option is reduction of a residual property right for certain cases, patronage administration or voting trust may be agreed for the time of distress of a corporation, lock-up agreements, etc.. All such solutions may prevent bankruptcy of a corporation or may establish positive incentives to encourage the stakeholders to start negotiating the problems and avoid hasty installation of formal insolvency proceedings – by the way, that is why some of these tools would change the balance of power in the corporation and would partly level out the information asymmetry. It should also be added, however, that such rules concerning possible joint action should be tested in respect of the provisions of the law of corporate groups, if/as imposed by national jurisdictions, because such conduct may amount to joint acting or even to acting of a group.[13]

The rules agreed to prevent possible failures, or to encourage their settlement often result from the fact that the original shareholders' agreement aims not only to arrange for the rules among shareholders, but also for the rules among investors expecting their subsequent exit. Shareholders thus often co-create wider rules for start-ups or various spin-off structures[14] which do not aim to strengthen the equity situation in the corporation but rather only investment positions. Such an assumption will also determine the tools elected, and it will logically presume that it is in the interest of the investor to find a solution that will reduce the negative exposition of a corporation to distress during the time of crisis. While the residual owner bear the risks of a project failure from the very nature of its position, a party having a fixed-claim or quasi-fixed-claim may anticipate or decrease such risks.

**13** Cf., for example, the German law of corporate groups (*Konzernrecht*) contained in the Aktiengesetz (AktG 1965), the Czech law of corporate groups in the Czech Companies Act – see, e.g. *Havel* Czech Corporate Law on its Way, ECFR 2015, p. 32 an., or "Proposal to Facilitate the Management of Cross-Border Company Groups in Europe" in ECFR, Vol. 12, Issue 2, 2015, p. 299 – 306, or German version in ZGR 4/2015, str. 507 an., or the relevant parts of the draft European Model Company Act.

**14** Especially with these structures it is becoming more obvious that contractual regulation of their activities and governance is more significant that the mandatory law, as rule, a simplified law of private limited liability companies, also see *Hansmann/Kraakman* The Contractualization of Organizational Law, l.c., p. 756 an.

# C. Corporation in distress and influence of distress on its conduct

There is no doubt that distress of a corporation will not mean that such a corporation is already bankrupt in the eyes of the law. In other words, distress of a corporation is a wider concept which is more of an economic nature and which will be legally considered and further specified as bankruptcy as soon as it is to be settled formally. From such a perspective, the concept of distress of a corporation focuses on the period when a corporation is approaching a condition or is in a condition when it may be expected that it will be unable to *"realize a rate of return on invested capital that (...) is significantly greater than the prevailing market rates in similar investments"*[15]. Such a condition may be caused by a whole range of internal or external circumstances, and it basically results in a corporation being unable to reach its goal that was set out and presented to its investors at the beginning. The distress itself is a period of change, it may occur quickly or it may take places in various stages by partial economic failures at the beginning, through threatening bankruptcy, with the final actual bankruptcy. When discussing a corporation in distress, however, its respective stages must always be well- identified because what may be arranged for at the time of threatening bankruptcy, may not be agreed at the time of actual bankruptcy, etc. It should therefore be strictly distinguished if a corporation is only undergoing some problems that might still be settled and which were foreseeable, or if it is already in the stage of *threatening bankruptcy*, which is often subject to legislative definitions, or whether it is already in the condition that amounts to bankruptcy under national legislation which is basically connected with the mandatory initiation of formal insolvency proceedings. The identification and description of a particular stage of distress are important *ex ante* not only in order to propose a solution and to implement it, but also to determine a standard of care to be pursued by the management.

A fatal manifestation of distress of a corporation is its bankruptcy considered legally, since it is the gate for mandatory installation of insolvency proceedings. Usually, bankruptcy might have two forms, in particular *balance sheet test* rendering a proportionate value of the corporation's assets and its liabilities taking into consideration a presumption of *going concern value*, a *cash flow test* examining the corporation's ability to meet its liabilities when due. The two of the categories are specifically defined in various jurisdictions which also distinguish

15 *Finch* Corporate Insolvency Law, l.c., p. 124.

their various modifications basically concerning the temporary nature of distress (*liquidity constraints,* or also a German solution of *Liquiditätslücke*[16], which was also adopted e. g. by the Czech insolvency law). However, it should be noted that various variations of bankruptcy, or its possible sub-classification into various lighter stages, are possible only if it is not the case of *systemic bankruptcy.* Defensive schemes which are laid down by the law or agreement will therefore be applied only if a particular distress does not amount to a systemic failure of a corporation which must be settled within involuntary collective proceedings.

Discussions about a corporation in distress should also involve a very important argument that with a developing crisis of a corporation the intended interest to be pursued by the corporation's management will change. While at the beginning of the life of a corporation it is supposed to pursue the interest of a corporation itself, or its residual owners, the more the legally defined bankruptcy is coming close, the more it is to be necessary to take into account the creditors' interests, while upon entering into formal insolvency proceedings the latter will already prevail[17]. This is important not only to identify the overall focus of governance of a corporation in distress, but especially to determine the nature of fiduciary duties of the management (and sometimes also those of owners). While admitting a standard difference between *duty of care* and *duty of loyalty,* it still may be argued that whereas a duty of care is not expected to change as to its content (although certain obligations are added/modified), a duty of loyalty obviously shifts toward safeguarding the claims and interests of creditors. While in the early stages of distress of a corporation it is still possible to use an argument of defending a corporation itself, or its productivity, with a decreasing chance of rescue of a corporation the management must focus more on the liquidation benefit for creditors. At the same time, however, interests of shareholders and owners might split, because the closer the actual influence of creditors upon the assets of the corporation, the lesser the willingness of owners to take care about the interests of creditors[18]. Hence, on all sides of the originally

16 Based on the case law of the Federal Court of Justice, the German Institute of Auditors *(Institut der Wirtschaftsprüfer in Deutschland E.V. – IDW)* prepared a standard for the evaluation of existence of reasons to install insolvency proceedings, (so called IDW S 11 – https://www.idw.de/idw/idw-aktuell/idw-s-11-zur-insolvenzreife-ergaenzt/99362) – also see Entwurf eines IDW Standards: Beurteilung des Vorliegens von Insolvenzeröffnungsgründen (IDW ES 11), https://www.hoeher-consulting.de/wp-content/uploads/2015/02/Entwurf-IDW-Standard-Insolvenzer%C3%B6ffnungsgr%C3%BCnde-ES11.pdf.

17 Also see, for example, the English decision in Brady v. Brady – cited according to *Griffin* Company Law, Harlow: Pearson Longman, 1994 (2006), p. 315, see https://www.lawteacher.net/cases/company-law/brady-v-brady.php

18 *Jackson* The Logic and Limits of Bankruptcy Law, l.c., p. 122 an.

"uniform" firm there will appear behavioural defects of decision-making (behaviour), moral hazard will increase, mutual trust will decrease, aversion toward risk or loss is modified, negative sentiment is growing, etc..

Standards of care applicable in this stage of the life of a corporation will operate with a force of heteronomic law, as an exogenous fact, and, in general, they do not attempt to hide the fact that they are intended to protect especially the interests of creditors, which are still on a weaker side of the information asymmetry. That is why the law contains rules which allow to examine the pre-insolvency period retrospectively, and that is again relevant for the related utilization of contractual models designed to settle distress. Such tools examine the conduct of a corporation allowing to find if the principle of equal treatment of creditors was not interfered with, of if some them were not put into advantage or were not disadvantaged (compare, for example, *preference law*[19], *actio Pauliana* in the German, Austrian, Swiss or Czech insolvency law). A more general aim of such rules is to decrease a chance of moral failure of individual creditors and the management who would attempt to eliminate or damage a possibility of foreseeable collective proceedings by enforcing their partial individual claims[20].

## D. Settling distress of a corporation

First of all, there is a rule that the sooner the management admits the fact that something wrong is going on with the economic results of their corporation, the better the whole problem may be settled, and, as a rule, the more the creditors are willing to cooperate. Such a position of the management will also ensure that the management will remain in office and thus will be "dominating the negotiations". By the way, a whole range of corporate and insolvency law rules have exactly such an *ex ante* effect which is to encourage such an early or preventive intervention. This may partly remind us of an advantage of the white chessman because the mode of acting by the management will give a corporation a chance to determine the further course of its negotiations and processes. Obviously, it should be added that a duty to divert/prevent bankruptcy is included in the fiduciary duties (under a duty of care), hence, the acting of the management is often a matter of duty rather than choice.

Real indicators of a corporation falling in distress should be certainly sought in the period where it is obvious that it is not, or will not be, able to pay its debts

19 l.c., p. 123.
20 l.c., p. 125.

when due[21], nevertheless there is a whole range of similar indicators – a problem with dominant client, a significant drop of margins, geopolitical restrictions of markers, etc. Some reasons are internal, including managerial failure, others are external, i.e. not caused by a corporation at all. In all cases, however, the corporate management system must be able and enabled to identify the problems and evaluate them.

A whole set of solutions is available, ranging from the soft ones to the very strict ones, and until the company falls into a systemic problem when the influence of creditors is growing significant (including, for example, acceleration of debts), it is a matter of a corporation which of them will be used. Solutions may be divided into informal and formal, internal solutions employing corporation's own resources, corporate group solutions, external solutions employing third persons' aid, formal solutions outside the regulation of insolvency proceedings, or insolvency solutions with various variants of simplified processes. Each decision brings its own transaction costs and it will depend on the actual condition of a corporation which costs are reasonably internalized or economically feasible for a particular solution.

As was outlined before it is already at this moment when the processes of corporate protection which were foreseen in the shareholders' agreement may be activated, and when the management may be able to ask the shareholders for help from the company's share capital, or other persons from the same corporate group. It is logical that such a solution will not always decrease the overall debt burden of a corporation, but the debts of shareholders may be subordinated either on a SHA or statutory basis, which will significantly change the overall economic balance of a corporation. Such models may also be handy to settle some transitional problems. It is quite obvious that other steps will also be necessary *within internal restructuring* of the business of a corporation (change of production activities, change of employee's portfolio, discontinuation of the operation of loss-making operations, etc.), which should be evaluated, proposed and implemented by the management, and in this stage jurisdictions expect co-involvement of the general meeting, or shareholders in the whole process.

A special case suggested above is a possibility of *rescue by an intervention within a corporate group*, which may bring a whole range of efficient solutions. Corporate-group aid need not take place only in form of a direct financial support, but also, for example, in the reconstruction of the structural ranking of a corporation within the activities of a corporate group, in the support of custom-

21 *Finch* Corporate Insolvency Law, l.c., p. 213.

er-supply relations within a corporate group, proclamation of support to be rendered to a corporation by its parent company (for example by using a letter of comfort, various forms of guarantees) etc. However, the rule applies that if there is no special regulation of corporate groups on a national level, the corporate interest is still the primary interest pursued by the management, and it is not substituted by the interest of a corporate group. That is also why the reconstruction of a corporate group must be performed within contemplations and steps aimed to divert/prevent the bankruptcy of a corporation rather than to prefer the interests of a corporate group or any of its members. Although still not being at the stage of bankruptcy, the protection of the creditors' interests starts to strengthen, and so the ultimate goal of the whole restructuring process should be their protection from a corporation falling into bankruptcy.

## E. Informal stabilization agreements

However, in many cases distress of a corporation is too serious to avoid the interference of creditors in its settlement. If such procedures were not arranged for in advance in a shareholders' agreement in some respect, for example, in relation to the financing bank, they should be a matter of further negotiations. National jurisdictions do not usually provide any specific instruments for these purposes, so the basic framework is delimited under the law of contract and its enforceability, by protection of creditors from preferential or harmful acting of a corporation, and, of course, by a threat/alternative of involuntary installation of formal proceedings in the case of legal bankruptcy. A significant legal as well as factual problem of this rescue processes is the fact that they presume voluntariness (agreement), which means that the creditors should not be forced to any of them against their will[22]. Moreover, in many cases the whole process will not be aimed to find a solution to settle the crisis, but already to prepare a corporation and its creditors to a related, although formal, but still, to a certain extent, pre-arranged solution ("*pre-pack approach*"[23]).

The willingness of creditors to act will be the lesser the closer the formal bankruptcy will be including the risk of installing collective formal proceedings. At the same time, a corporation involved in negotiating an informal solution with

**22** With the exception of specific processes which are admitted, for example, in the UK (part. 26 of CA 2006) or Canada (Companies Creditors' Arrangement Act 1985, consolidated version 2017) – see hereinafter.

**23** Possible survey of some of the solutions may be found in *Xie* Comparative Insolvency Law, The Pre-pack Approach in Corporate Rescue, Cheltenham: Edward Elgar, 2016.

the creditors will be approaching the phase close to "*financial distress*", and within internal processes of institutional creditors it will be settled within "work-out"[24], which means that it will treated differently from a sound corporation – creditor's willingness to look for a solution will be different as well as conservativism, etc.

It is certainly possible to negotiate with the creditors on a bilateral basis, i. e. to look for an *ad hoc* solution (e. g. to postpone maturity, to agree instalment schedules, to remit (a part) of a debt, to agree settlement of mutual claims and liabilities, etc.). Such solutions are mostly possible only in the initial stages of the crisis, or in its softer forms because later they will raise a risk of putting particular creditors in advantage and, in general, they will not be systemic; however, they are often similar to the arrangements that are involved in more extensive stabilization agreements.

However, if a corporation is already in the stage of actual financial distress, it is generally not possible to find a solution on a bilateral basis and it is therefore necessary to take systemic measures and more complicated legal instruments, such as standstill agreements. Such agreements are produced under the law of contract, so we are still in the informal process, but there are new standards arising which, similarly as in *lex mercantoria*, define a certain framework for such agreements and their negotiations. Probably, the most well-known "codified" framework is the "*London Approach*" which originated in the 70-ties of the 20$^{th}$ century on the British market and which is defined, for example, by the British Bankers' Association as "*a non-statutory and informal framework introduced with the support of the Bank of England for dealing with temporary support operations mounted by banks and others lenders to a company or group in financial difficulties, pending a possible restructuring*"[25]. This model of settling distress of a corporation is well elaborated and it presumes gradual process lasting for several months which is aimed to find the reasons of distress and their possible informal removal or preparation of possible subsequent formal proceedings[26].

---

24 "*An undertaking or plan intended to resolve a problem of indebtedness esp. in lieu of bankruptcy or foreclosure proceedings.*" (Merriam-Webster's Dictionary of Law, 2016).

25 *Xie* Comparative Insolvency Law, The Pre-pack Approach in Corporate Rescue, l.c., 22, also see, e. g., http://www.bankofengland.co.uk/archive/Documents/historicpubs/qb/1993/qb93q1110115.pdf.

26 For details cf., e. g. *Xie* Comparative Insolvency Law, The Pre-pack Approach in Corporate Rescue, p. 23 an., or *Finch* Corporate Insolvency Law, l.c., p. 219 an.

The process of reconstruction itself based on a standstill agreement consists in procedural and subsequent steps[27] – first of all, there should be defined a specific period (*standstill period*) in course of which a corporation (debtor) will undergo a thorough analysis (also in order to determine if a going concern value exists). During that period creditors must refrain from taking individual steps aimed to enforce their receivables, debtor's proceedings will be coordinated and controlled by creditors, or their professional advisors (including possible installation of crisis management), and subsequently a particular solution of a crisis will be gradually formulated and implemented, including possibly new funding etc.

Readers might be struck by a question how the possible solutions outlined above concerning an informal settlement of distress of a corporation are related to the shareholders' agreements. It was suggested before that a part of these solutions may be contained already in the shareholders' agreements themselves, especially if they are agreed upon not only among the shareholders, but also with a participation of other persons, typically investors. The relevance that can be found here is much deeper, however. Stabilization agreements are arrangements aimed to settle the crisis in which a corporation and its creditors are involved, nevertheless, their function is not exhausted thereby, because, in fact, they also contain rules for the company's governance, rules for possible subordination of residual rights of shareholders, they introduce the shareholders' obligation to pool up additional capital for a corporation, etc. Even the shareholders themselves are parties to stabilization agreements and these agreements define their mutual relations as well. So stabilization agreements are arrangements drawing on the experience with shareholders' agreements, including, for example, *non-disclosure agreements* (NDA) which derive therefrom. A stabilization agreement may be considered as an SHA-like institute, in other words, as an arrangement resembling the shareholders' agreement, although it is obvious, and should be remembered, that they still belong to a domain of general law of contract.

# F. Standstill agreements

As suggested above, a standard rescue instrument of an informal kind is a standstill agreement. Negotiations on such agreements are always preceded by the

27 Cf. e.g. INSOL Statement of Principles for a Global Approach to Multi-creditor Workouts (2000) – http://www.turnaround-sa.com/pdf/Lenders.pdf.

creditors considering if they can trust a corporation and if it is free of systemic sentiments on the part of the management or shareholders. At the same time, it is necessary to decide if there is a risk that at the time of negotiations a corporation will be subject to the (hostile) raids of invaders, or if it is going to face other aggressive methods that are basically not intended to remedy distress of a corporation. If mutual aversion is present already at the time of commencement of negotiations, or if it is obvious that there will be a tendency to "rip to pieces" the assets of a corporation, further process would only be a waste of time and money.

If some basic trust exists, however, it will be possible to start negotiating an agreement. The first thing is to agree on a *standstill period*, i.e. a period during which a corporation will be "protected"[28] from the devastating steps of creditors – that period will basically take 6–12 months and it is built on the presumption of *lege artis* conduct of the parties and on the absence of existence of legal bankruptcy. During such a period, a corporation will undertake to perform, or to have it performed by selected specialists, *an independent business review – IBR*. Such a review is aimed to provide all the stakeholders with some relevant information about the business operation, business strategies and problems related thereto, to describe the reasons of distress and recommend a basic set of restructuring measures. Such an analysis will also involve legal due diligence, financial due diligence and commercial due diligence with the whole analysis being focused not only on the examination of the past, but especially on the future. A corporation, or its management, will undertake contractually not only to provide assistance, but also to render all the necessary information, documents or explanations. The findings of the analyses will lead either to further fulfilling of a standstill agreement, its modification, or to its termination and initiation of formal proceedings.

Beside the particulars and goals of these agreements mentioned above, a standstill agreement will, as a rule, also contain other covenants:

- rules of joint procedure of creditors in order to settle distress of a corporation;
- postponement of maturity of principals of specific debts;
- fixing new amount of interests and agreement on remitting late-payment interests;

28 Protective schemes agreed for such purposes are contractual schemes and they differ from "schemes for protection against creditors", which sometime allow for insolvency regulations – e.g. the Czech moratorium pursuant to Section 115 InsA, that provides for time-limited defence against a compulsory insolvency petition.

- waiver of original interests exceeding the scope of a new agreement if the overall agreement is successful;
- agreement on new financing for a clearly and precisely defined purpose, including a covenant on its securing – new financing will basically be aimed to complete a particular activity of a corporation that may potentially bring new resources or improve an overall economic situation of a corporation;
- defining new obligations of shareholders and a corporation, in particular:
  - obligation of internal funding in order to maintain the workforce capital of a corporation;
  - obligation to retain the workforce indebtedness below a defined limit, or below a defined default period;
  - subordination of shareholders' claims;
  - restriction of a possibility of structural changes of the assets of a corporation without a consent of the parties to the agreement;
  - restriction of a possibility of shareholders' structuring of a corporation without a consent of the parties to the agreement;
  - prohibition of distribution of dividends among shareholders, members of the group or the management, without a consent of the parties to the agreement;
  - structured information duty exceeding the framework regularly ensured during audits of a corporation – a corporation often undertakes to perform the full disclosure;
  - requirement to retain EBIDTA and CAPEX within a defined range.
- definition of specific activities of a corporation which will be performed in a special regime and on a preferred basis, including, for example, an obligation to sell a part of the assets, etc.;
- definition of crisis management and establishing its obligation to submit a restructuring plan;
- definition of conditions precedent and subsequent for the agreement so that it could be guaranteed, if possible, that it will be fulfilled on condition that the requirements specified in advance are met;
- definition of an obligation of a corporation to bear the costs of the restructuring process, including a possible restructuring fee;
- non-disclosure agreement.

The particulars mentioned above will obviously vary on a case-to-case basis, and the agreement will often contain actual legal steps of restructuring, because the position of a corporation will become clear in course of negotiations. As to its kind, it is an innominate contract so its content must always be defined according to the needs of a corporation and its creditors. A fatal moment of its existence which, in general, results in its winding-up, is bankruptcy in terms of law, and an obligation related thereto to install formal insolvency proceedings. As suggested above, a standstill agreement must not put into unreasonable advantage particular creditors at the expense of others, and it must not harm other creditors involuntarily, otherwise there is a threat of subsequent application of defence by the insolvency practitioner, but it is also possible that it will violate fiduciary obligations of the management. Creditors involved in the standstill agreement will seek and initiate a joint action, but by doing so they should not be establishing, or they should be trying not to establish, a group within the meaning of the law of corporate group. The requirements for negotiation and formulation of such an agreement are therefore rather demanding and they require participation of external advisors, which will cause relatively high costs. It is therefore possible to conclude that such kinds of informal restructuring are applied in big companies which have complex corporate financing that presumes long-term solutions[29].

## G. Formal (non-insolvency) solution (pre-pack approach)

As mentioned below, beside informal process of rescuing a corporation in distress, and beside formal insolvency proceedings, in some jurisdictions there might be available another formal solution which joins elements of stabilization agreements and formal judicial process. The most significant form of such a solution is known in the English law, in the regulation entitled *Arrangements and Reconstructions* according to part. 26 Companies Act 2006 (similarly, the Canadian Companies' Creditors Arrangement Act). As to its function, it may be seen that this English solution is an alternative to pre-packed reorganization, as is known in Chapter 11 of the US Bankruptcy Law and as was adopted by a range of European countries. Nevertheless, it is taken out of the insolvency solution itself and the English law-maker finds it relevant in relation to mergers and divisions. This formal solution is based on that creditors and a debtor will agree on a certain solution of distress of a corporation (arrangement), which will be submitted to the court that will summon a meeting of creditors to negotiate it. If a majority in number representing 75% in value of the creditors or class of creditors or members or class of members (as the case may be) agree a compromise or arrangement, the court may, on an application under this section, sanction the

29 *Xie* Comparative Insolvency Law, The Pre-pack Approach in Corporate Rescue, p. 61–62.

compromise or arrangement. Such a solution will be binding upon all creditors, even upon those that did not take vote or voted against it, and upon a corporation itself. The court may also determine other conditions which will have to be met within the fulfilment of the approved agreement[30].

Wider efforts to settle this issue may be identified also on the level of Community Law. An overall economic situation of entrepreneurs in the EU and a partial disharmony of preventive measures have made the European Commission to submit, beside a recast regulation on the insolvency proceedings[31], a draft directive regulating, inter alia, preventive restructuring[32]. The process proposed is aimed to equip the European environment with a rescue solution which will, inter alia, allow of temporary suspension of enforcement of individual claims, and also suspension of an obligation to install formal insolvency proceedings (recital No. 18). As to its content, the draft directive is inspired by both the British as well as U.S. approach because it presumes a possibility of both majority approval of a negotiated restructuring plan (using 75% majority), as well as a possibility of *cross-class cram down mechanism*. Without attempting to analyse this proposal closer at this moment, it is obvious that it presumes a possible gradual formalization of otherwise informal stabilization agreements, with the rules, such as "*early warning*" (Article 3), to be possibly also included in the shareholders' agreements.

## H. Formal (insolvency) solution

Only to clear up the context, if formal insolvency proceedings have been installed, further settlement of distress of a corporation is a matter of formal court proceedings, although European jurisdictions offer, beside clearly formal liquidation bankruptcy proceedings, also some reorganization procedures which employ much of the processes and procedures described above. The solution it-

---

**30** For a literary description compare especially *Xie* Comparative Insolvency Law, The Pre-pack Approach in Corporate Rescue, p. 59 an., or *Finch* Corporate Insolvency Law, l.c., p. 324 an.
**31** Regulation (EU) 2015/848 of the European Parliament and of the Council of 20 May 2015 on insolvency proceedings – http://eur-lex.europa.eu/legal-content/EN/TXT/?uri=OJ:L:2015:141:TOC.
**32** Proposal for a DIRECTIVE OF THE EUROPEAN PARLIAMENT AND OF THE COUNCIL on preventive restructuring frameworks, second chance and measures to increase the efficiency of restructuring, insolvency and discharge procedures and amending Directive 2012/30/EU – http://eur-lex.europa.eu/legal-content/EN/TXT/?uri=CELEX:52016PC0723.

self is, however, inevitably collective, not presuming any separate agreements with creditors, and its economic background is already different in many cases.

# I. The role of shareholders' agreements at the time of rescue of a corporation

It may be expected that shareholders' agreements are mostly formed to ensure or increase a possibility to reach the intended benefits of a sound corporation. For such an obligation distress of a corporation or its bankruptcy represent a significant event that will change both its original incentives as well as its future content.

In considerations about the role of shareholders' agreements in the period of settling distress of a corporation it is necessary to distinguish not only the formality or informality of this process, but also whether corporations themselves are or are not parties to such agreements. Because if it is only an agreement among shareholders or other third persons (typically including the management or creditors), it is an agreement standing outside a direct influence of a corporation, or insolvency practitioner, and its life continues further, although it is often indirectly affected. However, if the shareholders' agreement is built on the wider participation of a corporation, then it is already an agreement that has or may have a direct relation to the settlement of a corporation's distress. We should therefore pose a question if such an agreement may be interpreted as "*executory contract*", i.e. a contract that is subject to special treatment. A classic Countryman's definition states that it is "*a contract under which the obligations of both the bankrupt and the other party to the contract are so far unperformed that the failure of either to complete performance would constitute a material breach excusing the performance of other*"[33]. Similarly, it presumes to standardise article 12 of the draft directive quoted above on the framework for preventive restructuring – executory contracts means contracts between the debtor and one or more creditors under which both sides still have obligations to perform at the moment the stay of individual enforcement actions is ordered[34]. The logics of a special

33 *Countryman* Executory Contracts in Bankruptcy (part. I.), 57 Minn. L. Rev. 439 (1973) – available, inter alia, in Hein online – http://heinonline.org/HOL/LandingPage?handle=hein.journals/mnlr57&div=25&id=&page=.

34 From the fact that shareholders' agreements or stabilization agreements are innominate contracts (*contractus innominati*), it follows that they are, at the same time, synallagmatic contracts, i.e. contracts with mumutual performance.

approach to these agreements is based on that these agreements are a mixture of assets and liabilities, at least hypothetical, which may have significance for the value of the assets of a corporation or its going concern value[35]; and an element of possible transaction costs associated with an automated termination of these agreements is significant as well. If we derive from the above definition of the executory contract, in the case of existence of shareholders' agreements which also involve a corporation itself[36], it is possible to defend a conclusion that such an agreement may be considered as executory contract, although its concrete content will have to be always examined separately.

Within an informal rescue solution on a contractual basis, shareholders' agreements are obviously not affected. Nevertheless, as was pointed out before, a whole range of arrangements contained in stabilization agreements interferes not only with a corporation itself and its management but also with the position of its shareholders. It may therefore be concluded that the covenants of such agreements directly or indirectly derogate the provisions contained in shareholders' agreements and the creditors should be notified of their existence within disclosure procedure, or within in-good-faith negotiations[37].

If the crisis of a corporation is settled formally, i.e. by mandatory engagement of third persons and a court, the role of shareholders' agreements with the involvement of a corporation will have to be examined from a point of view of their potential nature of executory contract, because various jurisdictions might provide concrete solutions for such cases. At the same time these agreements will be terminated within bankruptcy proceedings with liquidation as unnecessary or consumed. In the case of a rescue insolvency solution, it will always depend on a particular rescue solution, although even here it is not possible to expect survival of shareholders' agreements. All such cases, however, have a common characteristic in that the shareholders' agreements involving a corporation, in general, do not terminate automatically, but they require an intervention of an authorised person, unless it is an executory contract.

---

35 Also compare considerations in *Jackson* The Logic and Limits of Bankruptcy Law, Washington: BeardBooks, l.c., p. 105 an. nor *Baird* Elements of Bankruptcy, 4th. Ed., New York: Foundation Press, 2006, p. 129 an.

36 At this moment it is possible to consider the fact that if also the management or creditors are the party they act as private parties rather than on the account of a corporation, so their participation is, from a point of view of the role of agreement at the time of rescue of a corporation in distress, similar to the participation of shareholders.

37 Obviously, subject to the condition that this will not interfere with the legitimate expectation of other stakeholders, for example, based upon non-disclosure clauses.

Shareholders' agreements which do not involve a corporation as its party are not affected by formal insolvency solution and they are basically discharged by performance. Rescue plans might contain possible exceptions if they also modify the shareholders' structure of a corporation at the same time, etc. Other mechanisms built on the principle of SHA-like institutes are often a part of such rescue plans, especially when the shareholders become creditors by capitalising their own claims and the whole process is supposed to be aimed at gradual sale of the business of a corporation, etc.

## J. The role of stabilization agreements at the time of rescue of a corporation

To complete the picture it should be pointed out that the fate of stabilization agreements definitely ends on the moment when formal proceedings are commenced, at the latest, although they still may become a basis for the subsequent rescue solution (e.g. for the British arrangement or reorganizing plans, etc.). Until that moment, however, it is an obligation which contains sufficiently robust solutions available in case they are modified and/or amended.

Josef Bejček

# Shareholders' Agreements between the Law of Contract and Competition Law

**Table of Content**



## A. Introduction

Originally, shareholders' agreements were intended as a tool to influence disposition rights to business shares in so called private (not publicly traded, *closely held*) registered corporations and to ensure, via conditions laid down additionally, protection against unwanted changes in the personal structure of a corporation by transfer or passage of business shares,[1] especially against a hostile takeover.[2] Later, even wider possibilities of their use developed in *corporate governance*,[3] since they introduced the rules which were not made public in articles or memoranda of association, whereby there developed a *de facto* parallel subsystem of corporate governance of a contractual (*inter partes)* rather than corporate legal nature.

1 *Kramer* Shareholder Agreements In Succession Planning, 2005, p. 22. Function of shareholders' agreements of closely-held corporations (whose shares are not tradeable on the public markets) may even include an establishment of guaranteed market with shares not tradable publically.
2 Cf. *Betoncel* Abwehrmaßnahmen gegen feindliche Übernahmen im slowenischen Wirtschaftsraum. Zbornik rad. Sveuč. u Rij. Ekon. fak., God. 23, vol. 2, 2005, p. 279.
3 Cf. *Looney/Levitt* Shareholder Agreements for Closely Held Corporations. Business Entities 2003, no. 6, p. 20 etc.

**Prof. Dr. Josef Bejček,** CSc. Masaryk University in Brno.

https://doi.org/10.1515/9783110517026-007

Shareholders' agreements represent an interface between the contractual and corporate law. In extreme cases, by subsidiary shareholders' agreements the content of formal corporate documents may be reduced only to the "pure statutory minimum" which need not be much informative as to the actual distribution of power in a corporation (in contrast to the so called "subsidiary" shareholders' agreements).

Moreover, some arrangements among shareholders (for example, concerning joint exercise of voting rights, division of votes, prohibition of competition, etc.) may interfere with the protected public interests. They may even amount to tax delicts, offences, but also, for example, to prohibited agreements distorting competition, or they may involve elements of takeover of control by one competitor over another without due notification and necessary approval (inadmissible concentration of competitors). By some of these delicts membership of participants in one corporation may only create suitable conditions and might not have any impact on the activity and internal corporate governance as a whole, but may only affect the activities of their shareholders (for example, shareholders' agreements amounting to unfair competition). These do not have a corporate law dimension.

Some shareholders' agreements (for example, those concerning the joint exercise of voting rights), however, may influence the positon of a corporation as a whole, including the relations among shareholders, without such a change being observable from outside and without it even being known to third parties. This may apply not only to the agreements with the participation and "supervision" of majority shareholders, but also agreements of minority shareholders who may thereby acquire a *de facto* control over the competitive behaviour of a corporation. A *de facto* control may also be acquired by so called veiled control of competitive behaviour of a corporation by a competitor that would otherwise be subject to a permission of competent anti-trust authorities.

In general, shareholders' agreements are in compliance with the principle of autonomy of its members, and there is basically no reason to show them to shareholders unless they violate or deny the rights of other shareholders and creditors of a corporation[4] and general private-law corrective measures of contractual freedom[5] or its public-law restrictions. Shareholders' agreements actual-

4 Similarly *Hornstein* Stockholders'Agreements in the Closely Held Corporation. 59 The Yale Law Journal 1056 (1950). The author pleaded for further restriction of shareholders agreements already in the fifties, and defended the position that would treat shareholders' agreements as binding instruments enforceable through the courts.

5 For example, if shareholders participating in a shareholders' agreement attain the blocking minority or another relevant voting minority quorum, in exercising their share-bound rights

ly regulate not only the mutual relations among shareholders toward one another, but also relations of shareholders or their groups toward a corporation. The higher flexibility of shareholders' agreements associated with avoidance of the publicity of covenants which would become a part of articles creates, on the other hand, an information asymmetry and a detriment resulting therefrom to the shareholders who are not involved. Coordination of voting among shareholders is considered as a standard way of ensuring the operation of a corporation in a certain manner which is best to meet the investment goals and expectation of shareholders, although it would only be an agreement binding exclusively its parties.[6]

Shareholders' agreements are considered as manifestation of a contractual principle (contractual liberalism) in corporate law which is subject to more extensive regulatory interventions by the law, or to the content of articles required by the law.[7] Opting for a more liberal or stricter supervisory approach to the shareholders' agreements in favour of liberalization is sometimes treated as a sign of maturity of legal systems (beside a possibility of admitting foreign law for their application).[8] Corporations in which shareholders' agreements are employed are sometimes considered as better protectors of investors and their value correlates positively with the fact that their shareholders are bound by shareholders' agreements.[9]

Shareholders' agreements may be considered as an instrument where a clash of various private-law and public-law interests is to be balanced. One of the basic goals of shareholders' agreements is to protect the ownership of the business share. This is relevant in general, but especially with small and medium businesses having a form of joint stock companies – where the shareholders' agreements may prevent the unwanted transfers and passages of shares, and eliminate the threat to the well-established cooperation among shareholders related thereto, including division of powers in corporate governance.[10]

---

they will have to take into reasonable account the interests of other shareholders in relation to a corporation. Cf. *Schüppen/Schaub* Münchener Anwaltshandbuch Aktienrecht, München 2010, § 11 note 4.

**6** Cf. *Sealy* Case and Comment. 51 The Cambridge Law Journal, 439 (1992).

**7** *Duffy* Shareholders' Agreements and Shareholders' Remedies Contract Versus Statute? 20 Bond Law Review issue 2 (2008).

**8** Cf. *Pulec* Legal Restraints on the Use of Shareholders'Agreements for Structuring Foreign Investment Deals in Russia, 45 Cornell International Law Journal, 516 (2012).

**9** *Carvalhal* Do shareholder agreements affect market valuation? Evidence from Brazilian listed firms, 18 Journal of Corporate Finance 919 (2012).

**10** Similarly *Sund/Bjuggren* Protection of ownership in family firms: post-sale purchase clauses and management perspective, 33 Eur J Law Econ, 367 (2012). See also *Lavelle* Drafting Share-

Moreover, shareholders' agreements may[11] stabilize corporate *status quo* and division of powers among founders; they may maintain a special structure of a corporation even disregarding protection against competitors[12] (including special categories of members or rights of key persons); they deal with questions of legal succession (for example, they may legitimately prevent the shares falling into the hands of competitors[13], but, on the contrary, they may even establish a union with competitors); in certain situations they will ensure mandatory acquisition of shares; they may allow of responding to the government priorities and policy; they may specify the role of the corporate management in relation to the shareholders; they may grant special personal rights to shareholders which would not be enforceable under the articles[14]; they may regulate relations among shareholders not related to the general corporate governance; they may regulate the organization of joint ventures; they may contain purchase options and instructions thereto; they may regulate the right of veto; they may contain provisions to regulate pre-emption rights to new shares; they may deal with procedures to resolve the deadlock situations and internal corporate conflicts; they may provide for the issues of rewarding and procedural measures; they may regulate private dispute settlements; they may protect rights of minority shareholders; they may protect confidentiality. As may be seen from the above list, the scope of shareholders' agreements is rather wide.

This treatise is focused especially on the interface between contract and competition law, and thus it is marginally linked to the issue of the borderline between the law of contract and the corporate law which is dealt with by the co-authors. It analyse certain competition-law-related problems of shareholders'

---

holder Agreements for the Closely-Held Business, 4 Depaul Business Law Journal, 109 (1991/1992). The influence of shareholders' agreements is emphasised in relation to the composition of governance bodies which is in the imminent interest of shareholders of so called private limited companies.

**11** According to *Duffe* (supra note 11), p. 4.

**12** So called *lock-up-agreements* may prevent shareholders from the sale of shares in the case of a takeover bid. *Stand still agreements* bind the proponents to stop their participation in a corporation. Compare *Schlitt/Ries* in Münchener Kommentar zum AktG, 3rd edition 2011, § 33 note 112, 113.

**13** Compare *Painter* Stock Transfer Restrictions: Continuing Uncertainties and a Legislative Proposal. 6 Vill. L. Rev. 48 (1960).

**14** *Painter* Stock Transfer Restrictions: Continuing Uncertainties and a Legislative Proposal. 6 Vill. L. Rev. 50 (1960) Holmes' opinion is cited as follows "*Stock in a corporation is not merely property. It also creates a personal relation analogous otherwise than technically to a partnership. Notwithstanding decision under statutes...there seems to be no greater objection to retaining the right of choosing one's associates in a corporation than in a firm.*".

agreements and point out potential risks. However, I do not analyse corporate legal nuances of the topic, conflict-of-laws-related questions of shareholders' agreements or general content and formal aspects related to their execution.

Competition-law influences may be exerted, in particular, by the shareholders agreements concerning a joint exercise, modification or restriction of voting rights, or personnel structure of statutory bodies or the corporate management (that may establish the substance for the *control* of competitive behaviour of another competitor) and those laying down obstacles to the penetration of unwanted third persons among the existing shareholders.[15]

The object of shareholders' agreements may also involve controversial obligations of the parties to *waive competitive behaviour* toward a corporation. By means of shareholders' agreements, legally-independent entities may attain such a degree of influence over the strategic behaviour of a target corporation that may even amount to its takeover and control of its competitive behaviour ("secret", "creeping", "de facto" or "virtual" *merger*[16]). By means of shareholders' agreements it is possible to control a joint cooperative undertaking that may violate (as a kind of *competition-restricting agreement*) a prohibition of cooperation among competitors.[17]

## B. Control influence

*Sideletters* do not represent *structural* change of entities operating on the relevant market, but only the *inter partes* obligations; functionally, however, they may be paralleled with the structural changes although they do not have the "real rights" effect.[18] Informality, privity and flexibility make the process of

---

**15** In German law, so called *change of control* clause is treated as civil partnership (see *Mock* Germany B.II.4.).

**16** Cf. for example *Cohn* The Non-Merger Virtual Merger, 26 Delaware Journal of Corporate Law, 1 (2004).

**17** Contrary to the absolute turnover limits laid down by anti-trust regulations of the EU and Member States as the threshold that must be met (bottom threshold) of possible interference with the process of concentration, with a cartel-establishing shareholders' agreement such a threshold is not established, and it therefore may occur more frequently. The only rule that will be employed is a "*de minimis*" rule with cartels not involving so called strict (*per-se* prohibited) agreements.

**18** This metaphoric concept is used by *Stanislava Černá* in her article Sideletters of capital shareholders. Obchodněprávní revue 2011, No. 1, p. 2. However, the concept of "sideletters" has a wider contractual meaning than just shareholders' agreements. Not only that they represent a clash of corporate and contractual loyalty, but also public-law loyalty (e. g. interest to pro-

amendment of shareholders' agreements rather simple, so it is difficult to determine if they enable achieving the control influence upon a corporation which somehow presumes some long-term perspective (permanence). The defining features of shareholders' agreements also include latency of their possible unlawfulness and complicacy of its proving in respect of third persons affected by such agreements.

The intensity of impact exerted through shareholders' agreements may range from influence, through acting in concert to uniform management (corporate group). Corporate law has finer concepts than anti-trust law to identify the range and intensity of these aspects of influence upon the conduct of a corporation. It is primarily aimed to protect minority shareholders and third persons. Anti-trust law, on the other hand, has a different priority and it aims at a different goal – protection of the competition.

What is considered dangerous from this point of view is already the fact of creation of a *possibility* of control of another competitor. The concept of control does not necessarily presume the accomplishment of a possibility to exercise the controlling influence upon the activities of another undertaking, but rather its mere potentiality. The subjective side (intention)[19] itself is irrelevant. *Obtaining* control also logically and naturally means that such a controlling option of influencing the competitive behaviour of another competitor *had not existed before.*[20] Obtaining control means that one or more undertakings acquire the power, on a legal or factual basis, to take strategic decisions for one or more other undertakings.[21] Earlier the European Commission had stated that to obtain a *de iure* control over a joint stock company it will suffice to acquire 50 % majority share with voting rights plus 1 vote[22]. This is so if the articles of a corporation

---

tect the competitive environment). Articles of a corporation may contain mere contractual (non-corporate) elements. In theory, the corporate nature of shareholders' agreements enables to accomplish that which the corporate law (or, for example, competition law) denies.

**19** For example in the Decision of the Commission of 5 October 1992 in the case of *Air France/ Sabena*.

**20** That is why the change of control from single to joint and from joint to single is not considered as obtaining control because it actually does not imply a structural market change.

**21** Cf. *Faull/Nikpay* The EC Law of Competition, Oxford 1999, p. 210. The concept of "undertaking", however, should be not understood within the meaning of the former Czech "bulk substantive" understanding pursuant to Section 5 of the Commercial Code; undertaking in terms of the European case law is any entity (economic unit) regardless of its legal form which is involved in the economic life including non-profit aims.

**22** Decision of the Commission of 11 January 1993 in the case IV/M. 296 *Crédit Lyonnais/BFG Bank*, also Decision of the Commission of 5 September 1994 in the case IV/M. 492 *Klöckner&Co. AG/Computer 2000 AG.*

do not place any obstacles to such majority being treated as qualified majority, blocking minority with the right of veto, etc.[23]

Agreements on the joint exercise of voting rights among minority shareholders may, in fact, establish a similar situation as in the case of the acquisition of the majority share in a corporation, hiding the actual power structure established contractually without any changes to formal shareholders' structure. If it is realistic to expect long-term duration of such an agreement, the control may amount to a possibility of exercising the controlling influence over the activities of another undertaking.

For example, a minority shareholder with shares of a competitor's joint-stock company may enter into a shareholders' agreement with other minority shareholders on the joint exercise of voting rights in that competitor's joint-stock company without occurrence of the change of ownership of shares. They may silently acquire a *de facto* joint control over a joint-stock corporation and obtain control over its competitive behaviour. Agreements among minority shareholders concerning the joining of votes in voting about substantial economic and commercially strategic issues, or concerning the selection of members of corporation's bodies, may meet the element of the concept of control.[24]

Well-organized minorities may attain the controlling influence by means of agreed blocking covenants and veto rights – especially if they are exercised on a permanent and long-term basis. Even without performing such agreements it is possible to identify the controlling influence of the holders of blocking rights. Such rights may consist in agreeing special quora to take decisions in the relevant panels on the strategic business issues. Mere existence (which must be permanent, however) of such rights of veto will suffice.[25]

**23** Nevertheless, control is quite indefinite concept, both from a legal point of view as well as from an economic point and it attains its real content only in particular context. Its manifestation is also admitted by means of shareholders' agreements. Cf. *Reddick* Joint ventures and other competitor collaborations as single entity "undertakings" under US law, 8 European Competition Journal 350 (2012). For example, in terms of "circular definition", control also means shareholders' agreements concerning the election of directors allowing some entities to control a corporation. Sc. *Enriques/Gatii* Creeping acquisitions in Europe: enabling companies to be better safe than sorry, 15 Journal of Competition Law Studies 77 (2015). Control may be positive (being manifested as sufficient possibilities to accomplish a particular goal), but even negative will suffice (blocking minority sufficient to prevent the accomplishment of a goal).

**24** *Immenga/Mestmäcker* in Immenga/Mestmäcker, EU Wettbewerbsrecht, 5[th] editon 2012, Einleitung note 54.

**25** *Immenga/Mestmäcker* (supra note 25) Einleitung note 98 including references to the relevant sources.

Such conduct may become anti-competition-relevant only in the case where such a "creeping concentration" would substantially interfere with the competition, i. e. if statutory requirements for exceeding the turnover of involved competitors have been met (intervention threshold for anti-trust authorities to control any joint acting at all).

The impact on the competitive behaviour of a *controlled* competitor[26] must always have the quality that is critical, decisive, hence controlling.[27] A position may therefore be partly justified where the Czech lawmaker did not explicitly mention the feature of intensity of influence which the controlling entity exerts.[28]

*The controlling influence* upon the conduct of a competitor will depend on a particular situation in a given case. It need not amount to a simple-majority or even two-third-majority of votes in the decision-making bodies of a corporation since other votes may be so fragmented that a controlling packet of shares may be much smaller (of course, with a possibility of correction by the articles).[29] Also specific rights reserved for shareholders' minority (such as preferential votes capable of deciding about the half of members of the board of directors and thereby determine the commercial strategy of a corporation whose shares are subject to the acquisition[30]) may influence the behaviour of a competitor.

Controlling influence upon a competitor through daughter companies controlled by the competitor who is controlling its competitor this way should also be treated as indirectly exerted controlling influence. Distinguishing direct and indirect (i. e. mediated by another entity) controlling influence has only

---

**26** Cf. Section 12 subsection 4 para. b of the Czech Act on Restraints of Competition (ZOHS).
**27** Pursuant to Section 12 subsection 3 in fine ZOHS.
**28** Cf. *Dvořák* Kontrola spojování soutěžitelů., 2002, p. 18 – 19. The lawmaker actually did not define the term "control", but even the "influencing" of the competitive behaviour implies that such influence is allowed within the potential control (i. e. *possibility* of influence of the *controlling entity*; the concept of control may hardly be interpreted otherwise).
**29** Cf. the case heard by the German Bundeskartellamt, case No. BkartA, Beschl. v. 7.12.2001 – B9 – 114/01, *Krieger/Möbel Walther.* Obtaining control meant the acquisition of 47.5 % share in a joint-stock corporation by a sole entrepreneur. Business shares of other shareholders were rather diffuse and none attained 25 %, moreover, the corporation owned 10 % of equity shares, and an average attendance of general meetings was ranging below 90 % of voting rights. References to the Czech Office for the Protection of Competition decision in even more strict conditions (where a gain of 28 % shares was treated as obtaining control with simultaneous staffing of several positions in the supervisory board of a target corporation – S 121/95, or 17.7 % shares with simultaneous staffing of majority of positions in the board of directors – S 116/98, etc.) see *Dvořák* (supra note 29) p. 23 – 24.
**30** Cf. *Bellamy/Child* European Community Law of Competition. 5th edition 2001, p. 367 with reference to Case M. 794 *Coca-Cola/Amalgamated Beverages GB*, OJ 1997 L218/15.

an *analytical* rather than practical relevance and both cases are subject to the *same* legal regime.

It is not only the nominal number of shares (votes), but also if a group of shareholders or a shareholder alone may block some of the relevant decisions of the competitor (e.g. even by mere absence during the general meeting or another important body of a corporation).

Even so called *personal union* in statutory bodies of a competitor or so-called *control by articles or shareholders' agreements* could be considered as concentration of competitors. Nevertheless, if two shareholders agree to the veto right in an important question, i.e. they actually "control" one another regardless of the proportion of their business shares, it is not possible to conclude that one is controlled by the other (there would not exist a controlling influence on the acting of the other competitor); however, both may *jointly control* a third competitor deprived of its competitive independence.

A possibility of control means a possibility to exercise *controlling* influence upon *acting* of a controlled competitor. A business entity can hardly be reasonably expected to assume a *controlling* position over another competitor without being able to determine its *competitive* behaviour, i.e. behaviour in the competition. Illogical seems to be the contrary hypothetic alternative – not have control over all *competition-relevant* behaviour of another competitor (i.e. not to determine or not to influence it significantly), and simultaneously to treat such a competitor as a controlled competitor. It may therefore be concluded that a possibility of controlling of another competitor implies a possibility of determining its *competitive* behaviour or its influencing in a significant (controlling) manner. Such a possibility is to be identified not only in the wording of articles or memoranda of association, but also from other agreements among shareholders, including so called shareholders' agreements (if they are available to the authorities).

The controlling potential need not be manifested in form of a majority share in a corporation. Beside articles[31] a majority shareholder may be restricted in its voting rights also by shareholders' agreements on, for example, voting for a particular candidate on whom the parties of "syndicate agreement" have agreed in advance. On the contrary, thanks to a shareholders' agreement on the exercise of voting rights a majority shareholder may exercise the voting rights of some other minority shareholders and may act with some other persons in harmony with the aim of electing all members of the board of directors of a joint stock company

---

**31** For example, restriction of the highest number of votes.

whose articles require for such a person a high qualified majority of voting shareholders.[32]

Shareholders' arrangements which could be treated as having a competition-relevant impact must establish a real possibility of controlling influence upon the competitor's behaviour. This should be examined in each particular case and, depending on the finding, it is necessary to decide if such potential influence amounts to controlling influence or not. Control is a concept of a *qualitative* nature. It is not possible to make a normative conclusion concerning its existence on the level of the law, but only a conclusion on the application level, in other words, by considering all the circumstances of the facts and the law of a particular case. A conclusion will depend on a *qualitative* evaluation of the influence of one person upon another *always* (without having a support of legally irrebuttable presumptions), and not quite rarely on an evaluation which is hypothetical (evaluation of future *possible* control influence upon the competitive behaviour of another competitor).

A clue to the evaluation of such an impact may be indicators employed in the European control of competitors' mergers. According to these indicators it is not the control of transaction and procedures leading only to a transitional possibility of control that are qualitatively relevant, but only those that establish a permanent or long-term possibility of control. Only long-term changes of control relations will be considered as competitors' concentration.[33] The aspects of long duration and permanence are not excluded even with shareholders' agreements. This is because the form is not the decisive factor – in contrast with the (structural) impact upon the market structure. However, it must include determination (that means influencing in a controlling manner), rather than a mere influencing of the competitive behaviour.[34]

---

**32** It is presumed here only to be the shareholders' agreement among shareholders of the same corporation rather than a possibility of one shareholder of another corporation entering into an agreement with a person from outside a corporation for whom it will be a tool to exercise its controlling influence over a joint-stock company.

**33** Similarly *Neruda* Získání možnosti kontroly nad podnikem jako forma spojení podléhající povolení soutěžního úřadu. Právní rozhledy 2005, No. 4, p. 115 and a synoptical commentary about such criteria is supplied by Mestmäcker/Schweitzer Europäisches Wettbewerbsrecht, 3rd edition 2014, 1, Kapitel note 11 f.

**34** Under the last mentioned extensive interpretation, however, even gaining minority voting rights would have to amount to concentration, i.e. the voting rights that may operate as blocking minority during the voting at a general meeting or as a necessary part of a qualified majority during major decision-making. This would be contrary to the protective purpose of control of concentration from a competition point of view.

It is obvious that shareholders' agreements are not excluded from the range of possible forms of obtaining control over an undertaking of another competitor and they may be an alluring/attractive, but also tricky, way of evading anti-trust prohibitions. If shareholders' agreements are concerning the staffing of the corporation's bodies, it is necessary to distinguish the *influencing* of nomination itself or election of candidates from the control via personal unions.[35] In practice, these are manifested by personal connections due to which one entity obtains control over another one (presuming the exceeding of turnover threshold and the fact if it amounts a competitors' concentration at all). It is an open concentration which will be disclosed to the public, of course, on the moment of entering the change of the composition of statutory bodies of a corporation into the business register, at the latest.

## C. Agreements concerning voting rights and minority shares in a corporation as a form merger?

Voting rights agreements[36] concluded especially among minor shareholders are a legitimate tool to increase their influence in pursuing their own interests. They may even grow into "*voting pools*" to accomplish particularly agreed goals. They may establish so called blocking minority, and, in theory, also qualified majority thanks to the agreement between the minority and the other shareholders. The blocking minority itself does not establish a possibility of joint control; many other factual circumstances in relation to the exercise of voting rights would have to be examined.[37]

Discussion has developed lately about the potential danger of obtaining control over other competitors detrimental to the competitor through the acquisition

**35** In some countries shareholders' agreements concerning conditions of exertion of control over a joint undertaking are forbidden and they are treated as void (as it is, for example, in Russia. Cf. be careful about joint venture, EURO E15 of 13 October 2008).

**36** Pursuant to Section 78 subsection 2 paragraph i) of the Czech Act on Corporations (ZOK) persons that have entered into an agreement on the exercise of the voting rights are considered as persons acting in concert on a rebuttable basis.

**37** Similarly *R. Neruda* in the cited paper (Právní rozhledy 2004, No. 1), p. 2.

of minority shares.[38] Concerns arise, supported by the economic arguments, that even “non-decisive” control obtained due to a minority share in the business of a competitor may significantly restrict the competition. The European legislation has not provided for any measures against the control of concentrations in its Regulation No. 139/2004.

Structural links are established by the fact that a competitor that has a minority share in a business of its competitor will no longer behave as if not having such a share because it is also interested in good results of its competitor from which it gains profit. Thus, competition parameters are suppressed, such as price, production quantity, quality and extent of investment into innovation – which, at the end of the day/eventually, decreases consumers’ welfare.[39] The rate of interest of a minority shareholder in the results of its competitor will be proportionate to its share in its competitor’s business.

In this respect, an agreement among minority shareholders may be detrimental to the competition (regardless of whether they are direct competitors of the main shareholder or even other stakeholders) if it coordinates their activities in their competitor’s joint-stock company. The controlling influence of the concentration of competitors cannot be excluded but such a concentration would have to meet the statutory requirements (especially, meeting the lower turnover threshold necessary for the origination of a power of anti-trust authorities to examine the concentration of competitors). It would be much more probable to take it as a an agreement distorting competition (concerted practice) which is not subject to quantitative criteria in contrast to the supervision over concentration of competitors (with the exception of *de minimis* rule).

Thanks to shareholders’ agreements among minority shareholders, minority shareholders may have not only a “passive” financial interest in the economic results of their competitor’s business, but they may also partly control it with various degrees of intensity until its “de facto takeover”. This may be very dangerous from a point of view of the competition. One entrepreneur may even have more than one minority share in various companies of its competitors – as a result, a competition-harmful cumulative effect of diversified partial control may become manifested.[40] However, revealing of the acquisition of a competition-det-

---

**38** In 2013 the European Commission launched public consultations on a possible gap in the regulation of competition concerning the acquisition of minority shares. Cf. *Competition Policy Brief* October 2014, Issue 15.

**39** Cf. an informative article of *Nejezchleb* Nabývání minoritních podílů z hlediska hospodářské soutěže. Obchodní právo, 2015, No. 11, p. 392ff.

**40** A case was described where Ryan Air had the biggest minority share in its competitor Air Lingus which enabled Ryan Air to block the joining of Air Lingus with its strategic business part-

rimental minority share by a competitor is very difficult, and revealing of an even more dangerous shareholders' agreement is even more difficult if not completely impossible.

The acquisition of minority in a competitor's business itself may not be considered as concentration of competitors, despite of the extensive interpretation of the concept of "controlling influence", unless some special rights are accompanying the minority share.

Shareholders' agreements among minority shareholders may operate as "intensifiers" of the position of minority shareholders and may render them such force and influence upon decision-making that will not be proportionate to their business shares. What should be examined here is if shareholders' agreements are intended to provide legitimate protection of minority shareholders, or if the protection framework is exceeded and it is rather aimed at the strategic influence upon decision-making of a target corporation.[41] It is also important to examine the factual position of a target corporation, such as a probability of gaining majority at the general meeting because of the absence of the other shareholders and their fragmentation, history of absences at general meetings, probability of some shareholders voting jointly due to structural, economic or family ties (of course, including the existence of shareholders' agreements), should the minority shareholder pursue similar activities as a target corporation or if it behaves only as financial investor.[42]

Hence, joint control may originate not only in consequence of the acquisition of a control packet of shares, but also as a result of the acquisition of minority shares under certain circumstances, such as shareholders' agreement concerning joint exercise of voting rights in the context indicated above. It is to be de-

---

ners (*Nejezchleb*, supra note 40, p. 401, including relevant references to sources). However, such an effect could be eventually pro-competitive – prevention of pooling and concentration of competitors that would be unfavourable for Ryan Air, but also for consumers – or anti-competitive (if the said concentration brought significant effect for consumers without substantial interference with competition).

**41** Cf. *Nine/Fréget/Beauchataud* Minority interests require attention. International Financial Law Review, October 2008, p. 35–38 (available at http://www. iflr. com/Article/2025672/ France-Minority-interests-require-attention. html).

**42** According to the sources cited above, in France even 20% shareholders' share was officially considered as exclusive control if a minority shareholder operated in the same or similar area as a target corporation and if other shareholders were financial investors. By analogy, it could be possible to assume that it will suffice to reach even a mere 20% share of votes coordinated by an agreement on the joint exercise of voting rights among minority shareholders whose individual business shares are substantially lower.

tected if minority shareholders have a strong joint interest which makes them exercise their rights toward a corporation without going against each other.

As a matter of principle minority share in a corporation does not establish control of competitive behaviour of a corporation. The fact that it does not amount to the concentration of competitors (for example, because turnover threshold has not been met for an intervention of anti-trust authorities, or interference with competition due to the obtained control would not be substantial) does not imply that the acquisition of minority shares or agreements concerning voting rights cannot have anti-competitive goals or effect.

A competitor's share in its rival's corporation will enable its access to the strategic and sensitive information, shareholders' agreements may facilitate the silent coordination of competitors' behaviour, they may restrict competition also by agreements of shareholders concerning restriction or prohibition of competition, agreements on pre-emptive rights may operate as a *de facto* obstacle to the entry or to the restriction of market dominance of a competitor, etc. Minority shares and shareholders' agreements among minority shareholders are therefore quite controversial in terms of competition law, especially when it comes to the entry of competitors and their influence upon decision-making of a target corporation which seems formally negligible at first sight.

A prohibition of separate transfer of voting rights pertaining to shares[43] along with a possibility provided for in the articles to restrict the voting rights by specifying the highest number of votes of one shareholder or totally for a shareholder and persons controlled by it[44] may interfere with one of the features of capital-based corporations – a business-share-based participation in the management of a corporation. It is one of the major instruments of the protection of minority shareholders and determination of basic formal influence relations inside a corporation.

Such a restriction of voting rights by the articles may be avoided by a shareholders' agreement concerning a joint exercise of voting rights by means of which the upper limits of influence laid down by the articles may actually "dissolve", and some shareholders may become majority shareholders or *de facto* qualified-majority shareholders.

Since, as a matter of fact, shareholders' agreements need not be necessarily concluded among all shareholders, but only among some of them, the balance of power inside a corporation may theoretically change to the competition-relevant degree of control acquisition even without any publicity of such an agreement.

43 Pursuant to Section 281 subsection 4of the Czech Act on Corporations (ZOK).
44 Cf. Section 353/2 ZOK.

The lack of transparency of the situation resulting from the conclusion of such agreements will occur not only in relation to third persons standing outside a corporation (including anti-trust authorities), but also for non-engaged shareholders of the same corporation. So there may occur competition-law-relevant control by a non-transparent method of changing the relation toward the voting rights.

There may therefore occur a secret "de facto fusion/merger" which need not have a form of structural (formal) market change, but it may have similar consequences, although it is basically a behavioural change, if it lasts sufficiently long to affect (interfere with) competition on the relevant market *substantially.* It should be pointed out that the major criterion for the application of anti-trust law to such concentrations is a turnover threshold, otherwise the practises will be considered as competition-irrelevant. Nevertheless, this will not exclude such agreements violating other regulations.[45]

If a shareholders' agreement concerning the exercise of voting rights meets the criteria for the concentration that is subject to the supervision of anti-trust authorities it will imply, inter alia, a public notification duty in respect of such an agreement (a duty to file a motion to commence proceedings to permit the concentration of competitors) pursuant to applicable competition law regulation. Shareholders' agreements are confidential *per se*, but the public arm may reach over them this way.

A question of probability of being sanctioned for a separate administrative delict of failure to notify a concentration of competitors is, obviously, another thing and the shareholders involved must assess that risk within their overall risk assessment. It has become a public secret that lots of concentrations that were supposed to have been submitted for approval to anti-trust authorities took place without such a consent (especially because of transaction costs or just because "the matter was so urgent"). However, that may not always pay.[46]

---

**45** Cf. for example Sections 17 and 20 of the Czech Bank Act No. 21/1992 Coll., as amended. A consent of Czech National Bank to the acquisition of even an indirect business share by the bank (through controlled persons) is required mainly because of the departmental security supervision rather than to protect the competition; hence, it is not subject to a turnover threshold as in the case of notification of anti-trust authorities in respect of the concentration of competitors.

**46** In February 2013 the Czech Anti-Trust Office imposed a fine on the ground of the fact that the company failed to apply in 2002 (!) for a permit of a merger which occurred in order to obtain non-notified control over another competitor through borrowed shares (the name of the company – Karel Holoubek Trade Group). A turnover thresholds for the intervention were very low in the past, so a whole range of concentrations was subject to a notification duty, which would today fall beyond the office's competence. For more details, compare Arthur Braun. An old merger, a new punishment. Lidové noviny of 19 March 2013, p. 16. A similar case of sanction imposed

Relying on the assumption that shareholders' agreements do not meet the requirement of permanence and long duration of a change of control need not be quite safe.

# D. Prohibited Shareholders' Anti-Competitive Agreements

Some shareholders' agreements may oscillate on the borderline between obtaining control over an undertaking of another competitor (if a turnover threshold for intervention is exceeded) and an agreement restricting competition.

Competitors may establish a concentrative joint-venture (fulfilling all functions of separate economic entity and independently operating on the market) and they may agree[47] in the shareholders' agreement that when deciding on all questions related to the competitive behaviour of a joint undertaking it is always subject to the unanimous consensus. Another alternative is an agreement on that a minority shareholder in a joint undertaking will have a right of veto ensuring them the standard protection. This might be important during decision-making concerning a business goal and its changes, or concerning other competition-relevant decisions (for example, concerning an intention to merge with another competitor). In such a case the minority shareholder has, thanks to the right of veto entrenched in the shareholders' agreement, joint control over a joint business, and this will amount to a form of concentration of competitors that is subject to the rules commented on above.

Competitors that are shareholders of the same corporation may also use it as an opportunity to coordinate certain aspects of their competitive behaviour (coordination of a joint undertaking, for example, for joint research and development purposes, for joint distribution and sale of their products, etc.). In such a case, its founders remain on the market even after its establishment, and

---

with a big time span after the implementation of non-notified concentration occurred in Slovakia. M-Market company failed to notify the acquisition of exclusive control over a part of ZDROJ-VOPO company, but it continued to control it for almost 5 continuous years. Afterwards, the Anti-Trust Office granted its consent with concentration, on the one hand, but it sanctioned the control acquirees by a lower fine for a delict of failure to apply for a consent in time. Cf. Concentrations: PMÚ (Slovak Anti-Monopoly Office) imposed a fine do EUR 40,720.00 for a failure to meet the obligation to notify the concentration, in Aktuality (on line). The Anti-Monopoly Office of the Slovak Republic 2013, issued on 22 September 2015, cited on 28 November 2015.

47 As stated in *Neruda* Společný podnik jako spojení soutěžitelů z pohledu práva na ochranu hospodářské soutěže. Právní rozhledy, 2004, No. 1, p. 8f.

they operate on the market as separate competitors. Their joint-venture is intended only as a form of coordination of their competitive behaviour. From a competition-law viewpoint, a cooperative joint-venture is treated as separate competitor, unless it is controlled by its founder or its founders jointly. In the case of (joint) control, a joint-venture along with its controlling entities are considered as single competitor.

Shareholders' agreements among founders may define and specify such forms of coordination, and they might meet the criteria for agreements distorting competition. They will obviously be subject to a general *de minimis* rule as well as exceptions from the prohibition of cartel agreements. Alternatively, a so called prioritization option may be applied to them.[48]

The difference between a concentrative joint-venture and a cooperative joint-venture consists,[49] inter alia, in that in a case of a concentrative joint-venture the potential prohibition requires substantial distortion of competition, whereas with a cooperative joint-venture, on the contrary, only such agreements are not prohibited, whose impact on competition is negligible, or those meeting the statutory conditions for being exempt from the prohibition; hence, in order to satisfy the elements of agreements distorting competition, even an "ordinary" (not specifically qualified) distortion of competition will suffice.

In a concentrative joint-venture, joint decision-making, planning and coordination of economic and competitive activities are not prohibited, because joining ensues in the origination of a new, separately-deciding competitor (not inevitably also a legal entity!), that is exempt in this area from the operation of the prohibition of agreements distorting competition.[50] On the contrary, a coordinative joint-venture will coordinate the separate partial economic interests and activities of its stakeholders in their common interest at the expense of the competition, since in other (non-coordinated) areas they basically remain separately-acting and independently-planning entities. A cooperative joint-venture generally do not go beyond the prohibition of cartel agreements.

---

**48** Cf. Section 21 subsection 2 ZOHS. For details that are not immediately related to shareholders' agreements references may be done to the relevant specialist and commentary literature.
**49** Exceeding the statutory turnover threshold for intervention.
**50** In the decision of the Czech Office for the Protection of Competition case No. ÚOHS – S 75/2015/KS-5582/2015/840/LBř of 27 February 2015 it is stated, inter alia, that a joint-venture established on the ground of the Shareholders' Agreement among Acelor Mital Ostrava, a. s., et al, and TAURON Polska et al. does not amount to the concentration of competitors that is to be subject to a permission of the Office, because the Target company TAMEH Holding having its registered office in Poland does not show sufficient commercial independence from its parent companies and cannot be considered as fully functioning joint-venture. The Target company will not fulfil all functions of a separate economic entity within the meaning of the relevant regulation.

The purpose of shareholders' agreements may also include variously defined (as to time, territory, merits) *prohibitions of competition.*[51] A shareholders' agreement concluded by shareholders of a newly founded joint venture, or even an undertaking in which the shareholders – competitors – acquired a share, which would prohibit mutual competition among the shareholders may be considered as a severe anti-competition restriction comparable to the division of market. Hence, even a *de minimis* rule will not apply to it. However, a prohibition of competition which would only cover partial aspects of a joint-venture could have a character of so called admissible *ancillary restraints.*

A practical question is whether the conflict with public law results in invalidity of concentration-establishing shareholders' agreement.[52] This can hardly be affirmed. Even if it could be possible in the case of shareholders' agreement establishing a cartel, its party may hardly protest against the invalidity of such a cartel agreement (*nemo turpitudinem suam allegare potest*). Employment of the leniency policy could be considered if statutory requirements were met.[53] Actually, it would be an exemption from the above rule prohibiting the parties taking advantage of their own unfair conduct (*turpitudo*).

On the other hand, enforcement of covenants restricting competition contained in the shareholders' agreements by a civil action is contrary to their social purpose and the intentions and meaning of the law. Legal acts are in general void if they are contrary to the law in terms of its intentions and meaning.[54]

It is beyond any doubt that cartel agreements violate the law, and being as such they are, no doubt, void. It might be disputable with agreements below the

---

**51** These commonly occur as so called *ancillary restraints* in relation to the sale of an undertaking which are accepted if they are imposed upon the seller. They are treated as admissible attenuation of conditions (impact) of the change of control of an undertaking. With a prohibition of competition of a rational buyer it could be problematic, since such a prohibition is not substantiated as to its merits in contrast with a prohibition of competition imposed upon the seller. It is only one of the evidence that any restriction of business and competition need not be void and prohibited under all circumstances, because otherwise it would be necessary to sacrifice the principle which forms only the basis of the rule to the rule itself, which would be in conflict with the sound legal principles. Cf. *G. H. H.* Contracts in Restraint of Trade: Agreement by Retiring Stockholder, 8 California Law Review 440 (1920).

**52** This resembles by its very nature the grounds of an application for examination of a preliminary question of SDEU in the case "Crehan" (Judgment in the case C-453/99 *Courage Ltd versus Bernard Crehan* and *Bernard Crehan versus Courage Ltd et al.*), where the obligated person rejected to perform under the exclusive sale contract which was according to him in conflict with the law as a cartel agreement.

**53** Cf. Section 22ba subsection 1 ZOHS.

**54** I.e. Section 580 subsection 1 of the Czech Civil Code.

*de minimis* threshold to which the competition law does not apply at all.[55] Since such negligible agreements are not in conflict with the law, the principle of preference of their validity would apply.

Potential application of the premise that the application of the private law is independent from the application of the public law[56] to cartel agreements (in support of the assertion of their validity) is absurd, eventually. Otherwise, it would have to be possible to enforce, by a civil action, such agreements which may qualify as criminal acts.[57]

Due to the form of shareholders' agreements, competitors may also violate other rules protecting competition. Competitors may, for example, exchange sensitive commercial information and thereby eliminate or remove uncertainty about the future conduct of competitors that is contrary to the law. In each particular case, it would be necessary to consider, by the nature of information and frequency and mode of its exchange, if it amounts to anti-competitive exchange of sensitive commercial information veiled by the pretention of obligations imposed in the shareholders' agreement.

This, however, is another topic.[58]

# E. Conclusion

From a point of view of protection of competition, shareholders' agreements are significant especially when examining the competitive behaviour in relation to the concentrations of competitors. Their relationship toward agreements distorting competition (cartels) is more marginal, because, as a matter of fact, they will be about coordination of the behaviour of competitors who own a joint share in another competitor. A "classical" coordination of the competitive behaviour above this range need not be a shareholders' agreement.

The relevant criterion for the application of the anti-trust law also to the concentrations effected by shareholders' agreements is the lower statutory turnover threshold of the concentrating competitors; otherwise, the practices are irrelevant in terms of antitrust. That, however, does not mean that such "below-threshold" agreements may not violate other legal regulations.

55 Agreements whose impact upon the competition is negligible are not treated as prohibited.

56 I.e. Section 1 subsection 1 of the Czech Civil Code.

57 By the way, conclusion of cartel agreements is regularly a criminal offense.

58 Cf. Instructions for the application of Article 101 of the Treaty on the Functioning of the European Union on agreements concerning horizontal cooperation agreements – 2011/C 11/01.

A shareholders' agreement may meet the criteria for joint control not only by acquiring a controlling packet of shares, but also as a result of the acquisition of minority shares under certain circumstances – especially if it is of sufficiently long duration to be able to influence (interfere with) competition on the relevant market *substantially.*

A shareholders' agreement may establish a "de facto fusion/merger", that need not necessarily be of a nature of structural (formal) market change but it may rather have similar consequences although the change itself amounts only to a mere behavioural change.

It should be examined, on a case-to-case basis, if an understanding of shareholders having a form of shareholders' agreement that is alleged to be competition-relevant has provided for a real possibility of influencing the competitor's behaviour in a significant (controlling) manner. From the anti-trust-law point of view, even the potentiality of influence is legally relevant.

# National Reports

Marie-Agnes Arlt

# Austria

## Table of Content



Austrian law distinguishes – like the major part of legal systems – between companies/partnerships (*Personengesellschaften*) and corporations (*Kapitalgesell-*

**Dr. Marie-Agnes Arlt,** LL.M. (NYU)

https://doi.org/10.1515/9783110517026-008

*schaften*). The major forms are the private or civil partnership pursuant to the Austrian Civil Code (ABGB) (*Gesellschaft bürgerlichen Rechts*), the general business partnership (*offene Gesellschaft*) and the limited business partnership (*Kommanditgesellschaft*). Most important forms of corporations are the company with limited liability (*Gesellschaft mit beschränkter Haftung*) and the stock corporation (*Aktiengesellschaft*). As in Germany, shareholders' agreements are of relevance for all forms, whereby they are often of importance for larger companies and, in particular, for stock corporations and companies with limited liability.

Like in Germany (see Mock, 280), usually the rules and principles of company law (civil companies) apply since shareholders' agreements often constitue civil law companies (see below (B.I.)).[1]

# A. Nature of Corporate Law Regulation

In general, the Austrian corporate law follows the principle of the freedom of contract (*Vertragsfreiheit*) whereby – depending on the specific form of the company – various restrictions apply. As a consequence thereof, the flexibility of the Austrian corporate law is dependent on the specific company. However, in general, the shareholders of any company are – with certain restrictions – free to supplement the articles of association by shareholders' agreements.

Under Austrian law, shareholders are, hence, in general entitled to establish and – to a certain extent – individualize the corporate charter of "their" company.[2] This right is, of course, not unlimited but follows – depending on the type of the corporation at hand – legal rules and guidelines. As a principle, the flexibility of shareholders of companies (*Personengesellschaften*) is higher than the one of corporations whereby there is, in addition, a great difference between companies with limited liability and stock corporations. In general, legal restrictions and limits are usually drawn in light of minority shareholder and creditor protection.

The corporate charter/articles of association is/are qualified as an agreement among the (existing) shareholders which is also binding for future shareholders.[3]

1 Please note that this article in general focuses on corporations since shareholders' agreements are usually of higher relevance for this type of corporations.

2 See with respect to stock corporations *e.g. Kalss* in Kalss/Nowotny/Schauer, Gesellschaftsrecht (2017) n 3/54.

3 See e.g. *Schauer* in Kalss/Nowotny/Schauer, Gesellschaftsrecht (2017) n 1/68 et seq.

Usually, the articles of association contain various organisational and cooperative provisions whereby the mandatory minimum content is determined by law.[4]

Depending on the legal form, the applicable laws either limit the shareholders' opportunity to individualize the corporate charter or allow shareholders to amend the statutory regulation(s) on corporations.

For example, the right of shareholders of listed stock corporations to indivudualize the articles of association follows stricter rules in comparison to shareholders of private companies.

The flexibility associated with companies (*Personengesellschaften*) goes hand in hand with the fact that articles of association of this type of companies ususally do not have to be concluded in writing and in general do not have to be submitted to the companies register while articles of association of corporations must be concluded in writing and submitted to the commercial register.

The Austrian stock corporation act – in contrast to for example the German stock corporation act[5] – does not contain explicit provisions which only allow for regulations deviating from statutory law to the extent it is explicitly allowed for by law and for the supplementation to the extent that the legal provisions are not exclusive (*Grundsatz der Satzungsstrenge*). Austrian prevailing doctrine and case law nevertheless follows this concept to a certain extent.[6] Hence, articles of association of stock corporations do not allow for an unlimited flexible individualization but only for a restricted possibility for a supplementation or deviation. This concept was, however, criticized by newer Austrian doctrine.[7] In 2013, the Austrian Supreme Court also followed the critical academic statements when it decided on the validity of certain provisions in articles of associations, which amended applicable non-mandatory corporate laws.[8] Pursuant to this judgment, the extent of the shareholders' rights to amend applicable corporate law by articles of association is dependent on the question whether the company is a "private" limited stock corporation or a listed stock corporation.[9] Shareholders of

4 See with respect to stock corporations *e.g. Kalss* in Kalss/Nowotny/Schauer, Gesellschaftsrecht (2017) 3/55 et seq.

5 See Mock, page 281.

6 *Kalss* in Kalss/Nowotny/Schauer, Gesellschaftsrecht (2017) n 3/57 et seqq.

7 See Kalss in Kalss/Nowotny/Schauer, Gesellschaftsrecht (2017) n 3/59 with further references; see also OGH 8.5.2013, 6 Ob 28/13f.

8 OGH 8.5.2013, 6 Ob 28/13f.

9 See OGH 8.5.2013, 6 Ob 28/13f; see in this context also *E. Gruber* in Doralt/Nowotny/Kalss, AktG 2. Auflage (2012) § 17 Rz 34; *Ch. Nowotny*, Satzungsstrenge im österreichischen Aktienrecht? in FS Doralt (2004) 411 (416); *Haberer* Zwingendes Kapitalgesellschaftsrecht (2009) 13; *Kalss* in Kalss/Nowotny/Schauer, Österreichisches Gesellschaftsrecht (2017) n 56 et seqq.; *Kalss/Probst*

"closed" (i. e. non-listed) companies therefore have a broader range to create a corporate charter, which is individually customized to the needs of the company and its shareholder structure. This result is reasonable and serves the needs of non-listed stock corporations. In addition, also the Austrian legislator started to distinguish more and more between listed and non-listed stock corporations.

The situation is different for companies with limited liability (*GmbH*). Target groups of this company type are usually family businesses or other businesses whereby the shareholders intend to have a decisive influence on the management and organization of their company. Of course, this does not mean that the size of the business is limited. In fact, Austrian companies with limited liability are used for all sizes and often are large companies. Further, in terms of companies with limited liability, the "relationship" between the shareholder and the company is closer compared to the one of (minority) shareholders of listed companies. This principle is reflected in the possibility to tailor the corporate charter of a company with limited liability. Hence, laws applicable to this type of companies (i. e. the *GmbHG*) follow the principle of freedom of scope (*Gestaltungsfreiheit*)[10], leading to the broad but not limited right to amend the applicable national laws. Amendments and supplements of the statutory law are permitted unless they violate mandatory (corporate) law.[11] This differentiation goes hand in hand with the fact that it is prohibited to list shares in Austrian companies with limited liability on a stock market.

Once articles of association are agreed upon, the change thereof also follows strict rules which shall protect the existing (minority) shareholders and – depending on statutory law and/or contractual provisions – require the acceptance of all or a (qualified) majority of the shareholders.[12] Hence, it is also possible to customize the articles of association in the course of the business, provided that the requisite majority agrees thereto.

---

Familienunternehmen (2013) Rz 4/5 ff; *Haberer/Zehetner* in Jabornegg/Strasser, AktG, 5th edition (2011) § 62 Rz 36; *Kalss* Zur Satzungsstrenge des Aktienrechts, ecolex 2012, 559.

**10** See *Kalss* Wie sichtbar muss ein Syndikatsvertrag sein in FS *Koppensteiner* (2016) 155; OGH SZ 48/133; OGH 8 Ob 253/75; *Koppensteiner/Rüffler* GmbHG³ (2007) § 4 Rz 19; *Kalss* Anmerkungen zur Privatautonomie in der GmbH in Kalss/Rüffler, Satzungsgestaltung in der GmbH – Möglichkeiten und Grenzen (2005) 13; *Harrer* in Gruber/Harrer, GmbHG §§ 49, 50 n 19 et seqq.

**11** *Nowotny* in Kalss/Nowotny/Schauer, Gesellschaftsrecht (2017) n 4/128 et seq.

**12** The requisite minimum quorum usually depends on the subject matter of the resolution. It is, to a certain extent and under certain circumstances, also possible to change the requisite majority with respect to an amendment of the articles of association.

# B. Regulation of Shareholders' Agreements

## I. General Remarks

Shareholders' agreements are not subject to specific rules or specific statutory laws; thus, the general rules and provisions on contract law and – as the case may be – corporate law apply. It is the common understanding of legal doctrine and case law that shareholders' agreements are a permissible agreement among all shareholders or parts thereof.[13] Shareholders' agreements, thus, do not need a specific permission by laws or articles of association; it is at the discretion of the shareholders to decide whether they want to arrange and/or organize their coexistence and cooperation. In addition, there are no rules on the form of the agreement (*Formfreiheit*), *e.g.* no notarial deed is usually mandatorily required.[14] Hence, shareholders' agreements can be concluded in a more flexible and, thus, also faster manner. Further, shareholders' agreements do not have to be disclosed to the public.[15] Hence, they leave more room for provisions requiring confidentiality and sensitiveness.[16]

Shareholders' agreements are continuing obligations (*Dauerschuldverhältnis*) and are usually qualified as non-disclosed companies organized under the Austrian Civil Code (civil law company; *Gesellschaft bürgerlichen Rechts*).[17] Such civil law companies normally do not appear or participate in or act on the market (towards third parties) but remain undisclosed (*Innengesellschaft*).[18]

---

**13** *Harrer* in Gruber/Harrer, GmbHG (2014) §§ 41, 42 n 151; *Koppensteiner/Rüffler* GmbHG³ § 39 n 19; *Kalss/Probst* Familienunternehmen n 4/13.

**14** However, it has to be noted that certain subject matters might trigger the need for a notarial deed (for example if the shareholders' agreement already contains an offer to transfer the shares in a company with limited liability); see OGH 28.8.2003, 8 Ob 259/02z. In contrast to shareholders' agreements, the form of articles of association is dependent on the type of the company; while articles of association of companies ususally do not request a specific form, strict rules apply to articles of associations of corporations.

**15** See below B.III.

**16** See for example, *Kalss/Probst* Syndikatsverträge in Familienunternehmen – rasch überprüfen!, GesRZ 2015, 154; *Artmann* Die Auslegung von Personengesellschaftsverträgen, einschließlich Syndikatsverträgen in Artmann/Rüffler/Torggler, Die Verbandsverfassung (2013) 34 et seq.

**17** See for example OGH 17.9.2014, 6 Ob 35/14 m; RIS-Justiz RS0079236 [T6, T7]. The qualification as a civil law company has, of course, legal consequences, *e.g.* with respect to the termination of the shareholders' agreement.

**18** It is in general also possible that shareholders' agreements are mere contracts to which the rules on civil law companies do not apply.

Since the general principles of civil law apply, it is at the discretion of the parties how they intend to customize the provisions of the shareholders' agreements, *e.g.* it has to be decided who the parties of the agreement are and/or whether the company shall be informed about the existence[19] and/or the content of the agreement and whether – which is rarely the case – the agreement shall be structured as third party beneficiary contract (*echter Vertrag zugunsten Dritter*) to the benefit of the company.[20] Therefore, there is a broad range of possibilities allowing shareholders for a rather flexible arrangement.

## II. Scope of Shareholders' Agreements

The typical purposes of shareholders' agreements, among other things, are the organization of the relationship between the (member-)shareholders, their strategic combined voting, the exit of shareholders as well as the transfer of shares. In addition, it is often intended to provide for regulations of profit distribution (*Gewinnausschüttung*) and financing obligations (capital increasing measures, shareholder contributions etc.) which shall normally only establish an obligation between the parties and shall not directly entitle the company to trigger or enforce financing obligations. By shareholders' agreements, the participating shareholders also have an opportunity or leverage to gain more influence in a company irrespective of their actual shareholding in the company. Rights to nominate members of the managing and/or supervisory board (*Nominierungsrechte*) or proceedings regarding the choice or nomination of key personnel as well as other organisational regulations often accompany such power balance provisions.

Key components of shareholders' agreements are the regulation of voting and the balance of the power. It is possible, for example, to empower one shareholder to make a decision and instruct all other shareholders in terms of their

---

The qualification as civil law company has, of course, different consequences, e.g. the termination of civil law comapnies follows other rules than the termination of mere contracts.

In this context see also Mock, 284 et seqq whereby similar principles also apply to Austrian shareholders' agreements.

**19** Of course, applicable mandatory laws have to be considered, *e.g.* certain disclosure requirements exist in case of listed stock corporations.

**20** In such case, the company would be in a position to enforce for example financing obligations (see below B.VII).

votes.[21] In this context, an important motivation or background of such agreements is the prevention of a stalemate or disagreement within the company (in particular with respect to general meetings and the passing of resolutions). In fact, a shareholders' agreement which regulates combined voting usually leads to a situation where conflicts have to be solved prior to the relevant shareholders' assembly; the voting result of resolutions passed in the shareholders' assembly is therefore often predetermined in case of the shareholders' agreement dealing with combined voting.[22] An agreement which is customized to the specific needs and interests can also facilitate the common conduct in case of conflicts between shareholders and can guarantee a mechanism to find an agreement or "decision" within the shareholders, resulting in a situation where resolutions cannot be frustrated.

Shareholders' agreements are, in fact, an important way to regulate the co-existence and cooperation between shareholders. In practice, articles of association are often plain vanilla agreements not providing for detailed provisions amending the applicable law. Thus, in such case articles of association are often not customized to the specific needs of the company's shareholders. Individual situations are as a consequence thereof rarely reflected within the articles of association. While shareholders obviously normally do not take advantage of the broad range of potential regulations with respect to the – publicly available – articles of association, they often agree upon side-contracts, *e.g.* shareholders' agreements, which allow for a tailor-made solution without being in the spotlight of third parties (including competitors or potential investors).[23] They are also of relevance in situations where shareholders do not want to show the actual distribution of power within the shareholders. In case of family businesses or in the course of a succession planning, it shall potentially not be disclosed to third parties (market participants, competitors, employees, business partners, etc.) that (still) one specific shareholder remains – at least for a certain period of time – in the decisive position and pulls the strings behind, although such family member/shareholder already transferred parts of his shares to his/her successors.

---

**21** See e.g. *Jud* Syndikatsverträge – Regelungsgegenstände, Regelungsprobleme, Regelungsgrenzen in Artmann/Rüffler/Torggler, Die Verbandsverfassung (2013) 43 with further references; *Heidinger/Schneider* in Jabornegg/Strasser, AktG[5] § 16 Rz 5; see also for example OGH 13.10.2011, 6 Ob 202/10i.

**22** See e.g. *Harrer* in Gruber/Harrer, GmbHG (2014) §§ 41, 42 n 149 et seqq.

**23** See *Kalss* in Koppensteiner FS (2016) 156; *Fleischer* Vergleichende Corporate Governance in der geschlossenen Kapitalgesellschaft, ZHR 179 2015, 404, 419.

Of course, shareholders' agreements can also give the leeway to establish an informal corporate codex, a family business charter or a constitution in which a code of ethics or conduct may be determined. While such provisions might appear to be, in the first instance, of low priority, the finding of common standards and codes of conducts can prevent misunderstandings and, as a positive statement, can facilitate to find a common understanding how to run the business.

## III. Disclosure/Non-disclosure/Confidentiality

In the vast majority, shareholders' agreements (*i.e.* its content and/or its existence) are not publicly disclosed. Since shareholders' agreements are not submitted to and published by the commercial register, third parties do not become easily aware of the fact that the shareholders are contractually bound by additional agreements (unless the articles of association contain a reference to an existing shareholders' agreement).[24] Hence, in case of non-disclosed shareholders' agreements, their existence could merely be perceived by an analysis of the (combined) voting or the facts of the case at hand. Thus, the non-disclosure bears the risk for a new shareholder or investor of a misjudgement regarding the actual power structure within the company.

Often, shareholders' agreements are subject to non-disclosure and confidentiality provisions. While articles of association of corporations are disclosed and – to a certain extent – examined by Austrian courts, shareholders' agreements can be designed as "shadow agreements", only known to their parties and not subject to an automatic examination of courts.[25]

The situation is different with respect to listed stock corporations. Pursuant to Section 243a para 1 n 2 UGB (Austrian commercial code) listed corporations have to disclose and publish the fact that a shareholders' agreement exists as well as its essential content. By this regulation, it is guaranteed that the capital market is informed about the fact that there are strategic (or other) alliances and that the influence of certain shareholder (groups) is catalyzed through an agreement. This information is, thus, prized-in by the capital market. It is also consequent to provide for a disclosure obligation for listed stock corporations, since

24 Articles of associations of corporations are submitted to the commercial register and, thus, publicly available. Articles of associations of registered companies are, however, not submitted to the commercial register.

25 As mentioned, this only applies to corporations while the articles of association of companies (e.g. OG and KG) are not publicly available.

shareholders' agreements may also trigger obligations pursuant to the Austrian Takeover Act.[26]

In the recent past, it became, however, more usual that the corporate charter mentions or refers to the existence of shareholders' agreements. Since a reference to the existence of the shareholders' agreement within the articles of association results in a disclosure thereof to third parties, potential investors and, more important, potential new shareholders make their decisions on a more informed basis. As a consequence thereof, a potential new shareholder cannot allege that he/she was not informed about (i) the fact that the voting power of his shares might be "diluted" and (ii) – depending on the information which is disclosed – that acquisition rights of other shareholders or limitations on the transferability of the shares exist. Such disclosure might, hence, lead to a situation where – although the third party is not bound by such agreements – this third party is not held bona fide when acquiring the share in violation of such restrictions.[27]

## IV. Conflict between articles of association and Shareholders' Agreements

Shareholders' agreements are only binding its parties, while articles of association are binding also – to a certain extent – external third parties as well as future shareholders.[28] If new shareholders are, however, not concluding an agreement with the shareholders being parties to the shareholders' agreement, they will not become a party to the shareholders' agreements.[29] Depending on the purpose of the shareholders' agreement, there might be a contractual obligation for transferring shareholders to transfer the obligations to the new shareholder and guarantee that he becomes party to the agreement.[30]

As a consequence thereof, articles of association in general prevail shareholders' agreements (in particular towards third parties). In case of a discrepan-

---

**26** See *Winner* Die 1. Übernahmeverordnung, RdW 1999, 509 with further references. See also below B.8.

**27** See for example *Frenzel/Gero* Die Absicherung syndikatsvertraglicher Überbindungspflichten durch Satzungsgestaltung bei der GmbH, GesRZ 2016, 264; *Kalss/Probst* Syndikatsverträge in Familienunternehmen – rasch überprüfen!, GesRZ 2015, 156; *Jud* in Artmann/Rüffler/Torggler, Die Verbandsverfassung (2013) 45 et seq; see also OGH 30.8.2000, 6 Ob 174/00g.

**28** See, however, B. III.

**29** See B.III., D.II.

**30** See C.6.

cy or contradiction between the articles of associations and shareholders' agreements, the provisions of the articles of association have to be applied.[31] However, resolutions passed by shareholders contradicting the articles of association are not in any event or automatically null and void. It has to be differentiated: In the case that the resolution is qualified as a selective amendment/breach of the articles (*punktuelle Satzungsdurchbrechung*), the resolution is valid unless it is (legally binding) challenged. If the resolution is not successfully challenged, the resolution remains valid although it is in contradiction to the provisions of the articles of association.[32] Examples for such selective resolutions are: resolutions on the retention of profits or resolutions which are resolved on the basis of a quorum which is not in compliance with the provisions of the shareholders' agreement.

## V. Parties to Shareholders' Agreements

As noted, parties to the shareholders' agreement are all or parts of the shareholders of a company. The company itself is usually not party to the agreement and not bound by its provisions.

It is, however, possible that the company becomes – at least to a certain extent – party to the agreement. For example, companies may be bound by provisions regarding the financing of the company or the obligation of shareholders to make contributions. Certainly, it is not possible to circumvent applicable mandatory (corporate) law or to bind the company regarding voting or the nomination/appointment of the management board, the supervisory board or other organs of the company.[33]

## VI. Duration of Shareholders' Agreements

There are, in general, no specific restrictions with respect to the duration of shareholders' agreements. Hence, the duration respectively the right to terminate

---

**31** See *Kalss* Zur Zulässigkeit eines Hinweises auf einen Syndikatsvertrag in einem GmbH-Vertrag, GesRZ 2013, 344 et seq.

**32** See *Kalss* Zur Zulässigkeit eines Hinweises auf einen Syndikatsvertrag in einem GmbH-Vertrag, GesRZ 2013, 344 et seq; *Kalss/Probst* Familienunternehmen, Rz 4/85; *Winner* in MünchKomm AktG$^3$ § 179 Rz 229; *U. Torggler* Die Satzungsdurchbrechung und ihre (Dauer-)Wirkungen in Artmann/Rüffler/Torggler, Die Verbandsverfassung (2013) 79 et seqq.

**33** *Kalss/Probst* Syndikatsverträge in Familienunternehmen – rasch prüfen!, GesRZ 2015, 155.

the shareholders' agreements depends on the qualification of the agreement as mere contract or as civil law company. In most cases, shareholders' agreements are, as mentioned, structured as continuing obligations whereby the right to terminate the agreement is usually (strictly) limited. In this context, the Austrian Supreme Court decided that shareholders' agreements, which are concluded for an indefinite time, are usually qualified as civil law companies. Hence, the right to terminate the civil law company respectively the shareholders' agreement can be restricted to the extent that the parties are merely entitled to terminate the agreement for good cause.[34]

Pursuant to the Austrian Civil Code (ABGB) this only applies to civil law companies which remain "internal" civil law companies (*Innengesellschaft*). If the civil law company is also acting on the market (which is normally not the case), the termination rights, however, can only be limited by extending the grace period; other limitations would be invalid (see Section 1209 Austrian Civil Code).[35]

In a situation where a shareholders' agreement is qualified as a "mere agreement", the right to terminate follows the general principles of civil law which restricts such limitations to a certain extent.

## VII. Need for shareholders' agreements in partnerships?

There is no distinction between partnerships/companies (*Personengesellschaften*) and corporations regarding shareholders' agreements. Applicable law of partnerships allows, however, in general for more flexibility so that the range of agreements is broader than for corporations. Since the articles of association of partnerships are usually not disclosed to the public, it is more likely that the relevant provisions are already included therein.

**34** See OGH 28.04.2003, 7 Ob 59/03 g; OGH 14.09.2011, 6 Ob 80/11z.

**35** Initially, Section 1209 Civil Code was amended by BGBl I 83/2014. This new Section 1209 Civil Code, however, did not differentiate between non-disclosed and publicly-acting civil companies resulting in a situation where shareholders' agreements could easily be terminated by its parties. This fact was heavily criticized since such termination right would foil the nature and purpose of shareholders' agreements. For this reason, the Austrian legislator amended again Section 1209 Civil Code by allowing for limitations of the parties' termination right at least with respect to non-disclosed companies (BGBl. I Nr. 43/2016).

## VIII. Relevant statutory laws for stock corporations

As mentioned above, shareholders' agreements of listed corporations are subject to disclosure requirements.[36] Section 243a para 1 n 2 UGB (Austrian commercial code) provides that stock corporations (i) whose shares are listed within the meaning of Section 1 para 2 Stock Exchange Act 2018 (BörseG 2018)[37] or (ii) which issued other securities on such market and whose shares are traded via a multilateral trading system pursuant to Section 1 number 24 WAG 2018 (Securities Supervision Act 2018) have – to the extent known to the management of the company – to disclose all limitations of voting rights or the transfer of shares also if they are part of shareholders' agreements.

Further, shareholders' agreements may also trigger obligations under the Austrian Takeover Act, leading, under certain circumstances, to a mandatory takeover bid (*Verpflichtung zur Abgabe eines öffentlichen Angebots*). Pursuant to Section 22 para 1 of the Austrian Takeover Act, a mandatory takeover bid must be made if a shareholder gains (actively or passively[38]) direct or indirect control over the target company whereby such obligation only applies with respect to the first gaining of control or change of control.[39] The relevant threshold amounts to 30 % whereby certain obligations are already triggered even before this threshold is met. Since Austrian Takeover Law does not refer to the acquisition of ownership but the gaining of control, also shareholders' agreements might enable a shareholder or a group of shareholders to gain control.[40] As a consequence, shareholders' agreements might be qualified as acting in concert of their parties, resulting again in the trigger of obligations under the Austrian Takeover Act.

---

**36** See B.III.

**37** In terms of the new Austrian Stock Exchange Act (BörseG 2018) see *Arlt/von Schrader*, Das neue Börserecht. BörseG 2018: Einführung, Neuerungen und Grundlagen, 2018.

**38** Passive control is in general also relevant with respect to the application of Austrian takeover law; however, in a situation where a shareholder gains passively control but could not expect to do so when acquiring the shares and without taking an action promptly prior to gainin control, the shareholder is merely obliged to inform the takeover commission (*Übernahmekommission*) but is not obligated to make a takeover offer. *Jud* in Artmann/Rüffler/Torggler, Die Verbandsverfassung (2013) 55 et seq.

**39** See *Diregger/Kalss/Winner* Das österreichische Übernahmerecht – Ein Gesamtüberblick$^2$ (2006) n 11, 177; *Winner* Das Pflichtangebot nach neuem Übernahmerecht, ÖJZ 2006, 660.

**40** See *Kalss/Oppitz/Zollner* Kapitalmarktrecht $^2$ (2017) § 24 n 33; *Jud* in Artmann/Rüffler/Torggler, Die Verbandsverfassung (2013) 52 with further references.

Since 3 January 2018, the new Austrian Stock Exchange Act 2018 provides for delisting regulations which also might lead to a mandatory offer.[41]

Also with respect to delisting resolutions, parties to shareholders' agreements can be qualified as shareholders acting in concert.[42]

## IX. Selection of Case law

The Austrian Supreme Court (*Oberster Gerichtshof*) rendered numerous judgements regarding shareholders' agreements on various occasions. The following judgments might be of interest and relevance:

- OGH 28.04.2003, 7 Ob 59/03 g; OGH 14.09.2011, 6 Ob 80/11z: as mentioned above, the Austrian Supreme Court decided on the permissibility of contractual restrictions of the termination rights.
- OGH 26.02.2008, 1 Ob 180/07p: The Austrian Supreme Court ruled that shareholders' agreements have to be considered when assessing a potential change of control. The judgement was rendered in the context of the question whether a landlord is entitled to increase the rent. Pursuant to Section 12a MRG (*Mietrechtsgesetz*), a landlord is entitled to increase a rent to the appropriate level (pursuant to Section 16 MRG) whenever the legal or economic influence (possibilities) within a corporation[43] (*e.g.* by a sale of shares etc.) changes.

  Usually, shareholders' agreements are not relevant in this context and do not limit the rights of the landlord. In the case at hand, however, the Austrian Supreme Court decided that there is no change in the possibility to take economic influence if – prior the acquisition of shares in a corporation with limited liability – the acquirer was already party to the shareholders' agreement. The parties, however, complied with the agreement and concluded the agreement three years prior to Section 12a MRG getting into force. Further, there was no evidence that the agreement was concluded in order to avoid the applicability of Section 12a MRG.
- OGH 26.08.1999, 2 Ob 46/97x: In general, shareholders' agreements are mere agreements between their parties and supplement the articles of association. As a consequence thereof, shareholders' agreements do, however, not inter-

41 See *Arlt/von Schrader*, Das neue Börserecht. BörseG 2018: Einführung, Neuerungen und Grundlagen, 2018.

42 This fact becomes relevant with respect to the challenge of the offer; see *Arlt/von Schrader*, Das neue Börserecht. BörseG 2018: Einführung, Neuerungen und Grundlagen, 2018.

43 This provision also applies to entrepreneurial partnerships (*Personengesellschaften*).

fere with the corporate organisation resulting in votes casted in breach of the shareholders' agreements being valid. This leads to a situation where a resolution remains valid and cannot be challenged on the argument of a breach of the shareholders' agreement.[44] In its judgment 2 Ob 46/97x, however, the Austrian Supreme Court decided that under certain circumstances an infringement of the shareholders' agreement shall nevertheless be legally relevant and may lead to the voidability of resolutions passed against the provisions of the shareholders' agreement.

Provisions of shareholders' agreements shall only be relevant *(Durchgriff des Syndikatsvertrages)* (i) in a situation where all shareholders are party to the shareholders' agreements and (ii) with respect to corporations which are structured and organized in a "personalized" (*personalistisch*) manner, *i.e.* the corporation is dominated by its shareholders and the shareholders' agreement concretizes the fiduciary duties (*Treuepflicht*). The Austrian Supreme Court in particular mentions that the principles developed in this judgment shall apply to corporations with a (very) limited number of shareholders and where all shareholders are, to a certain extent, relevant to the company (*i.e.* each individual shareholder is important to the company; the company is, therefore, dependent on each individual shareholder and their common consistent intent (*Wille*)).

- OHG 13.10.2011, 6 Ob 202/10i: In 2011, the Austrian Supreme Court rendered another judgment in this context.[45] In this judgment, the Austrian Supreme Court decided that the cooperative parts of articles of association have to be interpreted in an objective manner. It was further stated that a shareholders' resolution cannot be challenged on the basis that the resolution was passed in violation of the shareholders' agreement, unless the shareholders' agreement and the commitment therein is merely concretizing the fiduciary duty (*Treuepflicht*) among the shareholders.[46] In the case at hand, it was, however, also relevant that not all shareholders of the company were also party to the agreement.

  It appears therefore that the Austrian Supreme Court is willing to only accept an objective interpretation of articles of association. In light of the fact that there are different types of corporations and that the influence and role of

---

44 See for example OGH 5.12.1995, 4 Ob 588/96; 6 Ob 9/93 = ecolex 1993, 605.

45 See *Harrer* in Gruber/Harrer, GmbHG §§ 41, 42 n 154 who qualifies the judgment as a requisite correction of the above mentioned judgement. However, see also *Jabornegg* Auslegung der Satzung von Kapitalgesellschaften in Artmann/Rüffler/Torggler, Die Verbandsverfassung (2013) 12 et seqq.

46 See *e.g.* Koppensteiner/Rüffler, GmbHG$^3$ § 39 Rz 21.

the shareholders varies from company to company, it would not be understandable why the actual intent of the shareholders should be ignored or be irrelevant without assessing the specific facts of the case at hand. For example, if no change in the (founding) shareholders took place and all of them are members to the shareholders' agreements, why should the specific interest of the shareholders be irrelevant with respect to (i) the interpretation of the articles of association and (ii) the voidance of a resolution which was passed in violation of the shareholders' agreement?

# C. Forms of Shareholders' Agreements

Since the content and scope of shareholders' agreements are highly dependent of the "underlying" company, there is a huge variety of shareholders' agreements in legal practice. Nevertheless, there are certain scopes of shareholders' agreements which are ususally addressed. In the following sections, usual contents shall be discussed.

## I. Voting agreements

Voting rights and the regulation of combined voting are usually essential parts of shareholders' agreements. As mentioned above, there are various ways to regulate voting rights, their exercise and/or the decision-making process regarding the casting of votes. Typical shareholders' agreements provide for regulations in particular on the decision making process, the weight of votes and the proceedings in case of disagreements.

In order to ensure that agreements on the casting of votes are not breached, some shareholders' agreements provide for certain control mechanisms. There are two main options: granting of proxies and voting trusts. In the first case, the member shareholders can grant a general proxy to a certain member of the shareholders' agreement (*e.g.* the president of the syndicate). Of course, such proxy follows – like all powers of attorney – strict rules and, thus, cannot be unlimited.[47]

In terms of voting trusts, the shares are transferred to a trustee. Such trustee becomes, as a consequence thereof, the owner of the shares but is bound by the

47 See *Jud* in Artmann/Rüffler/Torggler, Verbandsverfassung (2013) 49.

instructions of the beneficial owner.[48] Since the transfer of shares in a company with limited liability requires a notarial deed, a voting trust construction in such situation is rather complicated and not flexible.

## II. Shareholders' agreements and management instructions

In general, the management board (stock corporations) or the managing directors (companies with limited liability) run the daily business whereby the individual shareholders are not entitled to give instructions. Of course, there are differences between stock corporations and companies with limited liability.

The management board of stock corporations is entirely and mandatorily independent. Pursuant to Section 70 of the Austrian Stock Corporation Act, the management board manages the business of the company at its sole discretion. Neither the supervisory board nor the shareholders' assembly are entitled to instruct the board.

The situation is rather different with corporations with limited liability. In general, the shareholders of corporations with limited liability are entitled to give instructions. However, instructions can only be given through resolutions passed by the general assembly or by all shareholders (in writing whereby certain exemptions apply). If shareholders' agreements shall deal with instructions, they have, again, to provide for proceedings with respect to the passing of resolutions. It is not permissible that shareholders' resolutions or the shareholders' agreement entitle one (or a group of) shareholder(s) to give instructions.

## III. Shareholders' agreements as coordination to enforce shareholder claims

In terms of companies with limited liability, claims, which the company has against its board members or its shareholders, have to be enforced by the company itself (Section 48 GmbHG). Individual shareholders are in general not entitled to enforce claims. Only under certain circumstances, shareholders are entitled to (immediately) enforce claims of the company. Of course, the shareholders may instruct the management board and, under specific circumstances, the supervisory board to claim for damages. Further, minority shareholders who hold

48 *Tichy* Syndikatsverträge, 193; *Torggler* Vertragliche Gestaltung zur Wahrung des Gesellschaftereinflusses, GesRZ 1990, 191; *Jud* in Artmann/Rüffler/Torggler, Verbandsverfassung (2013) 49.

at least 10 % of the share capital or a nominal capital of EUR 700,000 are entitled to directly claim for damages if the company refuses to take action (§ 48 para 1 GmbHG).

The enforcement of claims of stock corporations follows a similar logic. In general, claims have to be enforced by the company itself. The stock corporation is represented by the management board or, if this is not possible, the supervisory board. The boards are obliged to enforce a claim if an according resolution is passed by the general assembly. In addition, pursuant to section 134 et seq. Austrian Stock Corporation Act, also minority shareholders with a share representing at least 10 % of the share capital (alone or together) are entitled to enforce a claim.

Shareholders' agreements can therefore deal with the enforcement of claims in different manners. Generally, the agreement can provide for mechanisms with respect to the decision-making process resulting in the syndicate deciding on whether the company itself is instructed to enforce a claim.

## IV. Shareholders' agreements on financing the company

In general, no shareholder of an Austrian corporation is – besides his obligation to pay in the share (capital) of the company – obliged to make addition financial contributions to the company (apart from his initial capital contribution), unless such obligation is provided for in the articles of association or other relevant agreements. Hence, it is at the discretion of the shareholders to agree on finance obligations within the articles of association.

Another option is to agree on financing obligations within shareholders' agreements. In this case, the financing obligation is only binding towards the parties to the agreement but does not bind the shareholders towards the company. Hence, unless the shareholders' agreement is qualified as a third-party beneficiary contract (*echter Vertrag zugunsten Dritter*) to the benefit of the company, only the parties to the agreement (*i. e.* the shareholders) can enforce the financing obligation whereby new shareholders who do not participate in the syndicate or the company cannot rely on such obligation. The difference is in particular of relevance in case of an insolvency of the company, since the liquidator/insolvency administer is not empowered to enforce a shareholders' agreement.[49] In this context, it is noteworthy that, pursuant to the Austrian Supreme Court, provi-

---

**49** See above C.VIII.; *Kalss/Probst* Syndikatsverträge in Familienunternehmen – rasch prüfen!, GesRZ 2015, 156.

sions on financing obligations (*Vereinbarungen über Zuschüsse*) can be concluded without triggering the necessity for a specific form (*e.g.* no notarial deed must be concluded).[50]

Shareholders' agreements can also provide for regulations with respect to capital increases or capital decreases whereby such provisions usually deal with questions of the obligation to participate in the capital increase/capital decrease and/or the consequences if a shareholder is not able to or does not want to participate in the capital increase.

Again, shareholders' agreements have to comply with relevant applicable laws. In case of listed stock corporations, the range of potential provisions is more restricted than for companies with limited liability.

## V. Shareholders' agreements and Austrian Law of groups

Austrian statutory corporate law does not provide for a specific law of groups (*Konzernrecht*). The Austrian legislator of course recognizes the existence of corporate groups; several specific statutory provisions deal with questions of groups and Austrian doctrine and case law derives specific regulations from the general corporate and civil law principles.[51] Shareholders' agreements are a general tool to coordinate the conduct of shareholders (exercise of voting rights and other rights) and, thus, are also a possibility to support the combined voting and conduct within corporate groups. Also, with respect to groups, shareholders' agreement can of course not be used to circumvent mandatory laws or violate applicable laws. For example, it is not possible to undermine fiduciary duties or duties of loyalty which shareholders have towards their company.[52]

## VI. Shareholders' Agreements on the (Limitation of the) Transfer of Shares

In general, provisions on limitations of the transfer of shares can be incorporated either in the articles of association, bylaws or shareholders' agreements. The ad-

**50** OGH 17.09.2014, 6 Ob 35/14 m.

**51** See *Haberer/Krejci* Grundfragen zum Konzernrecht in Haberer/Krejci, Konzernrecht (2016) n 1.46 et seqq; *Schima/Arlt* Leitung und Überwachung – Corporate Governance im Konzern in Haberer/Krejci, Konzernrecht (2016) n 9.1 et seqq.

**52** See *Jud* in Artmann/Rüffler/Torggler, Die Verbandsverfassung (2013) 50 with further references.

vantage of incorporating such provisions in the articles of association is their binding effect on (potential) new shareholders and third parties. Since the articles of association are disclosed and publicly available in the commercial register, it is assumed that a shareholder and third parties are informed about its content and, consequently, of transfer limitations therein. Thus, a potential acquirer is also bound by such limitations. A third party therefore does not deserve legal protection if it intends to acquire a share by violating a transfer limitation provision in the articles of association.

In addition to such restrictions, it is also common to agree upon drag along clauses, tag along clauses and shoot out clauses. Again, such clauses can be incorporated in the articles of association as well as in shareholders' agreements. In general, provisions contained in the articles of association do not contain the entire regulations but are supplemented by the shareholders' agreement or they are merely incorporated in the shareholders' agreements.

In terms of limitations being part of the articles of association, the flipside of the coin is, of course, the fact that third parties are also informed about the existence of such limitations and do have better knowledge about the power balance within the company.

As soon as shareholders' agreements are concluded, it is very likely that the parties to the agreement also provide for certain protection provisions which shall prevent that a third party becomes shareholder of the company without getting member of the syndicate. At the same time, in a situation where shareholders bind themselves through shareholders' agreement, it is also very likely that the shareholders do not want third parties to become shareholders without having certain control mechanisms in place (*i.e.* limitation of transferability, rights of approval etc.).

## VII. Shareholders' Agreements on the Constitution of the Corporation

Shareholders' agreements may contain provisions relating to constitutional and/ or organizational questions to the extent that mandatory law does not require a certain form. In shareholders' agreements, shareholders may for example agree on the right of a specific shareholder to appoint directors or members of boards, capital measures (*e.g.* the obligation to recapitalize the company, financing obligations) and other organisational structures (*e.g.* the implementation of bylaws). As mentioned above, such provisions are only binding on the parties of the shareholders' agreements. They do, however, not bind the company or other third parties. Even if the company becomes party of the shareholders' agreement, it cannot be bound by all obligations. For example, the company cannot be bound by provisions regarding the nomination of board members. It is also not possible to bind the company with respect to obligations regarding the passing of resolutions.

## VIII. Shareholders' Agreements in pre-insolvency situation

Usually, the company is not party to the shareholders' agreement and, thus, the company is not bound by the agreement.[53] As a consequence thereof, the bankruptcy of the company does not automatically affect the shareholders' agreement. Under certain (limited) circumstances, the shareholders' agreement may, however, be qualified as a third party beneficiary agreement (*echter Vertrag zugunsten Dritter*).[54] Such qualification would allow the company and – in case of a bankruptcy – the insolvency trustee/liquidator to claim for the compliance with the obligations of the shareholders' agreement. For example, if the shareholders agreed upon an obligation to finance the company, the insolvency trustee would be entitled to enforce such finance obligation.[55] This is, of course, not in the interest of the shareholders. It is therefore rare and not advisable to shape the agreement in a manner allowing the company to pursue the shareholders.

Of course, the shareholders' agreement itself may deal with certain aspects of pre-solvency situations; however, such shareholders' agreements hardly exist in practice. It is more common that the shareholders' agreements provide for specific consequences in case of a bankruptcy of the company.

---

**53** See OGH 17.09.2014, 6 Ob 35/14 m.

**54** See OGH 22.7.2009, 3 Ob z2/09y. In light of the consequences of such qualification, it is – in case of doubt – not assumed that a shareholders' agreement shall be qualified as a third party beneficiary contract (see *Kalss/Probst* Syndikatsverträge in Familienunternehmen, GesRZ 2015, 156.

**55** The situation is of course different if an agreement with the company or the articles of association provide for a financing obligation. As an alternative, the shareholders therefore agree on such obligation only in shareholders' agreements resulting in a situation where – in case of bankruptcy – the shareholders prevent additional finance obligations.

# D. Legal Effects of Shareholders' Agreements

## I. Legal Effects on the Corporation

As mentioned, shareholders' agreements are not part of a corporate charter (*Trennungsprinzip*).[56] The difference is evident: the corporate charter binds the existing and also future shareholders and third parties; the shareholders' agreement merely binds its parties. New shareholders therefore do not automatically become parties to the shareholders' agreement, unless the member shareholders and the new shareholder agree on the new shareholder becoming party to the agreement.[57]

Further, a resolution, which is made in breach of the shareholders' agreement, is not *ex lege* null and void. As mentioned above, the case law of the Austrian Supreme Court is strict in this context and limits the right of shareholders to challenge resolutions based on the argument that it was passed in violation of the shareholders' agreement.[58]

In general, shareholders' agreements do not have an effect on the interpretation of the corporate charter.[59] However, this principle should not apply to all companies to the same extent. As already mentioned above, it should be differentiated between listed stock corporations and personalized corporations whereby the boundaries are not constant or whether corporations are constructed in a manner which is closed or which is very open towards the market. At least as long as all shareholders of the company are also party to a shareholders' agreement and the company is structured in a very personalized manner, it is not understandable why the articles of association should not be influenced by a shareholders' agreement and/or the articles of association are interpreted in an objective manner rather than taking into account the real intent of the parties as of the time of the conclusion of the agreement.[60]

As long as interpretation relates to questions, which merely concern the (founding) shareholders and members of the shareholders' resolution, it appears to be fairer and appropriate to also consider the specific intent of the parties

---

**56** See *Tichy* 43 et seqq.
**57** See *Tichy* 40 et seqq.
**58** See B.IX, D.III.
**59** See above B.IX.
**60** See *Jabornegg* in Artmann/Rüffler/Torggler, Die Verbandsverantwortung (2013) 1 et seqq; *Told* Bericht über die Vormittagsdiskussion in Artmann/Rüffler/Torggler, Die Verbandsverfassung (2013) 39 et seqq who summarizes the different views of academics in the context of the discussion about the invitation of articles of association.

rather than relying on an objective interpretation. In case third parties are involved, an objective interpretation appears in any event to be the appropriate solution.

## II. Legal Effects on the Shareholders

In general, shareholders' agreements are a separate agreement from the articles of association, even though they are – from an economic point of view – a unified construct. As a consequence thereof, the acquirer of a share in a company becomes party to the articles of association, but not automatically a party to a shareholders' agreement. In fact, the acquirer might even not be informed about the existence of such agreement among (all other or certain) shareholders. Even if the shareholders' agreement obliges its parties to transfer the obligations of the shareholders' agreement to an acquirer of a share (or parts thereof), the third party is not obligated to become a member of the syndicate.

Usually, shareholders' agreements contain explicit rules on the transfer of shares and the duty to ensure that an acquirer agrees to and becomes party to the shareholders' agreement. Such obligation is also flanked by the obligation that the members of the syndicate accept a new member (whereby, of course, limitations and an interplay of entitlements to give consent etc. apply).

The possibilities range from mere transfer restrictions (approval requirements etc.), contractual provisions prohibiting the transfer of shares to a non-member of the shareholders' agreement, to more or less detailed references to the shareholders' agreement within the articles of association.[61]

## III. Consequences of a Breach of the Shareholders' Agreements

As a general rule, shareholders' resolutions violating the shareholders' agreement are binding and cannot be successfully challenged merely on the fact that one (or more) shareholder(s) breached the provisions of the shareholders' agreement.

61 See e.g. *Frenzel/Gero* Die Absicherung syndikatsvertraglicher Überbindungspflichten durch Satzungsgestaltung bei der GmbH, GesRZ 2016, 260 et seqq.

In a decision of the Austrian Supreme Court in 1999[62], the Austrian Supreme Court, however, sentenced that in case of a strongly "personalized" company with limited liability (*ausgeprägt personalistische GmbH*), a resolution might be challenged if it is in breach of a shareholders' agreement, which was concluded upon all shareholders. The right to challenge a resolution in such situation is only a conceivable solution if the structure of the company is personalized (limited number of shareholders; all shareholders are parties to the agreement; the company is depending on the shareholders etc.).[63] To date, it is not finally decided whether a challenge of a resolution can be based on the fact of a breach of a shareholders' agreement.[64]

Shareholders, however, have certain fiduciary duties against all other shareholders (*Treuepflicht*). A breach of the shareholders' agreement might therefore lead to a breach of such fiduciary duties resulting in a successful challenge of the resolution.[65]

Further, a violation of the shareholders' agreement may entitle other shareholders to obtain compensation for damages. Shareholders may also enforce the shareholders' agreement (*e.g.* with respect to financing obligations).

A violation of the shareholders' agreement does not in any event affect the membership in the corporation. Depending on the gravity of the violation and/or the contractual provisions it may, however, form the basis for an exclusion of the shareholder. It might of course also trigger contractually agreed upon provisions obliging a shareholder to transfer its share to (the) other shareholder(s).

# E. Enforcement of Shareholders' Agreements

## I. Contractual "enforcement provisions"

Since a shareholders' agreement is a "normal" contract, it is at the discretion of the parties to provide for enforcement mechanisms. The range of such clauses is broad. Mechanisms could be, for example, contractual penalties (in addition to

**62** OGH 26. October 1999, 2 Ob 46/97x; see above B.IX.

**63** See OGH 26. October 1999, 2 Ob 46/97x; *Jabornegg* Auslegung der Satzung von Kapitalgesellschaften (AG und GmbH), in Artmann/Rüffler/Torggler, Die Verbandsverfassung (2013) 8 et seqq.

**64** See above B.IV.

**65** See OGH 26 October 1999, 2 Ob 46/97 x; see also *Walch* Verstoß gegen einen omnilateralen Syndikatsvertrag als Anfechtungsgrund eines Gesellschafterbeschlusses, GES 2015, 159 et seqq.; critical *Koppensteiner/Rüffler* GmbHG$^3$ § § 39 number 21.

or as a minimum compensation for damages), the obligation to transfer the share or the temporary suspension of participation in shareholders' resolutions.

Depending on the design of the contractual penalty, a contractual penalty has two effects: on the one hand, it provides (monetary) compensation (without bearing the full burden of proof) and, on the other hand, it is a tool to influence the conduct of the parties to the shareholders' agreement. Thus, it is essential to draft a well-balanced penalty clause which incentivises the parties in the right manner.

Since a compulsory exit of a shareholder is one of the most extensive interference with the property of a shareholder (it might be comparable to an expropriation), it should remain the last resort and consequence. It is important to find a balance between the interest of the shareholder with respect to receive compensation, remain in the company and defining the reasons for a termination or exclusion for good cause.

## II. Court proceedings and injunctive relief

Obligations resulting from shareholders' agreements are usually enforceable via court proceedings. Pursuant to the prevailing opinion, shareholders' agreements are enforced by action for performance (*Leistungsklage*).[66] Consequently, also a specific casting of votes can be enforced in front of a court. In a situation, for example, in which a resolution cannot be challenged on the grounds of a violation of the shareholders' agreement, the shareholders could be obliged to pass a contradictory resolution which sets aside the previous resolution.[67] As mentioned above[68], it is not a clear-cut-case to challenge a shareholders' resolution on the argument that it was passed in violation of the shareholders' agreement; legal doctrine and case law are not entirely consistent in this context.[69] As a consequence thereof, there is a high risk that a resolution is legally bindingly passed albeit it infringes the agreement.

In a situation where such infringement is foreseeable, the enforcement of the agreement could be procured by help of an injunctive relief (*einstweilige Verfü-*

66 OGH 28.4.2003, 7 Ob 59/03 g, JBl 2003, 869; *Koppensteiner/Rüffler* GmbHG$^{3}$ § 39 Rz 22; *Harrer* in Gruber/Harrer GmbHG, §§ 41, 42 n 155.

67 See *Harrer* in Harrer/Gruber, GmbHG §§ 41, 42 n 155 et seqq with critical notes.

68 See B.IX.

69 See above D.III.; OGH 2 Ob 46/97x; 6 Ob 292/10i; *Jabornegg* in Artmann/Rüffler/Torggler, Die Verbandsverfassung, 8 et seqq, 12 et seqq; *Told* Bericht über der Vormittagsdiskussion in Artmann/Rüffler/Torggler, Die Verbandsverfassung, 39 et seqq.

*gung*). In light of the normal duration of court proceedings, such injunctive relief appears to be the most efficient way.[70] Preconditions of an injunctive relief are the preliminary proof (*Bescheinigung*) of a claim (*Anspruch*) and a risk (*Gefährdung*).[71] Whether the preliminary proof of claim is successful depends in particular on the design of the provisions contained in the shareholders' agreement as well as the question, whether all proceedings contractually agreed upon were met. The claiming shareholder has to further provide preliminary evidence that a binding resolution pursuant to the provisions of the shareholders' agreement was passed as well as the content thereof. In the next step, it has to be proven that an issuance of an injunctive relief is in the prevailing interest of the claiming shareholder. In this context, the Austrian Supreme Court resolved that the relevant question is if (i) the allowance of an interim protective measure or (ii) its omission is more likely to cause an irrevocable harm.[72] The balancing of interests in the context of an injunctive relief is a special measure, since usually an injunctive relief should not cause irrevocable consequences.[73] In addition, the claiming party also has to provide preliminary evidence of a concrete risk, *i.e.* such risk must not be an abstract possibility but an actual threat must be evidenced that the defending party will not comply with the passed shareholders' agreement and cast its vote in violation thereof.

## III. ADR Mechanisms

In a shareholders' agreement, it is also permissible to agree upon alternative dispute resolution mechanisms, such as arbitration proceedings or the obligation to open mediation proceedings. Arbitration clauses are in general permissible, however, certain preconditions have to be met.

---

**70** *Oberhammer* Einstweiliger Rechtsschutz zur Durchsetzung von Stimmpflichten in Artmann/Rüffler/Torggler, Die Verbandsverfassung (2013) 65.

**71** *Oberhammer* Einstweiliger Rechtsschutz zur Durchsetzung von Stimmpflichten in Artmann/Rüffler/Torggler, Die Verbandsverfassung (2013) 65.

**72** OGH 28.04.2003, 7 Ob 59/03 g RdW 2003,452 = ÖJZ-LSK 2003/180 = EvBl 2003/163 S 760 – EvBl 2003,760 = GesRZ 2003,291 = JBl 2003,869 = ecolex 2003,844 = Wallisch, ÖZW 2004, 55 = Zackl, ÖJZ 2005, 12 = MietSlg 55.814 = SZ 2003/45 = Zackl, JAP 2004/2005/13 S 50 – Zackl, JAP 2004/2005, 50.

**73** See *König* Einstweilige Verfügung im Zivilverfahren$^4$ (2012) n 2/53 et seqq; *Oberhammer* Einstweiliger Rechtsschutz zur Durchsetzung von Stimmpflichten in Artmann/Rüffler/Torggler, Die Verbandsverfassung (2013) 65 et seq.

### 1. Mediation

Shareholders conclude the shareholders' agreement often attempting to prevent conflicts and to define proceedings guaranteeing to find binding agreements and securing a well-balanced decision-making process. By shareholders' resolutions shareholders usually intend to better cooperate and to collaborate in order to facilitate the success of the company. In situations where shareholders are not only mere co-owners of the company but have a relationship to each other, *e.g.* family members in a family-run business or friends, respectively colleagues, who formed a start up together. In this context, it makes sense to also agree upon a conflict resolution mechanism which is an upstream process. Mediation proceedings are tailored to lead conflicting parties to a win-win situation by finding the main reasons for their conflict(s). Successful mediation further helps to develop options preventing conflicts in the future. It becomes therefore more and more common to include mediation clauses in business agreements and thus also in shareholders' agreements. Since shareholders remain parties of the shareholders' agreement and members of the same company, it makes sense to prevent court proceedings, while it is therefore preferable to initiate mediation proceedings prior to court proceedings.

### 2. Arbitration clauses

Since court proceedings are public and arbitral proceedings remain non-public, shareholders' agreements often also provide for arbitration clauses. It is generally recognized that claims arising out of shareholders' agreements can be subject to arbitral proceedings.[74] Precondition is, however, that all members of the shareholders' agreement validly agree upon the arbitration clause. In case of a dispute, it has, however, to be kept in mind whether all parties to the shareholders' agreement also have to be party to the proceedings. Pursuant to a decision of the Austrian Supreme Court, it is a question of the subject matter (claim) whether all parties have to be involved in the proceedings.[75]

---

74 OGH 22.10.2010, 7 Ob 103/10p.
75 OGH 22.10.2010, 7 Ob 103/10p.

Tom Matthijs

# Belgium

## Table of Content



**Tom Matthijs,** White & Case LLP, Belgium with contributions from *W. Van de Wiele.*

https://doi.org/10.1515/9783110517026-009

## A. Regulation of Shareholders' Agreements

A shareholders' agreement is a "contract" whereby two or more shareholders[1] typically agree on certain arrangements in relation to their shareholding in a company (such, as for example, share transfer restrictions, governance rules, voting agreements, information rights, etc.) This means that general Belgian contract law applies to shareholders' agreements, e. g. regarding the formation of the contract, content of the contract, evidence and formal requirements, as well as with respect to the interpretation of the contract.[2] Belgian contract law is set out in the Belgian Civil Code.

Shareholders' agreements do not qualify as a specifically regulated type of contract under Belgian law; there is no specific Belgian law containing an all-encompassing regulation with respect to shareholders' agreements under Belgian law.[3] Rather, the relevant legal provisions are spread out over various legal provisions, to be supplemented with interpretations by case law and legal doctrine. As a result, the content and object of a shareholders' agreement will be determined *inter partes* and will depend heavily on the objectives pursued by the relevant parties (e. g., stability of shareholding, reinforcement of the position of the minority shareholder(s), facilitate an exit through an IPO or a sale of 100 % of the shares, etc.).

The Belgian Company Code contains a number of mandatory provisions that have to be complied with when entering into shareholders' agreements. We will discuss these legal provisions in more detail below, but can highlight the following categories:[4] (1) provisions with respect to transfer restrictions,[5] (2) provisions with respect to voting agreements[6], (3) rules regarding the appointment of direc-

1 It is not required under Belgian law that shareholders' agreements are entered into by all shareholders. Moreover, shareholders' agreements can also be entered by shareholders and third parties, it being understood that such type of agreements will have different legal consequences because article 551 of the Belgian Company Code is generally not considered to be applicable on such category of agreements.

2 *J. Pattyn* Aandeelhoudersovereenkomsten – overdrachtsbeperkingen en stemafspraken in een niet-publieke nv, in Bibliotheek Handelsrecht Larcier – Vennootschaps- en Financieel Recht, Gent, Larcier, 2012, nr. 7 (hereafter referred to as *Pattyn* Aandeelhoudersovereenkomsten).

3 Ibid.

4 Ibid.

5 Article 510 et seq. Belgian Company Code.

6 Article 551 et seq. of the Belgian Company Code.

tors[7] and (4) provisions regarding the exclusion from profits and the exemption from contributing to losses.[8]

In addition to the general provisions of the Belgian Company Code, certain specific financial and other legislation has to be taken into account as part of the legal framework applicable to shareholders' agreements,[9] such as for example:

- the laws and regulations on the disclosure of major shareholdings;[10]
- the laws and regulations on public takeover bids, including the regulations with respect to mandatory takeover bids;[11]
- the laws and regulations with respect to the shareholdings in certain regulated companies such as banks,[12] investment firms[13] and insurance companies[14]; and
- competition law provisions.[15]

The 2009 Belgian Code on Corporate Governance (the "**2009 Code**")[16] for listed companies contains certain recommendations with respect to shareholders' agreements with a view to increase transparency and good governance. The following recommendations are specifically worth noting:

---

**7** Article 518 § 3 of the Belgian Company Code.

**8** Article 32 of the Belgian Company Code.

**9** *Pattyn* Aandeelhoudersovereenkomsten. nr. 7.

**10** The Law of 2 May 2007 regarding the disclosure of major shareholdings in companies admitted to trading on a regulated market (*Loi du 2 mai 2007 relative à la publicité des participations importantes dans des émetteurs dont les actions sont admises à la négociation sur un marché réglementé et portant des dispositions diverses/ Wet van 2 mei 2007 op de openbaarmaking van belangrijke deelnemingen in emittenten waarvan aandelen zijn toegelaten tot de verhandeling op een gereglementeerde markt en houdende diverse bepalingen* and the *Arrêté royal du 14 février 2008 relatif à la publicité des participations importantes/ Koninklijk besluit van 14 februari 2008 op de openbaarmaking van belangrijke deelnemingen*).

**11** The Law of 1 April 2007 regarding public takeover bids (*Loi du 1 avril 2007 relative aux offres publiques d'acquisition/Wet van 1 april 2007 op de openbare overnamebiedingen* and *Arrêté royal du 27 avril 2007 relatif aux offres publiques d'acquisition*).

**12** The Law of 25 April 2014 regarding the status and supervision of credit institutions (*Wet van 25 april 2014 op het statuut van en het toezicht op kredietinstellingen en beursvennootschappen*).

**13** Ibid.

**14** The Law of 13 March 2016 regarding the status and supervision of insurance and reinsurance companies (Loi du 13 mars relative au statut et au contrôle des entreprises d'assurance ou de réassurance. *Wet van 13 maart 2016 of het statuut van en het toezicht op de verzekerings- of herverzekeringsondernemingen*).

**15** Belgian Code of Economic Law.

**16** See http://www.corporategovernancecommittee.be/sites/default/files/generated/files/page/corporategovukcode2009.pdf (last consulted: 18 September 2017).

- listed companies disclose in their corporate governance charter the key elements of voting rights and special control rights of majority shareholders, and, if those majority shareholders act in concert, a description of the key elements of existing shareholders' agreements[17];
- listed companies should have a rigorous and transparent procedure for an efficient appointment and re-appointment of directors[18]; and
- the board of directors of a listed company should endeavor to have the controlling shareholders make a considered use of their position, respecting the rights and interests of minority shareholders as well as the provisions of the 2009 Code.[19]

The corporate governance code for non-listed companies, updated in May 2017[20] (the "**Code Buysse III**"), contains a specific chapter on the role of shareholders in non-listed companies.[21] This chapter emphasizes the importance for the shareholders' agreement to agree on the following matters in a shareholders' agreement[22]:

- exit provisions;
- share transfer restrictions (including, permitted transfers, pre-emption rights, rights of first refusal and price determination mechanisms); and
- composition of the board of directors.

This contribution focuses on the private limited liability company ("*société anonyme/naamloze vennootschap*") and the private limited liability company ("*société privée à responsabilité limitée/besloten vennootschap met beperkte aansprakelijkheid*"). These are the two types of legal forms commonly used for commercial companies in Belgium. Various other types of legal forms exist (although the new Belgian Company Code will simplify and reduce the number of legal form). While the general principles set out herein may also be relevant for these other legal forms, specific mandatory rules would need to be checked in order to determine their impact on the content and structure of the relevant shareholders' agreements.

**17** See recommendation 8.4 of 2009 Code.

**18** See recommendation 4.1 of 2009 Code.

**19** See recommendation 8.11 of 2009 Code.

**20** See http://www.codebuysse.com/downloads/CodeBuysseIII_NL.pdf (in Dutch; last consulted 18 September 2017).

**21** See chapter 7 of Code Buysse, p. 42–45.

**22** See recommendations 7.5 to 7.7 of Code Buysse III.

# I. Shareholders' agreements and the articles of association

Shareholders' agreements are generally permitted under Belgian law if and to the extent their object does not violate public order ("*ordre publique*") or provisions of Belgian mandatory law. In principle, shareholders' agreements do not have to be specifically mentioned in the articles of association or by the shareholders' meeting.

Practitioners are frequently asked to advise on whether a certain arrangement agreed between shareholders should be documented in the shareholders' agreement, the articles of association or both. The answer depends on the factual circumstances of each case, but the following considerations are in our view relevant:

- **Confidentiality** – The company's articles of association are published by extract in the Belgian Official State Gazette. Furthermore, any interested party can obtain a copy of the articles of association of a company at the relevant registry of the commercial court. The confidentiality of the company's articles of association (including all arrangements set forth therein) can therefore not be guaranteed. The existence and content of shareholders' agreements can be and is often protected through confidentiality provisions.
- **Legal effect versus third parties –** Share transfer restrictions set forth in a shareholders' agreement are in principle not enforceable ("*tegenwerpbaar*"/ "*opposable*") against third parties (including the company or any purchaser of shares).[23] This rule does not apply when the third party knew, or reasonably should have known (if it acted as a reasonable, diligence and prudent third party placed in the same circumstances), of the relevant share transfer restrictions. The Belgian Supreme Court has ruled that a sale of shares may be declared void if concluded in violation of share transfer restrictions where the purchaser is (as a third party) responsible for such violation on the basis of third party complicity.[24] Restrictions set forth in the articles of association benefit from a higher degree of enforceability in view of the disclosure in respect of such restrictions.[25]
- **Duration** – Arrangements set forth in a shareholders' agreement are valid for a specific duration (which is either the duration of the shareholders' agreement itself, or the specific duration contained in the shareholders'

23 Cf. article 1165 of the Belgian Civil Code.

24 Cass. 27 April 2006, *Pas.*, 2006, p. 976.

25 For completeness purposes, it should be noted that the Supreme Court has decided that no legal presumption of knowledge follows from the fact that an act has been published in the Belgian Official State Gazette. See Cass. 5 May 1976, *Pas.* 1976, I, p. 957.

agreement for a specific arrangement), whereas arrangements set forth in the articles of association will continue to apply until they are amended or until the company is wound up.

- **Formalism** – The articles of association can generally[26] be amended by an extraordinary shareholders' meeting, approving any amendment with a 75 % majority, provided more than half of the share capital is present or represented.[27] The extraordinary shareholders' meeting must be organized before a notary public (which triggers certain costs that are becoming payable by the company). Shareholders' agreement can be amended without any formalism, either via the consent of all parties or, if the shareholders' agreement provides for such mechanism, via the application of an amendment procedure (pursuant to which the required number of shareholders approves the amendments).
- **Director liability** – The directors of the company are liable on a joint basis, both *vis-à-vis* the company and any third parties, for any violation of the Belgian Company Code and the articles of association of the company.[28] The Belgian Company Code does not contain a similar sanction for a breach by the company of a contract.
- **Parties** – Finally, it should be noted that shareholders' agreements (compared to the articles of association) allow for greater flexibility with respect to their scope *ratione personae*. There is no legal requirement that all shareholders become a party to the shareholders' agreement, whereas all shareholders of a company automatically accept, and must adhere to, the company's articles of association.

A number of matters have to be mandatorily addressed in the deed of incorporation and the articles of association of the company (e. g., the corporate purpose, the duration of the financial year, etc.);[29] it would not be possible to validly deviate from these matters in a shareholders' agreement.[30] Furthermore, the Bel-

26 Specific thresholds and majority requirements apply for an amendment of the corporate purpose or any modification of the rights attached to different categories of securities. Reference is made to articles 287, 288, 559 and 560 of the Belgian Company Code.

27 Articles 286 (BVBA/SPRL) and 558 (NV/SA) of the Belgian Company Code.

28 Article 528 of the Belgian Company Code.

29 Article 69 of the Belgian Company Code (in general) and article 453 of the Belgian Company Code (with respect to the *société anonyme*).

30 We note that article 453 of the Belgian Company Code also includes a reference to transfer restrictions with respect to the shares of the company as a matter to be addressed in the articles of association; however, legal doctrine accepts that this only relates to transfer restrictions with respect to the shares imposed by the company itself and not to transfer restrictions agreed upon

gian Company Code includes certain "default provisions" and allows companies to introduce specific provisions modifying the application of these default provisions, e.g. in principle, a capital increase is to be decided upon by the shareholders of the company, but the articles of association can introduce authorized capital, permitting the board to increase the capital of the company within certain parameters;[31] when drafting the shareholders' agreement one will thus need to determine whether the matter to be addressed is not a "reserved matter" to be addressed by the shareholders' meeting through an amendment of the articles of association.

## II. Duration of shareholders' agreements

In general, there is no limitation on the duration of shareholders' agreements. The duration of shareholders' agreements can, at the option of the parties, be limited or unlimited.

According to Belgian law, agreements entered into for an unlimited duration can be terminated at any time, subject to a reasonable notice period.[32] Practitioners usually prefer to include an end date in shareholders' agreements in order to avoid any legal uncertainty which may arise as a result of a party giving notice of its intention to terminate the shareholders' agreement. While there is no clear legal basis for this, it is sometimes argued that contracts with an extremely long duration, i.e. more than 99 years, are not permitted under Belgian law.[33]

## III. Case law

There is an elaborate body of case law with respect to various aspects of shareholders' agreements. We have included references to some examples of this case

---

between the shareholders and not imposed by the company (see *Pattyn* Aandeelhoudersovereenkomsten, nr. 20 and the references to legal doctrine therein).

**31** See *Pattyn* Aandeelhoudersovereenkomsten, nr. 20 for a more detailed discussion in this respect.

**32** Cass. 16 oktober 1969, *RCJB* 1970, 529–530, noot *M. Papier-Jamoulle*. See also *Culot, H., Culot, L., De Cordt, Y., Gollier, J.-M., Hannouille, A., Konings, N., Magnus, F., Parisis, G., De Pierpont, G. Van de Velden, K., Wolff, S.*, "Chapitre 6 – Transferts de titres " in Société anonyme, Bruxelles, Bruylant, 2014, (143) 159.

**33** *Claeys/Phang* Van bepaalde duur naar onbepaalde duur en terug, *TPR* 2008, 394.

law in the context of discussions on more specific topics as part of this contribution.

### IV. International or cross-border shareholders' agreements?

There are no specific laws or regulations applicable to international or cross-border shareholders' agreements. The general rules of international private law are relevant in this respect. Shareholders located in a country other than Belgium are not required to appoint an agent in Belgium for purposes of entering into a shareholders' agreement. Note, however, that in the context of legal proceedings, foreign claimants not established in a member state of the European Union may be required to issue a *cautio judicatum solvi* (security for purposes of any judgment pronounced against them). On a contractual basis, parties may also agree on an election of domicile in Belgium and the appointment of a process agent in Belgium. As to the law applicable to a shareholders' agreement, the parties would in general be free to choose the law applicable to their contract (subject to the rules of international private law as per the Rome I Regulation). However, certain matters regarding the functioning of the Belgian company will remain governed by Belgian law as *lex societatis* of the Belgian company. Therefore, for reasons of consistency, the choice of Belgian law would need to be considered for a shareholders' agreement with respect to a Belgian company.

## B. Forms of shareholders' agreements

### I. Shareholders' agreements on voting rights

#### 1. Kind of voting agreements

Shareholders' agreements regarding voting rights typically relate to the appointment (and dismissal) of directors and the dividend policy of the company.[34] Agreements regarding certain specific "ad hoc" matters are also concluded.[35] With respect to a public limited liability company ("*naamloze vennootschap*" / "*société anonyme*") and a private limited liability company ("*besloten vennootschap met beperkte aansprakelijhkheid*" / "*société privée à responsabilité limit-*

34 *Pattyn* Aandeelhoudersovereenkomsten, nr. 184.
35 Ibid.

*ée*"), the Belgian Company Code expressly recognizes that shareholders' agreements with respect to voting rights are legally permitted, provided that these agreements comply with a number of conditions.[36] Generally, the agreements must be limited in time and always be justified based on the corporate interest.[37] The following voting agreements are null: (1) agreements contrary to provisions of the Belgian Company Code, (2) agreements whereby a shareholder commits to vote according to the guidelines issued by the company, a subsidiary of the company, or one of the corporate bodies of these companies, and (3) agreements whereby a shareholder commits itself towards these companies (the company or subsidiaries of the company) or corporate bodies of these companies to approve the proposals of said corporate bodies.[38] The shareholders' agreements contrary to article 510 and 511 of the Belgian Company Code (with respect to the transfer restrictions) are also considered null.[39]

While the agreements must be "limited" in time, the Belgian Company Code does not provide for a fixed maximum term. The duration must be "reasonable" in view of the personal interests of the shareholders.[40] Initially, the legislation imposed a duration of maximum 5 years, but this limitation to 5 years was abolished in 1995, as this maximum duration was not sufficiently adapted to the practice: many shareholders' agreements with respect to voting agreements are concluded as part of joint venture operations with respect to industrial operations that can extend over a period of 15 to 20 years.[41] While the agreements must be "limited" in time, this does not mean that the agreements must be for a "short" duration.[42] The permitted duration needs to be assessed on a case-by-case basis. Despite some authors taking a more conservative position,[43] the majority of legal doctrine takes the view that a duration of 20 years for voting

---

**36** Article 281 § 1 of the Belgian Company Code and Article 551 § 1 of the Belgian Company Code.

**37** Ibid.

**38** Article 551 § 1 of the Belgian Company Code.

**39** Article 551 § 2 of the Belgian Company Code.

**40** See, among others, *Coibion* Les conventions d'actionnaires en pratique, Bruxelles, Larcier, 2010, p. 81; *M. van der Haegen* Les conventions d'actionnaires (pacte de votation, clauses d'agrément et de préemption), in JEUNE BARREAU DE BRUXELLES (ed.), Evolutions récente et perspective du droit des sociétés commerciales et de l'entreprise en difficulté, Bruxelles, Ed. Jeune Barreau de Bruxelles, 1996, p. 12.

**41** Parl. St. Senaat 1993–94, nr. 1086/2, 185, H. DHONDT, artikel 551 in Wet en Duiding –Economisch Recht, Deel 6, Vennootschappen, Larcier, 2014.

**42** *Pattyn* Not.Fisc. *M.* 2015/6, nr. 42.

**43** *Clottens* Proportionaliteit van stemrecht en risico in kapitaalvennootschappen, Kalmthout, Biblo, 2012, p.141, number 137; B. FERON, "Les conventions d'actionnaires après la loi du 13 avril 1995", *TBH* 1996, 699 j. 685.

agreements can be reasonable, depending on the relevant facts.[44] The requirement to limit the duration of the agreement in time should also be construed in conjunction with the legal requirement that the agreement be in the corporate interest.[45] Even though the agreement with respect to voting rights must be limited in time, this does not prevent a prolongation of the agreement. The prolongations should however be for a fixed term.[46]

Shareholders' agreements with respect to voting rights must "*always be justified by the corporate interest*". The use of the word "always" in the legal provision means that the determination of whether the agreement is in the corporate interest must not only take place at the time of the conclusion of the agreement, but that in order to remain valid, the agreement must remain within the corporate interest throughout the lifetime of the agreement, taking into account changing factual circumstances.[47] It is therefore possible for a voting agreement to be valid at the time of entering into such voting agreement and subsequently become invalid as a result of changes in the company's circumstances. The concept of "corporate interest" is not defined by the Belgian Company Code and has triggered debate among legal authors regarding the extent to which other interests (e.g., rights of creditors, employees, etc.) should be considered in addition to the patrimonial interests of the shareholders. The Belgian Supreme Court (*Hof van Cassatie/Cour de Cassation*) considered in 2013 that the corporate interest is determined by the collective lucrative interest of the actual and future shareholders of the company.[48] The courts will however only be entitled carry out a "marginal review": this means that only voting agreements that are manifestly contrary to the corporate interest can be nullified.[49] It is recommended to include "review clauses" in shareholders' agreements that provide a mechanism to review and adapt clauses taking into account changing circumstances.

---

44 *Pattyn* Aandeelhoudersovereenkomsten, nr. 134 ; *P. de Wolf* Les pactes d'actionnaires: intérêt et contraintes générales, Séminaire Vanham & Vanham, 17 mars 2016, p. 5; A. COIBION, *Les conventions d'actionnaires en pratique*, 81.

45 *Pattyn* Not.Fisc. M. 2015/6, nr. 42.

46 *I. Corbisier* La société et ses associés in Droit des sociétés: les lois des 7 et 13 avril 1995, Bruxelles, Bruylant, 1995, 179; *P. van Hoogten* Aandeelhoudersovereenkomsten na de wet van 13 april 1995, *DAOR* 1997, 51.

47 *H. Dhondt* artikel 551 in Wet en Duiding –Economisch Recht, Deel 6, Vennootschappen, 2014; *M. Wyckaert* "Overdrachtsbeperkingen en stemrecht" in JAN RONSE INSTITUUT (ed.), De nieuwe vennootschapswetten van 7 en 13 april 1995, Kalmthout, Biblo, 119, 113.

48 Cass. 28 novembre 2013, *TRV* 2014, p. 286.

49 *K. Geens* De bescherming tegen de bescherming – De jurisprudentiële bescherming van de minderheidsaandeelhouder tegen de door de meerderheid opgezette beschermingsconstructires in De bescherming van de minderheidsaandeelhouder – bijzonder nummer *TRV* 1988, II-20.

The Belgian Company Code does not allow any agreement pursuant to which any shareholder(s) would be (entirely) excluded from all profits or (entirely) exempt from contributing to losses.[50] This rule is considered to be of public order and any deviation is therefore null and void.

While this has been proposed "*de lega ferenda*" in Belgian legal doctrine, the current position adopted in Belgian law is that it would not be possible to have an arrangement whereby one shareholder has "multiple votes."[51] The principle of "*one share – one vote*" is considered to be a principle of mandatory law and public order; it is not possible to contractually deviate from this principle in a shareholders' agreement.[52]

## 2. No voting trusts

Generally, a "voting trust" can be described as an arrangement in which "corporate stockholders transfer their shares to a trustee for purpose of creating a voting block", whereby the shareholders typically still receive dividends under such arrangement.[53] Under Belgian internal law, the concept of trust is as such not legally recognized.[54]

---

**50** Article 32 of the Belgian Company Code.

**51** *Pattyn* Aandeelhoudersovereenkomsten, nr. 204.

**52** At the time of drafting this article, the Belgian Minister of Justice has announced its intention to modernize and re-codify Belgian company legislation (see: https://www.koengeens.be/beleid/hercodificatie-basiswetgeving/hercodificatie (last consulted: 18 September 2017). Multiple voting rights could become a possibility in private limited liability companies (SPRL / BVBA) and non-listed public limited liability companies (SA / NV). In listed public limited liability companies, the voting rights of "loyal" shareholders are expected to be legally limited at double the amount of voting rights to which they would be entitled pro rata to their shareholding. See also *Delvoie* "Daar is Nessie! Naar meervoudig stemrecht in NV en BVBA", *TPR* 2015, 985–989 for an extensive discussion regarding this topic under Belgian law.

**53** Black's Law Dictionary.

**54** *Storme* https://www.law.kuleuven.be/personal/mstorme/trust.pdf, explaining that while the trust does not exist as a separate legal concept in Belgium, there are certain trust-like arrangements; See also M. *Storme "Vertrouwen is goed, dual ownership is beter. Elf essentialia bij de invoering van een trustachtige figuur of fiduciaire overeenkomst in het Belgische recht"*, *R.W.* 1996–97, 137 v., *"La confiance est bonne, mais un dual ownership est préférable. Onze éléments essentiels à prendre en considération lors de l'introduction d'une figure similaire au trust ou contrat fiduciaire en droit belge"*, in Le trust et la fiducie / De trust en de fiduciaire overeenkomst, Bruylant Brussel 1997, p. 277 v.

Certain other mechanisms are however relevant. Issuing share certificates with respect to shares in a private limited liability company (BVBA)[55] or a public limited liability company (NV)[56] is allowed. These share certificates allow the creation of a split between the legal ownership and the economic benefits of the shares. The issuer of the share certificate will remain the legal owner of the shares and will continue to be entitled to exercise voting rights. The holders of the share certificates will be entitled to all the economic benefits of the certificates. A private foundation (*private stichting/fondation privée*) can, under certain circumstances, be used as a vehicle for certification of shares.[57] We also note that specific rules apply with respect to proxy voting and proxy solicitation.[58]

## 3. Binding instructions to the corporation

In a public limited liability company (NV) and private limited liability company (BVBA), the shareholders' meeting has powers regarding certain reserved matters only, while the other "residual matters" are within the powers of the board of managers or board of directors of the company.[59] The reserved matters are set out in the law.[60] It is possible to provide, in the articles of association of the company, that certain additional matters are "reserved matters" within the power of

**55** Article 242 of the Belgian Company Code.

**56** Article 503 of the Belgian Company Code.

**57** R. VAN BOVEN, "De Belgische private stichting als certificeringsvehikel: onbekend is onbemind", *TEP* 2014, afl. 2, 108 – 146.

**58** Article 549 § 1 of the Belgian Company Code.

**59** Article 257 of the Belgian Company Code (BVBA), article 522 of the Belgian Company Code (NV).

**60** The reserved matters can be summarized as follows: (1) Nomination and revocation of directors, including the determination of the remuneration (if any) of the directors (Articles 517 and 518 of the Belgian Company Code); (2) Nomination and revocation of the statutory auditor, including the determination of the remuneration of the auditor (articles 130, 134 and 135 of the Belgian Company Code); (3)Approval of the annual accounts, determination of the profits and the discharge of the directors (Article 554 of the Belgian Company Code); (4) Modification of the articles of association (Articles 531 and 558, al. 1 of the Belgian Company Code); (5) Modification of the share capital (Articles 603 and 612 of the Belgian Company Code); (6) Modification of the rights attached to the different categories of certificates (Article 560 of the Belgian Company Code); (7)Mergers, scissions, or similar operations (articles 697, 710, 720, 733 and 748 of the Belgian Company Code); (8) Decisions offering a third party rights which may affect the company's assets, where the exercise of such rights depends on a change of control or the launching of a public offer (cf., article 556 of the Belgian Companies' Code); (9) dissolution (article 561 of the Belgian Companies' Code).

the shareholders' meeting, e.g. a requirement to approve certain specific type of transactions.[61] As the shareholders' meeting only has powers with respect to the reserved matters, the "binding instructions" the shareholders' meeting can give to the corporation would be limited to these reserved matters. While there are certain individual shareholders' rights, such as a right (subject to certain conditions) to request points to be included on the agenda of the shareholders' meeting, and a right to ask questions,[62] there is as such no right for individual shareholders to give binding instructions to the corporation.

## 4. Shareholder claims

There is a specific "derivative action" allowing minority shareholders to start a proceeding in the name of the company with respect to the liability of the directors.[63] Minority shareholders must hold at least 10% (BVBA) or 1% (NV) of the shares in order to start such proceedings. There are a number of disadvantages related to such proceedings: the requirement to advance the cost of the proceedings, the fact that the result of the proceedings will only indirectly benefit the shareholders (the action is in the name of the company) and possible evidentiary issues.[64] Belgium has introduced a regime for class actions, but only certain recognized consumer organizations are allowed to initiate them.

## 5. Financing agreements

Various types of financing agreements can exist. Shareholders often provide financing under the form of shareholder loans. Typically, shareholder loans are on a contractual basis subordinated to other loans granted to the company. From a tax perspective, issues regarding thin capitalization may need to be considered. Only in very exceptional situations, e.g. abuse, have courts decided to impose a

---

**61** *Braeckmans/Houben* Handboek Vennootschapsrecht, nr. 727, also for discussion on the limitation on the external effects (effects regarding third parties) of such an extension of the powers of the shareholders' meeting.
**62** Article 274 of the Belgian Company Code (BVBA) and article 540 of the Belgian Company Code (NV).
**63** Articles 290 – 291 of the Belgian Company Code (BVBA) and articles 416 – 417 of the Belgian Company Code (NV).
**64** *Braeckmans/Houben* Handboek Vennootschapsrecht, Antwerpen, 2012, nr. 661.

subordination of a loan by a corporate insider (shareholder/director) by an order of the court, where such subordination was not contractually provided for.[65]

### 6. Law of groups

While there are certain Belgian legal provisions with respect to relationships between group companies, as well as case law in this respect, there is no general "law of groups" under Belgian law. We note that the directors of a Belgian company always have to take into account the corporate interest of the individual company. While they can take into account the interest of the group in assessing the interest of the individual company, they cannot sacrifice the interest of the individual company for the benefit of the group. This principle also has to be taken into account when assessing whether certain arrangements are in the corporate interest (see above with respect to voting agreements and below with respect to agreements limiting the transfer of shares). The interest of the individual company cannot be sacrificed for the interest of the broader group. This is a factual assessment that will need to be made on a case-by-case basis.

## II. Shareholders' Agreements and the limitation on the transfer of shares

Drag along and tag along provisions are very common in Belgium and are considered valid provided they respect article 510 of the Belgian Company Code. This article allows share transfer restrictions (such as, drag along and tag along provisions) if they are limited in time and "always justified" in the corporate interest of the company. If the share transfer restrictions follow a pre-approval clause or a right of first offer, then the applicability of the share restrictions may not lead to the impossibility to transfer shares in a public limited liability company for more than 6 months. The period is automatically shortened if the 6 months period would be exceeded. Shoot out (or shot-gun) clauses are seen in rare occasions, often in a specific joint venture context where parties agree in advance on a way to resolve deadlocks.

65 *Fransis* "Achterstelling" in X., Voorrechten en hypotheken. Artikelsgewijze commentaar met overzicht van rechtspraak en rechtsleer, Algemene bepalingen, I. Achterstelling, 1–45 (p. 45).

## III. Shareholders' Agreements on the constitution of the corporation

The appointment of directors is a matter reserved for the shareholders' meeting of a limited liability company. In principle, every shareholder is free to nominate directors, which are then appointed by the shareholders' meeting with a simple majority. Accordingly, the boards of directors of Belgian limited liability companies do not necessarily represent a proportional picture of the shareholding of the company – as a matter of principle, the majority shareholders will be able to decide on the composition of the board.[66]

In order to mitigate unwanted consequences deriving from the above principle, shareholders' agreements often grant nomination rights to shareholders. As a result, it is possible to mirror the shareholding of the company at the level of the board of directors, or to allow the representation of one or more minority shareholders at the same time.

The flexibility of the shareholders to agree by contract on the composition of the board of directors of a limited liability company is limited by the binding rule that the shareholders' meeting is the only body competent to appoint the directors. This rule would be violated if the shareholders' meeting were not offered a choice between various candidates. In practice, clauses including a nomination right for one or more shareholder(s) should therefore be drafted such that the relevant shareholder nominates either two candidates for each mandate reserved for such shareholder at the board of directors, or at least a number of candidates which exceeds the number of mandates reserved for the shareholder.[67]

Shareholders could make amongst themselves certain agreements regarding the capital of the company. However, any decisions regarding the capital of the company should be approved by the meeting of shareholders or by the board (based on authorized capital).

The shareholders' agreement could include certain agreements between shareholders regarding organizational matters, such as e. g. certain practical matters regarding the organisation of shareholders' meetings.[68] However, it will need to be assessed whether any such agreements relate to matters reserved to the shareholders' meeting and do not violate any mandatory law rules.

**66** *Coibion* o.c., 93.
**67** *Pattyn* Aandeelhoudersovereenkomsten, nr. 196.
**68** *Pattyn* Aandeelhoudersovereenkomsten, nr. 221.

## IV. Shareholders' Agreements in a pre-insolvency situation

### 1. Non-petition clauses

Non-petition clauses are clauses prohibiting (or otherwise restricting) the right of a party to commence insolvency proceedings against a company. In light of public policy considerations regarding Belgian insolvency law, there is legal uncertainty regarding the validity and enforceability of such clauses.[69]

### 2. Standstill agreements

This depends on the circumstances. It would be possible to include shareholders' agreements as part of standstill agreements. Considerations regarding "hardening periods" will have to be taken into account: certain transactions between a company and counterparties in the period leading up to insolvency may be voidable.

# C. Legal effects of Shareholders' Agreements

## I. Legal effects on the corporation

### 1. Interpretation of the corporate charter?

As a principle, shareholders' agreements (concluded between shareholders only and not included in the articles of association of the company) do not affect the articles of association of a company. A shareholder can therefore in principle not obtain the nullity of a shareholders' decision taken in violation of the shareholders' agreement.

The shareholders' agreement is nonetheless a legal fact relevant for the company to the extent that it could not reasonably have been unaware that such shareholders' agreement exists (for example, if the articles of association include a reference to the shareholders' agreement). In such case, the company could po-

69 *Cloquet* Les Novelles, 2ed., nr. 1119 (stating that such clause is contrary to public policy and not enforceable); different opinions exist: see Répértoire pratique du droit belge, t. 5, 1950, nr. 171 (and the references); see also A. *Prum* (red.) La titrisation, Louvain-Neuve, 2008, p. 70

tentially be held liable if it could be viewed as having contributed to a breach under the shareholders' agreement.

Occasionally, shareholders' agreements are also concluded by the company or in the presence of the company. In such case, shareholders' agreements have legal consequences for the company and the company would also be bound by the provisions in the agreement applicable to it.

## II. Legal effects on the shareholders

Shareholders' agreements often contain restrictions on the assignability or transferability of rights and obligations arising from such shareholders' agreement. In the absence of any specific provision or restriction in the shareholders' agreement, shareholders are in principle allowed to transfer the rights (but not the obligations) arising from the shareholders' agreement. A debtor can only transfer its obligations with the consent of its creditor.

Shareholders' agreements can indeed create additional obligations of the shareholders' party thereto. In particular, where the relevant company is a listed company, the disclosure obligations with respect to major shareholdings (i.e. the Belgian law[70] based on the implementation of the European Transparency Directive[71]) will have to be taken into account. Specific disclosure obligations also apply in the context of a public tender offer bids.[72] In addition, in certain regulated industries (such as financial institutions[73] and insurance companies[74]), ad-

---

**70** *Loi du 2 mai 2007 relative à la publicité des participations importantes dans des émetteurs dont les actions sont admises à la négociation sur un marché réglementé et portant des dispositions diverses/ Wet van 2 mei 2007 op de openbaarmaking van belangrijke deelnemingen in emittenten waarvan aandelen zijn toegelaten tot de verhandeling op een gereglementeerde markt en houdende diverse bepalingen and the Arrêté royal du 14 février 2008 relatif à la publicité des participations importantes/ Koninklijk besluit van 14 februari 2008 op de openbaarmaking van belangrijke deelnemingen.*

**71** Directive 2004/109/EC of the European Parliament and of the Council of 15 December 2004 on the harmonisation of transparency requirements in relation to information about issuers whose securities are admitted to trading on a regulated market and amending Directive 2001/34/EC (as amended).

**72** *Loi du 1 avril 2007 relative aux offres publiques d'acquisition/Wet van 1 april 2007 op de openbare overnamebiedingen and Arrêté royal du 27 avril 2007 relatif aux offres publiques d'acquisition.*

**73** *Wet van 25 april 2014 op het statuut van en het toezicht op kredietinstellingen en beursvennootschappen.*

ditional disclosure obligations regarding major shareholdings may apply. For purposes of the relevant disclosure obligations, the relevant parties to a shareholders' agreement may indeed, depending on the content of the agreement, be deemed to be "acting in concert". Finally, shareholders' agreements may have an impact on the identification of "ultimate beneficial owners" for purposes of the applicable anti-money laundering regulations.

Pursuant to Belgian law, shareholders' agreements do not have to be published or registered in a public register. Shareholders often choose to enter into a shareholders' agreement (as opposed to implementing the relevant rules in the articles of association) precisely because a shareholders' agreement allows for secrecy and confidentiality. If the shareholders' agreement is included as part of the articles of association of the company, then the shareholders' agreement will become public as part of the official corporate documents of the company.

## III. Consequences of a breach of the Shareholders' Agreements

The principle under Belgian contract law for any breach of contract is "reparation in kind". However, monetary compensation can be requested and obtained if reparation in kind is not possible (e. g., if shares have been sold in violation of share transfer restrictions agreed in a shareholders' agreement, by a shareholder to a third party acting in good faith (i. e., a third party who had no, and could not reasonably have had, knowledge of the share transfer restrictions).

### 1. Challenging the resolution of the shareholders' meeting

The Belgian Company Code includes a limitative list of grounds on which the decisions of the shareholders' meeting can be challenged: (i) a formal irregularity, (ii) a violation of the rules regarding the functioning of the shareholders' meeting, (iii) an excess or abuse of power, (iv) the exercise of suspended voting rights, and (v) any specific nullity grounds expressly referred to in the Belgian Company Code.[75] It is not possible to obtain the nullity of a decision of a shareholders' meeting on any other grounds.[76] The articles of association cannot exclude

74 *Wet van 13 maart 2016 op het statuut van en het toezicht op de verzekerings- of herverzekeringsondernemingen.*

75 Article 64 of the Belgian Company Code.

76 *D. Van Gerven* Handboek Vennootschappen, Algemeen Deel, 2017, nr. 347.

grounds of nullity provided for by the Belgian Company Code, but can add additional grounds for nullity.[77] Therefore, to the extent a shareholders' agreement is included in the articles of association of the relevant company, it could provide for nullity grounds with respect to decisions of the shareholders' meeting. However, in the absence of any provisions in the articles of association, a violation of the provisions of a shareholders' agreement will not form a basis for nullity of the decisions of the shareholders' meeting.[78] It may be possible to seek compensation under the form of damages, but not the nullity of the decision of the meeting. We note that this is the traditional position, but that this position has been criticized in legal doctrine by authors arguing that it should be possible to obtain nullity of the decisions.[79] It is however unclear what the legal basis for this (minority) position would be, and this position also does not seem to be supported by case-law at this stage.[80] Finally, we note that according to legal doctrine it should be possible to obtain an injunction from a court (combined with a penalty payment in case of non-compliance with this injunction) if there are indications that a shareholder will commit a breach of the shareholders' agreement.[81] This would require the shareholders' agreement to be sufficiently precise and leave no margin of appreciation for the shareholders as to the possible exercise of the voting rights in the specific relevant circumstance.

## 2. Effect on the membership in the corporation

In principle, the violation of shareholders' agreements does not affect the membership in the corporation of the shareholder in violation. There could be an indirect effect in certain specific circumstances. For private limited liability companies (BVBA) and public limited liability companies (NV)[82] not having made a public appeal to savings, there is a specific judicial procedure allowing the expulsion of a shareholder in case of conflicts between the shareholders (in which case a copy of the shareholders' agreement will need to be provided to

---

**77** Ibid.
**78** *Pattyn* Aandeelhoudersovereenkomsten, nr. 187.
**79** Ibid.
**80** Ibid.
**81** Ibid.
**82** Article 334 et seq. of the Belgian Company Code (BVBA) and article 635 of the Belgian Company Code (NV). In order to start the legal proceedings for expulsion, the shareholders initiating the procedure must hold a sufficient number of shares to meet the relevant thresholds.

the court[83]). The expulsion procedure is only possible if there is a "justified reason".[84] Whether there is a justified reason warranting the expulsion of a shareholder is a factual assessment to be made by the court, whereby the court will take into account the corporate interest.[85] A serious breach of a shareholders' agreement could, depending on the factual circumstances, be considered as a "justified reason".[86]

## D. Enforcement of Shareholders' Agreements

Shareholders' agreements typically include a number of contractual provisions regarding the enforcement of the agreement. In order to enforce an agreement, an enforceable court decision or arbitral decision will in principle be required.

**Compensation for damages** – Parties to the agreement may claim damages for breach of contract in respect of a shareholders' agreement. Parties will have to demonstrate that the conditions for a claim are fulfilled, i. e. the existence of a breach of contract, the damage and the causal link. Note that unless there is an intentional breach of contract, the damages are limited to damages that could be foreseen at the time of the conclusion of the contract.[87]

Shareholders' agreement governed by Belgian law often contain contractual penalties which automatically apply (without any obligation to proof damages) if there is a breach of contract. The court is, however, allowed to mitigate (by its own motion or as requested by the defaulting shareholder) the consequences of any such contractual penalty, if the penalty "manifestly" exceeds the amount which the parties could determine as compensation for the damages resulting from the non-performance of the agreement.

It is permitted to include arbitral clauses in shareholders' agreements; a point of attention in this respect is to verify that all parties concerned are party to the agreement, including the company itself.[88]

---

**83** Cf., article 639 of the Belgian Company Code.

**84** Articles 334 and 340 of the Belgian Company Code (BVBA); article 636 of the Belgian Company Code (NV).

**85** *Braeckmans/Houben* Handboek Vennootschapsrecht, nr. 1447.

**86** *Braeckmans/Houben* Handboek Vennootschapsrecht, nr. 1448.

**87** Article 1150 of the Belgian Civil Code.

**88** See for example Gent 14 April 2014, *DAOR* 2014/11, 120; See also *A. Francois, L. Vandenbempt en T. Van de Gehuchte* Art. 334–342 en 636–644, X., Vennootschappen en verenigingen. Artikelsgewijze commentaar met overzicht van rechtspraak en rechtsleer, Boek VI, Titel VI, Hfdst. I en II, 1–79 (79 p.) – April 2011, p. 121 and references for a further discussion of arbitration clauses in the context of shareholders' agreements.

Ivens Henrique Hübert

# Brazil

## Table of Content



## I. Nature of Corporate Law Regulation

Two types of corporate entities are more often used in Brazilian practice: the so-called *sociedades limitadas* (Limitada) and the *sociedades anônimas* (SA).[1] There are other types of corporate entities regulated by law, which are essentially equivalent to partnerships, but they are nearly nonexistent in practice. Over 99% of all corporate entities registered in Brazil are either a Limitada or a variation of this model, the so-called EIRELI, which is its single-member form. The

1 For the purpose of this report, the words "company" and "corporation" will be used indistinctly, although the latter shall be preferred. If there is a need to distinguish the corporate types, the name of the respective corporate form (SA or Limitada) shall be used. The same applies to differences between stocks and shares, or stockholders and shareholders. We have preferred to use shares and shareholders indistinctly, referring to all kinds of companies.

**Dr. Ivens Henrique Hübert**, Andersen Ballão Advocacia - German Desk, Brazil

https://doi.org/10.1515/9783110517026-010

SA-type is on the other hand relevant because it is the model for big closed and stock corporations.

The regulation of the Limitadas[2] is based on a vast contractual freedom, which enables shareholders to define the regulation of the corporate charter as they may wish, while they only have to follow some mandatory standards foreseen in law. Although it is true that statutory law regulates the Limitadas in a much more extensive way since the enactment of the Civil Code of 2002, which brought a new regulation on this corporation type, the principle of contractual freedom still prevails.

The SAs on the other hand are subject to a much more extensive regulation, with several mandatory provisions arising from Federal Law 6.404/76 (hereinafter LSA). Notwithstanding that, there is no such provision as, for instance, in German corporate law, § 23 Abs. 5 AktG, which sets forth that the bylaws can only deviate from the stock and closed corporation law if so explicitly provided. In comparison to such a provision, Brazilian LSA contains several mandatory rules, which apply to companies irrespective of what is written in the bylaws, but it generally allows shareholders to deviate from the law whenever this is not expressly forbidden. In this sense, even issues which are not expressly regulated by law can be included in the bylaws.

Apart from that, there is no general restriction to shareholders, in any corporation type, to amend the normative regulation on corporations outside of the corporate charter. Generally, shareholders are entitled to do so, as long as they do not provide for matters which are not allowed by law to contract, as, for instance, voting regarding the accounts of the corporation and other similar issues which are not subject to negotiation.

## II. Regulation of Shareholders' Agreements

Only in the law of the SAs (which encompasses both closed and stock corporations) there are special provisions regulating shareholders' agreements. These provisions are set forth in Art. 118 LSA[3], which states, among other things, that shareholders' agreements regulating certain matters must be observed by the corporation, provided that the agreement is filed by the shareholders at its head office. These specific matters referred to in Art. 118 LSA, that cause the

2 Roughly, one could compare the Limitadas with the GmbHs in Germany, the private companies in England or the LLCs in the United States.

3 See Annex, below.

shareholders' agreement to be binding to the corporation, are (i) the purchase and sale of shares as well as special rights regarding the acquisition of shares, (ii) the exercise of voting rights and (iii) the exercise of control of the corporation.

Apart from these matters – and in the law of the Limitadas anyways –, all shareholders' agreements can be freely settled by shareholders but are not binding to the corporation. In this sense, they are solely subject to general contract law.

Thus, it is possible to refer to two different types of shareholders' agreements in relation to the regulation they are subject to: shareholders' agreements which are expressly regulated by the LSA and others that are subject to general contract law.[4] The latter are those agreements related to Limitadas or other company types, or otherwise related to SAs but dealing with matters which are not set forth in Art. 118 LSA or if the agreement has not been duly registered in the corporation's head office. Since the sole legal provision regarding shareholders' agreements is contained in the law regarding closed and stock corporations (LSA), and it does not apply to all shareholders' agreements related to shareholders of such corporations, it is possible to state that there are no other distinctions provided by law between shareholders' agreements – as, for instance, between partnerships and corporations or between closed and stock corporations – except this one, related to the shareholders' agreements that fall within the scope of Art. 118 LSA and those which do not.

As to what refers to the shareholders' agreement expressly regulated in LSA, it is not necessary for them to be expressly admitted in the bylaws or by the shareholders' meeting. Besides, Brazilian law on closed and stock corporations (LSA) does not establish any restrictions on the duration of the shareholders' agreements. In fact, Art. 108, § 6 LSA sets forth that the shareholders' agreement which contains a provision defining a term or a condition for its termination can only be terminated according to such contractual provisions. This means that in such cases the agreement cannot be terminated before the occurrence of such conditions. Apart from that, it is commonly discussed whether a shareholders' agreement can be established in such a way that it could not be terminated while the condition of shareholder persists.[5] This would certainly not be allowed when the agreement deals with pre-emption rights or other option rights to pur-

---

**4** See *Abrão* in Ulhoa Coelho, Tratado de Direito Comercial, vol. 4, Acordos de Acionistas Típicos e Atípicos, 2015, p. 53.

**5** *Carvalhosa* Acordo de Acionistas, 2015, p. 64; *Eizirik* A Lei das S/A Comentada, vol. 1, 2011, p. 719.

chase shares, since such agreements must be limited on time because of the restrictions to the sale that they create. However, when it deals with voting rights or about the exercise of control, it is commonly understood that agreements that cannot be terminated, except by virtue of a just cause, are valid.[6] Notwithstanding that, it is commonly understood that an excessively long term could itself be a reason for termination, when the cause that justified the agreement is nonexistent anymore.

Finally, Brazilian law has no provisions on international or cross-border issues related to shareholders' agreements. Generally, Brazilian law is, in comparative terms, still weakly connected to other jurisdictions. This is also the case in regard to shareholders' agreements.

## III. Forms of Shareholders' Agreements

Shareholders' agreements can basically deal with any matters, as long as those are deemed lawful. There are thus some matters that cannot be regulated by such agreements, since they represent, expressly or implicitly, a fraud or a violation of law. This is the case for instance, when the agreement has the practical effect of establishing an "acquisition" of voting rights by one of the contracting parties, in a way that the other party would neither have a right to interfere in the decisions, nor would have rights to terminate the agreement.[7] This would happen when one of the parties receives powers to vote for the others in all and every matter concerning the corporation, without having the shareholders' agreement specify in detail which are these matters and what the respective directives of voting are. It is also unlawful to stipulate that voting rights are to be exercised according to the instructions given by the management or the supervisory board or by people who are not shareholders. Besides, the definition of voting rights related to approval of accounts and other issues in which voting is not a result of a free choice, but rather derive from the exercise of the duty of care, is forbidden. These and any other unlawful matters cannot be the subject of a shareholders' agreement.

As to what refers to typical shareholders' agreements which fall under the scope of Art. 118 LSA, they can only refer to the matters expressly provided for in that article. Meaning that, even if such agreements are registered in the corporation's head office, only the issues set forth in Art. 118 LSA will be binding

6 *Carvalhosa* Acordo de Acionistas, 2015, p. 65.
7 *Carvalhosa* Acordo de Acionistas, 2015, p. 84.

to the corporation. These matters are basically of three different sorts: agreements on (minority) voting rights, on the limitation for the transfer of shares (lock-up agreements) and on the exercise of control of the corporation.

In the following items, the different forms of shareholders' agreements will be analysed disregarding whether such agreements fall into the rule of Art. 118 LSA or not, aiming to facilitate a comparative perspective with other national systems.

## 1. Shareholders' Agreements on Shareholder Rights

Brazilian law differentiates between basically two sorts of Shareholders' Agreements regarding voting rights. One of them is the agreement established by the shareholders in relation to the exercise of control of the corporation. It presupposes the agreement between shareholders that are jointly capable of exercising the control of the corporation. As per Brazilian law, control of the corporation is defined as the possibility of permanently deciding corporate matters by voting on general meetings and by appointing the managers and members of the supervisory board, along with the effective use of such power.[8] In this sense, the control power of the corporation is considered a corporate body, with special fiduciary duties towards the corporation. Such agreements usually refer to voting rights, but they commonly also encompass other matters related to the structuring of a controlling block of the corporation.

The other is the shareholders' agreement of minority shareholders, who have no control over the corporation. As to what refers to such shareholders' agreements, they can be established by any minority shareholders, including holders of preferential shares. Minority shareholders are defined, as per Brazilian law, in opposition to controlling shareholders.

This differentiation is relevant because there are different consequences arising whether voting rights are settled by a minority group or by a controlling block. As per Art. 118, § 8 LSA, any vote which is against what has been settled on a shareholders' agreement of a closed and stock corporation duly registered in its head office shall be disregarded by the chairman of the shareholders' meeting. This rule is applicable to all shareholder's agreements, irrespective of its re-

8 Art. 116, LSA: *"A controlling shareholder is defined as an individual or a legal entity, or a group of individuals or legal entities by a voting agreement or under common control, which: (a) possesses rights which permanently assure it a majority of votes in resolutions of general meetings and the power to elect a majority of the corporation officers; and (b) in practice uses its power to direct the corporate activities and to guide the operations of the departments of the corporation".*

lation to minority or controlling groups. However, Art. 118, § 8 LSA also states that the chairman of the supervisory board or of the management board shall not count votes of directors appointed by shareholder groups when they are against the content of a shareholders' agreement which has been duly registered in the corporation's head office. Although the provision does not differentiate the cases, it is generally understood that it only applies to agreements related to the control of the corporation. This is because, differently from controlling shareholders, minority shareholders have no direct relation to the directors they have appointed, since they do not owe fiduciary duties to the corporation in the same extent as a controlling shareholder.[9] Thus, minority shareholders have no possibility of interfering in administrative decisions in any extent, while controlling shareholders can do that as long as the issues discussed by the management board are not related to the day to day business. Minority shareholders do not hold a "power-duty of control", thus their voting rights can only be exercised within the shareholders meeting. Differently from the shareholders' agreements related to the exercise of control, they are not binding on the administrative bodies of the corporation, such as the supervisory or the management boards, even when minority shareholders contract for the purpose of appointing members of the management and supervisory boards.[10] An agreement between minority shareholders which aims to establish directives to the action of a director appointed by such shareholders would be considered invalid.

Having said that, it is common for both controlling and minority groups to enter into pooling agreements for the exercise of votes, which will be exercised in ordinary as in extraordinary meetings, and, in the case of the controlling group, also in the meetings of the supervisory or of the management board. The agreement often sets forth that shareholders shall convene on previous meetings, in order to decide how they will vote in the corporation shareholders' meeting and how directors who were appointed by the controlling shareholders' group may vote in the meetings of the supervisory or the management boards. In the preliminary meetings to decide how the group shall vote, decisions are usually taken by majority and requisites of unanimity are deemed invalid, since this

---

**9** Nevertheless, Art. 115 LSA states general duties of all shareholders towards the corporation: *"The shareholder shall exercise the right to vote in the corporation's interest; the right to vote shall be deemed abusive if it is exercised with the intent to cause damage to the corporation or to other shareholders, or of obtaining an advantage for the shareholder or for a third party to which neither is entitled, and which results or may result in damage to the corporation or to other shareholders."*

**10** *Carvalhosa* Acordo de Acionistas, 2015, p. 117.

would affect the decision-making-process within the corporation.[11] When the shareholders' agreement is related to the control of the corporation, the controlling block is considered as an intern body of such corporation and its decisions are taken in such preliminary meetings. The regularity of its decisions depends on the observance of formal proceedings regarding the calling of the meeting and its conduction, as set forth in the shareholders agreement. Statutory rules regarding the calling of the shareholders meeting[12] are applicable if the agreement is silent about the matter.

As to what refers to minority shareholders, as per Art. 141 § 7 LSA[13] it is possible for them to appoint directors and members of the supervisory board through a system of multiple voting, as long as they gather at least 10 % of the voting capital. Notwithstanding that, the controlling shareholder shall always have at least the simple majority of the respective board, so that, under certain circumstances, the number of seats has to be increased, in order to fit all members. In this sense, shareholders' agreements often set forth the rules for the appointment and election of these directors to be elected by the minority group. Apart from that, such shareholders' agreements can also deal with the definition of a common standard of conduct regarding dissent towards the controlling block and the management. Finally, agreements on voting rights can serve for the election of an incumbent board and an incumbent management with a simple majority in those companies in which control is dispersed. In this sense, the main goal of such agreements on minority rights is the formation of a cohesive minority, organized for the defence of their interests as a group. Through these shareholders' agreements, minority shareholders holding at least 5 % of the capital can, for instance: a) represent the corporation as claimants (Art 159 § 4 LSA), b) order a complete inspection of the books of the corporation (Art. 105 LSA); c) call general meetings, when the corporation's directors

---

**11** *Carvalhosa* Comentários à Lei de Sociedades Anônimas, vol. 2, 2003, p. 525.

**12** LSA, Arts. 121 to 131.

**13** Art 141 LSA: *"Whether or not provided for in the bylaws, when electing the members of the administrative council, shareholders representing at least one-tenth of the voting capital may request that a multiple voting procedure be adopted to entitle each share to as many votes as there are council members and to give each shareholder the right to vote cumulatively for only one candidate or to distribute his votes among several candidates."* (...) § 7: *"Whenever the election of the board of directors is conducted through multiple voting and the holders of common shares or preferred shares exercise the right to appoint a member of the board, the shareholder or shareholders bound by voting agreements representing more than fifty percent of voting shares shall have the right to appoint the same number of members appointed by the remaining shareholders plus one, regardless of the number of board members specified in the bylaws"*.

do not comply with their request (Art. 123 LSA), as well as reach several other quorums as set forth by law.

Besides such agreements regarding the obtainment of such quorums, contracts between preferential and ordinary shareholders, which enable the first ones to acquire certain rights that would not be granted to them by the bylaws, are also common. In Joint Ventures, it is also usual that controlling and minority shareholders agree on certain rights, which the latter would not have otherwise as a result of law or of the bylaws, e.g. veto rights or a strategic position in the management.

Shareholders' agreements on voting rights can also regulate renounces to specific rights, as, for instance, the renounce to subscription rights on capital increase, the suspension of withdrawal rights in case of changes of the corporation's bylaws or even the suspension of multiple voting regarding the election of directors and members of the board. Such renounces cannot be settled in general terms, but must refer, on the contrary, to specific topics and/or situations. A general renounce of shareholders' rights is not admissible under Brazilian Corporate law. Generally, open clauses can be considered void, for instance should there be a general submission of the contracting shareholders to the decisions of one of them.[14]

In this sense, Brazilian authors usually recognize in such agreements regarding minority voting rights a characteristic of accessory agreements to the bylaws, which differ from the agreements regarding the control of the corporation. The latter are considered a part of the very essential structure of the corporation, since they regulate what, as per Brazilian Law, is considered a specific body of the corporation, i.e., its control. On the other hand, agreements on minority voting rights enable minority shareholders to better fulfil their surveillance tasks, assuring the lawfulness and regularity of the acts of the management and, in this sense, establishing a counterweight to the power of control. They have no direct relation to the interest of the corporation. The corporation is neither a signing party nor a third party with special interests in these agreements, as they are only related to the exercise of rights of the minority shareholders. They serve, in this sense, for the implementation of individual rights of the shareholders, which can only be achieved by virtue of these agreements. Nevertheless, the exercise of voting rights as they are established in the shareholders' agreement must observe general obligations of good faith, especially in regard to the submission of the action of the shareholders to the interest of the corpora-

14 *Eizirik* A Lei das S/A Comentada, vol. 1, 2011, p. 708.

tion.[15] They cannot be interpreted or exercised in a way that would signify systematic and permanent opposition and obstruction to the corporation's interests.[16]

## 2. Shareholders' Agreements on the (Limitation for the) Transfer of Shares

Apart from agreements regarding voting rights, it is also common to settle agreements on the limitation for the transfer of shares. Brazilian closed and stock corporation law also expressly refers to this sort of lock-up agreements in Art. 118 LSA, as one of the matters that might be binding on the corporation and its directors, or even on third parties, as long as some formalities are observed. This sort of shareholders' agreements is usually related to pre-emption or option rights in regard to the purchase and sale of shares or convertible bonds, or to restrictions to the sale of shares for a certain period of time. These agreements are deemed as accessory to the corporation's structure, since they only involve interests of the shareholders and not immediately of the corporation. Notwithstanding that, the corporation may be a contracting party of such agreements, when the pre-emption right to purchase shares or other convertible bonds is granted to her. The main purpose of such shareholders' agreements is to restrain the free circulation of shares, whether existent or still to be issued. Thus, they often serve to enhance the effectiveness of the shareholders' agreements on voting rights, for instance by forbidding the sale of shares while the agreement is in force or through the institution of pre-emption or option rights for purchase or sale of shares between the contracting parties.

According to general principles of contracting law generally accepted in Brazil, a general prohibition on the sale of shares of one shareholder or the permission of sale to third parties conditioned to the approval of the other shareholder is only deemed valid if such agreement is limited in time. There is no consensus as to the maximum period of time acceptable, but it is generally understood that such limitations should not surpass one or two years. Because of that, it is more common to settle pre-emption rights on the purchase of shares, since this mechanism preserves the general rights of shareholders to leave the corporation and can thus be settled for a longer period of time. According to such clause (right of first refusal), a shareholder who has an offer to purchase her shares coming from

**15** See Art. 115 LSA (footnote 8, above).

**16** *Carvalhosa* Acordo de Acionistas, 2015, p. 117.

a third party must firstly offer her shares for sale to the other shareholders on the very same conditions. The other parties to the agreement have a deadline to exercise their pre-emption right, as set forth in the shareholders' agreement. If they do not exercise their right to purchase, the seller is free to sell the shares to third parties.

The fixation of a price in the shareholders' agreement is not of the nature of such pre-emption rights. The price is indicated by the seller when he offers his shares to sale and the purchasers must accept such conditions, if they want to exercise their pre-emption rights. A counter-offer of the purchaser is strange to such agreements, even though the seller may opt to negotiate with her. The fixation of the price in the shareholders' agreement would probably also be considered void if such price would substantially differ from the current economic value of such shares. On the other hand, it is common that such clauses establish criteria for the apportionment of the shares at sale. It is also possible that only part of the shares of the shareholders, and not all of them, be included in the deal regarding the rights of preference to purchase.

Under Brazilian practice it is also usual that the corporation is a signing party in such agreements regarding pre-emption rights to purchase shares, since according to Art. 30 LSA the corporation can acquire its own shares under certain conditions, as long as its capital would not be compromised. In this case, the corporation could be a formal part to the shareholders' agreement and the management board could opt to purchase shares in order to avoid the entrance of new shareholders.

Besides such pre-emption rights, shareholders' agreements under Brazilian Corporate Law often contain call and put options, i. e., options to buy and to sell shares. Differently from pre-emption rights, option clauses already contain the main conditions for the purchase and sale agreement to be executed, as the quantity and kind of shares and its price – or at least a mechanism to calculate it –, as well as the conditions of payment. Call and put options are thus understood as right granted in favour of one or more of the shareholders, who only need to choose, when certain conditions are given, whether to purchase or to sell the shares as agreed in the option clause. Such price settlement is subject to general restrictions as set forth in law, as, for instance, the limitations arising from the *rebus sic standibus* clause[17] and the general prohibitions to unlawful enrichment, to leonine clauses and to abuse of rights.[18] The general standard of be-

17 Arts. 478 to 480 Código Civil.

18 Superior Tribunal de Justiça, REsp 1620702 / SP , Recurso Especial 2016/0090145 – 5, Relator: Ministro Ricardo Villas Bôas Cueva.

haviour of shareholders in this sense is the duty of objective good faith, as established in the Brazilian civil code (Código Civil).[19] Considering the fact that most of the conditions, including the price, are given in advance, option clauses are meant to be of short validity and could be deemed as invalid if they were established for longer periods, as for instance 5 or 10 years.[20]

Among such option rights, tag along and drag along clauses are very common in shareholders' agreements. According to tag along clauses, the seller can only sell its stake to the purchaser when he convinces the purchaser to also acquire the shares of those shareholders of the agreement that intend to sell its shares jointly. Brazilian stock corporation law contains a specific regulation on tag along rights, which is applicable in the case of takeovers.[21] According to it, purchasers of a shareholding that would grant them the control of the corporation are obliged to offer to all other owners of shares with voting rights an option to purchase their shares for at least 80 % of the price offered for the acquisition of control. Notwithstanding such statutory tag along right, it is common to settle such right also in closely held corporations and private companies, whether the offer is related to the takeover of the corporation or not. If tag along rights in case of takeover of listed corporations are settled contractually, the statutory provision of Art. 254-A functions as a minimum acquisition price, which can be increased contractually.

Drag along clauses are also common in agreements under Brazilian law. Authors often mention that in such case a call option for a purchaser of shares should observe the minimum standard set forth on Art. 254-A LSA, so that the price for the purchase of the shares of other shareholders who are parties to the agreement must be of at least 80 % of the price offered for the first shareholder (usually a shareholder with a major stake).[22] Besides, drag along clauses should be also of short validity, since they contain a duty of shareholders to sell their shareholding. While observing such general limitations, drag along clauses are considered within the frame of private autonomy and thus considered as valid.

---

**19** Arts. 187 and 422 Código Civil.

**20** *Carvalhosa* Acordo de Acionistas, 2015, p. 303.

**21** Art. 254- A LSA: *"The direct or indirect transfer of control of a publicly-held corporation can only be effected under the condition that the purchaser agrees to conduct a public offer to acquire the voting shares owned by the remaining shareholders. The offer price for such shares shall be at least eighty per cent (80 %) of the amount paid for the voting shares comprising the controlling block."*

**22** *Carvalhosa* Acordo de Acionistas, 2015, p. 314.

Other agreements regarding limitations to the free transferability of shares are equally common. Thus, in listed corporations bring-along clauses, by which a minority group with conditions to control the corporation with dispersed capital compromises itself to sell its shares along with other minority groups for a bidder that intends to own a bigger stake in order to acquire effective control of the corporation, are often used. Besides, different sorts of shoot out clauses are common, mainly in joint ventures. In such cases, the general limits of contractual law, as mentioned above, apply accordingly.

## 3. Shareholders' Agreements on the Constitution of the Corporation

As mentioned on point 1, above, agreements related to the exercise of control of the corporation differ from general minority voting agreements because of its specific nature. In fact, in case the shareholders' agreement deals with the control of the corporation, it is considered as an extension of the bylaws, in a way that there is a unity between the bylaws and the shareholders' agreement. Those agreements are substantially considered as part of the constitution of the corporation[23], as the shareholders' agreement regarding the control provides stability for the corporation's strategy. By way of such an agreement, shareholders create a communion of interests, through which they can jointly appoint directors and members of the board or previously define the decisions which will be taken by their voting in the general meeting. The shareholders' agreement regarding the exercise of control enables shareholders to achieve such a controlling position which they would not have otherwise and it thus provides stability to the corporation by creating a block of control. Under Brazilian stock and closed corporation's law, the power of control assumes the character of a corporation's body, with the purpose of controlling it on a permanent basis.[24] The controlling party or parties are embodied with special fiduciary duties[25] towards the corporation. This is why, according to Art. 118, § 8 LSA, both the management and the board shall observe the content of the agreement regarding the control of the corporation in the definition of its general strategy. Even in corporations in which there is no board, the management is bound to the agreement in what refers to strategic decisions taken by the controlling shareholders.

---

**23** *Carvalhosa* Acordo de Acionistas, 2015, p. 167.

**24** See footnote 12, above.

**25** *Carvalhosa* Acordo de Acionistas, 2015, p. 219.

Shareholders' agreements regarding the control of the corporation must define its subject in detail, specifying what are the matters in which the controlling shareholders will exercise their control power on a joint basis. Additionally, clauses of such shareholders' agreements cannot invade the field of competences of the directors or of other corporate bodies. An agreement regarding the control of the corporation must take into account the interest of the corporation. Generally, all shareholders must observe the interests of the corporation while exercising their rights. This is a general provision, which aims to bind all shareholders to the common interest of the shareholders as a whole. For the shareholders in a controlling position, on the other hand, Brazilian stock and closed corporation law stipulates much stronger and more enforceable fiduciary duties. Specially, such shareholders cannot use its position abusively, as per Art. 117 LSA.[26] In this sense, Art. 118 § 2 LSA states that the shareholders' agreements cannot be invoked in a way to exempt shareholders of their responsibilities towards the interest of the corporation or their special position of control.

Shareholders' agreements of controlling shareholders can thus interfere in the structure of the corporation in many ways, either by appointing members of the supervisory or of the managements boards, but also by defining the main features of the constitution of the corporation beforehand, such as the capital and the organization structure in general. Also capital increases and capital reductions can be regulated to some extent by shareholders' agreements. In this sense, especially in joint ventures, shareholders define the form of contributions and of the services to be rendered to the corporation by each of the shareholders. They also agree on the destination of profits, by way of the payment of dividends or capital reductions. Finally, shareholders' agreements have also reflexes on controlled corporations, so that it is possible to organize whole groups of companies by way of them.[27]

## 4. Shareholders' Agreements in pre-insolvency situation

Shareholders Agreements with the specific purpose of bankruptcy averting are quite rare under Brazilian law. Nevertheless, there are no absolute restrictions to such agreements and they can occur when shareholders structure plans in order to recover the corporation. Such agreements do not fall under the regula-

**26** Art. 117 LSA: *"A controlling shareholder shall be liable for any damage caused by acts performed by the abuse of its power"*.

**27** Tribunal de Justiça de São Paulo (TJSP), Apelação Cível Nr. 161.344–1/9, Relator: Desembargador Ney the Mello Almada, 11/26/1992.

tion of Art. 118 LSA und thus they are in no way binding for the corporation, unless she is also a signing party to such agreement.

Such shareholders' agreements can often define that shareholders shall contribute with capital to the corporation in crisis or that they will assume specific liabilities towards third parties. On the other hand, agreements that harm creditors in an explicit or implicit way tend to be deemed as void and can cause the shareholders to be held jointly liable for some liabilities of the corporation.

# IV. Legal Effects of Shareholders' Agreements

## 1. Legal Effects on the Corporation

An agreement signed by shareholders has no direct impact on the bylaws or on the corporate charter. In joint ventures or in partnerships and private companies this might be different, when all the shareholders or partners are also parties to the shareholders' agreement. In such cases, the interpretation of the corporate charter may be directly affected by the content of the shareholders' agreement. On the other hand, when the shareholders' agreement is not signed by all shareholders, then there is no direct connection between such agreements.

However, there are two possibilities of a shareholders' agreement having legal effects on the corporation: a) the corporation also being a signing party to the agreement or b) through the procedure set forth on Art. 118 LSA. As for the first case, there are generally no restrictions for a corporation to be part of a shareholders' agreement. This will be commonly the case when the shareholders' agreement deals with obligations or rights of the corporation, such as, for instance, pre-emption rights or call options relating to shares of the signing shareholders. Besides, a corporation can also be signing party – as she substantially is – in shareholders' agreements regarding the control of the corporation. In such cases, the corporation can be the holder of specific obligations, as much as this is generally allowed by law.

On the other hand, the shareholders' agreement is binding to a closed or listed corporation, as mentioned above, whenever it deals with the specific matters expressly set forth in Art. 118 – minority voting rights, structuring of the corporation's control or limitation to the transfer of shares –, and provided such shareholders' agreement is duly registered in the corporation's head office. In such cases, the corporation is obliged to observe and follow the agreement under any circumstances. This also leads the corporation's bodies to specific obligations in case of breach of the agreement by one of the parties. [28]

## 2. Legal Effects on the Shareholders

According to Art. 118, § 7 LSA, shareholders can grant powers to a proxy to represent them in general and special meetings, and such powers can have a longer validity as those generally allowed under Brazilian stock and closed corporation law, which is of one year.[29] This proxy shall represent the shareholders of the agreement according to what has been settled in the shareholders' agreement or according to the decisions held on the previous meeting of the shareholders.

Apart from that, the shareholders' agreement also explicitly produces effects towards third parties (other than the corporation), as long as the agreement is registered in the book of shares and in the shares certificates.[30] Such shares which are related to a shareholders' agreement cannot be sold in stock exchange or over-the-counter markets, as per Art. 118, § 4 LSA.

Shareholders' agreements can also grant rights to shareholders and third parties regarding the acquisition of shares. This is the case, for instance, of drag along clauses. According to the conditions set forth in the agreement, such duties towards third parties are binding for all or some of the signing shareholders.

Nevertheless, the elementary obligations of the shareholders cannot be assigned by way of a shareholders' agreement. Shareholder's rights to dividends or voting rights, for instance, cannot be permanently transferred to other shareholders by way of an agreement.

It is also important to mention that a shareholder agreement may place the shareholder in a position undertaking obligations that he would not have otherwise. This is the case when the shareholders' agreement results in the formation of a controlling group. The shareholders participating in such agreement will then assume special fiduciary duties towards the corporation, in a way that they must always act on behalf of the interests of all shareholders, not only on behalf of their personal interests, and can be held liable for the abuse of its control position.

---

**28** See below, item IV 3).

**29** Art, 126, § 1, LSA: "*A shareholder may be represented at a general meeting by a proxy appointed less than one year before, who shall be a shareholder, a corporation officer or a lawyer; in a publicly held corporation, the proxy may also be a financial institution*" (...).

**30** Art. 118, § 1 LSA (see annex, below).

## 3. Consequences of a Breach of the Shareholders' Agreements

Brazilian stock and closed corporation law provides some specific consequences for the case of breach of shareholders' agreements. Specifically, there are mechanisms of self-protection, related to the effects of votes issued in the general meetings by the shareholders and even by directors within the meetings of the management and supervisory boards. Such mechanisms are mainly related to the concern of Brazilian Law with the stability granted by the figure of the controlling shareholder. In this sense, Brazilian law encourages shareholders to join others through agreements in order to form a cohesive block of control that can provide such stability. Since the control itself is considered a corporate body, it has also authority over directors appointed by this group.

Specially, voting agreements, as per Art. 118 §§ 8 and 9 LSA, if duly registered in the corporation's head office, will have the effect of: a) votes expressed in a general meeting being disregarded, when they are against the content of the shareholders' agreement or the decisions taken in the preliminary meeting of the contracting parties; b) votes expressed by directors in their respective bodies, as long as they were appointed by shareholders in a position of control through a shareholders' agreement and the issue is not related to the ordinary business, also being disregarded, when they are against the express content of the shareholders' agreement or the decisions taken in the preliminary meeting of the contracting parties; and c) shareholders who are parties of a shareholders' agreement on voting rights or directors appointed by them being able to vote with the shares of absent shareholders or of those who have abstained from voting, if they are also parties to such agreement and have failed to vote in accordance to what has been settled in the shareholders' agreement or in the preliminary meeting. If necessary for the decision about counting such votes or not, the corporation might require clarification regarding the content of certain clauses of the shareholders' agreement to its members.[31] In this sense, voting rights can be directly enforced, giving shareholders the opportunity of requiring to the chairmen of the shareholders meeting, of the supervisory board or of the management board, that any votes which are contrary to the content of a shareholders' agreement or a shareholders' resolution passed according to it, be disregard. Besides, shareholders or directors can vote in lieu of those shareholders or directors who have not been present or have refrained from voting according to the

31 Art. 118, § 11 LSA (see annex, below).

content of the shareholders' agreement or the resolutions taken in the previous meeting held by the shareholders in agreement.

Such self-protection mechanism aims basically to protect shareholders' agreements executed with the purpose of setting the control of the corporation. However, also a shareholders' agreement that deals with voting rights of minority shareholders is enforceable at least at the level of the shareholders' meeting. As to agreements regarding the limitation to the transferability of shares, Brazilian stock and corporations law also provides mechanisms of self-protection, which can be exercised if the shares are duly registered in the in the book of shares and in the shares' certificates. In such cases, third parties cannot invoke their good faith in order to enforce the transference of the shares.

When it comes to agreements that do not fall within the scope of Art. 118 LSA, the only consequence in such case is the possibility of claiming damages.

## V. Enforcement of Shareholders' Agreements

Besides the possibilities of self-protection, as referred to above, Brazilian stock and closed corporation law provides specific performance mechanisms.[32] In relation to voting rights, it is possible to claim for an injunction in order to count votes that were not given by shareholders according to a shareholders' agreement or a preliminary meeting. In the case of agreements related to the limitations to the transferability of shares, preliminary injunctions are also possible, in order to guarantee the rights established in the agreement and so to avoid purchase or sale of shares performed in disrespect to what has been settled and has been registered in the corporation's head office and in the share's certificate and in the book of shares.

Apart from these remedies, damages and contractual penalties foreseen in the agreement can also be claimed. Especially for such agreements which are not within the scope of Art. 118, LSA, contractual penalties are relevant mechanisms for such enforcement. Brazilian law basically defines contractual penalties as liquidated damages, so that damages that surpass the amount of the penalty can only be claimed if this is specifically mentioned in the agreement.

Alternative dispute resolution mechanisms are often used in shareholders' agreements, especially in joint ventures or other agreements in which the parties

---

32 Differently from other jurisdictions, specific performance is considered the general rule on enforcement in Brazil, while damages should only be claimed when specific performance is not possible.

do not come from the same jurisdictions. Arbitration has become increasingly common in Brazil since the nineties, when the arbitration law came into force. Meanwhile there are several well known arbitration chambers in Brazil, some of them with long experience in managing corporate law disputes. More recently, mediation procedures have also become more common, since a mediation law came into force in 2015.

# VI. Annexes

## 1. Federal Law 6.404/76 (LSA)[33]

Art. 118. Shareholders' agreements regulating the purchase and sale of shares, preference to acquire shares, the exercise of voting rights, or the exercise of control must be observed by the corporation when filed in its head office.

§ 1. The commitments or encumbrances resulting from such an agreement may only be enforced against a third party after the agreement has been duly entered in the register books and on the share certificates, if any.

§ 2. Such agreements may not be invoked to exempt a shareholder either from liability when exercising his right to vote (article 115) or from the power of control (articles 116 and 117).

§ 3. Under the terms of the agreement, shareholders may make provision for the specific performance of the commitments undertaken.

§ 4. Shares registered under this article cannot be traded on a stock exchange or in the over-the-counter market.

§ 5. The administrative bodies of a publicly held corporation shall include in their annual report to the general meeting information concerning any provisions on profit reinvestment or dividend distribution policy contained in shareholders' agreements filed with the corporation.

§ 6. A shareholders' agreement with a term that depends on a certain condition may only be denounced according to its provisions.

§ 7. The mandate granted under the terms of a shareholders' agreement to render a vote against or in favor of a resolution in a general or special meeting may have a term that exceeds the term provided for in § 1 of Article 126 hereof.

---

33 The English version of this legal provision, as well as all other legal provisions of the LSA cited in this text, derive from the English version that can be found on the website of the Brazilian Stock Exchange Agency (*Comissão de Valores Mobiliários* – CVM), under http://www.cvm.gov.br/export/sites/cvm/subportal_ingles/menu/investors/ anexos/Law-6.404-ing.pdf [access on 3/12/2017].

§ 8. The president of the meeting or of the decision making body of the corporation shall not compute a vote that infringes a duly filed shareholders' agreement.

§ 9. Failure to attend a general meeting or meetings of the corporation's management bodies, as well as failure to vote on matters specified in the shareholders agreement by any party or by members of the board of directors elected under the terms of the shareholders agreement assures the damaged party the right to vote with the shares belonging to the shareholder who is absent or remiss and, in case of a member of the board of directors, by the board member elected by the votes of the damaged party.

§ 10. Shareholders bound to the shareholders' agreement shall indicate, in the act of filing, a representative to communicate with the corporation to render or to receive information upon request.

§ 11. The corporation may request the members from the agreement to elucidate its clauses.

Bohumil Havel

# Czech Republic

**Table of Content**



## I. Nature of Corporate Law Regulation

It is quite obvious that after the Czech society opened and liberated from the trap of the communist régime, it quickly started to adopt the legal standards and conventions of its neighbours, in particular, those of Germany and Austria[1]. That trend was strengthened not only by the fact that the Austrian law had significant-

1 Originally, through these jurisdiction, and afterwards also through the contractual and corporate standards known in the English practice – they were introduced by the lawyers of foreign law offices (also see *Hopt, K., J.* Comparative Company Law in Reimann, M., Zimmermann, R., The Oxford Handbook of Comparative Law, Oxford, OUP, 2006, p. 1169 an.)

**Doc. JUDr. Bohumil Havel PhD.** is a researcher of the Institute of State and Law of the Academy of Sciences of the Czech Republic (www.ilaw.cas.cz), a member of the Scientific Board of the Centre for Restructuring and Insolvency of *Harry Pollak of the University of Economics* in Prague (http://iem.vse.cz/cri/english/), and a lecturer in Bankruptcy Corporate Governance at the Law Faculty of the *Charles University* in Prague; he also works as counsel in the law office of PRK Partners Prague. The work was supported (partly) by the grant project APVV-0809-12.

https://doi.org/10.1515/9783110517026-011

ly influenced the Czech law until the end of 1950[2], but also by the fact that German entrepreneurs used to be, and still are, the major investors in the Czech Republic. All these facts played the role in the process of adoption of the new Civil Code (Act No. 89/2012 Sb. (Coll.)[3] – hereinafter also referred to as "CC"), which derived especially from the Austrian, German and Swiss experience in the area of the law of contract. Similarly, the new Company Law Act took inspiration from abroad (Act No. 90/2012 Sb./Coll./[4] – hereinafter referred to also as "CompA"), and so it adopted a whole range of instruments that are quite common in Europe.

New private law derived from the intention of significant strengthening of the autonomy of the will and from the principle that every autonomous right must be within the limits of the law, good morals, public order and constitutionality. While this intention is present rather strongly in the law of contract, the rules regulating legal entities or corporations intensively lean on the mandatory law, i.e. statutory law. In this sense, the Czech doctrine basically concludes that the fundamental existential features of a corporation, including the basic definition of competences of corporate bodies, are mandatory/statute-based which means that they cannot be modified by the will of shareholders. The Czech corporate law, however, does not contain any specific provisions that would lay down the mandatory or dispositive nature of statutory rules and it is satisfied with a general statement concerning the limitation of the autonomy of the will of legal acts. The German concept of *Satzungsstrenge*, which is also partly followed by the Austrian case law, was not adopted by the Czech law, although the regulation of joint stock companies was quite inspired by the German Act on the joint stock companies (*Aktiengesetz*). A doctrinal consensus prevails that while the questions of status and basic structure of a corporation are statute-defined, the rules determining the conduct of shareholders are more of a dispositive nature, unless the rights of minority shareholders guaranteed by the law have been interfered with[5].

---

2 Until 1918 Czechoslovakia was a part of the Austrian-Hungarian Empire and even after the establishment of an independent state it adopted the previous (Austrian) private law.

3 English translation – http://obcanskyzakonik.justice.cz/index.php/home/zakony-a-stanoviska/preklady/english.

4 English translation – http://obcanskyzakonik.justice.cz/index.php/home/zakony-a-stanoviska/preklady/english.

5 It also admitted that corporations are instruments of the law of contract in many respects and the restrictions imposed by the law are placed especially to protect creditors, minority shareholders, and to ensure reasonable/sound corporate governance, cf., for instance, *Ronovská/Havel* Kogentnost úpravy právnických osob a její omezení autonomií vůle, nebo vice versa? Obchodněprávní revue, Prague, 2/2016

The questions of interpretation of the law or internal regulations of a corporation are perceived in the same way. Whereas the Act is interpreted in a more objective manner taking into account the meaning and purpose of particular rules, the articles and shareholders agreements are interpreted more subjectively, taking into consideration the intended and expressed will of the parties (see hereinafter).

The fundamental statutory provisions of the corporate law do not contain any specific regulation of agreements which are therefore subject to the general law of contract contained in the Civil Code. That is why no specific regulation of shareholders' agreements exists, nevertheless, there is no doubt that they may be created and they are quite common in practice. However, statutory law indirectly influences the content of shareholders' agreements through some of its rules by, for example, modifying the voting rights in some cases, or guaranteeing independence of corporate bodies, regulating fiduciary duties of corporate bodies, regulating acting in concert and possible delictual consequences of detrimental influence within the group, etc. It is also generally admitted that some specific rules may either be incorporated in the articles, above that which is required to be included in them by statute, or in the separate shareholders' agreements[6]. While the articles are always accessible to the public, shareholders' agreements are taken as contracts and their accessibility to the third parties is up to the parties. Shareholders' agreements, however, are not allowed to introduce any rules that would interfere with the mandatory – statutory rules when it comes to the maintaining of the constitution of a corporation. Hence, it is not possible to introduce, for example, such rules that would restrict fiduciary duties and independence of authorised statutory bodies that would establish "self-regulation" in a corporation, i.e. its bodies would act in accordance with its will. A question of potential consequences of those covenants that would exceed the said limit is disputable, too – while a part of experts tend to consider such covenants void, another group claims that they will not cause a change of statutory law, but will be binding *inter partes*, and disputes might be settled within the delictual law. Case law also records cases inspired by the German law where a particular shareholders' agreement of all shareholders whose content was in conflict with the articles resulted in their one-only change (ad hoc breakthrough of the articles[7]), meaning that such an agreement will pierce a prohibition to transfer shares foreseen by the articles.

---

6 Beside the literature mentioned hereinafter, also see *Černá* Vedlejší dohody (sideletters) společníků kapitálových společností, Obchodněprávní revue, Prague, 1/2011.

7 Ruling of the Supreme Court of the Czech Republic, case ref. 29 Cdo 2254/2007.

Shareholders' agreements basically serve to ensure the functioning of a corporation with a particular goal and are the elements of a more general concept of *joint ventures*. In the Czech practice there may be found almost all possible forms of shareholders' agreements that may be found abroad (rules for the exercise of voting rights, rules for the staffing of corporate bodies, rules for a particular kind of corporate governance, pre-emption rights to shares, tag/drag along, deadlock settlement, and the like). It should be added that the Czech corporate law is liberal when it comes to the question of creation of various kinds of business shares (in limited liability company) and shares of stock (in joint stock company), and there are lots of rules that are commonly included in the shareholders' agreements, which connects them directly to a particular kind of a business share or a share of stock contained in the articles.

Although this report deals with the current Czech law, it should be mentioned that in the period from 1991 until 2013 the previous Commercial Code was in force[8], which was more restrictive and its interpretation tended to lay down the mandatory character of the said rules. Nevertheless, even then it was beyond any doubt that shareholders' agreements were a permitted type of legal conduct and that they were rather common in the legal practice.

## II. Regulation of Shareholders' Agreements

As it has already been mentioned the Czech law does not contain specific provisions for shareholders' agreements, so their existence, as well as content, are a matter of the general law of contract. Their conclusion and performance are not a matter of corporate law, nor need they be foreseen in the articles or corporate decisions – a corporation itself even need not know of their existence at all. The limits of the content of shareholders' agreements are laid down by the general law of contract and they are identical with those applicable to any other contract. The specific limitation to the content of shareholders' agreements is an obligation to maintain the functions of a corporation, hence it is not possible to agree effectively such rules that would interfere with the basic constitution stones of a corporation and statutory powers of its bodies.

Since shareholders' agreements bind only its signatories or those that acceded thereto, their existence is always somehow connected with the existence of the shareholders' position. Whereas in the case of a transfer of shares a new shareholder is automatically bound by the articles, with the shareholders' agree-

8 Act No. 513/1991 Sb. /Coll./.

ments it would require the assignment of the agreement or another similar legal act[9]. The Act itself basically does not contain any rules for the duration of shareholders' agreements – it is therefore left for the parties to agree thereon.

Parties to the shareholders' agreements are shareholders, but not rarely also a corporation itself or members of its bodies. In the cases where it is a corporation or its bodies that enter into a shareholders' agreement, status rules laid down by the law must be paid more attention. In the Czech practice there may also be found such cases where a third person becomes a party to a shareholders' agreement, for example an investor, without it being a shareholder (typically within spin-off structures or project companies).

In general, the Czech corporate law distinguishes 4 types of corporations – general partnership and limited partnerships (jointly referred to as personal companies) and a private limited liability company and public limited liability company/joint-stock company (jointly designated as capital/registered companies)[10]. The general regulation for all of them is the same although it is obvious that the regulation of personal companies shows a higher degree of non-mandatory rules. Similarly, the same regulation of corporate groups applies to all types of companies. In the Czech law the rules for shareholders' agreements do not differ by the respective types of companies, nevertheless, a particular regulation may be stricter and more detailed with capital companies, which may obviously influence the content of such agreements. In practise, shareholders agreements are mostly negotiated in the context of capital companies.

Generally speaking, the same rules apply regardless of whether a corporation is closed-held or whether its shares are listed on a regulated stock-exchange market. Nevertheless, listed corporations have another duty imposed by the public capital market, which means that the existence of such agreements may establish their notification duty linked to the existence of control, etc.

Similarly as in many other jurisdictions that do not have special provisions for shareholders' agreements, these agreements are not submitted to courts in case of disputes. This is often due to the intended confidentiality, and in many times and/or more frequently it is because disputes arising out of these agreements are settled in arbitration proceedings, or shareholders' agreements themselves foresee and provide for particular dispute-settlement procedures. That is why the case law contains only decisions concerning fragmented issues of share-

9 The Czech law allows both the assignment of a claim as well as the assignment of the whole agreement or its part, including the assignment to order (Section 1895 – Section 1900 CC).
10 We are leaving behind the cooperative, various forms of collective investments (SICAV, limited partnership with shares) and other alternatives of treating foundations or trusts established under the Civil Code as businesses.

holders' agreements, such as problems of controlling/influential conduct, pre-emptive rights, voting rights agreements, etc. Such jurisdiction, however, is not being separated specifically for shareholders' agreements, it only examines if a particular arrangement is or is not contrary to the law. Paradoxically, the courts even avoid using the concept of shareholders' agreement itself, although this might be so because they have not been made to do so, yet. For the same reasons as those mentioned in respect of the absence of specific regulations, the Czech law does not contain any specific rules for international and cross-border shareholders' agreements, although in practice shareholders' agreements whose parties involve entities from various jurisdictions is quite common. If such agreements are negotiated/executed with participation of foreign investors, the whole contractual framework is often governed by a foreign law (choice of law, typically the English law). In the case where the governing law is sought in the situation where the parties did not indicate otherwise, the Czech Act on the Private International Law and Procedure/Conflict of Laws Act will apply (Act No. 91/2012 Sb./Coll./[11]), or the Rome I Regulation[12] and Brussels Ia Regulation[13]. In this context it is interesting that although discussion is pending in Czech expert discuss concerning the application of an exception pursuant to Article 1 section 2 paragraph f) of the Rome I Regulation, the Czech Supreme Court did subject an agreement on the transfer of business share between a Czech and Austrian parties to that Regulation[14]. Analogically, it is possible to presume that disputes arising out of shareholders' agreements involving a cross-border element will not be subject to the exemption mentioned above and will be governed by the Regulation.

# III. Forms of Shareholders' Agreements

## 1. Shareholders' Agreements on Shareholder Rights

The most frequented issues dealt with by shareholders' agreements are those concerning the exercise of the voting rights. Although the previous Commercial

11 English translation – http://obcanskyzakonik.justice.cz/index.php/home/zakony-a-stanoviska/preklady/english.

12 Regulation of the European Parliament and of the Council (EC) No. 593/2008 on the law applicable to contractual obligations.

13 Regulation of the European Parliament and of the Council (EC) No. 1215/2012 on the jurisdiction and recognition and enforcement of judgments in civil and commercial matters.

14 Judgment case ref. 29 Cdo 2842/2013 and section case ref. 29 Cdo 1029/2014.

Code modelled by the German law of joint-stock company prohibited a whole range of such agreements, the new Act has waived those rules and it only provides for the protection against the negative influence within the group and standards of fiduciary duties[15]. Nevertheless, what is inferred therefrom is the inadmissibility of such voting agreements that would result in self-regulation, i. e. shareholders undertaking to vote according to the instructions of the corporation itself[16]. Another disputable point is an arrangement concerning so called right of appointment – right of shareholder to directly appoint one member of board of directors; case law tends to admit that the powers of corporation's bodies are to be defined solely by the statute and the assignment of such competences to another person or body should not be permitted[17]. In practice, however, the same goal may be achieved by introducing cumulative voting (Section 354 an. CompA), special voting type of shares, etc. Since the law does not provide for any concrete solutions, various models are used in practice – pooling voting, but the experts are more-or-less reluctant toward the employment of a voting trust as is known in the U.S. law – due to the essential inseparability of the voting right from the ownership of a share. This discussion is quite agitated today since there have been concurrently admitted shares without voting rights or various forms of fiduciary custody of shares, fiduciary securing assignment of ownership, securing agent, etc., which also results in numerous variations for shareholders' agreements concerning the voting rights.

As has already been mentioned several times, one of the restrictions to the shareholders' agreements is the existence of the law of corporate groups. In Section 71 an. CompA the Czech law relinquished the original German model of the law of corporate groups and introduced a different regulation inspired by the French case law (so called *Rozenblum* concept)[18]. Shareholders' agreements containing covenants concerning joint corporate governance may be treated as manifestations of influence or control, in response to which the Act established a duty to remedy the possible harmful consequences thereof. However, the general

---

**15** Cf. also *Janošek* Dohody o výkonu hlasovacích práv, akcie bez hlasovacích práv, sistace hlasovacích práv akcionáře (nejen) na základě ujednání stanov. Obchodněprávní revue, Prague, 2016, No. 4, p. 109 and subs.

**16** *Dědič/Lasák* Akcionářské dohody v praxi v České republice in *Csach/Havel et al.* Akcionářské dohody, Prague: Wolters Kluwer, 2017, p. 51.

**17** Cf. especially rulings of the Supreme Court of the Czech Republic, case ref. Cpjn 204/2015.

**18** Cf. *Havel* Czech Corporate Law on its Way, ECFR, vol. 12, no. 1, 2015, p. 32 and subs. or *Čech* Neues tschechische Recht für faktische Koncerne – vom deutschen Konzernrecht zu Rozenblum oder ein dritter Weg? in Hommerlhoff, P., Lutter, M., Teichmann, Ch. (Hrsg.), Corporate Governance im grenzüberschreitenden Konzern, De Gryuter, Berlin, Boston, 2017, p. 67 and subs.

rule is that no one is authorised to give binding instructions to the company's bodies, but for strategic guidelines, which entitles the corporation's management to reject such instructions. A major exemption from this rule is the existence of a corporate group[19], where the controlling (dominant) entity may issue instructions to the controlled (dependant) person which are treated as binding under the majority doctrine[20]. Such instructions, however, must be issued for concrete situations, they must pursue the interest of the corporate group as a whole and if some damage is caused it must be remedied within the corporate group as a whole.

## 2. Shareholders' Agreements on the (Limitation for the) Transfer of Shares

Shareholders often specify, already in the articles themselves, whether their corporation is to be held closely or openly, and for that reason they incorporate the fundamental rules for the transfer of business shares and particular shares of stock already in these statutory instruments. Nevertheless, in the case where such rules are not intended to be the same for all shareholders or to be available to the public, they are placed in the shareholders' agreements. The most frequent among such covenants are the rules on the pre-emptive rights which the Czech case law treats as restriction to the transferability of the shares of stock or business shares if they are contained in the articles, and it is not permitted to transfer them without first-refusal procedure taking place[21].

Other forms and variations of the right of pre-emption or other similar tools (drag/tag along clauses) are not regulated by the law, nevertheless, since the law of contract is basically dispositive, they are permitted and commonly used. However, it is always necessary to consider if such rules should not be preferably in-

**19** The concept of corporate group is defined in Section 79 CompA:

(1) One or more entities subject to single management (the "dependent person") by other person or persons (the "dominant entity") shall form a corporate group with the dominant entity.

(2) Single management shall mean the influence of the dominant entity on the activities of the dependent entity aimed at coordination and conceptual management of at least one of the important components or tasks within the corporate group's business activities, in order to ensure a long-term promotion of the corporate group's interests under the corporate group's single policy.

**20** Cf. especially *Havel* Commentary to Section 79, in Štenglová/Havel et al. Zákon o obchodních korporacích. Komentář, 2[nd] issue, Prague, 2017.

**21** Cf. the ruling of the Supreme Court of the Czech Republic, case ref. 29 Cdo 2811/99.

corporated in the articles and as such connected with the transferability restriction, or if they should be agreed in terms of the property rights.

Similarly, there is no blocking to the specification of the rules for a potential corporation's deadlock. In practice all possible shoot out clauses are admitted, nevertheless, less aggressive solutions are usually opted for. If these agreements are to have an influence upon the position of a shareholder in a corporation the paramount imperative is that a corporation should treat all of its shareholders equally and that no one should be excluded from a corporation against their will, unless the law or articles foresees and clearly provides for such a situation in advance. Such rules are therefore incorporated also into the corporation's articles.

## 3. Shareholders' Agreements on the Constitution of the Corporation

Another significant purpose of shareholders' agreements is to establish rules for a joint course and management in the extent that is either not permitted by general corporate rules, or, although admitted, the parties want the rules to be confidential and associated with various sanctions (contractual fines). It is therefore quite common also in the Czech practice that the statutory rules for corporate governance are supplemented and detailed in the shareholders' agreements. Hence, shareholders' agreements specify a degree of participation of particular shareholders in the corporation's bodies, they establish extra-statutory bodies of shareholders which supervise the corporation's management (various forms of steering committees, etc.). This is often a kind of response to the types of business shares or shares of stock defined in the articles and it also co-modifies a standard of governance of a corporate group. Partial agreements may make up, alongside the articles, a contractual peel around the corporation which may push forward the interpretation of loyalty and interest to be pursued by the members of corporate bodies. In the light of the statutory regulation of the interest of a corporate group mentioned above (Section 79 CompA), the Czech doctrine admits a wider interpretation of loyalty of corporate bodies in these cases[22].

On the other hand, so called right of appointment – i.e. the right to appoint a particular member of a corporate body by a particular shareholder (see above)

**22** Cf. *Havel* Commentary to Section 81, in Štenglová/Havel et al. Zákon o obchodních korporacích. Komentář, 2nd issue, Prague, 2017.

– is controversial. In practice it is often solved by a combination of the force of voting rights of particular shareholders, etc., which means that the effect is functionally similar[23]. Moreover, it should be mentioned that this year employee's co-determination was returned to the Czech law of openly-held corporations/joint-stock companies without any discussion of experts and obviously only for political reasons.

## 4. Shareholders' Agreements in pre-insolvency situation

From an economic point of view, shareholders' agreements are also motivated by the shareholders' effort to prevent future economic problems. That is why they may also provide for the rules for gradual financing (especially with start-ups), additional capital investments in the case of economic problems, etc. The Czech law admits and employs so called extra contribution beyond the registered capital which means an option, or even an obligation, to contribute to the corporation's equity during the time when a corporation incurs some loss, etc. (Section 162 and subs. CompA for private limited liability company) – such rules, however, must be contained in the articles should they establish an obligation to pay an extra contribution. Supplementary provisions are therefore added to shareholders' agreements, including rules for shareholders' loans, rules of approval of external funds, etc. It should be added that the Czech insolvency law subordinates shareholders' claims in the case of bankruptcy, but only those claims that are related to the position of the shareholders (dividends, etc.) – so it does not admit the full equitable subordination. If the shareholders also have claims arising out of loans, etc., they must (may) register them within insolvency proceedings and such claims will be discharged in the order of sequence laid down by the Insolvency Act.

In general, shareholders' agreements are agreements only among shareholders, and so they last even when the corporation falls insolvent – however, their effectiveness is actually limited, because the management of a corporation may be taken over by an insolvency practitioner/trustee in bankruptcy. Similarly, a general meeting's powers may be suspended in certain cases and their competences may be assumed by an insolvency practitioner. It will always depend on whether a corporation's insolvency is settled by bankruptcy with a liquidation or rescue re-structuring. Where a corporation itself is a party to a shareholders'

23 Also see *Dědič/Lasák* Akcionářské dohody v praxi v České republice in Csach/Havel Akcionářské dohody, Prague: Wolters Kluwer, 2017, p. 59.

agreement such an agreement may be treated as executory contract and it will be administered pursuant to the law (compare also the chapter on Shareholders Agreement Arrangement in Pre-insolvency and Insolvency Law).

The Czech law, in harmony with the European practice, employs various forms of stabilization agreements in all cases of preventing insolvency or another economic crisis. Principles of shareholders' agreement are reflected in such agreements in many respects, especially in the wording of standstill agreements or lock-up agreements. Such types of agreements, however, differ from ordinary shareholders' agreements especially by their purpose (to rescue a crisis), a period of their duration which is usually limited to 6–12 months, and with participation of biggest creditors (banks etc.). Along with shareholders and corporations as parties there also appear significant institutional creditors. The Czech law also lays down the limits of such agreements, which are typically the problems of their possible nullity (*actio Pauliana*). Another discussion in respect of such agreements concerns a question if creditors might exert significant influence in a corporation through such agreements in terms of the law of corporate groups.

# IV. Legal Consequences of Shareholders' Agreements

## 1. Legal Consequences on the Corporation

The Czech doctrine also deals with the questions of interpretation of shareholders' agreements, and/or interpretation of the articles in the light thereof[24]. It is admitted, by analogy with the German doctrine, that the interpretation of shareholders' agreement is on the borderline between the objective and subjective interpretation and a kind of corporation is also pointed out. Shareholders' agreements are therefore more likely to influence the interpretation of personal corporations rather than the capital/registered companies. A general tendency is that the articles that are available to the public should be interpreted separately from such agreements. Nevertheless, since a corporation is a tool based on the law of contract, in certain cases, especially in the case of conflicts, a shareholders' agreement may help in finding a reasonable content of the articles.

24 *Ronovská/Havel* Povaha a pravidla výkladu (nejen) zakladatelských právních jednání soukromých korporací, Právní rozhledy, Prague, 18/2016.

As has already been mentioned, shareholders agreements will be more important if a corporation or its bodies are the parties thereto. In such a case, however, such influence is caused by the fact of being a party to the shareholders' agreement itself, rather than some wider interpretation approach.

## 2. Legal Consequences on the Shareholders

As a shareholders' agreement operates in a regime of the law of contract, it is possible to employ its tools unless their employment is excluded by the shareholders' agreement itself. By adopting a new Civil Code, the situation has simplified largely and the changes as to the parties to a shareholders' agreement need not be done by combinations of several acts. A party to a shareholders' agreement may assign its rights (assignment – Section 1879 an. CC), or it may assign the whole agreement, or its wider part (assignment of agreement – Section 1895 an. CC). As has been mentioned above, within the assignment of agreement it is also possible to include a transfer to order and to transfer an agreement by endorsement (Section 1897 subsection 2 CC). These options may also be supplemented, for example, by automated termination of participation in the shareholders' agreement on the moment of termination of the share in a corporation. A shareholder that is not a party to the shareholders' agreement is not affected thereby unless acceding thereto (including an accession agreement etc.).

Shareholders that enter into a shareholders′ agreement basically indicate that they are acting in concert or even creating a group. These questions, as has been mentioned in section III. 1, are regulated by the Czech law of corporate groups, and there may also occur cases of joint acting where that fact becomes significant. Similarly, there may occur related obligations pursuant to the Act regulating the capital market[25] – typically a duty to notify a share pursuant to Section 122 and subseq. of that Act. In the case where a shareholders' agreement is not available to the public it is quite frequent that the acting in concert does not have to be notified, or a statement is made that it does not qualify as acting in concert. For this reason, but also due to a whole range of other reasons, the Czech law does not establish a duty to publish shareholders' agreements. These agreements therefore often include a non-disclosure agreement (NDA) and sanctions for a breach of a confidentiality duty.

25 Act No. 256/2004 Sb. (Coll.).

## 3. Consequences of a Breach of the Shareholders' Agreements

Even in the Czech practice it is possible to find some complicated and long-term shareholders' agreements which are subject to foreign jurisdictions, and they are therefore created as a "complex" world. Nevertheless, there are also simple agreements which rely on quite detailed provisions of general contractual law which implies that in the case of a breach of the agreement there are available contractual rules for remedies for immediate consequences of the breach as well as the rules for the compensation of damage, etc. The Czech law admits substantial and non-substantial breach of contractual obligations based on which it has imposed a duty to remove the consequence of the breach, or has established a right to withdraw from the contract. Obviously, if damage results from the breach the law imposes a duty to compensate. Nevertheless, shareholders' agreements mostly supplement these rules by contractual fines, suspension of rights of the breaching party, etc.

As shareholders' agreements are a part of the world of the law of contract, a direct link between the breach of a shareholders' agreement and the position of a shareholder is not expected. Should there occur a breach of an obligation pursuant to a shareholders' agreement, the position of a shareholder is not changed, unless the rules corresponding thereto would be included in the articles. In order to intensify the effectiveness of shareholders' rights, its philosophy often projects into the articles and a breach may bring suspension of the voting right, activation of call option, etc.

The rules for competences of a general meeting are perceived more as statutory, depending on the jurisdiction, however, it is admitted that the articles may also be amended by agreement of all shareholders outside the regime of general meeting. This procedure is restricted in use due to the fact that lots of general meeting's decisions require a form of notarial deed, but shareholders' agreements need not even have a written form. There were cases of one-off piercing of the articles where a shareholders' agreement changed the articles *ad hoc* (see above). Nevertheless, none of them indicated that a breach of a shareholders' agreement could establish a right to review a decision of the general meeting. From a doctrinal point of view, such a possibility may not be excluded because, for example, with shared participation of a corporation in the shareholders' agreements there may be agreed some rules that will be so united that a breach of a shareholders' agreement may be viewed as a breach of the articles. There is also a rule that the existence of a shareholders' agreement may be known to all the shareholders and their acting that is in breach thereof may be considered as acting against good morals, which may interfere with the legality of the general meeting. Further development, however, is a matter of case law/ courts.

## V. Enforcement of Shareholders' Agreements

The same as it is in other aspects of the life of shareholders' agreements, even its enforceability is fully governed by the law of contract. Shareholders' agreements are not treated as consumers' contracts, so they are not subject to the general limits of consumer protection. The enforceability of a shareholders' agreement is identical with any contract for repeated performance. The parties may therefore generally request the performance of obligations by filing an action to enforce the performance, they may execute the final judicial decision, etc. However, other contractual mechanisms may be agreed as well, because judicial procedures are formalized and time-demanding. That is why other "coercive" schemes have been introduced alongside contractual fines and rules concerning damages (restriction of rights of the breaching party, activation of the transfer of the position, strengthening of the rights of other parties, etc.). As it has been mentioned before, such schemes are often connected with the wording of articles and a breach of a shareholders' agreement may also be treated as the reason to restrict the voting right or the share in profit, it may be the reason to remove a member of a corporation's body from office, or it may be the reason to active call options, etc. The same as in the case of deadlock, in the Czech practice, too, it is possible to find standard instruments that are utilized in Europe.

Dispute settlement is basically left with general courts. Nevertheless, in the case of more complicated shareholders' agreements procedures such as conciliation, mediation or ADR, are often used. The Czech law does not impose any specific restrictions in this respect, so there is a possibility to opt for a third person to settle disputes, to use a qualified mediator, or to submit a dispute to an arbitration tribunal (not only Czech[26], but also foreign[27]).

---

26 To the standing Arbitration Tribunal of the Economic and Agricultural Chamber of the Czech Republic – http://en.soud.cz/.

27 UNCITRAL rules are therefore used, both LCIA and ICC. London, Vienna, Stockholm or Paris are used as arbitration venues.

Professor Mette Neville

# Denmark

## Table of Content



**Professor Mette Neville,** Department of Law, Aarhus, University, Denmark

https://doi.org/10.1515/9783110517026-012

# A. The nature of company law regulation

In Denmark there is general principle of freedom of contract in company law. This means that as point of departure there is freedom to choose between different forms of incorporation,[1] and there is freedom to determine the content of the company's contracts (for example the articles of association and shareholders' agreements). Freedom of contract is limited only by the mandatory provisions of companies' legislation, general legal principles and suchlike.[2] Thus, the extent of freedom of contract depends on the extent of mandatory regulation. The Companies Act, which governs public and private limited companies, contains the most mandatory rules, while for example partnerships are very little governed by legislation, so that freedom of contract in partnerships is primarily only limited by general legal principles.[3]

Companies legislation stands at the top of the hierarchy of corporate law. Then come the company's articles of association. As for shareholders' agreements, page 840 of the Danish Parliamentary Company Law Report 1498:2008 states that a shareholders' agreement may not conflict with companies' legislation or the company's articles of association. Thus, a hierarchy of sources of law stands behind the reform of companies' legislation, in which shareholders' agreements rank below the legislation and articles of association. However, this has been questioned in legal theory,[4] since the whole point of shareholders' agreements is to go into greater detail or even to vary the articles of association. Shareholders' agreements are often intended to give relations within the company priority over the articles of association, and this is directly expressed in provisions on priority in the agreement.[5] The Company Law Report also seems to

---

1 However, in some professions there can be some restrictions requiring a certain profession only to be carried on using a specified corporate form. For example, the business of banks and mortgage lending institutions must be carried on by public limited companies. On the other hand there can be restrictions whereby some professions may not be carried on in the form of a limited company; this applies to pharmacies. For further on this, see *Fode/Munck* Valg af selskabsform, 2016, p. 55. In practice this kind of restriction on freedom of contract is limited nowadays.

2 *Kruhl* Ejeraftaler, 2011, p. 79; and *Gomard et al.* Almindelig kontraktsret, p. 15.

3 Other than a few provisions in the Act on Certain Commercial Undertakings, partnerships are still governed by general legal principles.

4 See *Kruhl* Ejeraftaler, 2011, p. 102; *Jensen* in Neville/Sørensen (eds.), Den nye selskabslov, 2009, pp. 181–208; and *Werlauff* Selskabsret, 2016, p. 439.

5 Prior to the introduction of Section 82 of the 2010 Danish Companies Act it was assumed that it was possible to agree the priority; see e. g. *Sørensen* Joint Ventures, p. 549; and *Nørgaard/Werlauff* Vedtægter og aktionæroverenskomster, 1995, p. 89.

acknowledge this elsewhere, as it stated: *"In a shareholders' agreement shareholders may agree that the agreement shall take priority over the articles of association in relations between them"* (unofficial translation).

# B. Regulation of Shareholders' Agreements

In Danish law shareholders' agreements are ordinary private law agreements, and there is no special requirement as to their form. Shareholders' agreements are not required to be registered and are thus not publicly accessible; see further in section V.3.1.

Despite the widespread use of shareholders' agreements by Danish companies, until the 2010 Companies Act there was no substantive regulation of them. The first legislative regulation of shareholders' agreements was made in the new Companies Act, BEK No 172 of 22 February 2010.

## I. The law prior to 2010

Before 2010 there was some uncertainty about whether shareholders' agreements were binding on companies and, if so, under what conditions. However, it was the prevailing view of both academics and practitioners that shareholders' agreements entered into by all the shareholders, which had a clear content and had been notified to the company, could be asserted at the company's general meetings so that the chairmen of such meetings should ensure that the decisions of general meetings were in line with the shareholders' agreement.[6] Among others, this is supported by the judgment of the Danish Supreme Court in U 1996.1550 H.[7]

---

**6** See *Werlauff/Nørgaard* Vedtægter & Aktionæroverenskomster, 1995, p. 65; and *Bernhard Gomard*'s article in Scandinavian Studies in Law, 1972, p. 97 ff. This view has also been put forward (without reservation) in *Werlauff* U 2008 B 207; *Andersen* U 2008 B 425; and *Werlauff* U 2009 B 119.

**7** From which it follows that a shareholders agreement in a private company can have a legal effect for the company if all the members of the private company are covered by the agreement.

## II. Regulation of Shareholders' Agreements under the 2010 Companies Act

With the comprehensive reform of Danish company law by the 2010 Companies Act, Section 5 an Section 82 of the Act introduced substantive regulation of shareholders' agreements. The aim was to clarify the law. Shareholders' agreements are defined in Section 5(6) as: *"An agreement governing the ownership and management of the company entered into between the shareholders."*[8] According to Section 82 of the Companies Act, shareholders' agreements are not binding on the company or on resolutions passed at general meetings.[9] Thus shareholders' agreements are now clearly distinguished from articles of association. This means, for example, that a majority at a general meeting can refuse to comply with a shareholders' agreement that governs voting, without incurring any consequences under company law. It does not matter that all the shareholders' are parties to the agreement, whether the agreement is clear and unambiguous, or whether the shareholders' who are in breach of the agreement openly admit that the voting is in breach of the agreement. The chairman of the general meeting is legally obliged to uphold voting that may be in breach of an agreement. This applies to shareholders' agreements requiring certain decisions to be made unanimously or that each shareholder has a right to nominate a member of the board, for whom the other shareholders are obliged to vote in favour of at the general meeting; see section III below.

Section 82 of the Companies Act does not in itself restrict the freedom to enter into agreements; it only governs whether such agreements can be binding on the company. This means that, as previously, shareholders may enter into such agreements, and that a breach of an agreement can have consequences for the parties to the agreement under civil law and in particular under contract law, but it does not affect the legality of decisions made at a general meeting or their registration in the IT system of the Danish Business Authority.

---

**8** For further on the definition of a shareholders agreement in the Companies Act, see *Jensen* in Neville/ Sørensen (eds.) Den nye selskabslov, 2009, pp. 181–208 (at. 197). The author rightly criticises the provision as being unclear and giving rise to problems of definition. It is assumed that Section 82 does not apply to shares pledged as security if the pledgee obtains the voting rights for the shares pledged; see also *Müller/Werlauff* Vedtægter & Ejeraftaler, 2010, p. 83.

**9** According to the commentaries on the draft law – L 170 of 25 March 2009 – this was only a codification of the existing law, so the Act did not provide transitional provisions for this. However, as stated above, since there was a general view among legal scholars that shareholders agreements could be binding, subject to certain conditions, the view expressed in the commentary does not seem to be correct. The assumption in the commentaries have also been criticised by *Jensen*, among others, in Neville/Sørensen Den nye selskabslov, 2009, p. 182.

Since shareholders' agreements typically concern enduring company matters without a time limit, shareholders' agreements are also typically for an unlimited period.[10] There has been a discussion in theory about whether a shareholders' agreement that does not include a specific provision on termination can be terminated by giving a normal period of notice, as is the case with other agreements, including partnership agreements.[11] For this reason a provision on termination is usually included in shareholders' agreements and the great majority of these provide that they shall be for an unlimited period. In principle, such provisions must be respected. However, circumstances can develop in such a way that it would clearly be unreasonable to hold the parties to the agreement. In this case it is possible to try to have an agreement set aside under the rules of Danish contract law, for example Section 36 of the Contracts Act, according to which the courts can amend or terminate an agreement in whole or in part if it would be unreasonable or contrary to good business practice to enforce it. Decisions made under Section 36(1) must have regard for the circumstances in which an agreement is entered into, the content of the agreement and subsequently arising circumstances.

Section 82 applies to private limited and public limited companies covered by the Companies Act.[12] This means it applies to both closed corporations and listed companies. This has been criticised, particularly in relation to its application to SMEs (closed corporations). For example, in its submission to Company Law Reform Committee, the Danish Bar and Law Society criticised the proposed provision and recommended that shareholders' agreements should be binding under company law on non-listed companies if the agreement is clear and covers all or the greater part of the shareholders.

---

**10** However, shareholders agreements can be intended to serve a specific purpose, for example entering into a joint venture for the construction of a hotel. In these cases the agreement will automatically lapse when the aim of the agreement has been fulfilled and the rights and duties of the parties have been exhausted; see *Kruhl* Ejeraftaler, 2011, p. 277.

**11** *Kruhl* Ejeraftaler, 2011, p. 278.

**12** The provision does not apply to other forms of associations such as partnerships, limited partnerships, cooperatives etc., which are not governed by legislation in Danish law. These are primarily governed by the agreements entered into by their members and by general legal principles. See *Fode/Munck* Valg af selskabsform, 2016, p. 72.

## C. Forms of Shareholders' Agreements

In Denmark there is widespread use of shareholders' agreements to supplement companies legislation and articles of association. Research into Danish private limited companies has shown that the shareholders had entered into shareholders' agreements in the majority of companies.[13] In many SMEs the real regulation of the shareholders mutual rights and obligations are to be found in a shareholders' agreement, while the articles of association only contain the minimum of information required by the Companies Act.[14] Shareholders' agreements typically govern the following:[15]

a) Business goals
b) Administrative rights, i.e. the influence of the shareholder, for example by exercising voting rights;
c) Financial rights, i.e. the right to a share of the company's capital and profits, primarily dividends and the proceeds of liquidation; and
d) Rights of disposal, for example the right to dispose of shares by selling them, pledging them as security etc.

The content of shareholders' agreements will obviously depend on their purpose and the nature of the company, and they also reflect the fact that the legislation does not fulfil all the company's needs for regulation, particularly in the case of SMEs. Most SMEs have an ownership structure where there are one or a few shareholders who are themselves wholly or partly involved in running the business.[16] In such companies the shareholders' agreement will usually aim: to ensure the desired balance of power; that the shares are not disposed of without some form of control; and to create a general framework for the company's operations.[17] This means they will often contain provisions restricting the right to transfer shares, an obligation to vote for a given composition of the company's board of directors, rules on exits from the company, provisions on dividend policy[18] etc. A number of shareholders' agreements also contain provisions on how

---

13 *Neville* in Neville/Sørensen (eds.) Den nye selskabslov, 2009.

14 *Jensen* Den nye selskabslov, p. 183; and *Lego Andersen* – Aktionæroverenskomster, 2000.

15 *Werlauff* Selskabsret, 2016, p. 435; *Schans Christensen* Kapitalselskaber, 2015, p. 204.

16 On ownership and management structures of Danish SMEs, see *Neville* in Neville/Sørensen Company Law and SMEs, 2010, p. 248 and *Bennedsen* Ejerledelse i Danmark, rapport 1, 2015.

17 *Kruhl* Ejeraftaler, 2011, pp. 45–67; and *Krüger Andersen* Aktie- og anpartsselskabsret. Kapitalselskaber, 2017, p. 183.

18 For example, some shareholders agreements contain provisions stating that it is not the intention to pay dividends during the first three years of the company's operations.

the company's activities are to be financed, including that financing shall be secured from the company's own means or that the parties are bound to invest further or provide security for loans from third parties. Other provisions can deal with an expanded right to information,[19] winding up the company etc.

## I. Shareholders' Agreements on shareholders' rights

### 1. Voting rights

Shareholders' agreements typically regulate the shareholders' rights, including in particular their voting rights and thus their power in the company. Research into shareholders' agreements carried out in 2011 showed that 89 % of agreements regulated the parties' voting rights, usually by varying the majority principle in the Companies Act.[20] SMEs shareholders' agreements often contain provisions requiring important strategic and financial decisions to be taken unanimously, or by giving the parties a veto right over such decisions. These are nearly all intended to protect minority shareholders.[21] Shareholders' agreements often require the following decisions to be taken unanimously:
(a) adopting the budget for the following financial year, which must be approved before the end of the current financial year,
(b) changing the company's business strategy,
(c) major investments or disposals,
(d) starting new activities or restricting existing activities,
(e) entering into tenancy agreements,
(f) appointing and dismissing personnel,
(g) taking up, changing or increasing a loan,
(h) providing loans or extending credit beyond normal business credit, and

19 The Danish Companies Act only provides for a limited right to information. According to Section 102 of the Companies Act individual shareholders have a right to ask questions at the general meeting about matters that are relevant for understanding the annual accounts, annual report and the company's situation in general. The board and the management can refrain from giving information if doing so could result in substantial harm for the company. This limited right to information applies to both large and small companies. This is why shareholders agreements sometimes provide for an expanded right to information, for example requiring individual shareholders to give information about important matters and/or an obligation to answer all questions. Such provisions on disclosing information are often supplemented by an expanded obligation of confidentiality about the circumstances of the company.

20 *Kruhl* Ejeraftaler, 2011 p. 52.

21 Cf. A questionnaire-based study (Neville 2003) of 350 respondents.

(i) changing the company's bank etc.

These decisions are often referred to the shareholders, even though a number of them would typically be decisions for the board of directors; see Section 111(1) of the Companies Act. According to Act, the board has three main responsibilities:
1) It is responsible for the company's overall and strategic management;
2) It must arrange for a proper organisation for the company;
3) It has financial responsibilities, including ensuring that there is adequate capital and risk management controls; and
4) It must ensure that the executive board performs its duties properly.

For example, a change of strategy will normally require a board decision, as will any decision to take a loan etc. In some shareholders' agreements important decisions are left to the board, but the board is required to take such decisions unanimously.

In addition to provisions on unanimous voting and veto rights, which are the usual ways in which smaller companies vary the standard rules on majorities, the majority principle in large public companies may be departed from where voting rights are exercised either by a person who is not the owner of the shares in question or when rules bind shareholders to vote in a particular way. In practice, in most cases shareholders use binding provisions on voting, whereby the shareholders bind themselves to vote in a particular way.[22] Such provisions are used, for example, to concentrate the influence of a number of shareholders to achieve a significant or dominant position, as in cases where agreements over voting rights are entered into to avert a hostile takeover. There can also be such voting cooperation with a view to taking over another company.[23] While it is permissible to enter into binding voting agreements, these are of a private law character and pursuant to Section 82 of the Companies Act they cannot be enforced at the company's general meeting.[24]

---

22 *Werlauff* Selskabsret, 2016, p. 438.

23 *Krüger Andersen* Aktie- og anpartsselskabsret. Kapitalselskaber, 2017, p. 184. See also U 1999.1036 H, which reproduces an agreement concerned with the takeover of another company.

24 Pursuant to Section 80 of the Companies Act it is possible to give a power of attorney, but in this case the requirements under Section 80(2) of the Companies Act apply, the power must be in writing and 12 months' notice must be given. If there is a requirement to regulate voting rights in the articles of association, either to concentrate power or to ensure the dispersal of power, in such a way as to have an effect for the company, this can be done by introducing multiple voting rights (see Section 46 of the Companies Act) or by introducing voting limits (see Section 107(2). For further on this, see *Krüger Andersen* Aktie- og anpartsselskaber. Kapitalselskaber, 2017, p. 407.

Agreements for the transfer of voting rights can also be for the *permanent* transfer of voting rights to another shareholder or a third party. Such agreements are often called irrevocable powers of attorney. Directions are usually given about the exercise of such voting rights.[25] Since shareholders' agreements are not enforceable at general meetings, it is questionable whether they should be classified as powers of attorney since, under Section 80(1) of the Companies Act, all shareholders are entitled to attend general meetings by proxy and Section 82 on shareholders' agreements is not intended to alter this.[26] Consequently the chairman of the meeting must allow attorneys to vote if they can present a written and dated power of attorney.[27] However, since Section 80 of the Companies Act requires powers of attorney to be revocable at any time, a provision on the irrevocability of a power of attorney must normally be categorised as a provision in a shareholders' agreement. In cases of doubt the chairman of the general meeting must decide.

It is not possible to get round Section 82 by making the company a party to an agreement or by informing the board of directors of the agreement.[28]

## 2. Economic rights and duties

Economic rights are another of the fundamental rights of shareholders, for example a right to dividends. According to Section 180 of the Companies Act the general meeting decides on the distribution of dividends. However, the general meeting cannot decide to distribute dividends for a greater amount than that proposed or accepted by the company's board, regardless of what the articles of association or shareholders' agreement provide. The board is responsible for ensuring that the company has adequate capital provision, so the board must either propose or approve the level of any dividend. In Danish shareholders' agreements, especially those in SMEs, the dividend policy is often governed by the shareholders' agreement. For example, agreements in SMEs sometimes contain guidelines for when the company can declare a dividend. In companies shareholders' agreements restrict the right to dividends, for example by linking dividends to a minimum level of solvency, while others contain restrictions on the timing of dividends.

---

**25** *Werlauff* Selskabsret, 2016, p. 437.

**26** *Werlauff* Selskabsret, 2016, p. 437; and *Jensen* Ejeraftaler in Neville/Sørensen (eds.) Den nye selskabslov, 2009, p. 199 ff.

**27** *Jensen* Ejeraftaler in Neville/Sørensen (eds.) Den nye selskabslov, 2009, p. 210.

**28** *Werlauff* Selskabsret, 2016, p. 441.

Shareholders' agreements can also include provisions on the shareholders' financial obligations. Shareholders limit their liability by paying up on their shares and cannot be made subject to further obligations except by a unanimous decision; see Section 107(1) of the Companies Act. This is the starting point, but it is often departed from in SMEs by provisions in shareholders' agreements on the company's financing. For example, these can require shareholders to take on further obligations. This can include provisions by which the parties agree that all shareholders will be obliged to give the company's creditors security in proportion to their shareholdings in connection with setting up the company or the future expansion of the company's activities. The maximum amount of any security to be given can be stated and a shareholders' agreement and can include provisions that taking substantial loans shall require unanimity; see above.[29]

## II. Shareholders' Agreements on the transfer of shares

Unlisted companies usually have few shareholders who typically participate in the management of the company.[30] In companies which have few shareholders and which are wholly or partly managed by the shareholder(s), the success or failure of the company is highly dependent on cooperation between the shareholders. For this reason such companies have a vital interest in being able to control who shall be shareholders. Section 48 of the Companies Act contains a declaratory rule on the free transferability of shares. The free transferability of shares is most suited to companies where the shareholders are passive investors and there is separation of ownership and control, and a transfer of shares will not usually influence the operation and management of the company. Moreover, the free transferability of shares is a fundamental condition for the proper functioning of a securities market so that securities regulations limit companies' restrictions on share transfers. However, the principle of free transferability is often inappropriate and it is derogated from in virtually all articles of association and/or shareholders' agreements in SME's by the inclusion of restrictions on

---

**29** Another example of provisions concerning the company's financing are those according to which the shareholders are bound to vote for an increase of the company's capital to cover losses from previous years or the current financial year. Decisions to increase the capital are made pursuant to Section 106 of the Companies Act and must be must be passed by at least two-thirds of the votes cast as well as at least two-thirds of the share capital represented at the general meeting.

**30** 67 % of Danish public and private companies have one shareholder, and only one in ten have three or more shareholders; see *Bennedsen* Ejerledelse i Danmark, rapport 1, 2015.

share transfers, usually in the form of pre-emption rights or requirements for the consent of the other shareholders. Such terms are often included both in the articles of association and the shareholders' agreement. The articles contain a brief formulation corresponding to that in the Companies Act,[31] while the more detailed guidelines and provisions are included in the shareholders' agreement. However, many smaller companies articles' take the form of minimum articles[32] with restrictions on share transferability only included in the shareholders' agreement. A study of 72 shareholders' agreements in 2011[33] showed that 96 % of them contained provisions on pre-emption rights in the event of the transfer of shares while 24 % of them contained provisions requiring the consent of the other shareholders.

In addition to stating the circumstances that will trigger a pre-emption right (assignment, succession or the assignment of voting rights), provisions on the transfer of shares often address the question of the valuation of the shares,[34] with guidelines for how the purchase price should be assessed.

On consent clauses, shareholders' agreements sometimes contain a rule on what will trigger a requirement for consent (assignment, succession etc.). On the other hand, it is unusual for such a provision to list the conditions under which consent can be refused, but there is often a provision requiring the shareholders' agreement to be complied with. There is almost never a provision on justification or on alternative means of exiting the company if the board refuses its consent.[35]

In relation to restrictions on the transfer of shares in shareholders' agreements, Section 82 of the Companies Act requires the company to list changes of share-ownership in the company's register if there is free transferability under the articles of association, even if the transfer takes place contrary to a provision in the shareholders' agreement.[36]

In addition to the provisions on the transferability of shares directly referred to and to some extent regulated in the Companies Act (Section 67 on pre-emption and Section 68 on consent) if they are included in the articles of association,

---

**31** If provisions are included in the articles of association restricting the transferability shares in the form of a requirement for consent or a pre-emption right, Sections 67 and 68 of the Companies Act apply.

**32** The website of the Danish Business Agency publishes a minimum articles, but it does not meet the needs of companies with two or more shareholders.

**33** *Kruhl* Ejeraftaler, 2011, pp. 57–66.

**34** See *Kruhl* Ejeraftaler, 2011, p. 61.

**35** On problems concerning consent clauses in general, see *Neville* Samtykkeklausuler in Hyldestskrift til Jørgen Nørgaard, 2003, p. 935–965.

**36** *Werlauff* Selskabsret, 2016, p. 440.

many shareholders' agreements contain other provisions on the transfer of shares that are not governed by the Companies Act. Drag-along and tag-along clauses are examples of such provisions. These are usually standard provisions whereby a private equity fund, business angel or the like[37] buy into the company. The 2011 study of shareholders' agreements in SMEs showed that 25 % of the agreements contain tag-along clauses. A 'tag-along clause' is a clause under which, if one shareholder wants to sell their shares to a third party, the other shareholders have a right to sell their shares on corresponding terms.[38] In some cases (44 % of the shareholders' agreements studied) tag-along clauses are only triggered by the transfer of control, involving more than 50 % of the voting rights. In other cases (23 %) something more than the transfer of control is required. And in yet other cases (33 %) any transfer of shares, regardless of the amount of voting rights, triggers a tag-along clause. As for 'drag-along', 15 % of the shareholders' agreements contained drag-along clauses, under which if one of the shareholders wishes to sell their shares the other parties are bound to sell their shares on corresponding terms. In the same way as with tag-along clauses, the obligation to sell is often triggered by a transfer of control (45 %), or by more than the transfer of control (28 %) or by any transfer at all (27 %).[39] In practice the two kinds of provisions are often linked, and of the 25% of agreements that contained a tag-along clause, in 44 % of the cases this was combined with a drag-along clause.

## III. Shareholders' Agreements on the constitution of the corporation

Under the Danish Companies Act the board of directors or the supervisory board of a public limited company are elected by a majority of the shareholders at the company's general meeting; see Section 120 of the Companies Act. For private companies no rules are laid down about who is to elect or nominate members of the board of directors or the supervisory board. This means that shareholders in private limited companies are free to decide in the articles of association whether a majority of the board members, the supervisory board or the management shall be chosen by others than the shareholders. In many companies, especially SMEs, there is often a desire that all the shareholders should have an

37 *Andersen* Etablering af Private Equity Funds, NTS 2005:4, p. 90 ff.
38 *Kruhl* Ejeraftaler, 2011, p. 64.
39 Ibid., p. 65.

influence on the company's overall management. There often are provisions in shareholders' agreements which derogate from the principle in the legislation, for example by providing that individual shareholders or groups of shareholders shall have a right to nominate one or more members to the board whom the other shareholders are bound to vote for at the general meeting.[40] For example, such provisions can be formulated as follows:

"The company's board shall consist of four member elected at the general meeting, who shall be nominated by the parties to this agreement as follows:

- A shall nominate two members
- B shall nominate two members.

The parties' nominations for members of the board shall be laid before the other parties prior to the general meeting. The parties are obliged to vote[41] for the nominated board members unless there are important commercial objections to doing so."

With the introduction of Section 82 of the Companies Act a company will no longer be bound by such agreements and the chairman of the general meeting cannot base decisions on them. See below in section V.6. on the possibility of moving such provisions to the articles of association.

Since the board is responsible for the overall strategic management of the company, the shareholders will often seek to bind the board in the exercise of its powers. This is often done by means of a provision in the shareholders' agreement requiring each shareholder to use their influence to ensure that the board members nominated by them and elected at the general meeting are made aware of the agreement and are bound to comply with its provisions in the exercise of their powers. Such provisions raise the question of whether the shareholders have powers to give instructions to the company's board and management. There are significant differences between the Member States on the extent to which national company laws allow shareholders to have either direct control over the company's operations or only indirect control by means of board appointments.[42] Under the Danish Companies Act the general meeting is the com-

**40** *Schans Christensen* Kapitalselskaber, 2015, p. 265.

**41** See *Müller/Werlauff* Vedtægter & Ejeraftaler, 2010, p. 82.

**42** According to *Gerner-Beuerle, Paech* and *Schüster's*, "Study on Directors' Duties and Liability", prepared for the European Commission DG Market, April 2013, p. 118, this depends on whether the shareholders are seen as the source of corporate power, with the directors being agents whose authority to make decisions on behalf of the company is delegated from the shareholders, or whether the directors receive their powers directly from statutory authorisation. This

pany's supreme body and has the right to take decisions on any company matter, unless the Act provides that such a decision is a matter for the board and/or the management.[43] A majority of shareholders can thus intervene in the management of the company at the general meeting, even concerning the company's day-to-day management.

Another question is whether an individual shareholder who has a right to make a nomination to the board can give instructions to 'their' board member about how they should act.[44] In principle this is not allowed. The role of a board member is independent and the shareholders cannot bind board members (or members of the supervisory board) by means of a shareholders' agreement in relation to the boards obligations under the Companies Act, for example to protect creditors by ensuring competent management of the company.[45] According to the Committee Report 1498/2008 on the Modernisation of Danish Company Law, p. 840: 'the company law rules are based on an assumption that the shareholders exercise their influence at the company's general meeting and that the responsibilities of board members are their personal responsibilities, so that board members are not subject to instruction'. That said, the situation will often be different in practice, as long as the interests of creditors are protected. For example, in SMEs if the board does not manage the company in line with the shareholders' interests the career of a board member will be short.

determines whether the shareholders have a right to instruct the management or intervene in strategic decisions.

**43** This is the case, for example, with the payment of dividends. The general meeting decides on dividends, but the meeting may not decide to pay a larger dividend than that proposed or approved by the board; see Section 182 of the Danish Companies Act. This is because the board is responsible for ensuring that the company has adequate financing; see Section 111 of the Companies Act. Another example is the appointment of the executive management. The power to appoint the management of a public company is a matter for the board, pursuant to Section 111(1) of the Act, and this is in line with the responsibility of the board to ensure that the company has a has an appropriate organisation; see Section 111.

**44** *Werlauff* Aktionæroverenskomstens retsvirkning for generalforsamling og bestyrelse, U 2008 B 207 ff.; *Lego Andersen* Mere om aktionæroverenskomstens retsvirkning for generalforsamling og bestyrelse, U 2008 B 425 ff.; and *Werlauff* Ejeraftalers selskabsretlige virkning, U 2009 B 119 ff.

**45** *Schans Christensen* Kapitalselskaber, 2015; *Werlauff* Ejeraftalers selskabsretlige virkning, U 2009 B 119; *Werlauff* Selskabsret, 2016, p. 440; and *Bang Sørensen/Jensen* Ejeraftaler efter selskabslovens § 82, NTS, 2009:4, p. 84.

## IV. Shareholders' Agreements in a pre-insolvency situation

In 2010 the Danish Parliament adopted a number of amendments to the Insolvency Act. Among other things, a new Part 1 A was introduced; see Sections 10 to 15b of the Insolvency Act. This means that if a debtor is insolvent they can either be declared bankrupt or, at the request of either the debtor or a creditor, they can enter into a reconstruction proceeding; see Section 11(1) of the Insolvency Act. The new rules on reconstruction were included with the aim of improving the chances of survival of undertakings that are in financial difficulties. The Act is aimed at improving the framework for effectively supporting the efforts of undertakings seeking reconstruction in order to limit the losses of creditors where this is a clear alternative to bankruptcy proceedings.[46] At the same time Part 1 A repealed the previous rules on the suspension of payments. The new reconstruction rules make distinct changes to the previous rules. Some of the most important of these are that, while a suspension of payments could only be requested by the debtor, reconstruction proceedings can also be initiated by a creditor. However, the debtor must, in principle, agree to this; see Section 11 (3) of the Insolvency Act. If the debtor is a company it is the central management organ (the management board or the supervisory board) that decides this. In the case of companies, reconstruction proceedings can be initiated without the agreement of the debtor (see Section 11a(3) of the Insolvency Act), in which case the administrator of the reconstruction automatically takes over the management of the business[47]; see below.

In reconstruction proceedings an administrator is appointed and it is envisaged that the administrator will play a more active role than was the case with the supervision of a suspension of payments. A plan must be drawn up for the reconstruction (see Section 11c of the Insolvency Act) which will be adopted unless a simple majority of the participating creditors vote against the plan and the proposal to carry out a reconstruction; see Section 11e of the Act. The requirements for the creditors' participation in a reconstruction proposal are thus less stringent than the previous rules on a compulsory agreement. Once reconstruction proceedings are initiated a request for reconstruction cannot be withdrawn; see Section 11e of the Act.[48] Reconstruction proceedings can lead either to a declaration of bankruptcy, compulsory arrangement with creditors or a transfer of the business. During reconstruction proceedings to which the debtor has agreed,

---

**46** See Betænkning 1512:2009 om Rekontruktion mv., p. 26 et seq.; *Petersen/Ørgaard* Konkursloven med kommentarer, 2013, p. 134 et seq.

**47** *Petersen/Ørgaard* Konkursloven med kommentarer, 2013, p. 176.

**48** *Petersen/Ørgaard* Konkursloven med kommentarer, 2013, p. 192.

the debtor will usually retain access to their assets, but the company may not make any major decisions without the consent of the administrator, and the payment of any debts may only be made in accordance with the bankruptcy order, unless payment is necessary in order to avoid loss; see Section 12 of the Act. Under Section 12c of the Act, there are a number of restrictions on creditors' rights to seek satisfaction of their claims from the debtor's assets during reconstruction proceedings. This is a precondition for a reconstruction being successful.

As stated above, the debtor retains control and the company's management continues to manage, subject to restrictions on their right to make such decision or dispositions as follow from the reconstruction agreement. The administrator or claimants that represent more than 25 % of the total known amount that gives a voting right can ask the bankruptcy court to authorise the administrator to take over the management of the company. This provision is aimed at situations where the claimants and/or the administrator disagree with the business decisions of the debtor (in practice, the company's management), or where the debtor does not wish to cooperate with the reconstruction plan or proposals put forward by the administrator. However, this provision could also be applicable in other circumstances, for example if the administrator or claimants do not have confidence in the debtor acting in good faith to implement the plan or if they find that the debtor is resisting the work of reconstruction. The same applies if the debtor's management resigns and new management is not appointed quickly. If the bankruptcy court grants the request the administrator will replace all the management organs and, *pari passu*, will have the obligations and responsibilities that follow from Section 111 of the Companies Act. However, the administrator will not take over the role of the general meeting. Under Section 12(6) of the Insolvency Act, if the debtor is an association registered by the Danish Business Authority, an administrator who has taken over the management of an undertaking may not make decisions on matters that should be dealt with at a general meeting, other than the election of the auditor.[49] The commentary on the Act refers in particular to decisions to amend the articles of association. This means that the administrator may not make decisions on raising or reducing the company's capital, for example. This provision means that the general meeting keeps its role as the company's highest authority, but even if all the shareholders agree the general meeting may not adopt a valid decision without the agreement of the administrator. The extent of the powers of an administrator are not clear from the Act, and the *travaux préparatoires* only contain a few

49 *Petersen/Ørgaard* Konkursloven med kommentarer, 2013, p. 209.

short comments which are a matter of debate among legal academics.[50] It is outside the scope of this contribution to discuss the extent of the provision in greater detail.

As for the significance of shareholders' agreements in the event of a reconstruction, in SMEs such agreements often contain provision which can have a major impact on the possibility of implementing the measures necessary for a reconstruction, for example the requirement for unanimity for important decisions such as capital increases, capital reductions or the sale of significant parts of the business. This raises the question of the extent to which such agreements must be respected in connection with reconstructions. When there is a reconstruction there will often be a need for additional capital, and banks imposing a condition that, if their involvement is to continue, the shareholders must contribute additional capital. If there is to be a capital increase, then unless the board has been authorised to increase the capital, such a decision must be taken by the general meeting, and according to Section 157 (together with Section 106) of the Companies Act, such a decision must be taken by a two-thirds majority. However, shareholders' agreements often contain provisions whereby decisions such as increases of capital require the unanimity of the shareholders. This means that a single shareholder will be able to prevent a capital increase that is essential for ensuring a reconstruction. Since the general meeting has retained its decision-making powers, subject to the restrictions referred to above, a shareholders' agreement should presumably not be treated differently whether or not there are reconstruction proceedings. According to Section 82 of the Companies Act, this means that an agreement cannot be enforced by the shareholders at a general meeting.

However, shareholders' agreements not only contain provisions on decisions taken at general meetings. In SMEs, including family-owned companies, shareholders' agreements often contain provisions whereby decision that are typically a matter for the management organ, such as the sale of parts of the business, sale of the company's real property, appointment of personnel etc., must be made by the shareholders, often by a unanimous decision; see the example given above in section III.1.1a. Since shareholders' agreements are not binding

**50** It has been discussed whether Section 12(6) comply with Article 25(1) in the Directive 77/91/EØF. According to Article 25, the General Assembly has the power to increase the share capital. See for the discussion *Hansen/Krenchel* Dansk Selskabsret 2, 2014, p. 724, *Hansen* Rekonstruktørens kompetence i selskabs- og grundretlig belysning, Ugeskrift for Retsvæsen 2010B.401, *Christensen* Nogle spørgsmål om ledelsesovertagelse, Ugeskrift for Retsvæsen, 2011B.117; *Bang-Pedersen/Christensen/Sommer/Madsen/Mylin* Rekonstruktion – teori og praksis, 2011, p. 193; *Petersen/Ørgaard* Konkursloven med kommentarer, 2013, p. 209.

on the company (see Section 82 of the Companies Act), they will presumably not be binding on an administrator who has taken over the management of the company. This also suggests that in this situation the protected interests are less those of the shareholders and more those of the creditors.

# D. Legal Effects of Shareholders' Agreements Legal Effects on the Corporation

## I. Shareholders' Agreements as an aid to interpretation

While a shareholders' agreement may not be enforceable against the company, they may nevertheless play a role in relation to the company in some circumstances. For example, shareholders' agreement may have an indirect role in the interpretation of the company's articles of association.[51] In principle the articles of association must be interpreted objectively,[52] that is in accordance to the wording of the provisions. In smaller companies, where all the shareholders have taken part in drawing up the articles of association and where there has been no change in the identities of the shareholders, there is not the same need for consideration of new shareholders so that subjecting the provisions of the articles to an interpretation according to their purpose is not excluded when seeking to determine their intention; see e.g. U 1994.234 H.[53] In these cases it must be assumed that the shareholders' agreement will be one of the aids to interpretation if the intentions of the parties' articles of association are to be determined.[54]

51 *Jensen* Ejerftaler in Neville/Sørensen (eds.), Den nye Selskabslov, 2009, pp. 181–208 (p. 193).
52 *Nørgaard/Werlauff* Vedtægter og aktionæroverenskomster, 1995, p. 34 et seq.
53 *Nørgaard/Werlauff* Vedtægter og aktionæroverenskomster 1995, p. 37: *Neville* Samtykkeklausuler in Kristensen/Iversen/Werlauff (eds.): Hyldestskrift til Jørgen Nørgaard, 2003, p. 935–965; and *Jensen* in NTS 2007:3, pp. 106–124.
54 *Jensen* Ejerftaler in Mette Neville & Karsten Engsig Sørensen (eds.), Den nye Selskabslov, 2009, pp. 181–208 (p. 203).

## II. The significance of Shareholders' Agreements for the formation of corporate groups in Danish law

According to the Danish Companies Act, shareholders' agreements can also be taken into account in determining whether a corporate group exists. Under Section 7 of the Act there will be a corporate group either when a parent company owns more than half the voting rights or has control of another company pursuant to Section 7(3) of the Act. Under Section 7(3), control exists if the parent company has:

1) the power to exercise more than half of the voting rights by virtue of an agreement with other investors;
2) the power to control the financial and operating policies of a business under any articles of association or agreement;
3) the power to appoint or remove the majority of the members of the supreme governing body, and this body has control of the business; or
4) the power to exercise the actual majority of votes at general meetings or an equivalent body and thus the actual control of the business.

As can be seen, the control referred to under points 1 to 3 can be derived from the provisions of a shareholders' agreement.[55] If it is determined that a group exists, the provisions of the Companies Act on corporate groups must be complied with, as well as the requirement under Section 109 of the Financial Statements Act for corporate groups to submit a group financial statement and for subsidiary companies to give information about closely related parties under Section 98 C of the Act and information in connection with takeover bids; see Section 107a of the Act.

55 *Werlauff* Selskabsret, 2016, p. 442, states that Section 7(3), nos 1–4, of the Companies Act on the formation of a corporate group can only operate as intended if at least some of the elements of a shareholders agreement nevertheless actually bind the company and that in this case Section 82 of the Act must be derogated from to a sufficient extent on the basis of the principle of *lex specialis*.

# E. Legal effects on the shareholders

## I. Publication and registration of Shareholders' Agreements

In principle, a shareholders' agreement is a private agreement and, in contrast to the articles of association, it neither must nor can be made public.[56] Since a shareholders' agreement is not valid against third parties who act in good faith, the shareholders may have an interest in making third parties aware of the agreement, so the actions of a third party will no longer be excusable on the ground they were acting in good faith. This will ensure the enforceability of agreements against third parties. Thus, the practice has arisen of including provisions in the articles of association stating that a shareholders' agreement has been entered into, for example restricting the transferability of shares. However, it was argued in the *travaux prêparatoires* to Section 28 that, according to the practice of the Danish Business Authority the articles of association cannot refer to a shareholders' agreement.[57] Some legal scholars dispute whether the Business Authority can refuse the registration of provisions that link articles of association to shareholders' agreements.[58] However, the Authority does allow a link to be made between private law agreements and a company's articles, for example in connection with provisions on pre-emption rights. The same is the case with consent clauses (Section 68 of the Companies Act), under which a company must consent to the transfer of shares. Here it can be stated that guidelines in the shareholders' agreement will be followed.[59]

---

**56** *Kruhl* Ejeraftaler, 2011, p. 79. In connection with the introduction of Section 82 of the Companies Act the parliamentary committee considered whether a shareholders agreement could be binding on the company, and whether there should be a requirement to make such agreements public as in the case of the articles of association. Since the committee confirmed that shareholders agreements are agreements between the parties involved which, in contrast to the articles of association, and that company law is not relevant to their validity, the committee was of the view that there was no reason to introduce a requirement to publish such agreements; see the Report 1498/2008, p. 282. However, shareholders agreements in listed companies which are significant to assessing prospectuses must be described in the prospectus, in so far as the company is aware of them.

**57** See Vejledning om Ejeraftaler (Aktionæroverenskomster) published by Erhvervsstyrelsen, July 2010.

**58** *Kruhl* Ejeraftaler, 2011, p. 107 ff.

**59** See Vejledning om Ejeraftaler (Aktionæroverenskomster) published by Erhvervsstyrelsen, July 2010, p. 3.

## II. The significance of Shareholders' Agreements for others than the parties

A question can arise about the significance of a shareholders' agreement in relation to an acquirer of shares, for example. This is a complex and much debated issue in Danish law.[60] In the case of a transfer of shares to a third party, where the transferor has entered into a shareholders' agreement that gives the other shareholders' rights such as a pre-emption right, tag-along rights, redemption rights etc., it must be assumed that the shareholders' agreement can be enforced against a transferee if they knew or ought to have known about the agreement.[61] The interesting and much debated question is whether there can be situations where a transferee of shares acting in good faith is bound by a shareholders' agreement. Martin Cristian Kruhl has written in detail on this subject in *Ejeraftaler*, 2011, p. 254 f., with references to, among other things, the judgments U 1960.304 H and U 1998.1743 Ø. He assumes that Section 65 of the Companies Act[62] either directly or analogously means that disposition rights such as pre-emption rights can benefit from the protection of rights *in rem* if the measures taken to protect such rights include making a declaration to the company or to the keeper of the company's register of shareholders.[63]

As for provisions in a shareholders' agreement on administrative rights, such as a binding agreement on voting, these do not concern the disposition of shares and are thus presumably not covered by Section 65 of the Companies Act, either

---

**60** *Kruhl* Ejeraftaler, 2011, p. 107 ff., with references.

**61** *Gomard* Aktieselskabsret, 1970, p. 269; and *Werlauff* Generalforsamling og beslutning, 1983, p. 241.

**62** Section 65(1) of the Companies Act states: *"Any transfer of a share that has not been issued through a securities centre, or for which no share certificate has been issued in ownership or by way of security, will only be effective against the creditors of the transferor if the limited liability company or the keeper of the register of shareholders (see section 50(3)) has received notice of such transfer from the transferor or the transferee"*. Section 65(2) states: *"Where a shareholder has transferred the same share to more than one transferee and the share is governed by subsection (1), any subsequent transferee takes priority over prior transferees once the limited liability company or the keeper of the register of shareholders (see section 50(3)) has received notice of the transfer to the subsequent transferee, provided that the subsequent transferee acted in good faith when the company or the keeper of the register of shareholders received the notice"*.

**63** *Schans Christensen* Kapitalselskaber, 2015, p. 263; *Andersen* Paradigma – Aktionæroverenskomster, 2000, p. 47; and *Johansen* Forkøbs- og køberettigheders tinglige beskyttelse in U 2010 B 245, where it is also stated that Section 82 of the Companies Act does not prevent the notification of a pre-emption right.

directly or analogously.[64] In theory it is assumed that a transferee who is either aware or ought to have been aware that the transferor was bound by a shareholders' agreement, and that, as will usually be the case, the agreement will prevent the transfer of the shares without maintaining a binding agreement, cannot oppose an agreement on voting rights even though the transferor has not imposed such a condition on the share transfer and even if the transferee has not undertaken to respect the agreement.[65]

While a shareholders' agreement is an agreement under private law, it can be relevant to a number of shareholders' obligations.

## III. Mandatory offers

Section 44–46 of the Law on Capital Markets[66] contains the Danish provisions on mandatory offers. In the same way as with the formation of a corporate group, the obligation to make a mandatory offer can be triggered if, for example, provisions in a shareholders' agreement establish control by a shareholder or a group of shareholders. There will be an obligation to make a mandatory offer if there is the transfer of a shareholding in a company that has one or more classes of shares that are traded on a regulated market or an alternative investment market to a transferee or to persons who act in concert. In such a case the transferee must give all the shareholders in the company the possibility of disposing of their shares on the same terms if the initial transfer means that the transferee obtains control of the company; see Section 44(2). Under Section 44(2) control will exist if the transferee directly or indirectly has at least one third of the voting rights of a company, unless in special circumstances it can be shown that such ownership does not give control. Moreover, under Section 44(2) there will be control if a transferee who does not have at least one third of the voting rights in a company has control over at least one third of the voting rights by virtue of an

64 *Lego Andersen* Aktionæroverenskomster, 2000, p. 49, argues that administrative rights should be treated in the same way as rights to dispose of shares, since a decision to the contrary would result in a law based on abstract principles. For a criticism of this see *Kruhl* Ejeraftaler 2011, p. 258.

65 *Gomard* Aktieselskabsret, 1970, p. 269; *Nørgaar/Werlauff* Vedtægt- og aktionæroverenskomster, 1995, p. 75; and *Kruhl* Ejeraftaler, 2011, p. 260. However, see *Schaumburg-Müller/Werlauff* Vedtægter og ejeraftaler, 2010, p. 96, who seem to believe that shareholders agreements cannot be enforced against transferees, whether or not they are acting in good faith.

66 Lov nr. 650 of 816 2017. On mandatory bid see *Section* 44–46.

agreement with other shareholders or powers to appoint or dismiss the majority of the members of the company's Board of directors or Supervisory Board.

## IV. Making public major shareholdings

Shareholders' agreements are also relevant to the obligation to make public the existence of significant shareholdings; see Section 38–44 in the Law on Capital Markets which applies to listed companies, and Section 28a of the Companies Act which applies to unlisted companies. While, in principle, the obligation to give information under Section 28 is linked to the ownership of shares, under Section 28a to these are added shares whose voting rights belong to an undertaking that is controlled by that shareholder, as referred to in Section 7 of the Companies Act. Thus, according to this, control can be based on the provisions of an agreement.

## V. Consequences of a breach of a Shareholders' Agreement

As can be seen from the above, pursuant to Section 82 of the Companies Act a shareholders' agreement cannot be enforced at the company's general meeting, so it is not possible to challenge a resolution of a general meeting on the ground that it is contrary to a shareholders' agreement. However, while a shareholders' agreement is not enforceable at a general meeting, it is binding on the parties to it and must be complied with by them. If a shareholders' agreement is breached, an injured party can invoke the usual remedies for breach of contract[67] in civil proceedings or in arbitration in so far as the agreement provides for this; see part V. The extent to which a breach of a shareholders' agreement will be relevant to the continued participation of the defaulting shareholder will depend on the content of the agreement. Provisions are often included in such agreements whereby in the event of a serious breach of an agreement, the other shareholders are entitled to buy the shares of the defaulting shareholder at a reduced valuation.

67 *Schaumburg-Müller/Werlauff* Vedtægter og ejeraftaler 2010, p. 105 et seq. and *Schans Christensen* Kapitalselskaber, 2015, p. 239.

# F. Enforcement of Shareholders' Agreements

As stated above, where there is a breach of a shareholders' agreement, an injured party can usually claim remedies in civil proceedings before a court or arbitration tribunal, in so far as the agreement provides for this. There follows a review of such remedies.

## I. Compensation

If a party breaches a shareholders' agreement, the injured parties can claim compensation. In order to obtain compensation the general conditions for obtaining compensation must be fulfilled,[68] including there being a loss suffered by the claimants. In practice loss can be difficult to prove, for example from the lack of payment of a dividend or the failure to appoint the agreed management.

## II. Termination of the agreement

Breach of a shareholders' agreement can also give the injured parties a right to terminate the agreement. According to the general rules of the law of obligations, the termination of an agreement because of its breach requires the breach to have been material[69] and the claim to be made without undue delay. A time limit for making a claim can be included in the agreement.[70]

Whether it is appropriate to terminate the agreement will depend on the consequences of the defaulting party no longer being a party to the agreement. Whether a breach will affect the defaulting shareholder's participation in the company will depend on the content of the agreement. As an alternative to termination, shareholders' agreements often contain provisions stating that a material breach of the agreement will lead to a right to acquire the defaulting shareholder's shares at market price, subject to a discount for the breach.

---

**68** In addition the loss that must have been suffered by the injured parties, the party in breach must have acted culpably, the loss must be accountable to their actions and there must be a causal connection between the culpable acts of the party in breach and the loss of the injured parties. On the conditions for claiming compensation for breach of contract, see *Kruhl* Ejeraftaler, 2011, p. 223 ff.

**69** *Gomard* Obligationsret Del 1, 2016, s.37 et seq.

**70** *Kruhl* Ejeraftaler, 2011, p. 228.

## III. Judgment for specific performance

In principle the injured parties will be able to claim specific performance, under which the defaulting party can be required by a court to exercise their voting rights in accordance with the agreement, and this can be enforced by a bailiff. However, this approach is little used in practice as it requires a judgment of the court, which is both costly and involves delay, so that judgment will first be given, after the breach has occurred.

## IV. Injunction

If, prior to a general meeting, there is a suspicion that one of the parties will breach the shareholders' agreement, it may be possible to obtain an injunction and thereby prevent the casting of votes in breach of the agreement or to prevent a sale of shares contrary to the agreement. However, this requires the conditions in chapter 40 of the Administration of Justice Act to be met.[71] The imposition of an injunction only affects future voting; it does not make it possible to retrospectively enforce voting in compliance with an agreement. An injunction is a less powerful measure than an order for specific performance, but it allows measures to be taken more quickly.

## V. The significance of a breach of an agreement for the imposition of sanctions under the Companies Act

While a shareholders' agreement is a private law measure whose breach is subject to the civil law, it is assumed that a breach of an agreement can be relevant to the imposition of sanctions under the Companies Act. According to Section 362(2) of the Act, 'If any shareholder has, intentionally or by gross negligence, caused a loss to the company, other shareholders, the company's creditors or other third parties, and there is a risk of continued abuse, the court may order that shareholder to redeem the shares belonging to the shareholder who suffers a loss at a reasonable price which is to be fixed with regard to the company's financial position and the circumstances of the case.' Under Section 362(2) the court has powers to require a defaulting shareholder to sell their shares to the injured shareholders. It is clearly stated in the *travaux préparatoires* to the pro-

71 *Schaumburg-Müller/Werlauff* Vedtægter og ejeraftaler, 2010, p. 208.

vision that: 'even though shareholders' agreements cannot affect the validity of the decisions of a company under company law, the breach of such an agreement can have company law consequences, as a breach can be taken into account in assessing whether a shareholder is in gross breach of their obligations to the other shareholders in the company; see Section 377 of the Companies Act.

## VI. The regulation of breaches in the Shareholders' Agreement

Since the usual remedies for breach often have the same effect for breaches of shareholders' agreement as for breaches of other kinds of agreement (see above[72]), sanctions for breach are often governed in the agreement in order to ensure that the desired power structure can be maintained. Often there are provisions on conventional fines or provisions that injured shareholders have the right to buy the shares of the defaulting shareholder, possibly at an advantageous price, or that the injured shareholders have a tight to sell their shares to the defaulting shareholder.[73]

Another possibility is to transfer some of the provisions currently found in the shareholders' agreement to the articles of association, for example provisions on pre-emption rights, tag-along and in particular provisions on special majorities etc.[74] However, not all kinds of provisions can be transferred to the articles without further thought, and there is often a strong desire not to make public the content of a shareholders' agreement. Moreover the Danish Business Authority requires the provisions to be relevant to the articles of association.[75]

---

**72** *Kruhl* Ejeraftaler, 2011, p. 228.

**73** *Schans Christensen* Kapitalselskaber, 2015, p. 266.

**74** *Schans Christensen* Kapitalselskaber, 2015, p. 240 et seq.

**75** See *Krüger Andersen* Aktie- og anpartsselskabsret. Kapitalselskaber, 2017, p. 181; *Hansen* Ejeraftaler og hensynet til tredjemands indsigt i selskabet, Nordisk Tidsskrift for Selskabsret, 2012:1, p. 31 and *Kruhl* Nogle bemærkninger til Søren Friis Hansen, Nordisk Tidsskrift for Selskabsret, 2012 3:4, p. 43.

Rafal Zakrzewski

# England and Wales

**Table of Contents**



## I. Nature of Corporate Law Regulation

The main sources of English (and Welsh) law relating to companies are the Companies Act 2006, and the body of case law developed by the courts. Publicly traded companies are also subject to securities laws stemming from the Financial Services and Markets Act 2000, regulations made under that Act and the rules included in the FCA Handbook such as the Listing Rules, the Prospectus Rules, and the Disclosure and Transparency Rules. The securities laws imple-

---


**Dr Rafal Zakrzewski**, Solicitor (England & Wales), BA LLB (UQ), DPhil (Oxon)



https://doi.org/10.1515/9783110517026-013

ment relevant EC Directives. Shareholders' agreements may also trigger competition law consequences under EC and national law.[1]

The Companies Act 2006 stipulates that every company must have articles of association, which must be registered with the registrar of companies at Companies House.[2] The articles of association are characterised as an agreement among the shareholders which is also binding on future shareholders. Their purpose is to regulate the day to day internal management of the company: they govern the relationships between the board of directors and the shareholders and amongst the shareholders themselves.

Usually the articles of association either apply by default[3] in the model form prescribed by regulations made under the Companies Act,[4] are adopted as modifications to that model form[5] or are adopted in a free standing alternative form. The articles of association registered by a company must be contained in a single document and be divided into numbered paragraphs.[6] The model articles deal with the following management and administrative matters: directors' powers and responsibilities, decision-making by directors (including directors' meetings and conflicts of interest), appointment of directors, shares (including their issue and transfer) and distributions of funds, decision-making by shareholders (including procedures for shareholders' meetings), administrative matters and directors' indemnity and insurance.

The articles of association are registered at Companies House and are open to inspection by the public.[7] Section 33 of the Companies Act 2006 provides that the articles of association bind the company and its members to the same extent as if there were a contract on the part of the company and of each member to

1 However competition law aspects of shareholders' agreements are outside the scope of this chapter.

2 Companies Act 2006, s 18(1).

3 Companies Act 2006, s 20.

4 The Companies (Model Articles) Regulations 2008 (SI 2008/3229). Standard sets of articles have been prescribed by regulations for the three most common types of companies: private companies limited by shares; private companies limited by guarantees; and public companies. Formerly these were Tables A to F of the Companies Act 1985.

5 Companies Act 2006, s 19(3). See, for example, the model articles of association for early stage investments published by the British Venture Capital Association at http://www.bvca.co.uk.

6 Companies Act 2006, s 18(3).

7 However, third parties not affected by limitations in the articles of association unless they deal with the company in bad faith – Companies Act 2006, s 40; but shareholders are not third parties for these purposes: *EIC Services v Stephen Phipps* [2004] EWCA 1069.

observe those provisions.[8] New shareholders are automatically bound by this statutory contract contained in the articles.

The shareholders can amend the company's articles of association by special resolution,[9] that is, a resolution passed by a 75% majority of votes at a general meeting or by written resolution.[10] A shareholder cannot be forced to contribute more money to the company by an amendment to the articles which he or she does not consent to.[11] It is possible for articles to contain "provisions for entrenchment" which provide that specified provisions of the articles may be amended or repealed only if conditions are met, or procedures complied with, that are more restrictive than in respect of a special resolution, for example, by requiring unanimous consent of the shareholders.[12] It is also possible to entrench provisions in the articles by employing one of three other mechanisms. First, voting rights may be weighted, for example, by stipulating in the articles that the shareholder's voting rights increase in respect of certain matters such as the removal of a director.[13] Secondly, by creating class rights such as by stipulating that a certain matter is a class right attaching to certain shares; it can then only be amended by a special resolution passed by the relevant class, i.e. by a 75% majority of that class.[14] Finally, it is possible to entrench rights by contract, that is, by undertakings as to voting set out in a shareholders' agreement.

Freedom of contract prevails and shareholders are generally entitled to agree in the articles of association of their company whatever they see fit.[15] For example different classes of shares, with different voting rights and different entitlements to dividends and a return of capital may be set out in the articles, and the articles may provide for anti-dilution protection through the issue of new shares. They may also regulate transfers of shares in detail, including by setting

---

**8** Thus shareholders can clearly sue the company under the articles and vice-versa, but some doubts have been expressed as to whether shareholders can sue each other under the articles of association: *Welton v Saffrey* [1897] AC 299; *Hickman v Kent or Romney Marsh Sheep Breeders' Association* [1915] 1 Ch 881; cf *Hurst v Crampton Bros (Coopers) Ltd* [2002] EWHC 1375 (Ch). Of course no such doubts exist in respect of shareholders' agreements.
**9** Companies Act 2006, s 21(1).
**10** Companies Act 2006, s 283.
**11** Companies Act 2006, s 25.
**12** Companies Act 2006, s 22.
**13** *Bushell v Faith* [1970] AC 1099.
**14** Companies Act 2006, s 630.
**15** Articles of association, as well as shareholders' agreements, are generally exempt from judicial control under the Unfair Contract Terms Act 1977.

out tag-along and drag-along rights.[16] The articles may also provide for other bespoke matters such as borrowing limits, and permissions for directors to share information with shareholders who nominated them for appointment. Commercially sensitive or very complex matters are not regulated in the articles of association. Instead shareholders often agree side-contracts, such as shareholders' agreements, to implement bespoke and confidential solutions without revealing their arrangements to third parties, including competitors, potential investors, customers or employees.

In order to understand the rationale and need for shareholders' agreements, it is first necessary to consider what rights a shareholder, in particular, a minority shareholder in a private company, would have vis-a-vis the company and the other shareholders as a matter of general corporate law, and assuming only the model form articles had been adopted. For these purposes, a minority shareholder is someone who cannot prevent the other shareholders from controlling the composition of the board of directors and the management of the business. In the absence of special rights such control will be with the holders of a simple majority of voting rights – because they can appoint directors by an ordinary resolution. As a matter of common law doctrine, a minority shareholder cannot sue for a wrong done to the company or in respect of an internal irregularity where the majority can lawfully ratify it.[17]

As a matter of general corporate law, a minority shareholder has some limited "negative control"; he or she has the ability to prevent the passing of certain resolutions (for example, if the minority holds more than 25 % of voting rights, it can block special resolutions such as those proposing changes to articles or a winding up of the company). Holders of fifteen percent or more shares of a class can bring an action objecting to an alteration of those class rights.[18] A minority shareholder also has certain specific statutory rights, including a statutory pre-emption right requiring offers of new shares for cash to be made to existing shareholders on a pre-emptive basis[19] and the right of holders of five percent or

**16** See, for example, the model articles of association for early stage investments published by the British Venture Capital Association at http://www.bvca.co.uk.

**17** Thus a minority shareholder cannot effectively complain in respect of breaches of authority by directors or breaches of duty by directors because of the so-called rule in *Foss v Harbottle* (1843) 2 Hare 461.

**18** Companies Act 2006, s 633.

**19** Companies Act 2006, s 561. In the case of private companies, this right can be excluded in the articles of association.

more of the company's shares to requisition a general meeting or instigate a written resolution.[20]

The minority shareholders also have some rights to bring an action to obtain relief from an English court in particular circumstances. First, the minority can bring a common law action alleging fraud on the minority, namely, that an alteration of the articles is not bona fide for the benefit of the company as a whole.[21] Secondly, they can bring petitions for relief on the ground of "unfairly prejudicial conduct" under section 994 of the Companies Act 2006; for example, due to a failure to pay dividends without good reasons or mismanagement by the directors or misappropriation of assets. If the case is made out, the court may make such order as it thinks fit; for example, and perhaps most importantly in this context, for the petitioner's shares to be purchased by the majority. Thirdly, the minority has a right to petition for winding up on the "just and equitable" ground under section 122(1)(g) of the Insolvency Act 1986; for example, due to deadlock[22] or due to breach of some formal or informal agreement between the shareholders.[23] Finally, a minority shareholder may be able to bring a derivative claim on behalf of the company under section 260 of the Companies Act 2006. A derivative claim is a proceeding for a wrong done to the company which seeks relief on behalf of the company. Such claims may be brought after obtaining the court's permission.

In the context of a minority shareholders' statutory causes of action, it is also necessary note that the existence and content of a shareholders' agreement is taken into account as a relevant consideration in determining whether the statutory remedies ought to be granted: a shareholders' agreement can be treated by the court as being exhaustive of a minority shareholder's rights and remedies. This can be said to promote certainty.

As the above shows, the rights of a minority shareholder are not extensive. The balance that is struck by the default legal rules is usually inappropriate for a minority shareholder. Additionally the court actions referred to above involve a good deal of discretion on the part of the court: they can be uncertain, drawn out and expensive. Therefore shareholders will commonly insist on having their rights supplemented in a shareholders' agreement before subscribing for shares in the company or acquiring them from another shareholder.

**20** Companies Act 2006, ss 292 and 303.

**21** *Allen v Gold Reefs of West Africa Ltd* [1900] 1 Ch 656.

**22** *Re Yenidje Tobacco* [1916] 2 Ch 426.

**23** *Ebrahimi v Westbourne Galleries Ltd* [1973] AC 360.

# II. Regulation of Shareholders' Agreements

## 1. General Remarks

Shareholders' agreements are not subject to any specific legal regulation. The generally applicable rules of contract law apply. They are simply contracts enforceable on ordinary contract law principles. Shareholders' agreements do not need to be permitted by the articles of association or any bylaws of the company. It is left to the shareholders to determine whether they want to regulate the relationship between them by further supplementing the general rules of corporate law and the provisions of the articles of association which have been adopted by the company. The doctrine of freedom of contract allows the parties great latitude in determining the content of the matters they wish to regulate in a shareholders' agreement. A shareholders' agreement can be a contract between all of the shareholders or just a sub-set of them. For example, in the case of a management buy-out transaction, employee shareholders may be excluded from the shareholders' agreement that is entered into between the investment fund and the management shareholders.

Unlike articles of association, there are no rules as to the form in which a shareholders' agreement is to be entered into or the way in which it may be amended. Consequently shareholders' agreements can be entered into and amended in a more flexible and informal manner.[24] But like all contracts they cannot be varied without consent of all the parties, unless they provide otherwise. Additionally since they are not registered with Companies House and hence not disclosed to the public, they can remain confidential between the parties.

Since the general principles of contract law apply, the parties are free to decide what matters they wish to regulate by means of a shareholders' agreement, and whether to inform the other shareholders or the company itself of the existence or the content of the agreement. Hence in theory there is almost an infinite range of possibilities as to what can regulated in a shareholders' agreement and how. However, in practice the content of shareholders' agreements is shaped by problems that minority shareholders would otherwise face if there was no such agreement in place. First, minority shareholders often complain of poor management by the majority or that they are completely excluded from management and from important decisions in respect of the company. Secondly, they have limited

24 Shareholders' agreements can also be amended informally through the conduct of all the parties thereto: *Euro Brokers Holdings Ltd v Monecor (London) Ltd* [2003] EWCA Civ 105.

access to information regarding the company; in a private company they only have a right to annual audited accounts and to inspect minutes of general meetings (not directors' meetings).[25] Thirdly, in private companies minority shareholders often have no freedom to transfer their shares to third parties.[26] Fourthly, minority shareholders may complain about the lack of dividends being paid and therefore having a limited participation in profits.[27] Fifthly, the majority may pay its connected parties excessive remuneration under services contracts or as remuneration for holding the office of directors. Sixthly, the majority may operate a competing business and thereby not put sufficient resources into growing the company's business. Consequently shareholders agreements often contain provisions addressed towards each of the above problems.

## 2. Scope of Shareholders' Agreements

Shareholders' agreements are an important tool for regulating the ongoing relationship between shareholders in respect of the company. They are supplemental to the articles of association. By utilising a shareholders' agreement, a minority shareholder can increase its influence on the management and future direction of the business of the company. The shareholder can secure for itself the right to nominate directors to be appointed to the company's board of directors or perhaps even nominate key personnel of the company.

The typical matters that are regulated by shareholders' agreements in respect of private companies include, among other things: the regulation of governance rights, the exercise of voting rights and decision making (including vetoes of major decisions), rights to receive information regarding the company's business, provisions regarding the transfer of shares to third parties and the exit of shareholders. In addition, shareholders' agreements also usually regulate: the distribution of profits, the provision of finance to the company (most commonly through capital increases or shareholder loans), and related party transactions.

---

**25** In a public company minority shareholders have greater access to information because of regulation: the Listing Rules place continuing disclosure obligations on listed companies and the City Code on Takeovers and Mergers tries to ensure that in respect of a takeover bid shareholders are treated fairly and equally.

**26** For example, under article 26.5 of the model articles, the board of directors has a discretion to register a transfer of shares by a shareholder.

**27** The model articles make the payment of dividends a decision of the board of directors.

Non-compete provisions and other restrictive covenants are also often included in private company shareholders' agreements.[28]

Many of the above matters can also be regulated in the company's articles of association. It is often a matter of convention, market practice or a particular client's or legal practitioner's individual preference as to whether particular rights are regulated in the company's articles or a shareholders' agreement. The factors that dictate whether it would be more appropriate to regulate a particular matter in a shareholders' agreement or the company's articles include the following. First, dealing with a matter in a shareholders' agreement preserves confidentiality; articles on the other hand are filed with Companies House and open to public inspection. Secondly, shareholders' agreements are used to confer rights which would not be enforceable in the articles; i.e. "personal rights" conferred on shareholders not in their capacity as shareholders; e.g. certain personal rights such as to be a professional adviser to the company or to be paid for providing other services.[29] Thirdly, shareholders' agreements are used to regulate "relationships between shareholders" which are not related to the administration of the company, such as obligations not to compete with the company. Fourthly, shareholders' agreements have traditionally been used to protect minority rights (such as the power of a minority shareholder to veto certain actions which the company may take). This is because the shareholders' agreement, being a contract between the parties, requires all parties to agree to any changes, as opposed to the articles which may be amended by a special resolution. This point is now less of a concern than before the Companies Act 2006 was enacted because section 22 of that Act has made it easier to entrench minority rights in the articles. Fifthly, another advantage of embodying rights in a shareholders' agreement as opposed to articles of association is the administrative ease of amending a shareholders' agreement – there is no need to pass resolutions or to file anything. Finally, in an international context, a shareholders' agreement gives the parties freedom to choose the law by which their agreement will be governed and to select the appropriate means and forum for dispute resolution.

---

**28** Shareholders often want to protect their investment by not having other shareholders preferring their own interests by competing with the company or taking advantage of opportunities it generates. Restrictions typically include: covenants not to compete; covenants not to solicit customers; and covenants not to solicit employees. Such restrictions will be restricted by scope of activities, geographic area and duration. However, as a matter of English law, such restrictions must be justified as reasonable in the interests of the parties and the public or they will be declared void: *Dawnay Day & Co* [1997] IRLR 442.

**29** *Hickman v Kent or Romney Marsh Sheep Breeders' Association* [1915] 1 Ch 881, 900.

In contradistinction it is more appropriate to regulate a matter in the articles of association rather than in a shareholders' agreement when the parties want all shareholders to be automatically bound without requiring new shareholders to execute a separate document. Additionally a shareholders' agreement may be simply impractical where the company will have an excessively large number of shareholders.

## 3. Disclosure / Non-disclosure / Confidentiality

Generally it is not necessary to disclose the content or even the existence of shareholders' agreements. Subject to the observations made below, they do not have to be submitted for registration in the companies register at Companies House. Therefore third parties are usually not aware of the fact that the shareholders are contractually bound by agreements which impose obligations in addition to the articles of association.

While articles of association are disclosed because they must be registered with Companies House and therefore are easily accessible to third parties, shareholders' agreements usually contain non-disclosure and confidentiality clauses which cover their content and existence and confidential information relating to the company. It is important to note that there appears to be no implied right to disclose information that is covered by such a clause in order to allow an effective sale of a shareholder's shares. Therefore, if the shareholders' agreement contains a confidentiality clause which does not permit disclosure of confidential information to potential purchasers, the shareholder will not be able to make such a disclosure, even if this is proposed to be done subject to a non-disclosure agreement.[30]

It is important to be aware that an agreement agreed by all the shareholders (or a class of them) and which would not otherwise be effective for its purpose unless passed by a special resolution must be registered with Companies House.[31] It will then be publicly available. The case of *Re Duomatic Ltd*[32] decided that where all shareholders are a party to it, a decision or an agreement may have effect as a corporate act, that is, it may have effect as a resolution of the general meeting of the company. Consequently if a shareholders' agreement to which all the shareholders are parties overrides the provisions of the articles

**30** *Richmond Pharmacology Ltd v Chester Overseas Ltd & Ors* [2014] EWHC 2692.
**31** Companies Act 2006, ss 29 and 30.
**32** [1969] 1 All ER 161.

of association, it would have the effect of a special resolution and amend the articles of association. Therefore it would have to be registered. A failure to do so is a breach of the Companies Act punishable by a fine. To prevent the need to register the shareholders' agreement, a provision is sometimes included that in the event of a conflict with the articles of association, the shareholders shall use their voting rights to amend the articles. The effect of this is considered to be that the shareholders' agreement does not itself amend the articles and hence the requirement to register it does not arise.

A shareholders' agreement could also trigger other registration requirements. Under Part 21 A of the Companies Act 2006, companies need to record details of their ultimate beneficial owners and controllers (persons exercising significant control or "PSCs") and that information has to be filed on the public register at Companies House with an annual confirmation statement. Non-compliance is a criminal offence for the company and the PSCs, who will also not be able to enjoy their rights as members (including to vote, receive dividends or transfer their shares). A person is a PSC in relation to a company if directly or indirectly that person: owns more than 25 per cent of the shares or has the right to exercise more than 25 per cent of the voting rights in the company; has the right to appoint or remove a majority of the board of directors; or has the right to exercise, or actually exercises, significant influence or control over the company (whether directly, or by exercising significant influence or control over a trust or firm that is not a legal person and which satisfies one or more of the other criteria). For the purposes of these rules, if shares or rights are held by different people but are subject to a "joint arrangement" under which they will exercise their rights jointly in a way predetermined by the arrangement, then each of those people will be treated as holding the combined shares or rights. Accordingly a shareholders' agreement which contains provisions that meet this test (for example, if it gives a group of shareholders control over the appointment or removal of a majority of the board of directors) will have the effect of requiring information on the relevant persons as PSCs to be filed with Companies House.

## 4. Conflict between Articles of Association and Shareholders' Agreements

As with any other contract, a shareholders' agreement only binds the persons who originally agreed to be bound by it and any other persons who subsequently agree to be bound (for example, by executing a deed of accession). Shareholders' agreements usually impose a contractual obligation on the transferring shareholder to ensure that the new shareholder accedes to the shareholders' agreement and thereby becomes a party to it. Articles of association on the other hand automatically bind future shareholders to their provisions.

Inconsistencies between the provisions of the shareholders' agreement and the articles of association are usually regulated by an express provision in the shareholders' agreement. Most commonly the shareholders' agreement will state that in the event of any inconsistency the obligations under the shareholders' agreement will prevail, or there will be a further assurance provision requiring steps to be taken and voting rights exercised to bring the articles into compliance with the shareholders' agreement. This will usually be effective between the parties in their capacity as a shareholders as a matter of contract law. As discussed above, if all shareholders are party to the shareholders' agreement, and it overrides the articles of association, it may require registration with Companies House as a constitutional document.

However the default position is that in the absence of an express provision, the articles of association will normally prevail in the event of a conflict; in such a case, terms are unlikely to be implied into the shareholders' agreement to override the articles of association, particularly where the apparently inconsistent provision grants powers to the directors rather than to the shareholders.[33]

## 5. Parties to Shareholders' Agreements

The parties to a shareholders' agreement are usually all of the shareholders of the company; however, as already noted above, any of group of shareholders could enter into such a contract to the exclusion of other shareholders.

Practice varies as to whether the company itself is included as a party to the agreement. On the one hand, a company may be excluded so as not to be bound by its provisions. This will mean that the shareholders would have no right to sue the company directly for a breach of the shareholders' agreement. If it is not a party to the shareholders' agreement, the company would also not obtain any rights under the agreement, unless the Contracts (Rights of Third Parties) Act 1999 applied (and as a matter of practice it is standard to exclude the application of this Act in commercial contracts). This prevents a liquidator from asserting such rights, for example, the right to obtain financing from the shareholders, in the event that the company became the subject of insolvency proceedings.

**33** *Dear v Jackson* [2013] EWCA Civ 89.

A shareholders' agreement is enforceable against company where it is a party, but this is subject to the limitations noted in *Russell v Northern Bank Development Corp.*[34] If the company is a party to the shareholders' agreement, it is not possible to circumvent relevant applicable mandatory corporate law so as to bind the company regarding the exercise of its statutory powers; the company cannot fetter its statutory powers by entering into inconsistent contractual obligations. "Statutory powers" are presumed to include any matter the Companies Act requires to be resolved upon by a general meeting, including matters requiring a special resolution such as alteration of capital, alteration of articles and winding up or matters requiring an ordinary resolution such as the removal and appointment of directors. In effect, the board of directors cannot deprive the shareholders of their powers to make decisions in respect of such matters by entering into contracts in respect of these matters.[35]

Nonetheless there are a number of reasons why shareholders may wish a company to be a party to the shareholders' agreement. First, they may wish to bind the company to restrictions on the conduct of its business that are imposed on it in the shareholders' agreement, such as not to exceed specified borrowing limits or not to dispose of certain valuable or key assets. If the company is a party to these obligations, it can be potentially subjected to an injunction if there is a breach or threatened breach of them. Secondly, for similar reasons, the shareholders may want to bind the company to an undertaking to give effect to the decision-making arrangements in the shareholders' agreement. Thirdly, the shareholders may wish indirectly to force the directors to give effect to the arrangements as to the conduct of the company's business that are set out in the shareholders' agreement; otherwise the directors will be able to argue that their directors' duties require them to exercise independent judgement and to act to promote the success of the company as a whole rather than necessarily acting in line with what the shareholders' agreement envisages should be done.

## 6. Duration of Shareholders' Agreements

There are no restrictions with respect to the duration of shareholders' agreements. Such agreements are usually structured as perpetual obligations which are expressed to continue until such time as there is only one shareholder left

---

34 [1992] BCLC 1016 (HL).

35 But in some cases the company could still be liable in damages to a third party in respect of such a contract: *Punt v Symons* [1903] 2 Ch 506.

in the company. Rights that will lead to an end of the agreement in this way are contained in the exit provisions, that is, put and call options which allow one shareholder to buy out another in the event of certain defined events occurring. As a matter of general contract law, it would be possible to terminate a shareholders' agreement if the other party repudiated the agreement by indicating that it is no longer bound by it or committed a breach of a term which went to the root of the contract.

## 7. Distinction between Partnerships and Corporations regarding Shareholders' Agreements

Relations between partners in a traditional English law partnership and relations between shareholders in an English company are regulated in fundamentally different ways. Whereas shareholders are considered to be in a position similar to arms' length contracting parties (meaning that no duties of good faith or loyalty are automatically implied into their relationship), partners are held to be in a fiduciary relationship with one another. Consequently the relationship between partners is subject to numerous duties implied as a matter of law, a shareholders' agreement on the other hand is a simple contract with very limited scope for the implication of terms. However in recent times there have been instances where terms requiring the parties to act in good faith relative to each other have been implied into commercial agreements.[36] But even where such obligations to act in good faith have been expressly included by the parties in a shareholders' agreement, they have been given a narrow construction only requiring the parties to act honestly.[37]

## 8. Relevant Statutory Laws for Public Companies

The Disclosure and Transparency Rules in the FCA Handbook aim to provide the markets with information about the control of voting power in publicly traded companies. "Control" is defined by s.89 J FSMA 2000 so as to include not only people who hold the majority of voting rights or the right to appoint the board of directors, but also those who control the voting rights in another person because of a shareholders' agreement, or who exercise a dominant influence

**36** *Yam Seng Pte Ltd v International Trade Corp Ltd* [2013] EWHC 111 (QB).
**37** *Re Coroin* [2013] EWCA Civ 781.

over the company. Thus where such control is acquired through a shareholders' agreement the public company and the voteholder will be required to provide relevant "voteholder information", being information relating to the proportion of voting rights held under common control, to the Financial Conduct Authority (FCA) to make the control of the company transparent to the markets. In particular, voteholder information must be provided by persons acquiring control over shareholdings crossing thresholds of 5 %, 10 %, 15 %, 20 %, 25 %, 30 %, 50 % and 75 % of the total number of shares in an issuer.

A shareholders' agreement in respect of shares in a publicly traded company may also trigger obligations under the City Code on Takeovers and Mergers. Pursuant to Rule 9 of the Code, a mandatory takeover bid must be made if a person and "any persons acting in concert" acquire shares carrying 30 % or more of the voting rights of a target; or if any such concert parties who together hold not less than 30 % but not more than 50 % of the voting rights increase their holding. Rule 9 requires a mandatory offer to be made in cash, or to be accompanied by a cash alternative, and at the highest price paid by any such concert party for any interest in shares of the relevant class during the twelve months prior to the announcement of the offer. Since the touchstone is acting in concert, shareholders' agreements relating to voting or control would be likely to cause holdings to be aggregated for the purposes of triggering this Rule, resulting in the triggering of obligations under the Code.

## 9. Specific Regulation of International or Cross-Border Shareholders' Agreements

There is no specific regulation of international or cross border shareholders' agreements which are governed by English law. They are simply subject to the same principles as any other contract. In fact, it is not unusual for English law to be used to govern shareholders' agreements even though the company to which they relate is not incorporated in England but in an overseas jurisdiction. It is particularly common for such English law shareholders' agreements to be entered into in relation to companies incorporated in developing markets jurisdictions. This is because of the advantages of using English law and litigating in English courts in an international commercial context.

# III. Forms of Shareholders' Agreements

## 1. Shareholders' Agreements on Shareholder Rights

### a. Voting rights

A core component of shareholders' agreements is the regulation of voting rights: shareholders may be bound to exercise their rights in particular ways or not to exercise them in particular ways. In *Russell v Northern Bank Development Corp*,[38] the House of Lords confirmed that shareholders' agreements can effectively bind shareholders among themselves to exercise their voting rights in the agreed manner in the future.

Restrictions on the exercise of voting rights are key parts of shareholders' agreements. As mentioned previously, shareholders' agreements usually require voting rights to be exercised by the parties in a manner that is consistent with the obligations laid down in the agreement. Typically articles of association regulate the voting process itself, whether at meetings or by the circulation of written resolutions. Shareholders agreements usually supplement the minority's voting rights by reserving certain matters for decision with a higher majority than a simple majority of 50 %+1 votes. For example, certain categories of decisions may require a higher, say 66.66 % or 75 %, majority or unanimous consent.

Thus a shareholders' agreement may give a shareholder (or director appointed by it) negative control over a matter (i.e. a power to veto or block a reserved matter) or it may give such a person positive control (i.e. the power to force a decision through). In a so-called 50:50 or deadlock joint venture company, many or even all matters may be left in a potential deadlock with no-one having positive control – both parties having only negative control.

Often two levels of decision making are regulated in a shareholders' agreement: board decisions and shareholder decisions. Generally the articles of association give the board of directors (acting by simple majority) the power to manage the company, but certain board matters may be specified in the articles or a shareholders' agreement as capable of being vetoed by directors appointed by a particular shareholder or class of shareholder. Additionally certain matters ("reserved matters") are usually withdrawn from the authority of the board and left to a shareholder vote or specified as requiring the consent of a particular shareholder or class of shareholder. Practically it is said to be somewhat easier to get decisions on director reserved matters than shareholder reserved matters be-

38 [1992] BCLC 1016 (HL).

cause directors will have greater knowledge about the business and so will be better placed to make quick decisions.

Reserved matters (whether at board or shareholder level) usually include: changes to dividend policies; the issue of new shares and introduction of new shareholders; amendments to the articles; winding up of the company; and related party transactions with any of the shareholders. They may also include: substantial changes to the company's business; corporate mergers and acquisitions; major capital expenditures; major borrowings; major disposals; and transactions outside of the ordinary course of the company's business. The objective is to ensure that the decisions most likely to affect the value of the shareholders' stakes in the company are reserved, but that the veto rights do not impinge on the day-to-day running of the company.

Various voting thresholds to allow action to be taken in respect of such reserved matters may be imposed: they may require unanimous consent of the board or shareholders (i.e. everyone has veto); they may require a super-majority (set at a level so that a specified minority can block the decision); or they may require a decision taken with the prior written consent of a particular shareholder or the director appointed by it or the consent of the majority of one class of shareholders or directors appointed by one class of shareholders.

Where someone is empowered to veto particular decisions that would otherwise be passed by a majority on general corporate law principles, an important consequence of such provisions is the risk of a stalemate or irreconcilable dispute within the company. This then leads to the need for detailed deadlock provisions to be added in the shareholders' agreement which will assist in resolving such a stalemate situation, or, less drastically, will act as a disincentive for the creation of such a situation.

Mechanisms commonly employed for the resolution of deadlocks include the following. First, the dispute may be escalated internally to senior officers of the shareholders, but the disadvantage is that this will not resolve a genuine commercial disagreement. Secondly, the dispute can be sought to be resolved externally by expert determination (or, for example, an independent member of the board could be given a casting vote). The disadvantage of expert determination is that, apart from the delay, cost and uncertainty involved, it amounts to the delegation of a business decision; and an external party may not be the best person to make such a decision. There may be no right answer. For example, one shareholder may require a large dividend to be declared but the other may want the money to be reinvested for the company to grow. Such a dispute is not just a matter of sound business judgement but a conflict of contrary interests which an expert is not necessarily well placed to resolve.

The third possible mechanism for resolving decision making deadlocks is through the forced sale and purchase of shares in the company, that is, put and call options. One variant of this mechanism is a "Russian Roulette" clause (a buy and sell offer). Pursuant to this clause a shareholder makes an offer to buy out or sell to the other shareholder; the other shareholder can accept this offer to buy or sell at the same price. The advantage is that the shareholder that initiates this mechanism is forced to place a fair value on the shares in question. The disadvantage is that it only works properly where: there are two parties; the parties have roughly equal access to funding; the amounts at stake are not excessive for either party; and neither party brings something unique to the company necessary for its continued success. Another variant of the mechanism is a "Texas or Mexican Shootout" clause. Pursuant to this clause a shareholder makes an offer to buy out the other shareholder, that other shareholder can reject it by serving a counter-notice making a higher offer to buy out the first party, and so on (an auction process commences). Another variant requires the shareholders to submit sealed bids for each other's shares with the person who values the shares the highest being the winner. The disadvantages of this approach is that it is more prone to misuse where one shareholder does not have the funds or desire to buy, as it would take a significant risk if it made a counter-offer at an increased price. The other disadvantages mentioned above also apply. Another variant is to force a sale of the relevant shares to a third party or the company itself. Yet another potential deadlock resolving mechanism that is sometimes used is to place the company in voluntary liquidation if the deadlock cannot be resolved in any other way. The disadvantage is that this may not be the best way of realising value; the company's value may be greatest if it is sold as a going concern. One overriding commercial difficulty with deadlock and the above resolution mechanisms is that a deadlock can be contrived or manufactured to opportunistically take advantage of them.

In the case of public companies in a takeover context, it is possible for shareholders to grant irrevocable undertakings or commitments to the prospective bidder to accept an offer or to vote in a particular way, including in favour of a resolution to approve or to give effect to a scheme of arrangement. Before making a public offer, the bidder will want to know it will be likely to succeed. It will seek irrevocable undertakings from more significant shareholders that they will accept or vote in favour of the offer. These may be "hard", being an undertaking to accept the bid irrespective of competing offers, or they may be "soft", being not binding if a higher offer emerges. The Takeover Code requires irrevocable commitments to be disclosed to the market.

### b. Instructions

The board of directors are vested with the right and obligation to manage the day-to-day business of the company. The Companies Act 2006 imposes a duty on a director always to exercise his or her independent judgment in relation to any company matters that require his or her decision.[39] It is a fundamental principle of English corporate law that the individual shareholders are not entitled to give the directors instructions on such matters. A director who agrees to always act on an appointee's instructions irrespective of the company's interests would be in breach of his or her duties to the company.[40]

If a shareholder controls or directs a company's activities and its decision-making processes, it may become liable for such acts as a de facto or shadow director.[41] A de facto director is a person who acts as a director without having been formally appointed as a director. A "shadow director" of a company is a person in accordance with whose directions or instructions the directors of the company are accustomed to act (but a person is not deemed a shadow director by reason only that the directors act on advice given by him in a professional capacity).[42]

A de facto director[43] or shadow director[44] can owe director's or fiduciary duties to the company, and of course would bear unlimited liability for a breach of those duties. If the company runs into financial difficulties, such a shareholder could, for example, also be exposed to misfeasance proceedings under the Insolvency Act 1986[45] or to disqualification proceedings under the Company Directors Disqualification Act 1986.[46]

---

**39** Companies Act 2006, s 173.

**40** *Re London & South Western Canal Ltd* [1911] 1 Ch 346.

**41** *Smithton Ltd v Naggar* [2014] EWCA Civ 939 involved an unsuccessful attempt to claim that a director of a holding company was a de facto or shadow director of a joint venture or subsidiary company on the basis of his actions and the rights conferred by a shareholders' agreement.

**42** Insolvency Act 1986, s 251. Similar definitions are to be found in the Company Directors Disqualification Act 1986, s 22(5) and the Companies Act 2006, s 251. As for the application of the definition see *Secretary of State for Trade and Industry v Deverell* [2001] Ch 340, [24]–[36]; *HMRC v Holland* [2010] UKSC 51; *Mckillen v Misland (Cyprus) Investments Ltd* [2012] EWHC 521 (Ch), [67]; and *Smithton Ltd v Naggar* [2014] EWCA Civ 939, [32].

**43** *Re Canadian Land Reclaiming and Colonizing Co* (1880) 14 ChD 660, 670.

**44** *Vivendi SA v Richards* [2013] EWHC 3006 (Ch); [2013] BCC 771.

**45** For instance, for fraudulent trading under s 213 or for wrongful trading under s 214 of the Insolvency Act 1986.

**46** Company Directors Disqualification Act 1986, s 6(3C).

### c. Coordination to enforce shareholder claims

Claims which a company has against its directors, shareholders or third parties generally have to be enforced by the company itself. Thus the decision to sue usually has to be made by the board of directors of the company. This is a fundamental principle of English corporate law known as the rule in *Foss v Harbottle*.[47] Generally shareholders are not entitled to enforce such claims of the company. However, under certain circumstances, shareholders are entitled to enforce through a statutory derivative action the claims of the company against its directors arising from negligence, default, breach of duty or breach of trust. Under Part 11 of the Companies Act 2006, the court has a discretion in appropriate circumstances to allow shareholders to continue a derivative claim in their own name on behalf of the company, unless the wrongs of the directors that they complain of have been ratified in accordance with the procedure prescribed by section 239 of the Companies Act 2006. As with other matters concerning the rights of shareholders, a shareholders' agreement could be entered into between two or more shareholders to deal with the pursuit of a derivative action.

### d. Agreements on financing the company

It is a fundamental principle of English corporate law that no shareholder of a limited liability company is obliged to make financial contributions to the company over and above his or her initial contribution to the capital of the company. This is the principle of limited liability. Nonetheless the shareholders are at liberty to commit to additional obligations to finance the company. If this is done, it is usually agreed within shareholders' agreements rather than in articles. A financing obligation is only binding on the parties to the agreement and would not give the company rights against the shareholders, unless the company was also a party to the shareholders agreement or it acquired rights against them as a third party under the Contracts (Rights of Third Parties) Act 1999. Whether or not the company had a right to enforce a shareholder's obligation to provide finance would be critical in the event of the insolvency of the company because a liquidator could then step into the shoes of the company and enforce the relevant obligations under the shareholders' agreement on behalf of the company.

Shareholders' agreements often regulate financial contributions by stipulating that additional financing may be requested or required by the company. They

47 *Foss v Harbottle* (1843) 67 ER 189.

also regulate when it would be payable and sometimes impose caps on the amounts of such obligations (if any). A shareholders' agreement may entitle and require the shareholders to participate in capital increases or new shareholder loans, and stipulate the consequences if a shareholder is not able to or does not want to participate in the capital increase or shareholder loan. Such increases in share capital or shareholder loans usually require proportionate contributions or, if a shareholder cannot comply with the requirement for additional finance, they may lead to a dilution of his or her stake or trigger a default exit mechanism.

Other issues that a shareholders' agreement may provide for in respect of the financing of the company include: veto rights on capital increases; specified pre-agreed amounts and timetables for contributions to be made; provisions for emergency funding to be provided by one or more shareholders if the company is facing a liquidity crisis (often on particularly favourable terms for the funding shareholder); and provisions as to how and when the company may borrow from third parties.

Another financial matter that is often regulated in shareholders' agreements is the policy as to the payment of dividends by the company. The default rule is that dividends are not payable until such a payment is recommended by the board of directors and approved by a general meeting of the company's shareholders.[48] This may be unacceptable for minority shareholders who may require a commitment from the majority shareholder that dividends will be paid when specified objective criteria are satisfied.

### e. Law of groups

English corporate law does not provide for a law of groups (*Konzernrecht*). Each English company in a corporate group is treated as an entirely separate and distinct legal entity.[49] A director always owes his or her director's duties to the company of which he is a director and does not have any duties to other companies in its group or to their creditors. As Templeman LJ stated in *Re Southard Ltd: "A parent company may spawn a number of subsidiary companies, all controlled directly or indirectly by the shareholders of the parent company. If one of the subsidiary companies to change the metaphor, turns out to be the runt of the litter and declines into insolvency to the dismay of its creditors, the parent company and*

48 Companies (Model Articles) Regulations 2008 (SI 2008/3229), Schedule 1, Article 30.
49 *Salomon v A Salomon & Co Ltd* [1896] UKHL 1.

*the other subsidiary companies may prosper to the joy of the shareholders without any liability for the debts of the insolvent subsidiary."*[50] Only in very limited and exceptional cases will the courts disregard the separate legal personality of a company and look beyond the corporate veil of incorporation, namely, where the company is being used as a "facade" to conceal the true principals of the transaction or where the company is being used to "evade" a legal duty owed by the true principals.[51]

## 2. Shareholders' Agreements on (Limitations regarding) Transfers of Shares

The identity of shareholders and their continued commitment to the business that is being conducted by the company are usually of critical importance. The parties want to ensure their co-shareholders are fully committed and that their skills and resources are applied to growing the company's business. Consequently limitations on the transfer of shares are often agreed between the shareholders.

In the case of private limited liability companies, limitations on the transfer of shares are incorporated either in the articles of association or in shareholders' agreements. The advantage of incorporating such limitations in the articles of association is that the transfer limitations will be automatically binding on third parties who subsequently acquire shares in the company. This is because the articles of association are deemed to be a contract to which all of the shareholders are parties.

The most common limitation on transfer in a private limited liability company is a provision giving the board of directors' discretion to register a transfer of shares.[52] While this may be appropriate for closely held companies, it is unlikely to be satisfactory for minority financial investors, such as funds, for whom liquidity and an exit will be of paramount importance. Hence it is not unusual for the shareholders to agree detailed transfer provisions. These may comprise lock-in periods, rights of first offer or rights of first refusal, drag-along clauses, tag-along clauses and, in the event of a deadlock, shoot-out clauses. Shoot-out clauses were already discussed above but the others will now be considered.

**50** [1979].

**51** *Prest v Petrodel* [2013] UKSC 34.

**52** Companies (Model Articles) Regulations 2008 (SI 2008/3229), Schedule 1, Article 26(5).

The range of limitations on transfers that shareholders might agree in the articles or a shareholders' agreement will now be discussed, starting with the most restrictive and ending with the least restrictive:

1. Absolute prohibition on transfers – the shareholders may agree that one, some or all of the shareholders cannot transfer their shares at all until the company is wound up.
2. Prohibition on transfers for a specified "lock-in" period – the shareholders may agree that one, some or all of the shareholders cannot transfer their shares for a specified period of time or until a particular event happens. Such a "lock-in" ensures a minimum period of commitment to the company. For example, in a management buy-out, private equity investors may require this to lock in management shareholders.
3. Transfers permitted subject to "pre-emption" by other shareholders – Rights of pre-emption are a popular mechanism for controlling transfers because, in effect, there is an in-built valuation mechanism (namely, what a third party is willing to pay) and it gives the remaining parties discretion or flexibility as to whether to allow the transfer to proceed or to step-in and acquire the shares. Such rights of "pre-emption" may take the form of:
   a. rights of "first refusal" – this is the right to step in and buy on the same terms before an identified third party is permitted to do so;[53] the disadvantage of such rights is that third parties may not be interested in engaging in due diligence and negotiations if they know that such a right exists or they may require a break fee to compensate them for their efforts; or
   b. rights of "first offer" – this requires the shareholder who wishes to transfer its shares to offer them first to the other shareholders, if they decline to buy them, the offering shareholder can then sell them within a specified period of time (a clear market period) for a price no less than was offered to the other shareholders; the disadvantage of this right for the other shareholders is that they lose control over the identity of the third party who will become their fellow shareholder.
4. Transfers permitted to specified persons – for example, to the other shareholders, to related parties, to parties who are specifically named (on a so-called "white list") or who fit a particular description.
5. Transfers permitted with the consent of the other shareholders or of the board of directors.

---

53 *AstraZeneca UK Ltd v Albemarle International Corp* [2011] EWHC 1574 (Comm).

6. Transfers permitted if the entire shareholding is transferred or if a minimum percentage shareholding is retained (for example, to allow syndication by a private equity investor).
7. Transfers permitted with a right to "drag-along" and/or to "tag-along":
   a. a right to "drag-along" allows a majority shareholder to force the minority shareholder to sell its shares to the same purchaser on the same terms and conditions as the majority shareholder is receiving; this right can raise concerns regarding non-arms' length transactions or transactions at an undervalue (but including a right of pre-emption addresses that risk to some degree);[54] or
   b. a right to "tag-along" allows a minority shareholder the option to sell its shares to the same purchaser as the majority shareholder is selling to, again, on the same terms and conditions as the majority shareholder is receiving.
8. Finally, shares could be allowed to be freely transferable.

One risk to the enforceability of transfer provisions (such as drag and tag rights) in a shareholders' agreement stems from the obligations of a UK company to keep a register of persons exercising significant control (PSC) under Part 21 A of the Companies Act 2006. Under Part 21 A, a restrictions notice can be issued by the company to a shareholder who has not provided sufficient information rendering any transfer of such shareholder's shares void. If such a restrictions notice is in place, it would prevent transfer provisions, such as drag and tag rights, from operating in accordance with their terms.

## 3. Shareholders' Agreements on the Constitution of the Corporation

Shareholders' agreements may contain provisions concerned with constitutional or organisational matters. To protect his or her investment in the company, a shareholder may insist on a right of veto in respect of any changes in the capital structure of the company or changes to the company's constitution. A shareholders' agreement may also provide that a particular shareholder may have a right

54 In the absence of a drag-along right: (i) Part 28 of the Companies Act 2006 would have to be relied on to squeeze out the minority shareholder but this would require a takeover offer accepted by 90 % of the majority shareholders and would involve a right of objection and the exercise of discretion by the court, alternatively (b) a scheme of arrangement could be conducted under the Companies Act 2006, but again this would require an application to court.

to appoint a certain number of directors to the board of the company. A shareholder will often require a right to appoint and remove one or more directors because the shareholder wants to exercise management control, to influence such control or at least to monitor the performance of the company.

As already noted, such provisions will only bind the parties to the shareholders' agreement. However the shareholders are permitted to bind themselves as how they will exercise their voting rights in the future. So provided that shareholders who control a sufficient number of shares to at least form a relevant majority are party to the shareholders' agreement, provisions of this nature, such as regarding the right to have a certain number of directors appointed, will be effective.

But as also already noted, if the company is a party to the shareholders' agreement, the company cannot effectively bind itself by obligations which involve a restriction on the statutory powers of the shareholders to decide certain matters by resolutions.

## 4. Shareholders' Agreements in Pre-insolvency and Insolvency situations

As a general rule, a shareholders' agreement is treated in the same way as other contracts in the case of the insolvency of one of the shareholders who is a party to it or the insolvency of the company itself.

In the context of insolvent shareholders, one legal risk which sometimes comes up in the case of shareholders' agreements is the enforceability of call options which would allow the insolvent shareholder to be removed from the company by the other shareholders. The shareholders' agreement may provide that an insolvency of a shareholder shall be a trigger for a call option for the shareholder to sell its shares to the other shareholders. This should generally be enforceable if the consideration to be paid for the shares is specified to be their market value at the time the option is exercised, however, enforceability would be subject to the powers of the liquidator to disclaim onerous contracts. Sometimes attempts are made to impose a discount on the market value of the relevant shares in such situations. But this would be unenforceable under English insolvency law since it would infringe the anti-deprivation principle which provides that an arrangement will be void if it is triggered by insolvency and its commercial objective is to remove an asset from an insolvent's estate that would otherwise be capable of realisation for the benefit of its creditors generally.[55]

If the company is not party to the shareholders' agreement, the insolvency of the company will not directly affect the shareholders' agreement. As already noted above, if the company is a party to the shareholders' agreement or the Contracts (Rights of Third Parties) Act 1999 applies, a liquidator could step into the company's shoes and enforce any rights that may have been conferred on the company under the shareholders' agreement.

An additional insolvency risk to consider in the context of shareholders' agreements is that a shareholder who acts as a director (without actually having been appointed to that office) may be considered to be a de facto director or a shareholder on whose directions or instructions the directors habitually act may be considered to be a shadow director of the company.[56] A shareholder who acts in this way pursuant to a shareholders' agreement could thereby incur liability to the insolvent company's creditors for fraudulent or wrongful trading under the Insolvency Act 1986[57] or such a shareholder may become liable to the company for breach of fiduciary duty.

# IV. Legal Effects of Shareholders' Agreements

## 1. Legal Effects on the Corporation

Shareholders' agreements are distinct from the company's articles of association. The articles of association bind the existing and future shareholders of the company, whereas a shareholders' agreement only binds the parties to it. New shareholders do not automatically become parties to the shareholders' agreement, unless the current shareholders and the new shareholder agree for the new shareholder to become a party to the agreement, which they can do by entering into an entirely new contract or by including the mechanics for such a new contract in the shareholders' agreement itself in the form of an accession clause and a pro forma accession deed set out in a schedule.

As separate contracts, shareholders' agreements ought not to have any effect on the interpretation of the articles of association. However this is subject to two possible exceptions. The first is the *Duomatic* principle, already discussed above,

**55** *Belmont Park Investments Pty Ltd v BNY Corporate Trustee Services Ltd* [2011] UKSC 38.
**56** See the discussion under the "Instructions" section above.
**57** Insolvency Act 1986, ss 213 and 214.

pursuant to which an agreement between all the shareholders could be effective to amend the articles of association. The second exception is that if two or more persons agree amongst themselves, whether in a shareholders' agreement or otherwise, that a particular meaning is to be given to a particular provision of the articles of association then, as between those persons only, that meaning will be binding on them pursuant to the doctrine of estoppel by convention.

## 2. Legal Effects on the Shareholders

As already stated, shareholders' agreements are a separate agreement from the articles of association. The acquirer of shares in a company automatically becomes bound by the articles of association, but does not automatically become a party to a shareholders' agreement. However shareholders' agreements almost invariably require a selling shareholder to ensure that the new shareholder will agree to become a party to the shareholders' agreement and to be bound by its terms.

The legal effects of shareholders' agreements as far as securities laws are concerned have already been discussed above.[58] In the case of publicly traded companies, they may trigger certain obligations based on "acting in concert" provisions.

Shareholders' agreements do not have to be published or registered in a public register, subject to the exceptions already discussed.[59]

## 3. Consequences of a Breach of a Shareholders' Agreement

A violation of a shareholders' agreement would entitle the innocent shareholders to damages for any losses suffered by them as a result of the breach of contract. Damages for such breaches of contract are generally awarded on the expectation measure: the innocent party is to be put into the position that he or she would have been in had the contract been duly performed. The innocent shareholders could also seek injunctions or specific performance. These remedies are dealt with in greater detail in the next section.

Generally shareholders' resolutions which violate the shareholders' agreement are binding and cannot be successfully challenged merely because a share-

58 See Section II(8) "Relevant Statutory Laws for Public Companies".

59 See Section II(3) "Disclosure / Non-disclosure / Confidentiality".

holder breached the provisions of the shareholders' agreement. However the private law remedies summarised above would be available against the infringing shareholder. A violation of a shareholders' agreement, being merely a breach of contract, would not in itself affect the continuing membership in the company of the shareholder in question. However shareholders' agreements often provide for a call option allowing the innocent shareholders to buy out the shareholder who has breached the shareholders' agreement (this is further discussed below).

It should also be kept in mind that violations of the shareholders' agreement (whether through the passing of inconsistent shareholders' resolutions or other actions or omissions which breach the agreement) could also potentially form the basis for a claim that the company be wound up on the "just and equitable" ground under section 122(1)(g) of the Insolvency Act 1986 or for relief on the ground of "unfairly prejudicial conduct" under section 994 of the Companies Act 2006.[60] However one must also note that the existence and content of a shareholders' agreement is taken into account by the court in determining whether one of these statutory remedies ought to be granted. A shareholders' agreement may be treated as exhaustive of a minority shareholder's rights and remedies. Such an approach may be said to promote certainty in commercial affairs.

Finally, it must be noted that perhaps the most commercially important consequences of a breach of a shareholders' agreement are likely to be embodied within the terms of the shareholders' agreement itself. Shareholders' agreements often provide that in the event of a breach of the shareholders' agreement the innocent shareholders are entitled to trigger a call option requiring the guilty shareholder to sell his or her shares in the company to them at a discount to their market value at the relevant time. It used to be thought that such provisions fell foul of the English law prohibition on contractual penalties. But recently the Supreme Court reshaped the unenforceable penalty doctrine in the case of *Cavendish Square Holding BV v El Makdessi.*[61] This case involved a transaction whereby Cavendish purchased from Mr Makdessi the majority shareholding in a target company involved in the international advertising and marketing business. Mr Makdessi retained about 20 % of the shares in the target company. A put option was included in the shareholders' agreement which provided that Mr Makdessi had to sell these shares at Net Asset Value (NAV) if he was in breach of the non-compete undertaking in the agreement (that is, in effect he would re-

60 *Re A & BC Chewing Gum* [1975] 1 All ER 1017, where a breach of a shareholders' agreement (viz. the repudiation of a right to appoint a director) was a reason for winding up the company on the "just and equitable" ground.
61 [2015] UKSC 67.

ceive nothing for the sale of goodwill if he competed with the company). Mr Makdessi admitted to breaching the non-compete undertaking but argued that the large discount embodied in the put option made it a penalty and as such unenforceable under English law. The Supreme Court disagreed, and in doing so to some extent rewrote the law on what amounts to an unenforceable contractual penalty. The court held that he had to sell his shares at the low NAV price pursuant to the put option because the discount imposed in the event of a breach protected the legitimate interests of the counterparty to the shareholders' agreement.

## V. Enforcement of Shareholders' Agreements

Obligations and rights arising from shareholders' agreements are generally enforced through court action; however alternative dispute resolution mechanisms are also often employed. For example, sometimes, especially in an international context, the parties may opt for disputes under or in connection with the agreement to be resolved through arbitration. Shareholders' agreements also sometimes contain requirements for the parties to engage in mediation, or at least friendly discussions between senior management, before formal steps are taken to commence litigation or arbitration.

The most common remedy for breach of a shareholders' agreement, and one that is available as of right, is an award of damages which are intended to compensate the innocent party for any reasonably foreseeable losses that have been suffered as a result of the breach of contract. The innocent party is entitled to be financially put into the position that he or she would have been in if the contract had been performed in accordance with its terms. Such losses can include costs incurred and the loss of expected profits. However the right to recover damages is subject to any exclusions and limitations that the parties have agreed – any caps and limitations will be given effect to by the English courts as the parties are generally free to allocate the risks and consequences of breaches of contract as they see fit.

Additionally, so-called "equitable remedies" such as injunctions and specific performance may be available in the court's discretion. That is, they involve a residual choice on the part of the court as to whether to grant or refuse the remedy in the particular case.[62] An injunction is simply an order that replicates a negative obligations, that is, an obligation "not to do" something. For example,

62 R Zakrzewski, *Remedies Reclassified* (OUP 2005), Chapter 6.

an obligation not to compete with the company's business could be enforced by means of an injunction that would prohibit such conduct. Similarly an obligation not to vote in a particular way could be enforced in this way.[63] An order for specific performance is a court order that replicates a positive contractual obligation, that is, an obligation "to do" something. For example, an obligation to vote in a particular way when a vote on a given matter is taken could be enforced by specific performance.[64] Similarly put and call options and drag-along and tag-along rights which are often included in shareholders' agreements would also be enforceable by means of orders for specific performance.[65] An order for an injunction or specific performance is a particularly powerful remedy because disobedience constitutes contempt of court, so a recalcitrant defendant can be committed to prison for disregarding such an order.[66]

**63** *Greenwell v Porter* [1902] 1 Ch 503.

**64** *Puddephatt v Leith* [1916] 1 Ch 200.

**65** A call option in a shareholders' agreement was enforced by an order for specific performance in *Euro Brokers Holdings Ltd v Monecor (London) Ltd* [2003] EWCA Civ 105.

**66** For further details of English law remedies such as damages, injunctions and specific performance and the methods for their enforcement, see R Zakrzewski, *Remedies Reclassified* (OUP 2005).

Sebastian Mock

# Germany

## Table of Content



---

**PD Dr. *Sebastian Mock*,** LL.M.(NYU), Universität Hamburg, As far as reference is made to the German Civil Code (*Bürgerliches Gesetzbuch*) or the Closed Corporation Code (*GmbH-Gesetz*) this country report is based on the official translations provided by the German Federal Ministry of Justice (available under https://www.gesetze-im-internet.de/englisch_bgb).

https://doi.org/10.1515/9783110517026-014

German law distinguishes like the majority of the legal systems in the world between companies (*Gesellschaften* or *Personengesellschaften*) and corporations (*Körperschaften* or *Kapitalgesellschaften*). The major forms of companies are the private or civil[1] partnership (*Gesellschaft bürgerlichen Rechts [GbR]*), the general business partnership (*offene Handelsgesellschaft [oHG])* and the limited business partnership (*Kommanditgesellschaft [KG]*). The major forms of corporations are the closed corporation (*Gesellschaft mit beschränkter Haftung [GmbH]* and its sub-form the *Unternehmergesellschaft haftungsbeschränkt [UG]*) and the stock corporation (*Aktiengesellschaft [AG]*). Shareholders' agreements are generally important for all these forms of companies and corporations. Since the majority of business entities in Germany are corporations, shareholders' agreements are especially relevant in this area. However, a unique feature of German company/corporate law is that the rules and principles of company law apply in the context of the law of corporations since shareholders' agreements usually constitute a civil partnership.[2]

# A. Nature of corporate law regulation

In German company law, generally – without being explicitly stated in company law legislation – the freedom of contract applies allowing the members of companies to design the articles of association of the company as they see fit. However, the members of companies are not limited to use the articles of association of the company to regulate their relationships. In fact, the principle of freedom of contract also applies in regard to shareholders' agreements governing the rights and duties of shareholders outside the articles of association. Therefore, in German law members of companies can basically choose to address their relation-

1 The term *civil* refers to the fact that German company law distinguishes between general (civil) and commercial partnerships.
2 See B.II.1. for further details.

ship in the articles of association or in a separate shareholders' agreement. This applies to all kind of companies and therefore especially to small and closed corporations (*Gesellschaft mit beschränkter Haftung [GmbH] and Unternehmergesellschaft haftungsbeschränkt [UG]*) and to all other forms of companies. However, the articles of association and shareholders' agreements have different legal effects[3].

An exception to these rules is provided by German stock corporation law (*Aktiengesetz*) which limits this freedom for the shareholders of a stock corporation (*Aktiengesellschaft [AG]*). Pursuant to Section 23 subs. 5 German Stock Corporation Law[4] the articles of association can only deviate from the provisions of the German Stock Corporation Law if the German Stock Corporation Law explicitly permits it. This so-called *Satzungsstrenge* is based on the idea of shareholder protection since the stock corporation is basically designed as an anonymous corporation where single shareholders do not have the necessary bargaining power to enforce their interests.[5] In addition, the *Satzungsstrenge* is supposed to allow shareholders to buy shares of the stock corporation without having the burden of examining all provisions of the articles of association since a basic protection is already guaranteed (*idea of standardization*).[6] However, this *Satzungsstrenge* does not limit the shareholders to close shareholders' agreements since the *Satzungsstrenge* applies only to the articles of association of the corporation.[7] Therefore, the freedom of contract also applies to shareholders' agreements closed by shareholders of stock corporations.[8] Nevertheless, the shareholders cannot replace the articles of association of the corporation with a shareholders' agreement. If the shareholders address certain issues in a share-

---

**3** See D. for further details.

**4** Section 23 subs. 5 German Stock Corporation Law (*Establishment of the Articles*) states: *"The articles may contain different provisions from the provisions of this Act only if this Act explicitly so permits. The articles may contain additional provisions, except as to matters that are conclusively dealt with in this Act"*.

**5** See *Arnold* in Kölner Kommentar zum AktG, 3rd edition 2011, § 23 note 130; *Hüffer/Koch* Aktiengesetz, 12th edition 2016, § 23 note 34.

**6** See e.g. *Hüffer/Koch* (supra note 5), § 23 note 34; *Pentz* in Münchener Kommentar zum AktG, 4th edition 2016, § 23 note 6.

**7** See e.g. *Hüffer/Koch* (supra note 5), § 23 note 47; *Pentz* (supra note 6), § 23 note 200f.; *Ulmer* liber amicorum Röhricht, 2005, p. 633ff., 650ff.; *Noack* Gesellschaftervereinbarungen bei Kapitalgesellschaften, 1994, p. 116; *Vedder* in: Grigoleit, AktG, 2013, § 23 note 9.

**8** Federal Court of Justice as of 27.10.1986 – II ZR 240/85, NJW 1987, 1890, 1891; Federal Court of Justice as of 7.6.1993 – II ZR 81/92, BGHZ 123, 15, 20 = NJW 1993, 2246; Federal Court of Justice as of 15.3.2010 – II ZR 4/09, NJW 2010, 3718; Federal Court of Justice as of 22.1.2013 – II ZR 80/10, NZG 2013, 220; see also *Hüffer/Koch* (supra note 5), § 23 note 45.

holders' agreement which are supposed to be governed by the articles of association the shareholders' agreement has no binding effect. In that way, the *Satzungsstrenge* has a limiting effect for shareholders to close shareholders' agreements. See also D.I. for further details.

# B. General regulation of shareholders' agreements

## I. Lack of a specific regulation – Application of the freedom of contract

The general importance of shareholders' agreements in the practice of German company law is not reflected by the actual regulation since German company law hardly regulates shareholders' agreements. In fact, shareholders' agreements are not specifically addressed in German company or corporate law but only governed by general civil and commercial law. Even the terminology for shareholders' agreements in German law is not consistent since the terms *Gesellschaftervereinbarungen* (shareholders' agreements), *satzungsergänzende Nebenabreden* (supplementary agreement to the articles of association) or *schuldrechtliche Nebenabrede* (contractual supplementary agreement) are used without actually describing different kind of agreements.[9] In fact, these different terms already reflect the distinctive feature of shareholders' agreements as an instrument being based in two different worlds (contract and/or company law).[10]

In German law members of companies are not limited to close shareholders' agreements or need a specific approval by the other members or by the management of the company. Consequently, shareholder's agreements are basically governed by general contract and company law and are therefore generally admissible. Due to the general lack of a specific regulation addressing shareholders' agreements shareholders are basically free to address any issue in the agreement and to design these agreements as they set fit. The only limitation set by general contract law is that the shareholders' agreement cannot violate a statutory prohibition (Section 134 German Civil Code[11]) or be contrary to public policy (Section

9 See e.g. *Hüffer/Koch* (supra note 5), § 23 note 45 with an overview on the terminology.
10 See Part A–B.
11 *Section 134 German Civil Code (Statutory prohibition) states:*
*" A legal transaction that violates a statutory prohibition is void, unless the statute leads to a different conclusion."*

138 German Civil Code[12]). Unfortunately, so far there is only a rather limited case law stating that shareholders' agreements can violate public policy[13] or good faith. However, there is growing debate in German company law whether especially shareholders' agreements limiting the transferability of shares or the exit from the company especially in the context of shoot-out clauses are contrary to public policy since they usually limit the freedom of the shareholders in a serious way.[14] See also C.II. for further details.

## II. (General) status of shareholders' agreements in German law

Because German law hardly[15] provides specific rules on shareholders' agreements the general principles and provision of the German Civil Code apply. In this regard one has to distinguish between shareholders' agreements on voting rights (see B.II.1.), shareholders' agreements on the limitation for the transfer of shares (see B.II.2.) and shareholders' agreements on the constitution of the corporation (see B.II.3.).

### 1. Shareholders' agreements as civil partnerships

Shareholders' agreements are in the majority of cases[16] – pursuant to Section 705 German Civil Code[17] – considered as a private or civil partnership (*Gesellschaft*

---

**12** *Section 138 German Civil Code (Legal transaction contrary to public policy; usury) states: " (1) A legal transaction which is contrary to public policy is void.*

*(2) In particular, a legal transaction is void by which a person, by exploiting the predicament, inexperience, lack of sound judgement or considerable weakness of will of another, causes himself or a third party, in exchange for an act of performance, to be promised or granted pecuniary advantages which are clearly disproportionate to the performance."*

**13** See e.g. Federal Court of Justice as of 22.1.2013 – II ZR 80/10, NZG 2013, 220 regarding an agreement between the corporation and a shareholder forcing to transfer his shares to the corporation in case of the termination of the contract with any consideration.

**14** See e.g. *Schröder/Welpot* High Noon in Nürnberg – Neues zum Texan Shoot-out, zum Russian Roulette und zu anderen Klauseln der alternativen Streitbeilegung im Gesellschaftsrecht, NZG 2014, 609; *Schulte/Sieger* "Russian Roulette" und "Texan Shoot Out" – Zur Gestaltung von radikalen Ausstiegsklauseln in Gesellschaftsverträgen von Joint-Venture-Gesellschaften (GmbH und GmbH & Co. KG), NZG 2005, 24; see also *Elfring* "Deadlock" beim paritätischen Equity Joint Venture, NZG 2012, 895.

**15** For the few specific rules in stock corporation law see B.III.

**16** See B.II.2. for the "remaining" cases.

*bürgerlichen Rechts [GbR]*) in German law since the shareholders agree to promote the achievement of a common purpose by making a certain contribution. This is especially the case for voting agreements[18] (common purpose = *coordinated execution of the voting rights according to the resolutions of the partnership* by making a certain contribution = *voting rights*) but also applies in the case of shareholders' agreements on the constitution of the corporation[19] (common purpose = *change or uphold the current constitution of the corporation* by making a certain contribution = *their influence usually voting rights*).

Although the civil partnership is considered as a (specific) form of contract in the German law of obligations also elements of company law apply putting it from a conceptual point of view between contract and company law. This is especially the case regarding the termination of the civil partnership and the duties of its members. While under German contract law a revocation of a contract results in the duty of the parties to return everything they received to the other party (Section 346 German Civil Code[20]) a civil partnership can only be terminated by the parties resulting in its winding-up (Section 738 German Civil Code[21]) as it is typical for all kind of companies and corporations. Also, the regulations for the termination of the civil partnership are rather strict in the case that the articles of association of the civil partnership states a specific duration since then a termination prior to the expiry of that period is only admissible if there is a com-

---

**17** Section 705 German Civil Code (*Contents of partnership agreement*) states:

*"By a partnership agreement, the partners mutually put themselves under a duty to promote the achievement of a common purpose in the manner stipulated by the contract, in particular, without limitation, to make the agreed contributions"*.

**18** See C.I.1. for further details.

**19** See C.III. for further details.

**20** Section 346 subs. 1 German Stock Corporation Law (*Effects of revocation*) states:

*"If one party to a contract has contractually reserved the right to revoke or if he has a statutory right of revocation, then, in the case of revocation, performance received and emoluments taken are to be returned."*

**21** Section 738 German Stock Corporation Law (*Winding-up of the partnership on retirement*) states:

" *(1) If a partner retires from the partnership, then his share in the assets of the partnership accrues to the remaining partners. The latter are obliged to return to the retiring partner under the provisions of section 732 the items he transferred to the partnership for use and to exempt him from joint debts and to pay him what he would receive in case of winding-up if the partnership had been dissolved at the time of his retirement. If joint debts are not yet due for repayment, then the remaining partners may provide the retiring partner with security instead of exempting him.*

*(2) The value of the assets of the partnership is, to the extent necessary, to be determined by means of an appraisal*".

pelling reason (Section 723 subsection 1 sentences 2 German Civil Code[22]). If the civil partnership is not set up for a definite period of time each partner can terminate it at any time (Section 723 subsection 1 sentences 1 German Civil Code[23]). Since this usually does not reflect the interest of the parties of a shareholders' agreement they usually agree that the shareholders' agreement can only be terminated if there is a compelling reason which is also very often further described in the agreement. Also, the parties usually agree that the termination of the agreement by one party results in a continuation of the civil partnership with all remaining parties since a termination without such a clause in the shareholders' agreement results in a dissolution of the civil partnership. Regarding the duties of the parties the (additional) duty of loyalty of shareholders (*Treuepflicht*) applies providing certain limitations for the members of the civil partnership for the execution of their rights.

It also has to be noted that the formation of a shareholders' agreement – as a civil partnership – does generally not require a certain form or the fulfilment of specific formal requirements. This is even the case, if a provision contained in the shareholders' agreements could also be included in the articles of association requiring a certain formal procedure to be changed.[24] Although it is therefore possible to conclude shareholders' agreements orally in the legal practice these agreements are usually done in writing.

### 2. Shareholders' agreements as mere contracts

Shareholders' agreements can also constitute mere contracts (without the application of the rules on civil partnerships[25]) since in their agreement the shareholders do not necessarily agree to promote the achievement of a common purpose. This is especially the case for shareholders' agreements on the limitation for the transfer of shares[26] often being found in companies or corporations

**22** Section 723 subs. 1 sentences 1 and 2 German Stock Corporation Law (*Termination by partner*) states:

*" If the partnership has not been set up for a definite period of time, then each partner may terminate it at any time. If a period of time has been determined, then notice of termination prior to the expiry of that period is admissible if there is a compelling reason".*

**23** See supra note 12.

**24** See e.g. Federal Court of Justice as of 15.3.2010 – II ZR 4/09, NZG 2010, 988 stating that shareholders can agree on the amount of an appraisal right for the membership in a closed corporation (GmbH) in a shareholder agreement or in the articles of association.

**25** See B.II.1.

**26** See C.II.

owned by families or other (closed) group. Also, the formation of these contracts does not require the fulfilment of a certain formality. However, if these agreements relate to shares of closed corporations *Gesellschaft mit beschränkter Haftung [GmbH]* usually the participation of a notary is required if the agreement creates the obligation to transfer the share (Section 15 subs. 4 German Closed Corporation Law[27]).[28]

### 3. Shareholders' agreements in the articles of association

Although shareholders are generally free to conclude shareholders' agreements they do not necessarily have to use this form of agreement. In fact, they are also free to use the articles of association to coordinate their rights and duties even if these additional provisions apply only to single shareholders. This is especially the case for shareholders' agreements dealing with limitations for the transfer of shares[29] since then not only the actual but also the future shareholders are bound by such a clause. See also D.I. for the impact of shareholders' agreements on the articles of association.

## III. Specific regulation in stock corporation law (*Aktienrecht*)

A specific regulation of shareholders' agreements exists in stock corporation law. However, these are only two indirect regulations on shareholders' agreements which only refer to voting agreements (*Konsortial-*, *Pool-*, *Stimmbindungs-* or *Syndikatsverträge*). According to Section 136 subs. 2 German Stock Corporation Law[30] a contract that establishes an obligation for a shareholder to exercise

**27** Section 15 subs. 4 German Closed Corporation Law (*transfer of shares*) states:

*"An agreement establishing the shareholder's obligation to transfer a share shall likewise require notarial form. However, an agreement concluded without such notarial form shall become valid once the transfer agreement is concluded pursuant to subsection (3)."*

**28** See e. g. *Fastrich* in Baumbach/Hueck, GmbHG, 21st edition 2017, § 15 note 33 with further references.

**29** See C.II.

**30** Section 136 subs. 2 German Stock Corporation Law (*Exclusion of voting rights*) states:

*"An agreement whereby a shareholder undertakes to exercise voting rights in accordance with the instructions of the company, the management board or the supervisory board of the company or a controlled enterprise shall be null and void. An agreement whereby a shareholder undertakes to vote for the respective proposals of the management board or supervisory board of the company shall likewise be null and void".*

his voting rights in accordance with the instructions of the company, the management board or the supervisory board of the company or a controlled enterprise shall be void. Moreover, the so-called vote buying[31] is a criminal offence according to Section 405 subs. 3 No. 2 German Stock Corporation Law[32]. In both cases the contract is void pursuant to Section 134 German Civil Code[33].[34] However, it has to be noted that both provisions are generally regarded as being obsolete or at least being problematic.[35] This is especially the case since they were introduced during the reform of German stock corporation law in 1937 and are basically influenced by a rather strict and limited understanding of the stock corporation in general.

Moreover, it has to be noted that Section 405 subs. 3 No. 2 German Stock Corporation Law does not apply to the closed corporation.[36] Consequently, the closed corporation lacks completely a specific regulation on shareholders' agreements. However, a contract according to which a shareholder binds himself to execute his voting right according to the wishes of a non-shareholder in return for a payment is considered as a violation of public policy (Section 138 German Civil Code[37]) and therefore void.[38]

---

**31** Voting buying is generally understood as a contract between a shareholder and a third party under which the shareholder promises to vote in the general meeting in a certain way for being paid by the third party (see e.g. *Schaal* in Münchener Kommentar zum AktG, 3rd edition 2011, § 405 note 94 ff.).

**32** Section 405 subs. 3 No. 2 German Stock Corporation Law (*Administrative Offences*) states: *"Whoever uses shares of another person which he has acquired by granting or promising special benefits to exercise rights at a shareholders' meeting or a separate meeting... shall be guilty of an administrative offence;"*.

**33** See supra note 7.

**34** See Higher Regional Court of Hamm as of 3.2.2014 – 8 U 47/10, BeckRS 2015, 00257 for a violation of Section 405 subs. 3 No. 2 German Stock Corporation Law and see *Schröer* in Münchener Kommentar zum AktG, 3rd edition 2013, § 136 note 81 for a violation of Section 136 subs. 2 German Stock Corporation Law.

**35** See e.g. *Herrler* in Grigoleit, AktG, 2013, § 136 note 28.

**36** OLG Nuremburg as of 23.8.1988 – 1 U 3651/87, GmbHR 1990, 166; see also *Zöllner/Noack* in Baumbach/Hueck, GmbHG, 21st edition 2017, § 47 note 8.

**37** See supra note 9.

**38** *Hüffer/Schürnbrand* in Ulmer/Habersack/Lübbe, GmbHG, 2nd edition 2014, § 47 note 85; *K. Schmidt* in Scholz, GmbHG, 11th edition 2014, § 47 note 45; *Zöllner/Noack* (supra note 26), § 47 note 114.

## IV. International shareholders' agreements – conceptual fractions between German and European law

Because German law already lacks a coherent regulation of shareholders' agreements in general also international shareholders' agreements are not specifically addressed in German law. In fact, also international shareholders' agreements are considered as civil partnerships on which – in the case of a stock corporation – the specific provisions of the stock corporation law (Section 136 subs. 2, 405 subs. 3 No. 2 German Stock Corporation Law[39]) apply. However, this understanding of shareholders' agreements as civil partnerships[40] – and not as mere contracts – conflicts with the conceptual distinction of contracts and companies in European private law. This is especially the case regarding the Rome-I-Regulation (EC/593/2008) since its Article 1 subs. 2 lit. f) exempts *questions governed by the law of companies* from its scope of application. While under German law shareholders' agreements – at least the ones being civil partnerships[41] – are probably considered as a *question governed by the law of companies* – therefore not being covered by the Rome-I-Regulation[42] – such an interpretation of Article 1 subs. 2 lit. f) Rome-I-VO is not compelling since the Rome-I-Regulation has to be interpreted autonomously without a direct reference to national law.[43] The same problem arises under the Brussels-Ia-Regulation (EU/1215/2012) since its Article 24 No. 2 establishes an exclusive jurisdiction – among other issues – for proceedings which have as their objects the validity of decision of organs of companies at the seat of the company. By considering a shareholders' agreement as a *company* instead as a *contract* far more limitations apply. See also Part A.II. (*Shareholders' Agreements from a European private international law and an international civil procedural law perspective*) for further details.

39 See supra B.III. for further details.

40 See B.II.1.

41 See B.II.1.

42 However, see Federal Court of Justice as of 13.9.2004 – II ZR 276/02, NJW 2004, 3706 regarding a silent partnership under Sections 230 ff. German Commercial Code.

43 *Kindler* in BeckOnline-Großkommentar, 2017, Article 1 Rome-I-Regulation note 56; *Martiny* in Münchener Kommentar zum BGB, 6th edition 2015, Article 1 Rome-I-Regulation note 71.

# C. Forms of shareholders' agreements and limitations

As in all modern jurisdictions there is also in German law a huge variety of shareholders' agreements in legal practice. Besides shareholders' agreements on shareholder rights and duties (see C.I.) and shareholders' agreements on the (limitation for the) transfer of shares (see C.II.) also shareholders' agreements on the constitution of the corporation (see C.III.) are common. A rather unchartered territory are shareholders' agreements in pre-insolvency situations (see C.IV.) which are of a growing importance.

## I. Shareholders' agreements on shareholder rights and duties

The most important form of shareholders' agreements on shareholder rights and duties are voting agreements (see C.I.1.). But also, other rights like the right to enforce claims of the company by the shareholders (see C.I.2.) and duties like the duty to finance the company (see C.I.3.) can be subject of a shareholders' agreement. In contrast, the coordination of rights of the shareholder to give instructions to the management of the corporation is of almost no importance since such rights exists only in the German law of corporate groups (see C.I.4.).

### 1. Voting Agreements

#### a. Forms of Voting Agreements

The most common form of shareholders' agreements are vote pooling agreements (*Konsortial-*, *Pool-*, *Stimmbindungs-* or *Syndikatsverträge*) in which the shareholders agree to exercise their voting rights according to the resolutions being based on a majority among the participating shareholders. For these voting agreements, which constitute a contract the law of the civil partnership applies (*Gesellschaft bürgerlichen Rechts* – Sections 705 ff. German Civil Code)[44] since the shareholders agree to peruse a common interested (exercise the voting rights) by contributing something (the obligation to exercise the voting rights ac-

44 See B.II.1.

cording to the majority of the partners) to the general civil partnership.[45] These general civil partnerships are not registered and are therefore not public. Neither do they have to be made public to the other shareholders or to the management of the corporation. Also, these general civil partnerships do not exercise the voting rights themselves. In fact, the partners of this civil partnership (= the shareholders of the corporation) exercise the voting rights themselves but are bound on a contractual basis by the resolution of the general civil partnership on how to exercise them.

Moreover, also spontaneous voting agreements are common in German legal practise but are not relevant from a legal point of view since they are usually not binding.[46] These spontaneous voting agreements usually occur in shareholder meetings when some of the shareholders come to a spontaneous consensus on certain issues. In contrast to the general civil partnership the shareholders usually have no intent to bind each other.

Finally, voting agreements can also be concluded as unilateral voting agreements (*einseitige Stimmbindung* or *Ad hoc-Koalitionen*) when one shareholder agrees to exercise his voting rights according to the directions of another person.[47] In this case, general service contract law (*Auftragsrecht* – Sections 662ff. German Civil Code) applies since unilateral voting agreements constitute only an obligation of the shareholder to exercise the voting rights. Therefore, also in this case the shareholder does not transfer the voting right to another person. In this context, also the limitation set by public policy (Section 138 German Civil Code) have to be considered.[48]

### b. Restrictions and limitations

Voting agreements are generally admissible in German corporate law.[49] If a shareholder is excluded from voting, he cannot conclude a voting agreement with other shareholders since this would circumvent the prohibition of voting.[50]

---

**45** See e.g. BGH as of 24.11.2008 – II ZR 116/08, Z 179, 13, 29 = NJW 2009, 669; *Schröer* (supra note 23), § 136 note 59ff.

**46** See e.g. *Schröer* (supra note 23), § 136 note 62.

**47** See e.g. *Schröer* (supra note 23), § 136 note 63; *Spindler* in K. Schmidt/Lutter, AktG, 3rd edition 2015, § 136 note 39.

**48** See B.III for further details.

**49** Recognized since RGZ 133, 90; later also the Federal Court of Justice confirmed this case law BGH as of 29.5.1967 – II ZR 105/66, Z 48, 163, 166ff. = NJW 1967, 1963; see also *Schröer* (supra note 24), § 136 note 64 with further references.

**50** Federal Court of Justice as of 29.5.1967 – II ZR 105/66, BGHZ 48, 163, 166ff. = NJW 1967, 1963; see also *Spindler* (supra note 37), § 136 note 38.

Such a prohibition of voting can especially occur when the shareholder resolution affects the shareholder himself (Section 136 German Stock Corporation Law[51]). Besides this rather specific limitation additional limitations do not apply.

The only (explicit) limitation for voting agreements is the prohibition of the so-called vote buying (Section 405 subs. 3 No. 2 German Stock Corporation Law) which applies, however, only to shareholders of stock corporations. This prohibition is based on the idea that shareholders should not sell the influence on the corporation to people outside the corporation since the voting right should be linked to the (capital) participation in the corporation.[52] Moreover, German stock corporation law still applies a rather strict prohibition for splitting shares or the rights of shares (Section 8 subs. 5 German Stock Corporation Law[53]). According to this principles shareholder cannot transfer the voting rights separately but only together with the shares. Therefore, voting agreements can only establish the obligation of the shareholder to exercise the voting rights in accordance with the majority resolution of the parties of the voting agreement.[54] Finally, voting agreements have no effect in takeover law if the articles of association of the corporation states so (Section 33b subs. 2 sent. 1 No. 2 Securities Acquisition and Takeover Act[55]).

---

**51** Section 136 subs. 1 German Stock Corporation Law states:

*"No person may exercise voting rights on his own behalf or on behalf of any other person in respect of a resolution concerning ratification of his acts, his discharge from a liability, or enforcement by the company of a claim against him. Voting rights arising from shares that may not be exercised by the shareholder himself pursuant to sentence 1 may also not be exercised by any other person".*

**52** See also B.III. for further details.

**53** Section 8 subs. 5 German Stock Corporation Law states:

*"Shares shall not be divisible".*

**54** See *Mock* in Großkommentar zum AktG, 5th edition 2016, § 8 note 202ff. with further references.

**55** Section 33b subs. 2 sent. 1 No. 2 Securities Acquisition and Takeover Act states:

*"The following provisions shall apply following the publication of the offer document pursuant to section 14 (3) sentence 1:*

...

*2.during the period for acceptance of a takeover bid, voting agreements shall have no effect at the general meeting deciding on defensive measures, and multiple-voting shares shall carry only one vote each."*

## 2. Coordination of shareholders to enforce claims (of the corporation)

Also, shareholders can coordinate to enforce claims of the corporation. Such a right is generally accepted in German company law as the so-called *actio pro socio* (*Gesellschafterklage*) which permits a shareholder to enforce a claim of the corporation in his (own) name. However, this right is only generally accepted in the case law and not expressly regulated. Only in stock corporation law an explicit provision (Section 148 Stock Corporation Code) addresses the *actio pro socio*. Pursuant to Section 148 Stock Corporation Code[56] shareholders holding

56 Section 148 Stock Corporation Law (*Court Procedure for Petitions Seeking Leave to File an Action for Damages*) states:

*"(1) Shareholders whose aggregate holdings at the time of filing the petition equal or exceed one per cent of the share capital or amount to at least 100,000 euros, may file a petition for the right to assert the claims of the company for damages mentioned in § 147(1) sentence1 in their own name. The court shall give them leave to file such action for damages if*

*1. the shareholders furnish evidence that they or, in the case of universal succession, their predecessors in title have acquired the shares before learning about the alleged breaches of duty or alleged damage from a publication;*

*2. the shareholders demonstrate that they in vain filed a petition to the company requesting to institute the necessary legal proceedings itself within an appropriate period of time;*

*3. facts exist which give reason to suspect that the company has suffered a loss as a result of improprieties or gross breaches of the law or articles; and*

*4. no overriding interests of the company exist which would prevent the assertion of such damage claim.*

*(2) The regional court of the company's registered seat shall decide on the petition seeking leave to file such action. If the regional court maintains a chamber for commercial matters, such chamber shall have jurisdiction in lieu of the chamber for civil matters. The state government may by regulation transfer jurisdiction for several regional courts to one regional court if such transfer is required to ensure uniformity of decisions. The state government may transfer such power to the state ministry of justice. The statute of limitation for the claim at issue is stayed by the filing of such petition until the petition has been dismissed by a final and binding decision or the period allowed for bringing an action has expired. Before rendering its decision, the court shall provide the other party with an opportunity to comment on the matter. Such decision may be appealed immediately. Appeals on points of law are not permitted. The company shall be made a party in the judicial proceedings deciding on the petition pursuant to paragraph (1) as well as in such action for damages.*

*(3) The company may assert its claims for damages itself at any time; as soon as the company files such action, all pending proceedings instituted by the shareholders concerning that particular damage claim become inadmissible. The company may decide to take over a pending action in which its own damage claims are being asserted by another party in its current state at the time when the action is taken over. In the event of sentences 1 and 2, all former petitioners or claimants shall be joined as parties.*

one percent or 100.000 € of the shares of a stock corporation can file for a petition allowing them to enforce certain claims of the stock corporation. Although Section 148 Stock Corporation Code permits shareholder to file for an *actio pro socio* alone or together with other shareholders its does not state how shareholders actually coordinate. It is, however, accepted by legal scholars that a coordination of shareholders to file for an *actio pro socio* has to be considered as a civil partnership (Section 705 German Civil Code) since the shareholder agreed to peruse a common interested (= to bring an *actio pro socio*) by contributing something (= their shares and if necessary funds to finance the law suit) to the general civil partnership.[57] However, it has to be noted that the organization of such a civil partnership and especially its role in procedural law is rather unclear. This is the case since so far, no practical application of the *actio pro socio* under Section 148 German Stock Corporation Law or case law exists although it was already introduced in 2004.[58]

---

*(4) If the petition is granted, the action may only be brought before the court with jurisdiction pursuant to paragraph (2) within three months from the date on which the decision has become final and binding, provided that the shareholders have one more time to no avail requested the company to institute the necessary legal proceedings itself within an appropriate period of time. The action shall be brought against the persons specified in § 147(1) sentence 1 with the aim of obtaining compensation for the company. Interventions by shareholders are not permitted after the petition has been granted. If more than one such action is brought, they shall be consolidated in order to be heard and decided together.*

*(5) Such judgement shall be binding on the company and all other shareholders even if the action is dismissed in the judgement. The same shall apply to a settlement to be made pursuant § 149; however, such settlement shall only be effective in favour of or against the company after the permission to file an action has been granted.*

*(6) The person filing the petition shall bear the costs of the judicial proceedings if and to the extent that the petition is dismissed. If the petition is dismissed for reasons of opposing interests of the company, of which the company could have informed the petitioner prior to filing the petition but failed to do so, then the company shall reimburse the petitioner for the costs. In all other respects, a decision on the allocation on costs will be rendered in the final judgement. If the company files an action itself or takes over a pending action brought by shareholders, it shall bear all costs incurred by the petitioner until such time and may, except for the three-year waiting period, withdraw its action on the conditions set forth in § 93 (4) sentences 3 and 4 only. If the action is dismissed in whole or in part, the company shall reimburse the claimant for the costs to be borne by them unless the claimant obtained the court's permission to file an action by making false statements intentionally or by gross negligence. Shareholders acting jointly as petitioners or party shall only be reimbursed for the costs of one attorney unless the engagement of another attorney was necessary to prosecute the action".*

**57** See *Mock* in Spindler/Stilz, 3rd edition 2014, § 148 note 54; *Schröer*, (supra note 24), § 148 note 7.

**58** *Mock* (supra note 47), § 148 note 6 with further references.

### 3. Agreements regarding financial contributions to the company or corporation and other obligations of shareholders

In German company law the obligation to finance the company is usually set out in the articles of association of the company or being based on a contract between the company and the (future) shareholders to acquire the shares. However, shareholders are also free to agree on (future) contributions to the company. These obligations of shareholders are usually linked to certain events (milestones) or generally being based on the financial needs of the company. For the creation of such an obligation for the shareholders basically two different options are possible. First of all, such an obligation can be based on a (separate) contract between the shareholder and the corporation. Moreover, the shareholders can also reach an agreement together forcing all of them to contribute additional funds to the corporations. Whereas in the first option the company has a direct claim against each shareholder, the shareholders can (usually) not force each other to contribute additional funds to the corporation but – with the exception of the *actio pro socio* – depend on the management of the company to enforce these claims. If the shareholders reach an agreement among each other to contribute additional funds to the corporation such a contract has to be considered as a civil partnership (Section 705 German Civil Code)[59]. Moreover, the shareholders can also conclude a contract forcing them to increase the capital of the company.[60] These principles also apply to all other obligations of shareholders.[61]

### 4. No authority of shareholders to give binding instructions to the management of the corporation

Finally, a coordination of shareholders to give binding instructions to the corporation does not exist in German company law because shareholders do generally not have the right to give binding instructions to the management of the corporations outside the shareholders meeting. This is the case for all forms of companies and corporations. However, especially in the case of the closed corporations and companies the articles of association can provide such a right. If such

59 See B.II.1. for further details.

60 See B.II.3.

61 See (for the stock corporation) *Bungeroth* in Münchener Kommentar zum AktG, 4th edition 2016, § 54 note 33; *Henze* in Großkommentar zum AktG, 4th edition 2004, § 54 note 55.

a right is provided for several shareholders or members of the company or (closed) corporation a coordination by the shareholders constitutes a civil partnership (Section 705 German Civil Code)[62] to which the general principles apply. It also has to be noted that in the case of the stock corporation the articles of association cannot provide shareholders with such a right since the board of directors (*Vorstand*) runs the corporation independently (Section 76 German Stock Corporation Law).

## II. Shareholders' agreements on the (limitation for the) transfer of shares

Another common form of shareholders' agreements are agreements on the transfer of shares which are especially common in small and closed corporations (*Gesellschaft mit beschränkter Haftung [GmbH]*) and are usually called *schuldrechtliche or satzungsergänzende Nebenabreden*[63]. These agreements on the transfer of shares can limit the transfer of shares (*Verfügungsbeschränkungen*) or create preemption rights for certain shareholders (*Vorkaufsrecht*). In this context drag along clauses, tag along clauses or shoot out clauses are also common and have a growing influence in legal practice. However, is has to be noted that German company law does not specifically address such clauses. Also, so far there is hardly any case law on this kind of shareholders' agreements since these agreements usually contain arbitration clauses in order keep them confidential. The major problem of these clauses in German company law is whether these clauses have to be considered as being void because they are contrary to public policy (Section 138 German Civil Code[64]) since they excessively limit the freedom of the shareholders to leave the company and being adequately compensated. However, so far, no case law exists actually stating that such a clause is contrary to public policy.[65]

Limitations for the transfer of shares are not only found in small and closed corporations (*Gesellschaft mit beschränkter Haftung [GmbH]*) but also in the stock corporation (*Aktiengesellschaft [AG]*) especially in stock corporations being held by a family or closed group of persons. In these cases, the shareholders' agreement usually states that the shareholders can sell the shares only to

62 See B.II.1. for further details.

63 See also B.III for further details.

64 See supra note 9.

65 See e.g. OLG Nuremburg as of 20.12.2013 – 12 U 49/13, NZG 2014, 222 stating that a so-called Russian-Roulette-Clause is not contrary to public policy.

certain persons (usually members of a family or other (closed) group).[66] In company law limitations for the transfer of shares are theoretically not necessary since in German company law shares of companies are not transferable since their transfer constitutes a change of the articles of association requiring the approval of all shareholders (Section 717 German Civil Code[67]). However, the shareholders of a company are free to allow a free transferability of the shares in the articles of association or to limit this free transferability with the respective limitations.

## III. Shareholders' agreements on the constitution of the corporation

Shareholders' agreement can also deal with aspects of the constitution of the corporation and bind the shareholders concerning their rights to appoint board members, to change the constitution of the corporation, to change its capital structure and also to establish the obligation to contribute additional capital in the context of a capital increase.[68] Also, these shareholders' agreements constitute a civil partnership (Section 705 German Civil Code) to which the general principles apply.

## IV. Shareholders' agreements in pre-insolvency situation

Finally, shareholders' agreements can deal with certain aspects of pre-insolvency situations. In German company law, such shareholders' agreement so far hardly exists since in German insolvency law the influence of shareholders before and after the opening of insolvency proceedings is rather limited. However, shareholders' agreements in pre-insolvency situation often exist in the context of

---

**66** See e.g. Administrative Court of Frankfurt/Main as of 4.11.2015 – 7 K 4703/15.F, NZG 2016, 913 = AG 2016, 336; see *Rück/Heusel* Zu den Grenzen der Beteiligungstransparenz bei Aktienerwerbsmöglichkeiten in Gesellschaftervereinbarungen, NZG 2016, 897 ff. for further details.

**67** Section 717 German Civil Code (*Non-transferability of partner rights*) states:

*"The claims to which the partners are entitled against each other under the partnership relationship are not transferable. Excepted are the claims to which a partner is entitled in his management to the extent that their satisfaction may be demanded prior to the winding-up of the partnership, and the claims to profit sharing or to what the partner is owed on the winding-up."*

**68** For the creation of an obligation to contribute additional funds (without increasing capital) see C.I.3.

shareholder loans since often especially in the case of closed corporations (*Gesellschaft mit beschränkter Haftung [GmbH]*) shareholder loans have to be subordinated to avoid overindebtness (Section 19 German Insolvency Act) and the corresponding duty to file for bankruptcy (Section 15a German Insolvency Act). In this context, it is important to keep in mind that a subordination in German insolvency law constitutes a contract for the benefit of third parties (= the creditors – Section 328 German Civil Code) which can only be terminated if all creditor agree or the overindebtness does no longer exist.[69] Therefore, a shareholders' agreement dealing with a subordination of loans or other claims always involves the rights of third parties and does not constitute a mere contract between the shareholder but – as the articles of association – a contract considering the interest of third parties.

# D. Legal effects of shareholders' agreements

## I. Legal effects on the corporation

German company law distinguishes for the interpretation of the articles of association between articles of association of companies and corporations. Whereas the articles of association of companies are interpreted according to the true intention of the founding members of the companies, for the articles of association of corporations an objective standard of interpretation applies.[70] Therefore, the interpretation of articles of association of corporations is not based on the intention of the founding members but on how an objective and neutral person would understand the articles of association.[71] In that regard, the interpretation of articles of association of corporations follows the same approach as the interpretation of laws in Germany. Taking these principles into account shareholders' agreements do generally not have an impact on the interpretation of articles of association of corporations.[72] This is even the case if all shareholders are a party of the shareholders' agreement since the content of the shareholders' agreement does not necessarily equals the understanding of the articles of asso-

---

**69** Federal Court of Justice as of 5.3.2015 – IX ZR 133/14, BGHZ 204, 231 = NJW 2015, 1672; see also *Mock* JZ 2015, 520 ff. for further details.

**70** See e.g. *Mock* Gesellschaftsrecht, 2015, p. 47 f.; *K. Schmidt* Gesellschaftrecht, 4th edition 2002, p. 87 ff. with further references.

**71** See e.g. *K. Schmidt* Gesellschaftrecht, 4th edition 2002, p. 87 ff. with further references.

**72** *Hüffer/Koch* (supra note 5), § 23 note 47.

ciation of the corporation by a neutral and objective party.[73] However, shareholders' agreements can – in rather rare occasions[74] – have an impact on the articles of association if the founding members of the corporation were aware of such a shareholders' agreement.[75] Similar, in the case of companies, shareholders' agreements have an impact on the interpretation as far as they reflect the intention and objective of the founding members of the corporation. This does necessarily require that all founding members are parties of the shareholders' agreement since it only then reflects to certain extent the intention and objectives of the founding members.

Finally, in German corporation law it remains unclear whether a shareholders' agreement in violation of the articles of association has to be considered as being void or at least being – in that regard – not enforceable. Although especially some legal scholars[76] are in favor of such a limitation it has not been accepted by the case law. Nevertheless, German corporate law applies the principle of *Satzungsdurchbrechung or Satzungsüberlagerung* (partial replacement of the articles of association) according to which a violation of the articles of association constitutes only its (admissible) replacement if the violation has only an internal effect and does not interfere with the external interaction of the corporation with the public and does not limit the interest of future shareholders.[77] This is especially relevant for distribution of profits not being in accordance with the provisions of the articles of association[78] but not the case if the articles of association limited the duration of the term of board members and the shareholders pass a resolution appointing some board members for a longer period.[79] However, it has to be noted that the existing case law is more or less fragmentary and is far from providing a coherent set of rules in this context.

**73** See D.IV.1. on the influence of a shareholders' agreement by all shareholders on shareholders' resolutions.

**74** This case law (see note 64) is based on sport associations where other associations have to be a member on order to engage in certain sports.

**75** Federal Court of Justice as of 2.12.1974 – II ZR 78/72, BGHZ 63, 282, 290 = NJW 1975, 771.

**76** See e.g. *Arnold* (supra note 5), § 23 note 181; *Pentz* (supra note 6), § 23 note 196.

**77** Federal Court of Justice as of 7.6.1993 – II ZR 81/92, BGHZ 123, 15 = NJW 1993, 2246; see also *Koch* Höherrangiges Satzungsrecht vs. schuldrechtliche Satzungsüberlagerung, AG 2015, 213 ff.; *Priester* Schuldrechtliche Vereinbarungen zur Gewinnverteilung bei der AG, ZIP 2015, 2156 ff.

**78** Regional Court of Frankfurt/Main as of 23.12.2014 – 3 – 05 O 47/14, NZG 2015, 482ff. stating that a shareholders' agreement cannot alter the rules for distributions set out in the articles of association.

**79** Federal Court of Justice as of 7.6.1993 – II ZR 81/92, BGHZ 123, 15 = NJW 1993, 2246.

## II. Legal effects on the shareholders

Since shareholders' agreements are regarded as civil partnerships (Section 705 German Civil Code)[80] the rights created by the shareholders' agreement are generally not transferable (Section 717 German Civil Code[81]). However, the parties of such an agreement are free to permit a free transfer of these rights. Also, the obligation arising from the shareholders' agreements can generally not be transferred to another party. Such a transfer requires the consent of all parties of the shareholders' agreement and of the party acquiring this obligation (Section 414 German Civil Code[82]). It has to be noted that in practice such a transfer of rights or obligations of a shareholders' agreement are rather rare.

Generally, the conclusion of a shareholders' agreement does not change the rights and obligations of the shareholder of a corporation. However, in capital market law additional requirements apply since a shareholders' agreement can constitute a so-called *acting in concert*. Pursuant to Section 33 German Securities Trading Act shareholders of listed corporations must notify the corporation and the German Federal Financial Supervisory Authority (*Bundesanstalt für Finanzdienstleistungsaufsicht [BaFin]*) when they acquire 3, 5, 10, 15, 20, 25, 30, 50 or 75% of the voting rights of the corporation. If shareholders conclude a voting agreement, such an agreement can constitute an *acting in concert* requiring the parties of the voting agreement to notify the corporation and the German Federal Financial Supervisory Authority (*BaFin*) when all the voting rights of the parties of the shareholders' agreement (together) reach the threshold of 3, 5, 10, 15, 20, 25, 30, 50 or 75% (Section 34 subs. 2 German Securities Trading Act[83]). The same principle applies in German Takeover Law when a shareholder

**80** See B.II.3. for further details.

**81** See supra note 32.

**82** Section 414 German Civil Code (*Contract between obligee and transferee*) states:

*"A debt may be assumed by a third party by contract with the obligee in such a way that the third party steps into the shoes of the previous obligor".*

**83** Section 22 subs. 2 German Securities Trading Act states:

*"Any voting rights attached to shares in the issuer whose home country is the Federal Republic of Germany which belong to a third party shall also be attributed to the party subject to the notification requirement in full if the party subject to the notification requirement or its subsidiary coordinates with such third party, on the basis of an agreement or in another manner, its conduct in respect of the issuer; agreements in individual cases shall be excluded. Coordinated conduct requires that the party subject to the notification requirement or its subsidiary and the third party reach a consensus on the exercise of voting rights or collaborate in another manner with the aim of bringing about a permanent and material change in the issuer's business strategy. Subsec-*

must make a public offer to all other shareholders to acquire their shares if one – or several shareholders *acting in concert* – gains the control of the corporation (Section 30 subs. 2 German Takeover Law[84]) which is the case when one shareholder acquired more than 30% of the voting rights. Besides, shareholders' agreements on the transfer of shares can also be relevant for the notification requirements of Section 33 ff. German Securities Trading Act if they provide the right for one shareholder to acquire shares of another shareholder under certain conditions since this qualifies as an instrument in the meaning of Sections 38 f. German Securities Trading Act.[85]

Shareholders' agreements are no subject to any mandatory publication or registration since they are regarded as civil partnerships (Section 705 German Civil Code)[86]. Moreover, shareholders' agreements often but not necessarily include a confidentiality clause. Therefore, it is usually impossible for outsiders to become aware of a shareholders' agreement unless the parties of that agreement make it public. An exemption to these principles is found in capital market law under the *acting in concert* since in this case the shareholders have to publish the amount of their own and the voting rights of the other parties of the shareholders' agreement.

---

*tion (1) shall apply mutatis mutandis to the calculation of the percentage of voting rights held by the third party."*

**84** Section 30 subs. 2 Securities Acquisition and Takeover Act states:

*"Any voting rights attached to shares in the target company which belong to a third party shall also be attributed to the offeror in full if the offeror or his subsidiary coordinates, on the basis of an agreement or in another manner, his conduct with such third party in respect of the target company; agreements in individual cases shall be excluded. Coordinated conduct requires that the offeror or his subsidiary and the third party reach a consensus on the exercise of voting rights or collaborate in another manner with the aim of bringing about a permanent and material change in the target company's business strategy. Subsection (1) shall apply mutatis mutandis to the calculation of the percentage of voting rights held by the third party".*

**85** See e.g. Administrative Court of Frankfurt/Main as of 4.11.2015 – 7 K 4703/15.F, NZG 2016, 913 = AG 2016, 336 denying this condition being met in the case. See *Rück/Heusel*, Zu den Grenzen der Beteiligungstransparenz bei Aktienerwerbsmöglichkeiten in Gesellschaftervereinbarungen, NZG 2016, 897 ff. for further details.

**86** See B.II.3. for further details.

## III. Shareholders' agreements and law of groups ("*Konzernrecht*")

In German law shareholders' agreements corporate an impact on the law of groups (*Konzernrecht*). First of all, a shareholders' agreement can provide a controlling influence for one party of the agreement regarding the corporation. As a consequence, this corporation would be considered a controlled enterprise (Section 17 subsection 1 German Stock Corporation Law[87]) which would lead to an application of the rules on the so-called *faktischer Konzern* (*de facto group of corporations* – Sections 311 ff. German Stock Corporation Law).[88] Moreover, shareholders' agreements can be used to rebut the presumption of control (*majority owned enterprise*) of Section 17 subsection 2 German Stock Corporation Law[89] which applies when an enterprise holds a majority shareholding of another enterprise.[90] This requires that the shareholders' agreement (partly) shifts the control one party has due to its majority holding to another party or to all party together. The idea behind such an agreement is to avoid the application of the rules on the so-called *faktischer Konzern* (*de facto group of corporations* – Sections 311 ff. German Stock Corporation Law).

However, it has to be noted that these rules of the law of groups solely apply to the stock corporation as being the controlled entity. They do not apply to all forms companies and especially not to the closed corporation (*Gesellschaft mit beschränkter Haftung [GmbH]*).[91]

---

**87** Section 17 subsection 1 German Stock Corporation Law (*Controlled and controlling enterprise*) states:

"*Legally separate enterprises over which another enterprise (controlling enterprise) is able to exert, directly or indirectly, a controlling influence, shall constitute controlled enterprises*".

**88** *Bayer* in Münchener Kommentar zum AktG, 4th edition 2016, § 17 note 73; *Emmerich* in Emmerich/Habersack, Aktien- und GmbH-Konzernrecht, 8th edition 2016, § 17 note 26; *Hüffer/Koch*, (supra note 5), § 17 note 6.

**89** Section 17 subsection 2 German Stock Corporation Law (*Controlled and controlling enterprise*) states:

"*A majority owned enterprise shall be presumed to be controlled by the enterprise with a majority shareholding in it*".

**90** *Bayer* (supra note 73), § 17 note 99; *Emmerich* (supra note 73), § 17 note 40; *Hüffer/Koch* (supra note 5), § 17 note 22.

**91** Federal Court of Justice as of 5.6.1975 – II ZR 23/74 (*ITT*), BGHZ 65, 15, 18 = NJW 1976, 191; Federal Court of Justice as of 16.9.1985 – II ZR 275/84 (*Autokran*), BGHZ 95, 330, 340 = NJW 1986, 188; Federal Court of Justice as of 17.9.2001 – II ZR 178/99 (*Bremer Vulkan*), BGHZ 149, 10, 16 = NJW 2001, 3622, see also *Altmeppen* in Münchener Kommentar zum AktG, 4th edition 2015, Vorbemerkungen zu § 311 note 78 ff. with further references on the discussion in Germany.

## IV. Consequences of a breach of the shareholders' agreements

### 1. Shareholders' agreements on voting rights

The consequences of a breach of shareholders' agreements on voting rights are rather limited in German company law. Since shareholders' agreements are civil partnerships (Section 705 German Civil Code)[92] one consequence of a breach is the right of the other parties to terminate the agreement since usually the parties explicitly state such a termination right in the agreement.[93] Moreover, the other parties of the shareholders' agreement can claim damages from the dissenting shareholder under general contract law (Section 280 subsection 1 German Civil Code[94]). However, usually they lack a clear and determinable damage since the violation of the shareholders' agreement does not correspond with a monetary damage of the other shareholders.

In contrast, there are no legal consequences of a breach of the shareholders' agreement for the corporation. The other shareholders can therefore especially not challenge the shareholders resolutions which were affected by the shareholders' agreement. The vote of each shareholder is completely valid even if this vote constitutes a violation of the shareholders' agreement. However, if all shareholders of the corporation are parties of the shareholders' agreement, the violation of the shareholders' agreement enables each shareholder to challenge the shareholders' resolution.[95] Nevertheless, it has to be doubted whether this case law (being only based on a closed corporation) still applies since it does not sufficiently reflect the difference between the articles of association on the one hand and the shareholders agreement on the other.[96] Also, the membership

**92** See B.II.3. for further details.

**93** See B.II. for further details.

**94** Section 280 subs. 1 German Civil Code (*Damages for breach of duty*) states:

*"If the obligor breaches a duty arising from the obligation, the obligee may demand damages for the damage caused thereby. This does not apply if the obligor is not responsible for the breach of duty".*

**95** Federal Court of Jusice as of 20.1.1983 – II ZR 243/81, NJW 1983, 1910, 1911; Federal Court of Justice as of 27.10.1986 – II ZR 240/85, NJW 1987, 1890, 1892 stating that an agreement of all shareholders has to be considered as an agreement of the corporation. See on this case *Ventoruzzo/Conac/Goto/Mock/Notari/Reisberg*, Comparative Corporate Law, 2015, p. 425 ff. with a translation of the first case.

**96** E.g. *Goette* in Henze/Timm/Westermann, Gesellschaftsrecht, 1995, p. 113, 119 ff.; *Hüffer/Koch* (supra note 5) § 23 note 47; § 243 note 10; *Pentz* (supra note 6), § 23 note 202.

of the shareholder and his rights and duties because of that membership are not affected by his violation of the shareholders' agreement.

## 2. Shareholders' agreements on the transfer of shares

The violation of shareholders' agreements on the transfer of shares – as an independent contract between certain shareholders[97] – constitutes a breach of contract resulting in the right for the other party to terminate the contract (Section 323 subsection 1 German Civil Code[98]) or to claim damages (Section 280 subsection 1 German Civil Code). Moreover, the parties can – if the conditions set out in the respective clause are met – also claim a performance of the party being in breach of the shareholders' agreement. Since the limitation of the transfer of shares is only being set out in the contract – creating a mere obligation – the actually transfer of the shares is not effected by the violation (Section 137 German Civil Code[99]). Therefore, the shareholders can effectively transfer their shares despite the fact that they are bound by are contract not to do so.

If the limitation of the transfer of shares is part of the articles of association a violation might also result in an exclusion of the party violating the respective provision. Moreover, in this case the transfer under the violation of the respective clause is not effective.[100] Therefore, the shareholders cannot effectively transfer the shares if the respective clause in the articles of association prohibits or limits the transfer.

---

**97** See supra B.II.2. for further details.

**98** Section 323 subs. 1 German Civil Code (*Revocation for nonperformance or for performance not in conformity with the contract*) states:

"*If, in the case of a reciprocal contract, the obligor does not render an act of performance which is due, or does not render it in conformity with the contract, then the obligee may revoke the contract, if he has specified, without result, an additional period for performance or cure*".

**99** Section 137 German Civil Code (*Prohibition of dispositions in a legal transaction*) states:

"*The power to dispose of an alienable right may not be excluded or restricted by a legal transaction. This effectiveness of an obligation not to dispose of such a right is not affected by this provision*".

**100** See *Fastrich* in Baumbach/Hueck, GmbHG, 21st edition 2017, § 15 note 47; see also Federal Court of Justice as of 28.4.1954 – II ZR 8/53, BGHZ 13, 179 = NJW 1954, 1155 (obiter).

### 3. Shareholders' agreements on the constitution of the corporation

Finally, the breach of a shareholders' agreement on the constitution of the corporation results in the right of the other parties to terminate the agreement since usually the parties explicitly state such a termination right in the agreement (Section 723 German Civil Code[101]). Also, (theoretically) the other parties can claim damages which, however, requires a clear and determinable damage which usually does not exist.

## V. Impact of void shareholders' agreements

### 1. Shareholders' agreements on voting rights

When a shareholders' agreement is void, it cannot create any obligation for the shareholder to exercise the voting rights in a certain way. Therefore, the shareholder can exercise his voting rights without any limitations. Consequently, the exercise of the voting right and the shareholder resolution itself is valid and cannot be subject to any claim. This also applies if the shareholder exercised his voting right assuming that he was bound by a voting agreement.[102] Therefore, the shareholder cannot claim that he would have voted differently if he knew that the voting agreement was void.[103]

### 2. Shareholders' agreements on the transfer of shares and on the constitution of the corporation

When it comes to shareholders' agreements on the transfer of shares and on the constitution of the corporation the consequences of void agreements are determined by general civil law. Therefore, the parties are not bound by these agreements and can reclaim anything that they performed expecting that these agreements were valid. The same applies for shareholders' agreements on the constitution of the corporation.

---

**101** See supra note 13.

**102** Higher Regional Court of Nuremburg as of 17.1.1996 – 12 U 2801/95, AG 1996, 228; see also *Hüffer/Koch* (supra note 5) § 136 note 29; *Schröer* (supra note 24), § 136 note 85.

**103** See also *Hüffer/Koch* (supra note 5) § 136 note 29; *Schröer* (supra note 24), § 136 note 85 with further references.

# E. Enforcement of shareholders' agreements

## I. Shareholders' agreements on voting rights

Since shareholders' agreements on voting rights merely create an obligation to vote in accordance with the agreement the options for an enforcement of these agreements are rather limited.[104] Although the other parties of the shareholder agreement can enforce the voting agreements this enforcement can usually not be obtained in time since the meeting of the parties of the voting agreements takes usually place only a few days before the actual shareholder meeting. Even the enforcement by preliminary rulings (*einstweiliger Rechtsschutz*) is rather difficult since this requires that the other shareholders know that the dissenting shareholder will not exercise his voting rights in the shareholder meeting in accordance with the agreement. Besides these practical problems it is also not absolutely clear whether such a preliminary ruling is admissible or not, since such a preliminary ruling is considered as an inadmissible intervention in internal affairs of the corporations. Moreover it actually completes the proceedings forcing the judge to decide the complete matter already in the preliminary ruling.[105]

Also, the other instruments of civil law are rather limited in their effect. This is especially the case for the duty to pay damages (Section 280 subs. 1 German Civil Code[106]) for the dissenting shareholders since these cases usually lack a clear and determinable damage because the violation of the shareholders' agreements does not correspond with a monetary damage of the other shareholders.

The most common and probably most effective tool to enforce voting agreements are contractual penalties which are generally admissible in German law (Section 340 German Civil Code[107]). However, German civil law sets a serious limitation in this regard since a judge can reduce a disproportionately high penalty to a reasonable amount (Section 343 subs. 1 German Civil Code[108]). Therefore, a

---

**104** For an overview see *Schröer* (supra note 24), § 136 note 87 ff.

**105** *Schröder* (supra note 24), § 136 note 92.

**106** See supra note 79.

**107** Section 340 German Civil Code (*Promise to pay a penalty for nonperformance*) states:

*"If the obligor has promised the penalty in the event that he fails to perform his obligation, the obligee may demand the penalty that is payable in lieu of fulfilment. If the obligee declares to the obligor that he is demanding the penalty, the claim to performance is excluded."*

**108** Section 343 German Civil Code (*Reduction of the penalty*) states:

*"If a payable penalty is disproportionately high, it may on the application of the obligor be reduced to a reasonable amount by judicial decision. In judging the appropriateness, every legit-*

legal uncertainty remains that a contractual penalty will not be upheld by the courts.

### II. Shareholders' agreements on the transfer of shares and on the constitution of the Corporation

In the context of shareholders' agreements on the transfer of shares and on the constitution of the corporation the enforcement is usually more simple. This is case since for the enforcement of these agreements time is not as much as an issue as it is for voting agreements. Therefore, the parties of such an agreement can enforce this agreement and claim specific performance. Moreover, the violation of these shareholders' agreements often creates damages for the other parties of the agreement which must be compensated by the violating shareholder.

## F. Summary

German corporate law is rather blind when it comes to shareholders' agreements since they are hardly regulated. Due to the general principle of freedom of contract shareholders' agreements are generally admissible and only limited by general principles of civil law in certain occasions. Although having legal effect and being binding for the parties the enforcement of shareholders' agreements is very weak since these agreements only create an obligation for shareholders to exercise his rights in a certain way. This is especially the case for voting agreements where an enforcement in a timely manner is almost impossible. However, the enforcement of shareholders' agreements on the transfer of shares and on the constitution of the corporation is more simple since the legal consequences of general civil law for a violation of these agreements apply and provide a sufficient framework for the enforcement.

---

*imate interest of the obligee, not merely his financial interest, must be taken into account. Once the penalty is paid, reduction is excluded".*

Georgios Psaroudakis

# Greece

**Table of Content**



## A. Nature of Corporate Law Regulation

There is no special legislation on shareholders' agreements in Greek law.[1] The law of public corporations (Law 2190/1920 on societés anonymes, the abbrevia-

1 With the exception of art. 26(2) of Law 959/1979 on maritime companies. Maritime companies are a variation of public corporations, which has been providing for more flexibility to address the particular needs of maritime commerce. The above-mentioned provision explicitly affirms the validity of vote-related shareholders' agreements in maritime companies. It has never been suggested that this could support an argument *a contrario* against the validity of such agreements in other corporations. It is rather an explicit rule to foster clarity (for which there

**Ass. Prof. Dr. Georgios Psaroudakis,** Aristotle University of Thessaloniki

https://doi.org/10.1515/9783110517026-015

tion for which in Greek is AE), as well as the law of both forms of private corporations (Law 3190/1955 on limited liability companies, i.e. EPE by their abbreviation in Greek, and art. 43 *et seq.* of Law 4072/2012 on private companies, i.e. IKE by their abbreviation in Greek) do not contain any provisions of the kind. Neither is any such provision to be found in partnership law, which is contained in art. 249 *et seq.* of Law 4072/2012.

Shareholders' agreements are only mentioned in other provisions (in particular, art. 32(2)(d1) of Law 4308/2014 on Greek Accounting Standards, art. 2(e) and art. 7(1) of Law 3461/2006 on takeover bids, art. 10(a,b) of Law 3556/2007 on transparency in listed companies), that attach legal consequences (consolidated financial accounting, mandatory bid, reporting of major holdings) to such agreements (among other arrangements that bring about the same consequences) without directly regulating their validity or content. One might argue that the basic validity of shareholders' agreements is implicitly recognized by such other provisions, as it is taken for granted that these agreements do bind shareholders and that the situation so arising must be further regulated. However, this argument is not ultimately convincing, as such provisions could also respond to the fact that shareholders might abide by such agreements (which would thus be practically relevant), even if they were under no legal obligation to do so. Indeed, gentlemen's agreements, that have been made non-binding by the parties, are caught by these provisions.

This is not at all to say that shareholders' agreements are not legally binding; this is only to say that the basis for their binding force is not to be found in the above-mentioned provisions referring to them in the context of other regulatory concerns. In particular, in the absence of any specific statutory regulation, shareholders' agreements are generally valid on the basis of the general freedom of contract (art. 361 of the Greek Civil Code)[2] and the lack of a prohib-

---

may had been more need at the time of adoption of the said Law, almost four decades ago, than today) in this particular area.

2 Athens Court of Appeal 8129/1977, NoB 1978, 1075; Athens Court of First Instance 3265/1991, EEmpD 1992, 444; Athens Court of First Instance 569/2007, EEmpD 2008, 76; Veroia Court of First Instance 304/1998, NoB 2000, 1604; *Antonopoulos* Law of public corporations and limited liability corporations, 4th edn. (Sakkoulas, Athens-Thessaloniki 2012) p. 51; *Georgakopoulos* Company Law vol. 3 (Athens 1974) p. 329; *Marinos* Shareholders' agreement and corporate charter, ElD 2008, 677; *idem* Case comment to Athens Court of First Instance 569/2007, ChrID 2008, 551–552; *Michalopoulos* Issues relating to shareholders' agreements, EEmpD 1992, 348, 353; *idem* Modern tendencies in the law of public corporations: From the strictness of the statute to interaction with shareholders' agreements, EpiskED 2008, 963, 971; *Mitsou* in Antonopoulos/Mouzoulas (eds.), Public corporations vol. I (Sakkoulas, Athens-Thessaloniki 2013) art 2 n 43; *Perakis* Contractual restrictions of the shareholder's voting rights (Athens 1976) p 117; *idem*

ition. This basic validity of shareholders' agreements has not been in any doubt on the part of case law or legal scholarship.

But the validity of shareholders' agreements is limited by the general clauses of the Civil Code, in particular the good faith principle in art. 288 and the prohibition of abuse of rights in art. 281,[3] the prohibition of excessively one-sided contracts in art. 179, as well as by an implied prohibition of circumscribing corporate law. While the reference to these general provisions of the Civil Code is uncontroversial and symmetrical to the recognition of shareholders' agreements as an expression of the general freedom of contract, to which these provisions provide intrinsic limits, the reference to the risk of circumscribing corporate law is a bit more questionable and has not been further clarified by case law. In particular, if shareholders' agreements only apply among shareholders and do not affect the legal position of the corporation itself, as will be further analysed below, then it is not immediately clear how corporate law may be circumscribed by them. Further analysis[4] is required in order to determine whether this may happen in some limited circumstances.

It should also be mentioned here that the law of public corporations (i.e., Law 2190/1920) is in principle mandatory, meaning that the corporation's statute may not deviate from it, except for the cases, in which such deviation is made possible by the said Law.[5] While this mandatory nature of its provisions is not explicitly provided for in this Law, it is a well-established feature of public corporations law in Greece,[6] standing against the background of the wide range of interests in the proper functioning of the public corporation and the need to protect shareholders who cannot influence management. Recent amendments to the Law 2190/1920 (in particular the major amendments made in 2007) increased the instances in which discretion is granted to the corporation's statute, in particular

in Perakis (ed.), Law of Public Corporations (3rd edn. Nomiki Bibliothiki, Athens 2010), Introduction para. 13; *Spyridonos* The protection of minority shareholders from shareholders' agreements, DEE 2004, 641.

3 The "good morals" (*gute Sitten*) principle in art. 178 of the Civil Code is also mentioned in this context: see e.g. *N. Rokas* Commercial companies, 7th edn. (Nomiki Bibliothiki, Athens 2012) p 230. However, it is the good faith principle that should be applied to intra-corporate matters, as it is better suited to pre-existing legal relationships, while art. 178 should rather be applied to matters arising between previously unrelated parties and relating to broader considerations: see generally *Voglis* Risks relating to the concretization of general clauses, DEE 2003, 757, 762.

4 See below at III.1.1.

5 See, among others, *Perakis* in Perakis (ed.), The Law of Public Corporations, Introduction para. 13; *Psychomanis* Law of commercial companies (Sakkoulas, Athens-Thessaloniki 2013) pp 192–3; *N. Rokas* (n 3) p 232.

6 See eg *Antonopoulos* (n 2) p 7.

using the methods of opting-in and opting-out. However, this does not alter the principle of non-deviation from the law unless otherwise stated.

This principle, taken together with the practical reality that most Greek AEs (public corporations) are very closely-held and thus value flexibility and direct contact among shareholders, explains why shareholders' agreements are important in Greek law: They bridge the gap between strict legal structure and factual closedness.[7] Indeed, there is a rich discussion on shareholders' agreements in legal scholarship, as well as a fair (if not high, given the discrete nature of such agreements) number of reported cases.

The other types of corporations and partnerships generally follow the principle of freedom of contract as to the internal workings of the corporation or partnership,[8] as the case may be (with limits derived from general limitations of freedom of contract and from the fundamentals of each corporate form). Therefore, there is much more leeway there as to the formation of the corporate charter, which may reduce the incentive to have recourse to further contractual arrangements.[9] In the (rather unlikely, in Greek practice) case of a multi-membered, less personal corporation (EPE or IKE) or partnership, shareholders' agreements might still arise, though again rather in corporations than in partnerships.

# B. Regulation of Shareholders' Agreements

## I. Validity across legal forms

As mentioned, there is no specific regulation on shareholders' agreements in Greek corporate law and it is rather general contract law that applies. It should also be noted that there exists a rather arcane criminal provision in art. 59 of Law 2190/1920, being inspired by the (outdated) analogy between "shareholder democracy" and democracy in the political sense,[10] and prohibiting the "sale of

7 Cf. *Giotaki* Case comment to Athens Court of First Instance 5565/2003, EEmpD 2004, 525, 530–1; *Marinos* Shareholders' agreements between contract and corporate law (P.N. Sakkoulas, Athens 2011) pp 8, 31–32; *idem* ElD 2008, 677; *Mitsou* (n 2) art 2 n 40.

8 See eg *N. Rokas* (n 3) pp 52, 528, 580.

9 *Marinos* Shareholders' agreements (P.N. Sakkoulas, Athens 2011) p 26; *Mitsou* (n 2) art 2 n 40.

10 It has been remarked that the tendency, especially in Romanic legal orders, to prohibit or limit agreements on the exercise of voting rights (cf. generally on this issue in French law eg *Viandier* Observations sue les conventions de vote, JCP G 1986 I 3253), has been informed by a par-

vote" by shareholders in public corporations. In particular, this provision criminalizes the offer and receipt of "special advantages" in order to abstain or vote in a particular manner in the shareholders' meeting. Already in 1962 the proviso has been added that such behaviour is only prohibited, if it occurs "on improper grounds". Therefore, clauses on voting in the shareholders' meeting as part of a shareholders' agreement are in principle valid, as this provision does not introduce (at least not any more) a ground for invalidity. The reason is that it does not explain itself what grounds are regarded as improper, but rather sets a (criminal) sanction for the case it is independently found that an agreement is improper.[11] Moreover, it does not seem to have any relevance in actual Greek practice[12], though it could relate to cases of naked bribery.

As also mentioned, the starting point is that shareholders' agreements are valid in all corporate forms as an exercise of the general freedom of contract (art. 361 of the Greek Civil Code). As will be further discussed below, there is a rather clear separation between the contractual relation among the contracting parties on the one hand and the corporate regulation and decision-making (corporate charter and decisions of the corporation's organs) on the other. It follows from this separation that the validity of these agreements does not depend on their admission in the charter or by the shareholders' meeting. Indeed, the charter cannot even contain a prohibition on shareholders' agreements; that would be invalid, as it would encroach on the shareholders' freedom of contract in their horizontal relations.[13]

The present analysis applies in principle to partnerships and close corporations as well. There is no difference between them and public corporations as to the validity of such agreements. However, shareholders' agreements are mostly discussed in the context of corporations (indeed typically public corporations that are, as mentioned, very common in Greece, even if most of them are not actually listed), and this is also where case law arises, given that the more personal nature of partnerships and close corporations and of their charters tends to preempt the need for further contractual arrangements. In theory, there may be

---

allel drawn between such voting rights and the voting rights of citizens: see among others *Marinos* (n 9) pp 21–22.

**11** *Perakis* (n 2) p 116.

**12** For similar (if not identical) discussions on the French and German criminal provisions of the kind see above, *Černá* p. 56 and *Mock* p. 287 respectively.

**13** *Perakis* (n 2) p 118, who also explains that such a clause could be re-interpreted as a shareholders' agreement itself (a meta-agreement, as it were), binding the founders who included it in the charter. This does not render future agreements invalid; it may subject the parties to such future agreements to contractual remedies on the basis of the former agreement.

more interest for such agreements in a partnership with capital-oriented features (such as a broad application of majority voting, indeed possibly on the basis of share, rather than following the unanimity principle, which applies by default under art. 253 of Law 4072/2012, or at least the "one person one vote" principle); it is under such circumstances that, for example, a "voting trust" may make sense. However, given the very small size and closely-held nature of partnerships in actual practice in Greece, this may a point of rather theoretical interest. In a similar (though not identical) vein, the practical need for shareholders' agreements is smaller in the case of the legal forms of EPE and IKE too.

## II. Duration

There are no restrictions on the duration of shareholders' agreements that would be specific to them. In this case as well, general contract law applies. On this basis, if their duration is indefinite (or so long, e.g. exceeding twenty years, as to be tantamount to indefinite), it should be accepted that shareholders have an implicit termination right, indeed without the need to invoke a "significant reason" for termination (art. 767 of the Greek Civil Code[14]).[15] Untimely termination might lead to an obligation of the terminating shareholder to compensate the rest. In case of definite duration, the better view is that there is, here too, still a termination right, provided that a "significant reason" exists. This right is based on art. 766 of the Greek Civil Code, if the agreement is qualified as a partnership.[16] But it is also arguable that the same applies irrespective of the exact qualification of the agreement, in the sense of a general right of termination for significant reason in all long-term contractual relations.[17]

14 That is, if the agreement is qualified as a partnership, as it typically would be in case of such duration: see n 26.

15 *Marinos* (n 9) p 71; *Perakis* (n 2) p 221.

16 *Perakis* (n 2) p 221. Another issue to be taken note of in this context, in particular if the agreement is qualified as a civil partnership, is that according to Greek case law the termination is valid even if there is actually no significant reason; the only consequence of the lack of significant reason is that the partner who exercised the termination right is liable for damages: see e.g. Areios Pagos 700/1973, EEmpD 1974, 199; Athens Court of Appeal 8129/1977, NoB 1978, 1075, and in the particular context of shareholders' agreements Athens Court of First Instance 5001/1971, EEmpD 1971, 545. This further facilitates termination.

17 *N. Rokas* (n 3) p 231. See also, as to the general discussion on this issue, *Filios* General law of obligations (4th edn. A.N. Sakkoulas, Athens-Komotini 2007) p 576; *Psychomanis* The placement of perpetual bonds by Greek banks, DEE 2010, 863, 864; for a different view see *Georgakopoulos*

In any case, it is advisable to regulate duration in the agreement itself, for otherwise unwanted consequences might arise, in particular on the basis of the law on civil partnerships. For instance, the death of a party to the agreement leads according to art. 773 of the Greek Civil Code to the termination of the partnership (in other words here, of the agreement), if not otherwise provided for in the partnership contract.[18]

## III. Case law

Individual aspects of the case law on shareholders' agreements are analysed below. As a general observation, the validity of shareholders' agreements is not questioned in principle.[19] Much discussion relates to their effects. The prevailing view is that these agreements are only relevant to the "horizontal" relation among their parties, as opposed to the functioning of the corporation. In particular, in case of violation of the agreement by one of the parties, e. g. by voting in a different manner than agreed upon or by transferring shares in a manner that is incompatible with the related agreement, other shareholders have contractual remedies, but the violating shareholder's action remains valid vis-à-vis the corporation: The resolution of the shareholders' meeting which was passed with the vote of this shareholder is not void or voidable, the transfer of shares has been effected. In other words, a strict separation between the contractual and the corporate is upheld.[20]

Actually, it is this separation that seems to make it easier for case law to affirm the general validity of shareholders' agreements, as it disproves the argument that shareholders' agreements generally circumscribe the law or the corporate charter.[21] In particular, shareholders' agreements do not lead to the same effect as a provision of the same content in the corporate charter, as they do not affect the validity of a corporate measure but rather merely lead to contractual remedies among the parties.

---

The law of long-term obligations (Athens 1979) p 171. It should be noted that the issue has not been dealt with in this generality by case law.

**18** See also *Marinos* (n 9) p 72; *Perakis* (n 2) p 222.

**19** See n 2.

**20** See the discussion below at IV.3.

**21** See in this vein Athens Court of First Instance 3265/1991, EEmpD 1992, 444; see also *Kefaleas* Shareholders' agreements in public corporations, EEmpD 1971, 179, 183 – 184.

## IV. Cross-border shareholders' agreements

There is not much discussion on cross-border shareholders' agreements and the law applicable to them. The issue does not seem to have arisen in case law.[22] The above-mentioned separation between the contractual and the corporate level would suggest that Greek courts would tend to bring shareholders' agreements within the scope of the Rome I Regulation, as this separation suggests that the exception of corporate matters from the field of application of the Regulation in art. 1(2)(f) thereof would not apply. Of course, this is in principle a matter of uniform interpretation of the Regulation; but the lack, under national law, of direct influence of the contract on the functioning of the corporation is significant for the qualification of the contract as per art. 1(2) of the Regulation, in particular its lack of corporate nature.[23] It should also be noted that, even if qualified as partnerships, these agreements are civil partnerships with no autonomous organization, so that they do not fall under the said exception on that basis either.[24]

In this context of the Rome I Regulation, it is clear that shareholders are free to determine governing law as per art. 3. If no such clause has been included, then applicable law comes down to the "closest connection" of the contract with a country according to art. 4(4) of the said Regulation. This may well ultimately be the law of the company's seat, not because the *lex societatis* is applicable as such, but rather because it also happens to be the proper *lex causae*. However, depending on the circumstances, it is not impossible to reach a different conclusion on the *lex causae* of the contract, in particular if all parties are resident in the same country, which is different from the country of the corporation's seat, and the contract is rather related to transactions with shares than to the corporation as such, eg to the workings of its organs.[25]

---

**22** As noted by *Perakis* Case comment to Athens Court of Appeal 8129/1977, NoB 1978, 1077, this judgment could have analyzed the law applicable to the agreement in question (as the corporation was Greek but the shareholders were domiciled and had concluded the agreement abroad), but it took the application of Greek law for granted instead.

**23** Cf. above, Csach p. 95.

**24** *Martiny* in MünchKomm-BGB (6th edn Beck, Munich 2015) Rom I-VO Art 1 n 70.

**25** For a similar (but not identical) view see *Perakis* NoB 1978, 1078, who suggests that agreements relating to voting in a single shareholders' meeting are very closely connected with the corporation and thus subjected to the *lex societatis*, while this is less certain in case of longer-term agreements. However, the latter agreements may indeed develop "a life of their own", but this is still closely related to the *societas*.

# C. Forms of Shareholders' Agreements

## I. Shareholders' Agreements on Shareholder Rights

### 1. Functioning and limits of agreements on voting rights

Agreements on the exercise of voting rights ("voting consortia") are the most common form of shareholders' agreements reported in case law. As the case is with regard to shareholders' agreements generally, they are not regulated explicitly, but they are generally thought to be valid. Actually, these agreements may be civil (i.e., non-commercial, as they do not have any market presence of their own) partnerships themselves (in which the shareholders participating in the agreement are partners),[26] not to be confused with the corporation (or partnership), to the voting rights in which they refer. Indeed, the contracting parties are thought to contribute, by means of their concerted voting, to a common objective, which is (generally speaking) a stable influence on the corporation's affairs.

It is possible, as an exercise of the general freedom of contract, to adopt a variety of arrangements as to the scope and functioning of such agreements. In particular, they may refer to the exercise of all voting rights or merely to some, narrowly or broadly defined, decisions of the shareholders' meeting. It is also conceivable to adopt a rule of "internal majority", according to which all shareholders have to vote "externally" (i.e., in the shareholders' meeting) as the majority among them has voted "internally" (i.e., in the meeting of the shareholders participating in the agreement), or a rule of unanimity, requiring the consent of all contracting parties for them to vote for a particular decision in the shareholder' meeting (effectively granting an "internal" veto to each of them, though this would be a rather troubling solution, as examined below), or another combination of such rules, e.g. differentiating among decisions or granting particular veto rights to some shareholders. It is noteworthy that, in the (rather improbable, as a practical matter) case of a shareholders' agreement

---

**26** Athens Court of Appeal 8129/1977, NoB 1978, 1075; Athens Court of First Instance 5001/1971, EEmpD 1971, 545; *Kefaleas* EEmpD 1971, 182; *Marinos* (n 9) p 65; *Michalopoulos* EEmpD 1992, 352; *Perakis* (n 2) pp 181–182; cf. above, *Mock* p. 286. It is mentioned in this discussion that this qualification as partnership does not apply in all cases, but may vary depending on the circumstances. However, it does seem to be the proper way of dealing at least with long-term agreements relating to the exercise of voting rights and thus with a concerted influence on the management of the corporation.

with no determination of the internal decision making, a rule of unanimity could be thought to apply on the basis of art. 748 of the Greek Civil Code on civil partnerships. This might of course lead to paralysis, as the parties could fail to reach any decision, so that each might be left to decide on their own how to vote in the corporation; this is why it is important to regulate decision making within the voting consortium.

Such agreements are designed to stabilize the balance of influence among shareholders. In particular if the contracting parties hold a majority (or, in any case, a working majority) in the shareholders' meeting, such an agreement may lead to results that would not be achievable otherwise: For instance, that a majority of the contracting parties may control decisions in the shareholders' meeting although it falls short of a majority in the latter. Similarly, a shareholder holding a veto power among the contracting parties may effectively block decisions, using the votes of these other parties too, without commanding a majority in the shareholders' meeting.

From the point of view of the corporation, this is acceptable as a consequence of the decision made by the contracting parties, exercising the freedom of contract among them, to commit their voting rights to their collective decisions. As discussed elsewhere in the present analysis, it should be recalled that the company is not directly affected by such commitments, votes in violation of them are valid, and enforcement of the agreements is played out among shareholders, and not them and the company. This also applies the other way round: The content of the agreement is in principle valid, even if it could not be made content of the charter.[27] For example, an obligation of the shareholder to always vote as decided by a larger group is obviously not a permissible clause for the charter, but it is a typical clause of shareholders' agreements.

In any case, it is often remarked that such agreements may not be incompatible with fundamental features of the corporate (or partnership) form involved. An example would refer to an agreement, according to which a particular person is guaranteed a seat at the board (or even the CEO's seat) for life, in the sense that all other shareholders are always obliged to vote for it as a board member; this is said to contradict the principle of free revocability of board members as per art. 19(2) of Law 2190/1920.[28] It has also been suggested that a general una-

27 *Marinos* (n 9) pp 176–180. Sometimes the formulation is used that shareholders' agreements may not contradict mandatory provisions of law: see e.g. Thessaloniki Court of First Instance 213/1983, EEmpD 1984, 605. But, if read in context (see n 28 and the corresponding text), this formulation may be related to the circumstances of particular cases, in which the shareholders' agreement provided for arrangements that would directly influence the corporation itself.
28 Cf. *Michalopoulos* EpiskED 2008, 985; *Perakis* (n 2) p 136.

nimity requirement within the voting consortium, which may lead to paralysis in the functioning of the corporation itself, is fundamentally incompatible with the majority principle in public corporations and the efficiency principle underlying it.[29] Lastly, the appointment, by virtue of a shareholders' agreement, of an "observer" by the minority, who would have access to all affairs of the corporation, is also invalid, as it would alter its organizational structure and would introduce a minority right which is unknown to public corporation law.[30]

This view introduces a distinction between "simple" mandatory rules of corporate law, that do not however restrict the permissible content of shareholders' agreements as such agreements do not directly affect the corporation, and, as it were, qualified mandatory rules, of such fundamental importance for the corporate form that even the factual and indirect influence of shareholders' agreements on the manner that shareholders vote is thought to be potentially inadmissible.[31] The distinction is obviously hard to apply[32] and bears the risk of inconsistency, as the same argument (that the influence on the contracting parties' voting is ultimately relevant to the corporation itself) could also be made more broadly. In any case, it is a distinction that needs to be taken note of, as part of the discussion in Greek law on this issue; moreover, similar results may often be reached on the basis of a different criterion, namely the prohibition of excessive restriction on the rights of the contracting parties. Against this background, the obligation to never vote for revoking the board membership of a particular person may be invalid (or valid only as long as no significant reason to do otherwise is put forward) not so much because it is incompatible with art. 19(2)

---

**29** *Marinos* (n 9) p 163; *Spyridonos* DEE 2004, 645. On the other hand, in the absence of a clause on decision-making, a unanimity rule (deemed inadmissible by these authors) would probably apply on the basis of art. 748 of the Civil Code, as already mentioned in the text; against such background, this argument ultimately suggests that a clause on (majoritary) decision-making is necessary for the validity of the agreement. It is also noteworthy that the latter author goes even further, suggesting that even the mere fact that a majority within the consortium (which is though a mere minority in the corporation) may impose its views in the shareholders' meeting, contravenes the basic majority principle in corporation law. However, shareholders' agreements only bind the internal decision by the shareholder on the way of exercising its voting right, while majority requirements at the corporate level are not affected: *Perakis* (n 2) p 79. Moreover, such a view would ultimately render shareholders' agreements quite useless, as their main function (since they are deemed valid) is to introduce contractual arrangements whose content could not be included in the statute and develop direct results at the corporate level: cf. *Spyridonos* DEE 2004, 649, accepting that incompatibility with the statute is not a reason for invalidity of a shareholders' agreement.

**30** This has been held by Thessaloniki Court of First Instance 213/1983, EEmpD 1984, 605.

**31** Cf. *N. Rokas* (n 3) p 230.

**32** See also n 46.

of Law 2190/1920 on free revocability (given that shareholders are still able, from the point of view of the company, to vote for revoking board membership), but rather because it restricts their behaviour too much (in the sense that they personally have to deal with contractual sanctions, with no time or material restraints on the applicability of such sanctions).

Therefore, from the point of view of individual shareholders making such agreements, it is possible, though only in rather exceptional circumstances, to raise the issue of excessive restriction of their voting rights. In the most extreme case, and beyond examples mentioned above, an agreement that a shareholder will indefinitely refrain from participating at the shareholders' meeting, and thus would not exercise its voting rights at all, would indeed qualify as such an excessive restriction.[33] However, the fact that a shareholder steadily finds itself in the minority among the contracting parties, and thus unwillingly exercises its voting rights in a broad range of issues in support of decisions it would rather not support on its own, is inadequate to justify such a claim.[34] For this claim to be successful, it should be coupled with further circumstances, going clearly beyond the mere outvoting of the shareholder within the voting consortium. These may be either subjective circumstances of the shareholder, in particular extraordinary inexperience that the other contracting parties have taken advantage of (which would run afoul of art. 179 of the Greek Civil Code), or they may (again, exceptionally) be subjective circumstances referring to the other parties, in particular a behaviour in bad faith on their part, designed to harm the weaker party to the agreement.

The above-mentioned right of termination for significant reason should also be recalled in this context as a means of protection of the parties to the shareholders' agreement. Of course, as a practical matter, this right of termination may also be a source of uncertainty for all parties involved; in this sense, it seems to be advisable to limit the scope or duration of the agreement to the extent possible, as this reduces the shareholders' dependence on the collective will of the consortium, and thus makes it less probable to find a significant reason for termination.[35] This is a further aspect of the remark already made here, that it is generally useful to regulate the agreement's duration.

---

33 *Marinos* (n 9) p 164.

34 But cf. also *Marinos* (n 9) pp 164–165, who finds that comprehensively binding the application of voting rights for all decisions to the prevailing view in the voting consortium is invalid.

35 Cf. *Marinos* (n 9) p 198.

Lastly, the issue may be an excessively long, possibly indefinite, duration of the agreement.[36] As mentioned above, in the latter case the shareholder has a right of termination with no need to invoke a "significant reason".

## 2. Voting trusts?

Agreements on the exercise of voting rights only establish a duty in contract of the parties to vote in the manner prescribed by the agreement. It will be explained below that this duty is enforceable, but not without uncertainties and practical difficulties. Therefore, it is conceivable that there would be interest in arrangements that bring about more certainty that voting rights will be exercised in accordance with the agreement.

A voting trust might be understood in the strict sense of the term, in other words as a proper transfer of voting rights to a third party, so that the shareholder remains such but this third party is the holder of voting rights and exercises them as its own, though it may have an internal duty to the beneficial owner of such rights, i.e. the shareholder. Such an arrangement is not permissible in Greek law, given that shares are indivisible, in the sense that it is not possible to "break up" the share and have some of the rights derived from it be held by one party and others by another.[37] In other words, the original holder of voting rights is always the shareholder itself.

What is indeed permissible, is that a third party is authorized by the shareholders-members of a "voting consortium" to exercise their voting rights. This comes somewhat close to a voting trust but is not tantamount to it. Voting rights are still held by the shareholder and exercised (by a third person) in the name of the shareholder. It is also remarkable as a practical matter that the shareholder may rescind the authorization; this may be a violation of the shareholders' agreement, but also be valid vis-à-vis the company. It is also conceivable that the authorization is made irrevocable, as this is possible under art. 218 of the Greek Civil Code when the authorization does not merely serve the interest of the authorizing party: Here, it serves a community of interest among shareholders (as expressed in the shareholders' agreement[38]), who have authorized the

---

**36** Cf. *Spyridonos* DEE 2004, 649.

**37** See, among others, *Psychomanis* (n 5) p 316; *N. Rokas* (n 3) p 367. Co-ownership of shares is of course possible. But this is a different concept, in which co-owners hold together each right derived from the share, voting rights included, and make joint decisions on their exercise.

**38** See generally *Doris/Nezeriti* in Georgiades/Stathopoulos (eds.), Civil Code vol. 1B (2$^{nd}$ edn., P.N. Sakkoulas Athens 2016) art 218 – 221 n 20, explaining that the permissibility of an irrevoca-

same party (possibly one of them). However, it should be noted from the point of view of corporate law, here too, that an irrevocable authorization might again raise the question of excessive restriction of the shareholder's voting rights: The discussion on limiting the scope of the agreement and the corresponding authorization is important in this context as well.

A similar solution, again without being a voting trust in the exact sense of the term, is for shareholders to make a fiduciary transfer of their shares to a third party (who may actually be one of them), or to contribute them to a holding company or partnership.[39] The point is that voting rights (among other rights emanating from shares) are exercised directly by the transferee or the holding company or partnership, according to the arrangements agreed upon by the parties. The difference with a voting trust in the strict sense is that the transferee becomes shareholder and holds all related rights, not just voting rights.[40]

## II. The subject-matter of these shareholders' agreements

In order to set the background for an explanation of the typical subject-matter of shareholders' agreements on shareholders rights (in particular, rights relating to the governance of the corporation), it is useful to refer to the position of the shareholders' meeting within this governance. In particular, the shareholders' meeting is declared to be the "supreme organ" of the public corporation (AE) under art. 33 of Law 2190/1920, and there is no rule that would correspond to § 76 I of the German *Aktiengesetz*, which attributes the *Leitung* of the corporation to the board beyond doubt.[41] On the other hand, the shareholders' meeting is attributed competence (mainly) on the election and removal of directors, approval of the annual accounts and determination of the use of eventual profits, as well as on capital measures (capital increase and reduction) and structural corporate measures (merger, division, transformation, dissolution), while competence for the management and representation of the corporation rests with the board of directors as per art. 18 and 22 of the said Law. Moreover, there is a system of liability rules for directors that would be undermined by the admissibility of binding instructions on the part of the shareholders' meeting. Indeed, following

ble authorization depends on the relation underlying the authorization (which in the present case is the shareholders' agreement).

39 See *Marinos* (n 9) p 58; *Perakis* (n 2) pp 214–215; *idem* in Perakis (ed.), The Law of Public Corporations, Introduction n 13.

40 *Perakis* (n 2) p 215.

41 See on this above, *Mock* p. 295.

binding instructions would mean that directors themselves have in principle no liability for the result of such action (art. 22(2) of Law 2190/1920). It is nowadays acceptable that shareholders may also have, to the extent of their influence on corporate affairs, a duty of loyalty to the corporation,[42] out of which liability of their own may arise for the instructions to the directors issued by the shareholders' meeting. This alleviates the liability-related concerns,[43] though the problem remains that there are sophisticated procedural rules on the liability of directors, while corresponding rules would still need to be developed in the case of shareholder liability.

Thus, it is an open question[44] to what extent the shareholders' meeting may intervene in the field of competence of the board of directors and issue binding instructions to them as to the management of the corporation. This does not refer to the representation of the corporation vis-à-vis third parties, which falls certainly under the competence on the board, but rather on the internal competence to make management decisions. However, this uncertainty does not seem to have caused practical problems, which is also why there is not much related case law. The reason is probably that shareholders exercise (informal but potentially decisive) influence anyway thanks to their power to remove directors.[45] In any case, it seems reasonable to suggest that, while the shareholders' meeting may not simply substitute itself for the board, it may nevertheless issue instructions in particular cases.

Against this background, it is reasonable to say, as already suggested, that the main field of interest for shareholders making agreements on voting rights is the composition of the board of directors, as this is a formal decision which also enables the exercise of informal influence. The background for such agreements may be the appreciation of the personal qualities of the potential directors, but may also (or indeed foremost) be the proximity of these persons with one or more shareholder(s) and/or the interests and management policies that these persons stand for. In other words, the decision to vote for them may be informed by the balance of power emerging with their appointment, as well as by

---

**42** See for a monographic analysis *Karamanakou* The shareholders' duty of loyalty (Nomiki Bibliothiki, Athens 2013) *passim*. See also, among others, *Antonopoulos* (n 2) pp 245–246; *N. Rokas* (n 3) pp 374–377; *Triantafillakis* The interest of the enterprise as a rule of behaviour for public corporations' organs (Ant. Sakkoulas, Athens-Komotini 1998) pp 293 *et seq.*

**43** See *Psaroudakis* EEmpD 2003, 76–78.

**44** Cf. *Psaroudakis* Case note to Athens Court of Appeal 4864/2000, EEmpD 2003, 73, 74–75.

**45** On this point see *Psaroudakis* Acting in concert in börsennotierten Gesellschaften (Heymanns, Cologne 2009) pp 302–306, 400–401.

their expected strategy. Thus, this is not merely a decision on human resources, as it were, but the decision framing the future management of the company.

However, it is naturally possible, and indeed probable, that the agreement on the exercise of voting rights extends to other issues as well. Shareholders may wish to protect themselves against surprising structural measures (e. g. capital increases, mergers etc.) by including them in the scope of such agreements. Moreover, a typical source of tension within corporations, as well as a field of fundamental importance for both the functioning of the corporation and the position of shareholders, is to be found in the decisions on the use of profits, in particular in the choice between reinvestment by the corporation and distribution to shareholders. It is possible that shareholders' agreements refer to such votes as well. Lastly, as to the informal influence that such shareholders exercise on directors, its common exercise may be implied in an agreement on votes to elect and remove directors, or shareholders may explicitly refer to significant issues of the corporation's financial policy or organizational structure as matters in relation to which they will exercise their collective influence on the board.

As regards corporations of different forms (i. e., in the form of EPE or IKE, or partnerships), the increased flexibility as to their internal structure and their more personal nature suggest that shareholders have more leeway to issue binding instructions to the management, without the qualifications presented above as to the AE (or at least with significantly less qualifications[46]). Therefore, in this case shareholders' agreements have an at least equally broad field of application, with the added benefit that it is easier to make agreements on votes in the shareholders' meeting relating to such instructions to the management.

## III. Shareholders' agreements and the law of corporate groups ("Konzernrecht")

Shareholders' agreements are a method to exercise collective influence on the affairs of the company. It is therefore possible that such an agreement leads to the establishment of a corporate group, if one or more of its parties are regarded as controlling shareholders of the corporation that the agreement relates to (the latter being then the subsidiary). It should be noted in advance that the sole certain consequence of the establishment of a corporate group is the duty to publish consolidated accounts: a German-style *Konzernrecht* does not exist in Greek

46 Indeed, it has been remarked in the context of such corporations as well that there should be some room for autonomous action on the part of directors: *N. Rokas* (n 3) p 586.

law, neither does liability of the parent undertaking for debts of its subsidiary exist in principle, though it is not impossible to establish in very exceptional circumstances. In any case, one would need to examine the actual behaviour of the parent undertaking vis-à-vis the subsidiary's creditors, while the mere control of the latter is not adequate.[47]

As briefly mentioned in the beginning, art. 32(2)(d1) of Law 4308/2014 does refer to an agreement with other shareholders as a means to control the majority of voting rights in another corporation, so that the latter is deemed to be a subsidiary and consolidated accounts must be published. Therefore, shareholders' agreements may help establish the presence of a corporate group. Notably, the wording of this provision seems to refer to a single parent company; in other words, it seems to imply the dominance of a single shareholder within the group and, as a result, in the corporation (ie, in the subsidiary).

This is indeed possible, but it does not reflect the reality of all voting consortia. In other words, where a shareholder dominates the consortium, and if the consortium itself collectively owns a controlling percentage of voting rights, this shareholder becomes a parent undertaking. If this is not the case, then it needs to be examined whether a particular small group dominates the consortium, or the latter is internally balanced and no one dominates it. It is conceivable that, depending on such circumstances, there are more than one parent undertakings or, on the other hand, that no corporate group is established at all. Marginal cases may arise, such as when the agreement only refers to voting on some decisions within the competence of the shareholders' meeting but not all of them (though special attention should be paid to the decisions to elect and recall directors), or when other shareholders tend to violate the agreement, so that the practical influence of the (supposedly) dominant shareholder is smaller than expected. But there does not seem to be any case law on such cases.

## IV. Shareholders' agreements on (limitation of) the transfer of shares

As a general observation, there are two manners in which to introduce clauses relating to the transfer of shares and limitations thereon. One is to include these arrangements in the corporate charter, while the other is a shareholders' agreement. A look at the capacity of the charter to incorporate such clauses is

47 Out of the rich discussion on these issues, which goes beyond the scope of the present analysis, see indicatively Areios Pagos (plenary session) 2/2013, NoB 2013, 363.

useful here, in order to appreciate the extent of the practical need for shareholders' agreements.

As regards public corporations (in the form of AE), the former method (inclusion in the charter) seems to be available, according to art. 3(7) of Law 2190/1920, only in order to introduce clauses that require the consent of the corporation (either by decision of the board or by resolution of the shareholders' meeting) for the transfer or otherwise limit the transfer. A tag along clause (requiring that no shares are transferred by one shareholder until the chance is given to other shareholders to transfer their own shares under the same terms too[48]) would seem to fall under this rule and thus be a permissible part of the charter. The same would apply to limitations such as a right of first refusal offered to fellow shareholders generally or to a person to be determined by the corporation. But other variations, in particular those referring not to a limitation of the transfer but rather to a duty to transfer, or co-transfer, as the case is in drag along clauses (in which shareholders are required to follow the decision of their fellow shareholder to transfer shares), may not be introduced in the charter, as they are not mentioned as possible content of the charter in the said provision.

As regards other corporations (in the form of EPE and IKE), it is possible to include other kinds of clauses as well, given the broader leeway that parties have in designing the charter, though there does not seem to be any related case law. As regards partnerships, it is important that, by default and in the absence of any different clause in the partnership contract, the transfer of a partner's share requires the consent of everyone else. If so, the transfer is limited by definition. In particular, there is no independent need for a tag along clause, as every partner may anyway require that its own share is included in the transfer in order to grant its consent to it. If on the other hand this requirement of consent by all shareholders has been disapplied by the partnership contract, then it is still obviously possible to include milder limitations on transfer in the same. Moreover, as contractual freedom is paramount in the law of the partnership contract, in particular as regards the internal affairs of the partnership, it is indeed possible to include other kinds of clauses mentioned above in the partnership contract itself.

The conclusion is that clauses on the transfer of shares may be included in the corporate charter or partnership contract, as the case may be, with a significant qualification as regards public corporations; in the latter, the charter may only prescribe limitations of the transfer. This confirms that shareholders' agree-

48 This clause, and others referred to in the same paragraph, are mentioned by *Mitsou* (n 2) art 2 n 41.

ments are particularly relevant in public corporations, and the least relevant in partnerships. Of course, even in cases in which it is possible to insert the clause under discussion in the charter, the parties may prefer, and are not hindered in any manner, to make a shareholders' agreement, e.g. because the clause has been agreed upon and is meant to apply only among some shareholders rather than all of them.

As regards shareholders' agreements of the kind outside the corporate charter or partnership contract, they would be regarded as valid as a matter of freedom of contract, though it should be noted again that there does not seem to be much case law on such issues.[49] An important issue to be examined refers to the precise legal effect of such a clause as part of a shareholders' agreement.

To begin with, one should take into account that, for instance, a transfer of shares without the necessary consent by the competent organ of the public corporation, as provided for in the corporate charter itself, is invalid vis-à-vis the corporation. It is possible to suggest that the parties to this invalid transfer have a contractual duty, as regards the "horizontal" relation between them, to bring about a condition that will come as close as possible to an actual transfer: Under such a concept, the transferor, who remains shareholder in the eyes of the company, should seek guidance from the transferee as to the exercise of its rights, and should pass on to the transferee dividends received. In any case, even this uncertain interpretation of the transfer contract does not alter in any case the position of the corporation, which must still take note of the clause in its charter and thus ignore the invalid transfer contract and look at the transferor as shareholder.

On the other hand, the corporation does not, in this context either, take note of clauses in shareholders' agreements. Just like a vote in the shareholders' meeting remains valid, even if incompatible with the agreement, a transfer of shares is also valid and the corporation has to deal with the *transferee* as owner of the shares, even if the transfer has been in contravention of such an agreement.[50]

**49** Indeed, the view has been expressed that a duty to transfer in a shareholders' agreement (as in a drag-along clause) is invalid, as the expulsion of the shareholder, to which such a duty is equivalent, is unknown to the law of public corporations: *Marinos* (n 9) p 165. This view relates to the above-mentioned discussion on fundamental features of corporate law, with which not even shareholders' agreements may come into conflict. As remarked, it is difficult to draw bright lines in this respect. Regarding the present issue, it could be argued that it does not affect the functioning of the corporation as such, as opposed to the composition of its shareholding, and that it reflects its closely held shareholding, as the case may be; in this sense, it is arguably valid.

**50** *Antonopoulos* (n 2) p 52; *Kotsiris* Cooperative public corporation – Limitation of the transfer of shares – Secondary duties of shareholders, DEE 1997, 449, 451; *Marinos* (n 9) p 230; *Michalo-*

Beyond the typical separation between the corporate and the contractual level, which has already been highlighted, this also derives naturally from a general principle of Greek private law to be found in art. 177 of the Civil Code and applicable also beyond the context of corporations: That a contractual duty not to transfer a piece of (real or personal) property does not affect the validity of the transfer that the holder of this property does nevertheless conclude with a third party.[51]

However, it may be possible to actually make (further) transfer impossible by rendering such further transfer of shares a condition subsequent of the contract, by means of which the shareholder (ie, the original transferee and further transferor) acquired the shares in the first place. Then, by concluding a further sale of shares the shareholder would fulfill the condition subsequent and the shares would return to the original transferor.[52] Still, this requires a clause in the (possibly related as a factual matter, but in any case conceptually different) original sale contract rather than in the shareholders' agreement. More to the point of shareholders' agreements, such limitations of transfer may be (indirectly) enforced by means of contractual penalties.[53]

## V. Shareholders' Agreements in pre-insolvency situation

The varieties of shareholders' agreements on both governance and the financing of the corporation may indeed be used in order to avert insolvency. In this context, it is remarkable that shareholders may generally not be compelled in advance to grant fresh contributions to the corporation or partnership. This is a principle established in art. 745 of the Civil Code and applicable to all corporate forms (though deviations in the charter or partnership contract are permissible, except for public corporations).[54]

*poulos* EEmpD 1992, 355; *idem* EpiskED 2008, 974; *Perakis* (n 2) p 218; *Vervessos*, in: Perakis (ed.), Law of Public Corporations, art 3 n 34.

**51** An exception, based on art. 466 of the Greek Civil Code, refers to the assignment of claims, which is indeed void if the contract between the original creditor and the debtor includes a *pactum de non cedendo*. However, this provision is not applicable here, because the share is not in itself a claim against the company, but rather a complex relationship (giving rise to particular claims, among other things), and also because, even if it was dealt with as a claim, the shareholders' agreement is not made between the shareholder and the company.

**52** See (not with reference to shares, but stating the principle that is applicable here too) Areios Pagos 494/2009, ChrID 2011, 418.

**53** See below at V.

**54** See *N. Rokas* (n 3) p 56.

Moreover, such efforts to avert insolvency require capital measures: Typically, this encompasses a capital reduction, in order to absorb losses, and a capital increase for fresh contributions to be made. Capital measures require qualified majorities and are thus prone to the emergence of a blocking potential on the part of some shareholders. It is therefore useful for shareholders to have been bound in advance to support such measures under certain circumstances or when the majority of a voting consortium is for them.

Shareholders' agreements may thus, in Greek practice as well, be useful in establishing a contractual duty of shareholders to vote in favour of, and possibly also to participate, in the effort to improve the corporation's capital position and avert insolvency. This tends to not be separately discussed, but is rather a particular application of shareholders' agreements in general.

# D. Legal effects of Shareholders' Agreements

## I. Legal effects on the corporation

A remarkable issue is whether shareholders' agreements may affect the interpretation of the corporate chatter. This is an aspect of the broader discussion relating to whether there is a strict separation between the shareholders' agreement as a contract and the internal organization of the corporation or, rather, there may be some influence of the contract on the corporation.

As analyzed elsewhere in the present report, the starting point for this discussion in Greek law is, appropriately, that the two areas remain separate. Applied to the interpretation of the corporate charter, this suggests that it may not be influenced by a shareholders' agreement. Indeed, in a more general vein, it is established that the interpretation of the charter must be objective,[55] in other words may not be influenced by subjective understandings possibly emerging among shareholders.

The single exception that is conceivable relates to agreements in which all shareholders participate.[56] However, even in this case it should be taken into consideration that the corporate charter affects third parties as well, and that

55 *Kotsiris* Shareholders' agreement made among all shareholders as the basis of a sales contract for shares, EEmpD 2006, 237, 240; *Marinos* (n 9) pp. 212–221; *idem* ElD 2008, 685; *Psychomanis* (n 5) p. 206; *N. Rokas* (n 3) p. 225.

56 A case, in which it was accepted that agreements among all shareholders may be used in order to interpret the corporate charter, is Athens Court of First Instance 5723/2006, DEE 2006, 1145.

shareholders' agreements, as opposed to the charter itself, are not publicized.[57] For instance, it would not be acceptable to interpret the charter's provisions on the representation of the corporation, which are of much interest to third parties, on the basis of a shareholders' agreement that these third parties are not aware of, indeed without any fault of their own. In other words, this exception might only be applicable (and even this at first glance only) to provisions of the charter that are of interest to the parties of the shareholders' agreement alone, which may happen if they only relate to the internal workings of the corporation.

The problem with this argument is though that even organizational matters of the corporation without any direct influence on its transactions are of indirect interest to third parties. Creditors are potentially interested in the corporation's governance and its decision-making mechanism, as this influences the quality of decisions to be expected.[58] This ultimately collapses the distinction (for the purposes of the present discussion) between decisions of interest to third parties and "internal" decisions, and leads to the conclusion that the interpretation of the charter remains objective and that shareholders' agreements should not be made part of it.

## II. Legal Effects on Shareholders

Shareholders' agreements are binding on the parties to them. The rights and obligations arising from these agreements are separate to the legal position of the shareholder as such (though obviously related to it).[59] Therefore, the transfer of the shares does not by itself bring about a substitution of the acquirer to the rights and obligations of the transferor from the agreement.[60] A further agreement, which is conceptually separate from the transfer of the shares, is required for the latter result to occur. Indeed, this further contract, by virtue of which the transferee enters the shareholders' agreement, has to be made between this transferee and all other shareholders that have concluded the shareholders'

57 See also n. 59.

58 Cf. *Marinos* (n 9) p. 219.

59 The lack of any reference of statutory rules on corporate law (Law 2190/1920 and the corresponding statutes with regard to other corporate forms and partnerships) to shareholders' agreements is thought to express this separation: *Marinos* (n 9) p. 20.

60 *Antonopoulos* (n 2) p. 51; *Marinos* (n 9) p. 230, *idem* ElD 2008, 684; *idem* DEE 2007, 1150; *Michalopoulos* EpiskED 2008, 972 n. 41; *Perakis* (n 2) p. 233 (also noting that, given the lack of a requirement for formalities, the substitution may be concluded implicitly); *Spyridonos* DEE 2004, 647.

agreement. It is conceivable (though not necessary) that the shareholders' agreement contains terms that facilitate the entrance of a new party, e.g. by granting in advance the consent of the other shareholders to this substitution (while, possibly, at the same time requiring the parties to transfer their shares only on the condition that the acquirer also enters the shareholders' agreement).

Another result of the same privacy of contract, as applied to shareholders' agreement, is that there is, in principle, no publicity for such agreements, indeed neither any requirement to make them known to the general public nor any need to register them in a register of the corporation.[61] Indeed, it is not even required to conclude such agreements in writing, on the basis of the principle in art. 158 of the Greek Civil Code on the lack of such formalities, if not otherwise stipulated; of course, it may be practically advisable to have written evidence of the agreement.

This lack of publicity is a significant expression of the difference between the corporate and the contractual level, as publicity is a well-known feature of corporate law, while knowledge only *inter partes* is typical for contract law. The same difference is an important argument against broadening the legal effects of such agreements in a manner that would make them directly relevant to the corporation. Since they are not as transparent as corporate acts, they do not regulate the corporation as such.[62]

On the other hand, a degree of disclosure may be mandated in case of listed companies. In particular, art. 10(a) of Law 3556/2007 expands the disclosure obligation of art. 9 for significant shareholdings, so that it also applies to the collective shareholdings of parties that have agreed to apply their voting rights in concert and thus to adopt a lasting common policy as regards the corporation's management. This implements art. 10(a) of Directive 2004/109/EC in Greek law. It does not apply to all agreements, as it requires a connection to the management of the corporation and a lasting common policy on the basis of the agreement. Therefore, agreements that only relate to acquisitions, disposals etc. of shares are not caught by this provision.[63] Moreover, the same applies to agreements

---

**61** Athens Court of First Instance 3265/1991, EEmpD 1992, 444; *Marinos* (n 9) pp. 90–91; *idem* ElD 2008, 685; *Michalopoulos* EEmpD 1992, 356.

**62** Cf. *Marinos* (n 9) pp. 131–132; *idem* ElD 2008, 683; *idem* Case comment to Areios Pagos 1121/2006, DEE 2006, 1148, 1149; *Spyridonos* DEE 2004, 643–644; *Vervessos* Shareholders' agreement among all shareholders of the corporation and voidness of the shareholders' meeting resolution, EEmpD 2007, 928, 933.

**63** *Psaroudakis* Acting in concert in börsennotierten Gesellschaften (Cologne, Heymanns 2009) pp. 249, 391. This could be subjected to criticism, as the shareholding structure of the corpora-

that do not go beyond a single case of "momentary", or in any case very short-term, coordination.

It should be noted that the obligation to disclose applies whether coordination is based on a contract, which is obviously binding as a legal matter, or it is based on a non-binding agreement (or in any case binding as a factual matter at best, as the case would be in a gentlemen's agreement).[64] It is even more significant that it is only required that shareholdings themselves are publicized, with a reference to acting in concert as the reason for such publication. In other words, the fact that an agreement exists is made known, but the actual content of the agreement needs not be made known. This is also reasonable, given that disclosure of significant shareholdings, also when they belong to a single shareholder, does not require any further information on the shareholder's plans. In case of concerted action, it would be arguable that the parties, if required to disclose the fact that they coordinate, should at least have a right (rather than a duty) to explain what their coordination is about; this would be practically interesting in case of a comparatively narrow (though still relevant) agreement, in which case the parties might want to show that, despite disclosure, no all-encompassing coordination is taking place. However, there is no related practice at all.[65]

## III. Consequences of a Breach of the Shareholders' Agreements

As the case is in general contract law, parties to a shareholders' agreement have a claim against each other to refrain from any behaviour that would violate it and cease the violation, if it has taken place. The extent to which such claims are practically useful is discussed below (under V). Other parties also have a claim to damages against the one who violated the agreement, though its practical value is, again, often questionable and to be further discussed under V. On the other hand, such violation does not affect the corporation and its legal acts.

According to the view that seems to have prevailed in Greek case law and scholarship (though not without some discussion as to the proper handling of the issue[66]), even a shareholders' agreement among all shareholders is not tan-

tion, and potential changes to it (or the lack of such potential) is a significant issue in order to understand the basis for its further steps.

**64** *Psaroudakis* (n 63) p. 389.

**65** On these issues see *Psaroudakis* (n 63) pp. 403 – 410.

**66** For instance, the judgment of the Athens Court of Appeal 7119/2004, EEmpD 2005, 54, which was subsequently vacated by Areios Pagos 1121/2006 (see n 68), invoked the shareholders'

tamount to a provision in the corporation's charter;[67] this applies all the more to agreements that have not been concluded by the entirety of shareholders. The agreement's violation may bring about other consequences of the kind discussed above, but it is not a ground to challenge the validity of the corporate act under examination,[68] as the agreement is a contract, indeed among shareholders and not between them and the corporation,[69] and not a part of the corporation's internal order. Its factual importance in the affairs of the corporation may not produce a change in its legal quality as a "horizontal" contract.[70]

In particular, the agreement is not a ground for such challenge either as such or indirectly, i.e. as a basis for invoking the prohibition on the abuse of rights (art. 281 of the Greek Civil Code) and suggesting that the shareholder

---

agreement in question, among other things, in order to establish the invalidity of a resolution of the shareholders' meeting due to abuse of right on the part of the majority. In favour of regarding shareholders' agreements among all shareholders as relevant in corporate law, because they are thought to be part of the legal order developing at the corporation, see also Athens Court of First Instance 5723/2006, DEE 2006, 1145; *Giotaki* EEmpD 2004, 531–2; *Kotsiris* EEmpD 2006, 241 et seq.; *Mitsou* (n 2) art 2 n 51; *Varela* Case comment to Areios Pagos 1121/2006, DEE 2007, 586, 588–9; cf. also (if somewhat more reluctantly and with reference to extraordinary circumstances) *Vervessos* EEmpD 2007, 938–9. It is remarkable that this discussion in Greek law takes note of the judgments of the German *Bundesgerichtshof*, according to which shareholders' agreements among all shareholders could form a basis for the annulment of resolutions of the corporate organs: BGH NJW 1983, 1911; BGH NJW 1987, 1891; cf. also, for a view that goes even further and takes into account agreements among a qualified majority of shareholders as well, *Noack* Gesellschaftsvereinbarungen bei Kapitalgesellschaften (Mohr Siebeck, Tübingen 1994) p. 167. It is important though that these judgments have not been taken up by later German case law (see BGHZ 123, 15, 20), neither has this view prevailed in German scholarship: see e.g. *Ulmer* "Satzungsgleiche" Gesellschaftervereinbarungen in der GmbH?, in: Festschrift Röhricht (Otto Schmidt, Köln 2005) pp. 633, 635; *Winter* Organisationsrechtliche Sanktionen bei Verletzung schuldrechtlicher Gesellschaftervereinbarungen?, ZHR 154 (1990) 259, as well as above, *Mock* p. 302.

**67** This relates to the discussion on the nature of the charter itself, which, beyond being a contract among the founders, is organizing a legal entity (which shareholders' agreements obviously do not do): see *Marinos* ElD 2008, 680–2.

**68** See in particular Areios Pagos 1121/2006, ChrID 2006, 821 = DEE 2007, 583, which referred to an agreement among all shareholders on the composition of the board and held (though not without a dissenting opinion) that voting in contravention of the agreement did not affect in any manner the validity of this resolution of the shareholders' meeting. See also *Antonopoulos* (n 2) p. 52; *Marinos* ElD 2008, 679; *idem* DEE 2006, 1148–9; *idem* ChrID 2008, 552; *Michalopoulos* EpiskED 2008, 973; *Mitsou* (n 2) art 2 n 43; *Perakis* (n 2) pp. 193–4.

**69** *Michalopoulos* EpiskED 2008, 983.

**70** Cf. *Antonopoulos* (n 2) pp. 50–51; *Marinos* (n 9) pp. 92–95, 144; *Michalopoulos* EEmpD 1992, 354.

who violates this agreement is abusing its voting rights.[71] Although there has been a case (unrelated to shareholders' agreements as such) adopting the idea that the entirety of the members of the corporation is tantamount to the corporation itself,[72] which could support the relevance of agreements among all shareholders in corporate law as well,[73] later case law has not followed on this idea.[74]

Thus, decisions of the shareholders' meeting, which are based on votes by shareholders that are incompatible with contractual obligations that shareholders had assumed to each other, remain valid. Moreover, sales of shares that do not comply with terms of related agreements are also valid (which is also connected to the general validity of transfers of property despite pre-existing contractual duties of the transferor towards third parties, as per art. 177 of the Greek Civil Code).

Lastly, the breach of a shareholders' agreement does not, in itself, constitute a reason for the expulsion of the party from the corporation (or partnership), as it is not a breach of the corporation's regulation. Such expulsion is anyway not even possible in public corporations (AEs) under any circumstances. In other corporations and partnerships it is indeed possible on the basis of a significant ground. In cases of clearly personal nature of the corporation or partnership, it is conceivable that the breach of the agreement may contribute to the significant ground for expulsion. This would refer not to the breach of the agreement as such, but rather to the grave breach of confidence (if the case may be) among shareholders arising from the violation of the further agreement among them; but an argument based on breach of confidence would not be available in any such case, but would rather depend on the circumstances.

# E. Enforcement of Shareholders' Agreements

According to the better view, and as the case is with contracts in general, it is possible both to require actual compliance with the shareholders' agreement (which is the primary contractual claim) and to exercise a secondary claim to

71 Cf. n. 66.

72 Areios Pagos (plenary session) 26/1998, NoB 1999, 234 = EEmpD 1998, 553 = EpiskED 1998, 694 = DEE 1998, 851.

73 On the connection between this idea and the view that agreements among all shareholders are relevant for the corporation (notwithstanding the criticism) see *Marinos* (n 9) pp. 126–127; *Michalopoulos* EpiskED 2008, 977.

74 Even the dissenting opinion in Areios Pagos 1121/2006 (n 68), which supported the relevance of agreements among all shareholders in corporate law, did not cite this previous judgment.

damages for breach of contract, if the case may be. The issue becomes all the more important because of the validity in corporate law of acts that have been made in violation of a shareholders' agreement. Therefore, as corporate law cannot undo the violation once the shareholder has, eg, voted otherwise than provided for by the agreement, contractual claims and remedies are the only means at the disposal of shareholders against the party in violation of their agreement.

As regards actual enforcement, the other parties to the agreement may decide to seek a court judgment on the basis of art. 949 of the Greek Code of Civil Procedure that (when made final, and depending on the content of each shareholders' agreement) is substituted for the shareholder's vote[75] and directly imposes a vote according to the agreement,[76] or is substituted on the basis of the same provision for the shareholder's part in a sale of its shares and thus effects the sale of shares as per the agreement. It is also possible to seek a judgment that prohibits a sale of shares and imposes a potential penalty if the sale is made on the basis of art. 947 of the said Code. Importantly, these are proceedings among shareholders, while the corporation may not be involved, either as a petitioner or as a respondent.

Notably, it has not gone undoubted in the Greek discussion that actual enforcement is possible. There is some (indeed rather recent as well) support for the view that, due the nature of the behaviour required, no such claim exists and other parties may only raise a (secondary) claim for damages.[77] This view seems to be based on the separation between the corporate and the contractual level; it suggests that, given the lack of any corporate nature of shareholders' agreements, they may not be used to directly influence the behaviour of share-

**75** Actual enforcement should also be deemed to be available in case of agreements relating to the transfer (or non-transfer) of shares: *Mastrokostas* Techniques in order to maintain and control the changes of shareholding in the closely held public corporation, ChrID 2016, 481, 485. Indeed, actual enforcement would face less doubts in this case.

**76** It has been noted that, prior to the actual vote, a shareholder also has to follow the formalities for participating at the shareholders' meeting, so that its vote can be registered. Given that the shareholder in the present case has no interest in participating in order to cast a vote that has been imposed on it by the court, there is a need to apply art. 945 of the Code of Civil Procedure as well, which allows the petitioner to perform necessary acts (here the formalities prior to the shareholders' meeting, whose main aspect would in this case be to notify the corporation of the court's judgment) in lieu of the respondent (here the shareholder who does not comply with the agreement voluntarily): see *Perakis* (n 2) pp 206–212. It is true though that this is a burdensome enforcement procedure, let alone the legal uncertainties explained in the text below as regards preliminary injunctions.

**77** Athens Court of First Instance 5001/1971, EEmpD 1971, 545; Athens Court of First Instance 569/2007, EEmpD 2008, 76 = ChrID 2008, 549; *Antonopoulos* (n 2) p 53; see also *Vervessos* EEmpD 2008, 80–81, commenting on the respective judgment.

holders within the corporation's organs. However, it is one thing to influence the functioning of the organ as such and quite another to influence the vote of a member.[78] Indeed, if applied properly, this view would prohibit even the indirect influence on voting that comes from the menace of a claim for damages,[79] and would ultimately lead back to the older concept that shareholders' agreements are invalid altogether.[80] On the contrary, the argument made here for actual enforcement is reflected at the procedural level by the above-mentioned fact that these are disputes among shareholders, with no participation of the corporation.

But even if one accepts, as suggested here, that such a contractual claim exists, this does not mean that its exercise is without difficulties. The practical problem is that the injunction would be issued (and become enforceable, which requires either that no appeal has been filed or that it has been rejected) long after the shareholder has already violated the agreement; thus, the injunction may be useless. The solution to this is to request a preliminary injunction (or even, in Greek practice, of a preliminary order as per art. 691 of the Greek Code of Civil Procedure that comes before the preliminary injunction, as the latter may take some time too), pending resolution of the main case as such.

The main counter-argument against this use of the preliminary injunction, when it comes to the exercise of shareholders' voting rights, is that it might pre-empt the decision in the main case, while art. 692(4) of the Greek Code of Civil Procedure prohibits the "complete fulfilment" of the claim under examination at the stage of preliminary proceedings).[81] It is true that, according to the better view, this argument would ultimately not be decisive. In particular, when the shareholders' meeting is imminent and there is no time for a final injunction, the issuance of a preliminary injunction may indeed seem to cause this pre-emption. But the denial of a preliminary injunction equally pre-empts the result of the main case, as the decision on the final injunction is issued after the vote has been cast, so that it is useless. Under such circumstances, it is arguably

**78** See also *Perakis* (n 2) p 198.

**79** *Perakis* (n 2) p 199–200.

**80** As aptly remarked by *Marinos* ChrID 2008, 553–4; cf. also *idem* (n 9) pp 237–238.

**81** See *Marinos* (n 9) p 240; *Perakis* (n 2) p 213. As the preliminary injunction falls, among the various kinds of preliminary proceedings, under the "temporary arrangement of the situation" (art. 731–732 of the Greek Code of Civil Procedure), it is worth mentioning that there has been some controversy as to whether art. 692(4) is applicable at all to this kind of preliminary proceedings: see for instance *Mitsopoulos* The notion of "temporary arrangement of the situation" as a basic form of preliminary measure, ElD 2002, 1233, 1241. However, the view seems to have prevailed that art. 692(4) is applicable in this case too: Athens Court of First Instance 1552/2003, DEE 2003, 641; Athens Court of First Instance 6521/2015, Nomos Database; see also *Beys* Civil Procedure V (Athens 1983) pp 115–124.

necessary (at least if no other effective remedy exists[82]) to grant judicial protection by accepting in principle that the request for preliminary injunction is permissible and examining whether such an injunction should be issued in the particular case. But Greek case law has not been favourable to such arguments, accepting them only when non-pecuniary interests are at stake,[83] which is not the case here; therefore, it is more than doubtful that a preliminary injunction of the kind would be granted.

Beyond this (formidable in Greek practice, as already explained) argument against the use of preliminary injunctions as a means of enforcement, it is perhaps equally important that time constraints are such, that even the preliminary injunction would come too later for the petitioner. This is why other methods of enforcement become particularly important.

In particular, a secondary contractual claim for damages is available in principle. However, it is hard, or even impossible, to show damage. In particular, the other parties to the agreement must show direct damage to themselves, rather than the corporation, for instance because they have lost influence in it. But it is precisely this kind of damage that is extremely hard to quantify.[84] As it happens in such cases, parties may thus have recourse to contractual penalties as the most effective means of enforcement[85] (while fiduciary transfers of shares or transfers to a holding company may also be used to prevent violations in the first place). Such contractual penalties are acceptable on the basis of art. 404–409 of the Greek Civil Code; the party invoking them does not need to prove or to quantify actual damage, but only to show the breach of contract itself. In case of excessiveness, the penalty provided for in the contract may be reduced by the court.

In conclusion, while typical claims in contract may exist in any case of breach of shareholders' agreements, they are associated with such practical impediments that the inclusion of penalty clauses is advisable.

---

**82** As explained by *Beys* (n 81) pp 131–3, preliminary injunctions that pre-empt the final result should not be granted, even if their refusal renders actual enforcement impossible as mentioned in the present text, provided that another remedy (obviously, a claim for damages) exists. In the present case, a claim for damages exists in principle, though it is hardly practicable; in practice, the negative stance of Greek case law would probably prevail.

**83** Lamia Court of First Instance 401/2013, Nomos Database; see also *Beys* (n 81) p 133.

**84** Cf. *Marinos* ChrID 2008, 552; *Michalopoulos* EEmpD 1992, 355; *Perakis* (n 2) p 196.

**85** Athens Court of First Instance 5001/1971, EEmpD 1971, 545; *Georgakopoulos* (n 2) p 330; *Kefaleas* EEmpD 1971, 184; *Marinos* (n 9) p 58; *Mitsou* (n 2) art 2 n 45; *Perakis* (n 2) p 197, 214; *idem*, in: Perakis (ed.), The Law of Public Corporations, Introduction n 13.

Lastly, it is permissible to use alternative dispute resolution mechanisms in order to enforce shareholders' agreements. While the precise extent, to which corporate disputes may be dealt with in this manner, is disputed,[86] it follows from the separation between the corporate and the contractual level that this dispute does not affect shareholders' agreements, and the related issues arising among their parties. Omn the contrary, the use of such mechanisms sits well with the speed and discreteness required in the resolution of these disputes.[87]

**86** See *Perakis* General part of commercial law (Nomiki Bibliothiki, Athens 1999) pp 153–154.
**87** Cf. *Marinos* (n 9) p 24.

Tibor Tajti

# Hungary

## Table of Content



---

**Prof. Tibor Tajti (Thaythy),** Professor of law and Chair of the International Business Law Program at Central European University (CEU), Budapest, Hungary (http://www.ceu.edu). Contact: tajtit@ceu.edu . The author would like to express his gratitude to the following persons for the materials and email exchanges related to shareholders' agreements, *Gábor Baranyai*, adjunct professor of CEU Business School, *Laszlo Czirjak*, partner of the investment firm '*iEurope Capital*,' *Károly (Charles) Jókay*, executive director of the Hungarian-American Fulbright Commission, *Zoltán Marosi*, partner of the Oppenheim Law Firm, *Zsolt Okányi*, partner of the law firm Ormai és Társai – CMS Cameron McKenna LLP, as well as *Tekla Papp*, professor of law at Szeged University Law School.

https://doi.org/10.1515/9783110517026-016

# A. Introduction

Notwithstanding the small yet increasing number of cases and the availability of only a few scholarly publications with some empirical contents on shareholders' agreements, sufficient evidence is available to claim that shareholders' agreements play an important role in Hungary today. This, however, was not the product of prescriptive company law but rather organic growth and borrowing from more developed western jurisdictions given that during socialism, neither shares as investment vehicles, nor the corollary legal categories existed. The redirection towards market economy and capitalism somewhere in the 1990s made shareholders' agreements again of importance. It was not without a reason that essentially the only monograph devoted to this peculiar agreement published in 1996 underlined that "*notwithstanding the short history of shareholders' agreements, they are used by a large circle of [businesses] in [Hungary].*"[1] It ought to be mentioned, however, that shareholders' agreements were far from unknown in the pre-socialist Hungary, as proven indirectly even by the notorious 1948 Decree No. XXV. on Nationalization of some Industrial Enterprises.[2] Their appearance could validly be linked to the end of the 19th century, which represents the peak of Hungarian capitalism.[3]

This advancement notwithstanding, there are no governmental or industrial analyses or estimates, let alone official statistics (no matter how imperfect they could be) on this subject matter. Not unsurprisingly, this is primarily attributable to their confidential (secret) nature. Practicing lawyers and investors, however, confirm that while the first, post-1990 generation of shareholders' agreements were adapted versions of (typically) English shareholders' agreements, today that is not necessarily so anymore and complex versions, increasingly with locally-forged contents, are in use. Instead of taking over whole (or much of) model contracts, counsel today rather select and adapt model clauses only. Empirical data suggest as well that different approaches exist in some specific market niches and depending also on what the background of the investors is.[4] These post-

1 *Kolben* A szindikátusi szerződés [Shareholders'Agreements] (Közgazdasági és Jogi Könyvkiadó, Budapest 1996), Preface, at 9. Hereinafter: Kolben, 1996.

2 This Decree mentions shareholders' agreements in its section 15(2)(b) which foresaw that the terms and conditions of the continued validity, as well as the invalidation of shareholders' agreements will be regulated by a special governmental decree. The Hungarian title of the Decree is "1948. évi XXV. Törvénycikk egyes ipari vállalatok állami tulajdonba vételéről".

3 See *Krisztina Nagy Barna* Néhány gondolat a szindikátusi szerződésről jogtörténeti aspektusban in Opuscula Civilia, No. 2016/5, available at < http://akk.uni-nke.hu/uploads/media_items/2016_-evi-5_-szam_opuscula-civilia.original.pdf >; last visited on 21 Jan. 2017.

4 In the venture capital and private equity sectors, concurrent with an investment, the rights of shareholders' are defined in various agreements. In Europe, the more common approach is to use a unified shareholders' agreement while in the United States numerous parallel agreements accomplish the same goal. Often what is regulated in articles of incorporations in the US, with its business friendly corporate law base and with extensive case law, is only able to be enshrined in shareholders' agreements in Europe. This conclusion seem to be valid also for Hungary. It is a problem in Hungary (similarly to other Continental European jurisdictions) that the company law has so far been too restrictive, at least, adjudged from the perspectives of these sectors. As a result these investors often rely on a neutral jurisdictions, rather than Hungarian law, such as English or other Anglo-Saxon law for the shareholders' agreements. Interview with Las-

1990 developments, however, should not lead to the conclusion that students come out of law schools fully equipped with knowledge of the field.[5]

Last but not least, important questions remain obscure in this domain and thus the researcher may not often be in the position to provide firm answers. This is something that the reader should bear in mind when reading the ensuing elaboration. For example, given the continued high-prestige of English shareholders' agreements in Hungary, it would be of great interest to know whether shareholders' agreements are exploited as a protective shield against liability under such acts as the UK Bribery Act 2010[6] when Hungarian agents or subsidiaries are involved. Likewise, it would be interesting to see the discrepancy that inevitably exists between scholarship and prevailing business practices. Obviously, the former significantly lags behind developments primarily because the confidential nature of shareholders' agreements makes research and analysis next to impossible. A telling example are the co-sale (tag along)[7] rights of shareholders that

---

zlo Czirjak on 10th of January 2017, the founder and partner of 'iEurope Capital' (http://ieurope.-com), a US-based investment firm with offices both in Budapest and New York.

5 A notable exception seems to be the work of a few enthusiasts at the Debrecen Law School. See the articles of *Gergely Szabó* Gazdasági társaság a szindikátusi kötelemben, Céghírnök, No. 5 (May 2012), at 7–11 and Texas Shoot-out, avagy biztosítéki konstrukciók a szindikátusi kötelemben, Debreceni Jogi Műhely, 3/2012 (2012. július 1.), vol. IX., No. 3, available electronically at < http://www.debrecenijogimuhely.hu/archivum/3_2012/ > and *Krisztina Nagy Barna* A szindikátusi szerződés, Debreceni Jogi Műhely, 2015. évi (XII. évfolyam) 3-4. szám (Dec. 2015). Both last visited on 21 January 2017.

6 The Bribery Act 2010 (c.23) introduced in its Section 7 a new type of offence allowing for prosecuting of foreign agents or subsidiaries of commercial organizations incorporated in the UK, or of companies that carry on at least part of their business in the UK, not only for committing acts of bribery but also for *failure to prevent bribery.* Adding appropriately formulated defences – more precisely having in place "*adequate procedures designed to prevent persons associated with [the company] from undertaking such conduct*" – to shareholders' agreements might be a tool to protect oneself against such vicarious liability. While under the earlier legislation the prosecutors "*had to identify the directing will and mind within a company at the time on offence was committed and obtain evidence of that person's knowledge and involvement,*" under the 2010 Act they "*will need only to prove fault by an individual connected to a relevant organisation ... in order to engage this section.*" See *Aaronberg/Higgins* The Bribery Act 2010: all bark and no bite ...?, Archbold Review 6 (2010), at 8.

7 As defined by the British Private Equity and Venture Capital Association's Guide to Venture Capital Term Sheets (October 2007) – "*If a shareholder wishes to dispose of shares that are the subject of co-sale or tag along right, the other shareholders who benefit from the right can insist that the potential purchaser agrees to purchase an equivalent percentage of their shares, at the same price and under the same terms and conditions.*" *Id.* at 15. Document downloadable at: <http://www.bvca.co.uk/Portals/0/library/Files/StandardIndustryDocuments/Guide_to_VC_-Termsheets.pdf>; last visited on 29 December 2016.

according to practicing businessmen and counsel are widely used yet which escape commenting by scholars. These and similar objective factors should be borne in mind when reading the ensuing elaboration on the present-time position of shareholders' agreements in Hungary.

# B. Nature of Corporate Law Regulation

## I. The Civil Code of 2013: A Paradigm Shift

For the time being, Hungary has neither special legislation, nor a developed conceptual framework on shareholders' agreements. As these peculiar Janus-faced contracts, hybrids survive on the borderline of company and private law (obligations), a glance at those elements of the former that most intensely affect shareholders' agreements is a must. Here, however, we will limit our review to the last changes of Hungarian company law, a paradigm shift introduced with the passage of the new 2013 Civil Code of Hungary,[8] which did not result in addition of any provisions specifically on shareholders' agreements. This was the case though also with the earlier 2016 Company Act.

The two fundamental changes that indirectly affect shareholders' agreements concern the status and the basic characteristics of company law. On the one hand, as opposed to the earlier period when company law was enshrined in a distinct statute,[9] from 2013 company law is placed in Book Three of the Civil Code. With this, Hungary has joined the club of those European systems that have opted for **'integrated regulation of company law'.**[10]

**8** Hungary, in his modern history, had only two Civil Codes. The first, enacted during socialism in 1959 (Act No. IV. of year 1959 on the Civil Code), was replaced by a the new one only in 2013, after more than ten years of work on the new, market-economy-fitting version. The full reference to the new Civil Code is Law No. V. of year 2013 on the Civil Code ("*A Polgári Törvénykönyvről szóló 2013. évi V. törvény*") [hereinafter: Civil Code or Civil Code of 2013].

**9** The earlier Act of year 2006 No. IV on Commercial Companies (*A gazdasági társaságokról szóló 2006. évi IV. törvény*) was repealed by the 2013 Civil Code, stepping into force on 15 March 2014.

**10** As one of the comments mentions, such approach is applied in Italy, the Netherlands and Switzerland. See *Kisfaludi* Comments on Company Law, in: Lajos Vékás (editor in chief), Complex Commentary (Complex – partner of the Wolters Kluwer Group, Budapest, 1st ed., 2013), at 21 and 124 [hereinafter: Complex Commentary]. Besides the Complex Commentary, the HVG/ORAC Commentary (2013) is being used as well, named after its publisher (HGV/ORAC, Budapest, partner of the LexisNexis Group). The editor in chief of this was *György Wellmann*, the

On the other hand – and presumably more importantly from the point of view of our central theme – instead of the earlier prescriptive and detailed drafting, the drafters of new company law shifted to a company law dominated by default (dispositive) rules,[11] private ordering and the increased role of freedom of contract. As one of the Comments states "*posting dispositivity as the main rule [of Book Three on juridical persons] affects, directly or indirectly, all provisions of Book Three. The central novelty inherent to the change is that the rules of Book Three have become nothing more than models to parties wishing to use them, similarly to the rules on contracts.*" One of the repercussions of the volte face is that the "*founders of a company are entitled not only to decide on the fact of the establishment of the company but they may also (...) freely shape the rules of the operation of the juridical entity.*"[12]

## II. From Prescriptive Drafting to Private Ordering

This change is of crucial importance for shareholders' agreements because in the new, contract-dominated era, instead of dictating through mandatory norms, company law gives almost unlimited freedom to parties to forge solutions that in their view best fits their interests. Now, the counsel's primary function is not to 'tick the boxes' and satisfy, or react to, all the items prescribed by the law, but rather to be innovative and capable of engaging in legal engineering to best satisfy their clients' needs. In other words, the earlier **'era of prescriptive company law'** changed to the new that may conveniently be referred to as the **'era of private ordering'** or the **'era of three P's'** – known from contract law.[13]

---

judge of the Hungarian Supreme Court, named as Kúria (Curia). This Commentary will be referred to herein as HVG/ORAC Commentary.

11 As it is commonly known, the concept and designation of 'dispositive' or 'dispositivity' is unknown in common law systems, or it has a radically different meaning. The closest equivalent of what is a complex theoretical concept in civilian laws, is nothing more than a mere drafting technicality in common laws – embodied in the category of 'default rules.' *Farnsworth*, the doyen of US contract law, talked of the European concept as a 'term of art' when explaining what default rules of contract law are: "*European legal systems have long had terms of art to distinguish between rules of law that the parties can vary by express provision or usage and rules of that are beyond their power to modify.*" See *Farnsworth* Contracts (Aspen, 4th ed., 2004), § 1.10, at 37.

12 Complex Commentary, at 85–86.

13 See, for example *Burnham* Drafting Contracts – A Guide to the Practical Application of the Principles of Contract Law (Michie Company Law Publishers, Charlottesville, Virginia, 1993), at

The three P's denote the three tasks counsel should know how to satisfy and these are to PREDICT, to PROVIDE and to PROTECT the clients; in our case, shareholders concluding a shareholders' agreement. As the sheer number of mandatory norms has decreased as a result of the new approach, there are therefore fewer such restrictive statutory norms that might bind the hands of drafters of shareholders' agreements as well. Figuratively speaking, the doors to the imagination, creativeness of counsel and party freedom have thus been opened significantly wider by embracing this private ordering-focused approach in the 2013 Civil Code. At least, that is what one may presuppose. At any event, presumably years will be needed for a fuller understanding of what this shift denotes, a test period both for practicing lawyers and for judges or arbitrators.

## III. Deviation from Book Three of the Civil Code

Two points ought to be raised to provide the reader with a more complete picture on what is exactly meant by the above-mentioned shift to a model dominated by default (dispositive) rules. Or, in other words, in which cases may private parties deviate from the provisions of the Code? The first is that the new paradigm does not mean unrestricted freedom to bypass the provisions of the Code; limitations do exist first and foremost through explicit mandatory provisions in Book Three. The second is that one of the Book Three-related issues debated by scholars concerned exactly what the hinted at *dispositivity* denotes? In other words, there is no full consensus on what the dispositivity-related change concretely means.

As far as blackletter law is concerned, the formula employed by the Civil Code is made of two parts. On one hand, it proclaims as a general principle that the members, or founders, of juridical entities ("*jogi személyek*") *may* deviate from the Code's rules of Book Three on juridical persons in the corporate charter.[14] The deviations may be related to the internal relations of the members, their relation to the legal entity as well as to the operation and governance of the legal entity.[15] It is not clarified by the Comments why have only these three groups of issues been explicitly mentioned yet due to the breadth of their reach one could presume that essentially such formulation was meant to extend to all possible aspects of corporate existence. Of importance to our central topic is that such formulation provides the drafters of shareholders' agree-

93. According to this source, the three P's of contract drafting are: PREDICT what may happen; PROVIDE for that contingency and PROTECT your client with a remedy.

14 See § 3:4(1) and (2) of the 2013 Civil Code.

15 See § 3:4(2) of the 2013 Civil Code.

ments as well with almost unrestricted freedom, not just when desiring to conclude a shareholders' agreement, but also when tailoring these legal tools to their clients' needs.

The multi-pronged restrictions come in through two quite general provisions. Namely, after proclaiming the earlier mentioned general principle of *dispositivity*, the Code prohibits deviations in five specific instances.[16] The sanction in each case is the invalidity of the bypassing provision.[17] According to the first, shareholders or founders cannot depart from the Code when the Code itself prohibits that. Perhaps the best example is the Code's limitation of the available company forms ("*formakényszer*").[18] The second, third and fourth restrictions aim to protect the rights of creditors, employees and minority shareholders as enshrined in the respective provisions of the Code. There is a qualification, however, to the applicability of these limitations: namely, deviations from the Code rules in such cases would be prohibited only if the deviating provisions would '*manifestly infringe*' ("*nyilvánvalóan sérti*") the rights of creditors, employees and minority shareholders.[19] Needless to say, the indeterminacy inherent to such qualification cannot but be left to be resolved by courts. Last but not least, it is prohibited to deviate from such provisions that aim to ensure the legality of the operations of a company.[20]

---

**16** See § 3:4(3) of the 2013 Civil Code.

**17** See Complex Comments at 86.

**18** See § 3:89 of the 2013 Civil Code. According to this provision, four organizational forms are available for founding a commercial company ("*gazdasági társaság*") today in Hungary only. Though the joint stock company ("*részvénytársaság*" or Rt.) – in essence the local kin of the German "*Aktiengesellschaft (AG)*" or the French "*société anonyme (SA)*" – has two variants: the so-called 'closed' and the 'open' joint stock company. While in the case of the close joint-stock company the shares of the company are not listed on an organized exchange, in the case of the open they are. See § 3:211(1) and (2) of the 2013 Civil Code for the definition of these two forms of joint stock companies. This, in other words, also means that in Hungary it is not possible to establish a joint-stock company by raising capital on open markets. Rather, the company must first be founded as a closed joint-stock company and only after its shares – in the next stage – have been listed on a recognized exchange may the company tap the capital markets. See Complex Comments at 169.

**19** See § 3:4(3)(b) of the 2013 Civil Code.

**20** The Complex Commentary at 86–7 provides the following such example: the parties cannot agree that the right of the state to control the legality of the operations of the company will not apply to their company.

### IV. The *Dispositivity* Debate

Given that no company law has ever been based on *dispositivity* in Hungarian legal history, the volte face to the exact opposite of the earlier mandatory rules-dominated nature of company laws has proved to be one of the most debated issues among Hungarian scholars. However, as eventually the rule on the *dispositivity* of Book Three of the 2013 Civil Code has, neither been abandoned, nor changed, with the Amendments of the Civil Code passed 2016, three years after the enactment of the new Code,[21] here it suffices only to briefly sketch the main points of potential relevance to the topic of shareholders' agreements.

Admittedly, the most useful practical lesson from the debates is that the occasional drafting and linguistic imprecisions, or the provisions asking for interpretation, do create some uncertainty. In this sense *Sárközy* is right to claim that "*Book Three is full with provisions the language of which suggests that they are mandatory*"[22] when actually it is not necessarily so. This is critical from the perspective of shareholders' agreements in case of which one of the main concerns is exactly what questions may the parties modify.

## C. Regulation of Shareholders' Agreements or rather the Law on Shareholders' Agreements

### I. The Lack of Topic-Specific Regulation

As already hinted at, Hungary has, neither special legislation, nor a developed doctrinal concept on shareholders' agreements as of today. This, however, does not mean that they are not used in business life. Although no statistical data is available – partly because of the desire of parties not to disclose them – there are indirect evidences of their relatively wide exploitation. Suffice to point to the fact that, relative to the breadth of the topic of shareholders' agreements, a relatively meaningful number of high court decisions being focused on

---

21 See the Act No. LXXVII of year 2016 on the Amendment of Act No. V of year 2013 on the Civil Code ("*2016. évi LXXVII. Törvény a Polgári Törvénykönyvről szóló 2013. évi V. törvény módosításáról*").

22 *Tamás Sárközy* Még egyszer a Ptk. jogi személy könyve állítólagos diszpozitivitásáról [Once again on the *Dispositivity* of the Civil Code's Book Three on Juridical Persons], in: Gazdaság és Jog, No. 11 (Nov. 2015), pp. 8–14, at 8. [Hereinafter: *Sárközy* (Nov. 2015)].

or at least mentioning shareholders' agreements have been reported. Likewise, while it would be an exaggeration to state that the topic has already been exhaustively covered by scholarship, especially from a comparative perspective, publications do exist (as it may be seen also from the references in this paper).

Various industrial bodies as well speak of shareholders' agreements as being exploited in practice. For example, the Hungarian Private Equity and Venture Capital Association, in its 2012 opinion on the new Civil Code, speaks of shareholders' agreements as commonly used and important elements of the legal system.[23]

All this, in other words, means that general contract law as supplemented by the applicable case law and industrial practices are the source of law for shareholders' agreements in Hungary at the moment. Consequently, based on the venerable principle of contract law – the principle of the freedom of contract –, shareholders' agreements are legitimate categories of the Hungarian legal system. There are no provisions in the 2013 Civil Code, or other statute either which would make their conclusion contingent to inclusion into the corporate charter, bylaws or decision of the shareholder meeting. Likewise, there is no code or statutory provision that would impose restrictions on the duration of Shareholders' Agreements or that would provide for distinct rules for international or cross border Shareholders' Agreements.

## II. The Key Features of Shareholders' Agreements according to Present-Time Hungarian Law

Notwithstanding the lack of direct regulation, the key features of shareholders' agreement are generally agreed upon by both courts and scholars to a great extent thanks to a string of court cases involving them. Perhaps the most succinct definition, the holding of an Appeal Court judgment, deserves to be cited. It reads as follows:

> The shareholders' agreement is such an atypical contract that creates valid obligations for the parties to it and which should be performed according to the contents formulated by

23 See Magyar Kockázati és Magántőke Egyesület új Polgári Törvénykönyvvel kapcsolatos észrevételei (3 April 2012), section 2.3 at page 4. The text is available in Hungarian at < http://www.hvca.hu/wp-content/uploads/2012/05/Magyar-Kockazati-es-Magantoke-Egyesulet-eszrevetelei-az-uj-Ptk-tervezethez-120413.pdf >. Last visited on 28 Dec. 2016.

the parties. Consequently, the remedy for its breach is equal to the remedies available for breach of any other civil law contract: damages unless otherwise agreed upon.[24]

According to this unofficial, case law-based definition, the following three key features must be mentioned. Out of these, the first two are interlinked and represent in a sense the two sides of the same coin. Namely, *first*, the shareholders' agreement is an *innominate* contract meaning that it is not one of the contracts regulated and known by name in the Civil Code. Figuratively speaking, it is a 'no name' contract for the Code. Typically new types of contracts are innominate until they become so widely used that the lawmaker decides to name and regulate it as a separate type of contract to the Civil Code. Admittedly, this in dualist systems may be also the Commercial Code or other legislative act in jurisdictions without codes. In Hungary, for example, business format franchise had been an innominate contract until it was added to the 2013 Civil Code, whereby it morphed into a nominated one.

It is, *secondly*, an *atypical* contract as well given that its nature and key features make it ill-suited to any of the more venerable contracts known by the Civil Code and otherwise. Truth be told, although these two features are often reiterated in court decisions and in various pertaining publications, the exact meaning of what makes the shareholders' agreements atypical has not been fully explored yet. Perhaps the most determinative from that perspective, however, is its Janus-faced nature. Namely, as properly highlighted in the BDT2007.1671 judgment, the shareholders' agreement is, on the one hand, of accessory nature because its existence obviously is linked to the corporate charter, a higher ranking source of law. It is not that it may not contradict it but is resorted to exactly to regulate those questions of interest to shareholders that have been left out from the corporate charter, are only partially regulated by the former or may be regulated differently from what the charter provides.

On the other hand, it is also a contract that is independent from the corporate charter because it is different from it, at least, in three respects: parties to it, its contents and the remedies for breach. As far as the parties are concerned, while the corporate charter must be agreed upon by *all* shareholders (members or partners), a shareholders' agreement must not be unanimous, involving all shareholders. In this respect, Hungary does not seem to differ from other western

**24** *See* BDT2007.1671. The Hungarian language formulation reads as follows: "*A szindikátusi szerződés olyan atipikus szerződés, amely a szerződő felekre érvényes kötelmi jogi kötelezettségvállalást keletkeztet, és amelyet olyan tartalommal kell teljesíteni, ahogy azt a felek szabályozták. A kötelezettségvállalás megszegésének pedig ugyanaz a következménye, mint más polgári jogi szerződés megszegésének: eltérő kötelmi kikötés hiányában a kártérítés a szankció.*"

legal systems and both unanimous and non-unanimous shareholders' agreements are known even in the lack of sector specific regulations.

The two differ in two meaningful respects as regards their contents as well. *First*, although the contents of the two may (and normally do) relate to the same questions (e.g., appointment of officers, voting), the shareholders' agreements typically go broader. To take two examples from reported cases, they may foresee extension of a loan, [25] or making a sum of money available,[26] by one of the shareholders to another one under certain terms and conditions. *Secondly*, while the corporate charter's contents are fixed by law in Hungary, freedom of contract reigns in case of shareholders' agreements. Thus, albeit linked and similar, the corporate charter and the shareholders' agreement, at least in this country, contents-wise radically differ: while the first is about satisfying mandatory norms ("ticking the boxes"), the latter is not and is rather a contract "the contents of which is not fixed ["*kötött tartalma nincsen*"]." More precisely, the parties enjoy some freedom in the case of corporate charters as well given that although they must "tick all the boxes", the law provides them with choices. For example, they choose the name of the company, and unless deceivingly resembling with another already registered name,[27] the system will yield to the choice of the parties.

*Thirdly*, courts and scholars agree that the shareholders' agreement creates obligations. This, in other words, means that the shareholders' agreement is looked upon as contract, a legal category belonging to the law of obligations rather than to company law. The most important consequence of this feature is that the remedies for the breach of shareholders' agreements are the remedies applicable in the context of obligations, concretely damages.[28]

## III. Partnerships, Closed and Open Joint-Stock Corporations

No explicit rule exists specifically on shareholders' agreements related to any of the five company forms in Hungarian law, to wit unlimited and limited partnerships, limited liability companies and joint-stock companies (both the closed and the open variants). Hence, theoretically shareholders' agreements may be

25 See, e.g., the arbitral award Vb/02180 of the Arbitral Institution attached to the Hungarian Chamber of Commerce and Industry (2003) published by Complex Publisher as 2003/4.
26 See, e.g., the decision BH2015.285 in which an investor promised to extend 500 million HUF in return for becoming the shareholder.
27 See §3:6(1) of the 2013 Civil Code.
28 See BDT2007.1671.

concluded by the shareholders, partners or members of any of these. As no precise statistical data exists, it is impossible to tell in which industrial sectors or the shareholders' of which types of businesses typically resort to shareholders' agreements. The reported cases and other sources show that large and small as well as private and by-municipalities-owned businesses alike could be found among those having concluded shareholders' agreements.

Perhaps the most famous Hungarian shareholders' agreement was concluded by the Republic of Croatia (represented by the Government of the Republic of Croatia) and the MOL Hungarian Oil and Gas plc in 2003, a document that is now publicly available[29] given that a dispute, reported by the Hungarian media, arose a between the parties a few years ago, involving corruption charges against the CEO of MOL and eventually an ICSID arbitration that was lost by the Croatian side. [30] MOL is otherwise the holder of two large blocks of shares in the Croatian oil and gas company INA, which was acquired as part of the privatization of the latter. This shareholders' agreement, while demarcating the exercise of the rights of shareholders, aimed also to protect the interests of the Croatian side that planned to continue with the privatization of the company.[31] The shareholders' agreement of MOL and INA contains numerous standard clauses of shareholders' agreements, from a five year lock up provision (restricting the transfer of INA shares),[32] participation in the governance of INA[33] (including resolution of deadlocks),[34] dividend policy,[35] undertakings of the Hungarian party as far as future

**29** The English language text of the Shareholders' agreement can be downloaded from the following page of MOL-Group http://molincroatia.com/sites/default/files/SHA%2017–07–2003.pdf; last visited on 28 December 2016.

**30** See ICSID case MOL Hungarian Oil and Gas Company plc v. Republic of Croatia, case No. ARB/13/32 of 2 Dec. 2014. The case was launched after the relations of the two sides have deteriorated somewhere after 2009, when the CEO of MOL was accused of bribery of the former Croatian Prime Minister (who was convicted for having accepted bribe in Croatia). MOL claimed that due to a series of measures taken by the Croatian government "*designed to damage and impair [its] investment in INA*" In particular, as claimed by MOL, MOL was prevented from acquiring the INA Gas Trading Company contrary to earlier agreements (section 18), the acquisition of more than 50% of INA shares traded on the Zagreb stock exchange was also blocked (relying on Croatian pension funds, point 19); as well as forcing MOL to supply gas at artificially depressed controlled prices (section 20).

**31** See, for example, MTI (the Hungarian News Agency*)* MOL: a horvát kormánynak is előnyös a részvényesi megállapodás [MOL: the Shareholders' Agreement is Favourable also to the Croatian Government] from 2012, available electronically at <>. Last visited on 28 Dec. 2016.

**32** Croatia-MOL shareholders' agreement, section 11.

**33** Croatia-MOL shareholders' agreement, section 7.

**34** Croatia-MOL shareholders' agreement, section 14.

**35** Croatia-MOL shareholders' agreement, section 8.

explorations and entry into new markets is concerned,[36] a tag-along (co-sale) provision,[37] or dispute resolution.[38] Otherwise, MOL seems to regularly conclude shareholders' agreements with foreign companies in which it has stakes.[39]

Additionally, shareholders' agreements have been concluded not only by private companies but also by municipalities that formed businesses for provision of some services (e. g., water supply, funeral services[40]). Reported cases exist though also involving shareholders' agreements of Hungarian businesses and foreign investors.[41]

## IV. A Word of Caution on Terminology and Translation

Given that this article is in English, it is not of direct relevance that there is a discrepancy between the English and Hungarian nomenclature. Yet once one embarks on reading, checking or researching Hungarian language sources, it might be of help to know the following. *First*, as the topic of shareholders' agreements has escaped regulation so far, the related terminology is tainted with some level of indeterminacy as well. *Secondly*, as opposed to, for example, US law (more precisely the laws of the various States that regulate partnership and the law of corporations), Hungarian legal terminology uses different terms for the equity stakes one may have in the known types of business forms. The main divide is between joint stock companies on one hand, and the LTD as well as the two partnership forms on the other. Namely, while in case of the former the law speaks of 'shares' ("*részvény*") and 'shareholders' ("*részvényes*") in the context of partnerships 'membership stakes' ("*tagsági részesedés*") and

36 Croatia-MOL shareholders' agreement section 9.2.

37 Croatia-MOL shareholders' agreement, sub-section 9.1.1.

38 Croatia-MOL shareholders' agreement, section 15.

39 Besides the Croatian one, conclusion of a shareholders' agreement was reported on in MOL's bulletin MOLGROUP PANORAMA April 2015 (sixth) issue. This one was concluded related to MOL's interests in Kazakhstan by Cooperatieve KMG EP U.A., MOL Caspian Oil & Gas Ltd and the First Int'l Oil Corporation Ltd. The bulletin can be downloaded from <https://molgroup.info/images/molgroup/pdf/press_centre/publications/MOL_Group_Panorama_2015_April.pdf>. Last visited on 28 December 2016.

40 See, e. g., the decision of the Hungarian Competition Law Agency VEF 1996/5 in which eight municipalities (local governments) formed a new company that was supposed to provide funeral services for each of them.

41 See, e. g., case EBH2007.1617 where a Hungarian limited liability company concluded a shareholders' agreement with Russian investors, who promised not only to bring in new capital but also to ensure continuous supply of oil (10 thousand tons per month).

'members' ("*tagok*") and members and business shares ("*üzletrész*") in the context of LTDs. What may be a bit puzzling is that each of these may (and is often) translated to English as 'share' and those holding it 'shareholders.'

This digression to the idiosyncrasies of the nomenclature of Hungarian company law is then of impact on our central topic as well. Namely, as a consequence of the above, normally the general reference to shareholders' agreements is different and shareholders' agreements concluded by shareholders of a joint-stock company are named as "*részvényesi szerződés*" as opposed to the ones concluded by the partners and members of the other business forms – the "*szindikátusi szerződés.*"[42] Notwithstanding this dualism in Hungarian legal terminology, both should be translated as shareholders' agreements – a pattern we will follow in this paper, too.

## V. The Quintessential Role of the Case Law on Shareholders' Agreements

In the lack of explicit regulations on shareholders' agreements, the post-1990 case law, the relatively scarce yet existent scholarship and the pertaining industrial practices are the most important sources of law in Hungary today. Yet if one would like to find out what solutions are employed and what are those aims and goals that shareholders exploit shareholders' agreements for, court and arbitral cases are beyond doubt the most important tools. This notwithstanding that scholars as a rule fail to take a closer look at cases save for citing them in footnotes with a sentence or two in the main body of text. For this reason, this paper will try to fill the void by placing precedents in the centre of our discussion.

This is a bit unusual in Hungary as a civil law country where codes and statutory law are still the most important sources of law though the importance of high court decisions as a source of law has undoubtedly increased in the last

---

42 The origin of the attribute "*szindikátusi*" is not fully clear. According to the Dictionary of Foreign Originated Words [in Hungarian Language], this word – obviously the domesticated version of the term '*syndicate*' known by many other European languages – denotes "*common action by banks or companies to achieve a common goal, or to complete a common transactions, like issuance of bonds*". See *Bakos* Idegen szavak és kifejezések szótára (Akadémiai kiadó, Budapest ,2005). According to *Kolben*, most presumably the term was inherited from the pre-II WW period when the *syndicate* or '*szindikátus*' was a form of temporary associations that did not qualify as a company and which was formed only to issue certain securities *("emissziós ügylet"*). As this term figured also in venerable legal textbooks of two leading Hungarian scholars of the first half of the 20[th] century (*Károly Szladits* and *Ödön Kuncz*), rightfully *Kolben* concluded, that meant that the term has already then been more generally subscribed to. See *Kolben* at 12.

decade or so. The domain of shareholders' agreements is an excellent proof of that. For researchers it is salutary that, as a corollary, the number of reported court cases has increased as well, which do reveal details about shareholders' agreements, that are as a rule confidential. Moreover, the Supreme Court regularly adopts uniformity decisions ("*jogegységi határozat*") that are binding and published in the Hungarian Official Gazette.[43] A few of such unifying decisions have already dealt with shareholders' agreements (even if only obiter) yet what could be taken as indirect proof of the presence and prestige these peculiar agreements have gained in the meantime in Hungarian business life.

The increased importance of court cases does not seem to be a Hungarian peculiarity only. Some post-socialist countries went in this respect as far as making online publication of all court cases mandatory; notably this was the case in Ukraine.[44] In Hungary, today the number of publicized cases – though typically in abridged concise form only – is above one-hundred thousand no matter which of the commercial databases are looked upon and it continues to grow.

Besides court decisions, one should mention as well arbitral awards and decisions of the Hungarian Competition Agency as sources. Before proceeding to the synopsis of arbitral and competition agency cases, the following ought to be added related to the former. Namely, as it was of utmost importance for the drafters of the 2013 Civil Code to promote arbitration in the company law-context, explicit paragraphs were added in addition to the generally application arbitration act.[45] As one of the Commentaries states: "*Agreeing on dispute resolution by arbitration could equally be enshrined in the articles of incorporation and in the agreement of the parties to the dispute.*"[46] However, the arbitral agree-

---

43 For the English language pages of the Hungarian Supreme Court (now called "*Kúria*") *see* < http://www.lb.hu/en/uniformity-decisions >. Last visited on 28 December 2016.

44 See the Editors' Introduction in: Stefan Messmann & Tibor Tajti (eds.), the Case Law of Central and Eastern Europe – Enforcement of Contracts (European University Press, Bochum – Germany, 2009), pp. 14–19. The book, led by the realization of the increased importance of court cases in the Central and Eastern European region, takes a look at such novel fields of law and the related judgments as leasing, secured transactions or franchise. The Lithuanian chapter, written by *Lina Aleknaite*, for example, showed the problems these countries then on the road towards free market economy faced in grappling with such new legal challenges as pledging of company shares and the exact meaning of the related enforcement rights. Id. volume I, at 376 et seq. See also Stefan Messmann & Tibor Tajti (eds.), the Case Law of Central and Eastern Europe – Leasing, Piercing the Corporate Veil and the Liability of Managers and Controlling Shareholders, Privatization, Takeovers and the Problems with Collateral Laws (European University Press, Bochum-Germany, 2007).

45 See §§ 3:92 and 3:93 of the 2013 Civil Code.

46 Complex Commentary (2013), at 128.

ment in the shareholders' agreement does not extend onto disputes arising from the corporate charter, and vice versa.[47]

## VI. Cases Involving Shareholders' Agreements: Arbitration, Competition Authority and Constitutional Court Decisions

### 1. The "Reach" of Arbitration Agreements in Shareholders' Agreements

Although the number of reported arbitral awards involving shareholders' agreement is not big in Hungary, they are instructive in more respects. The low number of reported cases primarily is attributable to the fact that arbitral proceedings are in principle confidential as well, something crucial whenever disputes concerning shareholders' agreements are at stake.[48] While here the focus will be limited to a single reported case that dealt with such conventional issue of arbitral law as the arbitrability of disputes arising from shareholders' agreements, the reader is well-advised to note that some of the cases discussed hereinafter involved arbitration as well.

In the case decided by the Hungarian Supreme Court (BH1992.772), the parties concluded a shareholders' agreement to form an LTD and to "*fix the rights and duties of the parties to the agreement in-between themselves as well as with the company to be established, the governance principles and all other basic questions that are inevitable to ensure peaceful cooperation of the parties*

---

47 BH1997/1.; VB/95040. Cited also in *Auer/Balog/Jenovai/Juhász/Papp/Strihó/Szeghő* Atipikus szerződések [Atypical Contracts] (Opten Kft, Budapest, 2015), at 227. Hereinafter: *Auer et al* Atypical Contracts (2015). See also the arbitral case Vb 95.040 made by the Arbitral Institution attached to the Hungarian Chamber of Commercial and Industry. Here, the Hungarian partners concluded a shareholders' agreement with a foreign expert who promised to provide his expert services exclusively for the newly established company for 15 years. However, the arbitration agreement was added only to the charter of the newly founded company. Later, the foreign expert extraordinarily terminated its employment and caused damages to the company by stopping to provide the promised services. The arbitration tribunal found that it has no jurisdiction to hear the case related to breach of the shareholder's agreement. However, as the foreign expert has a few years after the foundation of the new company become a shareholder and thus the corporate charter applied also to him, the arbitral tribunal awarded damages for breaching the charter.

48 *Kolben* is of the opinion that in most cases shareholders' agreements foresee arbitration as dispute resolution method. Besides the traditionally cited advantages of arbitration over litigation (i.e., presumption that arbitration is shorter, cheaper and makes more expert decisions possible as industry experts may also serve as arbitrators), confidentiality is in his opinion the main reason. See *Kolben* (1996), at 98–99.

*in the future*." In other words, such wording of the shareholders' agreement, admittedly quite general, suggests that the parties' intention went beyond mere foundation of the LTD. An arbitration agreement opting for the standing Arbitral Tribunal of the Zurich Chamber of Commerce in case the disputes arising out of the shareholders' agreement cannot be solved amicably within 90 calendar days has also been added to it. Thereafter, the company was formed and the corporate charter was also passed by the shareholders' meeting of the new company, however, no dispute resolution mechanism was added to it. The dispute arose when one of the founders was excluded from the LTD by the decision of the shareholders' meeting of the LTD.

The issue was whether a Hungarian court or rather the Swiss arbitral tribunal has jurisdiction to hear the case. Needless to say, the parties disagreed. The claimant was of the position that the shareholders' agreement foresaw arbitration in Switzerland *only* for disputes arising from the shareholders' agreement, however, the shareholders' agreement had been fulfilled in the meantime by the fact of the founding of the LTD. Therefore, the arbitration agreement enshrined in the shareholders' agreement does not apply anymore to the disputes that arise from the corporate charter. As opposed to that, the respondent put forward that the shareholders' agreement is still alive, it governs the operation of the LTD in certain respects and as such it supplements the corporate charter. Moreover, no dispute resolution clause was added to the corporate charter exactly because the parties wanted to stick to the one in the shareholders' agreement.

The Supreme Court ruled that the arbitration agreement in the shareholders' agreement does not apply to disputes arising from the corporate charter for two main reasons. On one hand, the shareholders' agreement was primarily concluded to form the LTD. As that occurred, the shareholders' agreement has materialized. Moreover, the dispute was triggered by the claimant's exclusion as a shareholder by the already formed LTD's general meeting of shareholders. Thus, the dispute is based not on the shareholders' agreement but on the corporate charter. On the other hand, the shareholders of the LTD are different from the parties who have signed the shareholder's agreement. Consequently, as the parties to the corporate charter have failed to agree on arbitration, Hungarian courts have jurisdiction to adjudicate the case.

## 2. What do the Decisions of the Hungarian Competition Authority Reveal?

Interestingly, a few decisions of the Hungarian Competition Authority involved shareholders' agreements as well. Although the issue of these is not about the agreements themselves but rather about various anti-competitive behaviours, they are a valuable repository of empirical evidences from which certain conclusions could be drawn concerning in what situations and for what purposes have shareholders' agreements been resorted to. As these cases are focused on competition law, the shareholders' agreements-related facts are typically described in less detail. Two cases will be mentioned here briefly.

### a. Shareholders' Agreements on "*Coordinating*" the Relevant Market

As reported in a Supreme Court decision from 1996[49] – focusing on abuse of dominant market position by refusing to conclude a contract with a smaller company wishing to provide services on the relevant market – a shareholders' agreement was concluded by eight municipalities, a county and a county association. The agreement was concluded to found a company that would provide funeral services on the entire territory of the county (of *Somogy*) with the ultimate aim to ensure provision of appropriate quality services. As part of the agreement, the municipalities transferred onto the new company also the right to maintain the cemeteries subject to the restriction that the new company – obviously acquiring a dominant position on this market – may not restrict provision of funeral services to other businesses. As it may be presumed, the new company was found to have abused its dominant position; the fine imposed on it by the first instance court was eventually confirmed also by the Supreme Court.

In another case, starting as a fine imposed by the Competition Authority and finally adjudicated by the Budapest Capital Appeal Court in 2005,[50] the shareholders' agreement was concluded as well to form a new company yet for a different reason: to some extent resembling price fixing. Or, as both the corporate charter and the shareholders' agreement stated, to "*calm the fluctuation of prices stemming from the cyclicality of the market, by forming a new company.*" They agreed also to continuously "*reconcile*" their sales prices for each category of products and to reach an accord on the entry onto new markets either directly or via the new company. More concretely, the new LTD was essentially formed for sale of eggs and to act in concerted manner on the Hungarian market of eggs.

49 See VEF 1996/5.

50 See VEF 2005.54. The case reference number with the Hungarian Competition Authority is Vj-199/2005.

### b. Anti-Competition and Loyalty Clauses

The Hungarian literature makes mention of shareholders' agreements which contain anti-competition and loyalty clauses tailored for the specific needs of the company the shareholders of which are concluding the shareholders' agreement. These may be either in the form of various limitations obliging the shareholders not to work for or not to do business with a competitor. Alternatively, in practice such provisions are employed as well that allow doing business with a third partner subject to the precondition that quotations are to be acquired also from the company and if they are not less favourable than those of the competitors the shareholder must contract with the company.[51] As per a decision of the Supreme Court, the breach of such anti-competition clauses may lead to exclusion of a shareholder from the company. In a 1999 decision, that involved a shareholder which has been employed by a competitor company notwithstanding a loyalty clause, the Supreme Court ruled that the remaining shareholders were entitled to react by his exclusion from the company.[52]

## 3. Shareholders' Agreements before the Hungarian Constitutional Court: Decree No. 3078/2013 (III. 27.) of the Constitutional Court

Although the request to conduct a constitutional review was rejected by the Constitutional Court as not satisfying the entry conditions and thus no decision was passed on the merits of the claim, it is noteworthy that a dispute concerning a shareholders' agreement has reached this pillar of the Hungarian court system as well. It is a proof, at least, of the presence, and relatively important role shareholders' agreements play in contemporary business life of Hungary.

The reason why the affected shareholders found it worthwhile to turn to the Constitutional Court is instructive as well: protection of their constitutionally guaranteed right to property through the shareholders' agreement. Namely, the shareholders' agreement foresaw two interlinked sets of transactions, increase of the registered capital, issuance and immediate dematerialization of the new securities as well as accounting for certain deficiencies.

In the first phase, **focused on the increase of registered capital**, the first defendant had to convene a shareholders' meeting to increase the capital of the company and to issue registered shares (“*névre szóló részvény*”). The plaintiff

51 See *Lukács/Sándor/Szűcs* Új típusú szerződések és azok gyakorlata a gazdasági életben [New Types of Contracts and their Exploitation in Business Life](HVG-Orac, Budapest, 2003), at 34.
52 Legfelsőbb Bíróság Gfv. VII. 31.582/1999 – BH 2000/498. Reported in *Lukacs et al Id.*, at 34–42.

was nominated by the shareholders' meeting as the recipient of these new shares preconditioned on transfer of a specific amount of cash. The said shareholders' meeting passed also a decision on the dematerialization of all certificated securities.

In the second phase, as a consideration for the acquisition of these new shares, the plaintiff had to purchase the 100% and the 60% stakes in two distinct companies within the system; what was fulfilled. The dispute arose, however, related to the related obligation of the plaintiff, according to which he had the duty to return free of charge certain quantity of the mentioned newly issued shares if the capital of the purchased stakes in the two companies fell below the threshold of 1 million HUF. The shareholders' agreement and the decision referred to this last set of duties as **'accounting for stakes'** ("*elszámolás*"). As per the shareholders' agreement, if that happened, the stake-holdings of the involved parties in the first company would change proportionately as well.

The dispute arose when the first defendant – in a sense, shortening the process anticipated by the shareholders' agreement – registered a smaller number of dematerialized shares for the benefit of the plaintiff notwithstanding that the plaintiff performed all what was expected from it. More precisely, instead of 3765, it registered only 887 shares. The justification for this was that the difference was "*kept*" as a result of the mentioned 'accounting' as foreseen by section 24 of the shareholders' agreement.

In the view of the plaintiff, its right to property was infringed, *first*, by not transferring to him all the shares he was entitled to but only the difference remaining after the 'accounting.' The plaintiff started arbitration proceedings to annul the said section 24 of the shareholders' agreement and to compel the first defendant to register also the remainder of shares on his securities account. As the arbitral tribunal rejected these claims, court proceedings began that ended with an identical Supreme Court decision that was eventually attacked before the Constitutional Court. In the opinion of the Supreme Court, as the dematerialized securities were duly registered, the plaintiff's right to property was not infringed. It was a different story whether the 'accounting proceedings' were legally problematic yet that was an issue not decided upon by it. As already noted, the Constitutional Court rejected to hear the case.

# D. Forms of Shareholders' Agreements

## I. Shareholders' Agreements on Shareholder Rights

### 1. Voting Rights in Shareholders' Agreements

While it could hardly be supported by quantitative empirical data, voting rights presumably are one of the most frequent subject matters of shareholders' agreements.[53] As far as the statutory background is concerned, the new Civil Code's provisions on voting are pretty liberal, with very few interferences, in line with the paradigm change the Code made with respect to company law mentioned above. Thus, there is ample room for shareholder's agreements to fill this legislative void with contents.[54] The chapter on joint-stock companies, for example, proclaims as a general rule that the shareholders may exercise their rights through proxies, though subject to some explicit statutory limitations.[55] Besides the proxies that act in the name and for the account of the shareholder, there is another category of representative-voting: voting through the so-called 'shareholder-appointee' ("*részvényesi meghatalmazott*") who acts in his own name but for the benefit of the shareholder.[56] Simple internet research may easily track down forms containing specific rubrics for voting through representatives.[57]

---

53 See also *Kolben* 1996, at 103, who – also without any quantitative data and pointing to concrete cases – speaks of voting as a topic that "*occupies a special place*" in elaborations on shareholders' agreements.

54 See *Auer et al* Atypical Contracts (2015), at 228.

55 While § 3:255(1) of the Civil Code proclaims the general principle that shareholders may exercise their right through proxies, § 3:256 defines the shareholder-appointee. Two limitations are imposed on the general right to exercise rights through proxies. According to the first, directors, officers, supervisory board members and accountants cannot act as proxies (§ 3:255(1)). As per the second, if a shareholder is represented by more proxies and they vote or make declarations that contradict each other, the votes or declarations of all of them will be deemed null and void (§ 3:255(2)).

56 Complex Commentary at 185. Note that the 2001 Capital Market Act also regulates shareholder-appointees (§§ 150 – 155). However, while under the Civil Code anybody can act as shareholder-appointee if registered in the register of shares, as per the Capital Market Act only the securities account- or deposited securities-handling intermediaries, and the central clearing house ("*értékpapír-számlavezető, a letétkezelő, vagy a központi értéktár*") may contract for such function (§ 151(1)).

57 See, for example, the instructions on voting (including through proxies) of MOL Hungarian Gas and Oil plc. at < https://molgroup.info/images/molgroup/pdf/investor_relations/regulated_informations/MOL_AGM_2011_EN.pdf >; last visited on 29 December 2016.

As far as voting trusts are concerned, the following ought to be added. Although the 2013 Civil Code introduced for the very first time in Hungary's history the concept of 'trust' following the Anglo-Saxon concept, this trust was not forged for voting but for property and estate handling, be it in the context of financial services or inheritance.[58] Moreover, the company law that is now enshrined into the Civil Code in a much shorter version compared to the earlier law, does not specifically know for the concept of 'voting trust' either. However, cooperation of shareholders as to voting and versions of voting through an agent are not unknown in Hungarian practice, as mentioned in the previous section. The articles of incorporation, for example of the Hungarian Oil and Gas Company MOL, one of the largest businesses of Hungary, knows for the category of 'shareholder groups' which may be formed, inter alia, also for common voting.[59] The law on company groups and its rules on acquisition of dominant control recognizes as well various concerted voting agreements, which do resemble voting trusts.[60]

The reported cases display the following on voting. In one of the cases, five shareholders concluded a shareholders' agreement for acquisition of the controlling package of shares in a yet-to-be privatized company.[61] Besides foreseeing a duty to share all relevant information, damages for intentional or negligent breach of the shareholders' agreement, provisions on voting were also added. As per these, they should have strived for consensus in the first step and – if consensus could not be reached – was formal voting to be resorted to. For passing of decisions, four out of the five members had to cast an affirmative vote for the decision-proposal. At the general meeting of the company voting by a common representative was provided for as well, who – if not voting as per the instructions of the consortium members – would be liable for the damages caused.

---

**58** The newcomer trust agreement is regulated in Book Six on Obligations, meaning that it is perceived to be "only" one type of nominated contracts, notwithstanding that it was modelled after common law concept of trust that is not treating trust as a mere contract. *See* the Complex Commentary at 794. On the newly introduced Hungarian trusts see Tibor Tajti and Robert Whitman, Common Law Trusts in Hungary and Other Continental European Civil Law Systems, John Marshall Law Rev., vol. 49, No. 3 (Spring 2016), pp. 709–727.

**59** *See* section 10.1.2 (b) of MOL's Articles of Incorporation downloadable at: from https://molgroup.info/images/molgroup/pdf/befektetoi_kapcsolatok/tarsasagiranyitas/fobb_tarsasagiranyitasi_dokumentumok/molnyrt_alapszabaly_20160623.pdf; last visited on 20 Dec. 2016. Put simply, if more shareholders are voting together they will be treated as a 'shareholder group.'

**60** *See* 2013 Civil Code §8:2(2)(b).

**61** Case No Pf.II.20.010/2007/4. szám, decided by the Appellate Court of Győr. Text (in Hungarian) available on the webpage of the Court at <http://gyoriitelotabla.birosag.hu/sites/default/files/field_attachment/20010–2007–4.pdf>; last visited on 29 December 2016.

The dispute arose because one of the shareholders was excluded from the consortium at a meeting to which he was not invited.

In another case,[62] involving four shareholders (including a municipality), the shareholders' agreement – concluded after the company has already been formed – contained provisions foreseeing asymmetric right to nominate directors and a commitment to vote affirmatively at general meetings as far as the nominations of the so-called 'investor' shareholders were concerned. They also added that two directors, with joint authorization to sign, are to run the company. The dispute arose because a new director was elected yet without recusing one of the old ones, a duty that was otherwise explicitly foreseen *only* in the shareholders' agreement but not in the articles of incorporation. Fully in accordance with the prevailing view on the nature and legal effects of shareholders' agreements, the court concluded that "*given that the shareholders' agreement is an a-typical contract that is binding only on the parties to it [and that] the effectuated election of directors, contravenes neither the articles of incorporation, nor the law, it is of no relevance that it is contrary to the shareholders' agreement.*"

## 2. Right of Nomination in Shareholders' Agreements: Can Holders of Common Shares (Stock) have Different Nomination Rights?

As one could presume, voting agreements are often paralleled by provisions allocating the rights to nominate as well; as it was so in the preceding case. There are, however, cases in which the central issue was exactly about the right to nominate. In one of the reported cases[63] decided under the old 2006 Company Act, the issue was what the nature and exact meaning of the shareholders' right to nominate is and under what conditions they can be awarded to various classes of shareholders? In the case, only common shares were issued and according to the law in force, in such case, all shareholders were entitled to the same bundle of rights. Notwithstanding of such explicit provision in the law, however, the general meeting of shareholders passed three decisions according to which the right to make nominations to the management and supervisory boards, as well as for the accountant were attributed only to some specific classes of shareholders. Unfortunately, the publicly available summary of the case only mentions in that respect that "*section 6 of the shareholders' agreement enclosed to the file decidedly foresaw the method of nominations at the time of pri-*

62 Szegedi Törvényszék 6.G.40.256/2011/13.
63 Case No. BH1997.540 (Supreme Court file number: Legf. Bír. Gfv. X. 31.361/1996 sz.).

*vatization, moreover it also required transposition of those rules into the articles of incorporation."*

## 3. Binding Instructions to the Corporation: A Case with an Unanimous Shareholders' Agreement and a Planned Spin off

Scholars and the case law is in agreement that in principle no binding instructions can be foreseen in the shareholders' agreement to the company. The conditional language is due to the fact that unanimous shareholders' agreements may amount to binding instructions presuming no such supervening changes occur as change in the identity, stakes or interests of shareholders; though this question remains to be answered by the courts. In principle, however, nothing would prevent a shareholder not to vote according to, or not to fulfil his other obligations, from the shareholders' agreements. Similarly, the shareholder-director of a company may have to disregard what he promised in the shareholders' agreement if the law or the interests of the company would require that. This because of the mandatory rule in the Civil Code according to which the chief executive officer "*performs its duties independently having the interests of the company primarily in regard.*" In performing his duties, he is bound only by the applicable laws, the company's articles of incorporation and by the decisions of the highest decision-making body of the company; shareholders have no right to give instructions to him.[64]

Case law, again, brilliantly shows, that under some circumstances, the shareholders, indeed, may through the shareholders' agreement steer the hands of the company. In a recent case that reached even the Supreme Court ("*Kúria*"),[65] an unanimous shareholders' agreement was made by three partners, five years after the establishment of the company. The main function of the agreement was setting the terms and conditions for the future spinning off three activities conducted by three of the signatories of the shareholders' agreement. *First*, they declared in the agreement that each of them is running a distinct business activity as part of the common company (division), for what each of them has been allotted the necessary assets. *Secondly*, they agreed also that each division is to be accounted for separately in the future. And, *most importantly*, they amended the articles of incorporation simultaneously essentially transposing what they agreed upon in the shareholders' agreement. As suggested above,

**64** See § 3:112(2) of the 2013 Civil Code.
**65** Kúria Gfv.VII.30186/2013/6.

this case is unorthodox and binding the hands of the company was possible because an unanimous shareholders' agreement was at stake, the key elements of which were additionally added also to the company's articles of incorporation. However, the holding of the case was not about the validity of this arrangement but rather about a drafting mistake, or differing interpretation of the agreement by the parties. Namely, the agreement did not clearly formulate whether the book or rather the market value of the assets allocated to divisions is to be departed from when leaving the company.

## 4. Investments and Support for Small and Mid-Scale Enterprises

The publicly available text of the case decided in 2008[66] by the Regional Court of Capital-Budapest reveals another economically important form of the exploitation of shareholders' agreements: financing of small and mid-scale enterprises, the primary job-creators in Europe. Although unfortunately not all details could be learned from the publicized text of the decision, even the basic contours as put forward by the court – of the otherwise complex structure made of more interlinked agreements – is very instructive. The contracts underlying the scheme were concluded by three parties in August 2004 – besides a 'Shareholders' Agreement,' also Agreements named as 'Investment Contract' and 'Agreement on Establishment of Buy-Sell Rights' – as part of a 'Capital Enhancement Program for Small and Mid-Scale Companies.' As the shareholders' agreement stated, the ultimate goal was "*to ensure that [the Hungarian companies into which moneys are invested as part of the Program] remain competitive with small and mid-scale companies of the European Union in the long run.*" The parties were, on one hand, a financial institution providing capital and, on the other hand, two shareholders (owners) of two fully-owned LTDs.

Besides increasing the registered capital of the two LTDs and thus becoming a shareholder, the financial organization was granted also the right to buy or sell the stakes within five years from the day of the registration of any new acquisition. It was (allegedly) also stated in the shareholders' agreement that the financier engages in these investments with intent to make income ("*hozam*"). The court concluded as well, though without concretizing based on which provisions of the agreements, that the said option right was also a security for the financier. This on top of a clause in the Investment Contract according to which "*the funds received through increase of the registered capital are to be used exclusively*

66 Budapest Környéki Törvényszék G.40030/2008/16.

*for the implementation of the goals specified in the business plan [of the companies].*"

The dispute arose when roughly two years after the conclusion of the said agreements, the financier exercised its right to sell the stakes by delivering the required unilateral written declaration to the two shareholders as provided in the agreements, who have however failed to transfer the requested monies within the set 30 days deadline. As a reaction, the financier assigned the claim, and thus it participated in the court proceedings only as an intervener helping the assignee. The non-paying shareholders raised various objections, among which the claim that the above summarized amounted only to a preliminary contract not producing an unconditional immediate payment obligation was the most important. Yet each of their counts was rejected by the court.

## 5. Financing of the Corporation

A number of reported court and arbitral cases is related to financing; though some mentioning that only obiter.[67] Various disputes have arisen out of these as well.

In an arbitral case from 2003, the shareholders' agreement – concluded by the corporation itself and its shareholders in 1999 – provided that one of the shareholders (the future respondent) shall open a credit line of 380 thousand USD for the benefit of the corporation if the cash available to the corporation would drop below 100 thousand USD within two years from the signing of agreement. Besides this provision, the agreement had only two more credit-related provisions. While the first foresaw that the interest rate is to be calculated as per the formula USD LIBOR + 0.5 % per annum valid on the day of the withdraw-

67 See, e. g., the already mentioned BH2015.285 (Curia Gfv.VII.30.087/2015), which provided that one of the investors (in a three-membered company, including a municipality) was to 1) make 500 million HUF available to the company, 2) but having also the right to determine the form, terms and conditions, as well as the legal and accounting methods of the capital to be provided. The dispute arose related to one of the contributions made in a high-value immovable by the said investor; the value of which was determined by an external expert. A separate extraordinary general meeting of shareholders was convened for that reason, which passed a decision whereby in return for the transfer of the said immovable, the investor is to receive 15 new, publicly not traded shares, each in 20 million HUF denominations and that the registered capital of the company is increased by the same amount. The decision was split: three shareholders voted for and two against the decision. The issue to be decided upon by the Curia was, however, whether shareholders can vote by conference call at general meetings given that one of them voted that way at the meeting in question.

al of moneys from the credit line, the second required that the credit and the withdrawals be structured so that they would not fall under any governmental approval proceedings.

The cash of the corporation dropped below the threshold already in 2001 and the dispute arose from the refusal of the future respondent to open the credit line as per the shareholders' agreement. Instead of performing, the future respondent conditioned the credit line with all the other shareholders of the corporation providing the same amount of credit to the corporation. This made the claimant start the arbitration proceedings with the Arbitral Tribunal Attached to the Hungarian Chamber of Commerce and Industry asking an award in which the respondent would be ordered to perform and open the credit line for the benefit of the corporation.[68]

During the arbitral proceedings, the claimant put forward that it was an internationally reputed Hungarian enterprise with meaningful technological expertise and valuable intellectual property before the respondent had acquired a stake in it. Moreover, given the specificities of the sector, it was the respondent who encouraged the management of the corporation to make more investments and spend the cash because "*that is how the industry works and could prosper*". The respondent from its side added that the cash available in fact did not fall below 100 thousand USD and given that it did not participate in the management of the corporation it could not affect the cash movements.

The issue the tribunal was asked to answer was whether the mentioned provisions in the shareholders' agreement qualified as a credit contract based on which performance could have been ordered? As the shareholders' agreement contained only provisions on the interest rate, the upper limit of and a condition on the extension of the credit, the arbitral tribunal was of the opinion that these do not amount to anything more than a mere preliminary contract. Based on this the respondent could have been ordered only to negotiate to reach an agreement on the extension of the credit line. In the opinion of the tribunal, the evidences presented by the claimant were insufficient to make the tribunal infer the remainder of key terms conditions of a credit contract. In addition, the cash requested by the claimant was insignificant compared to the average cash flow of the claimant and – as stated by the respondent – the claimant-corporation and its directors have become unworthy of the credit as well.

68 The case number at the Arbitral Tribunal is Vb/021800.

## 6. Provision of Services or Assets to the New Company

There are shareholders' agreements that include provisions whereby one person, expert – shareholder or yet-to-become shareholder – promises to provide some specific expert services. In one arbitral case, a foreign expert signed the shareholders' agreement exactly to provide some very specific services (not specified in the publicly available text of the case), which were allegedly crucial for the newly established company.[69] Based on the agreement, besides a salary, he was entitled also to 30 % of the net profits of the new company and a right to purchase a 30 % stake in the company, which he did realize eventually. For an unspecified reason, however, he resigned unexpectedly and had terminated his employment with the company and simultaneously exercised his put rights: his shares were repurchased by the other shareholders.

In another Hungarian arbitral case,[70] trying to define also what goodwill means, the shareholders' agreement (concluded simultaneously with the articles of incorporation) foresaw transfer of various machines and rights – including 'goodwill' and the right to use the brand name – by a foreign partner, as well as the conclusion of the necessary additional agreements to implement the transfers. Concretely, a sales plus a brand licensing agreement were added to the package.

Two further points make the case interesting for us: both display questionable practices or unnecessary complications with unintended consequences, if not outright drafting mistakes for which counsel might be held potentially liable.[71] The first is the linkage of the four agreements, which formed a kind of

---

69 Arbitral case No. Vb 95.040, decided by the Arbitral Institution attached to the Hungarian Chamber of Commerce and Industry.

70 Arbitral case No. Vb 94.013.I decided by the Arbitral Institution attached to the Hungarian Chamber of Commerce and Industry.

71 The central issue of the case revolved, however, around what the exact meaning of 'goodwill' is yet as this is not directly related to the subject matter of shareholders' agreements, a brief account should suffice though obviously the parties' failure to properly fix what do they mean under 'goodwill' and what the related rights of the parties are, could also qualify as a drafting mistake. In the case, the goodwill was *sold* together with the sale of a business. As part of that the buyer acquired also the right to use the name X appearing in the name and brands of the seller. As the tribunal found, the Hungarian perception of goodwill was narrower from the one in international commerce because 1) was not identical with but could not be separated either from the trade name, 2) it could not be separated from the commercial activities of the seller either; 3) it referred also to other factors concerning the operation of the seller's business, and 4) it should include also the more-or-less stable circle of business clients.

unit not only because of cross-references but – as the tribunal determined – because "*notwithstanding that the parties to the contracts were not necessarily identical, (...) the parties' intention was to have regard to all the contracts when implementing them.*" The other concern that should be given serious attention to if opting for multiple agreements is that various agreements may not be in force for the same amount of time. Concretely in the case the shareholders' agreement ceased to exist due to governmental intervention while the other agreements did not.

## 7. Duty to Conclude Rent Contracts

The issue in an arbitral award was the relevance and impact of a shareholders' agreement on rental agreement which was foreseen to be concluded based on a shareholders' agreement. In the case, a new company was formed by the respondent by spinning off its maintenance units together with the employees. Also, a shareholders' agreement was concluded in which the respondent obliged himself, among others, to "*make available for rent, for indefinite period of time, those premises that are necessary for the operation of the claimant, [the newly formed company].*" A rent agreement was thereafter concluded by the parties foreseeing that the rent may be terminated only if proper reasoning is given.

As one may presume, not long after the rent agreement was concluded, the relations of the parties deteriorated leading to the termination of the rent by the respondent yet based on grounds none of which was accepted by the tribunal as legitimate. What is of relevance for us is that in interpreting the rent agreement the tribunal found it important to depart from the shareholders' agreement, especially as far as those questions were concerned for what there was no explicit rule in the rent agreement itself. It ruled that – given that the rent agreement served the implementation of the shareholders' agreement – the rent could not be terminated until the use of the premises in question had become either unnecessary for the materialization of the aims and goals of the shareholders' agreement, or until such circumstances had arisen that would have made the use of the premises impossible.

All this was, however, of importance to determine what the rights of the parties were given that the seller could not guarantee the exploitation of the goodwill anymore three years after the conclusion of all the interlinked agreements due to governmental intervention in the form of nationalization. Given that neither party could have been blamed for the so caused stalemate, the tribunal found that the provisions on impossibility ("*ellehetetlenülés*") apply. As the buyer has already paid full purchase price, he is entitled to get back a proportionate part of the price.

## 8. Shareholders' Agreements and the Law on Company Groups

Hungarian law on company groups is in many respects inspired by German *Konzernrecht* (law on groups of companies) and the pertaining EU laws.[72] It recognizes two types of company groups, recognized ("*elismert*")[73] and de facto ("*tényleges vállalatcsoport*")[74] groups, both subject to registration with the Company Registry.[75] These categories are based on the concept of control, which as per both, the old 2006 Company Act and the 2013 Civil Code may be acquired either via equity stakes, or by various contractual arrangements – including shareholders' agreements.[76] Of relevance is only the category of substantial control ("*meghatározó befolyás*") that exists if the dominant person is either in the position to appoint and remove the majority of directors or supervisory board members, or if based on an agreement with the members or shareholders these will vote as per the instructions of the controlling person or the controlling person will be empowered to vote on their behalf.[77]

Yet the story does not end here. Namely, because of the drafters' liberal approach, giving maximal room for default rules and thus to private ordering, what

---

72 See *Tamás Sárközy*, editor of the volume on juridical persons, in the HVG/ORAC Commentary of the new Civil Code (HVG/ORAC, 2013), at 872. For an overview of the new law on groups of companies in English in the 2013 Civil Code *Tekla Papp* in Keserű B. A. – Kőhídi Á. (eds.), Tanulmányok a 65 éves Lenkovics Barnabás tiszteletére (Publisher: Eötvös József Könyv- és Lapkiadó Bt., Széchenyi István Egyetem Deák Ferenc Állam- és Jogtudományi Kar; Budapest – Győr; 2015), pp. 601–630.

73 See 2013 Civil Code §3:49 which foresees the following preconditions for the registration and recognition of a group of companies: 1) the group must be made of one controlling (dominating) and at least three controlled members; 2) the group must have a common business policy based on a control agreement; 3) group members may be only joint-stock companies, limited liability companies, associations and cooperatives; 4) they must submit yearly consolidated financial reports, and 5) if more than one legal entity performs the functions of the controller they must define by contract who is going to perform the rights belonging to the controlling (dominating) entity.

74 See 2013 Civil Code §3:62 defining what a de facto group of companies means. According to this, any interested person may turn to a court to mandate the conclusion of a controlling agreement and for the registration of the group if 1) a controlling agreement was de facto existent among the affected companies, 2) for at least three consecutive years 3) without interruption. Moreover, the court may apply the rules on recognized and registered groups of companies, upon the request of the interested person, even in case of de facto groups.

75 See 2013 Civil Code §3:51(5).

76 See also *Kinga Pázmány* Konszernrendelkezések és a vállalatcsoportokra vonatkozó szabályozás, in Gazdaság és Jog, No. 2011/7–8, pp. 24–29, at 24.

77 This definition is in one of the last provisions of the 2013 Civil Code, in the part containing a few interpretative provisions in the concluding Eight Book of the Code, §8.2.

has been said about the paradigm shift in the realms of company law equally applies in this specific domain as well. In particular, although the pertaining provisions speak of a specific nominated contract as the alpha and omega of the entire system – the control (dominating) agreement ("*uralmi szerződés*") – they do not dictate what its contents must be and thus certain issues may be left to be regulated by shareholders' agreements.[78] Resort to shareholders' agreements – as secret documents – may be desirable because of two main reasons: on the one hand, the control agreements must be publicized,[79] and on the other hand, the court maintaining the Company Register exercises statutory control over the groups and on the implementation of the control agreements.[80] While in case of shareholders' agreements that court only exceptionally may render an injunction or specific performance (and thus damages are the normal remedies), for grave or repeated infringements of a control agreement the court may, upon the claim of any interested person, impose some measure or even dissolve the group.[81]

This applies in particular to *de facto* groups of companies, where exactly the provisions of a shareholders' agreement may in fact amount to control. When that happens, the law mandates the group to conclude the mentioned 'control agreement,' which is a particular nominated type of contract under the Civil Code.[82] This implies a sort of '**functional thinking**', expecting from the court to understand the economics of the governance and functioning of the involved companies.

---

**78** See 2013 Civil Code §3:50, which requires regulation of three categories of issues: 1) the name and seat of the controlling and controlled entities within the group; 2) description of the method of cooperation within the group and the most important elements of such cooperation, as well as 3) declaration of whether the group came into being for a fixed or a non-fixed period of time. The law imposes additionally three relatively general expectations that must be taken into account when drafting the control agreements, which are a) the restrictions imposed on the controlled entities within the group may not go beyond what is needed for the implementation of the common business goals, b) appropriate attention should be given also to the protection of the rights of controlled entities and of creditors, and finally c) the generally applicable rules on contracts should be equally applied to these controlling agreements.

**79** See 2013 Civil Code §3:51(3) and (4), which foresee that the controlling company must, eight days from the day on which the last decision on the approval of the controlling agreements was made, two times publish an announcement about the formation of the group; with at least thirty days lapsing between the two publications. The announcement must contain also the control agreement.

**80** See 2013 Civil Code §3:60.

**81** Id.

**82** The 2006 Company Act, that first regulated groups of companies in Hungary, essentially contained identical rules.

Reported court cases involving the law of groups of companies and shareholders' agreements exist as well. For example, in a case adjudicated still under the 2006 Company Act,[83] a shareholders' agreement was concluded by the owners of a group of companies (targets), the acquirer (investor) and another group of companies of interest aimed at acquisition of 100 % stake in some of the targeted companies. The dispute arose related to the potential liability of the sellers of targets for those losses that could not be covered in insolvency (liquidation) proceedings based on the rules of the liability of controlling stakeholders.

## II. Shareholders' Agreements Limiting Transfer or Selling of Shares

No specific statute has been so far passed on transfer, or limitation of the transfer of shares, stakes or memberships yet the generally applicable rules of company law,[84] competition (anti-trust) or the law on takeovers may come into picture. In fact, very few sources even mention tag-along, drag-along and similar tools on transfer of shares outside the context of topic of shareholders' agreements.[85] This applies also to the most important publications on shareholders' agreements that otherwise do focus on the known and possible subject matters of shareholders' agreements.[86]

It is noteworthy, however, that these clauses have been used in case of two big-ticket Hungarian companies. The first is the decree on the Hungarian government's acquisition of an equity state in the former national air carrier, MALÉV, which does foresee tag-along ("*együttértékesítési jog*") and drag-along ("*együttér-*

83 See the decision of the Curia No. BH 2015.10.437.

84 E.g., § 3:107(2) foreseeing the three cases in which a member or shareholder cannot be excluded from a company (e.g., no such proceedings can be initiated if there are only two members and/or shareholders).

85 One of the notable exceptions is the article of *Zoltán Czinkóczky* and *Károly Mike* Befektetővédelem – Társasági Jogi Szabályok a Kockázati Tőkebefektetések Tükrében in Iustum Aequum Salutare, vol. VIII, Nos. 3–4 (2012), pp. 43–61. Besides focusing on venture capital only (and not on shareholders' agreements), unfortunately, the article is focused on international developments and practices and contains very few points related to Hungary. For example, it does mention tag-along (p. 53) and drag-along clauses (p. 55) yet without reflecting on their use in Hungary.

86 See *Auer et al* Atypical Contracts (2015) at 227–28 with a non-laundry list of possible subject matters as well as *Kolben* 1996, parts 2, 3 and 4.

*tékesítési kötelezettség*") rights.[87] The second is the MOL-INA shareholders' agreement from 2003, which contains an asymmetric Clause 11 that makes transfer of shares subject to consent of the Croatian Government and some other preconditions that aim to ensure control by the Croatian side.

Though not in a shareholders' agreement but in the articles of incorporation, one reported case from 2011[88] does reveal, for example, that granting of the right of first refusal is not foreign to Hungarian business life. Here, the right was foreseen both for transfer of shares and also for increase of registered capital. In both cases, a written offer had to be made, which must have been reacted upon by existent shareholders within 30 days. They had a right to purchase shares proportionate to their shareholdings on specific dates.

In light of the extreme scarcity of data on this particular aspect of the topic, one ought to conclude that the development and more widespread use of these types of tools lags behind in Hungary compared to the others that have already been even tested either in courts or in arbitral proceedings. These may be taken as proofs that the law and practices on shareholders' agreement develop organically.

## III. Shareholders' Agreements on the Constitution of the Corporation

Shareholders' agreements that regulate questions related to constitution of a company are not unknown in Hungary; *Kolben* called these as '*Type A shareholders agreements*' to differentiate them from those dealing with questions popping up in the post-formation phase.[89] These regulate such issues as fixing the seat of the company, the aims and goals the partners desire to achieve, selection of the activities of the company, distribution of constitution-related costs, decision on whether to issue preferential shares and with what extra rights, and liability for damages for failed constitution of the company.[90] The reported cases unearthed occasionally quite complex arrangements in pre-formation shareholders'

87 See section 2(i) of the Governmental Decree 1051/2010 (II. 26) on Acquisition of Equity Stake by the Hungarian State in the Air Transport Closed Joint-Stock Company MALÉV (*1051/2010. (II. 26.) Korm. határozat a MALÉV Magyar Légiközlekedési Zártkörűen Működő Részvénytársaságban történő magyar állami tulajdonszerzésről).*

88 Case decided by the Appellate Court of the Capital (Fővárosi Törvényszék) No. G.40.745/2011/22.

89 *Kolben* 1996, Chapter Four points b/ and c/ as well as Chapter 18.

90 See *Auer et al* Atypical Contracts (2015), at 227.

agreements. The next three are especially interesting, the first for its extreme detail and versatility, the second for risks inherent to software as a contribution and the third for the detailed agreement on the way the main activity of the company is to be conducted (wholesale).

### 1. Multi-Legged Shareholders' Agreement Aimed at Exploitation of Immovables

A recent case decided by the Court of Justice of the Capital-Budapest, is particularly illustrative of the level of complexity shareholders' agreements could reach. This could be concluded based on the fact that the judgment had to be reported on 18 pages; something quite extraordinary for Hungarian standards.[91] The shareholders' agreement in question was a sophisticated, multiple-elements structure aimed at fixing five key aspects of the future company among only a few partners. Nothing more than a brief account of these could be made here.

*First*, it specified in great detail the *contributions* and the terms and conditions of their transfer. One of the main partners was to contribute with various immovables within 90 days from the signing of the agreement and subject to finding some replacement immovables. As opposed to that, the other was to supply only cash, 50% within 20 days from the conclusion of the articles of incorporation and the other half within a year from the registration of the company. It was the latter who breached the shareholders' agreement by failing to pay in the promised sums. Interesting solution was also the rule according to which (or at least that seems to have been intended) the first party's stake should at all times be higher by four million HUF than the stake of the others, to ensure his majority position.

*Secondly,* provisions were added to divide the appointment powers among the future shareholders. While the chief-executive officer was to be appointed by the first party and the accountant by another one, the appointment powers of the three-membered supervisory board were split among them. *Thirdly,* the first party had also a bankruptcy-liquidation preference proportionate to his contributions. *Last but not least,* the goals of the enterprise were also defined as formation of a project company for the exploitation of the contributed immovables. Plus, it was planned that the first party will spin off part of the business after a few years of operation. The litigation ended with the court ordering restitution.

91 Fővárosi törvényszék 26.G.41.390/2012/5.

## 2. The Software-Contribution Case[92]

In another case, involving a small company active in the media sector, the shareholders' agreement provided that one of the partners was to contribute with developing and then making available certain novel software to be used by the company for its activities. As opposed to the previous case, here the company had already been registered by the time the shareholders' agreement was made yet it was in a sort of incubator phase.

The dispute arose because the software supplied was different from what was promised and eventually could not be used by the company because lack of licenses. More precisely, the software was not a novel independent product developed by the partner but was a version of a software that was subject to licensing. As the partner had no license to use or make derivative products, it could not provide exclusivity to the company either. This was determined based on an expert testimony, accepted by the court as the determinative proof. Consequently, the value of the software was not few million HUF as claimed but zero. The court case was launched to exclude the partner, who additionally even made false statements to the general meeting of shareholders. The court decided for the plaintiff, excluded the partner and ordered him to pay the costs of the proceedings.

## 3. The Retail-Wholesale-Focused Shareholders' Agreement

In this case, the shareholders' agreement focused on the activity of the company, which was wholesale of household electronic appliances. In fact, the company was formed to help the retailer shareholders acquire the goods to be marketed by them at a discount. It was the shareholders' agreement which foresaw in detail how this was to occur. The gist of the process was that each of the retailer-shareholders had a right to order goods in the name of the company but for their use. They had to pay the related invoices one day before the due date.

The dispute arose because one of the shareholders abused the process (and thus breached the agreement) by ordering a larger quantity of goods in a shorter period of time and then leaving the company (the general meeting passed a decision on his exclusion). He was in the position to do that because two similarly named companies, with the same staff and seat, existed within the system. The court decided for the plaintiff confirming the exclusion.

---

92 Fővárosi Törvényszék G.40407/2009/44.

### 4. Shareholders Agreements Granting Right of First Refusal for Purchase of Immovables: the Budapest 'Western Railway Station' ("*Nyugati Pâlyaudvar*") Case

Although the central issue of the case was about the exercise of the right of first refusal,[93] it is worth mentioning because this entitlement was provided for in a shareholders' agreement. Concretely, the single founder established a single-shareholder company (which later was expanded to two members) and rented to it various immovables on the territory of the 'Western Railway Station' in the capital of Budapest. Although a shareholders' agreement was concluded by the two on the day of the formation of the company (1997), only the later (2002), shareholders' agreement granted the right of first refusal. According to this, the new company could trigger this right when the premises rented by it would be offered for sale.

The dispute arose between the parties related to the implementation of the said first refusal right given that the pertaining provisions did not spell out lots of details on that (e.g., whether increase of the registered capital is a precondition for the exercise of the first refusal right, or whether the right must be exercised by the company itself or another shareholder may do that instead of it). Otherwise, the right was foreseen because the founder wanted to ensure that the new company would not be forced to move its operations to another location should that be required by a newcomer shareholder in the future.

## IV. Shareholders' Agreements in Pre-Insolvency Situation

Similarly to such developed civil law countries as Germany, the level of bankruptcy stigma is extremely high in Hungary.[94] Additionally, the second chance

---

**93** BH2007.158 (Supreme Court decision No. Gfv.IX.30.262/2006).

**94** The gist of this phenomenon is superbly described by *Reinhard Bork*, the doyen of German insolvency in his recently published book. "*It is widely known and widely felt that in the business world, at least in Germany, insolvency is still viewed as a failure and the filing of an insolvency application as an admission of one's own failure – regardless of the actual cause. No manager wants to be confronted with his or her own shortcomings. As long as this emotional inhibition remains in place, it may require some convincing to persuade managers to attempt restructuring within an insolvency procedure. It may be tempting to disregard this fact as non-serious, but any earnest attempt to construct an efficient restructuring law must take it into account until there is evidence of a wide-ranging and sustained change in popular mentality.*" See *Bork* Rescuing Companies in England and Germany (Oxford University Press, 2012), section 1.12, at 24–25. He as well criticized German insolvency law because "(...) *German law forces the debtor into insol-*

– or fresh start[95] – philosophy embraced by the EU[96] is still something known only be very few businessmen. Consequently insolvency is normally looked upon as a phenomenon tainted with fraud, abuse and overreach. For these reasons, restructuring of insolvency businesses rarely works in practice[97] and an average Hungarian businessman does not believe as of yet that insolvency can have different outcomes but liquidation and loss of money. For these reasons, it should not come as a surprise that, neither empirical evidences, nor scholarly discussions exist on whether shareholders' agreements include provisions related to insolvency.[98] As nothing in Hungarian insolvency law prohibits conclusion

*vency proceedings and into the costs and delays that come with it, further reducing whatever value is left in the business.*" Id. section 7.30, at 81. See also Tibor Tajti, The Bankruptcy Stigma and the Second Chance Policy: the Impact of Bankruptcy Stigma on Business Restructurings in China, Europe and the United States. China-EU Law Journal (Nov. 2017), DOI10.1007/s12689-017-0077-z.

**95** As *Grant Gilmore*, a US commercial law expert put it related to US law, where the fresh start idea comes from: "*[t]he federal Bankruptcy Act is presumably based on the theory that it is desirable social policy to allow debt-burdened individuals and business enterprises the opportunity to make a fresh start.*" See *Gilmore* Security Interests in Personal Property (1965), at 1281.

**96** The last soft law instrument that once again emphasizes the importance of a desirable paradigm shift from a liquidation-dominated to a restructuring/reorganization-based one is Commission Recommendation of 12 March 2014 on a new approach to business failure and insolvency (L 74/65). The quintessence, obviously affecting also what and how shareholders think of insolvency, is expressed in this document as follows: "*The objective of this Recommendation is to ensure that viable enterprises in financial difficulties, wherever they are located in the Union, have access to national insolvency frameworks which enable them to restructure at an early stage with a view to preventing their insolvency, and therefore maximise the total value to creditors, employees, owners and the economy as a whole. The Recommendation also aims at giving honest bankrupt entrepreneurs a second chance across the Union.*"

**97** This was confirmed by *László Juhász*, the author of the two-volume Hungarian Insolvency Handbook ("*A Magyar Fizetésképtelenségi Jog Kézikönyve*," (Novotni Publisher, Miskolc, in 2014), undoubtedly one of the leading publications in the field of insolvency law in 2014, in which he concluded that 1) the efforts to spread a restructuring culture has proved not to satisfy the expectations, 2) while on average ten to fourteen-thousand liquidation proceedings were filed annually since the enactment of the new modern Insolvency Act in 1991, only ten to twenty reorganizations cases were attempted; moreover, almost all of them was a failure. Last but not least 3) the debtors have rather tried to negotiate with creditors one-by-one to find a way out of their financial difficulties to a great extent exactly because filing with an insolvency court was invariably taken by other creditors as a red flag. *Id.* volume I, at 145.

**98** One of the articles of very recent vintage is devoted exactly to the chances and desirability of domesticating a version of second chance policy promulgated by the EU Commission yet without going as far as pondering whether shareholders' agreements might have any function in that respect. See *János Bóka* A szerkezet-átalakítási eljárások és a fizetésképtelenség új megközelítése az Európai Unióban in Ádám Auer and Tekla Papp (eds.), A gazdasági világválság hatása egyes

of out-of-court agreements (workouts) between the debtor and (all or some of) its creditors,[99] it is not excluded that insolvency-related shareholders' agreements have already been made in this country. However, exactly because of the general hostility and incomprehension of insolvency as a phenomenon as well as of insolvency law as such, this would undoubtedly be a-typical, at least, at present time.[100] This may be concluded even from the relatively long list of possible subject matters of shareholders' agreements in the related few publications.[101]

# E. Legal Effects of Shareholders' Agreements

## I. Legal Effects on the Corporation

The basic principle is that a shareholders' agreement cannot contain a provision that is contrary to a mandatory provision of the Civil Code (which since 2013 contains also company law) or of the corporate charter given that in such case it would be treated as an invalid agreement producing no rights.[102] This follows from the fact that the corporate charter is the mandatory constitutive and thus superior legal act of companies that additionally must be made public – contrary to the confidential nature of shareholders' agreements. Consequently, shareholders' agreements are subordinated to and are looked upon as distinct from the corporate charter. Yet as they may supplement the corporate charter, they may be a source for interpretation of the corporate charter. Obviously however with stronger force in case of such unanimous shareholders' agreements that were

---

jogintézményekre Magyarországon és az Európai Unióban (Publication of the National University of Public Service, Budapest, 2016), pp. 243–269.

**99** Hungarian insolvency law is enshrined in the Insolvency Act passed in 1991, as amended more than ten times ever since. The Act does not regulate out-of-court agreements (workouts). Full reference to the Act is *1991. évi XLIX. Törvény a csődeljárásról és a felszámolási eljárásról* (Act No. XLIX of year 1991 on Restructuring and Liquidation Proceedings).

**100** For more details on Hungarian insolvency law in English see the chapter written by *Tibor Tajti* devoted to Central and Eastern Europe (Hungary, Lithuania and Poland) in Gerard McCormack and Reinhard Bork (eds.), SECURITY RIGHTS AND THE EUROPEAN INSOLVENCY REGULATION (Intersentia, Cambridge, 2017).

**101** See, e.g., *Auer et al* Atypical Contracts (2015) at 227–28 with a non-laundry list of possible subject matters. Here, neither the seven possible company founding-related items, nor the sixteen company-operation (i.e., already existent company) items include insolvency. *Kolben*'s 1996 monograph likewise fails to list insolvency.

**102** See *Auer et al* Atypical Contracts (2015), at 230–31. The relevant section in the Civil Code is § 6:95. See also the decisions of the Győr Regional Court of Appeal Pf. II. 20.010/2007/4 and Gf. II. 20.341/2010/6.

signed by identical shareholders. This is confirmed unequivocally by one reported case.[103]

Yet life may forge unusual fact patterns and outcomes, too. In one of the cases, the shareholders' agreement gave to the shareholder having merely 0.23 % stake the right to appoint one of the board members, who had to vote according to his directions.[104] The dispute arose as the minority shareholder failed to come to the general meeting where decisions were passed in his absence on the appointment of directors and increase of the capital. Not fully clear why, the court was of the opinion that a shareholders' agreement could not have even be concluded in the case and thus it did not take it into account when deciding the case; which otherwise depended on the interpretation of the pertaining provision in the articles of incorporation. The court concluded that the articles of incorporation may foresee a higher quorum threshold than what company law sets and thus the outcome of the case depended on the interpretation of the relevant clause in the articles of incorporation – without any regard to the shareholders' agreement.

**103** See, e.g., the decision of the Regional Court of Szeged No. 2014.156. The Court held that, first, "*the shareholders' agreement is not part of the articles of incorporation and as such it may not impose duties on the company as a distinct legal entity. The shareholders' agreement may bind only the signatory parties [...]. Secondly, such decision of the company's general meeting that contradicts the shareholders' agreement cannot be invalid because the shareholders' agreement is not determinative for the internal relations of the company and its infringement cannot amount to invalidity of the articles of incorporation.*" What makes this case interesting is not the holding though but the complexity of facts and the strategic manoeuvring the parties were engaged in; partly relying also on the shareholders' agreement. Interestingly, it was the 'appendix to the shareholders' agreement' – concluded in Milan (Italy) between the Italian shareholder having 73 % stake and a Hungarian shareholder with 33 % stake – that contained the most important provisions. It foresaw, among others, that key decisions are to be made exclusively by the general meeting (amendment of the articles of incorporation, duties and the remuneration of officers). For a valid decision, at least, the affirmative votes representing 70 % of the registered capital were needed. Moreover, each of the two directors had a right to nominate one officer with independent right to represent the company; including the right to effectuate entries with the company registry.

**104** The case was decided by the Appeal Court of Nyíregyháza, file No. G.40105/2011/11.

## II. Legal Effects on the Shareholders

### 1. Registration of Shareholders' Agreements in Hungary

For the time being there are no public registers for shareholders' agreements in Hungary. Further, the company register contains, neither information on the very existence, nor on the contents of shareholders' agreements. In other words, no public notice is provided to other participants of the market as a consequence of what obligations and/or rights may arise from them only for the parties to it. Both the reported cases and scholars agree on this point.

The only exceptions are shareholders' agreements concluded by municipalities as shareholders, which are made available to the public by placing the texts of the agreements on the Internet by the various county governmental offices ("*kormânyhivatal*").[105] This publication is made because public goods and interests are at stake and stems from the constitutional right of citizens to be informed about public affairs.[106] One could say that these shareholders' agreements are a combination of public and private law elements what makes them specific notwithstanding of what the basic rules applies also to them: they provide rights and obligations only for the signatory parties.

### 2. Transferability of Rights in Shareholders' Agreements

#### a. General Considerations on the Assignability of Rights

As far as the transferability of rights in shareholders' agreements are concerned, no reported case, commentary or scholarly publication seem to exist which would come forward with a formula on the transfer of rights and obligations

---

**105** See, for example, the shareholders' agreement concluded by fifty-six municipalities in the County of Pest at < http://docplayer.hu/22389767-Szindikatusi-szerzodes.html >; last visited on 28th of December 2016. These municipalities are the shareholders of a water-supply public utility company the main function is supply of water to the citizenry of the owner-municipalities. Besides provisions on voting, appointment of the supervisor and management boards, the agreement specifies which municipality contributed with what to the capital of the new business entity formed in 2012.

**106** In the case decided by the Curia the issue was the extent to which data protection laws apply in this specific context. In the case, the city of Pécs passed a decision to amicably terminate the privatization agreement of the water and sewage public utility company that had been concluded in 1995 with a French partner; the privatization "*package*" included a shareholders' agreement as well. The mayor and the municipality refused to reveal some related documents, which was adjudicated as lawful by the Curia. See Kúria Pfv.IV.21.705/2011/14.

from shareholders' agreement to another person that would be different from what the generally applicable rules on assignment dictate or what would follow from the very nature of these peculiar agreements. This follows also from a 2011 case that involves a shareholders' agreement through which two shareholders agreed on a joint share-acquisition plan, assignment of shares and a formula for dividing the obtained shares.[107] The same could be said also with respect to a 2009 cross-border case, to be discussed in more detail starting from the next paragraph, involving a Hungarian and an Italian partner as well as arbitration in Switzerland (Geneva). Here, the underlying shareholders' agreement concluded at the beginning of privatizations in Hungary in 1991 foresaw the transferability of registered shares held by the founders without imposing any restriction.

Still, some particular agreements may be contingent on who the persons involved are. In such instances, assignments may not be desirable by other shareholders. As Hungarian law is silent on this, for such eventualities the appropriate panacea are tailor-made provisions in the shareholders' agreement. For example, the 2003 MOL-INA shareholders' agreement prohibits all assignments in its Clause 18.

### b. The Effect of Shareholders' Agreements on Legal Successors: Is there a Duty to Inform Legal Successors on the Contents on the Shareholders' Agreement? [108]

A few publicized cases bring to the surface interesting issues on the effects of shareholders' agreements on shareholders. In one of the cases decided by the Supreme Court, one of the main issues was the impact of shareholders' agreements on legal successors of signatories of shareholders' agreements. Here, the shareholders' agreement was concluded by a Hungarian (Founder-Hungarian Company) and an Italian company as only founders of a new International Construction Company (hereinafter: Construction Company), which foresaw that the founders will abstain from any such activity on the territory of Hungary that would amount to competition with the newly established company (the anti-competition clause). What made things complicated is that the Founder-Hungarian company was foreseen to be wound up without a legal successor yet what did not take place; rather it was taken over by the government. This was an im-

**107** Case decided by the Appellate Court of the Capital (Fővárosi Törvényszék) No. G.40.745/2011/22.

**108** See the case BH2009.11.506 (Supreme Court file number: Legf. Bír., Gfv.X.30.154/2009).

portant fact because the Privatization Agency declared unilaterally at the time of the conclusion of the shareholder's agreement that the "*Hungarian side will not be in the position to stick to the anti-competition clause should different agreement be reached in the privatization process.*"

It is also of relevance that the shareholders' agreement provided that the Construction Company will come into existence once the Hungarian agency approves the articles of incorporations and that the shareholders' agreement will remain in effect until, either the Company is dissolved without a legal successor, or there will be at least two remaining shareholders to which the shareholders' agreement would apply. While the Construction Company came into existence validly, the planned cooperation did not materialize and the structure of shareholders has begun to change already from 1992. In particular, the legal successor of the Italian founder acquired all the shares in 1994, which were then transferred to a new Hungarian company as the sole shareholder (Company 'K'). Formally, however, neither the Founder-Hungarian, nor the Construction Company were wound up or liquidated.

Irrespective of this hectic period and the failed plans, Company 'K' launched arbitral proceedings in Geneva against the legal successor of the Italian founder-company for breaching the anti-competition provision in the shareholders' agreement after year 2000. Although the respondent raised as defence that the shareholders' agreement was no longer in force, the arbitral tribunal was of contrary opinion. Moreover, it ruled that the anti-competition prohibition equally applied also to subsidiaries breaching the anti-competition clause and consequently it awarded damages. The Hungarian Supreme Court took the position that the continued existence of the shareholders' agreement as decided by the Swiss arbitral tribunal had to be accepted as a *fact* and consequently it did not extend its analysis to that particular aspect of the case.

The Italian legal successor, having lost the Swiss arbitral case, sued the Founder-Hungarian Company, now government owned, claiming that the Swiss arbitral panel should have ordered the Founder-Hungarian company to pay the damages, which had failed to inform it about the contents of the shareholders' agreement – i.e., it breached its duty to inform. As per the Supreme Court's opinion, however, the Hungarian party had no duty under the shareholders' agreement to inform the legal successor of the Italian founder-company, neither continuously, nor on an ad hoc basis, especially as the legal predecessor of the plaintiff was one of the signatories.

### c. Contracting for Transfer of Shares: Do the new Shareholders Get also the Right to Participate in the Penalties Awarded for Breach of the Shareholders' Agreement? [109]

A recent reported case (with more changes in the identity of parties) decided by the Court of Appeal of Capital-Budapest is interesting because it involves two different types of legal succession-related issues: one related to transfer of obligations and the other one on rights from the shareholders' agreement. As far as the underlying shareholders' agreement is concerned, of relevance to the case were the following elements. First, it explicitly provided that if the issued registered shares are transferred, all rights and obligations from the shareholders' agreement are deemed to be transferred onto the acquirers as well. Secondly, it contained also an anti-competition clause (proscribing shareholders to engage in road construction) and penalties for its breach, as well as, thirdly, dispute resolution by arbitration in Switzerland.

The question whether and in what form are *obligations* from a shareholders' agreement transferred onto legal successors came up because the said anti-competition clause was breached by a legal successor company of one of the signatories to the shareholders' agreement; what made one of the shareholders to the shareholders' agreement launch arbitral proceedings. The Arbitration Centre of the Chamber of Commerce and Industry of Geneva awarded a substantial amount of penalties (2.8 billion HUF plus interest) to the claimant and held that the anti-competition clause applied equally to the legal successor company.

The issue of whether and in what form are *rights* from a shareholders' agreement passed onto the acquirers of shares was the subject matter of the Hungarian court case before us, which was launched as well by new – yet from the one winning the Swiss arbitration case – different shareholders. They claimed that the penalty (or part of it) awarded by the Swiss arbitral tribunal should be paid to them yet instead of a concrete sum of money "*they asked the court to issue a declaratory judgment proclaiming that they have become subjects to the shareholders' agreement in question.*" Although they lost the case for procedural reasons, the final distance court did not question their right. The court said that rather "*they have failed to prove why it would be necessary to make a declaratory judgment on their right.*"

Obviously, the case is illustrative what complications may arise even when the shareholders' agreement unequivocally proclaims that the acquirers of shares are transferred all rights and duties from the shareholders' agreement.

---

**109** See the case Fővárosi Ítélőtábla 5.Pf.21.851/2010/6. .

One may wonder whether the outcome would have been any different at all had the parties failed from putting that forward in the shareholders' agreement.

## III. Consequences of a Breach of the Shareholders' Agreements: The Three Theories

Given that shareholders' agreements are not regulated by primary sources of law in this country but are rather the product of case law and industrial practices, it should not come as a surprise that three different opinions have survived up until today on the consequences of the breach of Shareholders' Agreements. According to the most radical position, perceiving the shareholders' agreement exclusively as civil law contracts (obligations), no company law-type of consequences could follow from their breach under any circumstances.[110] Simply, shareholders' agreements conceptually do not belong to the realm of company law.

The middle position does not look upon shareholders' agreements as conceptually completely distinct from company law. Rather it departs from the presumption that – save voluntary implementation by the signatory shareholders – company law-type of consequences envisaged by shareholders' agreements may not be awarded by courts of law. Consequently, the only court remedy available for breach of shareholders' agreements are damages as the generally available remedy of private law.[111] Thus, for example, no court can order a shareholder to vote according to a voting arrangement in the shareholder's agreement.

Finally, as per the view of the proponents of the most lenient and thus most-permissive position – besides suing for damages – the duties foreseen by the shareholders' agreements may also be enforced in courts of law though only if they can in fact be implemented, are also in the interest of the other party/parties and the specific performance would not result in a complete deadlock of the enterprise due to excessive extra costs or other types of burdens.[112]

---

110 See *Auer et al* Atypical Contracts (2015), at 231.

111 *Id.* This position is attributed primarily to Professor *András Kisfaludi*, who was one of the drafters of the new Civil Code's company law part.

112 *Id.* This is position is attributed primarily to Professor *Attila Menyhárd*, another member of the new Civil Code's drafting team. The referred to position was expounded by the Professor in his article "A szindikátusi szerződés kikényszeríthetősége" in Acta Conventus de Iure Civili – Tomus X.; a publication of the Law School of Szeged, edited by Tekla Papp (Lectum Publisher, Szeged, 2009), at 254–255.

This last position is corroborated by one of the few cases not involving damages but exclusion of a signatory to a shareholders' agreement.[113] Here, the shareholder's agreement was concluded by four persons, one (the defendant, shareholder to be excluded) appearing in the shoes of an 'investor' and the other three (plaintiffs, controlling shareholders) as owners of immovables located in the capital Budapest. The agreement fixed that they form a project for construction of prime residential apartments, which is exclusively to be financed from their contributions and from a credit. It turned out soon, however, that additional sources of financing are needed as the financing bank asked for more self-financing and thus they passed a decision according to which each of the four shareholders is to pay in substantial additional amounts of money.[114] This, however, was not fulfilled by the defendant, notwithstanding multiple requests by the company and warnings that his failure to contribute was gravely endangering ("*nagymértékben veszélyeztette*") the project. Eventually litigation was started, which ended with his exclusion exactly having the project's aims and goals at sight. Although this decision was passed before the enactment of the 2013 Civil Code, it is still of relevance given that the Code took over almost intact the pertaining solutions from the 2006 Company Act.[115]

Finally, notwithstanding the differing opinions, of most practical importance is that Hungarian courts normally award only damages for breach of shareholders' agreements and this is therefore what one should primarily reckon with when pondering to go to court. Claiming other conventional private law remedies (e. g., declaration of the loss of a contractual right, penalties or forfeiture of moneys)[116] are not excluded either, yet do not seem to be frequent.[117] Reported cases

---

**113** Decision of the Appeal Court of the Capital Budapest No. Gf. 40386/2008/4.

**114** The amount at stake was substantial: one-hundred million Hungarian Forints (HUF). In December 2016 the exchange rate was about 310 HUF for one Euro.

**115** See §§ 3:107 and 3:108 of the 2013 Civil Code (sections 47 and 48 in the 2006 Company Act). While in principle exclusion of members and shareholders is possible, there are three exceptions: 1) two-member companies; 2) shareholder of an open-joint stock company (i. e., whose shares are publicly traded); and 3) the member or shareholder who possesses at least 2/3 of votes at the highest decision-making body. See § 3:107(2). The test is grave endangering of the achievement of the company's aims and goals. § 3:107(1).

**116** This conclusion is corroborated also by scholars yet typically without citing concrete cases. See, e. g., *Auer et al* Atypical Contracts (2015), at 231–32.

**117** Id. at 232. The Court of Appeal of Győr was the court that adjudicated in more of its decisions that "*given that the shareholders' agreement creates obligations, the breach of these obligations produces the same consequences as the breach of any other private law contract: unless other remedies are agreed upon, damages will follow.*" See the following decision of this court: Gf.II.20.118/2009/4; Pf. II. 20.014/2009/4; Pf. II. 20 010/2007/4.

though exist. Thus, a recent Hungarian court case was related to the award of penalties by the Arbitration Centre of the Chamber of Commerce and Industry of Geneva for breaching the anti-competition clause in a shareholders' agreement.[118]

# F. Enforcement of Shareholders' Agreements

## I. Arbitration of Disputes from Shareholders' Agreements

As one could have seen from the above selection of cases involving shareholders' agreements, there is no hindrance to resort to arbitration or any other form of alternative dispute resolution to resolve related disputes in Hungary. The relatively meaningful number of publicly available case summaries unequivocally proves that. The cases prove as well that courts stand ready to adjudicate disputes involving shareholders' agreements and – save some exceptions[119] – shareholders' agreements are looked upon as legitimate legal institutions of the Hungarian legal system.

## II. Damages as Most Typical Remedies for Breach of Shareholders' Agreements

As already hinted at, the most typical remedy available for breach of shareholders' agreements are damages. Most of the reported cases corroborate that given that typically they involve the question of the awarding and fixing the amount of damages. The cases, however, show as well how intricate and complex these issues may become when breach of shareholders' agreements are at stake. In one of the most illustrative cases – we may conveniently refer to it as the '*newspaper publishing case*'[120] – the task of the courts was to answer whether, and if yes, what amount of damages is to be awarded for breach that made the coming into being of the company impossible?

**118** Fővárosi Ítélőtábla 5.Pf.21.851/2010/6.

**119** See above, for example, the case decided by the Appeal Court of Nyíregyháza, file No. G.40105/2011/11.

**120** EH 2006.1428 (original number of the Supreme Court: Legf. Bír. Gfv. IX. 30.279/2005. sz.

## 1. The 'Newspaper Publishing Case' and Apportioning of Damages for Terminating Shareholders' Agreements before Registration of the Company

The facts of the case were as follows. As per the articles of incorporation (2 Aug. 1994), a limited liability company was to be founded by three shareholders for indefinite period of time and for publishing of newspapers. The plaintiff promised as well to provide, as an ancillary service though for remuneration, all that was necessary to make the newspaper appear. Before registering the company, they have concluded also a shareholders' agreement (17 Aug. 1994) in which it was specified what costs and expenditures the plaintiff could deduct each month from the income of the sold newspapers; the surplus was to be transferred monthly to the LTD. No profits could be distributed yet the plaintiff had a right additionally to a 25% lump sum as fixed costs.

A year later, they amended the shareholders' agreement (6 Sept. 1995), when besides decreasing the plaintiff's rights, they fixed as well that the profits and losses are to be borne by them in proportion to their stakes. On 2 January 1996, however, one of the partners (first defendant) terminated the shareholders' agreement for the alleged financial and economic failure of the business. The LTD was eventually not registered by the Company Register because the shareholders had failed to supply to the court some missing documents. Given that the plaintiff has by that time made substantial investments into the printing business but could not cover his costs and expenditures as the enterprise produced only losses both in 1994 and 1995, he sued for damages. The courts were to decide for what period of time and what amount of damages was the plaintiff entitled to? The termination was declared to be groundless.

The case went through more instances ending with revision by the Supreme Court, the two key findings of which were the following. The *first* was drafting-related. Namely, as the court stressed, the shareholder's agreement provided *only* for sharing of losses of the LTD but *not* that the other shareholders will cover the costs, expenditures and remuneration of the plaintiff if he will not be in the position to cover them from the income of the publication of the newspaper. Likewise, they could have, but did not include into the articles of incorporation provisions whereby the losses could have been covered also from the capital of the LTD or the additional contributions of the shareholders. As a result, the aggregate loss of the plaintiff had to be borne by the two defendants only in proportion to their shareholdings (first defendant 51%, second defendant 5%), minus the payments that had been effectuated to the plaintiff earlier.

The *second* issue, the reason why the holding of the case is cited and what impacts also the calculation of damages, was about the dependency of shareholders' agreements from the articles of incorporation. As the court correctly noted, the shareholders' agreements are ancillary to the charter and cannot exist without it and without the company. As in the case the registration of the company was rejected by the court that also meant that the partners had a statutory duty to cease the business activities. The implementation of the shareholder's agreement became impossible as a consequence of that as well. This fact should also be taken into account when apportioning of damages for unjustified termination of the shareholder's agreement. Fixing of damages in such cases is otherwise the task of courts.

## 2. Can a Director be Removed with Immediately Effect for Not Acting According to the Shareholders' Agreement? – Case on Sale and Lease-Back of Buses

A decision of the Curia (Supreme Court) from 2012[121] deserves a few lines notwithstanding that the publicized text of the decision reveals very little about the shareholders' agreement itself yet it deals with one particular aspect of enforcement of shareholders' agreements: the liability of directors that make contrary decisions. What is known from the decision related to the contents of the shareholders' agreement is, first, that it was concluded by two shareholders of a transport company (providing services also to some municipalities and thus presuming approval of the municipality on key decisions) and, second, that the managerial rights were allocated only to one of the shareholders.

What was quintessential is that the director of the transport company (the plaintiff) "*gravely neglected his duties*" as the chief-executive director of the company by concluding contracts (sale and lease-back agreements) bringing about a transaction that was "*contrary to the shareholders' agreement accepted by the general meeting.*" The CEO sued for he was removed from this position with immediate effect. While he won before the labour and the second instance court and back pay for one year was awarded to him together with interest, he lost the case on revision by the Curia (the Supreme Court), which ruled that due to his heightened duty of care ("*gondosság*"), "*he should have investigated and revealed all the important terms of conditions of the contracts concluded [and] in order to prepare and assist the employer to pass a reasonable and well-grounded decision, he should have informed the employer about these – normally before decision-making and especially when great-value contracts are at stake.*"

**121** EBH2012.M.11 (Kúria Mfv. I.10.409/2011).

# G. The Most Typical Anomaly: Conflicting Charter and Shareholders' Agreement and a Case on Excessive Limitation of Termination Rights

The analysis of shareholders' agreements-related cases is useful also to detect anomalies, misconceptions and drafting errors. Some of the reported cases, indeed, are instructive from that perspective. Undoubtedly, the lack of topic-specific regulation is partially attributable that these recur. Besides the cases discussed above – which should speak for themselves – let us close the review by taking a look at another Supreme Court case likewise involving the presumably most typical misconception: conflict of the articles of incorporation and the shareholders' agreement. [122]

As a preliminary caveat: the central issue of the case was not about shareholders' agreements *directly* but rather about the due process issue whether an arbitral tribunal has the power to declare *sua sponte* that a contractual provision is null and void; i.e., without giving the parties the right to be heard and present evidence? On that point the Supreme Court annulled the attacked arbitral award because the tribunal declared the termination clause in one of three interlinked contracts – named as 'Operations Contract' – as '*excessively limiting the right to terminate a contract.*'

What makes the case useful for us is the fact that it involves more interlinked contracts, one being exactly a shareholders' agreement besides the mentioned '*Operations Contract*' and the third document named as '*Frame Agreement*' ("*Keretmegállapodás*"). It needs to be highlighted that the shareholders' agreement contained also provisions on share subscriptions ("*Részvényjegyzési és részvényesi szerződés*").

Two main mistakes could be detected from the summarized facts of the case. The *first* was that the three legal documents were not fully coordinated notwithstanding that each of them seem to have had distinct roles in an otherwise complex venture (operation of water supply and sewage systems); involving a French group of companies, too. As per the original intention of the parties, while the Frame Agreement foresaw the founding of a new company for provision of these services, the Operations Contract provided the details about the technical operation of the water supply and sewerage system. The synchronization of the

---

**122** Supreme Court Decision EBH2011.2421.

three agreements, however, was far from perfect; perhaps best visible from foreseeing different types of dispute resolution methods.[123]

The *second*, more problematic solution was related to the asymmetric nature of the termination clause mentioned above. Namely, the termination clause enshrined in the shareholders' agreement provided that the Operations Contract can be terminated by (some of) the Hungarian parties[124] even in the lack of a breach of the contract by the French partner.

## H. Some Concluding Thoughts

In Hungary, like in most other European jurisdictions, the confidentiality of shareholders' agreements is a major obstacle for researchers. This is then topped by the historic fact that these *sui generis*, Janus-faced devices, surviving on the border-line of company and private law (obligations), have had a relatively short period of time available for development given that due to more than four decades of socialism – discarding them – the process had to be restarted essentially from scratch after the fall of the Berlin Wall. As the regulatory policy in the post-1990 period has consistently been not to interfere, organic growth – borrowing from western developed systems combined with local legal engineering – was the way for headways. Yet the relatively big number of reported court and arbitral cases, displaying the tendency of growth, is a good indicator that shareholders' agreements have gained solid foothold in this country by now. Moreover, they are employed not only when foreign partners are involved but also even when municipalities hold shares typically in public utility companies.

The shaping of the contours of the law on shareholders' agreements then is inevitably left primarily to courts and arbitrators. Although it can, neither be properly ascertained, nor claimed, yet many of the cases referred to above

123 While under the Operations Contract the agreed upon dispute resolution method was arbitration with the Permanent Arbitral Body of the Hungarian Chamber of Commerce and Industry, the shareholders' agreement opted for the kin arbitral institution of the Vienna Federal Chamber of Commerce and Industry. The dispute resolution clause in the Operations Contract excluded disputes from the shareholders' agreement. It was an issue also that the parties to them differed.

124 From the over-concise text of the reproduced judgment it is next to impossible to determine how many parties and in what role were they involved in the case. Unfortunately, this is not the anomaly only of this multi-party Hungarian decision, but is common to most of them. The problem is to a great extent attributable to the practice according to which the parties' names cannot be revealed but instead abbreviations and/or general references (plaintiff – defendant, claimant – respondent) are being used. This is primarily due to European data protection and privacy laws taken over by Hungary as well.

were undoubtedly cases of first impression, where the courts were those agents that were asked to comprehend and provide the necessary guidance, the longed-for-benchmarks, for the future unfolding of this specific area of law. Such constellation of the law and the pioneering role of susceptive practitioners coupled with the support of courts, however, should remind us also that surprises should also be expected in this domain given that especially in complex fact patterns it cannot be ascertained properly whether and with which provision of the new Civil Code are certain solutions in shareholders' agreements in conflict. The living topic of whether and how could present generations of shareholders bind the hands of the future generations, for example, is awaiting the courts to clarify.[125]

Scholarship, besides devoting insufficient attention to the topic, seems to have been constantly lagging behind developments; it has failed even to start a discourse on possible methods for research and analysis. Consequently, the topic of shareholders' agreements is quite obscure for many in the legal profession. As the rumours suggest, some scholars go as far as equating them with suspicious behind-the-scene deals of shareholders bordering with outright fraud, which as such should simply be curbed, if not prohibited by the force of law. The picture one may get by reading the – otherwise modest number of – publications on the topic is that the law of shareholders' agreements is static. Yet that is a false presumption if adjudged based on what practicing lawyers, financiers and investors claim, or if one takes more than a cursory look at the complex arrangements parties have created in practice – as unearthed by the reported cases. The cases are invaluable in this domain exactly for this and for two further reasons. On the one hand, they prove that mistakes are made in practice, a reason why reshuffling of the priorities of scholars and perhaps even of the regulators would be of importance; the latter could guide future development through prescriptive drafting – an approach that was rejected by the drafters of the 2013 Civil Code. On the other hand, the cases corroborate also that Hungarian busi-

125 Although past court decisions may have only persuasive force in Hungary, *Kolben* found it important to quote the related decision of the Curia from 1925, which points to the gist of the issue and reads as follows: "*Such agreements of shareholders that would mandatorily apply also to their legal successors, who thus would be restrained to vote according to their interests and as it would fit the changing business environment (...) cannot be enforced in courts of law.*" Decision of the Curia No. 3478/1925, cited by Kolben 1996, at 113. While such limitations were given partial green light in the United States in the famous Galler v. Galler case [Illinois Supreme Court, 203 N.E.2d 577, 1964), the position of Hungarian law is unclear as of yet. The author of this paper has tried to highlight these issues in his article "Vagyonvédelem, hagyatéktervezés és a szindikátusi szerződések" [Asset Protection, Estate Planning and the Shareholders' Agreements] in István Mándoki (ed.), A hagyatéki vagyontervezés – Estate Planning, Studia Notarialia Hungarica Tom. XVII (Budapest, 2015), at 79 – 93.

nessmen and their counsel are open to learn from the experiences of others as far as shareholders' agreements are concerned. For that reason, a pan-European project that would collect, analyse and systematize good and bad practices, solutions and the knowledge on shareholders' agreements should be welcome in this country.

Omer Kimhi, Achiad Harel and Yve Binestock

# Israel

## Table of Content



---

**Prof. Omer Kimhi,** University of Haifa, Faculty of Law
**Achiad Harel,** Partner, Amar Reiter Jeanna Shochatovitch & Co.
**Ive Binestock,** Associate, Amar Reiter Jeanne Shochatovitch & Co.

https://doi.org/10.1515/9783110517026-017

# A. Nature of Corporate Law Regulation in General

Israeli companies are regulated by the Israeli Companies Law, 5759–1999 (the "**Companies Law**"), which entered into effect on May 1999. The Law replaced the Israeli Companies Ordinance (New Version) 5743–1983 (the "**Companies Ordinance**"), which in turn was based on the British Mandate Companies Ordinance of 1929, and was perceived by many legal scholars and practitioners as deficient and outdated.[1] Before 1999, therefore, much of the Israeli corporate laws were based on court rulings (pursuant to the common law tradition), and one of the objectives of the 1999 Companies Law was the codification and modernization of the Israeli corporate laws.[2]

The fundamental viewpoint that governs the Companies Law – and has immense impact on the matter of shareholders' agreements at hand – is one which favors the autonomy of the individual will. Such viewpoint has several implications, the first of which is that the individual is free to incorporate, and he is independent in designing the nature and content of such incorporation. This outlook has an enormous effect on the way the company's Articles of Association and shareholders' agreements are regulated and interpreted by the courts. Another implication of this philosophy is the fact that most of the Companies Law's provisions are dispositive, *i.e.* provisions that the incorporating parties can deviate from, while only small part of the provisions is mandatory. This has a significant effect on the content of the incorporation documents, as will be more fully explained below.[3]

In the period during which the Companies Ordinance applied (i.e., before 1999), there were three sorts of incorporation documents: Memorandum of Association, Articles of Association ("AoA") and Shareholders' (or Founders) Agreements. Since the Companies Law entered into effect, the separation between the Memorandum of Association and the AoA was aborted, and nowadays the only fundamental document required for the establishment of a company and the only agreement regulated pursuant to the Companies law – is the AoA. Along

---

1 Joseph H. Gross, The New Companies Law 2 (4th Ed. 2007)
2 The Companies Law Bill – 5756, State of Israel Bills 2432, at 5.
3 *Supra note* 2, at 6.

with the AoA there are shareholders' agreements, which may be divided into two types: founders agreements – when the agreement is concluded prior to the establishment of the company, and shareholders' agreements – when the agreement is concluded after the establishment of the company (Henceforth, in this report, founders and shareholders' agreements together shall be named "**Shareholders' Agreements**").[4] These agreements, however, are voluntary in nature, and are neither necessary for the establishment of a company nor for its operation.[5]

As more fully described below, the use of any one of these corporate documents (the AoA or Shareholders' Agreements) is subject to a different set of rules and regulations and is intended to serve different purposes.

# B. Regulation of Shareholders' Agreements

## I. The Articles of Association as a Unique Contract (sui generis)

The AoA is the founding document of the Company. According to Israeli law, a company cannot be incorporated without an AoA,[6] and the AoA must remain in existence, albeit with possible amendments, throughout the company's life.

The Companies Law determines that the AoA is a contract among the company and its shareholders and among the shareholders themselves.[7] This means that, except when determined otherwise by the Companies Law or the courts, general contract laws will apply and the shareholders and company are bound thereby.[8] The contractual nature of the relationship between the shareholders also manifests itself in certain provisions of the Companies Law. Section 352 (a) of the Companies Law determines that the general laws which apply to the

---

4 While the AoA and Founders agreement are usually formed upon the incorporation of the company by its founding shareholders, a shareholders' agreement might be created in subsequent phases in the company's life span, between its shareholders at that time who did not take part in founding the corporation.

5 Irit Haviv Segal, Corporate Law in Israel 191(2007).

6 Section 15 to the Companies Law.

7 Section 17 (A) to the Companies Law; G. Procaccia, *The Appliance of Contract Law on the Memorandum and Regulations of a Company*, Eiunei Mishpat H 491;

8 The relevant laws are the Contract Law (General Part) – 1973, which deals, among others, with the formation of a contract, and the Contract Law (Remedies for Contract Breach) 1970 – which regulates the reliefs to which the party adversely effected by the breach of the contract is entitled to.

breach of a contract shall apply, *mutatis mutandis*, to the breach of a right granted to a shareholder towards the company or towards another shareholder pursuant the Law[9]; Section 192(c) of the Companies Law determines that the law which applies to the breach of a contract shall apply, *mutatis mutandis*, to the breach of a shareholders' duty to act in good faith towards the company and its shareholders, and to a violation of a shareholders' duty to avoid the deprivation of other shareholders; Section 193 of the Companies Law determines that the law which applies to the breach of a contract shall apply, *mutatis mutandis*, to the breach of an obligation of a controlling shareholder to act fairly towards the company.

The AoA, however, is not a regular contract. It is designed to regulate the legal relations among a relatively large number of parties, and it affects third parties, such as future shareholders, who did not take part in its formation. As a result of these characteristics, some of the rules that govern regular contracts do not apply to the AoA, and in certain respects the AoA is governed by specific (*sui generis*) rules.

First, the content of the AoA is, at least to some extent, limited by the Companies Law. Despite the "Freedom of Contracts" principle, which constitutes a fundamental principle in the Israeli legal system,[10] the Companies Law determines that there are certain issues that the AoA must address and there are certain issues the incorporating parties cannot contract out of. Section 18 of the Companies Law details the issues an AoA must address: the name of the company; the purposes of the company; details regarding the registered capital shares of the company; *and* details with regard to the limitation of liability of the shareholders.[11] Section 19 of the Companies Law allows the AoA to address supplementary discretionary issues: the rights and obligations of the shareholders and the company; instructions regarding the management of the company; *and* any other matter the shareholders see fit to regulate in the AoA. In addition, the Companies Law restricts the content of the AoA. The AoA cannot overrule certain mandatory provisions of the Companies Laws, and any attempt to do so will be considered null and void. Thus, for example, the incorporating parties cannot contract out of the officers' duty of loyalty towards the company or the duty to act in good faith to one another.

---

**9** Yechiel Bahat, Corporate Law- the New Corporate Israeli Law, 495 (12th Ed. 2011).
**10** Gavriela Shalev, Contract Law- General Part, Towards Codification of the Civil Law, 48 (2005); C.A 9323/04 *Meitzar Development Ltd. v. Partnership Building No. 17 Site no. 5* (Decision rendered on 23 July 2006).
**11** Section 18 of the Companies Law.

Another unique aspect of the AoA as a contract has to do with the mechanism that allows its change. Whereas the amendment of a regular contract requires the unanimous consent of all contractual parties, the amendment of an AoA is governed by a majority rule. The majority rule mechanism is required since the relationship between the incorporating parties (the shareholders) is long-lasting, and if a unanimous consent was required for each and every amendment, the company's ability to survive changing market conditions would be jeopardized.[12] Section 20(a) of the Companies Law sets the general rule that a Company's AoA can be amended through regular majority in the Company's general assembly, but shareholders can opt-out this general rule.[13] They can determine that the amendment of certain or all provisions of the AoA shall be made with a special majority or even a unanimous consent, and the Companies Law respects and enforces their choice.[14] The Law, however, requires the resolution that a certain provision shall be amended only with a special majority to be passed with the same special majority required for the aforesaid provision's amendment. [15] Thus, if the shareholders determine a provision according to which the amendment of a certain section must be made with a unanimous consent, such provision must also be resolved unanimously.

A third issue relating to the unique contractual nature of the AoA concerns its interpretation. According to the Israeli contracts laws, a contract should be interpreted pursuant to the parties' *subjective* estimated intent[16]. Such subjective estimated intent is derived from the language of the contract, but also from external circumstances within which the contract was created.[17] The courts estimate what were the intention and purposes of the parties when drafting the contract, and then interpret the contract accordingly – even if the written language of the contract does not perfectly coincide with such interpretation thereof.[18] The

---

**12** *Supra note* 5, at 192.

**13** Section 20(a)

**14** Section 20(a)

**15** Section 20(b)

**16** C.A 8239/06 Avron *v.* Plada (Decision rendered on 21 December 2008); C.A 4628/93 *The State of Israel v. Apropim Housing and Promotions (1991) Ltd.* (Decision rendered on 6 April 1995); Further Hearing 2045/05 *The Organization of Vegetables Growers, Agricultural Cooperative Corporation v. The State of Israel* (Decision rendered on 11 May 2006).

**17** Section 25(A) to the Contract Law; C.A 5856/06 *Levy v. Norkeit Ltd.* (Decision rendered on 28 January 2008); C.A 841/15 *Panorama the North a Construction Corporation Ltd. v. Undisclosed* (Decision rendered on 23 May 2016); C.A 5925/06 *Blume v. Anglo-Saxon Assets Agency (Israel 1992) Ltd.* (Decision rendered on 13 February 2008).

**18** C.A 4628/93 *The State of Israel v. Apropim Housing and Promotions (1991) Ltd.* P.D Vol. 49(2) P. 265.

same is not true with respect to the AoA. Here, especially with respect to public companies, the courts put more emphasis on the language of the AoA than on the subjective intent of the drafting parties of the AoA. External evidence, and in particular a custom (a conduct adopted by the parties that is not reflected in the wording of the AoA), cannot usually be used to interpret the AoA.[19]

## II. Shareholders' and Founders' Agreements

As mentioned above, since the legislation of the Companies Law, the AoA is the only mandatory document required for the incorporation and the operation of a company (the Memorandum of Association, existing in the Companies Ordinance, was cancelled). However, shareholders keep using shareholders' agreements to regulate their affairs.[20]

The Companies' Law does not refer to shareholders' agreements as corporate documents, and there are no specific provisions that separate them from any other regular contract. Thus, regular general contact laws apply to shareholders' agreements, and shareholders' agreements are binding solely on the persons which are explicitly made parties thereto. A person is not subject to a shareholders' agreement just because she bought shares in the company (as is the case with the AoA), but rather must explicitly agree to accept the terms of the shareholders' agreement (as is the case with respect to regular contracts). In addition, the amendment and interpretation of shareholder's agreements are performed pursuant to the regular contract rules, and there are no specific sections or provisions that these agreements must contain. The prohibition on opting out the mandatory provisions of the Companies Law, though, remains the same as with regard to AoA's.

The reasons for using shareholders' agreements instead of just using an AoA for addressing certain corporate issues vary.[21] In certain cases the legal issues addressed in shareholders' agreements are relevant only to some of the shareholders and not all of them, and so the creation of an agreement separate from the AoA is necessary. In other cases, it is a matter of convenience. Parties do not wish to submit the Agreement to the Companies' Registrar (as is the ob-

**19** HCJ 4222/95 *Platin v. the Cooperatives Registrar* [30 December 1998]

**20** Supra note 5, at 191.

**21** Since the AoA is defined not only as a contract between the shareholders and the company, but also as a contract among the shareholders themselves, most legal issues among the shareholders can, at least in theory, be regulated in the AoA, without the need for an additional document.

ligation with an AoA), they do not wish to include future shareholders in their agreement, the agreement is formed before the company is incorporated[22], etc.

In situations where there is a conflict between the AoA and a shareholders' agreement (founder's or shareholders' agreements), the general rules of interpretation apply. Pursuant to such rules, in the relation between the company and its shareholders, the language of the AoA has the utmost importance and the subjective intent of the shareholders is less relevant.[23] Thus, in this respect, and barring exceptional circumstances, the AoA shall prevail.[24] In the relations among the parties to the shareholders' agreement, the court may also address the estimated will of the parties, the date of the formation of the Agreement – when the later one may prevail – or specific arrangements which will usually supersede general ones. This is in addition to the considerations relating to the benefit and dynamic needs of the company, and the importance of flexibility in light of the company's need to adjust to the changing business reality and economy.[25]

## III. Public Companies Versus Private Companies:

With respect to shareholders'/founders' agreements, same rules apply to both public and private corporations. However, with respect to the Corporation's AoA, there are two main differences, which are important to emphasize: the interpretation of the AoA and the recommended "adopt or disclose" provisions.

We have already mentioned in section 1 above that the rules of interpretation of an AoA are different than those of a regular contract. Whereas in the interpretation of a regular contract courts emphasize the subjective intent of the parties, in the interpretation of an AoA the objective language is more important. This rule is especially important in public companies. In public companies the interpretation of an AoA shall never deviate from the language of the AoA, even when shareholders prove that their true will was different than stipulated thereunder.[26]

The second difference concerns the content of the AoA. Section 19(2 A) of the Companies Law recommends ***public*** companies to include several "best practice" corporate governance provisions in their AoA (the provisions are detailed in the first appendix to the Law). Companies are not obligated to include

22 Such agreement would usually be a founders agreement.

23 Supra note 1, at 92.

24 HCJ 4222/95 **Platin v. the Cooperatives Registrar** [30 December 1998]

25 Supra note 5, at 237.

26 CA 54/96 *Hollander v. The Innovative Dimension Software Ltd.* )Decision rendered on 23 December 1998(.

these "best practice" provisions, but they are required to disclose in their financial statements whether they have done so or not. The rationale of this mechanism is that the capital markets will favorably price the inclusion of the "best practice" provisions in the AoA, and that the disclosure will incentivize the public corporations to adopt the provisions even if they are not forced to do so. The "best practice" provisions include, *inter alia*, a requirement that the board shall be comprised of a certain portion of independent directors (a majority if there is no controlling shareholder, and a third if there is one), gender diversification in the board, mandatory board meetings without the presence of senior officers etc. Private corporations are not recommended to include these provisions in their AoA, and naturally they do not have to disclose to the public whether they have done so or not.

## C. Forms of Shareholders' Agreements

As mentioned above, there are three types of shareholders' agreements in Israel: the AoA, founders' agreements and shareholders' agreements.[27] Until now, we have described the regulation of these types of agreements, and in this part we elaborate on the main issues they deal with. Except if explicitly stated otherwise, all the provisions (types of agreements) below are respected and enforced by courts in Israel, and are especially common in private start-up (high-tech) companies.

We divide the issues into four parts: shareholders' rights, the transfer of shares, the constitution and management of the corporation and pre-insolvency issues.

### I. Shareholder Rights:

#### 1. Voting Rights and Voting Agreements:

In Israel, private companies (and private companies alone) can divide the corporation's share capital into different classes of shares, and assign each class of shares with different voting rights. Such classification must be provided for in

27 Since shareholders' agreement and founders agreement are materially similar except for the timing of their formation, then for the sake of convenience we shall refer to both of them hereinafter collectively as "shareholders' agreement".

the AoA, which should detail the different types of shares, and the different rights (including voting rights) each class has. Often, financial investors (such as angles or hedge funds) receive preferred shares, which have more votes per share than ordinary shares, and/or may have veto rights on certain issues.

As opposed to private companies, according to Section 46B of the Securities Law – 1968, the Israeli stock market can register companies for trade only if they have only one class of shares, which assigns an equal number of votes to all shares of the company. Section 46B does allow a registered company to issue preferred shares with a dividend preference, and to assign special voting rights to special shares held by the state (in case the government determined there is a special need for such special rights).

In addition, section 189 of the Companies Law allows shareholders, in both private and public companies, to have voting agreements made between them or any other agreements for collaboration. Such voting or collaboration agreements are subject to the shareholders' obligations prescribed by the Law, such as the obligation to avoid the abuse of their power in the company and the obligation to act towards the company and towards other shareholders in good faith.[28]

The voting agreement binds only the shareholders who are party to it, and it has no legal power towards the company itself or other shareholders not party to it.[29] As a result, in the event that one of the shareholders breaches the voting agreement and votes against the agreement, his vote shall be valid and binding, notwithstanding the breach of the shareholders' agreement thereby. In any such case, the only remedy of the shareholder affected by the breach would be compensation for damages caused thereto as a result of the breach.

It is also important to note that a shareholders' voting agreement is not binding on the board of directors. According to the law in Israel, board members (and corporate officers) have a fiduciary duty towards the company, and they must vote and act independently in good faith pursuant to what they believe is in the best interests of the company. Board members are not allowed to take voting instructions from shareholders (even the shareholders that appointed them), and they are also prohibited from reaching voting agreements amongst themselves.[30] Thus, shareholders cannot agree on the way the directors will vote in the board.

---

**28** Section 192 of the Companies Law;

**29** C.A 6041/15 *Ha'ama Ltd. v. Muler* (Rendered on 25 September 2016).

**30** Section 106 to the Companies Law.

### 2. The Right to Receive Information.

Section 184 of the Companies Law determines the shareholders' right to receive certain information from the company, and shareholders' agreements in private companies usually include a provision dealing with this right and broadening it.

The general right for information includes the right to review protocols and resolutions of the general meetings as well as any applicable documents and any document required in order to make a decision in a matter on the agenda of the general meeting.[31] The shareholders are also entitled to receive a copy from the company's AoA and copies of the financial reports[32]. Shareholders in private companies often contractually agree to receive additional information regarding the company, beyond what is prescribed in the Companies Law. They require information on issues such as the company's on-going business, intellectual property information, future projects the company may engage in and so on.

### 3. Preemption Rights.

When investors wish to protect their right to maintain and increase their share and control in the company they are often granted Preemptive Rights. Such rights grant the current shareholders in the company a priority during the issuance of new shares in the company, and provide them the right to participate in the issuance of shares, according to their *pro-rata* part in the Share Capital of the company. This right usually does not provide the shareholders with any discount or favored conditions, but merely the right to be offered the issued shares first and prior to a potential investor or new strategic partner or even a public offering, according to their share of investment in the company.

Section 290 of the Companies Law determines that, unless otherwise determined in the company's AoA, a private company, which includes only one type of shares, should first offer every shareholder the issued shares according to his *pro-rata* share in the share capital of the company. Only after a shareholder refuses the offer or does not accept the offer until the end of a defined period, the board of directors may offer the shares to an entity outside of the company. It is customary in many shareholders' agreements to limit the aforesaid Preemptive Right, in order to allow the company to issue shares and raise the capital necessary to achieve essential business objectives. Investing parties often wish to de-

**31** Sections 184 and 185 to the Companies Law.
**32** Id.

sign their own preemption mechanism, rather than rely on the generic mechanism set by law.

### 4. Dividend Preferences

Each shareholder is entitled to receive dividends according to the rights attached to its shares and subject to the company's decision to distribute dividends.[33]

A company, however, may issue special types of shares (in addition to the ordinary shares) which have dividend preferences and are usually named "Preferred Shares". Such shares grant their holders a priority in the distribution of dividends and preferences in the event of the company's liquidation, vis a vis the ordinary shareholders in the company.[34]

Notwithstanding the existence of preferred shares, it is not always possible to distribute dividends in a company. The Companies Law determines mandatory obligations regarding the distribution of dividends,[35] according to which a company that wishes to distribute dividends (regardless of whether there are preferred shareholders in the company or not) must first meet two conditions (i) the distribution of dividends shall jeopardize the company's ability to meet its obligations when they come due ("the solvency test"); *and* (ii) the company has sufficient profits for distribution, as detailed and defined under the Companies law or the distribution was approved by the court.[36] These conditions are mandatory, and cannot be contracted out in any shareholders' agreement.

## II. Limitation on the transfer of shares

As a general matter, the Israeli Companies Law determines that each share issued in a company is transferable.[37] This reflects the legislature's presumption

---

**33** Section 190 of the Companies Law.

**34** With regard to public companies, as explained earlier, a company which registers its shares for trade in the stock exchange may only have one type of shares. However, a year after the company was first registered for trade the company may issue also preferred shares, which entitle their holders to a preference with regard to the distribution of dividends (See, HADARA BAR-MOR, COMPANIES LAW 202–203 (2007)).

**35** Section 1 of the Companies law (under the definition of distribution); Sections 302–303 of the Companies Law.

**36** Sections 302–303 of the Companies law.

**37** Section 293 of the Companies Law.

that a share is an asset in the possession of the shareholder, and as such it may be transferred according to the shareholders' free will. The transferability of the shares allows shareholders to sell their shares to third parties, and thereby to realize their investment in the company.[38]

Nevertheless, the provision of the Companies Law determining that the shares are transferrable is subject to any agreement to the contrary between the shareholders. Section 294 of the Companies Law allows the company to determine limitations on the transferability of shares in the company, and shareholders in privately held companies often impose such restrictions.[39] Detailed herein is a summary of the sorts of provisions limiting the transfer of shares in a company, which are prevalent in shareholders' agreements and enforced in Israel.

### 1. Right of First Refusal.

The right of first refusal is common in shareholders' agreements. The purpose of the first refusal provisions is to prevent the entry of external and unwanted partners into the company, and allow the existing shareholders to increase their holding in the company if they wish to.[40]

Under a right of first refusal mechanism, a shareholder who wishes to sell his shares in a company is obligated to first turn to the rest of the shareholders in the company, and offer them to purchase his shares. Only after the other shareholders decline the offer to purchase the shares, the seller shareholder may make an offer to a third party according to the conditions determined in the first refusal mechanism in the agreement. Usually, a shareholder asking to transfer his shares is obligated to notify the rest of his partner shareholders and inform the other shareholders of the identity of the potential purchaser (in order to allow the other shareholders to prevent the entrance of any unwanted new business partners) and following the receipt of the offer from the poten-

**38** Joseph Gross, Yechial Bahat and Irit Haviv Segal assert that the possessional character of the ownership of shares is realized by the shareholder's liberty to use the shares, according to his discretion, which reflects a fundamental principle of the corporation of a company (together with the principle of the limitation of liability). See, Supra note 1, at 316, 487; Supra note 9, at 787–788 (the tenth edition, 2008); Supra note 5, at 155.

**39** Zipora Cohen, Company Shareholders – Causes of Action and Remedies, 279–283 (2008); the Supreme Court, Civil Appeal 6205/98 **Unger *Versus* Ofer** (Rendered on 15 July, 2001).

**40** Eyal Raz and Israel Shapiro, *The Revocability of an Offer Rendered within the Exercise of the Right of First Refusal in the Business Arena,* Corporations Vol. 9(2) 78 (2012).

tial purchaser, each of the shareholders shall have an exclusive and irrevocable right to purchase the transferred shares.[41]

A transaction made not according to the agreed upon mechanism in the shareholders' agreements (or Articles of Association, as the case may be) will have no legal effect; In Civil Case 44733–09–11,[42] the District Court determined that the right of first refusal applies to every sort of transfer of shares, whether in the manner of the sale of shares in actual fact or, as in this specific case, the sale of rights for shares deriving from convertible loans (loans which may be, under certain conditions, converted into shares of the company). The Supreme Court, in a decision rendered on August 2015,[43] supported the legal result in the District Court's ruling with regard to the wide interpretation of the first refusal right and its appliance on any transfer of any sort of rights to shares.

### 2. "Tag Along"("Co-Sale")

"Tag-Along" provisions provide a way to guarantee the Minority's right to participate in special and exceptional business opportunities of the majority shareholders. Minority shareholders fear a situation in which the majority shall realize a business opportunity, such as a merger, acquisition or IPO (i.e., some sort of "Exit") without including the minority therein. The "Tag Along" provisions, therefore, enable the minority to participate in any event by which an external purchaser or an existing shareholder asks to purchase a controlling part in the company.[44]

### 3. "Bring- Along" ("Drag-Along").

The "Bring-Along" provisions allow the majority shareholders to force the rest of the shareholders (the minority) to join the majority in a transaction for the sale of the entire issued and outstanding share capital of the company. This occurs when a purchaser conditions the acquisition of the company with purchasing the whole of the company's share capital. These provisions are intended to pre-

---

**41** Id.
**42** Civil Case 44733–09–11 *Erez Cochva Holdings (1999) Ltd. and others Versus Key Vesting Ltd.* (Rendered by the District Court of Tel-Aviv, the Economic Division, on 25.06.2013).
**43** Civil Appeal 6437/13 *Erez Cochva Holdings (1999) Ltd. and others Versus Key Vesting Ltd.* (Rendered on 02.08.2015).
**44** Supra note 5, at 213.

vent the minority shareholders from preventing the sale of the company (by using any voting rights they may have). The customary provision determines that when the holders of a certain percentage in the company (usually between 70–80%) are interested in selling their share in the company to a third party, they will be entitled to require the rest of the shareholders to join the sale under the same terms according to which the majority shareholders are selling their shares.

"Bring along" provisions are enforced in Israel, and the Companies Law even contain resembling provisions. With respect to private companies, sections 341–342 enable a forced sale of the minority's shares, in the event there is a majority of 80% of the shareholders who wish to sell their shares. The Law in this case allows shareholders to opt-out of this mechanism – deny the "Bring Along" mechanism altogether or determine a different mechanism (for example, determining a different majority) – which parties often do. With respect to public companies, sections 336–340 of the Companies Law determine that any sale to a third part of more than 90% of the shares of the company should be made by a tender offer to all of the shareholders and require minority shareholders to sell their shares in case 95% of the shareholders consented to the tender offer.

### 4. No-Sale Provisions.

No-Sale provisions are usually intended to make sure that the founders of the company do not sell their shares for a certain period of time, as their knowledge and acquaintance with the company's core capabilities is essential, at least for an initial starting period. This provision is usually requested by investors (e.g., in the framework of rounds of investment) and according to which, without their approval, the founders are not permitted to sell their shares in the company for a defined period of time, out of the notion that the founders are the core essence of the company and its product.

The limitation of time may range between a few months and a few years, depending of the circumstances surrounding the investment. In some cases, the limitation is gradual, and each set period of time, the founder is allowed to sell a defined part of his shares in the company.

## III. The Constitution and Management of the Corporation

### 1. Agreements for the Appointment of Directors.

One of the common agreements between shareholders is an agreement for cooperating with regard to the appointment of directors. In many cases the major shareholders agree on a certain key for the appointment of directors in the company, according to which the holding of a defined part of the company's share capital shall grant its owners the right to recommend the appointment of one or more directors.[45] Minority shareholders in private companies may also sometimes reserve their right to appoint a representative on their behalf to the board. Such agreement is usually due to the fact that the minority shareholder invested in the company, and wants to ensure his participation in the company's management, or in case the minority shareholder has special knowledge and expertise in matters relating to the company's activities.[46]

In some companies, the right to appoint directors is set forth in the company's AoA. Once such a right is determined in the AoA – the parties are not dependent on one another's votes in order to exercise their right for the appointment of directors on their behalf.[47] However, the determination of the shareholders' right to appoint directors in the company according to the shareholders' names may be considered as the creation of different share types in the company. This may be problematic for companies who wish to be listed in the stock exchange for public trading (i.e., to issue an IPO – Initial Public Offering), as public companies are only allowed to have one class of shares.[48]

### 2. The Funding of the Company.

For many shareholders it is important to regulate in the agreement the manner through which the company's operations will be funded during the lifetime of the company. There are a few ways to fund the company's activities and many shareholde's agreements include provisions regulating the shareholders' consent regarding this issue.

Shareholder loans are a relatively simple way to raise funds and finance the operations of the company. They are usually determined according to the *pro-*

---

**45** Amir Wasserman, Moty Yamin, Corporations and Securities 626 (2006)

**46** Id, at 628.

**47** Id, at 628.

**48** CA 6041/15 *Ha'ama Ltd. v. Muler* (Rendered on25 September 2016);

*rata* share of each shareholder in the share capital of the company, detailing the financial terms of the loans (e.g., the bearing interest, if applicable) and including the dates or other time frames or milestones regarding the return of the loans to the lending shareholder. This tool is usually arranged in separate shareholder loan agreements, executed between the shareholders and the company in addition to the shareholders' agreements.

An additional method is the raising of funds in consideration for shares in the company. Usually, however, when the company decides to raise funds through equity, the portion of the share capital of each of the shareholders who is not interested in investing additional funds in the company is diluted, and as a result their controlling power in the company is reduced. In this respect, many investors, especially sophisticated ones, and most commonly in the High-Tech industry (such as venture capital funds), insist on including anti-dilution provisions. In Ha'ama Ltd. *Versus* Orna Muler ("**Ha'ama**")[49], a ruling which will be discussed further on, the Supreme Court discusses whether an anti-dilution protection stipulated in a founder's agreement may bring to the cancelation of the company's resolutions and actions, which diluted the holdings of the "protected" shareholder, notwithstanding the protection provided thereto by an Anti-Dilution provision. The ruling determines that the court may refuse to enforce Anti-Dilution agreements which undermine the benefit of the company or which are not in good faith or which are used as an extortion instrument by the "protected shareholder" in his relations *vis a vis* the company.

### 3. Confidentiality; Intellectual Property; Non-Competition

It is also common practice to include Confidentiality, Non-Compete provisions and provisions regarding intellectual property of the company.

Confidentiality provisions prohibit the shareholders from disclosing any confidential information with regard to the company's business (as such term is defined under the specific agreement) – both during the period the person is a shareholder in the company and for a certain number of months or years thereafter (or, in many cases, indefinitely). Intellectual Property provisions include provisions according to which any and all intellectual property created by or in favor of the company – shall remain, at all times, the sole property of the company and the shareholder is banned from making any use or sale

---

49 *Id.*; Tomer Reif, *Diluting the Anti-Dilution Protection*, at http://www.globes.co.il/news/article.aspx?did=1001161447.

thereof– whatsoever– without the company's explicit consent. In Non-Competition provisions, shareholders undertake not to compete with the company or the company's business during their position as shareholders in the company and for certain duration of time (as agreed) thereafter.

## IV. Insolvency Situations

### 1. Pre-Insolvency

Shareholders in Israel may not contractually avert bankruptcy. The legal conditions for filing for bankruptcy are mandatory, and shareholders cannot prohibit the company, the shareholders or the creditors from filing when the conditions prescribed by the law are met.

### 2. Post-Insolvency Liquidation Preferences

Shareholder's agreements, however, can affect post-bankruptcy distributions to shareholders. In *private* companies, the parties may agree on liquidation preferences, which determine the priority among shareholders in case bankruptcy dividends are distributed (naturally, only in the rare cases the property of the bankruptcy estate is sufficient to afford such distributions to shareholders). These provisions usually result from the requirement of investors joining the company which wish to receive priority upon the distribution of funds in the event of the company's liquidation ("True Liquidation") or sale ("Deemed Liquidation").

This protection is usually granted by the issuance of preferred shares to the investors. There may be a few types of shares and the liquidation preference provisions stipulate the order of priorities amongst the different share types (i.e., who receives the proceeds first, second, third and so on, according to the amount of share types).

# D. Legal effects of Shareholders' Agreements

## I. Legal Effect on the Corporation:

The Supreme Court has lately determined, in Ha'ama Ltd. *Versus* Orna Muler,[50] that a company shall not be bound by a founders' agreement to which it is not a party. The court explained that the law does not acknowledge the legal obligation of a contract towards a company, when the company is not a party to such agreement and it did not ratify the agreement retroactively. The court clarified that even in cases where such founder's agreements were made between all of the company's founders, the company is not subject thereto.

According to the decision, a shareholder who sees himself adversely affected by a company's action, which contradicts an agreement made between such shareholder and another shareholder, cannot, on the basis of such agreement, invalidate the action lawfully made by the company's organs. Thus, with respect to the protection from the dilution – the subject matter of the case – it was decided that the injured shareholder may submit a law suit against the other shareholders (on the basis of contract law) – *i.e.*, the other parties to the agreement prohibiting the dilution of such shareholder – but the share issuance itself is not prohibited.

The court decision sets forth two ways to bind the company to a shareholders' agreement (in ways other than amending the AoA). The first, relevant only to private companies and to shareholders' agreements executed ***after*** the founding of the company, is a unanimous agreement between all shareholders of the company.[51] The second, relevant to all shareholders' agreements and to all types of companies – is the ratification, retroactively, of the agreement – even agreements entered into prior to the company's founding.[52]

---

**50** *Id.*

**51** See Section 76 to the Companies Law.

**52** The honorable judge Solberg determined, in a dissenting opinion, that in the event that the parties to the founders agreement are the only shareholders in the company and there are no third parties which may be adversely effected from the applicable matter agreed under the founders agreement, it is possible to bind the company with such consent, even without the explicit approval thereof (as required according to the majority opinion in the case and stipulated above). The honorable judge Solberg emphasized that specific conditions must be met in order for this to apply and which are composed of: (i) the full identity between the shareholders of the company at the current time and the shareholders who were parties to the consent; (ii) the consent which is to bind the company shall not have any adverse effect on any third party; and (iii)

## II. Legal Effect on Shareholders:

### 1. The assignment of a shareholders' agreement

Israeli contract laws allow the assignment of contracts to third parties, and shareholders' agreements are no exception.[53] The law, however, differentiates between the assignment of rights and the assignment of obligations. According to the Assignment of Obligations Law 1969, a right vis-à-vis a debtor is assignable with no need for the consent of the debtor,[54] whereas an assignment of an obligation towards a creditor is assignable only if the creditor consented to the assignment.[55] This means that if the shareholders' agreement contains obligations towards the other shareholders party to the agreement, their consent to the assignment of such obligation is needed. In addition, a frequently found clause in Shareholder Agreements is an Anti-Assignment clause. Such clauses prohibit the assignment of the agreement, unless all parties to the agreement gave their consent. If an anti-assignment clause exists, a shareholder cannot assign the contract, or any of the shareholders' rights thereof.

### 2. Capital Markets Obligations triggered by shareholders' agreements:

Israeli corporate laws, in particular in the case of public companies, contain various obligations that are triggered when a shareholders' holdings in a corporation reaches a certain percentage. These include, inter-alia, reporting duties, approval procedures in the general assembly,[56] obligations concerning tender offers and more.[57] It is, therefore, important to know when two different shareholders should be regarded as "holding in concert", and their holdings in the company should be counted together (as if they are one shareholder).

According to the Israeli Securities Law – 1968, holding in concert occurs when the holding of securities or their acquisition is done pursuant to an agreement for cooperation among the shareholders, which is made either in writing or

---

such consent shall not undermine the company and/or have any adverse effect on it, in any way, and shall adhere to the objectives of the Companies Law.

**53** Sections 1 and 6 of the Assignment of Obligations Law, 1969.

**54** Section 1 to the Assignment of Obligations Law 1969

**55** Section 6 to the Assignment of Obligations Law 1969

**56** Criminal Appeal 3891/04 *Arad Investments and Industry Development Ltd. v. The State of Israel* P.D Vol. 60(1) 294.

**57** Supra note 45, at 625.

orally.[58] The Supreme Court, however, recently made clear that not all shareholders' agreements will trigger the Securities Law condition for holding in concert, and that neither the law nor the courts have established clear guidelines as to the strength of the cooperation required to constitute such holding.[59] The court explained that the question of holding in concert requires both a factual and a legal inquiry, and such inquiry is made on a case by case basis. Clearly, though, to the extent the shareholders have a voting agreement, which requires them to vote together or to coordinate their votes, they will be considered as holding in concert, at least in those matters when their voting is agreed upon, and their holding will be counted together for the purposes of corporate laws obligations.

Moreover, the position of Israel's Securities Authorities is that unless there are special circumstances and significant evidence that prove otherwise – an agreement between shareholders for the appointment of directors shall deem such shareholders as holding in concert.[60]

### 3. The disclosure of shareholders' agreements

There is no general obligation to register shareholders' agreements (as opposed to the AoA) with the companies' registrar or to publish them. However, if the company is public, and depending on the content of the shareholders' agreement, there may be an obligation to disclose the Agreement pursuant to certain provisions of the Securities Laws.

### 4. The shareholders' ability to deviate from the Company Law.

As explained earlier, the fundamental viewpoint that governs the Companies Law is the one which favors the autonomy of the individual will. This means that the shareholders are free to design the nature and content of the incorporation, and they may contract out of many of the Companies' Law provisions. However, there are provisions in the Companies Law which are cogent, *i.e.*, they are binding upon incorporating parties and it is impossible to stipulate otherwise[61].

---

**58** Section 1 of the Securities Laws

**59** C.A 4154/14 *Hatzlaha" the consumer movement for society progress v. David Cohen* (Rendered on in 16.5.2017).

**60** Supra note 45, at 627.

**61** *Supra note* 2.

Most of the mandatory provisions apply to publicly traded companies, but some apply also to private ones.

Cogent provisions usually pertain to the Law's solutions to the agency problems generated by the incorporation or to the fundamental principles of corporate law. Examples for such cogent provisions are the obligation of a publicly traded company to appoint an oversight committee[62], and the stipulation that insurance and indemnification of officers and directors in the company with respect to breach of their fiduciary duty shall not be valid, unless provided in accordance with and subject to the provisions of the Companies Law[63]. Examples for issues regulated under the Companies Law as dispositive provisions are the majority needed for the amendment of the AoA[64], the timing for issuing invitations to the general meeting of the shareholders[65], and the requirement of the approval by the board of directors for a transaction between the company and one of its officers.[66]

## III. Consequences of a Breach of the Shareholders' Agreement:

As explained in section 2.1 above, a company's decision in violation of a shareholders' agreement (to which the Company is not a party) is binding and enforceable. The decision is not invalidated due to the violation of the Agreement, and the company cannot be deemed to be in breach of an Agreement to which it is not party.

A shareholder injured by a breach of a shareholders' agreement, however, does have a good claim against the breaching shareholder. The claim stems from the relationship between the shareholders party to the agreement, and not between the injured shareholder and the company. Correspondingly, the awarded remedy does not involve the company, only the shareholders themselves

62 Section 114 of the Companies Law.
63 Section 264 of the Companies Law.
64 Section 20 of the Companies Law.
65 Section 67 of the Companies Law.
66 Section 271 of the Companies Law.

# E. Enforcement

## I. Enforcement Mechanisms

Since shareholders' agreements are regular contracts, the way they are enforced is similar to any other contract. The injured party may go to court and ask for injunction, specific enforcement, damages or any other contractual (civil) remedies.

However, with respect to shareholders' agreements, a common remedy, either stipulated in the Agreement or mandated by the court is the buy-out.[67] Pursuant to the "Buy-Out" mechanism, under certain conditions or events the minority has the right to be "Bought Out" by the Majority, under terms and conditions set forth in advance. This "buy-out" mechanism allows the minority to "exit" an investment in case of unresolvable dispute with the majority,[68] and it relieves the majority's concern that it will not be able to exercise its control.

Another common solution in case of disputes is the "Buy Me, Buy You" mechanism ("**BMBY**"). The BMBY mechanism provides each of the disputed shareholders with the opportunity to either "Buy Out" or to be "Bought Out" by the opposing party.[69] Usually, in case both parties wish to buy out the other, the shareholder with the highest bid wins. This mechanism was recently used by the District Court in order to resolve a dispute between two shareholders, which both held an equal share in a private company.[70] The court provided detailed instructions to the company, according to which, within 14 days of the ruling, the BMBY proposal will be sent and within 14 days of the acceptance of the BMBY proposal, the proposed shareholder shall notify the proposing shareholder whether it elects to sell his shares in the company for such amount, or purchase the shares from the proposing shareholder for the same proposed price per share.

---

**67** Section 191 of the Companies Law determines that in any case of deprivation or fear of deprivation of the company's shareholders or any part of them, the court may provide instructions for the avoidance or removal of the deprivation, including with regard to the provision of instructions to the shareholders with regard to the management of the company or the purchase of shares in the company by one shareholder of the others. Courts take advantage of this section to order the buy-out of a certain shareholder in company, especially in cases of unresolvable disputes.

**68** Supra note 5 at 629.

**69** Id, at 214.

**70** Civil Case 16585–12–14 *Raichman v. Ulansky and Others* (Rendered on 07.02.2017).

## II. Alternative Dispute Resolutions

Arbitration or Mediation clauses are many times stipulated in shareholders' agreements. The identity of the arbitrator or mediator may be agreed between the parties in advance and stipulated in the agreement; alternatively, it could be stipulated that the parties will agree on the identity of the arbitrator or mediator within a certain amount of days. In Arbitration clauses it is usually stipulated that if the identity of the arbitrator is not agreed on between the shareholders within a certain amount of time, then the arbitrator shall be appointed by the Israeli Bar Association. It is also possible to determine that the arbitrator shall have certain expertise or qualification, according to the company's field of business or nature of the dispute, such as an engineer, attorney or accountant. [71]

It is common to determine that in any case of a dispute between the shareholders, they shall first try to resolve such dispute by a Mediation process, which shall assist the parties in order to reach an agreement. If after a certain amount time since mediation process commenced the parties do not reach an agreement, they can turn, either to Arbitration, or to the courts, as agreed in the shareholders' agreement.

**71** Arbitration Motion 32154–09–12 Poznanski v. Almond Investments Luxembourg S.A.R.L. (Rendered by the District Court of Tel Aviv on 17 March 2013).

Corrado Malberti

# Italy

## Table of Content



---


**Prof. Dr. Corrado Malberti** (LL.M. Chicago) and Professor of Commercial Law, University of Trento.



https://doi.org/10.1515/9783110517026-018

## A. Introduction

This chapter examines the rules governing shareholders' agreements in Italian law. After an introduction on the relationship between shareholders' agreements and company law (Part B), and a short description of the historical evolution of the legal framework for these arrangements in Italy (Part C), I present the principal sets of rules devoted to these contracts in this jurisdiction (Part D). More specifically, the rules governing shareholders' agreements can be divided into two different sets: one devoted to listed companies, and the other to public companies whose shares are not listed. In addition, I examine another distinction in Italian law between two different groups of companies whose shares are not listed, since some provisions are applicable to all public companies, whereas others are relevant only for companies that resort to capital markets. For all these companies, I investigate the rules governing the scope, disclosure and duration of shareholders' agreements. Moreover, I examine the sanctions resulting from violations of these rules.

Afterwards, in Part E, I examine the typical content of shareholders' agreements in Italy, and I present the issues raised by shareholders' agreements on voting rights and by those that introduce limitations on the right to transfer shares. Then, in Part F, I investigate the delicate issue of the more limited effects of shareholders' agreements, in particular compared to the effects of bylaws provisions. Part G concludes this chapter.

## B. Relationship between Shareholders' Agreements and Company Law

Until the enactment of Legislative Decree No. 6/2003 (hereinafter the Reform of Company Law of 2003 or the 2003 Reform), Italian company law was characterised by a somewhat limited degree of flexibility, and mandatory law played a central role. This approach changed partially with the 2003 Reform, which broadly promoted party autonomy for both public and private limited liability companies.[1]

---

1 On the role of party autonomy in the 2003 Reform see, for example, *Malberti/Ghezzi/Ventoruzzo* Comment on Article 2380 in F. Ghezzi (a cura di), Amministratori, in P. Marchetti et al. (diretto da) Commentario alla riforma del diritto societario, Giuffrè-Egea, Milano, 2005, p. 3 ff., at p. 30 ff.

While the scope of party autonomy has increased over the years, in practice many mandatory rules still exist in Italian company law. For example, the rules governing general meetings – such as the majority principle and the rules concerning the exercise of voting rights – cannot be freely amended,[2] even though the possibility of modifying majority thresholds or of issuing shares without, with limited, or with multiple voting rights grants a certain degree of freedom to shareholders in determining the majorities within a corporate body.

Another example of a mandatory provision that still characterises Italian company law is the prohibition of the so-called "patti leonini" (i.e. leonine partnerships), pursuant to Article 2265 of the Civil Code. This prohibition is applicable to all companies, and concerns all agreements whereby one or more shareholders are excluded from any sharing in the profits or losses of a company.[3]

Nevertheless, the limits and prohibitions mandated by company law, examined in the perspective of shareholders' agreements, would not be directly applicable to arrangements that are not incorporated in bylaws, since Article 1322 of the Civil Code recognises party autonomy in contracts. Therefore, one rationale for concluding shareholders' agreements can certainly be to ensure the validity of arrangements that, if included in bylaws, would be invalid.

Nor does the Civil Code give the parties to a shareholders' agreement absolute freedom to draft contractual terms that would violate company law. In fact, Article 1322 of the Civil Code must be examined in combination with Article 1344 of the Civil Code, which states that the cause of a contract is deemed illicit when the contract is a means to avoid the application of a mandatory provision.[4] The interplay between these two Civil Code provisions may be problematic, in particular in assessing to what extent a shareholders' agreement can be considered a means to avoid the application of mandatory company law provisions.

In this context, the two examples mentioned above – namely the arrangements on the exercise of voting rights and those on the exclusion of one or more shareholders from any profits or losses – have given rise to doctrinal dis-

---

**2** On the limits on party autonomy in company law after the 2003 Reform see, for example, *Notari* Le categorie speciali di azioni, in P. Abbadessa – G.B. Portale (diretto da), Il nuovo diritto societario. *Liber amicorum Gian Franco Campobasso*, Utet, Assago, 2006, vol. 1, p. 593 ff., at p. 610 ff.

**3** For a general overview of the role of the prohibition on the "patti leonini" see *Guidotti* Comment on Article 2265 in A. Maffei Alberti (diretto da), Commentario breve al diritto delle società, Cedam, Assago, 2017, 4th ed., p. 84 ff.

**4** See, for example, *Libertini* Limiti di validità dei patti parasociali, Rules Paper No. 2013–7, available at http://www.bafficarefin.unibocconi.it/wps/wcm/connect/9a5cf261-8958-43aa-8bdf-9ffe5cbb1ef0/libertini.pdf?MOD=AJPERES, visited on 7 August 2017, p. 18 ff., who also provides a detailed account of the other causes of invalidity of shareholders' agreements.

cussions[5] and abundant jurisprudence[6] that have evaluated case by case to what extent the same results that could not be achieved with a bylaws provisions were actually achieved with a shareholders' agreement. In that perspective, compared with bylaws provisions, the more limited the effects of a shareholders' agreement are, the more likely it will not be considered a means to avoid the application of mandatory provisions or to achieve other prohibited goals.[7] As we will see in the following pages, this is probably also the reason why the problem of the – more limited – effects of shareholders' agreements, compared with bylaws provisions, plays an important role in Italian company law.[8]

## C. Evolution of the Legal Framework for Shareholders' Agreements

### I. The Initial Approach of the 1942 Civil Code

Before the enactment of the Civil Code in 1942, the validity of shareholders' agreements was debated, and several court decisions declared arrangements concerning the exercise of voting rights to be inadmissible.[9] In the wake of this debate, the drafters of the 1942 Civil Code were well aware of the role shareholders' agreements may play for public companies; however, they preferred not to enact a specific regulation on this matter. The rationale for this choice is documented in the Explanatory Memorandum of the Civil Code, which, in a paragraph detailing the rules governing general meetings, acknowledged that the *"multiplicity of situations that would have had to be taken into account advised against an intervention on shareholders' agreements."*[10] The Explanatory Memo-

5 Cf., for example, infra n. 19, and the accompanying text.

6 In particular, on the exclusion of one or more shareholders from any participation in the profits or losses, see *Selleri* Comment on Article 2341-*bis*, in A. Maffei Alberti (diretto da), Commentario breve al diritto delle società, Cedam, Assago, 2017, 4th ed., p. 295 ff., at p. 298.

7 See Cass. civ., sez. I, 20 September, 1995, No. 9975, which clearly distinguishes between the obligations arising from shareholders' agreements and those deriving from company law.

8 Infra F.

9 See for example, Cass. civ., sez. I, 13 January 1932; Cass. civ., sez. I, 1 May 1934; Cass. civ., sez. I, 3 March, 1938, No. 706. Among the legal scholars, see *Vivante* Trattato di diritto commerciale. Le società commerciali, Vallardi, Milano, 1929, 5th ed., vol. II, p. 231, who argues that a shareholder may not validly bind himself to vote according to someone else's indications, since he must participate in the formation of the resolution of the general meeting with his free vote.

10 Relazione del Ministro Guardasigilli al Codice Civile, No. 972.

randum highlighted that, at that time, both the jurisprudence and the legal scholarship were debating shareholders' agreements.[11] In addition, this document also mentioned two different categories of shareholders' agreements; namely, those created to defend the shareholding structure of the company, and those concerning the exercise of voting rights.[12] Interestingly, the Explanatory Memorandum also stressed that the discussions on the admissibility of these arrangements principally concerned agreements on the exercise of voting rights.[13]

Apparently, the choice of not providing a specific regulation for shareholders' agreements was motivated by the difficulties in providing ex-ante a specific set of rules that would have been appropriate in all situations.[14] Therefore, it was considered preferable to leave it up to judges to evaluate the merits of these agreements.[15] Yet, with regard specifically to the shareholders' agreements concerning the exercise of voting rights in general meetings, the Explanatory Memorandum also said that some guidance to assess these arrangements could be found in the rules that restricted the exercise of voting rights in cases of conflict of interest.[16]

Even at this early stage of the evolution of the legal framework for shareholders' agreements, it is interesting to highlight the relevance these arrangements already had in the drafting of the 1942 Civil Code. It is also worth noting that, at that time already, the Explanatory Memorandum raised the question of the admissibility of shareholders' agreements on the exercise of voting rights.

## II. Evolution of the Legal Framework for Shareholders' Agreements up to Legislative Decree No. 58/1998

After the enactment of the 1942 Civil Code, the evolution of the legal framework for shareholders' agreements was mainly driven by jurisprudence,[17] and the ad-

---

**11** Id.
**12** Id.
**13** Id.
**14** Id.
**15** Id.
**16** Id.
**17** For example, as *Ascarelli* Limiti di validità dei sindacati azionari, in Foro. it., I, c. 175 ff., noted, Cass. civ., sez. I, 31 July 1949, No. 2079, provided some opening to the admissibility of shareholders' agreements on the exercise of voting rights, moving in the directions indicated by the Relazione del Ministro Guardasigilli al Codice Civile. Afterwards, Cass. civ., sez. I, 5 July 1958, No. 2422, made clear that, in fact, it was the possible conflict of interest between

missibility of many arrangements remained uncertain.[18] In particular, legal scholars debated the validity of agreements concerning the exercise of voting rights in which decisions were not taken unanimously but by a majority vote of participants.[19] These doubts were finally dispelled by a 1995 decision of the Cassazione that admitted the validity of these arrangements.[20]

In any case, the legislation enacted in the second half of the 20th century at least acknowledged the existence of shareholders' agreements, and some special laws even included specific provisions to regulate them. For example, Article 2 of the Law No. 416/1981 on publishing companies required the disclosure of shareholders' agreements that enabled the exercise of control on certain publishing companies. Reference to shareholders' agreements was also made by Article 27 of the Law No. 287/1990 (Competition Law), and by several other laws devoted to regulated industries. Interestingly, with regard to listed companies, Article 5-*bis* of Law No. 216/1976, which was introduced by Legislative Decree No. 90/1992, mentioned voting agreements and, under certain circumstances, also mandated their disclosure.[21]

## III. Enactment of the First Comprehensive Set of Rules on Shareholders' Agreements in Legislative Decree No. 58/1998

In this context that already recognised the existence of shareholders' agreements, even when concerning the exercise of voting rights, and admitted their validity, Legislative Decree No. 58/1998 (hereinafter the Consolidated Law on Finance or CLF) enacted the first comprehensive set of provisions on shareholders'

---

the company and the shareholders that could invalidate these agreements, even if, in a following decision (Cass. civ., sez. I, 25 January 1965, No. 136), it was also acknowledged that the risk of a conflict of interest was not the only grounds on which the validity of shareholders agreements could be challenged.

**18** Legal scholars, however, started examining shareholders' agreements. Among them, particular attention should be given to the seminal work of *Oppo*, who, in an Italy torn by the Second World War, published his research with two different titles: *Oppo* Contratti Parasociali, Milano, 1942; *Id.* Negozi parasociali, Milano, 1942.

**19** For a comprehensive analysis of the debate, see *Rescio* I sindacati di voto, in G.E. Colombo – G.B. Portale (diretto da), Trattato delle società per azioni. Assemblea, Utet, Torino 1994, vol. 3*, p. 485 ff., at p. 599 ff.

**20** Cass. civ., sez. I, 20 September, 1995, No. 9975.

**21** Cf. Cass. civ., sez. I, 20 September, 1995, No. 9975, which provides a catalogue of the legislation that, at that time, openly made reference to shareholders' agreements.

agreements. The scope of these rules, as in general that of the rules concerning public companies provided by the Consolidated Law on Finance, was limited to listed companies. However, as would be the case for other provisions of this legislation, the solutions adopted for shareholders' agreements in those companies would become a source of inspiration for the more general reform of company law that would be enacted in 2003.

The Consolidated Law on Finance recognised the general admissibility of shareholders' agreements for all listed companies, and it imposed certain obligations on shareholders that were parties to these agreements. To counter the criticisms of shareholders' agreements concerning voting rights, which were feared to be used as a tool to distort the governance of companies, particular emphasis was – again – given to the rules concerning the disclosure of such agreements.[22]

In addition, to avoid the risk that shareholders' agreements would be used to entrench shareholders and also limit the beneficial dynamics of the market for corporate control, the maximum duration of such agreements was limited. Moreover, a right of withdrawal from shareholders' agreements was given to the shareholders that wanted to tender their shares to offerors that made public offers to acquire the control of a company. This rule can be considered an antecedent of the EU's breakthrough rule.[23]

Without adding further comments on the legislation enacted in 1998, which will be examined in greater detail in its current wording in the next few pages, it is worth mentioning that the principal legal sanction for a violation of the rules on the disclosure of shareholders' agreements was to consider such agreements null and void. This sanction created several problems of interpretation and represented one of the most problematic aspects of the rules provided for listed companies by Legislative Decree No. 58/1998.[24]

In conclusion, the Consolidated Law on Finance was a decisive step in the evolution of the legal framework for shareholders' agreements. The fact that the scope of this legislation was limited to listed companies does not lessen

---

**22** For an overview of the state of development of the debate on shareholders' agreements at the time of the enactment of the Consolidated Law on Finance, see *Costi* I patti parasociali, in F. Bonelli et al. (a cura di), La riforma delle società quotate, Giuffrè, Milano, 1998, p. 113 ff.
**23** Cf. Article 11 of Directive 2004/25/EC.
**24** See *Costi* (n. 22), p. 126 ff., who provides an outline of the possible benefits of this sanction. However, see also *Macrì* Comment on Articles 122–123, in P. Abbadessa – G.B. Portale (diretto da), Le società per azioni. Codice civile e norme complementari, Giuffrè, Milano, 2016, t. II, p. 3842 ff., at p. 3864 ff., who today examines the challenging doctrinal implications of this sanction.

the importance of this legislation, which laid the groundwork for future changes in the legal framework for these agreements.

## IV. The 2003 Company Law Reform

In the years that followed the enactment of the Consolidated Law on Finance, the admissibility of shareholders' agreements was widely recognised even though legal scholarship maintained a somewhat more cautious approach.[25] The opportunity to extend the legislation in force for listed companies to all public companies (i.e. the *società per azioni* or s.p.a.) finally came with the broader reform of Italian company law enacted in 2003.

As has already been said, the approach adopted by the 2003 Reform was largely inspired by the solutions provided by Legislative Decree No. 58/1998, even though shareholders' agreements play a fairly different role in listed companies than in closely-held companies. In particular, the 2003 Reform provided a regulation on the duration of agreements and their disclosure. Interestingly, with regard to sanctions, the approach of the Consolidated Law on Finance, which considered undisclosed shareholders' agreements to be invalid, was not replicated in the Civil Code.

Probably the most interesting aspect of the Civil Code provisions on shareholders' agreements, apart from the definitive recognition of their admissibility for all public companies, concerned a more general aspect of the 2003 Reform, namely, the distinction made between three different categories of public companies: (a) those that are closely held, (b) those that resort to capital markets,[26] and

25 *Campobasso* Diritto commerciale. 2. Diritto delle società, Utet, Torino, 2001, 4th ed., p. 330 ff., who, a few years after the enactment of the Consolidated Law on Finance, provided a detailed account of the positions of legal scholars on this point.

26 The distinction between closely-held companies and companies that resort to capital markets is quite technical, and derives from the interplay between several provisions, namely, Article 2325-*bis* of the Civil Code, Article 111-*bis* of the Implementing and Transitory Provisions of the Civil Code, Article 116 of the Consolidated Law on Finance, and Article 2-*bis* of Consob Regulation No. 11971. These provisions only provide the criteria for determining whether a company resorts to capital markets, and the non-listed companies not falling in the scope of these criteria may be considered – at least for the purposes of this chapter – closely held. According to Article 2-bis of Consob Regulation No. 11971, a company resorts to capital markets if, jointly, (a) it has "different shareholders to the majority shareholders accounting for more than five hundred, overall holding at least 5% of the share capital"; and (b) it is not "eligible to draw up simplified annual financial statements under the first paragraph of Article 2435-bis of the Civil Code." However, these limits are considered to have been exceeded only if the shares, alternatively, (a) "have

(c) those that are listed. The distinction among these three different categories was also reflected in the rules concerning shareholders' agreements: for companies with listed shares, the applicable rules remained those provided by the Consolidated Law on Finance, while for companies that resort to capital markets but are not listed, as well as for closely-held companies, the rules governing shareholders' agreements were provided by the Civil Code. Lastly, with regard to the last two groups of companies, the principal difference between the rules applicable to companies that resort to capital markets and those that are closely held concerned the disclosure of shareholders' agreements, which was mandated only for the former and not for the latter.[27]

## D. Rules and Principles Governing Shareholders' Agreements in Italian Law

Having considered the historical evolution of the legal framework for shareholders' agreements in Italian law, we can now turn to an analysis of the rules currently in force, starting with those for listed companies. The Consolidated Law on Finance devotes two provisions to shareholders' agreements, Articles 122 and 123, which have been amended several times since their initial enactment in 1998. In addition, specific sanctions for the violation of those articles are provided in Article 193 CLF.

been the subject of a public subscription offer and sale, or payment of an exchange tender offer"; (b) "have been the subject of placement, in any form such may have been implemented, also with regards to qualified investors only"; (c) "are or have been traded on multilateral trading systems with the consent of the issuer or controlling shareholder or have been admitted to trading on regulated markets and subsequently been revoked"; or (d) "are issued by banks and purchased or subscribed by their offices or dependencies."

27 For more details on this distinction, see *Sciuto* Comment on Article 2325-*bis*, in P. Abbadessa – G.B. Portale (diretto da), Le società per azioni. Codice civile e norme complementari, Giuffrè, Milano, 2016, t. I, p. 135 ff.

# I. Legal Framework for Shareholders' Agreements in Listed Companies

## 1. Scope of the Rules on Shareholders' Agreements in the Consolidated Law on Finance

An important aspect of the legal framework for shareholders' agreements in listed companies is that of determining what type of arrangements may fall within the scope of the rules of the Consolidated Law on Finance. In that perspective, paragraph 1 of Article 122 CFL states that the provisions on shareholders' agreements in listed companies are applicable to agreements, concluded in any form whatsoever, that concern *"the exercise of voting rights in companies with listed shares and the companies that control them."* In addition, paragraph 5 of Article 122 CFL further adds that these provisions may also apply to agreements that (a) *"create obligations of consultation prior to the exercise of voting rights in companies with listed shares or companies that control them"*; (b) *"set limits on the transfer of the related shares or of financial instruments that entitle holders to buy or subscribe them"*; (c) *"concern the purchase of shares or financial instruments"* that entitle holders to buy or subscribe them; (d) *"have as their object or effect the exercise, jointly or otherwise, of a dominant influence"* on companies with listed shares or those that control them; or (e) *"are aimed at encouraging or frustrating the goals of a public offer to buy or exchange, including commitments concerning the non-participation in the offer."*[28] It is important to highlight that shareholders' agreements may be relevant not only if they directly concern a listed company, but also if they are concluded with regard to the shares of a company that controls a listed company.

The agreements mentioned in Article 122 CFL encompass a wide range of situations. A preeminent role is certainly played by agreements concerning the exercise of voting rights; this is understandable considering the long debate on their admissibility. However, the scope of this provision is not limited to these agreements alone, but also extends to other arrangements that may be relevant for the governance of companies, such as consultation agreements and those agreements whose goal is to exert a dominant influence on the company.[29]

---

28 For more details on these agreements, see *Macrì* (n. 24), p. 3848 ff.

29 With regard to the agreements concerning the exercise of voting rights in listed companies, it is also important to highlight that the simple conclusion of a shareholders' agreement on these rights is not considered – per se – as an action in concert, nor does it trigger the obligation to make a mandatory offer if the relevant shareholding thresholds are jointly crossed by the par-

In addition to these arrangements, the rules of the Consolidated Law on Finance apply to agreements that limit the transfer of shares in view of stabilising or maintaining a given shareholding structure. Moreover, agreements concerning the possible acquisition of shares are also concerned, even if no plans have actually been made on the subsequent exercise of voting rights or on the exercise of a dominant influence on the listed company.[30]

The last category of shareholders' agreements – i.e. those aimed at encouraging or frustrating public offers to buy or exchange – was introduced in the wake of a controversial takeover bid in which such a shareholders' agreement was concluded: Article 4 of Legislative Decree No. 229 of 2007 clarified that these arrangements may also fall within the scope of Articles 122 and 123 CLF.[31]

## 2. Duration of Shareholders' Agreements

If an agreement falls within the scope of Article 122 CFL, shareholders are not free to determine its duration. If the parties opt for a fixed duration, it may not exceed three years, and if a longer duration is indicated, the agreement shall be deemed to have been concluded for three years. However, in any case, shareholders are free to renew the agreement for an unlimited number of times at each expiration.[32]

Shareholders may also decide to conclude an agreement for an indefinite period of time. If this is the case, each shareholder enjoys a right of withdrawal by giving a six-month notice, and the exercise of this right is subject to disclosure.

Shareholders can also exercise their right of withdrawal when a public offer to acquire the control of the company is made. In this case, for both fixed duration and indefinite duration agreements, shareholders who want to tender their shares to a public offer may exercise their right of withdrawal without any notice. We have already seen the possible rationale for this rule: to avoid shareholders' agreements being used to entrench the position of shareholders with negative re-

---

ticipants in the agreement, at least as long as no acquisition of shares is made: see, for example, *Costi* Il mercato mobiliare, Giappichelli, Torino, 2016, 10th ed., p. 95.

**30** Cf. *Macrì* (n. 24), p. 3856 f.

**31** *Id.*, p. 3857; *Costi* (n. 29), p. 311.

**32** Cf. *Macrì* (n. 24), p. 3870 f., who also examines the controversial issue of whether a clause providing for an automatic renewal of the agreement, in the absence of an explicit repudiation, would be admitted.

percussions for the market for corporate control.[33] Here it should just be added that this mini-breakthrough rule plays an important role for Italian listed companies, since traditionally these companies have widely used shareholders' agreements as a control enhancing mechanism.

## 3. Disclosure of Shareholders' Agreements

In addition to the time limitation and to the possibility to exercise a right of withdrawal, another important constraint imposed on parties to shareholders' agreements is the obligation to disclose such agreements.[34] According to paragraph 1 of Article 122 CFL, within five days from its conclusion, the agreement must be: (a) communicated to Consob (the Italian financial authority); (b) published in an abridged version in the daily press; (c) filed with the business register of the place where the company has its registered office; and (d) communicated to the listed company.[35] It should also be mentioned that, as noted in the previous paragraph, the exercise of the right of withdrawal is subject to disclosure, as well.

In addition to these obligations, according to Article 128 of Consob Regulation No. 11971, other relevant events concerning shareholders' agreements must be communicated to Consob. More specifically, this obligation concerns amendments to the agreements, changes in voting rights relative to shares and financial instruments assigning rights to purchase or subscribe shares as a whole or individually contributed to the agreements, and information on the renewal or dissolution of agreements.[36]

The disclosure rules are onerous for shareholders and they do not distinguish between agreements that have been concluded by majority or minority shareholders. For minority shareholders that are just trying to coordinate their efforts at the general meeting, it may be particularly costly to undertake the disclosure procedure. In addition, market participants may be less interested in

33 Cf. *Picciau* Comment on Article 123, in P. Marchetti – L.A. Bianchi (a cura di), La disciplina delle società quotate, Giuffrè, Milano, 1999, t. I, p. 895 ff., at p. 923 ff., who also provides a critical evaluation of this rationale in light of the wording of this article.

34 However, it is also worth noting that the validity of shareholders' agreements is not linked to a provision of the bylaws, nor does it depend on the approval of the general meeting.

35 On the disclosure of shareholders' agreements in listed companies, see *Macrì* (n. 24), p. 3863 f.

36 It should be mentioned that, even if shareholders' agreements are subject to disclosure, this is not the case for the decisions that are taken by the participants in these agreements.

knowing of the existence of agreements concerning a limited number of shares. For these reasons, an amendment to the Consolidated Law on Finance recently introduced a waiver for the obligation to disclose the agreements that concern shareholdings totalling less than 3% (or 5% for SMEs as defined in the CFL) of the shares of listed companies. Therefore, not all shareholders' agreements concerning listed companies must be published, but only those concerning holdings that would give rise to the disclosure obligations for crossing shareholding thresholds.[37]

## 4. Sanctions Provided by the Consolidated Law on Finance

According to paragraph 3 of Article 122 CLF, if a shareholders' agreement has not been duly disclosed, it is to be considered null and void. This sanction is problematic, since it can hardly be reconciled with the general rules of the Civil Code on the invalidity of contracts.[38]

In addition to the general invalidity of the agreement, paragraph 4 of Article 122 CLF provides an additional sanction: the voting rights attached to the listed shares included in the agreement may not be exercised. In any case, if a resolution is taken in spite of this prohibition, its validity may be challenged, and also Consob would have standing in that action.[39]

Lastly, it should also be mentioned that paragraph 2 ff., of Article 193 CLF provide administrative sanctions in the event of violations of the disclosure obligations of shareholder's agreements mandated by the Consolidated Law of Finance. These sanctions consist of either: (a) a public statement indicating the subject or the person responsible for the breach and the nature of the same, when it features "scarce offensiveness or danger" and the infringement in question has ceased; or (b) an order to eliminate the infringements charged, with possible indications of the measures to be adopted and the deadline for compliance, and to refrain from repeating the offence, when the "said infringements feature scarce offensiveness or danger"; or (c) when a legal entity is responsible, a financial administrative sanction ranging from €10,000 to €10 million, or up to five per cent of the turnover when that amount is more than €10 million and the turnover can be determined, or, when a natural person is responsible, a financial

37 *Macrì* (n. 24), p. 3862 f.
38 Cf. supra n. 24, and the accompanying text.
39 *Macrì* (n. 24), p. 3867 ff.

administrative sanction ranging from €10,000 to €2 million.[40] These sanctions are applicable also when the voting rights attached to the shares involved in an undisclosed shareholders' agreement have been exercised in violation of paragraph 4 of Article 122 CLF.

## II. Legal Framework for Shareholders' Agreements in Non-Listed Companies

The legal framework for shareholders' agreements provided by the Civil Code is not applicable to listed companies. This conclusion derives from the general principle that excludes the possibility for a general law such as the Civil Code – even if it is more recent – to amend special legislation such as that provided for listed companies by the Consolidated Law on Finance.[41] Even applying this general criterion, it might still be possible to argue that the legislation provided in the Civil Code is applicable to shareholders' agreements involving listed companies, at least insofar as that legislation is not directly pre-empted by the special rules provided by the Consolidated Law on Finance. However, even in these more general terms, the applicability of the Civil Code provisions is expressly excluded by paragraph 5-*bis* of Article 122 CLF. Therefore, the two sets of rules applicable to listed and to non-listed companies, in principle, remain completely autonomous. [42]

### 1. Scope of the Civil Code Rules for Shareholders' Agreements

An important aspect of the Civil Code provisions on shareholders' agreements is that of their scope, which is narrower than that provided for listed companies by the Consolidated Law on Finance. Paragraph 1 of Article 2341-*bis* of the Civil

---

**40** According to paragraph 2.4. of Article 193 CLF, if the benefit obtained by the perpetrator of the breach as a result of the breach itself is above the maximum statutory limits indicated in the text, the financial administrative sanction would be increased up to twice the amount of the benefit obtained, provided that this amount can be determined.

**41** Cf. *Picciau* Comment on Articles 2341-*bis*-2341-*ter*, in M. Notari (a cura di), Costituzione – Conferimenti, in P. Marchetti et al. (diretto da) Commentario alla riforma del diritto societario, Giuffrè-Egea, Milano, 2007, p. 323 ff., at p. 329.

**42** *Picciau* (n. 41), p. 329; *Rescio/Speranzin* Comment on Article 2341-*bis*, in D.U. Santosuosso (a cura di), Delle società – Dell'azienda – Della concorrenza, in E. Gabrielli (diretto da), Commentario del codice civile, Utet, Assago, 2015, vol. 1, p. 725 ff., at p. 729 f.; *Selleri* (n. 6), p. 298.

Code mentions only three categories of arrangements that, if concluded in any form whatsoever, shall fall within the scope of these rules. These three categories are: (a) agreements that concern the exercise of voting rights in public companies or in the companies that control them; (b) agreements that limit the transfer of shares in public companies or in the companies that control them; and (c) agreements that cover the exercise, even jointly, of dominance over those same companies. Therefore, agreements concerning the prior consultation before the exercise of voting rights, or those concerning the concerted acquisition of shares, are not expressly mentioned in the Civil Code.[43]

In addition, another element of Article 2341-*bis* of the Civil Code that further narrows its scope is located in the very first words of this provision, where it is said that the relevant agreements for the application of this article are only those aimed at "stabilising the ownership structure or the governance of companies." It is evident that this general goal, which has also been considered applicable to the agreements concerning listed companies,[44] may give rise to some uncertainties, in particular with regard to the possibility of applying the provisions of the Civil Code to agreements concluded between minority shareholders.[45]

Finally, it is important to stress that the articles of the Civil Code concerning shareholders' agreements are part of the provisions on public companies. In light of that circumstance, the majority of legal scholars conclude that these rules are applicable only to public companies and, for example, not to private limited liability companies or partnerships.[46]

## 2. Duration of Shareholders' Agreements

With regard to the duration of shareholders' agreements, the Civil Code lays out rules similar to those for listed companies. Namely, if the shareholders' agreement has not been concluded for a fixed duration, each party enjoys a right of withdrawal by giving – in this case – a 180-day notice. If the agreement has been concluded for a fixed period of time, it may not last longer than five years.

Furthermore, the Civil Code provides that agreements concluded for a duration longer than five years shall be deemed to have been concluded for five

**43** *Perrino* Comment on Articles 2341-*bis*-2341-*ter*, in P. Abbadessa – G.B. Portale (diretto da), Le società per azioni. Codice civile e norme complementari, Giuffrè, Milano, 2016, t. I, p. 321 ff., at p. 328 ff.; *Picciau* (n. 41), p. 342 ff.; *Rescio/Speranzin* (n. 42), p. 731 ff.; *Selleri* (n. 6), p. 299 f.
**44** Infra n. 52, and the accompanying text.
**45** Cf. *Selleri* (n. 6), p. 300 f.
**46** *Picciau* (n. 41), p. 330 f.; *Rescio/Speranzin* (n. 42), p. 730 f.; *Selleri* (n. 6), p. 298 f.

years, and that shareholders' agreements may be renewed upon their expiration. Therefore, the principal difference on the rules concerning the duration between the Consolidated Law on Finance and the Civil Code lies with the possibility of having shareholders' agreements of a longer duration in non-listed companies.[47]

## 3. Disclosure of Shareholders' Agreements in Companies that Resort to Capital Markets

The Civil Code has a specific provision, laid out in Article 2341-*ter*, on the disclosure of shareholders' agreements in non-listed companies. The scope of this provision is narrower than that of Article 2341-*bis*, since it is limited only to the few companies that resort to capital markets but are not listed.[48]

Interestingly, the approach adopted in Article 2341-*ter* of the Civil Code is different from that provided for listed companies by the Consolidated Law on Finance. The disclosure of shareholders' agreements should take place via a communication to the company concerning the conclusion and the content of the agreement. Afterwards, the shareholders should be informed of the conclusion of the agreement at the first general meeting following this communication, since the information concerning the existing shareholders' agreements is to be reported to the participants at the general meeting with a statement made at the beginning of the meeting. Lastly, even the public should be informed of the conclusion of shareholders' agreements, because companies are required to report in the minutes of the general meeting the statement on the existence of shareholders' agreements made at the beginning of the meeting, and to file those minutes with the business register for publication.[49]

In conclusion, on the one hand, the rules applicable to the companies that resort to capital markets ensure the disclosure of shareholders' agreements, albeit not as promptly as for listed companies. It is also worth noting that Consob has no role to play in the disclosure procedure laid out in the Civil Code. On the

**47** On the duration of shareholders' agreements in non-listed companies, see *Perrino* (n. 43), p. 336 ff.; *Picciau* (n. 41), p. 350 ff.; *Rescio/Speranzin* (n. 42), p. 736 ff.; *Selleri* (n. 6), p. 302.
**48** Also for non-listed companies, the validity of shareholders' agreements is not linked to a provision of the bylaws, nor does it depend on the approval of the general meeting.
**49** *Perrino* (n. 43), p. 339 ff.; *Picciau* (n. 41), p. 363 ff; *Rescio/Speranzin* Comment on Article 2341-*ter*, in D.U. Santosuosso (a cura di), Delle società – Dell'azienda – Della concorrenza, in E. Gabrielli (diretto da), Commentario del codice civile, Utet, Assago, 2015, vol. 1, p. 741 ff., at p. 745 ff.; *Selleri* Comment on Article 2341-*ter*, in A. Maffei Alberti (diretto da), Commentario breve al diritto delle società, Cedam, Assago, 2017, 4th ed., p. 304 ff., at p. 305 ff.

other hand, for the companies that do not resort to capital markets, there are no general obligations to disclose shareholders' agreements.

### 4. Sanctions Provided by the Civil Code

The sanctions for failure to disclose shareholders' agreements involving companies that resort to capital markets are different from those for listed companies. Notably, the Civil Code does not declare such shareholders' agreements to be null and void – unlike for listed companies, which (as we have noted above) created some practical problems and proved to be a sanction difficult to frame from a theoretical perspective. Article 2341-*bis* of the Civil Code simply provides that, in the absence of a disclosure at the beginning of the shareholders' meeting, the owners of the shares concerned by the shareholders' agreement may not exercise their voting rights, and the validity of the resolutions of the general meeting taken with the decisive vote of these shares may be challenged.[50] This approach is more practical than the one for listed companies, and it reflects the evolution of the debate on the sanctions for the violation of the rules on shareholders' agreements that followed the enactment of the Consolidated Law on Finance.

## E. Content of Shareholders' Agreements

While discussing the scope of the rules provided by the Civil Code and the Consolidated Law on Finance, we have already mentioned which categories of agreements fall within the scope of the provisions on shareholders' agreements. However, this does not prevent shareholders from concluding other types of arrangements, as long as they do not violate the law.

A first example of such agreements is provided in Article 2341-*bis* of the Civil Code, which excludes from its scope the agreements pertaining to cooperation on the production or exchange of goods or services concerning companies entirely owned by the parties to the agreement.[51] Another example is given by agree-

---

**50** *Perrino* (n. 43), p. 343 f.; *Selleri* (n. 49), p. 307 f.; *Rescio/Speranzin* (n. 49), p. 752 ff., who also emphasise the Civil Code's different approach to that of the Consolidated Law on Finance with regard to the invalidity of the shareholders' agreement.

**51** *Perrino* (n. 43), p. 338 f.; *Picciau* (n. 41), p. 349 f.; *Rescio/Speranzin* (n. 42), p. 740 f.; *Selleri* (n. 6), p. 301.

ments that are not aimed at stabilising the governance of companies.[52] At least according to Consob, put and call agreements may fall into this category, since they may not aim to stabilise the ownership structure of companies.[53]

It is still debated if agreements not to vote for certain resolutions or not to sell shares always fall within the scope of the rules provided in the Civil Code and the Consolidated Law on Finance. This issue is discussed in particular for lock-up clauses during IPOs, and Consob has recognised that the function of these arrangements is different from that normally played by shareholders' agreements.[54]

## I. Shareholders' Agreements on Shareholder Rights

As already mentioned, the provisions on shareholders' agreements in both the Civil Code and the Consolidated Law on Finance are normally applicable to agreements concerning the exercise of voting rights. Interestingly, there is no reference in the legislation to the exercise of other shareholder rights; therefore, agreements on such rights may not fall within the scope of the agreements regulated by the law.[55]

In addition, we have already highlighted that the validity of agreements concerning the exercise of voting rights, in which decisions are taken not unanimously but by a majority vote of the participants, was debated until recently. In fact, the possibility of giving the majority of the parties to a shareholders' agreement the power to decide on the exercise of these rights for all the shares involved in the agreement was regarded as a potential violation of the rules on the general meeting.[56]

As previously said, these doubts were finally dispelled in an important decision that admitted a broader validity for shareholders' agreements on voting

---

**52** See *Macrì* (n. 24), p. 3859 ff., who highlights that this requirement is also applicable to listed companies, even though it is not expressly mentioned by the law. For a similar conclusion, see *Picciau* (n. 41), p. 335 ff., who argues that this requirement derives from the interpretation made by Consob of the provisions of the Consolidated Law on Finance. On the stabilisation requirement in general, see also *Selleri* (n. 6), p. 300 f.

**53** Consob, Comunicazione No. DEM/3077483 of 28 November 2003.

**54** Consob, Comunicazione No. DIS/29486 of 18 April 2000; Consob, Comunicazione No. DEM/3077483 of 28 November 2003; cf. *Picciau* (n. 41), p. 336 f.

**55** See, for example, *Macrì* (n. 24), p. 3858 f.; *Selleri* (n. 6), p. 301, who both make reference to the case of the agreement to present a list of candidates for the appointment to corporate bodies.

**56** Cf. supra n. 19 and n. 25, and the accompanying text.

rights.[57] This decision justified its conclusion by stressing the differences between shareholders' agreements and bylaws provisions, and by emphasising that the former do not have a direct effect on the latter: the shareholders that have agreed to cast their vote as indicated by the majority of the participants in the shareholders' agreement may still exercise their voting rights as they deem appropriate, at least as long as they are ready to face the liability deriving from their breach.

This decision is also interesting because it underlines an important feature of the Italian approach to shareholders' agreements: Italian scholarship frequently distinguishes between the different effects of shareholders' agreements and bylaws clauses, arguing that the former would bind only the parties that concluded them.[58]

A corollary of this approach is that, in principle, shareholders' agreements are far less likely to infringe any mandatory company law provision as long as their effects are limited to the contractual sphere alone and do not restrict shareholders' autonomy in exercising voting rights. On the one hand, shareholders' agreements cannot be considered a means to avoid the application of mandatory provisions if their effects are merely contractual and do not affect the organisational rules imposed by company law. On the other hand, shareholders' agreements may not give their participants the right to directly appoint persons to corporate bodies or the right to give binding instructions to directors,[59] since these clauses would alter the mandatory rules concerning the appointment of corporate bodies and those concerning the duties of directors.[60]

---

**57** Cass. civ., sez. I, 20 September, 1995, No. 9975; cf. supra C.II.

**58** See, for example, *Campobasso* Diritto commerciale. 2. Diritto delle società, Utet, Assago, 2015, 9th ed. (a cura di M. Campobasso), p. 340; and cf. *Libertini* (n. 4), p. 12 ff., who provides an assessment of the different corollaries and implications of this approach.

**59** These clauses may fall within the scope of the promise of the obligation or the fact of a third party as regulated under Article 1381 of the Civil Code, which states: "*A person which has warranted the obligations or action of a third party is required to indemnify the other contracting party if the third party refuses to be bound or does not perform the action.*"

**60** For a comparative analysis of this problem, and, more broadly, of shareholders' agreements, see *Guaccero* Patti parasociali e regole statutarie: una prospettiva comparata, in G. Carcano – C. Mosca – M. Ventoruzzo (a cura di) Regole del mercato e mercato delle regole, Giuffrè, Milano, 2016, p. 283 ff., at p. 298 ff.; *Portale* Patti parasociali con « efficacia corporativa » nelle società di capitali, in Riv. soc., 2015, p. 1 ff., at p. 4 ff.

## II. Shareholders' Agreements Limiting the Right to Transfer Shares

Shareholders' agreements limiting the right to transfer shares are common in Italy, even though the Civil Code allows companies to introduce such limitations in bylaws. Normally, shareholders prefer to introduce such limitations in bylaws to give them a broader effect. In fact, if included in the bylaws, limitations to the right to transfer shares become applicable to all present and future shareholders, they are not subject to time limits,[61] and transfers in violation of those limitations would be without effect vis-à-vis the company. However, certain limitations, such as those that would make the transfer of shares conditional upon the simple approval of a corporate body or of other shareholders, or those concerning limitations to transfers in case of death, are admitted in bylaws only if, in the event of a denied transfer, an exit right[62] is given to shareholders whose transfer of shares has been denied (Article 2355-*bis* of the Civil Code).[63] Moreover, these limitations may be introduced in bylaws by a majority vote, even though – at least as a default rule – a right of withdrawal should be accorded to the shareholders that did not approve that resolution.[64]

In contrast, limitations on the right to transfer shares included in shareholders' agreements (a) have a maximum duration of three or five years, (b) have effect only on the parties that concluded them, (c) may be modified – unless agreed otherwise – only with a unanimous agreement, and – importantly – (d) their breach would be irrelevant vis-à-vis the company and would justify only a claim for contractual damages. However, while bylaws are publicly available at the business register, shareholders' agreements ensure more confidentiality, since – at least when they concern shares of closely-held companies – their disclosure is not mandatory.

---

**61** With the exception of the clauses that prohibit any transfer of shares, whose duration, according to paragraph 1 of Article 2355-*bis* of the Civil Code, should be limited to five years.
**62** This exit right may even take the form of a right of withdrawal.
**63** See *Dal Soglio* Comment on Article 2355-*bis*, in A. Maffei Alberti (diretto da), Commentario breve al diritto delle società, Cedam, Assago, 2017, 4th ed., p. 438 ff., at p. 444 ff., 448 f.; *Ghionni Crivelli Visconti* Comment on Article 2355-*bis*, in D.U. Santosuosso (a cura di), Delle società – Dell'azienda – Della concorrenza, in E. Gabrielli (diretto da), Commentario del codice civile, Utet, Assago, 2015, vol. 1, p. 1021 ff., at p. 1029 ff., 1042 ff.; *id.*, Comment on Article 2355-*bis*, in P. Abbadessa – G.B. Portale (diretto da), Le società per azioni. Codice civile e norme complementari, Giuffrè, Milano, 2016, t. I, p. 660 ff., at p. 668 ff., 677 f.; *Stanghellini* Comment on Article 2355-*bis*, in M. Notari (a cura di), Azioni, in P. Marchetti et al. (diretto da) Commentario alla riforma del diritto societario, Giuffrè-Egea, Milano, 2008, p. 559 ff., at p. 575 ff., 606 ff.
**64** See, for example, *Stanghellini* (n. 63), p. 621 ff.

Among the limitations to the right to transfer shares, particular attention should be given to agreements that introduce the drag along, tag along and bring along of shares.[65] These arrangements are certainly admitted by Italian law, and they frequently appear in shareholders' agreements. In any case, it is not prohibited to include these types of arrangements in bylaws.[66] However, at least for drag along and bring along clauses, they are admitted in bylaws only as long as they comply with the same principles provided for the clauses that make the transfers of shares conditional upon the simple approval of a corporate body or of other shareholders. This means that in case of implementation of one of these clauses, the persons that are unwillingly bound to transfer their shares should not receive compensation that would be significantly lower than the value of their shares calculated according to the rules applicable in case of the exercise of the right of withdrawal.[67]

# F. Legal Effects of Shareholders' Agreements

Italian scholarship emphasises the different legal effect of shareholders' agreements and bylaws provisions. As previously stated, this is probably the result of the evolution of the judicial interpretation of the agreements concerning the exercise of voting rights, in light of a possible violation – by means of contractual arrangements – of mandatory company law provisions.[68]

Shareholders' agreements normally do not have effects similar to those of bylaws provisions: the former bind only the persons that concluded them, they do not hinder shareholders' autonomy in deciding how to cast votes, the

---

**65** The content of these clauses may vary, and any classification is generic and simply descriptive. Normally, drag along clauses enable shareholders (usually majority shareholders) to require one or more other shareholders (usually minority shareholders) to join them in the sale of their shares. Likewise, tag along clauses enable shareholders (usually minority shareholders) to join one or more other shareholders (usually majority shareholders) in the sale of their shares. Lastly, bring along clauses are similar to drag along clauses, with the difference that, in this case, the acquirers of the shares – and not those selling shareholders – can require one or more other shareholders – different from the ones that agreed to transfer their shares – to join in the sale: in these clauses also, the shareholders that decide to transfer their shares – and therefore activate the clause – must act so as to provide the transfer to the third party of the other shareholders' shares.

**66** See, for example, *Macrì* (n. 24), p. 3850 f.; *Perrino* (n. 43), p. 333 f.

**67** Massima No. 88 of 22 November 2005, in Consiglio notarile di Milano, Massime notarili in materia societaria, Milano, 5th ed., 2014, p. 305 f.

**68** See supra E.I., and cf. *Libertini* (n. 4), p. 4 ff.

resolutions of the general meeting that have been taken in their violation are valid and effective, and the remedy of specific performance cannot be invoked in case of breach, since the only available remedy would be that of damages.[69] This more limited effect of shareholders' agreements compared with bylaws provisions explains why courts consider comparable arrangements with greater leniency if they are included in shareholders' agreements: since shareholders' agreements may not achieve the exact same results as bylaws provisions, courts may evaluate them differently without fearing a violation of Article 1344 of the Civil Code.[70] In this perspective, since shareholders' agreements and bylaws are considered to be independent, it is also unsurprising that legal scholars exclude the possibility that shareholders' agreements may influence the interpretation of bylaws.[71]

However, even in the Italian legal system, this dichotomy between shareholders' agreements and bylaws provisions faces some challenges: for example, an issue debated by Italian legal scholars is that of the possibility that shareholders' agreements may become part of the document that incorporates the bylaws, without being granted the same effect as bylaws provisions. Some scholars accept this possibility, whereas others reject it.[72] To reconcile these different approaches, it has also been argued that the problem should be solved on the grounds of legal interpretation: namely, while it would be possible in principle to include shareholders' agreement clauses in bylaws, the fact that shareholders decided to include such arrangements in the bylaws should support the conclusion that, normally, these clauses should be presumed to have the same legal effects as the other provisions of the bylaws.[73]

---

**69** In some cases, shareholders' agreements may take a form similar to a voting trust. This purpose may be achieved, for example by appointing an irrevocable agent or by endorsing the shares to the person who will cast the vote in the general meeting. In these situations, the effects of shareholders' agreements are stronger than those that derive from a simple contract. On these arrangements, see, for example, *Rescio* (n. 25), p. 656 ff.

**70** *Libertini* (n. 4), p. 5 f.

**71** *Angelici* Le basi contrattuali della società per azioni, in G.E. Colombo – G.B. Portale (diretto da), Trattato delle società per azioni. Tipo – Costituzione – Nullità, Utet, Torino 2004, vol. 1*, p. 101 ff., at p. 158 f.

**72** On this debate, see, for example, *Perrino* (n. 43), p. 324 f.

**73** *Rescio* La distinzione del sociale dal parasociale (sulle c.d. clausole statutarie parasociali), in Riv. soc., 1991, p. 596 ff., at p. 639. This scholar confirmed this approach also after the Reform of Company Law of 2003, see *Rescio* I patti parasociali nel quadro dei rapporti contrattuali dei soci, in P. Abbadessa – G.B. Portale (diretto da), Il nuovo diritto societario. *Liber amicorum Gian Franco Campobasso*, Utet, Assago, 2006, vol. 1, p. 447 ff., at p. 475.

Certain recent judicial decisions have also challenged the clear distinction between the effects of shareholders' agreements and bylaws provisions. For example, in some cases, courts have issued injunctions to avoid a breach of contract, and ensured the performance of shareholders' agreements, ordering shareholders to cast their votes in the general meeting.[74] In any case, these challenges to the dominant paradigm prove that in Italy the legal framework for shareholders' agreements is still evolving, even if it is uncertain which direction this evolution could take, especially considering that, at least until now, the Cassazione has maintained its traditional approach, drawing a clear distinction between shareholders' agreements and bylaws provisions.[75]

# G. Conclusion

This chapter has examined the role played by shareholders' agreements in Italian law. After examining the relationship between shareholders' agreements and company law, I have provided a short description of the evolution of the legal framework for shareholders' agreements in that jurisdiction, and I have also examined the legislation currently in force. I have highlighted the importance of the rules devoted to shareholders' agreements in both listed and non-listed companies, and the emphasis that Italian law gives to the limited duration and the disclosure of such agreements.

This analysis showed that the evolution of the legal framework for shareholders' agreements is strictly related to the problem of their more limited effects compared with bylaws provisions. In fact, the broader jurisprudential recognition of the validity of shareholders' agreements on the exercise of voting rights was accepted based on the assumption that shareholders' agreements are binding only on the persons that concluded them, and that they may not influence shareholders' autonomy in exercising voting rights. Lastly, I have concluded this chapter mentioning some more recent jurisprudential evolutions that have begun to challenge the traditional approach on the limited effects of shareholders' agreements, nevertheless highlighting that the traditional approach remains predominant.

---

74 See Trib. Genova, 8 July 2004; Trib. Milano, 20 January 2009, and cf. *Libertini* (n. 4), p. 16 ff.
75 For some recent decisions that followed the traditional approach, see Cass. civ., sez. I, 5 March 2008, No. 5963; Cass. civ., sez. I, 2 August 2012, No. 13904, and cf., again, *Libertini* (n. 4), p. 17 f.

# H. Annexes

## I. Civil Code

### 1. Article 2341-*bis*

**Shareholders' Agreements**
1. The agreements, in whatsoever form concluded, which, in view of stabilising the ownership structure of the governance of a company:

a) concern the exercise of voting rights in public companies or in the companies that control them;
b) limit the transfer of shares in these companies or in the companies that control them;
c) have by object or effect the exercise, even jointly, of a dominance on the above mentioned companies,
   may not have duration longer than five years and they shall be deemed to have been concluded for such duration even if the parties provided for a longer duration; these agreements shall be renewable upon expiry.

Whether the agreement does not provide for a fixed duration, each party may withdraw by giving a one hundred and eighty days' notice.
The provisions of this Article are not applicable to the agreements functional to a cooperation on the production or exchange of goods or services concerning companies entirely owned by the parties in the agreement.

### 2. Art. 2341-*ter*

**Disclosure of Shareholders' Agreements**
In companies that resort to capital markets shareholders' agreements shall be communicated to the company and disclosed at the beginning of each general meeting. The statement must be recorded in the minute, which should be filed with the business register.
In the absence of the statement provided in the previous paragraph the owners of the shares to which the shareholders' agreement refers may not exercise their voting right and the resolutions of the general meeting adopted with their decisive vote may be challenged according to Article 2377.

## II. Consolidated Law on Finance

### 1. Article 122

**Shareholders' Agreements**

1. The agreements, in whatsoever form concluded, concerning the exercise of voting rights in the companies with listed shares and in the companies that control them, within five days from the conclusion shall be:

a) communicated to Consob;
b) published in excerpt in the daily press;
c) filed with the business register of the place where the company has its registered office;
d) communicated to the listed companies.

2. Consob shall provide in a regulation the means and content of the communication, the excerpt and the publication.

3. In case of violation of the obligations laid down in paragraph 1 the agreements shall be null and void.

4. Voting rights attached to listed shares for which the requirements laid down in paragraph 1 have not been complied with may not be exercised. In the event of violation, Article 14(5) shall apply. The challenge may also be filed by Consob within the time limit specified in Article 14(6).

5. This Article shall also apply to the agreements, in whatsoever form concluded, that:

a) create obligations of consultation prior to the exercise of voting rights in companies with listed shares or companies that control them;
b) set limits on the transfer of the related shares or of financial instruments that entitle holders to buy or subscribe them;
c) concern the purchase of shares or financial instruments referred to in letter b);
d) have as their object or effect the exercise, jointly or otherwise, of a dominant influence on such companies.
   d-*bis*) are aimed at encouraging or frustrating the goals of a public offer to buy or exchange, including commitments concerning the non-participation in the offer.

5-*bis*. Articles 2341-*bis* and 2341-*ter* of the Civil Code shall not be applicable to the agreements mentioned in this Article.

5-*ter*. The disclosure obligations indicated in paragraph 1 of this Article shall not apply to agreements, in whatsoever form they are concluded, concerning shareholdings totalling less than the threshold indicated in Article 120, paragraph 2.

## 2. Article 123

### Duration of Agreements and Right of Withdrawal

1. Where agreements referred to in Article 122 have a fixed duration, they may not have a duration longer than three years and they shall be deemed to have been concluded for such duration even if the parties provided for a longer duration; agreements shall be renewable upon expiry.
2. Agreements may also be concluded for an indefinite duration; in such case each party may withdraw by giving a six months' notice. Articles 122(1) and 122(2) shall apply to withdrawal.
3. Shareholders who wish to tender their shares to a public offer to buy or exchange made pursuant to Articles 106 or 107 may withdraw from the agreements referred to in Article 122 without notice. The withdrawal will have no effect if the transfer of the shares is not finalised.

## 3. Article 193

### Corporate Disclosures and Duties of Auditors, Statutory Auditors and Independent Statutory Auditors

(. . .)

2. Unless the fact is a criminal offence, in the case of failure to disclose major shareholdings and shareholders' agreements as provided respectively by Articles 120, paragraphs 2, 2-*bis* and 4, and 122, paragraphs 1, 2 and 5, and violation of the prohibitions established by Articles 120, paragraph 5, 121, paragraphs 1 and 3, and 122, paragraph 4, one of the following administrative sanctions is imposed on companies, entities and associations:

a) a public statement indicating the subject responsible for the breach and the nature of the same, when it features scarce offensiveness or danger and the infringement in question has ceased;
b) an order to eliminate the infringements charged, with possible indication of the measures to be adopted and of the term for compliance, and to refrain from repeating the offence, when the said infringements feature scarce offensiveness or danger;
c) a financial administrative sanction from ten thousand Euro to ten million Euro, or up to five per cent of the turnover when that amount is more than ten million Euro and the turnover can be determined pursuant to Article 195, paragraph 1-*bis*.

2.1. Unless the fact is a criminal offence, if the disclosures referred to under paragraph 2 are required of a natural person, in the case of breach one of the following administrative sanctions is applied:

a) a public statement indicating the person responsible for the breach and the nature of the same, when it features scarce offensiveness or danger and the infringement in question has ceased;
b) an order to eliminate the infringements charged, with possible indication of the measures to be adopted and of the term for compliance, and to refrain from repeating the offence, when the said infringements feature scarce offensiveness or danger;
c) a financial administrative sanction from ten thousand Euro to two million Euro.

2.2. For the breaches indicated under paragraph 2, the subjects who perform administrative, direction or control functions as well as the personnel, if their behaviour has contributed to determining the said breach on the part of the legal person, are subjected, in the cases contemplated by Article 190-*bis*, paragraph 1, letter a), to the administrative sanctions contemplated by paragraph 2.1.

2.3. In the case of a delay in making the disclosures contemplated by Article 120, paragraphs 2, 2-*bis* and 4, of no more than two months, the minimum statutory amount of the financial administrative sanctions indicated in paragraphs 2 and 2.1 is five thousand Euro.

2.4. If the benefit obtained by the perpetrator of the breach as a result of the breach itself is above the maximum statutory limits set out in paragraphs 1, 1.1, 2 and 2.1 of this Article, the financial administrative sanction is increased up to twice the amount of the benefit obtained, provided that this amount can be determined.

W.J.M. van Veen

# The Netherlands

## Table of Content



## A. Introduction

In practice, agreements between shareholders in which the rules that govern their collaboration within a company are laid down in detail are quite common. Such arrangements may relate to the manner in which the shareholders shall pass resolutions, the composition of the board of directors and the supervisory board, the allocation of control and profit, additional funding by the shareholders, dispute and 'dead lock' resolution etc. In the Dutch legal literature and case law, such agreements tend to be referred to as shareholders' agreements.

For a long time now, a great deal of attention has been paid in the literature to the phenomenon of the shareholders' agreement and the relationship between shareholders' agreements and Dutch company law. That is related to the fact that if such an agreement is in effect, the collaboration is governed by the company's Articles of Association on the one hand, and the shareholders' agreement on the

**Prof. dr. W.J.M. van Veen,** Professor of Corporate Law, VU University Amsterdam, Special Counsel Corporate Law at Baker & McKenzie Amsterdam, director of the ZIFO Institute for Financial Law and Corporate Law Amsterdam.

https://doi.org/10.1515/9783110517026-019

other. The collaboration, as a result, is governed by two types of legal rules: contract law on the one hand, and the law of legal persons – which also governs companies with share capital – on the other. That situation gives rise to many interesting questions, which arise primarily as a result of the fact that the law of legal persons (Book 2 of the Dutch Civil Code), is different in nature from contract law (Book 6 of the Dutch Civil Code). In this context I am referring primarily to the fact that contract law is primarily regulatory in nature, but the law of legal persons is largely mandatory in nature. This leads to questions as whether as a result, the parties are confronted with restrictions when they are shaping their collaboration in the form a company by means of a shareholders' agreement and, if so, what those restrictions are, and what, if any, the effect is of shareholders' agreement within the context of the company.

This contribution focuses on these questions and more broadly the interplay of shareholders' agreements and company law. The following analysis focuses on three central themes in the Dutch literature and case law in this particular field. The first is whether shareholders can bind themselves in a legally valid manner to exercise their voting right – and other rights and powers related to their shareholding – in a particular manner and, if so, whether any limits are to be observed in that context. The second theme is whether the mandatory nature of company law implies that contractual arrangements that are intended to lead to a particular result that cannot be achieved under company law by means of a regulation in the Articles of Association, are invalid or in any event unenforceable. The third theme, which is related to both of the other themes, concerns the impact of shareholders' agreements on governance. To what extent must the company, the company's bodies and the persons that are part of the organisation of the company, pay heed to a shareholders' agreement when they are carrying out their duties and exercising their powers and, if they fail to do so (or there is a risk that they will fail to do so), what, if any, legal remedies do the shareholders have available to enforce compliance?

In this contribution I will examine more closely the themes described above and the manner in which they have developed in Dutch law. I will not discuss the special and rather specific regulations that govern large companies in respect of which the statutory board regime (also known as the 'large company regime') applies.[1] That special regime is aimed at ensuring that the works council is involved in the appointment of members of the supervisory board or – in the event that the one-tier board model is applied – the appointment of non-execu-

1 See Articles 2:152 et seq. of the Dutch Civil Code in respect of public limited liability companies (NVs) and Articles 2:262 et seq. in respect of private limited liability companies (BVs).

tive directors, and at mitigating the influence of the general meeting on the composition of the supervisory board and the board of directors. Built into that regime is the rule that if the shareholders have agreed to collaborate and on the rules that govern their collaboration, the general meeting will retain its influence on the composition of the board of directors. In this article I will not address that fairly specific regime or rules concerning 'acting in concert' that apply to shareholders of listed companies. This contribution will focus on joint ventures and comparable forms of collaboration that have been given form through a company with share capital.

## B. Can the manner in which voting rights and other rights and powers under company law are exercised be the subject of a contract?

The question whether shareholders can legally bind themselves in respect of the manner in which they exercise their right to vote was a subject of discussion in the Dutch literature in the first half of the 20th Century. An objection that was put forward against the validity of voting agreements was that the voting right was granted to a member or shareholder in the interest of the 'community' of which he formed part and therefore, when exercising the voting rights, it was the interest of the joint members or shareholders, and not his own interest, that had to be expressed. A voting agreement pursuant to which a shareholder undertakes in advance to vote in a particular manner would therefore be contrary to public morals.[2]

However, in 1944 the Dutch Supreme Court rendered a ground-breaking Judgment in which it ruled that an agreement with respect to how the vote must be cast in the event of a deadlock in the general meeting of shareholders was, in principle, valid.[3] An important consideration that ensues from that Judgment is that the right to vote is granted to shareholders in order to serve their own interest in the company. The shareholder is free to use his right to vote, or refrain from using it. If the shareholder exercises the voting right, he may pursue his own interest in the company and therefore, in principle, he may also bind

2 See *C.J.J.M. Petit* Overeenkomsten in strijd met de goede zeden, thesis UL, Leiden, the Netherlands: Eduard IJdo 1920, pp. 203–204.
3 Dutch Supreme Court, 30 June 1944, NJ 1944/45, 465.

himself with respect to the exercise of his voting right. Thus, as a rule, voting agreements between shareholders are valid and enforceable.

In later Judgments the Dutch Supreme Court continued to render such decisions. In the Judgment in the case of *Destilleerderij Melchers*,[4] the Supreme Court ruled that for the assessment of the validity of the voting agreement in that case it did not matter that the agreement had been entered into for an indefinite term and that penalty clauses were agreed in order to safeguard the agreements and that irrevocable proxies to exercise the voting right were granted. In the *Aurora* Judgment, which the Supreme Court rendered a year later, the Court ruled more explicitly that agreements with respect to the exercise of voting rights between shareholders and third parties also were, in principle, valid. The Court went on to explicitly rule that agreements with regard to the exercise of the shareholder's right in respect of the appointment and dismissal of supervisory directors are also valid. That relates not only to the voting right itself, but according to the Court also to *"the rights that make it possible for him to achieve a vote in respect of any resolution"*.[5] Such rights can include the right to convene a shareholders' meeting and/or to put certain items on the agenda for such meeting. Thus, it is clear that other rights than voting rights can be the subject of a shareholders' agreement and, if they are, these agreements are indeed in principle legally binding.

Two caveats must be made in order to properly understand those two Judgments. The first is that the Supreme Court limited the freedom of shareholders to bind themselves with respect to the exercise of their right to vote at the general meeting in the sense that their doing so may not constitute an abuse of rights, and also that the agreement may not lead to any socially improper consequences.[6] I will discuss the limits on the permissibility of shareholders' agreements in more detail in sections 3 and 4 below.

The second caveat in this context is that the Supreme Court elucidated that a voting agreement has no effect on the validity of the vote itself. A vote that is cast in contravention of the agreements that were made is completely valid under company law.[7] The scope of that finding is broader in the sense that it does not relate exclusively to the voting right, but also to other rights and powers en-

4 Dutch Supreme Court, 13 November 1959, NJ 1960, 472.

5 Dutch Supreme Court, 19 February 1960, NJ 473. That case involved agreements between shareholders in the company's capital.

6 Dutch Supreme Court, 30 June 1944, NJ 1944/45, 465.

7 In this line of thinking lies that a shareholder under Dutch law cannot (unilaterally or by contract) renounce his right to vote or other rights ensuing from his shareholding. See further section 4 below.

suing from shareholding that are the subject of a shareholders' agreement. The shareholder in question may, however, be guilty of violating his contractual obligations towards the other party, and the other party therefore would have legal remedies available to enforce compliance with those obligations. In that manner voting agreements, and more generally agreements with respect to the manner in which a shareholder will exercise his rights or powers, in Dutch law actually do have an effect under company law. I will explain that in more detail in section 5.

In the Dutch literature there is also a discourse regarding the question whether managing directors and supervisory directors can bind themselves with respect to the manner in which they will exercise their powers. The background to this is that they have a different position in the company than the shareholders. Unlike the shareholders, the powers granted to them are not granted to serve their own interests. To the contrary: managing directors and supervisory directors are obliged to keep their own interests carefully separated from the company's interests and are obliged to be guided by and to act exclusively in the company's interest.[8]

For that reason, it is generally presumed that managing directors and supervisory directors are not free to conclude voting agreements. On the basis of the collective nature of their duties, as well as the fact that the positions of managing director and supervisory director are positions that are highly personal and non-transferrable, individual managing directors and supervisory directors are not permitted to bind themselves – and cannot do so in a legally enforceable manner – to vote in a particular way at meetings of the board of directors and the supervisory board, respectively.[9]

A different question is whether or not the joint managing directors or supervisory directors can bind themselves with respect to the manner in which the board of directors and the supervisory board, respectively, will carry out certain duties or exercise certain powers. I believe that to some extent they may. When they are carrying out their duties, managing directors and supervisory directors also have a certain amount of discretionary power, which implies that within certain limits they may make agreements about the manner in which they will exercise certain powers. In view of their legal duty and the position of trust that

**8** Article 2:129/239(5) and Article 2:140/250(2) of the Dutch Civil Code. It is expected that those provisions will be transferred shortly to Article 2:9 of the Dutch Civil Code for managing directors and Article 2:11 of the Dutch Civil Code for supervisory directors.

**9** In this respect, see *Dortmond* Stemovereenkomsten rondom de eeuwwisseling, inaugural lecture UL 2001, p. 25; *Asser-Maeijer* 2-III, no. 306; *Asser/Maeijer/Van Solinge/Nieuwe* Weme 2-II* 2009, no. 423; *van Veen* Boek 2 BW, statuten en aandeelhoudersovereenkomsten – stand van zaken en blik vooruit, ZIFO-reeks, part 2, Deventer, the Netherlands: Kluwer 2011, pp. 27–29.

they fulfil, that option is open to them only insofar as it is in the company's interest,[10] for example in a situation in which that is necessary in order for a transaction that is essential for the company to succeed. Moreover, because the duty of the board of directors and the supervisory board is collective in nature, the agreement would have to be entered into by all the managing directors and supervisory directors.[11]

In the case law that the Dutch Supreme Court has handed down, support for that approach can be found in that Court's Judgment in the case of *HVA v. Westertoren.*[12] The issue in that case was the fact that HVA's supervisory directors had made agreements with an intended strategic partner regarding the manner in which the supervisory board would be composed and remain comprised. The Supreme Court did not consider those agreements to be contrary to the law, from which it can be inferred that the Supreme Court did not wish to call into question the validity of the agreement. See further section 3 with respect to that decision.

Here I note that it is necessary to be appropriately reticent when such an agreement is entered into, because the management board or the supervisory board must be able to fulfil its duty with the necessary objectivity. If it is of the opinion that implementing an agreement is not in the company's interest, the statutory task description would oppose implementing the agreement.[13] That argues for having the agreement stipulate that, in situations in which a conflict with the statutory task description could arise, the management board/supervisory board and individual managing directors/supervisory directors cannot be held to what was agreed.

For the sake of clarity, in the rest of this analysis I will focus shareholders' agreements.

---

**10** In a comparable sense, see *van den Hoek* Variaties op de structuurregeling bij contract, in: Ondernemingsrechtelijke contracten, IVO series no. 14, Deventer, the Netherlands: Kluwer, 1991, p. 87.

**11** In this context, see also *de Kluiver/Meinema* Dwingend vennootschapsrecht na de Wet herziening preventief toezicht en de mogelijkheden van statutaire en contractuele afwijking en aanvulling, WPNR 6503 (2002), pp. 653, 654; Directors cannot conclude contracts on the exercise of authorities of the supervisory board and vice versa, because this would be at odds with the principle of autonomy. Within the same context *Bartman* WPNR 6809 (2009), pp. 688 et seq. and WPNR 6817 (2009), p. 849.

**12** Dutch Supreme Court, 19 March 1975, NJ 1976, 267.

**13** In this sense also *de Kluiver* De ondernemingsrechtelijke contractspraktijk: onderhandelen in de schaduw van de wet, Tijdschrift Contracteren 2001, p. 7–8.

# C. The mandatory nature of company law and the validity of Shareholders' Agreements under Dutch law

The fact that it is possible to enter into legally valid contracts with respect to rights and powers under company law does not imply that it is possible to do so without any limitation. One of the questions that has been a topic of much discussion in the Dutch literature is the question whether a result can be achieved by means of shareholders' agreements that is not possible by means of an arrangement in the Articles of Association because it is not permitted under company law.

In that discussion the central provision is that it is possible to derogate from the provisions stipulated in the law of legal persons, only insofar as that is apparent from the law itself (Article 2:25 of the Dutch Civil Code). Moreover, in cases in which it is permitted to derogate from the law, as a rule it is possible to do so only under or pursuant to the Articles of Association. Apart from certain exceptions,[14] the possibility to derogate by means of an agreement is not given. The question is therefore whether it is possible and valid to derogate by means of a shareholders' agreement from a provision stipulated in Book 2 of the Dutch Civil Code if that provision is mandatory in nature or if derogation from that provision is possible only by means of rules stipulated in the Articles of Association.

The background to this question is the fact that Article 3:40 of the Dutch Civil Code stipulates that legal acts – which include agreements – that are contrary to mandatory rules of law are null and void or subject to annulment unless a different interpretation ensues from the purport of the provision in question (Article 3:40(2) of the Dutch Civil Code). This gives rise to the question of what the provision stipulated in Article 2:25 of the Dutch Civil Code means in this context with respect to contractual agreements through which a legal situation is intended that is not permitted under company law or if the intended legal situation is permitted under company law on the condition that it is included in the Articles of Association. The essence of the question is ultimately whether it is the object of the mandatory system of company law that such contractual arrangements are null and void or subject to annulment.

14 See Article 2:92a/201a of the Dutch Civil Code with respect to the statutory possibility to buy out minority shareholders and Article 2:337 of the Dutch Civil Code with respect to dispute settlement rules.

In the (less recent) literature indeed various examples can be found of the interpretation that Book 2 of the Dutch Civil Code bars the validity of such contractual arrangements. That is expressed in the position that such contractual arrangements are null and void or subject to annulment. Such positions can be found for example with regard to agreements with respect to the determination of the price in the case of a voluntary or mandatory transfer of the shares (in which context the law mandatorily stipulated that the offering shareholder was entitled to a price determined by independent experts),[15] or with regard to contractual arrangements whose purpose is to stipulate that, in fact, every shareholder can appoint one or more managing directors (in spite of the fact that the law mandatorily stipulated that the appointment must be made by the general meeting of shareholders).[16]

No passages can be found in the parliamentary history pertaining to Article 2:25 of the Dutch Civil Code that elucidate what the legislature thought about the relationship between shareholders' agreements, Articles of Association and the law of legal persons in general or company law in particular. The passages in the explanatory notes to (the predecessor of) that article refer only to the relationship between the statutory provisions and the Articles of Association. The statutory system is aimed at providing clarity with respect to the question from which statutory provisions it is possible to derogate in the Articles of Association and from which statutory provision derogation is not possible.[17] There is no indication that this also was intended to restrict freedom of contract.[18] Thus, the legislative history leaves open the interpretation that Article 2:25 of the Dutch Civil Code and the related system of mandatory law does not have that purport.

---

**15** See, e.g., *Timmerman* Waarom hebben wij dwingend vennootschapsrecht, in: Ondernemingsrechtelijke contracten, IVO series no. 14, Deventer, the Netherlands: Kluwer 1991, p. 9 et seq.

**16** In sense see, e.g., *van Schilfgaarde* Contractuele structurering van bestuur en toezicht, in: Ondernemingsrechtelijke contracten, Deventer, the Netherlands: Kluwer 1991, pp. 15–16. See also *den Boogert* Aanpassing van Boek 2 BW voor joint venture-doeleinden?, AA 44 (1995), pp. 26 et seq. and *Maeijer* De stemovereenkomst van aandeelhouders, in: Recht zo die gaat (Van der Ploeg compilation), 1976, pp. 98 et seq. Since 2012, that limitation applies only in respect of public limited liability companies (NVs) and no longer in respect of private limited liability companies (BVs) (Article 2:242 of the Dutch Civil Code).

**17** See Ontwerpen van wetten op de vennootschappen en andere wijziging en aanvulling van de bepalingen omtrent de naamloze vennootschap, The Hague, the Netherlands: gebr. Belinfante 1929, pp. 40, 59.

**18** In this context see also *Meinema* Dwingend recht voor de besloten vennootschap, thesis UM, IVO series no. 43, Deventer, the Netherlands: Kluwer 2003, p. 26

Indeed, from a theoretical point of view that position is well arguable, in view of the fact that under Dutch law, Articles of Association on the one hand and shareholders' agreements on the other have fundamentally different characteristics that also are expressed in the statutory system. It is therefore not obvious and to a certain extent even illogical to put Articles of Association on par with shareholders' agreements for the application of Article 2:25 of the Dutch Civil Code.[19]

In this context, I point out that the Articles of Association determines the identity of the legal entity in terms of its name, registered office and objects and – as a supplement to the law – its internal organisation, including the rights, powers and obligations under company law of the parties involved in the organisation. Shareholders' agreements cannot attribute or remove rights or powers under company law. The statutory rules and the rules pursuant to the Articles of Association – possibly supplemented by regulations or resolutions having a general purport – are positive-law in nature in respect of the parties involved in the organisation.[20]A regulation in the Articles of Association has the same legal force as a statutory regulation in several ways. For example, a resolution that is in contravention of the Articles of Association is null and void, the transferability of shares can be restricted and temporarily precluded pursuant to the Articles of Association, and a violation of a formal requirement stipulated in the Articles of Association, for example in respect of casting a vote, will lead to nullity. A contractual regulation cannot have such effects.

Furthermore, in principle a regulation in the Articles of Association is binding in nature on any and all parties that are involved in the legal entity's organisation pursuant to the law or the Articles of Association. A contractual regulation, on the other hand, is binding only on those who are parties to it. A voting agreement or other agreement pursuant to which a shareholder binds himself with respect to the exercise of his rights or powers under company law need not also apply between or towards all the shareholders. In this context I would add that pursuant to Dutch law it is not possible to make a contractual regulation part of the regulations stipulated in the Articles of Association and/or furnish it with the legal force of a regulation stipulated in the Articles of Association by referring to the contractual regulation in the Articles of Association. That form of incorporation by reference is not permitted under Dutch law.

---

**19** I would refer the interested reader *van Veen* op. cit. (note 9), pp. 12–13.

**20** See further *Buys* Statuten, reglementen en besluiten beschouwen als algemene voorwaarden?, TVVS 1992, pp. 148–150.

The fundamental differences between Articles of Association on the one hand and shareholders' agreements on the other, also implies that the permissibility of shareholders' agreements need not be problematic. Articles of Association and shareholders' agreements can apply side by side without any problem because the legal nature of the two documents is fundamentally different under Dutch law. As a result there is no reason why Article 2:25 of the Dutch Civil Code and the related system of mandatory law should purport to restrict freedom of contract.

That conclusion is also expressed in the manner in which that issue has been treated in the relevant case law. There are many decisions in which the issue was the relationship between contract law on the one hand and company law (including regulations stipulated in Articles of Association) on the other. The casebook judgments on this point are the decisions rendered by the Dutch Supreme Court that were discussed in the preceding section with respect to the validity of voting agreements. Although that was not discussed in so many words in those Judgments, the implication of those judgments is that, in principle, regulations stipulated in shareholders' agreements on the basis of which individual shareholders can actually appoint their 'own' director are legally valid. The fact that Article 2:132 of the Dutch Civil Code in respect of public limited liability companies (NVs) (and previously Articles 2:242 of the Dutch Civil Code in respect of private limited liability companies (BVs)) does not permit that to be stipulated in the Articles of Association does not preclude that. The legislature has since implicitly acknowledged the validity of such agreements in Article 2:24a of the Dutch Civil Code.[21]

Another important decision in which the relationship between a mandatory regulation under Book 2 of the Dutch Civil Code and arrangements that are in contravention of it was addressed more explicitly is the above-mentioned decision that the Dutch Supreme Court rendered in the *HVA v. Westertoren* case.[22] In the case on which it was based there was no agreement between shareholders but rather between managing directors, supervisory directors and Socfin, a strategic partner of the company's. In these (inquiry) proceedings, one of the issues was the fact that the supervisory directors of HVA – in respect of whom the large

21 Article 2:24 of the Dutch Civil Code defines the term 'subsidiary'. That provision indicates that a majority of the voting rights in the general meeting can also be acquired by means of voting agreements. Article 2:24a of the Dutch Civil Code was introduced in 1988 in order to implement the Seventh Directive. The Directive does not oblige acknowledgement of the validity of agreements with respect to the appointment and dismissal of managing directors. The legislature did so of its own accord. See Parliamentary Documents II 1986/87, 19 813, no. 3, pp. 9–10.
22 Dutch Supreme Court, 19 March 1975, *NJ* 1976, 267.

company regime referred to in section 1 applied – had undertaken towards Socfin to ensure that the supervisory board would be permanently composed in a particular manner, in which context Socfin obtained the right to have a number of supervisory directors appointed in accordance with its advice and the right to object to an appointment of candidates in other vacancies. Although the large company regime prohibited, among other things, supervisory directors from being appointed on the basis of a binding nomination,[23] the Supreme Court ruled that the collaboration agreement 'in and of itself was not in contravention of one of the articles in the Dutch Commercial Code (*Wetboek van Koophandel*)'. It is clear from that Judgment that the Dutch Supreme Court accepts that, in principle, contractual arrangements that are intended to create a legal situation that is in contravention of mandatory provisions in Book 2 of the Dutch Civil Code and that as a result cannot be laid down in Articles of Association are not invalid for that reason, but indeed can be legally valid.

A more recent decision on the relationship between a contractual regulation and a mandatory regulation stipulated in Book 2 of the Dutch Civil Court, was rendered in the Judgment of the Court of Appeal of The Hague dated 7 August 2008.[24] In that Judgment the Court addressed the question of the validity of a contractual regulation with respect to the determination of the price of shares in a private limited liability company at the time of the mandatory transfer of the shares. On the ground of Article 2:195a(3) of the Dutch Civil Code, at that time the Articles of Association of a private limited liability company had to contain a regulation pursuant to which the offering shareholder, if he so requested, would receive a price from the party to which he could or had to transfer his shares that was equal to the value determined by one or more independent experts. At the time, the relevant provisions of Book 2 of the Dutch Civil Code were mandatory on that point.[25] However, in the case in question, as often is the case in practice, the shareholders' agreement contained a pricing regulation in contravention of the statutory provision. The shareholder in question argued that

---

**23** That still applies under the current law. See Article 2:158/268(4) of the Dutch Civil Code. Critical for that reason: J.J.M. Maeijer *op. cit.* (note 16), p. 99.

**24** *JOR* 2008/262 with commentary from Stokkermans. With respect to that decision see, e.g., *Nicolai* Contractuele regeling van de waardebepaling bij uitstoting, Ondernemingsrecht 2009, pp. 735 et seq. and *Steins Bisschop* Niets is meer zeker, zelfs niet het dwingend recht, TvOB 2010, p. 51.

**25** However, see Dutch Supreme Court, 21 January 2005, NJ 2005, 126, with commentary from Ma (*Hoffman v. Hoffman*), in which the Supreme Court did not consider the appointment of experts in accordance with Article 2:339 of the Dutch Civil Code necessary in the concrete circumstances of the case, in view of the pricing stipulated in the Articles of Association.

the contractual regulation was null and void, or in any event subject to annulment, because it was contrary to mandatory law.

The Court of Appeal of The Hague rejected that argument. In that context, the Court referred to, among other things, the development in the case law and the legislative proposal to increase flexibility of the law governing private limited liability companies. However, the Court of Appeal's principle consideration was the following:

The Court of Appeal agrees with Ramsley et al.'s argument that Article 2:195a (3) of the Dutch Civil Code stipulates a mandatory rule of law, on the understanding that that rule prohibits only the adoption of Articles of Association pursuant to which, in the case of a mandatory buyout, a shareholder receives a price for his shares that is lower than the actual value. Article 2:195 of the Dutch Civil Code does not stipulate anything with respect to agreements that contain such a regulation. (...) There is no valid reason why the principle of freedom of contract should stand down on this point.

Thus, the pattern that has developed in Dutch case law is that Article 2:25 of the Dutch Civil Code and the related system of mandatory law does not have the object of restricting freedom of contract. For that reason, it can be inferred from the case law that the fact that on the ground of Article 2:25 of the Dutch Civil Code it is not permitted to derogate from a statutory regulation in Articles of Association does not also lead to a prohibition against doing so by shareholders' agreement.[26]

## D. Limits on the permissibility of Shareholders' Agreements

The preceding section explained that the mandatory nature of company law does not have the object of combating contractual arrangements through which a result is achieved that could not be achieved by means of the Articles of Association. Of course, that does not mean that there are no limits whatsoever on the permissibility of agreements with respect to exercising rights and powers under company law. Pursuant to Article 3:40 of the Dutch Civil Code, agreements can be null and void if they are contrary to the law, public morals or public order. That applies equally in respect of shareholders' agreements. This is also referred to in the *Wennex* Judgment, which was discussed in section 2, in which the Dutch

**26** In this sense, see also District Court of Amsterdam, 15 October 2008, JOR 2009/124 (*Ixus Holding*).

Supreme Court explicitly ruled that, except in a case of an abuse of rights, a shareholder is free to bind himself with respect to the exercise of his right to vote at the general meeting, *"provided that that is not done in a manner or under circumstances through which the agreement would lead to socially improper consequences"*.[27]

There is a certain amount of consensus in the literature with respect to the nullity of certain types of agreements between shareholders. In broad terms this would include agreements whose object is to have a party cooperate in adopting a resolution that is contrary to the law, the Articles of Association, public order or public morals or whose object is to act (or refrain to act) in contravention of the law, Articles of Association, public order or public moral.[28] For the purpose of this contribution I will refrain from providing an in-depth analysis of the intricacies of Dutch law on the nullity of legal acts, but will focus on describing the main – partly overlapping – principles and the type agreements that as a result thereof are deemed not to be valid.

One principle in Dutch law is that a shareholders' agreement that is intended to harm the interests of the company and/or co-shareholders would be null and void because that would be contrary to public morals.[29] Such agreements are incompatible with the corporate-law principles of reasonableness and fairness stipulated in Article 2:8 of the Dutch Civil Code and the standards of due care that it comprises and that the shareholders must observe towards each other and the company.

A second principle of Dutch law is that the application of open standards of due care is not at the disposal of parties. An agreement granting a licence to violate statutory standards of due care is deemed to be non-binding.[30] The law of legal persons stipulates such a standard in Article 2:8 of the Dutch Civil Code, which stipulates the obligation to observe the principles of reasonableness and fairness in the mutual relationships between the parties that form part of the organisation of the legal person and the legal person itself. Any agreement whose content or object is to make compliance with the standard stipulated in

---

**27** Dutch Supreme Court, 30 June 1944, *NJ* 1944, 465.

**28** According to, among others, *van der Grinten* AAe IX, *1959–1960*, pp. 58–59; *Van Schilfgaarde/Winter/Wezeman* Van de NV en de BV, Deventer, the Netherlands: Kluwer, 16e printing (2013), no. 67; *Asser/Maeijer/Van Solinge/Nieuwe* Weme 2-II* 2009, no. 386; *Asser/Hartkamp/Sieburg* 6-III* 2010, no. 328.

**29** Idem *Maeijer* op. cit. (note 16), p. 100. *Stokkermans* Preliminary Advice of the Royal Dutch Association of Civil-law Notaries 2008, pp. 109–110.

**30** In this sense, see *Asser/Hartkamp/Sieburg* 6-III* 2010, no. 315 with respect to the principles of reasonableness and fairness in contractual relationships.

Article 2:8 of the Dutch Civil Code illusory would be non-binding. An agreement that is aimed at abrogating that standard, for example by having a shareholder waive in advance a claim to have a resolution nullified because it is in contravention of Article 2:8 of the Dutch Civil Code, is therefore also deemed to be non-binding.[31] For the same reasons standards with respect to conduct and duties, such as the rule that directors must perform their duties properly, cannot, by their nature, be evaded by contract.[32] For example, agreements that preclude directors' liability for performing their duties improperly in the case of an intentional act or omission or wilful recklessness are null and void.[33]

The third principle that I see is that a shareholders' agreement that is aimed at interfering with or even disrupting the proper functioning of the organisation of the legal person, are invalid. Agreements pursuant to which a party undertakes, for example, not to exercise supervisory duties, or not to do so properly, for example by agreeing to vote in accordance with instructions given by another party, are non-binding.[34] Agreements aimed at undermining the system of checks and balances laid down in the law or in Articles of Association, which is aimed at ensuring that the company functions properly, are likewise invalid.[35] An example of this would be an agreement between shareholders and managing directors pursuant to which the shareholders undertake to vote in accordance with the instructions given by the managing directors. If the validity of such agreements were to be acknowledged, that would essentially imply that the managing directors would be able to enforce at law that the shareholders will not avail themselves of their supervisory powers pursuant to the law and the Articles of Asso-

---

**31** The same applies to an agreement to waive the right to instigate an enquiry procedure with Enterprise Court at the Amsterdam Court of Appeals. In this sense, see also *Meinema* op. cit. (note 18), p. 56; and *Stokkermans* Het nieuwe BV-recht voor de praktijk, Preliminary Advice of the Royal Dutch Association of Civil-law Notaries (Koninklijke Notariële Beroepsorganisatie) 2008, p. 109–110. For an extensive discussion of waiver of rights, see *Meinema* op. cit. (note 18), p. 47.

**32** Cf. *Meinema* op. cit. (note 18), p. 27. In my opinion, the – unwritten – standard that the board of directors and the directors must focus on the interests of the legal entity when they are carrying out their management duties is comprised in the regulation stipulated in Article 2:9 of the Dutch Civil Code.

**33** In this sense, see also, e.g., *Wezeman* Aansprakelijkheid van bestuurders, thesis RUG 1998, IVO series no. 29, Deventer, the Netherlands: Kluwer, pp. 7–79. In my opinion, such agreements would also be invalid because they are contrary to a mandatory provision of law.

**34** In this sense, see also *De Kluiver/Meinema* op. cit. (note 11), p. 651.

**35** That is also supported by the parliamentary history. See further *Meinema* op. cit. (note 18), pp. 53–54.

ciation towards the managing directors.[36] Such agreements also have been declared invalid in the relevant case law.[37] The same fate would strike, I would argue, an agreement pursuant to which a shareholder undertakes in general and without reservation not to exercise his right to attend meetings and/or not to take cognisance of relevant information as that would result in de shareholder not being able taking part in supervising its management.[38]

In this context I would note that there is discussion in the literature about the validity of a contractual regulation pursuant to which a resolution to suspend or dismiss a director can be passed only if more stringent requirements are met than those permitted pursuant to Article 2:134/244(2) of the Dutch Civil Code. That Article stipulates that resolutions to suspend or dismiss a director may be subject to more stringent requirements only by an increased majority of two thirds of the votes cast that represent one-half of the issued capital. This gives rise to the question whether or not an agreement on the basis of which a larger majority, or even unanimous consent from the shareholders, is required for the dismissal or the suspension would be valid.[39]

In the recent case law, two district courts accepted the validity of such stipulations,[40] whereas a court of appeal avoided addressing that issue.[41] I believe that for the analysis it is relevant to take into consideration the fact that such a regulation is not at odds with the organisational structure. The general meeting retains the power to dismiss and suspend, and resolutions are adopted by the shareholders. In addition, such agreements are generally aimed at protecting the interests of a minority shareholder that participates with a substantial amount in the capital. Essentially, I am therefore of the opinion that this is a

---

**36** An agreement that would also fall within that scope would be an agreement not to exercise the right to information in accordance with Article 2:217 of the Dutch Civil Code. Cf. *Stokkermans* Preliminary Advice of the Royal Dutch Association of Civil-law Notaries 2008, p. 110. Another approach is that of *Blanco Fernández* Rechtmatigheidsgrenzen van stemovereenkomsten, *WPNR* 6626 (2005), pp. 517–518, who noted that the dualistic structure as such is not a fundamental principle of our company law. However, it is clear that that is not essence of my objections to such agreements.

**37** For an example, see Court of Appeal of Arnhem, the Netherlands, 8 March 1927, *NJ* 1927, pp. 1250 et seq.; Court of Appeal of Den Bosch, the Netherlands, 13 April 2004, JOR 2004/225. In the same sense, e.g., *de Kluiver/Meinema* op. cit. (note 11), p. 651.

**38** Such an agreement also conflicts with that relevant shareholder's obligation to observe the corporate standard of due care because it would render that obligation illusionary.

**39** See *Mohr* Spijkers: Ondernemingsrecht op de breuklijn van praktijk en wetenschap, Inaugural lecture UvA 1993, pp. 19–20, for an overview of proponents and opponents.

**40** District Court of Amsterdam, 16 January 2014, ECLI:NL:RBAMS:2014:193; District Court of Midden-Nederland, the Netherlands, 31 July 2015, ECLI:NL:RBMNE:2015:5677.

**41** Court of Appeal of Amsterdam, 13 January 2015, ECLI:NL:GHAMS:2015:55.

valid voting agreement, which is not aimed at disrupting the system of checks and balances but rather serves a legitimate interest in the mutual terms of collaboration between the shareholders.[42]

One specific type of voting agreement about which a great deal has been written is the 'vote buying' agreement. That is an agreement pursuant to which a shareholder undertakes, purely for the consideration offered in exchange, to vote in accordance with the instructions of the (generally highest) bidder or to allow his voting right to be exercised accordingly. A characteristic of vote buying is that as a result, the shareholder does not pursue his 'interest in the company'. If vote buying were considered valid, that essentially would mean that it would be acceptable and legally enforceable for control in the general meeting to be exercised without a coresponding equity participation. That would ultimately undermine the legitimacy of the general meeting (and the resolutions adopted in it) as such and as a result also the proper functioning of the company's organisation.[43]Therefore, the position that vote buying is impermissible is widely supported in the Dutch literature.[44]

On a more abstract note, the Dutch Supreme Court based the validity of voting agreements on the principle that a shareholder may serve his interest 'in the company' with the rights derived from company law. That formulation presumes a certain contextualisation and thereby normative framework, in the sense that in order to be valid there must be a certain degree of proportionality between what the shareholder has undertaken and the interest that he is pursuing. That assessment must be based on the specific circumstances of the case, in which context matters such as the term and terminability of the agreements play a role, in addition to the subjects to which it relates and to what and towards whom the shareholder has bound himself.[45]

In this context it is worth noting that an issue that formed part of the considerations that the Dutch Supreme Court put forward in the Judgments cited

---

**42** See further W.J.M. van Veen, 'Opnieuw: contractuele ontslagregelingen, doorwerking en het belang van de vennootschap', WPNR 2016 (7089), 20 – 23.

**43** *van Veen* op. cit. (note 9), p. 26.

**44** *van der Grinten* AAe IX, 1959 – 1960, p. 59; *Brenninkmeijer* Stemovereenkomsten van aandeelhouders, diss. KUN 1973, Deventer, the Netherlands: Kluwer, p. 164; *Asser-Maeijer* 2-III, nr. 288; *Van Schilfgaarde/Winter/Wezeman* op. cit. (note 28), nr. 67; *Asser/Maeijer/Van Solinge/Nieuwe* Weme 2-II*, nr. 384.

**45** *Löwensteijn* in Pitlo/Löwensteijn, Rechtspersonenrecht, 2nd printing (1986), pp. 266 – 267; *Meinema* op cit. (note 18), p. 195 – 197; *Maeijer* op. cit. (note 16), p. 101 – 102; *Asser/Maeijer/Van Solinge/Nieuwe* Weme 2-II*, nr. 385; *van Veen* op. cit. (note 7), pp. 26 – 27. For the record I would note that it is not necessary to address the question of whether the agreement substantively serves the intended interest well. That determination must be left to the shareholder.

above with respect to the validity of voting agreements was that the agreement intended to safeguard the agreements with respect to the resolution of disputes,[46] or the desired character of the company,[47] or a share transaction (and its implementation) between the shareholder and a third party.[48] Thus, the voting agreements in question serve an interest of the shareholder's in the outcome of the resolutions that are adopted or in the manner in which resolutions are adopted as such. An issue that formed part of the considerations that the Supreme Court put forward in the *Aurora* Judgment was explicitly that there was a certain degree of proportionality between the interest being pursued and the agreements that were made.[49] Here I reiterate that the fact that a voting agreement is entered into without any limitation in respect of its term and subject matter does not necessarily lead to the conclusion, in and of itself, that the agreement is invalid.[50]

Incidentally, I would note for the record that if a voting agreement is invalid it is not possible to demand in law that it be complied with. That does, however, not affect the fact that a vote that is cast in accordance with those (invalid) agreements is valid in principle.[51] A resolution that has been adopted in part on the basis of such agreements may, however, be subject to annulment.[52]

**46** Dutch Supreme Court, 30 June 1944, 465 (*Wennex*).

**47** Dutch Supreme Court, 13 November 1959, *NJ* 1960, 472 (*Destilleerderij Melchers*).

**48** Dutch Supreme Court, 19 February 1960, *NJ* 473(*Aurora*).

**49** For example, the Supreme Court ruled that option givers/shareholders had not undertaken towards Aurora in general to exercise their voting right to replace the supervisory directors of Olva, but rather exclusively to replace them in the event that the supervisory directors who were in office were to oppose the investigation that had to precede the transfer of the shares.

**50** Dutch Supreme Court, 13 November 1959, NJ 1960, 472.

**51** Unless, for example, it involves an abuse of power: Article 2:13(1) in conjunction with Article 3:13 of the Dutch Civil Code. In this sense, see also, e.g., *Mohr* op. cit. (note 39), p. 16; *Asser/Maeijer/Van Solinge/Nieuwe* Weme 2-II*, no. 387. Otherwise: *Blanco Fernández* Vennootschappelijke doorwerking van stemovereenkomsten, Ondernemingsrecht 1999, p. 148, who argues nullity of the vote. In view of the current provisions in the Dutch Civil Code on the nullity of votes I see no basis for that position.

**52** The resolution's being subject to annulment can be based on Article 2:8 of the Dutch Civil Code in conjunction with Article 2:15(1) of the Dutch Civil Code: contrary to the requirements of reasonableness and fairness.

# E. Shareholders' Agreements and corporate governance

## I. Effect of shareholders' agreements between shareholders

The starting point for a discussion of the interplay between shareholders' agreements and corporate governance, under Dutch law, is the observation that shareholders' agreements do not affect the allocation of rights and powers within the company. The allocation and assignment of rights and powers can be determined only under or pursuant to the Articles of Association with due observance of the statutory framework, not by means of an agreement. See sections 2 and 3.

In respect of the effect of shareholders' agreements, this means that they 'only' relate to the manner in which the right or power in question must be exercised. The right or power itself remains unaffected by the agreement. If a shareholder has acted (or there is a risk that a shareholder will act) contrary to the agreements that have been made, the other party has a number of legal remedies available, derived from the law of obligations, including demanding specific performance and/or compensation of damage.

An action for specific performance is of particular interest for this analysis, because it can also manifest in the context of company law. For example, if a resolution is adopted under company law as a result of acting in contravention of the agreement, it is possible to demand specific performance in the form that the shareholder in question shall cooperate with the revocation of the resolution and the adoption of a new resolution that is adopted in accordance with the agreement. Such a demand may also relate to the use of the powers that the shareholder has available in order to adopt resolutions, for example the power to convene the general meeting and the power to place an item on the agenda.[53] In the event that there are grounds on which to fear that a shareholder will not comply with the decision, the other party can request the court to rule that its decision will be deemed to be the vote (or, in appropriate cases: the other act that the shareholder has undertaken or is otherwise bound to perform) of the shareholder in question.[54]

A complication that may arise in this context is that the provisions in the shareholders' agreement may conflict with the provisions in the Articles of Asso-

53 Or the right to have such a meeting convened or to have items put on the agenda. Dutch Supreme Court, 19 February 1960, NJ 473, discussed in section 2. That case related to agreements between shareholders and the holder of options on shares in the company's capital.

54 Article 3:299 and Article 3:300 of the Dutch Civil Code.

ciation. That would be the case, for example, if unanimity were required for a particular resolution on the ground of the shareholders' agreement, but the Articles of Association require a majority of three-quarters of the votes cast for that same resolution. In these types of situations, it will have to be clear whether the shareholders intended (i) to have the regulation stipulated in the Articles of Association set aside the contractual regulation, (ii) to have the contractual regulation prevail over the regulation stipulated in the Articles of Association, or (iii) to have both regulations apply side by side. If it is not possible to determine that, it will be presumed that both regulations apply side by side.[55] In the Dutch case law no inherent hierarchy is assumed between the regulation stipulated in the Articles of Association and the contractual regulation.[56]

The Enterprise Court at the Amsterdam Court of Appeal (*Ondernemingskamer*) formulated that presumption in this a way that agreements that ensue from a shareholders' agreement "*cannot, in and of themselves, be cancelled out merely on the ground that resolutions under the rules of company law were adopted in the proper manner in a stricter sense*".[57]

## II. Effect of Shareholders' Agreements on the company (or its bodies)

In some cases, in order to ensure compliance with the arrangements stipulated in a shareholders' agreement, it is necessary to institute legal proceedings against the company. The question that then arises is whether the company and the company's bodies must also pay heed to the shareholders' agreement. In the Dutch literature this doctrine is known as 'the corporate-law effect of shareholders' agreements' (*vennootschapsrechtelijke doorwerking van aandeelhoudersovereenkomsten*).

There is ample case law that has been handed down in the Netherlands with respect to the *vennootschapsrechtelijke doorwerking* of shareholders' agreements. The pattern in that case law is that, in principle, the company, its bodies and others who are involved in its organisation must honour the agreements that the shareholders have made with each other and, if necessary, must actively ensure

**55** President of the District Court of Middelburg, the Netherlands, 14 April 1998, JOR 2000, 25 (VenV).

**56** That does not affect the fact that observance with the regulation stipulated in the Articles of Association is always a condition for the legal validity of the act in question. In view of the space that has been allotted to me I will not elaborate on that further.

**57** Enterprise Court at the Amsterdam Court of Appeal, 20 May 1999, NJ 2000, 199.

that they are complied with. If they fail to do so, depending on the concrete circumstances, that can be qualified as a tort,[58] a violation of the requirements of reasonableness and fairness required pursuant to Article 2:8 of the Dutch Civil Code,[59] and/or improper performance of their duties (Article 2:9 of the Dutch Civil Code).[60] That pattern is consistent from the District Courts up to the Dutch Supreme Court.

The corporate-law effect of shareholders' agreements transpires in Dutch law, through open standards, in particular the various standards of due care.[61] In the literature,[62] and case law handed down by a lower court,[63] the effect in question is sometimes subject to the condition that the company must be a party to the shareholders' agreement or must have implicitly accepted it. However, the fact that the effect transpires through open standards implies that that is not required.[64] That is evident from, for example, the Dutch Supreme Court's Judgment in the case of *Chipshol v. Landinvest*,[65] in which the Supreme Court ignored the company's defence that the arrangements stipulated in the shareholders' agreement did not concern it because it was not a party to that agreement. It is clear from many other decisions that the question of whether or not the company is a party to the agreement was not relevant in the context of the corporate-

---

**58** Dutch Supreme Court, 29 November 1996, NJ 1997, 345 (*Chipshol v. Landinvest*), in which a person was appointed supervisory director in contravention of the shareholders' agreement that he himself had participated in drafting.

**59** For example, Enterprise Court at the Amsterdam Court of Appeal, 8 May 2002, JOR 2002/112, with commentary from *J.M. Blanco Fernández* (*Versatel*); District Court of The Hague, 1 August 2012, ECLI:NL:RBSGR:2012:BX5922, *JOR* 2012/286, with commentary from *J.M. Blanco Fernández* (*Vanka-Kawat Holding BV*); District Court of Amsterdam, 16 January 2014, ECLI:NL:RBAMS:2014:193, JOR 2014, 157 (*RedBlue*).

**60** In exceptional circumstances directors sometimes may also be obliged, on the grounds of reasonableness and fairness, *not* to carry out the agreement between the shareholders, for example if they are unilaterally disadvantageous for the shareholder in question, who excusably was not aware that that was the case. See Court of Appeal of Amsterdam (Enterprise Court), 20 July 2001, JOR 2001/203 (*Nering-Plein*).

**61** For the record I would note that there can also be such an effect in the case of an agreement to which, in addition to shareholders, another parties involved in the organisation are parties. See, e. g., Court of Appeal of Amsterdam 21 January 2014, ECLI:NL:GHAMS:2014:91, *JOR* 2014/158.

**62** For example, *Bulten* De vennootschap en de geconstrueerde werkelijkheid, Ondernemingsrecht 2014/94, p. 475–476; Cf. *Timmerman* Wie moeten er meedoen?, WPNR 7028 (2014), p. 699.

**63** District Court of Rotterdam, 27 October 2010, ECLI:NL:RBROT:2010:BO4104, *RO* 2011/14 (*GS General Services v. X GmbH*).

**64** See *van Veen* op. cit. (note 9), pp. 33 et seq., SamenWerken in het ondernemingsrecht, Serie van wege het Instituut voor Ondernemingsrecht, part 80, Kluwer 2011, pp. 113 *et seq.* In the same sense see *J.M. Blanco Fernández* in his note to JOR 2012/286, in particular § 4.

**65** Dutch Supreme Court, 29 November 1996, *NJ* 1997, 345.

law effect.[66] The Supreme Court also commented on that in its recent ruling in respect of *Cancun*,[67] as in that ruling the Court referred to the obligation of the board of directors of a joint venture, when carrying out its duties to be guided inter alia by the nature and content of the collaboration agreed "*between the shareholders*".

Here I note that when the company has co-signed the shareholders' agreement, it is a matter of interpretation whether or not it can be considered to be a party to the shareholders' agreement or that it merely co-signed the agreement to express that has taken cognisance of it. See District Court of Amsterdam 5 July 2016, ECLI:NL:RBAMS:2016:4164, in which the court rejected the position of the company that it had become a party to the shareholders' agreement by co-signing the shareholders' agreement.

It is evident from the case law that the corporate-law effect can result in (i) an order to or prohibition against exercising rights or powers under company law in a particular manner;[68] (ii) nullification of resolutions;[69] and/or, in the context of inquiry proceedings, (iii) the determination that there is a well-founded reason to doubt correct policy or state of affairs, with the related possibility to make provisional measures;[70] or (iv) the determination that there has been mismanage-

**66** See, e.g., District Court of Middelburg, 14 April 1998, *JOR* 2000, 25 (*VenV*); Enterprise Court at the Amsterdam Court of Appeal, 20 May 1999, NJ 2000, 199 (*Versatel*); Enterprise Court at the Amsterdam Court of Appeal, 8 May 2002, JOR 2002/112, with commentary from J.M. Blanco Fernández (*Broadnet*); Enterprise Court at the Amsterdam Court of Appeal, 28 December 2005, JOR 2006/66 (*Gekas & Boot*).

**67** Dutch Supreme Court, 4 March 2014, ECLI:NL:HR2014:797, NJ 2014/286 (*Cancun*).

**68** See, e.g., Dutch Supreme Court, 29 November 1998, *NJ* 1997, 345 (*Chipshol v. Landinvest*): the board of directors were ordered to convene a general meeting, properly explaining that the agenda item would be the dismissal of a supervisory director; District Court of Amsterdam, 16 January 2014, ECLI:NL:RBAMS:2014:193, *JOR* 2014, 157 (*RedBlue*), in which the company was prohibited from dismissing in contravention of the shareholders' agreement.

**69** See, e.g., District Court of The Hague, 1 August 2012, ECLI:NL:RBSGR:2012:BX5922, *JOR* 2012/286, with commentary from *J.M. Blanco Fernández* (*Vanka-Kawat Holding BV*), which involved the nullification of a resolution that had been adopted by the supervisory board and the general meeting. Cf. Court of Appeal of Amsterdam 21 January 2014, ECLI:NL:GHAMS:2014:91, *JOR* 2014, 158, with commentary from Nowak, which involved nullification of a resolution that had been adopted by the general meeting of a private limited liability company and the board of directors of a foundation.

**70** See, *e.g.*, Dutch Supreme Court, 19 October 2001, ECLI:NL:HR:2001:AD5138, NJ 2002, 92 (*Skygate Holding BV*); Enterprise Court at the Amsterdam Court of Appeal, 8 May 2002, *JOR* 2002/112, with commentary from *J.M. Blanco Fernández* (*Versatel)*; Enterprise Court at the Amsterdam Court of Appeal, 28 December 2005, *JOR* 2006/66 (*Gekas & Boot*); Enterprise Court at the Amsterdam Court of Appeal, 31 December 2009, ECLI:NL:GHAMS:2009:BL3680, *JOR* 2010/60 with commentary from *Doorman*; Dutch Supreme Court, 25 February 2011, ECLI:NL:HR:2011:BO7067, *JOR*

ment, with the measures that may be attached to that.[71] Furthermore, a violation of a shareholders' agreement can lead to a forced takeover or transfer in the context of the statutory dispute settlement rules.[72]

In the *Cancun* Judgment that the Dutch Supreme Court recently rendered,[73] the corporate-law effect acquired an extra dimension. In that judgment, the Supreme Court ruled that in respect of joint ventures, the company's interest is determined in part by the continuous success of the company's enterprise and in part by the nature and content of the agreements that the shareholders have made with respect to the joint venture. In view of the fact that pursuant to the law, managing directors – and the same holds true for supervisory directors – must be guided by the company's interest while fulfilling their duties, the *Cancun* Judgment implies that in the case of joint ventures and other comparable forms of collaboration, the board of directors and the directors themselves must take into consideration the nature and content of the agreements that the shareholders have made with respect to their collaboration. If the company serves to give form to and implement the intended joint venture agreement, the board of directors and the directors themselves are obliged, on the ground of their statutory remit, to be guided, among other things, by the aim of realising that what the shareholders have agreed upon. If they are remiss in this respect, that will result in a higher risk of liability on the ground of improper performance of their duties.[74]

In this context it also should be noted that the Supreme Court ruled that the general standards of due care within the meaning of Article 6:162 of the Dutch Civil Code (tort law) are also interpreted in the light of the corporate-law reasonableness and fairness within the meaning of Article 2:8 of the Dutch Civil Code.[75] If a director acts in contravention of the shareholders' agreement and if, as a result, he harms a shareholder's interests, it will be more likely that that will be qualified as a tort towards that shareholder. That applies *a fortiori* in the event

---

2011/115, with commentary from *Doorman* (*Inter Access*); Dutch Supreme Court, 11 July 2014, ECLI:NL:HR:2014:1651 (*Novero Holdings*), with commentary from *P. Storm* Ondernemingsrecht 2014/130.

**71** See, e.g., Dutch Supreme Court, 4 March 2014, ECLI:NL:HR2014:797, *NJ* 2014/286 (*Cancun*).

**72** Cf. District Court of Rotterdam, 13 June 2012, ECLI:NL:RBROT:2012:BW8951 (*SEQ International/Eneco Wind*).

**73** Dutch Supreme Court, 4 March 2014, ECLI:NL:HR2014:797, *NJ* 2014/286 (*Cancun*).

**74** In this respect, see *van Veen* Vennootschapsrechtelijke doorwerking, bestuursautonomie en bestuurstaak bij Joint Ventures na 'Cancun', Ondernemingsrecht 2015–13, no. 88, pp. 441–449.

**75** See Dutch Supreme Court, 16 January 2007, ECLI:NL:HR:2007:AZ0419, *JOR* 2007/112, with commentary from Van Veen and Van Wechem.

that a provision intended to protect the shareholder has been included in the Articles of Association.[76]

Thus, it can be concluded that the shareholders' agreement to which all the shareholders are parties, is a powerful document from the perspective of corporate governance, even if the company is not a party to the agreement.

## III. The interests of the company and co-shareholders as correction

The effect of shareholders' agreements in relationships under company law was discussed in the preceding sections. In this section I will discuss another aspect of the interplay between company law and contract law: the effect of company-law norms in the contractual relationships. That could be thought of as the 'reverse corporate-law effect'. The fact that, as in the case of joint ventures, the shareholders have undertaken to collaborate in the form of a company with share capital can lead to a situation in which it is not possible to demand compliance with the shareholders' agreement.

Various examples of this can be found in the case law. The majority of those decisions relate to situations in which there was a threat to the continuity of the company or the enterprise affiliated with it. In such cases a dissident shareholder is expected to also take into consideration the company's interests. An excellent example of this is the Judgment rendered by the District Court of Middelburg dated 14 April 1998 (*JOR* 2000/23 (*VenV*)). Although the contractual requirement of unanimity to adopt the resolution in question was taken as the underlying principle, the invocation of that contractual stipulation was rejected on the basis of the following determination:

> *In view of the problems, without failing to appreciate Sandieson's interests as a shareholder, also in view of the obligation that ensues for it from the collaboration agreement to pursue the interests of all the shareholders, and in view of the responsibility that it also bears as a shareholder for the interests of other parties that have an interest in the company, such as employees, a constructive approach to possible solutions may nonetheless be expected of Sandieson.*

---

**76** See Dutch Supreme Court, 20 June 2008, ECLI:NL:HR:2008:BC4959 , *NJ* 2009, 21, *JOR* 2008/260 (*Willemsen/NOM*).

The Court went on to order *Sandieson* to cast its vote in favour of the board's proposal, and if it failed to do so the Judgment would take the place of the vote.[77]

A decision rendered by the Enterprise Court at the Amsterdam Court of Appeal took the same turn.[78] After formulating the basic assumption that, in principle, contractual agreements also had to be complied with, the Court ruled as follows:

> Furthermore, as things stand, but also apart from that, the joint venture nature of the collaboration between the original parties means that also Cromwild bears the obligation to promote to the best of its ability the realisation of a jointly supported policy (...) and it is not free, or in any event not in and of itself and not at all times, to give priority to its own interests.

Another decision that is worth mentioning in this context is the Dutch Supreme Court's decision dated 19 October 2001 (*NJ* 2002, 92 (*Skygate Holding B.V.*). In that case, the joint venture company urgently required additional financing. One of the joint venture partners (FTS) frustrated the adoption of a resolution to that effect, presumably because it could not finance an expansion of its equity investment. In the context of the inquiry proceedings injunctive relief was requested, which included having the company issue convertible loans. FTS objected to that relief, in part because it would have an irreversible effect on the agreed ratio in the blocks of shares in the joint venture company. However, the Supreme Court ruled that the conclusion from a reasonable weighing of the interests was that FTS could not block the issue by invoking the agreed existing ratios because without the issue the company would become insolvent and moreover the dilution that FTS feared need not occur if it were to decide to participate in the financing.

One last example I would mention is the Judgment of the Court of Appeal of Amsterdam dated 25 April 2002 (*JOR* 2002/128 (*Gorillapark*)), which also involved a company that urgently required supplementary financing. In that context the company drew up an investment plan, which was worked out in more detail in the "Second Amended Shareholders' Agreement". One of the shareholders, IIP, argued that it could not be expected to accept the investment plan because, compared with the existing shareholders' agreement, it provided for a less favourable anti-dilution clause. However, the Court of Appeal ruled that in view of the emergency situation that the company was in, IIP was acting in contraven-

77 With respect to a prohibition against voting, see, *e.g.*, District Court of Alkmaar, the Netherlands, 1 November 1989, ECLI:NL:RBALK:1989:AH2889.

78 Enterprise Court at the Amsterdam Court of Appeal, 20 May 1999, NJ 199 (*Versatel*).

tion of the principles of reasonableness and fairness towards the company (which was not a party to the agreement) and the shareholders who were parties to the shareholders' agreement. In this respect, the Court of Appeal found that on the basis of the corporate-law standards of reasonableness and fairness, the invocation of the original anti-dilution clause was unreasonable. Finally, the Court of Appeal confirmed the order that had been imposed on IIP in the first instance to act in accordance with the Second Amended Shareholders' Agreement.

Thus, it is clear from the relevant case law that the corporate-law standards of reasonableness and fairness stipulated in Article 2:8 of the Dutch Civil Code – both in a restrictive and in a supplementary sense – explicitly have an effect on the contractual relationships that ensue from a shareholders' agreement. Again, as the cited case law shows, the company need not be a party to the shareholders' agreement to have that effect.

# F. Conclusion

Under Dutch law, shareholders' agreements have full right of existence in addition to the regulations that the parties have laid down in the Articles of Association. A consistent pattern is discernible in the Dutch case law in which, often ahead of the doctrine, the validity of shareholders' agreements was presumed, also in the event that they are intended to create a legal situation that could not be achieved by means of a regulation in the Articles of Association (see section 3). Broadly speaking, agreements will only be deemed null and void if they aim at violating the law, directly or indirectly give licence to violate standards of due care with respect to exercise of powers and duties, or undermining the proper operation of the company, and/or are otherwise aimed at harming the interests of the company or other shareholders (see section 4). That cannot be considered an objectionable limitation of freedom of contract.

It can be concluded that the Dutch judiciary has not been readily inclined to presume that provisions under company law limit shareholders' freedom of contract with respect to how they wish to arrange their collaboration. Thus, if a shareholders' agreement is in force, the entirety of the regulations stipulated in the Articles of Association and the contractual arrangement governs the collaboration that is in effect between the shareholders. As a result of the fact that the effect of Articles of Association and shareholders' agreements is very different, shareholders can make custom-tailored agreements, and they have more influence on the legal effect of their agreements. That choice can be made, depending on the intended effect, by laying down certain agreements in the Articles of

Association and/or in the shareholders' agreement.[79] That inures to the benefit of flexibility and freedom to customise the agreed terms of collaboration.

Another set pattern in the case law is that the agreed terms of collaboration must be complied with and (therefore) it must be possible to effectuate them, either by means of an action for specific performance against the parties to the agreement (section 5.1), or on by means of an action against the company (and its bodies), known as the 'corporate-law effect' of shareholders' agreements (section 5.2). However, under some circumstances, demanding full compliance with certain agreed terms could frustrate or endanger the company or its enterprise. In such cases demanding compliance with the agreed term of collaboration would be contrary to the essence of what the shareholders have undertaken towards each other, *i.e.* to promote the success of the (corporate) collaboration and therefore contrary to corporate-law standards of reasonableness and fairness. In such cases the demand for compliance with the relevant provision in the shareholders' agreement is not honoured in the Dutch case law (section 5.3).

In sum: On the interplay between Articles of association and shareholders' agreements the Dutch judiciary appears to have been less conservative than the doctrine. The case law in the Netherlands concerning the interplay between Articles of Association and shareholders' agreements has developed steadily, well balanced and meritoriously for Dutch legal practice.

---

79 For example, if a right of first refusal is included in a shareholders' agreement non-compliance therewith would not render the shares non-transferrable, whereas right of first refusal stipulated in the Articles of Association would render the shares non-transferrable as long as the offering procedure is not complied with. Another example is that a breach of a contractual veto right would not render of the resolution in question null and void, whereas non-observance of veto right stipulated in the Articles of Association would render that resolution null and void. See for more examples section 3. It is beyond the scope of this article to discuss all the differences. I would refer the interested reader to *van Veen* op. cit. (note 9), pp. 16–18.

Łukasz Gasiński

# Poland

## Table of Content



---

**Dr hab. Łukasz Gasiński,** Faculty of Law, Warsaw University, LLM Columbia University, Partner, Weil, Gotshal and Manges, Warsaw Office

https://doi.org/10.1515/9783110517026-020

# A. Nature of Corporate Law Regulations[1]

## I. General concept regarding articles of association and the nature of a corporation

As in many other legal systems, there is also an ongoing debate in Polish law on the nature of a corporation and the limits of freedom of contract in corporate law. The Polish debate is quite similar to the one in other countries – there are two generally opposing views.

It is argued that a corporation is a contract; therefore, articles of association should also be regarded as a contract, but a specific one as they provide for the grounds for the creation of a corporation and are governed by a different set of rules than those governing a classic contract.[2] The opposite view is that a corpo-

1 Generally this paper deals with shareholders' agreements with regard to a joint-stock company (AG under German law) and not a limited liability company (GmbH under German law) in particular in the section devoted to the nature of corporate law. In the next section, when I refer to the corporation, it should be also deemed to be in reference to a Polish joint-stock company and in the situation in which I refer to a Polish GMBH it will be always mean a limited liability company. I will, however, refer to some instances of case law concerning the governing of shareholders' agreements which were established in a limited liability company. Worthy of note is the kind of peculiarity of Polish Supreme Court case law which limits the freedom of contract in such companies in a similar way as the Polish Commercial Code regulates the freedom of contract in a joint-stock company. Thus, any references to shareholders' agreements case law are justified as it is predictable that the Supreme Court will rule in the same way with respect to shareholders' agreements governing corporations.

2 S. Sołtysiński (w:) S. Sołtysiński, A. Szajkowski, A. Szumański, J. Szwaja *Kodeks spółek handlowych*, t. 3, Komentarz do artykułów 301–458, Warszawa 2008, s. 66 i nast., S. Sołtysiński (w:) *System prawa prywatnego, Prawo spółek kapitałowych*, 1.17 A, pod red. S. Sołtysińskiego, Warszawa 2010, s. 17–21, S. Włodyka (w:) *Prawo gospodarcze i handlowe, Prawo umów w obrocie gospodarczym*, t. 5, pod red. S. Włodyki, Warszawa 2001, s. 452, R. Potrzeszcz, T Siemiątkowski (w:) *Komentarz do kodeksu spółek handlowych, Spółka akcyjna i przepisy karne*, t. 1, pod red. R. Potrzeszcza, T. Siemiątkowskiego, Warszawa 2003, s. 24–27, J. Frąckowiak *Handlowe czynności kreujące*, PPH 2008, nr 12, s. 4 i nast., J. Frąckowiak (w:) *System prawa handlowego, Prawo spółek handlowych*, t. 2B, pod red. S. Włodyki, Warszawa 2007, s. 56 i nast., W. Popiołek *Akcja – prawo podmiotowe*, Warszawa 2010, s. 13, M. Romanowski (w:) *System Prawa Prywatnego, Prawo spółek osobowych*, 1.16, pod. red. A. Szajkowskiego, Warszawa 2008, s. 85–152, A. Szajkowski *Umowa spółki handlowej*, SP 2001, nr 3–4, s. 320 i nast., Ł. Gasiński *Umowy akcjonariuszy co do sposobu wykonywania prawa głosu w prawie polskim oraz amerykańskim*, Warszawa 2006, s. 17–22, D. Wajda *Obowiązek lojalności w spółkach handlowych*, Warszawa 2009, s.

ration is not a contract, but rather an institution. Therefore, the articles of association should not be regarded as a contract, at least from the date of the registration of the corporation with the registry court. Registration with the registry court transforms the articles of association from a contract into a different form of a legal act which can be defined as a "private legal act".[3] The prevailing theory is that a corporation is a contract or has contractual roots. Such theory has been well established in Supreme Court cases and is shared by many theorists. Consequently, the Supreme Court has several times referred to the view that articles of association are of a contractual nature and cannot be regarded as a "private legal regulation".[4]

## II. Limits on the principle of the freedom of contract in corporate law – articles of association

The general assumption that articles of association are of a contractual nature does not mean, by such simple statement, that the general principle of the freedom of contract should apply to the creation or amendment of articles of association. The Commercial Companies Code expressly allows for the application of the Civil Code, but only with respect to legal relations not regulated by the Commercial Companies Code. In the case of corporations, the Commercial Companies Code incorporates the German concept of Salztzunsstrenge (in Polish: *zasada ścisłości statutu*, in English: the principle of formal statute stringency) according to which it is possible to change a normative regulation only if the

73–75, R.L. Kwaśnicki *Swoboda w kształtowaniu treści umów i statutów spółek kapitałowych (na tle prawa niemieckiego)*, Warszawa 2010, s. 82–92, M. Goszczyk *Zmiany statutu i kapitału w spółce akcyjnej.* Artykuł 430–458 KSH. Komentarz, Warszawa 2009, s. 5, A. Opalski (w:) *System prawa prywatnego, Prawo spółek kapitałowych*, t. 17B, pod red. S. Sołtysińskiego, Warszawa 2010, s. 625. Zagadnienia te były również dyskutowane pod rządami Kodeksu Handlowego – zob. M. Goszczyk, *Charakter prawny statutu spółki akcyjnej*, Pr. Spółek 1997, nr 3, s. 10 i nast., S. Sołtysiński (w:) S. Sołtysiński, A. Szajkowski, J. Szwaja *Kodeks Handlowy.* Komentarz, t. 2, s. 60 i nast., A.W. Wiśniewski *Prawo o spółkach. Podręcznik praktyczny*, t. 3, *Spółka akcyjna*, Warszawa 1993, s. 33 i nast.; J. Okolski, J. Modrzejewski, Ł. Gasiński *Natura stosunku korporacyjnego spółki akcyjnej*, PPH 2000, nr 8, s. 1.

3 A. Opalski *O potrzebie systemowej analizy instytucji wspólnych dla zrzeszeń*, SPP 2009, nr 2, s. 97–113.

4 See, for example, the following rulings of the Supreme Court: Wyrok Sądu Najwyższego dnia 16 października 2008, III CSK 100/08, OSNC-ZD 2009, nr 1, poz.30, Wyrok Sądu Najwyższego z dnia 19 stycznia 2011 r., V CSK 223/10, LEX nr 688710, Wyrok Sądu Najwyższego z dnia 17 listopada 2011 r. III CZP 68/11, LEX nr 1049902, Wyrok Sądu Najwyższego z dnia 5 września 2012 r., IV CSK 2012 r., IV CSK 589/11, LEX nr 1232242.

Commercial Companies Code[5] allows it. The Polish regulator did not use the word "expressly", which allows for some speculation as to whether, in the absence of express permission to regulate something in a different manner, it is possible to reconstruct such authorisation as a result of the interpretation of the law. The libertarian view has developed the theory that the contractual roots of a corporation allow for the application of the principle of freedom of contract in certain cases, even in the absence of an express authorisation in the Commercial Companies Code. Some argue that such deviation from the Commercial Companies Code is possible even without express permission in the context of a technical regulation of the Commercial Companies Code, which does not serve to govern any fundamental values of corporate law but rather governs the technical details concerning a term of office or how supervision is performed in a corporation. [6]

The rigidness of the German concept pushed some scholars as well as the Supreme Court to look at the provisions of articles of associations from two different perspectives.[7] Basically, it is argued that the principle of formal statute stringency applies only to those provisions of articles of association that are defined as having a corporate nature (for example, provisions establishing the legal relations between different corporate bodies of a corporation), and that it does not apply to provisions that can be characterised as contractual ones (for example, provisions creating relations of which a good example would be a provision providing for a right of first refusal). Contractual provisions, in accordance with this theory, should be analysed from the contractual perspective of the principle of freedom of contract. This theory obviously allows for an extension of the

5 See Art. 304 § 3 and § 4 of the Commercial Companies Code – § 3. Where permitted by this Act, the company articles may contain provisions different from those provided in this Act. § 4. The company articles may contain additional provisions, save where it should transpire from this Act that exhaustive regulations are provided for therein, or where an additional provision of the company articles is contrary to the nature of the joint-stock company or good practice.

6 For example, the Commercial Companies Code provides that, except for certain situations, supervision over a corporation is performed by the supervisory board acting to¬gether and not by individual members of the supervisory board. Both forms of supervision are permitted in a limited liability company and, frankly speaking, there are not many arguments supporting the view that such supervision of a corporation should be allowed. Unfortunately, the Commercial Companies Code does not expressly allow for deviation apart from certain ex¬ceptions from the rule that the supervisory board members must act together in connection with the supervision of a corporation. It is argued that such freedom to deviate from the legal model can be recon-structed through interpretation. For more information on this, please see: Ł. Gasiński: *Granice Swobody kształtowania treści statutu*, Warsaw 2014, p. 184–192.

7 Wyrok Sądu Najwyższego z dnia 7 grudnia 2007 r., III CSK 195/07, LEX nr 465900.

boundaries of the principle of freedom of contract in a corporation, but it also creates certain ambiguity. The assignation of several provisions to one group or another may be difficult, and it will not always be crystal clear which of the principles – freedom of contract or formal statute stringency – should be applied.

The other consequence of the implementation of the principle of formal statute stringency is that provisions of articles of association (*dodatkowe postanowienia statutu*), which are in addition to the ones that are already envis-aged by the law, are permitted to the extent the Commercial Companies Code does not provide for complete regulation. For example, it is not possible to create new unnamed bodies within the corporate governance structure. Additional provisions related to the principle of the freedom of contract that are preceded by the wording 'in particular' are sometimes flagged by the Commercial Companies Code. For example there is no closed list of special rights that can be attached to privileged shares or individual rights of shareholders.[8] Another example of the provision that fails within the category of the additional provisions are provisions providing for the fulfilment of specific criteria in order to be appointed as a management board member or some additional buy-out obligations imposed on majority shareholders. Obviously, these additional provisions are subject to the other limitations of the principle of the freedom of contract.

In addition to the above-described limitations of the principle of the freedom of contract, any provision deviating from the law or any addition to articles of association (that is not expressly allowed by the law) needs to be in line with good rules of conduct ("*dobre obyczaje*" ("good morals", "fairness principle")) and the nature of a corporation ("*natura spółki akcyjnej*").

It is the fairness principle that allows one to not only look at the black-and-white letter of the law, but to also refer to certain values which exist irrespective of the written law. In the context of the principle of the freedom of contract, good morals are defined in principle as values that are protected in a given society and which do not allow certain areas of a person's activity to be encompassed by, or subject to, contractual law or which do not allow the entry into contracts in certain circumstances.

**8** See Art. 351, 354 of the Commercial Companies Code. It is argued that such broad regulation allows for rights such as veto rights, which are described as a "Golden Share". [For more information, please see Ł. Gasiński *Granice Swobody kształtowania treści statutu*, Warsaw 2014, p. 184–192. This view is not shared by the majority of Polish scholars; moreover, the most recent decision of the Supreme Court suggests that the attachment of veto rights to one share is rather not permissible under Polish law, in particular in respect of the State Treasury – Wyrok Sądu Najwyższego z dnia 23 września 2004, IC 713/03, OSNC 2005 nr 9, poz.160.

Another factor limiting the principle of the freedom of contract provided for in the Commercial Companies Code is a Polish innovation regarding discussions on the limits of contract.[9] The nature of a corporation is understood as the major characteristics of the corporation, such as the lack of the personal liability of the shareholders, the principle of equal treatment, the principle of proportionality, the majority rule principle, principles governing share capital, the minority protection principle, etc. Basically, not all deviations from these principles should be regarded as prohibited, but only those that are defined as blatant deviations. As this general concept is quite vague, its application is being discussed and questioned both in practice and in the theory of the law. Some even claim that the nature of the corporate clause, as one of the limits to the principle of the freedom of contract, should be removed from private law regulations. It is argued that it creates too much uncertainty and thus is not in line with free market principles.[10] Other critics of this clause assume that the concept of the "nature of the corporate clause" is nothing more than a "law clause" which is already incorporated into the principle of the freedom of contract. [11] The difference is that the nature of the corporate clause allows for the imposition of certain limits on the principle of the freedom of contract which are not expressly provided for in the Commercial Companies Code but rather reconstructed in the process of interpretation. The discussion with respect to the nature of a corporation is an important one given the fact that some commentators argue that such criteria are applicable to shareholders' agreements which are formed outside of articles of the association.

In order to provide an adequate picture of the principle of the freedom of contract in corporate law, it is necessary to state that the adoption of the princi-

**9** A similar criterion is expressly provided in the Civil Code, which espouses the nature of contractual relations that limit the principle of the freedom of contract. – Art. 3531 of the Civil Code – Parties entering into a contract may determine the legal relation at their own discretion, provided that its content or purpose does not prejudice the nature of the relation, a statute or the principles of community coexistence.

**10** Z. Radwański in: *Prawo cywilne – część ogólna*, red. Z. Radwański, t. 2: *System Prawa Prywatnego*, Warszawa 2008, p. 237.

**11** P. Machnikowski *Swoboda umów według art. 3531 KC. Konstrukcja prawna*, Warszawa 2005, p. 336. See, however, S. Wronkowska, Z. Ziembiński *Zarys teorii prawa*, Poznań 2001, p. 189. According to the findings of those authors: "However, accepting such principle – norm [the principle of the freedom of contract – Ł.G.] as prevailing and adopting the exceptiones non sunt extendendae interpretation principle, one should also assume that all regulations restricting the principle of the freedom of contract should, as regulations which establish exceptions, be interpreted exclusively in accordance with the language directives of interpretation, excluding any extensive interpretation".

ple of formal statute stringency does not eliminate freedom of contract as in many instances Polish law provides for the freedom to deviate from this law. For example, it is possible to incorporate in articles of association multiple voting shares (two votes per share), voting caps (even in a public corporation) or special shareholder rights. Consequently, it is argued that the adoption of the German concept (the principle of formal statute stringency) does not necessarily mean that the boundaries of freedom of contract are the same in Poland as they are in Germany.

# B. Regulation of Shareholders' Agreements

## I. Specific regulations on shareholders' agreements

Polish law does not provide for detailed and specific regulations regarding shareholders' agreements, which does not mean that there is no legal regulation at all or that Polish law ignores the existence of such agreements in practice.

## II. The regulation of shareholders' agreements in the Commercial Companies Code

The Commercial Companies Code does not explicitly set forth any general legal principles whereby such agreements are valid and binding, nor does it provide for a detailed obligation on how to draft such agreements or to take other actions to extend their applicability to the corporation itself, its governing bodies or any future shareholders. There is no general rule imposing an obligation to file a shareholders' agreement with the registry court, nor is there an obligation to publish its provisions. This does not mean that the Commercial Companies Code is completely silent on certain shareholders' agreements or that it ignores the existence of such agreements in practice.

The Commercial Companies Code regulates one of the aspects of shareholders' agreements and the consequences resulting therefrom. It provides a definition of a dominant company, which describes how one company can gain control over another company, and it provides that such control can be acquired as a consequence of the entry into a voting agreement. Regardless of the legal basis of control (through shares or voting agreements), the dominant entity is required to notify the controlled company of the fact of the acquisition of control.[12] This regulation is of a general nature and applies to all sorts of companies and partnerships.

The other aspect of the regulation of the issue of voting in shareholders' agreements that is provided for by the Commercial Companies Code is the regulation on pledges and usufructuary rights to shares. In both instances, it is permitted to transfer the voting rights to a pledgee or usufructuary right holder who is allowed to exercise voting rights attached to pledged or usufructuary shares, respectively. These specific mechanisms are allowed both with respect to a limited liability company[13] and a joint stock company. The main difference is that with respect to a joint stock company,[14] it is possible to contract it out in the articles of association, whereas in a limited liability company it needs to be contracted into the articles in order to allow the pledgee or usufructuary right holder to exercise voting rights attached to shares. As the pledgee or usufructuary rights holder is deemed to have the right to exercise voting rights in their own name and their right to vote from pledged or usufructuary shares is reflected in the shareholder register, it is fair to assume that Polish law recognises the transfer of a voting right attached to a share if it is connected with a pledge over or a

**12** See Art. 4 § 1 p. 4) – a payment card – this should be understood as a payment card within the meaning of the Payment Services Act of 19 August 2011 (Journal of Laws of 2016, item 1572).
**13** See Art. 187 § 1 and § 2 of the Commercial Companies Code – §1. The transfer of a share or, as the case may be, of part or a fraction thereof to another person, likewise the creation of a pledge or usufruct thereon, shall be notified by the interested parties to the company together with proof of the transfer or of the creation of the pledge or usufruct. The transfer of a share, or, as the case may be, of part or a fraction thereof, likewise the creation of a pledge or usufruct thereon, shall be effective against the company as of receipt by the company of a notification to this effect from one of the interested parties together with proof of performance of the act. § 2. The company deed may provide that the pledgee or usufructuary be authorised to exercise his voting right.
**14** See Art. 340 of the Commercial Companies Code – §1. The pledgee and usufructuary may exercise the voting right attached to that registered share or provisional certificate on which a pledge or usufruct has been established if this has been envisaged by the act in law by which the limited right in rem has been established and if the establishment of the right and the conferring of authority to exercise the voting right has been duly noted in the register of shares. § 2. A company's articles of association may provide for a prohibition on conferring a voting right upon a pledgee or usufructuary of a share, or may make the conferring of such right subject to the consent of a certain body of the company. §3. Throughout the period when those shares in a public company, on which a pledge or usufruct has been established, are entered into a securities account operated by a subject entitled thereto, pursuant to provisions concerning trading in financial instruments, the voting right attached to such shares shall be enjoyed by the shareholder.

right of usufruct to shares. It is something of an aberration that this Commercial Companies Code regulation is designed only for private companies and does not apply to public companies. This obviously does not mean that the establishment of a pledge over or usufructuary right to dematerialised shares is not allowed, but it means that the voting rights attached to such shares cannot be transferred to a pledgee or usufructuary rights holder. Such pledgee or rights holder would need to rely on a power of attorney if they wish to exercise the voting rights attached to the shares.

The mechanism that is related to voting agreements is exclusively designed for a public corporation. The Commercial Companies Code also allows for a shareholder holding a block of shares to vote in a different manner in respect of each of the shares. Basically, it means that one can vote in favour of or against a particular resolution based on the voting rights attached to the shares that the given shareholder has registered in connection with the meeting of the shareholders.[15] This regulation is meant to enable depositaries, investment firms, banks operating omnibus accounts and other financial institutions to express the will of the investors in the name of which such financial institution is holding shares. Basically, the assumption underlying such regulation is that an entity which is holding shares in the name of a beneficiary may enter into an agreement with the beneficiary and con-tract with him regarding how to exercise voting rights.

Apart from its very generic regulation of voting agreements, the Commercial Companies Code imposes a certain limitation on shareholders' agreements concerning the transfer of shares in a corporation.[16] As a general rule, the Commer-

---

**15** See Art. 411 of the Commercial Companies Code – a shareholder may vote differently in respect of each of the shares he or she holds.

**16** See Art. 337 and 338 of the Commercial Companies Code – Art. 337 § 1. Shares shall be transferable. § 2. A company's articles of association may make the disposal of registered shares contingent upon the consent of the company, or otherwise restrict the freedom of the disposal of registered shares. § 3. Where a company's articles make the transfer of shares contingent upon the consent of the company, the consent shall be given by the management board in writing on pain of being invalid, unless a company's articles of association provide otherwise. § 4. Where the company refuses consent to a transfer of shares, it shall indicate an alternative buyer. The time limit for indicating a buyer, the price or the manner of determining the same, as well as the manner of payment, shall be laid down in the company's articles of association. In the absence of such provisions, registered shares shall be freely transferable. The time limit for indicating a buyer shall not be longer than two months from the date of notification to the company of the intent to transfer the shares. § 5. Consent of the company shall not be required for a transfer of a share in connection with execution proceedings. § 6. The provisions of paragraphs 1 to 5 shall apply equally to the disposal of a fraction of a share. Art. 338 §1. An agreement restricting the disposal of a share or a fraction thereof for a definite time shall be admissible. Such restric-

cial Companies Code asserts the principle of the transferability of shares in a corporation; thus, the regulation of the admissible restrictions on the transferability of shares provided in the Commercial Companies Code is deemed to be an exception to such general principle. The transferability of shares can be restricted in both articles of association and shareholders' agreements. There are some differences in the regulation of transfer restrictions. Firstly, there are differences regarding the effect on the corporation and the shareholders depending on whether the restriction results from the articles of association or from a shareholders' agreement. However, this particular issue will be discussed in more detail in section IV. Secondly, articles of association may only provide for restrictions on the transferability of registered shares, while under shareholders' agreements both bearer and registered shares may be subject to transfer restrictions. Thirdly, shareholders' agreements may only be entered into for a limited period of time. Shareholders' agreements providing for a right of first refusal or for another priority right to acquire shares can be entered into for up to 10 years. Shareholders' agreements that impose other restrictions on the transferability of shares may not have a term longer than 5 years. The regulation regarding transfer restrictions in articles of association does not provide for such time limits, but this does not mean that such restriction may result in locking a shareholder into a corporation with no way out. If the articles of association provide for the obligation to obtain a corporation's consent prior to transferring shares, such articles also need to regulate in detail the consequences of the lack of such consent, i.e. the obligation to indicate an alternative buyer of the shares, the price determination process and the time frames within which to indicate an alternative buyer. If the articles of association fail to regulate such procedure, the transfer restrictions will be ineffective and the shares can be transferred without any limits.

In the past (the current iteration of the Commercial Companies Code in many respects mirrors the Commercial Companies Code from 1934) the regulation regarding restrictions on the transferability of shares included in shareholders' agreements resulted in questions as to whether other forms of shareholders' agreements were allowed. Such concerns were based on an a *contrario* reasoning: given the fact that the law expressly states that an agreement restricting the transfer of shares for a limited period of time is permitted and the law does not provide for similar express wording that other forms of shareholders'

---

tion on disposal shall not be imposed for more than five years from the date of execution of the agreement. § 2. Agreements providing for a right of pre-emption or other priority right to acquire a share or a fraction thereof shall be admissible. The restrictions on disposal arising under such agreements shall not continue in effect for more than ten years from the date of the agreement.

agreements are not permitted, it means that other forms of such agreements are not permitted. Such reasoning ignored the fact that corporate regulations were and are a part of private law and as a general rule, private law regulations cannot be regarded as a closed system of rules which does not allow for the creation of additional contractual relations. Such reasoning ignored the fact that corporate regulations were and are part of private law, and, as a general rule, private law regulations cannot be regraded as a closed system of rules which does not allow for the creation of additional contractual relations. On the contrary, private law allows, based upon the freedom of contract principle, the creation of other contractual relations which are not expressly provided for in the CCC regulation. Consequently, a regulation whereby only certain forms of shareholders' agreements are expressly allowed does not necessarily mean that other forms of shareholders' agreements are not.

However, the fact that the Commercial Companies Code imposes certain time limits on the duration of shareholders' agreements restricting the transfer of shares may be interpreted as an indication of an axiological preference with respect to other forms of shareholders' agreements. The basis for this reasoning is the observation that a corporation can be formed for an unlimited period of time and therefore certain rules governing articles of association are of a mandatory nature. In the case of a shareholders' agreement, the applicable rules are more flexible but at the same time, shareholders' agreements should not create contractual relations for an unlimited period of time that cannot be terminated or should not create overly long relationships. Basically, one may argue that the flexibility of a shareholders' agreement is independent of its scope and should always be offset by its limited term.

## III. The regulation of shareholders' agreements in public Law

Apart from the regulation of shareholders' agreements in private law, certain public law regulations also provide for the limited regulation of shareholders' agreements. The basic assumption underlying such regulation is the fact that the execution of a shareholders' agreement regarding voting may result in a change of control over the corporation or control over a large block of shares. Consequently, such regulation needs to impose a certain administrative obligation in connection with the execution of shareholders' agreements which mirrors the obligations imposed in connection with an acquisition of shares. This allows for the achievement of the primary goal, i.e. the avoidance of the situation in which someone enjoys the benefits of control over a large block of shares without the fulfilment of an administrative obligation.

As this text is focused on private law rules, below is an analysis of two regulations which I believe constitute good examples of how public law deals with shareholders' agreements.

## 1. Act on Public Offering, the Conditions Governing the Introduction of Financial Instruments to Organised Trading, and Public Companies

The first one is the Public Offering Act, which is applicable to all shareholders' agreements regarding public companies. Under Polish law, a public company is defined in a technical way as a corporation in which at least one share is dematerialised. One particularity under Polish law is that only shares subject to a public offering and/or listing may be dematerialised, i.e. only a public company can issue shares in dematerialised form.

The Public Offering Act sets forth disclosure obligations in connection with the acquisition of a certain percentage of shares in a public company.[17] It also requires the launch of a tender offer if the percentage of shares to be acquired results in crossing the thresholds of 33 % or 66 %.[18] In order to achieve the same level of administrative consequences in situations in which a certain block of shares is co-owned or controlled through shareholders' agreements,

17 Art. 69 p. 1 of the Public Offer -1. Whoever: 1) reached or exceeded 5,10,15,20,25,33,331/3, 50, 75 or 90 % of the total number of votes in a public company; or 2) held at least 5,10,15, 20,25,33,331/3,50, 75 or 90 % of the total number of votes in such company, and as a result of the decrease of such shareholding reaches, respectively, 5,10,15,20,25,33,331/3,50,75 or 90 % or a smaller percentage of the total number of votes shall be required to forthwith notify the Com-mission and the company thereof no later than within 4 business days of the day on which this person that learned about the change of the share in the total number of votes or, with due diligence, could have learned about it, and in the case of a change resulting from an acquisition of shares in a public company in a transaction concluded on a regulated market, no later than within 6 trading session days from the date of concluding the transaction.

18 Art. 73 and 74 1. Public Offering Act – Art. 73 1. Subject to paragraph 2, it shall be possible to exceed the threshold of 33 % of the total number of votes in a public company exclusively as a result of the announcement of an invitation to subscribe for the sale or exchange of shares in a company in a number ensuring the holding of 6 % of the total number of votes, save for a case when the threshold of 33 % of the total number of votes is to be exceeded as a result of the announcement of the invitation referred to in Article 74. 2. [...] Art. 74 1. Subject to paragraph 2, the threshold of 66 % of the total number of votes in a public company may be exceeded exclusively as a result of the announcement of an invitation to subscribe for the sale or exchange of all the remaining shares in such company.

the Public Offering Act provides for a detailed list of the situations which result in the requirement to dis-close information or to launch a tender offer.[19]

## 2. The Banking Law as an example of the regulation of shareholders' agreements related to a regulated entity

The regulations of the Banking Law require filings in connection with the acquisition of shares resulting in crossing certain thresholds[20] and grants the right to the Polish FSA to issue an objection to the acquisition of shares or the crossing of particular thresholds. The Banking law regulations assume that control over a bank or a large block of shares can be gained through shareholders' agreements executed at any level of the chain of companies holding shares in a bank. Consequently, the Banking Law requires the same sort of filing in connection with the exe¬cution of a shareholders' agreement as in the case of a planned acquisition of shares. If a bank or a large block of shares is controlled on the basis of a share¬holders' agreement between two or more entities, all that such entities need to do is make a filing with the Polish FSA.

**19** Art. 87 [ust.] 1 [...] p. 4), 5), 6) 1.Public Offering Act – 4) also by a proxy who, in connection with representing the shareholder at the general meeting of the shareholders, has been authorised to exercise the voting rights attached to the shares in a public company if that shareholder did not give a binding written instruction as to the manner of voting; 5) also jointly by all subjects united by way of a written or verbal agreement concerning the acquisition by these subjects of shares in a public company or by concordant voting at the general meeting of the shareholders or in pursuit of a unified policy towards the company, even if only one of these subjects undertook or intended to undertake acts resulting in the arising of these duties; 6) by subjects which enter into the agreement referred to in subparagraph 5 while holding shares in a public company in a number that would in total ensure the reaching or exceeding of a given threshold of the total number of votes specified in these provisions.

**20** Art. 25 [ust.] 1 and [ust]. 7 of the Banking Law – 1. Any entity intending to acquire or take up, directly or indirectly, shares or rights attached to shares in a domestic bank in a quantity allowing them to achieve or exceed the threshold of, respectively, 10 %, 20 %, one-third or 50 % of the total votes at the general meeting of the shareholders or of the bank's share capital shall in each case notify the Polish Financial Supervision Authority of the intended acquisition or taking-up of such shares. Any entity intending to become, directly or indirectly, a parent undertaking of a domestic bank other than by way of the acquisition or taking-up of the shares or rights attached to shares in a domestic bank in a quantity allowing them to hold the majority of the votes at the general meeting of the shareholders shall in each case notify the Polish Financial Supervision Authority of such intention. [. ] 7. The provisions of par. 1–6 and 9 apply accordingly if two or more entities act in agreement as to the exercise of the voting rights attached to shares at the thresholds referred to in par. 1, or the exercise of the rights of a parent undertaking of a domestic bank.

## IV. A general legal discussion on the Polish legal doctrine related to shareholders' agreements

The main question to be answered in this section is: What is the general approach to shareholders' agreements by Polish scholars? Given the fact that Poland was under a communist regime for nearly 50 years after World War II, discussions concerning commercial law issues were limited (even though the pre-war Commercial Companies Code was never completely abolished by the communists) and 'not extensively undertaken' both during the war and during the Communist-era post-war period. After the collapse of communism, theoretical discussions concerning commercial issues recommenced and were to a certain extent fuelled by the import of common law innovations into the practice of law in Poland. In the mid-nineties, some influential law professors published the first major post-war commentary, which also happened to reflect their professional experience.[21] It was the first time that shareholders' agreements were noted in a more detailed manner; from that point onwards, more elaborate discussions ensued. Certain of the results of these discussions were also reflected in the Commercial Companies Code and then in the administrative regulations governing public offerings or the acquisition of large blocks of shares in public companies or regulated entities (banks, insurers, brokerage houses etc.). The current mainstream status of the doctrine can be defined as the general acceptance of the principle that shareholders' agreements are allowed on the basis of the principle of the freedom of contract but are subject to the generally applicable limits on the principle of the freedom of contract. The following arguments have been raised in the relevant academic discussions: (i) Polish law does not expressly provide for a general prohibition on entering into shareholders' agreements, but only limits the duration of agreements restricting the transferability of shares; (ii) the principle of the freedom of contract has never been successfully questioned in respect of contractual relations governing the manner in which shareholders exercise their rights; (iii) Polish law, including the Commercial Companies Code, does not ignore the existence of shareholders' agreements, but regulates the consequences of the execution of such agreements; (iv) the need of the markets suggest that shareholders' agreements play an important role in the corporate world and facilitate many corporate relationships which are lawful; and (v) there are no arguments supporting the statement that shareholders' agreements are generally contrary to fairness principles or the nature of

---

**21** S. Sołtysiński in S. Sołtysiński, A. Szajkowski, J. Szwaja, *Kodeks Handlowy*, Komentarz. Tom II. Warszawa 1996, s. 41.

contracts (or the nature of a corporation since some scholars claim that such agreements should also be analysed from the perspective of such principle).

Consequently, the majority if not all mainstream scholars accept, as the starting point of the discussion, the principle pursuant to which shareholders' agreements are generally allowed.[22] Such a general statement does not mean that there are no areas of dispute among scholars or that, as a matter of fact, there are no limits on shareholders' agreements. The main discussion on the limitations on the principle of the freedom of contract with respect to shareholders' agreements focuses on the following points: (i) what is the relation between the regulation by the Commercial Companies Code of articles of association and shareholders' agreements, in particular in respect of the application of the principle of formal statute stringency to shareholders' agreements; (ii) what are the implications of the Commercial Companies Code regulations prohibiting certain actions (the issuance of a power of attorney to a management board member in a private company) or prohibiting the exercise of voting rights in certain situations (for example, a shareholder is not allowed to vote on matters that involve his personal liability towards the company); (iii) what are the implications of the principle (which principle is defended by some scholars) that a voting right cannot be transferred without the transfer of a share (and other corporate rights)[23]; and (iv) what are the consequences of shareholders' agreements entered into in order to avoid certain obligations resulting from articles of association, in particular whether such agreements are valid?

Generally, the legal doctrine does not claim that the same standards of the limits on the principle of the freedom of contract that govern articles of associ-

---

**22** S. Sołtysiński (w:) S. Sołtysiński, A. Szajkowski, A. Szumański, J. Szwaja, *Kodeks spółek handlowych*, tom III: Komentarz do artykułów 301–458, Warszawa 2013, s. 12, 26 i n.; M. Tarska *Zakres swobody umów w spółkach handlowych*, Warszawa 2012, s. 247; A. Opalski (w:) *Prawo spółek kapitałowych*, red. S. Sołtysiński, *System Prawa Prywatnego*, t. 17b, Warszawa 2010, s. 370; Ł. Gasiński *Umowy akcjonariuszy.*, s. 170; A. Szumański (w:) W. Pyzioł, A. Szumański, I. Weiss, *Prawo spółek.*, s. 666; A. Kidyba *Kodeks spółek.*, s. 658; J. Napierała (w:) A. Koch (red.), J. Napierała (red.), *Prawo handlowe*, Kraków 2002, s. 430; M. Michalski *Kontrola kapitałowa nad spółką akcyjną*, Kraków 2004, s. 538; R. Lewandowski, A. Pióro *Porozumienia akcjonariuszy*, Monitor Prawniczy 2008, nr 19, s. 1059. Takie stanowisko zajmowano też pod rządami kodeksu handlowego. Zob. np.: M. Spyra *"Związanie" prawa do głosu w spółce akcyjnej. Dopuszczalność, konstrukcja, skuteczność, Transformacje Prawa Prywatnego 2000*, nr 3, s. 87; J. Okolski, A. Opalski *Porozumienia akcjonariuszy*, Przegląd Prawa Handlowego 1999, nr 2, s. 8; M. Michalski *Ograniczenia w wykonywaniu uprawnień przysługujących akcjonariuszowi z akcji*, Prawo Spółek 2000, nr 7–8, s. 20.

**23** This principle is also described as the principle prohibiting the stripping of rights attached to a share – a share is defined as a nexus of rights linked to each other, and such nexus cannot be broken.

ation are applicable to shareholders' agreements.[24] In particular, mainstream doctrine does not share the view that the principle of formal statute stringency in its entirely applies to shareholders' agreements. Some scholars, however, argue that the nature of a corporation (which is a principle governing articles of association, and not contractual obligations, i.e. it is one of the criteria that forms the limits on the principle of the freedom of contract with respect to articles of association) establishes certain limits on the principle of the freedom of contract with respect to shareholders' agreements. Such view is based on the assumption that both articles of association and shareholders' agreements are linked to a corporation and that the relation between such legal link is so strong that certain limits on the provisions of articles of association (for example that no more than two votes may be attached to a share, or the general proportionality principle) should also limit the provisions of shareholders' agreements. The opponents of such a strict approach claim that there are material differences between shareholders' agreements and articles of association and therefore they are subject to different regimes. The objective of corporate law is to defend shareholders who may not be personally involved in the drafting of articles of association, on whom provisions of articles of association may be imposed by majority shareholders and those who are not in a position to question mechanisms that are unfavourable to them. A shareholders' agreement does not require such a level of intervention in respect of the principle of the freedom of contract as each party to a shareholders' agreement usually negotiates the provisions of such agreement; moreover, a shareholder does not become bound by the provisions of a shareholders' agreement simply by acquiring shares in a corporation. Pursuant to Polish law, as will be discussed in more detail later, a shareholders' agreement is only effective with respect to the parties thereto, and not with respect to the entire corporation or all of its shareholders. Moreover, there is no expressly provided normative basis which would permit the extension of the application of the principle of formal statute stringency over contractual relations outside of articles of association. On the contrary, the wording of the Commercial Companies Code suggests that strict corporate principles should be applied to articles of association and is silent on its applicability to contractual relations outside of articles of association.

The other question discussed is whether certain detailed rules restricting the exercise of voting rights should also be applied to shareholders' agreements. For

---

**24** Ł. Gasiński *Shareholders' agreements concerning the manner of exercising voting rights under Polish law and under US law* [Polish: *Umowy akcjonariuszy co do sposobu wykonywania prawa głosu w prawie polskim i amerykańskim*]. Warsaw 2006 C.H. Beck pp. XXXI, s. 170 – 174, 187– 199 (together with the literature indicated therein).

example, if a given shareholder is excluded from voting personally or as a proxy on certain resolutions,[25] this also means that he cannot enter into a shareholders' agreement for the purposes of binding other shareholders to vote as he wishes in respect of such restricted matters. The answer to this question is rather uncontroversial and suggests that such a shareholders' agreement is void.

The other interesting discussion concerning Polish law relates to the rule that it is not possible to dispose of voting rights without a simultaneous transfer of shares. The underlying principle is that all of the shareholders' rights create a kind of nexus that cannot be broken and it is not possible to strip certain rights, including voting rights, from a share or from each other. Some scholars claim that this principle can be interpreted two ways. The first way is that it is prohibited to enter into a transfer agreement the subject of which is the transfer of a voting right. The second interpretation assumes that agreements which only regulate the exercise of voting rights in certain situations can also infringe the principle of the prohibition on the disposal of voting rights. The second interpretation is based upon the observation that certain contractual relations create a situation similar to the disposal of voting rights. In deciding whether, in a particular situation, an agreement will result in the disposal of voting rights, one needs to analyse: (i) the time period for which the shareholders' agreement was entered into; (ii) the general purpose of the shareholders' agreement;[26] (iii) how the relevant decision-making process is structured; (iv) whether the agreement provides only one party with the right to require the other parties to vote in a certain manner; (v) the rights and obligations of each of the parties (to ascertain whether it is a balanced agreement); and (vi) how the execution of the agreement is secured (i.e. the scope of the agreement (matters subject to voting)). Depending on the outcome of such analysis, i.e. its duration, a lack of balance, no common decision-making, irrevocable proxy, excessive penalties or broad scope, it may result, according to some conservative views, in such voting agreements being declared invalid2fi. However, this conservative view is not shared by all scholars, and the criticism of such view has roots in two different assumptions.[27] The first assumption questions the existence of the general principle of prohibiting the transfer of voting rights in the absence of a transfer of

**25** See Art. 413 §1. A shareholder shall not, either personally or through a proxy or as another person's proxy, vote on the adoption of resolutions concerning its accountability to a company on whatever account, including on granting him a vote of acceptance, release from an obligation to the company, or a dispute between him and the company.

**26** A. Szumański (w): *Prawo papierów wartościowych...*, s. 300.

**27** M. Michalski *Dopuszczalność rozszczepiania uprawnień udziałowych z akcji*, Przegląd Prawa Handlowego 2008, nr 5, s. 35–42.

shares. Some scholars claim that such principle has never been articulated in any of the regulations and, to the contrary, certain provisions of the Commercial Companies Code suggest that a transfer of voting rights is possible even without a transfer of the ownership of shares. For example, it is possible to pledge voting rights. Accepting the theory that Polish law does not generally prohibit the transfer of particular corporate rights allows for the assumption that shareholders' agreements regarding voting cannot be questioned on the basis of such principle. Such criticism also comes from another angle. Some scholars accept the general principle pursuant to which it is not possible to dispose of voting rights without simultaneous transfer of shares, but they indicate that the rationale behind this principle does not effect validity of majority of the shareholders agreement. It protects the corporation against the situation in which some, who do not have enough economic interest in the corporation, gain disproportionate corporate control. If a shareholders' agreement does not create disproportionate control which is not backed by an economic interest, then such agreement is valid and binding. Consequently, most scholars ask for a very careful analysis by the judiciary before coming to the conclusion that a certain form of agreement is invalid.[28]

The last, but certainly not the least contentious, point which is subject to discussion and which was also subject to a Supreme Court judgment[29] is the question of how to react to a shareholders' agreement the purpose of which is to circumvent certain provisions of a company's articles of association. The general approach of legal scholars, which is also shared by the Supreme Court, is that articles of association possess a contractual character and therefore an agreement which is created to circumvent another agreement is not necessarily invalid. This may be the case, but only if in given circumstances such agreement also infringes the rule of law or fairness principles.

## 1. The case law on shareholders' agreements

The Polish legal system is not based on case law, in particular, judgments of the Supreme Court are not binding, but such judgments influence the practice and the ways in which jurisprudence develops with respect to a given issue. Based upon an analysis of the limited number of cases on shareholders' agreements,

---

**28** Ł. Gasiński Glosa do wyroku Sądu Najwyższego z dnia 6 lipca 2012 r., V CSK 354/11, *Z problematyki udzielania nieodwołalnego pełnomocnictwa do głosowania na walnym zgromadzeniu w związku z przedwstępną umową zbycia akcji*, LEX/el. 2014.

**29** Wyrok Sądu Najwyższego z dnia 19 stycznia 2011 r., V CSK 223/10, LEX nr 688710.

one may conclude that, unfortunately, there are some controversies and divergent court decisions. However the concept that shareholders' agreements, including shareholders' agreements regarding voting, are generally permitted has unfortunately not been adopted in all cases. Controversies arise in connection with shareholders' agreement regarding voting, whereas transfer restriction agreements and other agreements are not questioned or have not yet been tried before a Polish court. Polish jurisprudence has developed in two different directions while adjudicating on the topic of shareholders' agreements. The first theory was developed and has been upheld in two precedents and is based on the general assumption that all shareholders' agreements regarding voting are prohibited under Polish law. The second group of jurisprudence decisions is based on the assumption that shareholders' agreements regarding voting are generally permitted but that their enforcement may encounter certain difficulties.

The conservative view was developed for the first time by the Warsaw Appellate Court I Aca 630/05 dated 5 January 2006, which decided that an agreement pursuant to which a shareholder agreed on a one-time basis to vote on a matter in a particular fashion (one change to the articles of association) was invalid as it constituted a prohibited transfer of a voting right. As discussed above, such theory is controversial and the court definitely failed to distinguish between the obligation to exercise a voting right and an agreement pursuant to which a voting right is transferred. The case was decided with respect to a limited liability company; however, one may assume that similar argumentation would be made with respect to a joint stock company. Between the lines of the legal argumentation raised by the Warsaw Appellate Court one may read the suggestion that the case could have been decided differently if the articles of association of the limited liability company had reflected the fact that shareholders can enter into voting agreements. It can be interpreted that the Warsaw Appellate Court applied to shareholders' agreements regarding voting, per analogiam, similar requirements to those that are imposed by the Commercial Companies Code in the case of a pledge over shares or the establishment of a right of usufruct to shares in respect of a limited liability company. The response of the law practitioners to this conservative court decision has been to include a reference to shareholders' agreements in articles of association in order to cover the potential risks resulting from such decisions. The above-mentioned Warsaw Appellate Court judgment was heavily criticised by legal doctrine scholars, and certain scholars claim that such decisions will scare investors from subjecting joint-venture agreements to Polish law.[30]

**30** The "founding father" of the modern Polish company law (co-author of the Commercial

The other case which questioned the general validity of shareholders' agreements regarding voting was decided by the Supreme Court and was based on a similar principle and arguments. However, the factual background was more complicated and the shareholders' agreement regarding voting was entered into with respect to a transfer of shares and the exercise of voting rights in a private corporation. The background of the case can be summarised as follows. The claimant concluded preliminary share transfer agreements with several shareholders. In connection with these agreements, irrevocable powers of attorney to vote at the general meeting were granted. The preliminary agreements provided for a ban on the exercise of voting rights by the seller of the shares (the grantor of the power of attorney). Based on the preliminary agreements, the selling shareholders were paid an advance of one-tenth of the price of the shares set forth in the preliminary agreements. The agreements also provided for a contractual penalty equal to the purchase price for the shares to be paid in the event the grantor exercised the voting rights. The findings of the lower-instance courts also indicate that the company's articles of association provided for a restriction on the transferability of the shares (in the form of a requirement to obtain the consent of the supervisory board) and reserved the right of first refusal to purchase the shares in favour of the existing shareholders. The claimant intended to use the powers of attorney to implement changes to the composition of the supervisory board (he made a request for the convocation of an extraordinary general meeting containing that very item on its agenda), and in all likelihood intended, after making the changes to the composition of the supervisory board, to obtain the supervisory board's approval for the acquisition of the shares. The company did not grant the request to convene the extraordinary general meeting, nor did it permit the claimant holding the irrevocable powers of attorney to participate in an earlier general meeting. The company then sought the voidance of the irrevocable powers of attorney granted in connection with the preliminary agreements. The Supreme Court decided that the irrevocable proxy and the prelimina-

---

Companies Code and many commentaries on CCC) argues (S. Sołtysiński: S. Sołtysiński, A. Szajkowski, A. Szumański, J. Szwaja, *Kodeks spółek handlowych*, tom III: Komentarz do artykułów 301–458, Warszawa, 2013, s. 26): "The Appellate Court was incorrect in ruling that the provision of the agreement requiring the shareholder to vote in favour of a specific amendment to the articles of association of the company constituted a prohibited disposal [of the shares], as it led to a circum¬vention of the law (judgment of the Appellate Court of 5.1.2006, I ACa 630/05, OSA 2007, No. 10, item 33, p. 61). If the above-mentioned view, which challenges a transactional practice, became more prevalent, this could only lead to agreements regulating the exercise of voting rights being governed by foreign laws and subject to the jurisdiction of the courts (arbitration courts) of other OECD, in which the admissibility of such agreements is not open to doubt".

ry agreement were invalid as the result thereof was the illegal transfer of voting rights. It may be discussed whether from the fairness perspective the decision made in this case was the correct one; however, unfortunately, the arguments raised by the Supreme Court do not take into account the comprehensive legal analysis made by several academics. In particular, the Supreme Court incorrectly indicated that a general principle of Polish law is that any commitment to vote at a meeting of the shareholders is not generally permitted under Polish law.

It seems that at least in these two decisions the Polish courts misinterpreted the discussion among the academics or did not take into account the outcome or even the start of the discussion that the mainstream doctrine accepts the principle that shareholders' agreements are generally permitted.

As indicated above, the Polish courts have also taken a completely different approach and have assumed that voting agreements are, in fact, permitted under Polish law. In several cases, appellate courts have upheld that an investor in a limited liability company or in a joint stock company is permitted to agree to guarantee a certain result of the operation of the company.[31] For example, if he controls 70% of shares, such shareholder can undertake to increase the share capital and guarantee that the shares will be offered to a particular shareholder. In addition, the Supreme Court assumed that a shareholder can agree in a separate agreement to the manner in which a company is run, for example that it will distribute a certain percentage of the dividend to its shareholders and that it will not incur additional external debt.[32] It is clear that in both cases the courts strongly upheld the interpretation of the rule deriving from the principle of the freedom of contract. The general assumption of such interpretation is that agreements (which are not expressly provided for by law), including shareholders' agreements, are generally permitted. It is therefore assumed that someone claiming the general invalidity of a certain type of agreement must provide the court with the appropriate interpretation and in the case of any doubt, the principle of the freedom of contract prevails. Such approach with respect to shareholders' agreements is not only desired from the perspective of the practice of law, but is also built on a solid legal basis. Hopefully, the second approach will be finally adopted by Polish jurisprudence and will result in a more unified approach to shareholders' agreements regarding voting on the basis of the assumption that shareholders' agreements regarding voting are generally permitted.

Based on my own professional experience, it is fair to assume that the general validity of shareholders' agreements regarding voting under Polish law does

---

**31** Wyrok Sądu Apelacyjnego w Warszawie z dnia 16 lutego 2007 r. I ACa/749.05.

**32** Wyrok Sądu Najwyższego z dnia 7 maja 2009 r. III CSK/315.00.

not generate controversies in arbitration proceedings, which also explains why such agreements usually contain an arbitration clause.

### 2. Cross border Shareholder Agreements

Polish law does not provide for specific regulations regarding cross-border agreements. Shareholders' agreements are sometimes subject to foreign law, in particular English law.

# C. Forms of Shareholders' Agreements

## I. Shareholders' agreements regarding the rights of shareholders

As discussed in the previous section, there are no specific regulations regarding the different types of shareholders' agreements under Polish law. Generally, the scope of shareholders' agreements regarding the rights of shareholders is associated with the economic context in which such shareholders' agreements are entered into. Therefore, the section below describes the functions of shareholders' agreements together with the manner of the exercise of the shareholder rights regulated therein.

### 1. Shareholders' agreements regarding voting

Generally, in practice, more educated shareholders of both limited liability companies and joint stock companies enter into shareholders' agreements that govern voting rights in the case of joint ventures. However, it is not only the function of shareholders' agreements regarding voting with which Polish practice is familiar. In particular, shareholders' agreements regarding voting are entered into in connection with:

a) any private equity investment the purpose of which is to supplement a family-run company (start-up) with capital, but not to take over the full management of the given company. Such agreements usually contain clauses regarding the types of resolutions that require common consent, the consequences of a deadlock, etc. Basically, such agreements tend to regulate how the company is run;

b) joint ventures between sector investors in both public and private companies. A good example of such an agreement was the shareholders' agreement between the owner of a Polish broadcaster (publicly traded) and a French media group (Canal+) the purpose of which was to establish the rules regarding co-control over the publicly traded Polish broadcaster and the creation of a joint-venture of satellite operators. It also serves as a good example from a different perspective. The deal allowed for certain co-control or individual control over the entity in the given time period. Consequently, the detailed decision-making process within all the chains of the corporate holding was strictly regulated by the shareholders' agreement, including in respect of the approval of budgets, corporate resolutions, deadlocks, the distribution of dividends and the appointment of the management and supervisory board members;
c) shareholder disputes. The purpose of such agreements is usually the settlement of mutual claims along with the establishment of the detailed procedure for the corporate actions to be undertaken in the event of disputes, including in respect of the adoption of certain resolutions of the shareholders. A good example of such a situation was a settlement entered into between the Polish government and Eureco (Dutch investor) in connection with the privatisation agreement regarding a major Polish insurer (in fact, the largest insurer in Eastern Europe). As it was made public by both sides of the dispute, one could gain detailed knowledge of the subject of the agreement. The purpose of the agreement was to allow Eureco to dispose of the shares in the Polish insurer and to receive a certain amount of claimed damages from the Polish state. Basically, the agreement regulated how the parties thereto would support the launch of the IPO of the Polish insurer in which both parties would dispose of shares (all or nearly all of Eureco's shares), but with the Polish state disposing of only a certain amount in order to allow it to maintain control (the revenue generated from the disposal of shares by the Polish government was used to settle the claims of Eureco). The entire structure required several rounds of voting at the meeting of the shareholders, as well as appointments to the supervisory board of the company. In order to protect the voting mechanism, both irrevocable proxies and potential guarantee payments of certain lump sums were used;
d) M&A contracts which due to the timing required in connection with the regulatory approval (antimonopoly or financial supervision or other regulator) process need to address the problem of how the company is to be run during the time between the signing of the transaction and the closing of the transaction. Usually, such M&A contracts provide for constraints on the exercise of voting rights, for example, prohibitions on dividend distributions,

changes to the articles of association and the appointment of new supervisory board members;

e) restructuring processes. Usually, in a pre-insolvency situation when a restructuring plan assumes the issuance of new capital for cash or in exchange for debt, such insolvency plan is associated with a shareholders' agreement entered into by current or future shareholders; and

f) privatisation agreements. It had been the established Polish practice that privatisation agreements provided for certain commitments by investors irrespective of whether after the privatisation process (and the disposal of a certain number of shares to employees) the State Treasury would remain a shareholder of the privatised entity. Usually, such agreements provided for certain commitments regarding the investment strategy of the investors, including, but not limited to, an increase of the share capital, which meant that such agreements were basically a type of voting agreement with respect to the financing of the company.

## 2. Agreements on the appointment of members of governing bodies

Before getting into the details associated with shareholders' agreements governing the appointment of members of governing bodies, it is worth presenting a brief description of the approach to corporate governance by the Commercial Companies Code.

Polish corporate law is based upon a dual tier system, i. e. the management board has what is nearly an exclusive right to manage a company, while the supervisory board performs supervisory functions and does not represent the company (other than in connection with agreements with management board members or conflicts therewith). It is not permitted to be both a supervisory board member and a management board member at the same time. Therefore, shareholders' agreements can potentially stipulate the procedure for the appointment of both the management and supervisory boards.

The Commercial Companies Code provides that it is the meeting of the shareholders that appoints supervisory board members in a joint stock company and that it is the supervisory board that elects the management board. Both regulations can be altered in the articles of association, in particular, the right to elect management board members may be provided to the meeting of the shareholders or to particular shareholders. The Commercial Companies Code expressly authorises (in accordance with the principle of formal statute stringency) such alteration.

In a limited liability company, the management board is elected by the meeting of the shareholders unless provided otherwise in the articles of association. In "smaller" limited liability companies, it is not necessary to appoint a supervisory board as all of the shareholders have the right of individual supervision. If a supervisory board is envisaged by the articles of association, the right to appoint supervisory board members is granted to the meeting of the shareholders, which right can be altered by the articles of association.

Under Polish law, it is possible to include regulations in shareholders' agreements that are subject to a vote by the shareholders, including in respect of the appointment of members of governing bodies. It is quite usual for shareholders' agreements regarding joint ventures to have detailed provisions regulating the number of supervisory and management board members that may be elected by each of the parties to such agreement as well as provisions regarding the competencies of each of the elected members. The split of powers within a governing body usually reflects the character of a given investor or a particular scope of its activity. It is also not unheard of to have provisions protecting a minority investor in a public company and granting such minority investor the right to appoint one member of the supervisory or management boards. Such mechanism is frequently used in a Pre-IPO context when a majority investor, or the company offering shares, desires to have a reputable anchor investor such as, for example, the EBRD.

Sometimes such provisions are also reinforced by special rights granted to the shareholders under the articles of association. Under Polish law, it is permitted to include in articles of association a right to appoint /dismiss a given number of supervisory board members. The benefit of such solution is that such appointment / dismissal rights are effective with respect to the corporation and the shareholder must consent to a resolution depriving him of such rights.[33]

33 See Art. 354 of the Commercial Companies Code – §1. A company's articles of association may vest certain personal rights in an individually named shareholder. Such rights may relate in particular to the right to appoint and recall members of the management board and supervisory board, or the right to obtain from a company certain benefits. § 2. A company's articles of association may make the granting of a personal right to a shareholder contingent upon the provision of certain performances towards the company, the lapse of a certain period of time or the fulfilment of a certain condition. § 3. Limitations regarding the extent of rights to preference shares and on the exercise of the same apply respectively to personal rights granted to a shareholder. § 4. Personal rights granted to an individually designated shareholder expire no later than on the day when the holder of such rights ceases to be a shareholder of the company.

## 3. Voting trusts

Polish law does not regulate the institution of voting trusts. As discussed above, certain academics have openly expressed criticism with respect to the creation of a mechanism that can in effect play the same role as a voting trust. It does not, however, result in a situation in which mechanisms similar to those to a voting trust are not created in practice. I am not a supporter of such a conservative view and I believe that Polish law does allow for the creation of a legal mechanism that in practice is similar to a voting trust. For example, as discussed above, under Polish law, it is possible to establish usufruct rights to shares, including voting rights. Such an agreement can be associated with a detailed voting regulation on how to exercise voting rights and how any economic benefits deriving from shares will be distributed. The other way is to form a partnership and contribute shares in such partnership, provided that only one or a limited number of partners will have the right to represent and conduct the business of the partnership (including the exercise of voting rights). Consequently, there are many ways to create a mechanism which will work in a similar way to a voting trust.

## 4. Binding instructions issued to a company

The question of whether instructions included in shareholders' agreements regarding voting are binding on a company relates to the effect of shareholders' agreements and will be discussed in more detail below in section IV. For the purpose of the present discussion, at this point, it is enough to assume that under Polish law shareholders' agreements do not have a corporate effect of a nature similar to articles of association.

At this point, I would like to cover issues related to binding instructions under shareholders' agreements, i.e. whether a meeting of the shareholders has the right to provide a binding instruction to a management board. The situation differs depending on whether it is joint stock company or a limited liability company.

In respect of a joint stock company, neither the meeting of the shareholders nor the supervisory board may issue a resolution binding the management board.[34] The ideal assumption behind the rule is that a joint stock company

34 See Art. 3751 of the Commercial Companies Code – The general meeting and the supervisory board may not issue to the management board binding instructions as to the running of the affairs of the company.

has rather dispersed capital and therefore the management board should not be subject to a binding instruction of the meeting of the shareholders. Polish law does not provide for a different regulation with respect to private companies despite the fact that the above-mentioned rationale does not explain the application of such a strict rule to a private company. It must also be stressed that the general prohibition on issuing binding instructions does not preclude the supervisory board or the meeting of the shareholders from issuing a non-binding recommendation which may or may not be followed by the management board. Binding instructions need be distinguished from a management board's obligation to obtain the consent of the supervisory board or the meeting of the shareholders (pursuant to the law or the articles of association). If the management board fails to obtain such consent and enters into a transaction in connection with which consent was required by law, such transaction will be deemed void unless confirmed by the meeting of the shareholders or the supervisory board. If consent requirements derive from the articles of association, such transaction for which consent has not been obtained will be valid, but the management board members may bear personal liability for any damages resulting therefrom or be subject to corporate liability (which can, however, be waived).[35]

The regulations regarding a limited liability company do not provide for a limit on the right of shareholders to issue binding instructions to the company. Consequently, most academics assume that the meeting of the shareholders of a limited liability company is permitted to issue such instructions to the management board. As with a joint stock company, the articles of association of a limited liability company may provide for an obligation to obtain the consent of the meeting of the shareholders or the supervisory board. The requirement to obtain consent may also result from the regulations applicable to a limited liability company. The consequences of a lack of consent are the same as with a joint stock

35 See Art. 17 of the Commercial Companies Code – §1. Where this Act requires a resolution of the shareholders, the general meeting or the supervisory board for the company to perform an act in law, then an act in law performed without the required resolution shall be null and void. § 2. Consent may be granted before a company makes a declaration or after a declaration has been made, however, no later than within two months from the day when the company made the declaration. Confirmation expressed after making the declaration shall operate retroactively from the date of performance of the act in law. § 3. An act in law performed without the consent of the appropriate body of the company, in respect of which such consent is only required by the company's deed or articles, shall be valid, however, this does not preclude the liability of the members of the management board towards the company for a violation of the deed or articles of the company.

company and depend on whether the requirement was provided for by the articles of association or by the law.

The fact that shareholders cannot issue binding instructions to the management board does not mean that shareholders or co-investors do not enter into agreements pursuant to which one party commits to procure that the company will do something. If such commitment is constructed as a guarantee to achieve certain results and the shareholder fails to achieve such results (for example due to a refusal by the management board to act in a certain way), it can still be held liable under the agreement for the failure to achieve the desired results. Obviously, such obligation usually does not result in a specific performance claim, but rather is secured by penalty payments.

## 5. Agreements on the coordination of claims of shareholders

The Commercial Companies Code does not regulate agreements allowing shareholders to coordinate claims against a company or the exercise of minority rights (the right to require the management board to call a meeting of the shareholders, the right to require amendments to an agenda, the right to call for the appointment of a special auditor, the right to have the supervisory board elected by way of voting in separate groups, the right to challenge a resolution at a meeting of the shareholders, etc.). The only hint of such regulation is included in the Public Offering Act, which requires the notification of the existence of such an agreement.[36]

The Commercial Companies Code does not regulate agreements allowing shareholders to coordinate claims against a company or the exercise of minority rights (the right to require the management board to call a meeting of the shareholders, the right to require amendments to an agenda, the right to call for the appointment of a special auditor, the right to have the supervisory board elected by way of voting in separate groups, the right to challenge a resolution at a meeting of the shareholders, etc.). The only hint of such regulation is included in the

36 Art. 90 p. 2 of the Public Offer – The provisions of this Chapter, save for Article 69, Article 70, Article 87, paragraph 1, subparagraph 6 and Article 89, paragraph 1, subparagraph 1 – to the extent to which it concerns Article 69, shall also not apply in the case of the agreements referred to in Article 87, paragraph 1, subparagraph 5 entered into in order to protect the rights of minority shareholders in order for them to jointly exercise the rights set forth in Articles 84 and 85 hereof and in Article 385, paragraph 3, Article 400, paragraph 1, Articles 422, 425, Article 429, paragraph 1 of the Act of 15 September 2000 – Code of Commercial Partnerships and Companies.

Public Offering Act, which requires the notification of the existence of such an agreement.[37]

In connection with agreements the purpose of which is to allow minority shareholders to take actions against a company or the majority shareholders, it is worth mentioning a particular Polish mechanism – group voting in order to appoint one supervisory board member. This mechanism is provided for in the Commercial Companies Code and allows minority shareholders to appoint representatives to the supervisory board.[38] Basically, it works as described below.

Shareholders representing one-fifth of the share capital have the right to demand and place on the agenda of the next meeting of the shareholders an item regarding the appointment of the supervisory board using the voting in separate groups procedure. The management board is required to place such item on the agenda and during the next meeting of the shareholders the number of shares represented at the meeting of the shareholders is divided by the number of the supervisory board members. Shareholders that represent the minimum number of shares that will allow the election of one member may create a separate group to appoint such member and they may not participate in creating any other group. Shareholders who do not participate in any group elect such number of the supervisory board members that were not elected by the separate groups. One of the advantages of this mechanism is connected with the fact that there is a clear indication that such group voting prevails over any statutory provisions regarding the appointment of supervisory board members (for example, individual rights to appoint supervisory board members). In addition, during the voting on the appointment of the supervisory board members in separate groups, each share carries only one vote irrespective of any voting caps, special rights attributed to the shareholders or privileges attached to shares. The mechanism itself creates quite a lot of discussion in practice and the majority share-

**37** Art. 90 p. 2 of the Public Offer – The provisions of this Chapter, save for Article 69, Article 70, Article 87, paragraph 1, subparagraph 6 and Article 89, paragraph 1, subparagraph 1 – to the extent to which it concerns Article 69, shall also not apply in the case of the agreements referred to in Article 87, paragraph 1, subparagraph 5 entered into in order to protect the rights of minority shareholders in order for them to jointly exercise the rights set forth in Articles 84 and 85 hereof and in Article 385, paragraph 3, Article 400, paragraph 1, Articles 422, 425, Article 429, paragraph 1 of the Act of 15 September 2000 – Code of Commercial Partnerships and Companies.

**38** See Art. 385 of the Commercial Companies Code, §3 – §7 – §3. At the request of shareholders who represent no less than one-fifth of the initial capital, the supervisory board shall be elected by the next general meeting by a vote held in separate groups, even if the company's articles provide for a different manner of appointing the supervisory board. § 7. Failing the formation, at the general meeting referred to in paragraph 3, of at least one group capable of electing a supervisory board member, no election shall be held.

holders often try to prevent separate group voting from happening or undertake actions aimed at the dismissal of members elected by way of separate group voting. Several Supreme Court decisions have been issued in connection with this mechanism and, unfortunately, such rulings have not always protected minority shareholders in a sufficient manner.[39] The group voting mechanism is sometimes used by financial investors in public companies to gain access to information and to exercise supervision over a company if the majority shareholder fails to cooperate with a minority shareholder. In connection with planned cooperation on the enforcement of minority rights, institutional investors enter into a shareholders' agreement pursuant to which they coordinate and plan actions, in particular on how to exercise the right to have group voting and the election of a supervisory board member, as well as cooperation with respect to the appointment of a special auditor to audit the relations between the company and the majority shareholder

## II. Shareholders' agreements regarding limitations on the transfer of shares

As discussed in section II, Polish law in a very generic way regulates shareholders' agreements that limit the transfer of shares. Unfortunately, the Commercial Companies Code does not provide for a separate regulation concerning drag along clauses, tag along clauses and lock-up clauses. This does not mean that such clauses are not used in practice in Poland. On the contrary, in most joint venture contracts, certain types of these clauses are used depending on the economic context of the transaction. The lack of detailed regulation regarding such clauses results in such clauses being drafted so as to the meet the civil law requirements of particular mechanisms provided for by the Civil Code, such as the unconditional offer of a preliminary contract or the conditional agreement to buy/dispose of shares, to guarantee the obligation that a certain person acquires shares which are used for different types of option mechanisms, including through the use of drag along or tag along clauses.[40] These mechanisms are not

39 Wyrok Sądu Najwyższego z dnia 18 listopada 2008 r., II CSK 304/08, LEX nr 469611, Wyrok Sądu Najwyższego z dnia 13 grudnia 2007 r., I CSK 329/07, OSNC-ZD 2008/2/59, Wyrok Sądu Apelacyjnego z dnia 8 lutego 2005 r., I Aca 471/04, LEX nr 527490, Wyrok Sądu Najwyższego z dnia 21 stycznia 2005 r., I CK 505/04, OSNC 2006/1/10, Wyrok Sądu Apelacyjnego z dnia 30 marca 2004 r., VI Aca 771/03, OSA 2005/10/40.

40 Wyrok Sądu Najwyższego z dnia 11 marca 2016 r., I CSK 161/15.

absolutely perfect. Unfortunately, there are not many precedents concerning shareholders' agreements providing for option contracts.

Apart from shareholders' agreements regulating different forms of options allowing the shareholders to exit the company or change the shareholding structure, in practice, shareholders commit not to dispose of shares in connection with public offering processes, restructuring processes (entered into in connection with the restructuring of debt or the conversion of debt into share capital) or corporate restructuring processes. It is common capital market practice to conclude lock-up agreements pursuant to which the major shareholders agree not to transfer their shares for a specified time (between six and 18 months) after the completion of the public offering of the company's shares. A commitment of such kind is intended as a warranty for the investors so that they do not need to worry about a further sale of the shares on the market by major shareholders as such sale might affect the market price of the shares. In other words, the commitment of the major shareholders, and sometimes also the directors and officers, is conducive to conducting the offering and it is in the best interests of the company (understood as all of its shareholders), and is also intended to protect the interests of potential share buyers. Standstill agreements can serve as another example here; pursuant to such agreements, shareholders covenant to the company not to sell their shares for a specified time. Standstill agreements are intended to protect a company against a hostile takeover by tying "friendly" shareholders together with the company. Another example is presented by the placement of restrictions on the transferability of shares issued under management share incentive schemes. These restrictions serve to align the interests of a company with the interests of its directors and officers, that is, by tying certain individuals to the company for a long-term perspective. As discussed above, such agreements may be entered into for a limited period of time.

One of the more interesting precedents regarding restrictions on the transferability of shares provided for by shareholders' agreements was connected with a dispute between a joint stock company and some of its shareholders.[41] The shareholders were seeking the payment of compensation from a joint stock company in relation to an agreement restricting the transferability of shares. The context of the conclusion of such agreement was also interesting. According to the description of the case, the joint stock company was undergoing a restructuring process associated with the conversion of its debt into equity. The conversion was conditional on requiring certain shareholders not to sell or encumber their shares. The shareholders were granted compensation of PLN 500,000 per

41 Wyrok Sądu Apelacyjnego z dnia 6 sierpnia 2014 r., VI Aca 1673/13.

year under the agreement, with such amount being divided among the shareholders pro rata to the size of their respective shareholdings. The claimants did not sell their shares within the period contemplated in the agreement, whereas the company fulfilled its obligation to pay the compensation only in the first year of the effective term of the agreement. Thereafter, the company refused to pay the compensation and stated that the claimants had violated the social and economic purpose of the agreement. The breach allegedly involved certain actions on the part of the claimants' attorney-in-fact, who, as asserted by the company, made offers to the banks which executed the company's restructuring process to purchase some of the shares in the jewellery company. In the company's opinion, this obstructed the social and economic purpose of the agreement, which meant that the company was no longer under an obligation to pay the compensation. The appellate court upheld the validity of the agreement. The entry into the agreement was a condition to the restructuring process in connection with which the banks agreed to the conversion of the company's debt into equity. We can safely assume that the agreement was intended to safeguard the interests of the banks against a potential decline in the value of the shares as a result of their sale by some of the existing shareholders. Assuming that the restructuring process was designed to remediate the company's operations, we can conclude that the execution of the agreement was in the interest of the company, and thus in the interest of the shareholders viewed as a whole.[42]

It is also worth mentioning that given the possibility to include certain transfer restrictions in the articles of association of both a joint stock company as well as a limited liability company, the parties to a shareholders' agreement tend to reflect provisions on transfer restrictions in the articles of association, which results in strengthening the efficacy of transfer restrictions. An example of such practice was also the subject of a Supreme Court judgment. The articles of association that were subject to the Supreme Court's analysis imposed an obligation on a shareholder that crossed a threshold of 32% of the votes or shares to offer to the other shareholders to buy their shares. The court of lower instance ruled that such provision was invalid as it was contrary to the principle of formal statute stringency and the nature of a joint stock company. It claimed that the Commercial Companies Code provides for the exhaustive regulation of a reverse buy-back (sell out) and thus any additional provisions in this respect are not permitted. The Supreme Court did not share the view of the appellate court and ruled

---

**42** Ł. Gasiński *Glosa do wyroku Sądu Najwyższego z dnia 6 lipca 2012 r., V CSK 354/11, Z problematyki udzielania nieodwołalnego pełnomocnictwa do głosowania na walnym zgromadzeniu w związku z przedwstępną umową zbycia akcji*, LEX/el. 2014.

that the provisions of articles of association can be divided into two groups: (i) material provisions regulating relations among governing bodies and relations between the shareholders vis-a-vis the corporation; and (ii) formal provisions that may be included in the articles of association if they do not form "real" articles of association. The Supreme Court indicated that different principles apply to these different provisions. Only material provisions of articles of association are governed by the principle of formal statute stringency. Provisions establishing legal relations between shareholders are not subject to the principle of formal statute stringency and are instead subject to the principle of the freedom of contract. Consequently, the Supreme Court upheld the validity of the provisions requesting a shareholder crossing the threshold of 32 % of the shares or votes to buy shares from the remaining shareholders. The Supreme Court judgment seems to acknowledge the importance of the different option mechanisms that may also be included in articles of association. It would also be fair to assume that the Supreme Court would rather assume the validity of drag along or tag along clauses in a shareholders' agreement if properly drafted.

# D. Legal Effect of the Shareholders' Agreements

## I. Legal effect in respect of a corporation

The general principle of Polish law (which is assumed by both academics and the doctrine) is that shareholders' agreements do not bind a corporation in the same manner that articles of the association do, i.e. shareholders' agreements do not regulate or alter corporate relations in the manner that articles of association do. If there is a difference between articles of association and a shareholders' agreement, the articles will prevail over the shareholders' agreement. For example, if a shareholders' agreement provides for an obligation to obtain the consent of the meeting of the shareholders before making a particular disposal of assets, the company's management board is not bound by such provisions unless they are reflected in the company's articles of association. The same principle applies to other provisions of shareholders' agreements, i.e. provisions on the appointment of the members of the supervisory board will not affect the corporation unless pro-vided for in the articles of association. Consequently, the registry court competent for a corporation will not refuse to reflect a new appointment even if such appointment is in breach of the articles of association. There is also a significant difference between the legal consequences of a breach of articles of association and a breach of a shareholders' agreement. Generally, a breach of articles of association will result in corporate remedies, whereas a breach of the shareholders' agreement will result in contractual remedies. Shareholders' agreements do not form the corporation and do not result in the corporation altering the rights available under the articles of association.

## II. Legal effects of shareholders' agreements on shareholders

### 1. Transfer of rights and obligations under shareholders' agreements

The general principle under Polish law is that by virtue of the acquisition of shares, a shareholder does not become bound by a shareholders' agreement but only by the articles of association. In order to become bound by a shareholders' agreement, such shareholder needs to accede to the agreement (usually such accession requires the consent of the other parties to such agreement). The rights and obligations under a shareholders' agreement can be transferred subject to the general principles of the Civil Code, i.e. rights arising under a shareholders' agreement may be transferred without the prior consent of the parties to the agreement (unless it is set forth otherwise in the shareholders' agreement), and obligations under a shareholders' agreement may be transferred with the prior consent of the other parties to such agreement (unless it is set forth otherwise in the shareholders' agreement).

### 2. Other legal consequences of the shareholders' agreements

Please see section II.

## III. Consequences of a breach of a shareholders' agreement

The consequences of a breach of a shareholders' agreement are generally contractual in nature, i.e. such as certain rights under the shareholders' agreement, but do not affect the corporate legal relations. In order to better understand the legal effects of a breach of a shareholders' agreement, they must be compared against the legal effects of a breach of a company's articles of association. Depending on whether a certain provision is set forth in the articles of association of a joint stock company or in a shareholders' agreement, the consequences resulting from breaching such provision are of a different legal nature. This view can be illustrated by two examples – a breach of an agreement restricting the transfer of shares and a breach of a shareholders' agreement regarding voting.

### 1. Breach of the agreement restricting transfer of shares

The difference between a shareholders' agreement and articles of association can be illustrated by provisions restricting the transfer of shares. The view that agreements restricting the transferability of shares are only effective to the extent of establishing an obligation is commonly accepted in the legal doctrine. This concept was not, save for a few exceptions, challenged in the pre-war doctrine either. Shareholders' agreements do not form part of articles of association or alter articles of association to which a corporation is bound.

By virtue of Article 304 § 2 point 4 of the Commercial Companies Code, in regard to a joint stock company, a share transferability restriction becomes effective vis-a-vis the company itself, understood as a legal entity but also all of its shareholders. The setting forth of a provision restricting share acquisitions (e.g. making an acquisition conditional on the consent of the company) is deemed to cause any acquisition conducted contrary to the articles of association to be ineffective vis-a-vis the company. In other words, the company may refuse to enter the acquirer of its shares in its share register, as well as refuse to acknowledge such acquirer's right to exercise the rights attached to the shares, including the right to participate in the meeting of the shareholders. It is commonly accepted that in the event of a breach of the provisions of articles of association, we are dealing with suspended ineffectiveness within the meaning of Article 63 § 1 of the Civil Code. This article applies to both cases when the consent of a third party is required by law, as well as cases when such requirement is provided for contractually (in the articles of association). In the latter case, the admissibility of applying Article 63 § 1 of the Civil Code depends on whether or not the law grants authorisation to impose such restriction. In the case of share transferability restrictions, the legal basis is Article 304 § 2 point 4, Article 337 of the Commercial Companies Code, as well as Article 509 of the Civil Code in connection with Article 2 of the Commercial Companies Code.

In case of a breach of a shareholders' agreement, the legal situation is of a different nature. A breach of a shareholders' agreement restricting the transfer of shares only results in contractual consequences and does not result in the type of corporate consequences that result from an infringement of articles of association. This means that the company cannot refuse to reflect a transfer in the share register or refuse to acknowledge the authorisation of the given shareholder to exercise rights against the company. Such different consequences result from the fact that the shares are created by the articles of association and not by the shareholders' agreement. The parties to articles of association are authorised to define to a certain extent the rights attached to shares as well to modify the rules governing the transfer of such rights. Given the fact that pursuant to

Polish law a shareholders' agreement is not defined as a source of shareholders' participation in a company, such agreement cannot modify the scope of the rights attached to shares or influence the transferability of the shares in such a way that such modifications will have a binding corporate effect on the corporation and third parties pursuant to Article 57 of the Civil Code.[43]

An interesting issue related to a contractual transfer restriction is whether the concept of such agreements is only effective to the extent the establishment of an obligation would be affected if the company itself were a party to such agreement. In other words, could we assume that in such case the effectiveness of the agreement is broader, and the company would be entitled to refuse to enter into the share register a shareholder who acquired shares in breach of such agreement or refuse to permit a shareholder holding rights attached to bearer shares who acquired such shares in breach of the shareholders' agreement to participate in the general meeting. In my opinion, making a share transferability restriction commitment for the benefit of a company, as well as any commitments on the part of a company to observe the restrictions arising under such agreement, does not change the nature of the effectiveness of a shareholders' agreement. A shareholders' agreement will continue to be an agreement that does not bind the company in the corporate sense, which means that the company must, in principle, acknowledge an acquisition of its shares in a manner contrary to the shareholders' agreement. This, in my view, is supported by Article 304 § 2 point 4 of the Commercial Companies Code, which explicitly states that "The articles of association should contain provisions concerning: [...] 4) restrictions on the transferability of shares – otherwise being ineffective vis-a-vis the company". In other words, while shareholders' agreements are permissible, they do not have the corporate effect of binding a company understood as a legal entity and as all of its shareholders. Therefore, a company must accept the rights of a shareholder who acquired shares in the company in a manner contrary to a shareholders' agreement, even if the company itself is bound by the provisions of such shareholders' agreement.

---

**43** Art. 57 of the Civil Code – §1. An act in law can neither preclude nor limit the right to transfer, encumber, change or extinguish a right if in accordance with statutory law that right is transferable. §2. The above provision shall not preclude the admissibility of the obligation that the holder of the right shall abstain from making specified disposals of such right.

## 2. Right to challenge a resolution in case of a breach of a shareholder's agreement

The general principle under Polish law is that shareholders are not authorised to challenge a resolution of the meeting of the shareholders on the basis of a shareholders' agreement. The legal grounds for challenging resolutions of the meeting of the shareholders are stipulated in the Commercial Companies Code (Art. 422 and Art. 425 of the Commercial Companies Code), which does not provides for the possibility to make a specific claim in case of a breach of a shareholders' agreement but only for a breach of articles of association. Usually, it is underlined that unless a breach of a shareholders' agreement is also a breach defined in Polish law as a legal basis to challenge a resolution, such breach alone does not result in a legal right to challenge a resolution. There is an interesting court case which deviates to a certain extent from the common understanding of the legal grounds for challenging a resolution and which also illustrates that the Commercial Companies Code regulation on challenging resolutions can be interpreted so as to allow in certain cases the challenge of a resolution based on a breach of a shareholders' agreement. In one of the Supreme Court precedents in which the Supreme Court did not completely rule out the possibility of challenging a resolution in the case of a breach of a shareholders' agreement provided that such breach was also a breach of good morals (the fairness principle).

The Supreme Court issued its judgment based on the following situation. The shareholders and future investors in the company concluded an agreement on 12 May 2004 stipulating, among other things, the financing of the company (by way of the acceding investors granting a loan to the company), voting at the meeting of the shareholders and the profit distribution principles. The agreement stated that one-third of the profit would be used to repay the loans granted by some of the shareholders and that the remaining two-thirds would be distributed to the shareholders. On 21 December 2007, the extraordinary meeting of the shareholders adopted a resolution granting consent to the taking out of a credit facility to be earmarked for the repayment of the shareholder loans and to secure such credit facility. In a statement of claim filed on 18 January 2008 against the company, a minority shareholder demanded that the resolution be set aside on the grounds that it was contrary to good morals as it harmed the minority shareholders due to dividend payments being pushed forward in time as well as on the grounds of it being contrary to the agreement dated 12 May 2004. The Supreme Court did not agree with the claimant on the merits, but also decided not to challenge, in principle, the notion that a breach of good practice within the meaning of the Commercial Companies Code may involve a breach of the *pacta sunt ser-*

*vanda* principle through voting in a manner contrary to a shareholders' agreement:

> As a consequence of such line of thought, we come to the conclusion that a resolution may be challenged if it is contrary to a shareholders' agreement and, depending on what stance is adopted with regard to the construction of Article 249 § 1 of the Commercial Companies Code and if the existence of one of the two prerequisites are demonstrated as having occurred, i.e. harming the company's interests or being aimed at harming a shareholder.

Such a general statement of the Supreme Court may, unfortunately, be challenged. First of all, the adoption of such a pronouncement which de facto equates – for the purpose of challenging resolutions – a shareholders' agreement with the articles of association of a company leaves open the problem of explaining the potential differences between the shareholders' agreement and the articles of association in terms of their form, the parties thereto and other duties associated with the amendment or conclusion of both instruments. These differences are significant, because: (i) articles of association must be in the form of a notarial deed, whereas a shareholders' agreement does not need to be; (ii) articles of association are always binding on all of the shareholders, while a shareholders' agreement is only binding on those shareholders who are parties thereto – in other words, one cannot become a shareholder of a company without being a party to its articles of association, but not every shareholder needs to be a party to a shareholders' agreement; (iii) articles of association are registered by the courts and shareholders' agreements are not – analogously, an amendment of articles of association needs to be entered in the Register of Business Entities in order to be valid; and (iv) articles of association are available at the registry court, whereas a shareholders' agreement is not and is not required to be. In my opinion, these differences show a certain intention on the part of the legislators as to what may constitute a basis for challenging a resolution of the shareholders, i.e. which document should contain the rights and obligations of the shareholders with a view to ensuring that such rights and obligations are effective vis-a-vis all of the shareholders (and thus the company). Secondly, accepting the pronouncement of the Supreme Court indiscriminately (or at least without additional reservations) means that any adverse consequences of a breach of a shareholders' agreement would affect both those shareholders who are parties to such agreement, as well as those who are not. Such consequences could be independent of what percentage of the votes is represented by the shareholder asserting a breach of the shareholders' agreement. Thirdly, the wording of Article 159 of the Commercial Companies Code also contradicts the findings of the Supreme Court as such article states that special benefits and obligations which are to be granted to or required of the shareholders should be specified in detail in the articles of association, or else they shall be ineffective vis-a-vis the company. That provision should be taken to mean that the determination of a specific voting regime, which presents a certain burden on the exercise of voting rights by a shareholder, must be stipulated in the articles of association instead of any other document for such rights or obligations to be effective vis-a-vis the company (the entirety of its shareholders). In my opinion, in this way, the legislators determined that shareholders' agreements may have the same effect as articles of association (thus being able to provide a legal basis for challenging a resolution) to the extent that their provisions are reflected in the articles of association. This view is also supported by the systemic interpretation; in Article 304 § 2 of the Commercial Companies Code, a parallel solution is provided for with respect to joint stock companies.

# E. Enforcement of shareholders' agreements

The general principle under Polish law is that a contract is enforceable in accordance with its terms, i.e. usually a specific performance is available. This general statement does not mean that shareholders' agreements are easy to enforce under Polish law, which is in particular true in the case of shareholders' agreements regarding voting.

The legal basis for enforcement is set forth both in the Civil Code and the Civil Procedure Code. Under both regulations it is possible to ask the court to substitute the act of will of a person required under the contract to make an act of will. Such regulation allows, for example, the enforcement of shareholders' agreements which provide for certain options (call or put). In case of an option which is structured as a preliminary contract, if a party to such contract refuses to enter into the final contract, the other party may ask the court to substitute the other party and issue a judgment which will correspond to the final contract that the parties were supposed to enter into. In case of options structured in a different manner, i.e. irrevocable offers, the party in favour of which the option was granted simply accepts the irrevocable offer and in case of the refusal to transfer or buy shares, such party may make a claim for payment or for a transfer of the shares.

The situation is more complex in the case of shareholders' agreements regarding voting. In the precedent already described in section II, the Warsaw Appellate Court challenged not only the validity of voting agreements but also the possibility to claim a specific performance under such agreements. The Appellate Court in Warsaw pointed out that the Commercial Companies Code does not provide for the possibility to force a shareholder to vote in a certain manner (which, in the opinion of such court, might serve to support the view that the conclusion of shareholders' agreements regarding voting is not permissible). The Commercial Companies Code does not contain any provisions to that effect. This does not, however, mean that there is no legal basis for enforcing the performance of a voting agreement. The procedure to be followed when enforcing such claims is set out in Article 64 of the Civil Code. As mentioned above, in connection with Article 2 the Commercial Companies Code, the provisions of the Civil Code apply to corporate relationships in respect of matters not regulated in the Commercial Companies Code. The admissibility of enforcing the performance of a commitment to vote in a certain manner is an issue that gives rise to certain concerns in the legal doctrine. One cannot, however, a priori reject the possibility of enforcing claims under a shareholders' agreement regarding voting based on Article 64 of the Civil Code. The view that an act of casting one's vote constitutes a representation of will is quite commonly accepted in the doctrine, at least with regard to resolutions of the meeting of the shareholders that give rise to legal consequences. In the case under review, the commitment related to voting on a resolution amending the company's articles of association, and such resolution clearly does give rise to legal consequences. Consequently, the mere absence of a provision in the Commercial Companies Code setting forth a procedure for forcing a shareholder to vote in a certain manner cannot, per se, be seen as causing the enforcement of the performance of a shareholders' agreement regarding voting based on Article 64 of the Civil Code to be inadmissible.

The potential practical problems connected with the performance of a commitment to vote in a certain manner mean that the performance of such agreements is sometimes additionally safeguarded by a power of attorney. We even have to reckon with the admissibility of issuing irrevocable powers of attorney in such cases. The nature of the underlying relationship between the attorney-in-¬fact and the shareholder may support the argument that such power of attorney can indeed be granted. It is worth noting that the Commercial Companies Code does not limit such admissibility to revocable powers of attorney. Unlike in the case of the articles of association of a joint stock company, the articles of association of a limited liability company can exclude the right to grant a power of attorney to represent a shareholder at the meeting of the shareholders. If it does not, however, contain any provisions to that effect, it would be difficult to justify the view that there is no possibility to grant a power of attorney to participate in a meeting of the shareholders and exercise voting rights at the meeting of the shareholders, including an irrevocable power of attorney. The other way to secure the enforcement of such agreements is to provide for the payment of penalties in the case of a breach of a voting agreement.

**Definitions:**

| | |
|---|---|
| **Banking Law** | means the Act of 29 August 1997, the Banking Law. |
| **Civil Code** | means the Act of 23 April 1964, the Civil Code. |
| **Commercial Companies Code** | means the Commercial Companies Code. |
| **Public Offer** | means the Act on Offering and the Conditions for Introducing Financial Instruments to the Organized Trading System and on Public Companies. |

Radu Catană, Ioan Șumandea-Simionescu

# Romania

## Table of Content



**Prof. univ. dr. Radu Catană**, *Babeş-Bolyai University* Law School, Private Law Department; Center for Company Law & Corporate Governance, Cluj-Napoca, Romania.
**Ioan Șumandea-Simionescu**, PhD Student, *Babeş-Bolyai University* Law School, Private Law Department; Center for Company Law & Corporate Governance, Cluj-Napoca, Romania.

https://doi.org/10.1515/9783110517026-021

# A. Nature of Corporate Law Regulation

It must be noted that[1], although not expressly prohibited, extra-statutory agreements cannot expressly amend or come in direct contradiction with the provisions of the articles of incorporation or any imperative legal norms. Moreover, a change of a provision in the articles of incorporation through a private agreement between a group of shareholders will generate no legal effect in regard to the other shareholders, while for third parties the legal effects will be created depending on the disclosure levels as well the type of agreement, as we will discuss below.

Shareholders' agreements are those agreements concluded between the holders of equity interests in a company, with the aim of drawing up guidelines for the subsequent business of the company. The possibility of concluding (extra) statutory pacts is conferred under Romanian law on the principle of freedom to contract, i.e. to give birth to different legal relationships, observing imperative norms, public order and good morals.[2]

These shareholders' agreements may be included in the Company's Articles of Incorporation at the time in its creation or during the company's operation because of amendments to the Articles of Incorporation. Given the specificity of Romanian law, one of the advantages of a shareholder's agreement is the fact that in principle, it does not require any special form for validity. Also, this shareholder agreement can be considered a stabilizing element in those areas where shareholders can decide upon.[3] Moreover, since these conventions are unnamed contracts, there are no exact provisions on the exact type of clauses that they may include, thus offering greater flexibility.

The monistic concept of the New Civil Code, unifying the provisions of civil law with those of commercial law, brought together in its field the regulation applicable to societies. Thus, the provisions relating to the ordinary company, which are the common law applicable to companies, are complemented by those contained in Articles 197–224 C. Civ. regarding the legal entity, but also

**1** Preliminary considerations for the entire report: the issues and answers provided here are based on the research of the authors, which included: a sample group of articles of incorporation and shareholders' agreements of different types of companies (in the report identified as sample group or sample), relevant Romanian jurisprudence and doctrine. Under the current report, company law or general company law provision should be understood as referring to Law no. 31/1990 – Company Law.

**2** *Sandru* Pacte societare – clauze, pacte, intelegeri intre asociatii societatilor comerciale, Editura Universitara, Bucharest, 2010, pp. 15–28.

**3** Ibid.

those regarding the civil obligations. The Company Law further outlines the material guidelines. A variety of practical situations on extra-statutory agreements remain unregulated. The phrase "unless the articles of incorporation provide otherwise", which is at least 22 times stated in the company law, gives freedom to shareholders to lay down various solutions for various scenarios. Thus, the main issues on the negotiating table when drawing up corporate pacts, which can be included in the company's articles of association as well as in extra-statutory pacts, are related to the functioning of the company, the capital and the restrictions on the right of disposal on the shares, as well as the directors' relationship with the company.

Any company is constituted by a memorandum of association (Memorandum / Articles of Association, sometimes referred to as the Deed of Incorporation), which must be in writing and must be signed by all shareholders. In most cases, a private signature is sufficient, except for the limitations provided in Art. 5 § 5 of the Law no. 31/1990 (Company Law), when the act must be authenticated by a notary public. Apart from the articles of incorporation, the shareholders may also conclude an extra-statutory shareholders' agreement, which is not subject to disclosure. As it is no public, this contract between shareholders may not be opposed to third parties, unless it can be shown that third parties have knowledge of it (articles 50 – 52 of Law no. 31/1990).

As mentioned above, because these pacts are unnamed contracts, the shareholders may enter into such a covenant any provisions they deem necessary for the viability of the company, and there is no provision limiting the clauses to be included in an agreement.

Articles 7 and 8 of the Romanian Companies Law regulate the exact content of all provisions that must be included in articles of incorporations. Outside of these restrictions, articles of incorporation may include any provisions if they do not contradict directly applicable imperative norms.

# B. Regulation of Shareholders' Agreements

## I. Lack of a specific regulation

There is no express regulation that addresses the issue of shareholders' agreements. These are either governed by the Company Law provisions, if they are part of the articles of incorporation or by general contract law, if they are incorporated in private agreements between some or all shareholders.

In Romanian commercial law, shareholder pacts are mostly encountered in the case of companies that exceed a certain value, and less in the case of small-scale enterprises. The explanation lies in the fact that small-scale companies do not require an investment opportunity (and associated risk) that would cause associates to take advantage of implementing additional protective measures through extra-statutory arrangements.

It is a good idea that a shareholders' agreement is signed by all shareholders and is thus opposed to everyone; there are shareholders' pacts that are only signed by a shareholder, as well as situations where the provisions contained in a shareholders' pact may be opposable even to others than the shareholders of the future company.[4]The usefulness of a shareholders' agreement also derives from its flexibility, since although a shareholders' pact is a legally binding act for its parties (being governed, as any legal act, by the principle of *pacta sunt servanda*), it can be easily modified, when the conditions envisaged to sign it have changed without the need for any formalities. Instead, the amendment to the articles of incorporation involves difficult, lengthy and costly legal procedures (GSM, legal publicity etc.).

Articles 7 and 8 of the Romanian Companies Law regulate the exact content of all provisions which must be included in the articles of the incorporations. The articles of incorporation of the general partnership, of the limited partnership, and of the limited liability company shall thus contain at least (art. 7 of the Romanian Company Law): a) identification of the associates, in case of a limited partnership the active partners as well as the silent partners shall be clearly identified; b) the form, name, the headquarters; c) the company's object of activity, the field of action and the main activity; d) the subscribed and the deposited registered capital, with special mention of each associate's contribution, whether in cash or in kind, the value of the assets brought as contribution in kind and the way the evaluation has been made, in a limited liability company the number and the nominal value of all participating shares as well as the number of participating shares attributed to each associate for his contribution shall be specified; e) the associates who represent and manage the company or the independent administrators, be they natural or legal persons, the powers vested in them and whether they are going to exert the powers together or separately; f) each associate's part in profits and losses; g) location of its subsidiaries – branches, agencies or other offices of the same kind without legal personality; h) duration of the company; i) the method of dissolution or liquidation of the company as well as j) contribution to gains and loss.

4 *Sandru* Pacte societare – clauze, pacte, intelegeri intre asociatii societatilor comerciale, Editura Universitara, Bucharest, 2010, pp. 15–28.

While art. 8 of the Company Law stipulates that articles of incorporation of the joint-stock company or of the limited partnership by shares shall contain: a) identification of the founders; in case of a limited partnership by shares the active partners as well as the silent partners shall be clearly identified; b) the form, name, the registered office of the company; c) the company's object of activity, specifying the field of action and its main activity; d) the subscribed and deposited registered capital; e) the value of the assets brought as contribution in kind, the method of evaluation and the number of shares attributed against them; f) the number and nominal value of the shares, specifying whether they are registered or on bearer; where there are different categories of shares the number, nominal value and the rights conferred to each category shall be specified, as well as any restrictions in regard to transfer of shares; g) identification data of the first managers and directors; the special rights of administration and representation granted to some of them, including if they will exercise the rights separately; h) identification data of the first auditors; i) provisions regarding the management, functioning and control of the company by the statutory bodies; j) duration of the company; k) method of profit distribution and loss bearing; l) location of its subsidiaries – branches, agencies or other offices of the same kind without legal personality; m) special benefits conferred to any party participating the creation of the company or to transactions conducing to the incorporation at the time of incorporation or up to the moment the company is authorized to initiate activity, as well as the identity of the beneficiaries; n) the shares of the silent partners in a limited partnership by shares; o) the sums of money to be paid (or at least estimates) for operations re incorporation; p) method of dissolution and liquidation of the company.

As a result, any shareholders' agreements relating to the issues mentioned above have to be included in the articles of incorporation. Outside of the issues mentioned above, under general company law there are no express restrictions relating to shareholders' agreement not the need to include such provisions in the articles of incorporation or other documents of the company.

If shareholders' agreements are part of the articles of incorporation, then their duration is restricted to the existence of the articles of incorporation and thus directly correlated with the existence of the company (unless they are, of course, altered via GSM decision in accordance with the law). However, if the agreement is an extra-statutory one (and thus a contractual agreement), then there are no restrictions under the contract law directly relating to these issues outside of the scope of normal civil agreements.

## II. Distinction between partnerships and corporation

The main distinction we could find between partnerships and corporations regarding shareholders' agreement is one relating to scope. Under the Company Law, the former is under regulated compared to their corporate counterparts. Provisions relating to general partnerships tackle the minim regarding the issues of legal governance, providing for questions such as the powers of directors (art. 75–78, 88 CL), the responsibilities and the scope of power of shareholders (art. 79–85, 89 CL) etc. Outside of said provisions, the shareholders can agree through shareholders' agreements on any other issues relating to the management of the company. This is the purpose of such relaxed provisions. They offer flexibility for internal governance to make the company more attractive to entrepreneurs. Due to this, shareholders' agreements appear more frequently re such companies.

In corporations, due to stricter provisions, there is a more limited scope of issues on which shareholders can agree privately. This is not to say that such agreements are less frequent than those in general partnerships, but their scope is indeed diminished.

## III. Distinction between closed and stock corporations

The distinction between closed and stock corporations relates mostly to the degree of investor protection it offers. Stock corporation offer a clear framework for investor protection which set minimum requirements from which the agreements cannot derogate (fixed but small majorities, minimum provisions on transfer of shares etc.), but shareholders are free to introduce higher levels of investor protection. Closed corporation tend to offer a stricter framework of investor protection (higher levels of majority (absolute majority or even unanimity), difficult transfer of shares provisions) but it offers many more flexibility and incentive for shareholders to derogate from said provisions correlated with a lack of actual provisions. Of course, the higher number of provisions that regulate stock corporation as opposed to closed corporations should mean that shareholders' agreements tend to be more frequent in the latter, since shareholders have more room to manifest "corporate creativity" when drafting their articles of incorporation. However, the sample has shown that both types of companies frequently opt for shareholders' agreements. This could in part be due to the fact that shareholders on both sides feel they need to clarify or to implement provisions that suit their contractual needs which are not satisfied by the current legal framework.

There is relevant case law but it tackles specific issues relating to certain groups and types of shareholders' agreements and typically refers to enforceability. To avoid repetition, we will discuss the relevant case in each chapter below as it becomes relevant.

### IV. International or cross border Shareholders' Agreements

There is no specific regulation that directly addresses the issue of international or cross border shareholders' agreements other than those tackling cross-border contracts or issues relating to cross-border corporate events which may be directly related to the shareholders' agreement (cross-border mergers, *Societas Europaea* etc.).

## C. Forms of Shareholders' Agreements

### I. Shareholders' Agreements on Shareholders' Rights

The right to vote is recognized in doctrine and jurisprudence as the essence of shareholder status. The willingness of the shareholders must, in principle, be freely expressed and be a result of the debates within the General Assembly. This freedom implies the possibility that any shareholder has to change his/her decision during the general meeting, until the right to vote is exercised, i.e. at the conclusion of the debates.

However, the way the general assembly vote is exercised may be agreed upon by a share-holders' agreement. Conventions on the exercise of the right to vote have been denied and fought by the Romanian law until 2016 when, through the amendment to Law no. 31/1990, the former art. 128 was changed so that agreements on the exercise of the right to vote are allowed, except for those that imply compliance with the will of the directors or the society. The limitations in our current legislation have the purpose of avoiding situations where violations of power separations may occur, this being an intrusion of the executive bodies into the powers of the deliberative bodies, which constitutes a violation of the social interest, promoting the interests of the administrators or of other representatives to the detriment of society's interests.[5]

---

5 *Sandru* Pacte societare – clauze, pacte, intelegeri intre asociatii societatilor comerciale, Editura Universitara, Bucharest, 2010, pp. 163–167.

By corroborating the provisions of article 128 (1) with the provisions of article 101 of Company Law we conclude, however, that a convention on the exercise of the right to vote cannot lead to the renunciation of this right, neither by its abandonment nor by the transfer of the right dissociated from the rest of the social rights.[6] It is irrelevant the convention that would give an irrevocable mandate to another shareholder to vote in a determined manner, as such a "mandate" would be a void of content of the right to vote. However, the practice of the blank mandate, issued without indicating the meaning of the vote to be exercised by the trustee, is valid.

The question of voting agreements and disputes between shareholders in this regard was dealt with by the Romanian courts as well. In the case before the Brasov Court[7] a decision of the shareholders of a company by which it was decided: i) to amend the company's articles of incorporation, as well as ii) the approval of changes referring to the voting method (the vote by correspondence), to the incompatibilities, to the maximum share of the share capital which a shareholder can hold, as well as the revocation of directors, was attacked. The applicant, who became a shareholder in the defendant company after the decision was taken by the shareholders, requested the court to find the absolute nullity of the above-mentioned clauses and the nullity of a subsequent GMS decision (adopted in 2000), adopted considering the votes cast by correspondence. The Brasov Court partially upheld the applicant's claim, considering that only the clause on the correspondence vote was null and void because Law no. 31/1990 does not regulate such a method of voting for closed joint stock companies, but only for limited liability companies and even if the law does not prohibit this way of voting, from the interpretation of the provisions of art. 112 § 1 and art. 115 of the same law, it is necessary to have the personal presence of the shareholders or, possibly, by a representative according to the provisions of art. 124 (imperative legal norm) so their violation is sanctioned with absolute nullity. Since the Shareholders' Meeting of 2000 and the decision adopted on that date met the majority only because of the valid expression of votes by correspondence, the Court assessed – because of the nullity of that clause – that this judgment was also affected by relative nullity (annulment). Regarding the rest of the clauses whose invalidity was invoked, it was noted that they were modified following the decision of the initial GSM resolution, a judgment which had not been the subject of the proceedings; that, given the contractual

6 Ibid.

7 Decision of the Court of Appeals Brasov no. 49 of 31.01.2001 (Civil Sentence no. 918/C/04.07.2000 of the Brasov Tribunal).

nature of the documents of incorporation, shareholders may reduce or restrict the maximum share of shares they may hold (provided that that share falls within the quota maximum, not more than 5%, established by CNVM Regulation no. 6/1996) – through the determination of a smaller quota, taking into account the will of the shareholders: the same was said about the revocation of the directors.

The Court of Appeal dealt with the issue similarly to the tribunal. The Court rejected the applicant's appeal and partially upheld the defendant's appeal and considered the lawful and substantiated remedy of the case as nullity of the other clauses for which the applicant's action was dismissed and considered that if the legislator has established the maximum share level of 5% of the equity capital, any other share level below that threshold, which the shareholders have determined, is perfectly valid and legal. About the defendant's appeal concerning the nullity of the correspondence vote clause, the court of appeal considered that the substantive solution was correct; the texts of the special law concerning the presence of shareholders and the taking of decisions were imperative and excluding any discussion of other ways of voting. Thus, the courts established that, through agreements included in the Articles of Incorporation, the shareholders may both change the level of rights of holding if such agreements do not breach the legal provisions. It should be noted that the company in question was listed on the stock exchange and the issue of voting has been now settled through incorporation of different forms of voting in secondary legislation as well as changes in the mentality in regarding voting in the digital age.

At the bequest of the claimants, the case was reached to the highest court in Romanian, the Supreme Court of Cassation and Justice, and the decisions were overturned and sent to the lower courts for retrial. The decision was not justified, however, on the lack of merits of the findings of the lower courts' decisions on the issues mentioned above. The Supreme Court decided that the lower courts had not considered the difference between the annulment and the absolute nullity of the decisions. Thus, the court has decided that if an agreement is inserted in the Articles of Incorporation prior to the entry into the company of a shareholder in the company (as was the case here) the relative nullity is open only to shareholders who held their position at the time of the decision to change the Articles of Incorporation. As a result, the claimant could not claim the annulment of the decisions as well as the subsequent acts.

Under the Company Law, shareholders have various rights which allow a certain amount of control of the company. Shareholders' agreements usually deal with the co-ordination of the shareholders' rights. (A) GMS information right – conferred on any shareholder (requires access to annual financial statements, CA / auditors / censors reports, limited to the rest of the documents specific to society); b) the right to ask questions written prior to the AGM; c) permanent information right – granted to any shareholder (it provides access to the register of GSM deliberations as well as access to other constitutive acts of the company within the limits of the law); d) the right to vote – any shareholder based on the principle of one action – one vote. e) voting restrictions that act as shareholder protection measures; f) suspension of the voting right for the shareholder who is not aware of the payments, the obligation to abstain from voting – for the shareholder who is in conflict of interest (often the majority shareholder); e) the right to dividend if the requirements of the law are met; f) the right to bring an action for annulment of the decision of the General Meeting of Shareholders (GMS) – conferred on the shareholder who voted against or abstained within the AGM within the limits established by the law; d) the right of exit – protection granted to the shareholder who did not vote in favor of adopting the GMS decision.

The above rights are expressly stated in respect of closed stock corporations. Little regulation on this topic exists for other companies under general company law. As stated, shareholders may opt to include such rights in articles of association to enhance control (often seen in articles of incorporation of limited liability companies).

## 1. Voting trusts

A voting trust can be achieved in at least two ways under Romanian law. The first option available is the transfer of shares in a trust deed (fiduciary agreement). According to art. 773 Civil Code the trust deed is the legal operation whereby one or more constituents transfer real rights, debt rights, guarantees or other property rights, or a set of such rights, present or future, to one or more trustees who exercise them for a purpose determined for the benefit of one or more beneficiaries. These rights form an autonomous patrimonial mass, distinct from the other rights and obligations of the trustees so the transferred shares are protected by any form of force enforcement. In a trust arrangement, only banks, investment firms, brokerage companies, insurance/reinsurance companies, public notaries and/or lawyers can be trustees.

The advantage of the provision is that it is open to all companies and shareholders who wish to opt for such a trust. However, there are several disadvantages. Firstly, it implies an actual transfer of ownership of shares from the trustor (constituent) to the trustee for a certain amount of time. Parties of course can be regulated the way the shares and the voting rights will be dealt with but this is an *ex ante* control mechanism and the provisions prohibit intervention of the constituents in the management of the trustee during the existence of the trust deed. Unilateral termination of a trust deed is also difficult. Since the quality of trustor and the beneficiary can be held by the same person, this mechanism can be used full circle. Secondly, the trust must be signed before a public notary and since the tax for such proceedings is calculated regarding the value of the actual contract (and so the value of the actual shares transferred), the trust deed arguably becomes a costly endea-vor.

Another popular option is a so called "general or blank mandate" (art. 92 § 13 of the Law no. 24/2017 on issuers of financial instruments and market operations) which allows a shareholder to issue a general power of attorney by which it grants to a party the right to vote as they chose for a certain amount of time (a maximum of three years), allowing the representative to vote on all aspect of the GSM of one or more issuers identified in the power of attorney (either individually or as a general category), including decisions which imply rights of disposal. Of the two, the general mandate is indeed the more flexible and cost efficient since it implies little cost, easy termination and allows the party to draft the limits of the power of attorney. As with the above, the representative must be a lawyer or an authorized intermediary (brokerage companies or financial institutions) and the issuer of the mandate has to be their client. The clear disadvantage is that the provisions apply regarding the issuer of shares on capital markets (listed companies), severely limiting the scope of the provision. Moreover, there are strict regulations regarding conflict of interest correlated with the provisions re acting in concert, which can dissuade shareholders from using this type of agreement.

Regarding general company law, art. 128 of the Law no. 31/1990 provide that the voting right cannot be transferred and that any convention or voting trust by which the shareholder is obligated to vote in accordance with the instructions of the company or of the representatives of the company (directors, general managers etc.) is subject to annulment. While not forbidding voting trusts as such, the company law does restrict the parties which can take part in such an agreement.

## 2. Shareholders' Agreements on the coordination to enforce shareholder claims

Outside the provisions mentioned above regarding voting rights, there are no express provisions regulating shareholders' agreements regarding the enforcement of claims.

In situations where shareholdings held by shareholders are not equal, minority shareholders, in the desire to protect their investment in society[8], may propose (or even impose, if they are the company's financiers) to the majority shareholder certain conditions that they will have to are considered during the activity. In this respect, clauses regarding a) the quorum required for decision-making may appear in a shareholders' pact; of course, a shareholder holding a small share of the capital will want the decisions to be taken unanimously, and in the event that he cannot impose his point of view, it is advisable that at least the decisions on certain issues be adopted unanimously; b) rights and obligations of shareholders; c) the company's policy regarding the distribution / reinvestment of profits, etc., as well as d) any other clauses of possible checks and balances (including the increase of GMS attributions).

In the shareholders agreement clauses may be provided to limit the powers of directors and directors of the company so that minority shareholders are protected from the abuses of shareholders holding positions or exercising influence in the executive management of the company.

## 3. Shareholders' Agreements regarding the financing of the corporation

In the research provided, we have encountered either financing through infusion of capital correlated with issuance of shares or financing through loans. In this regard, two major pieces of legislation have given/will give a boost to the start-up and entrepreneurial environment in Romania: the business angel law and draft Law concerning the development of participative financing.

The draft follows another major development in the field of innovative financing, the Business Angel law (Law no. 120/2015) which offered significant tax relief to investors – individuals, companies are excluded – which opted to become shareholders in promising start-ups (i.e. SMEs) if they fulfil certain criteria (they are not linked to the company prior to the investing procedure, the value of the investment is between EUR 3000 and EUR 200000 and the share ownership of the angel investor does not exceed 49%).[9] The law offers benefits through exemption from dividend tax for 3 years to exemption for capital gains

8 *Sandru* Pacte societare – clauze, pacte, intelegeri intre asociatii societatilor comerciale, Editura Universitara, Bucharest, 2010, pp. 163–172, 193–198.

9 *Catana/Sumandea-Simionescu* Study On The Law Applicable to Crowdfunding – Country Report for Romania, Revue internationale des services financiers/International Journal for Financial Services, no. 4/2014, pp. 58–67.

tax if the transfer of shares is concluded after 3 years from the date of the investment.

It is worth mentioning that, in a recent study[10], Romania was a favored destination for entrepreneurs from the members states (in particular Italian nationals) taking into consideration the number of foreign shareholders in Romanian companies. This can also be seen in the sample pool studied. In companies where venture capital comes from other countries (as reflected in the share capital) financing clauses would often be correlated with investment protection mechanisms. We identified frequent tag along/drag along provisions (with stricter restrictions regarding the minority shareholder – usually the beneficiary of the investment), higher control through higher responsibilities for the GSM as opposed to the management as well as better agreement regarding director control. We also found that, while directors are better controlled, there is flexibility in the right of delegation. Under Romanian law, directors cannot delegate their rights to third parties unless it is allowed in the articles of incorporation (art. 71 § 1 Law no. 31/1990). In the sample studied, a large number had opted to allow delegation within certain parameters (caps or special control of the GSM etc.).

The concept of crowd investing or crowd lending has only recently been introduced in the Romanian legal paradigm through the draft Law concerning the development of participative financing – Crowdfunding (CL). As of 2017, the draft proposal is still being debated in the Chamber of Deputies of Romanian Parliament, after it has been approved in 2015 in the Senate. The Chamber of Deputies is the decision-making chamber which will make the final call as to the issue of this law.[11]

The courts have also been tasked with issues raised by financing clauses. The Bucuresti Tribunal, in its *Decision no. 172 of 2009*, viewed a case in which the claimants sued a company requesting that the court will find the absolute nullity of the contract of joint venture concluded between S (the Claimants inherited the rights and Obligations of S) and the company and, in subsidiary, to declare partial nullity of article 9 of the joint venture agreement signed between the

---

**10** *Siems/Schuster/Mucciarelli/Gerner-Beuerle* Why Do Businesses Incorporate in other EU Member States? An Empirical Analysis of the Role of Conflict of Laws Rules, p. 12, article accessible at: https://www.kcl.ac.uk/law/newsevents/eventrecords/Siems-Why-Do-Businesses-Incorporate-in-other-EU-Member-States-002.pdf. The authors provided the Country Report for Romania in the initial study for the European Commission – Study on the Law Applicable to Companies Final Report.

**11** *Catana/Sumandea-Simionescu* Study On The Law Applicable to Crowdfunding – Country Report for Romania, Revue internationale des services financiers/International Journal for Financial Services, no. 4/2014, pp. 58–67.

two persons mentioned. According to the article of the Articles of Association, dividends allocation will comply with those set out in the partnership contract, allowing the actual distribution to take place in two ways: firstly, dividends would be used to recover costs of incorporation of the company as well as the initial investment or secondly, upon completion of the first step, it would be equally distribution between the three partners.

The conclusion reached by the court is that the owners had temporarily departed from the law on the *pro rata* distribution of dividends to the amount of the share capital owned and agreed that the distribution of dividends would be made proportionally to the amounts that the company had been credited for initial expenses and investments. The first level court dismissed the requests on the ground that there are no clauses in the agreement that provided award of benefits to a single shareholder or exemption of a shareholder to participate in the losses and the value of the company (*lion's share* type clauses, prohibited under Romanian law). Throughout the period of recovery of financial investments, S received a fixed amount (250 USD) up to his death. However, at the time when it came for compensation for the investment made on land that now belongs to the claimants, they invoked the annulment of the contract of joint venture trying to dismiss such obligations under the contract mentioned above. Considering the above, the Court dismissed the appeal as unfounded.

## 4. Shareholders' Agreements and the law of groups ("*Konzernrecht*")

Currently Romania has not drafted a law to solely tackle the question of group relations. The closest definition on the issue of groups can be found in the new insolvency provision (Law no. 85/2014), art. 5 point 35 which stipulates that groups of companies are two or more interconnected companies, either by control or qualified holdings. The concept of control is central to the question of groups and the legislation that handles them, be it competition law, insolvency law, civil law or criminal law (especially anti-money laundering provisions – ultimate beneficiary theories).

In the sample analyzed, similar structures of control were identified. Where companies were linked in groups, shareholders' agreement reflected typical control structures such as higher responsibilities for GSM to control directors, while appointment of certain directors were vetoed or censured by the GSM or by the actual mother-company. An "insider" director was presented in the subsidiaries (member of the Board of both the mother and daughter company, or at least an inside man for the mother company). All the above would be frequently regulated through shareholders' agreements, especially when the shareholding structure was dispersed and provisions had to opposable to all present and future shareholders via the articles of incorporation.

## II. Shareholders' Agreements on the (Limitation for the) Transfer of Shares

These types of clauses have typically been used in medium and large companies, where conflict and interests reach higher levels. Regarding forced exit and compulsory redemption of shares, such provisions found their place in the Capital Market Law (L. no. 297/2004) – CML, art. 206–207 (and have now found their place in the new Law. no. 24/2017). In fact, these are cases of expropriation to accommodate private utility. Rule well known in the expropriation is that it is only for reasons of public policy or public interest, and these contractual arrangements do not justify such grounds. However, a case for such provisions can be made when considering efficient management.[12] Under the law, obligatory redemption (squeeze-out) allows shareholders to compel the minority to alienate holdings in their favor to gain full power in the company. The CML requires that the bidder holds shares representing more than 95% of the share capital or to purchase more than 90% of the shares concerned under the takeover bid. At the request of holder, the minority will be forced to alienate their financial instruments. For companies listed on the stock market, this operation can be done under the law. There are similar provisions that allow the minority shareholder to request the purchase of the shares by the majority holder to offer quick exit options.

In the research carried out, we identified clause / shareholders' agreement on preemptive rights and tag along / drag along / squeeze-out provisions.

Thus, in one analysis it was revealed that shareholders agreed on pre-emptive rights in further rounds of financing for all existing shareholders, pro rata. Any shareholder was entitled to exercise its right within 60 days from the decision of the GMS. If a shareholder does not exercise its right, rights of subscription for that round are transferred pro-rata to other partners, within a given day.

In addition, shareholders had the right of first offer at the same price on the same terms and under the same terms, in case of the sale by any shareholder of its shares in direct proportion to the share of capital held. In this case, if a partner wanted to sell its shares, he/she must first give its shareholders pro rata the

12 *Sandru* Pacte societare – clauze, pacte, intelegeri intre asociatii societatilor comerciale, Editura Universitara, Bucharest, 2010, pp. 199–213.

right to buy under the same conditions, including the redistribution of the parts of the offer which were refused by other shareholders within the procedure. Only if they are not purchased shareholders could sell them to third parties – in the same conditions as offered to the associates. Offers, including price, could be sent by email to all associate members and to the Company simultaneously. Shareholders had to exercise the right of first offer within certain days of receiving this notice and make the purchase and payment of the price within t + 10 days after acceptance of the offer.

Regarding drag-along rights, they were identified situations where the proceedings were drawn in the shareholders' agreement. Thus at any time after the passage of a period of six months from the signing of association articles, shareholder(s) owning at least 70 % of the shares (and not of the number of shareholders) or ii) after passing a period of 60 months from the date of signing the documents of incorporation, a majority of more than 50 % of the shares, (and not of the number of shareholders), but requiring the participation of at least two (2) shareholders, could (but were not be obliged) to request other shareholders to sell all holdings in the Company on the same terms and under the same conditions and to the same third party in good faith (Drag Along Right) and said shareholders would be forced to make, take or cause to be taken all steps to assist and cooperate with the sellers to achieve all aspects necessary, appropriate and desirable (including, without limitation, voting) to ensure that sellers will sell all of their shares (together with all the shares of other partners) on the same terms and under the same conditions and the same third party in good faith and in the timeframe requested by sellers. For drag along provisions to apply, sellers had to give notice to other partners at least 10 days prior to the signing of documents on the transfer of shares by which they would inform the participants of the activation of the Drag Along provisions as well as the price, terms and conditions of sale. Drag Along for exercising the right of sale price may not be less than either a fixed or a certain amount of times the company's income in the last 4 (four) quarters preceding the sale by which to inform them about this right of Drag Along and on the price, terms and conditions of sale. The Drag Along price could not be less than either i) a fixed sum or ii) x times the company's income of the last 4 (four) quarters preceding the sale.

We also encountered tag along rights inserted in shareholders' agreements of different types of which we synthesized a general mechanism. Thus, any shareholder would have the right (but not the legal obligation) to take part in any sale of shares carried by another shareholder *pro rata* to the number of shares held, in the same terms and conditions and to the same third party in good faith (Tag Along right). For tag along provisions to apply, the initial sellers had to give notice to other partners at least 10 days prior to the signing of documents on the transfer of shares by which they would inform the shareholders of the possibility of activation of the Tag Along provisions as well as the price, terms and conditions of sale. Notification must be submitted a certain number of days before the signing of documents on the transfer of shares. If other shareholders would not inform in writing or email the seller about the exercise of the right, within a few calendar days of receipt of the notification, the shareholder seller would be free to sell their shares under the terms and conditions notified to the other shareholders. If shareholders would exercise their right of Tag Along, informing him in this regard, the seller had to cooperate to achieve the sale of equity within the limits of the tag along provisions.

A relevant question can be raised regarding exit clauses which relate to companies using bearer shares (which are permitted under Romanian Company Law but are not often used anymore). As such a mechanism essentially uses a "cloak of anonymity", it is difficult the details the exact working of a possible drag along clause. A possible solution provided is to insert a transparency or disclosure clause in which the shareholder which holds the bearer shares would be required to disclosure ownership prior or at the time of the exercise of the exit clause.

Exit clauses mentioned above may be considered genuine pre-emption rights to acquire shares, where shareholders decide a transfer as valid to avoid placing others in society. However, exit clauses which involve in any way the access of third parties to the shares of a limited liability company will have to the validated through the positive shareholders' vote of at least ¾ of the capital of the company (art. 202 § 2 Company Law).

The Court of Appeal Cluj, in its *Decision no. 3 of 2008*, viewed a case in which they were faced with an application made by a claimant for exclusion from company of the shareholders-defendants since the shareholders had agreed to withdraw from society by not less than two meetings of shareholders (like a shoot-out/deadlock agreement).

Settling the case, the Court, considering the evidence provided in the case and applicable statutory provisions, considered the applicant's request as unfounded in terms of the grounds invoked. Thus, defendants cannot be excluded from a society under art. 222 of Law no. 31/1990 (Company Law) on the ground that the legal provision states expressly the exhaustive cases that may require exclusion of a partner and the situation presented does not fit into any of them.

Also, the contractual clause invoked at the last minute as the basis for an action "to find exit from the company" could not be considered by the court and such a defense is not only inapplicable, being introduced in articles of incorporation without the defendant's agreement, but it is also illegal because it falls beyond art. 222 of Law no. 31/1990 which strictly regulates and limits exclusion or forced exit from the company.

It was also considered that if the institution of exclusion is provided in company law, one cannot successfully promote an action for exit from society. Every shareholder is entitled to request an exit from the company and his will should be exercised freely and without a doubt in this regard. The statutory body can accept the request or not, of course. This statutory provision shows that shareholders have agreed to exit from their company by more than two meetings of shareholders and art. 226 of Law no. 31/1990 provides the situation in which a shareholder may withdraw from a society without specifying that one cannot provided in the constitution of the company other ways of exit from society.

About the exclusion of shareholders of limited liability companies, the provisions of art. 222 § 1 of Law no. 31/1990, determines an exhaustive list the cases of exclusion and the defendants do not fit into any of them. Inactivity in the company and the indifferent attitude of some shareholders may not constitute a cause of exclusion of the limited liability company, because this is not the case among the limitations provided by law.

The refusal of these partners to work together to achieve the smooth running of society itself (*affectio societatis*) can only be a cause of dissolution of the company and not associated with the sanction of exclusion.

The court found that the exit situations must be unambiguous and must be agreed by all members for exit to work, as presented in the memorandum through the agreement of all other partners, and when there is a lack of provisions, the partner can exit for justified reasons based on a judgment of the court.

So, while the court did validate a freedom for shareholders to agree upon creative ways to exit the company or to be forced out of the company, it did underline that such provisions had to be expressly included in the articles of incorporation.

In discussing exit rights, the Brasov Court of Appeal, in its *Decision no. 9 of 2009*, rejected the plea of a claimant by which he requested a finding of exit from the company, considering that in the minutes of a general meeting of shareholders, he said he intends to withdraw from company, and that according to the minutes, signed by all shareholders, the defendants unanimously agreed with the proposal to exit. The court found that the requirements for admissibility of the action under article 226 let. c of the Law no. 31/1990, which refers to a situation where the absence of provisions in the memorandum or where no shareholder agreement is reached, the shareholder can withdraw from the company via court proceedings, can only be used for good reasons, based on a decision of the court. Since the parties agree upon this exit right, the court dismissed the claimant's request, stating that while the exit did take place and was valid, it was not done by a court, but by the unanimous consent of the parties under Art. 226 lit. b of the Law no.31 / 1990.

The Cluj Court of Appeals, in its *Decision no. 9 of 2010*, viewed a case in which a General Meeting of Shareholders Decision was contested. The agreement stipulated that the shares in the company may not be transferred to other natural or legal persons outside the company and any transfer of shares by a shareholder can only take place based on a notification to the company (the notification had to comply with certain conditions), so that other shareholders would be able to make use of their right of preemption. If no shareholder or group of shareholders the company buys or expresses intent to buy, then the company may acquire its own shares directly in the terms and conditions provided by law and the regulation on acquisition of own shares. It was also decided that shareholders may cease to hold such a quality and the shares they hold can be removed and / or made available to the company (like a shootout provision) if: a) they cause or have caused property or financial damage to the company or encourages others to do such damage or help, aid, facilitate or instigate in anyway other people to produce such damages; b) if he/she transfers its shares to any natural or legal persons who are not shareholders of the company. The shareholders decided that the excluded shareholder exclude is entitled to receive from the Company an amount of money based on the number of shares withdrawn and/or seized and the price approved by the Board according to the internal regulation, shares which could be distributed to stakeholders within the company.

Thus, it was decided that the shares may not be transferred to other natural or legal persons outside the company and that any sale of shares without following the procedure established is invalid without the intervention of any courts or performance of any preliminary procedure, stating that the clause is enforceable fully and shareholders may cease to be a shareholder while the shares they hold can be removed and/or frozen. The claimant argued that the organization of the company remained essentially that of a joint stock company, and, for this form of organization, art. 222 of Law no. 31/1990 does not provide for the possibility of excluding shareholders. Without this legal possibility, he argued that court cannot recognize the shareholders' right to include in the memorandum a contractual arrangement that would allow the exclusion of a shareholder, regardless of the reasoning behind it.

Contractual freedom does not have an unlimited corporate scope. The law no. 31/1990 is one of the pillars on which any partner or shareholder of a company should look onto. Art. 969 § 1 of the then Civil Procedure Code provides that only "legally made agreements have force of law between the contracting parties". The above should not lead to the conclusion that the shareholder can produce a loss at the expense of company and not liable for damage caused or would be able to dispose of its shares to a third party. On the contrary, whoever causes damage, will answer for it, and a shareholder of a closed joint stock company will not be able to dispose of his shares outside of that company.

The court however held that current legislation does not provide a formal definition of a closed joint stock company. As a matter of practice, the company was defined as joint stock company whose constituent documents provide for restrictions on the free transferability of its shares and prohibits any distribution of securities to the public. This definition can be taken on, in accordance with art. 8 letter f of the law no. 31/1990, which stipulates that the articles of incorporation of a joint stock company can provide restrictions on transfer of shares. The essence of a closed company is the inability to transfer shares to persons outside the company and that owners of shares may not perform any form of advertising to sell their shares.

The decision to transform a joint stock company into a closed company belongs to the shareholders' collective will. It is a decision that cannot be reviewed by the court.

The law no. 31/1990 does not contain many references to a closed joint stock company. In fact, essentially the difference between an open and closed stock company, the court considered, is found only re how shares can be transferred. Shareholders may insert clauses restricting trading of shares, as required by art. 8 letters f of Law no. 31/1990. The remaining shareholders, by their own will, did not violate the property rights of the claimant by the clauses invoked. They exercised their own right to convert the stock company they belong to into a closed one.

Ownership is not an absolute right. Its exercise may be restricted either by law or assumed by the free will of the holder. Thus, by becoming a shareholder of a company, the claimant was considered to have understood and consensually obeyed the will of the majority shareholders. The law no. 31/1990 requires him to comply with the legal decisions made by a majority of shareholders.

Concluding on the above, the court held that opting for maintaining the quality of shareholder in a company closed, the applicant must comply with all the rigors arising from this status is important consequences on freedom of alienation of shares.

## III. Shareholders' Agreements on the Constitution of the Corporation

In accordance with the Civil Code, art. 1913 § 1, the appointment of directors, the organization thereof, the limits of the mandate and any other aspect of the company's management are established by contract or by separate acts. However, for most companies under the Company Law, the General Meeting of Shareholders has the sole right to appoint directors. Directors however have the right, under the law, to appoint the general manager/deputy general managers of the company. So, shareholders' agreements (if included in the articles of incorporation) can tackle the manner of appointment for the managers (e.g., the right of the GMS and not the directors) but it cannot give the power of appointment to a sole or group of shareholders. However, in the research group, we have found that majority shareholders tend to include a double majority to control an appointment together with a right to nominate. So, the shareholders have the right to nominate a candidate and an appointment is made with a majority of vote but the decision is final only upon final confirmation by said shareholder. To comply with good faith requirements, usually this right applies to only one such appointment (*one off inside man*).

The Cluj Court of Appeals, in its *Decision no. 201/2008*, viewed a case in which the parties signed a contract of sale of shares. Through this agreement the defendant had sold all his shares at an agreed transfer price of EUR 1.

Also in the agreement the parties had stipulated the following clause: under condition of termination with immediate and full effects, the transferee undertakes to keep on the current manager of company for a period of two years.

This clause was contested in front of the court. As stipulated in the contract, the clause made the transfer of ownership of shares from the transferor to the transferee conditional on keeping the transferor as director in the company. Under Romanian law, if the clause was not respected it is understood that the parties agreed re cancellation of the contract because of breach with all the legal effects applicable. As such a clause which terminates the assignment agreement is not prohibited by the rules of the Romanian Civil Code. According to the principle of freedom enshrined in the provisions of the Civil Code, people are free to enter into any agreement if they do not violate public order and morals.

And so, the court found that indeed the transfer of shares agreement was conditional on the maintenance of the director in his position. If such a condition was not fulfilled, contract law would apply and the contract would be terminated.

The Company Law no. 31/1990 does not prohibit the transfer of shares in a limited liability company to be subject to maintenance of an individual for a period as statutory manager of the company, even if said person is indeed the transferor, since the position of shareholder and director have separate attributes and cannot be confused or merged together.

Although the court agreed that the clause involved a clear limitation of the right of the new shareholder to appoint a director, the shareholder agreed to this freely in a contractual framework. In such circumstances, the Court held the clause as valid and rejected the claim of the transferee. The decision showed that shareholder agreements could validly limit the rights of a shareholder even is the other party had no holdings in the company, confirming that the right to appoint a director could be limited through a contractual framework such as a shareholders' agreement.

## IV. Shareholders' Agreements in pre-insolvency situation

There is no strict restriction that applies to agreements which tackle bankruptcy averting. However, shareholders must be weary of agreements in pre-insolvency situation since they are exposed to scrutiny through the provision of the Law no. 85/2014 on insolvency prevention procedure and the insolvency procedure (art. 117–122) if they have a fraudulent nature, within certain limitation.

The Supreme Court of Cassation and Justice (*Decision no. 4836 of December 5, 2012*) decided that, in accordance with art. 95 of Law no. 85/2006 on insolvency proceedings, any amendment to the articles of incorporation after the opening of insolvency proceedings must be included in the reorganization plan of the company subject to this procedure. In these circumstances, after opening insolvency proceedings, shareholders cannot agree upon any amendment to the articles of incorporation, as such changes are possible only during the normal operation and activity of a company or in an approved implementation of a legal reorganization plan. In the case the court heard, the company was part of a simplified insolvency proceedings (which excluded, under the insolvency law of the time – Law no. 85/2006 – the possibility of reorganization) and, therefore, as there was no reorganization plan, the transfer of shares could not take place since it involved a change of the articles of incorporation which was prohibited.

So, any shareholders' agreement has to take into consideration the above provisions. Outside these restrictions shareholders can typically coordinate their action and it is so recommended since they are usually all represented by a special proxy (special director).

# D. Legal Effects of Shareholders' Agreements

## I. Legal Effects on the Corporation

Shareholders' agreements usually aided the courts and the shareholders in interpreting the corporate charter by explaining or underlining certain provisions.[13] However, all interpretation of the articles of incorporation and the shareholders' agreement must be subordinated to the interest of the company and to the general imperative norms which apply. Shareholders cannot affect *affectio societatis* through such agreement since such a breach could result in the dissolution of the company (art. 227 of the Law no. 31/1990).

## II. Legal Effects on the Shareholders

The transfer of obligation and/or rights arising from the Shareholders' agreement to another shareholder is allowed under general contract law (of course applying when the provisions are not inserted in the articles of incorporation since then all shareholders are party to the agreement). If the transfer agreement implies movement of shares, then certain restrictions can apply (e. g. preemption right etc.). The transfer to a third party can only take place if the receiving party will become a shareholder in the company (since outside of this premise we cannot have a shareholders' agreement). If the agreement implies a transfer of shares, limitations may apply if it takes place in a limited liability company where third party transferors are subject of GSM approval as mentioned above.

If the Shareholders' Agreements tackle issues of voting rights or control and the company in question is listed on the Bucharest Stock Exchange, then the shareholders would fall under the capital market obligations, including acting in concert. This would include the application of European provisions on the topic as well as special disclosure and transparency requirements under the Romanian law (Law no. 24/2017).

Under general company law, there is no obligation of disclosure of agreements although this will generate a lack of opposability to third parties. However, under capital law requirements, certain restrictions apply. Under the Corporate Governance Code, the Bucharest Stock Exchange (BSE) listed companies must disclose corporate documents (including articles of incorporation) as

13 *Sandru* Pacte societare – clauze, pacte, intelegeri intre asociatii societatilor comerciale, Editura Universitara, Bucharest, 2010, pp. 44–46.

well as any and all transactions that might generate conflict of interests. Also, the independence of director can be affected by such agreements and such a situation must be disclosed if the parties involved consider the effects on independency as significant. Sibex (Sibiu Stock Exchange) has an excellent practice of creating a special section on the page of each issuer where extra-statutory agreements had to be disclosed. However, upon further research, no such disclosures of relevant importance were found. Since Sibex is in a merger procedure (via absorption) with BSE, it will be interesting to see if BSE will continue this practice.

## III. Consequences of a Breach of the Shareholders' Agreements

This topic was debated by the Romanian courts. The Cluj Court of Appeal, in its *Decision no. 359 of 2014*, viewed a case in which ONC and CR – shareholders of F SA – sign a contract for the transfer of shares, disregarding the articles of incorporation that require notification to the Board of Directors of the transfer and the right of preemption of the co-shareholders.

The applicant F SA, brought an action for annulment of the transfer contract, citing non-compliance with a statutory clause – art. 8 § 3.

The defendant makes a counterclaim seeking the annulment of the provisions of art. 8 § 3 and 6 of the articles of incorporation. He indicates that absence of notification does not entail any sanctions and that statutory clause invoked by the applicant (Article 8, § 3) has been and is used by directors for their personal goals as well as those of their family, so the provisions are far from being applied for the interests of other shareholders, as alleged. The directors of the company and its managers are part of the families of the majority shareholders, who make use of their position in the company to learn about potential transfers of shares and to encourage the sellers to transfer the shares to them, without making a public sale notification. Since the clause does not operate in the interest of the company, it leads to the conclusion that such a statutory clause is illicit. Proof of this is the fact that the claimant requested to be told the names of shareholders which notify the Board of the intention to sell and the directors had refused to communicate such information, although the price offered per share was higher. It follows without a doubt that this clause does not work in the interest of the shareholders, and it is just a clause used to facilitate the buying of shares by the managers in their own name or for their family.

The lower court granted the application and found the assignment agreement of the defendants invalid; the court rejected the counterclaim as unfounded in law. Regarding exceptions to lack of interest in promoting action, they were dismissed as unfounded, as a company has a standing interest to bring proceedings for a declaration of invalidity of a contract for the transfer of its own shares to hold a proper record of its shareholders in accordance with the articles of incorporation. Moreover, the court held that shareholders could agree on preemption rights and regulate them as such in the articles of incorporation.

The Appellate Court upheld the appeal of the initial defendant, and changed the judgment of the lower court in the sense that the request for summons considering the claimant as a company cannot invoke the absolute nullity of a contract it is not a part of, even it relates to a breach of the provisions of the articles of incorporation, it can only request a proper fulfilment of registration of transfer of shares in accordance with the articles of incorporation since the preemption rights belonged to the shareholders and not the company. While the clause in question was breached, the consequence is a lack of opposability of the contract regarding the company and not an annulment of the contract.

Based on said decision, we can determine that shareholders have the right to claim the annulment of the contract based on the breach of the shareholders' agreement while the company can only claim a lack of opposability of the agreement (the contract will produce no legal effects for the company for the time being).

As discussed in previous sections, through the *Decision of the Court of Appeals Brasov no. 49 of 31.01.2001 (Civil Sentence no. 918/C/04.07.2000 of the Brasov Tribunal)* the court had decided that if an agreement is inserted in the Articles of Incorporation prior to the entry into the company of a shareholder in the company (as was the case here) the relative nullity is open only to shareholders who held their position at the time of the decision to change the Articles of Incorporation. Thus, the claimant could not claim the annulment of the decisions as well as the subsequent acts.

Should a shareholders' agreement generate a potential conflict of interest for a certain point on the agenda of the GSM (for example), in accordance with art. 127 of the Company Law, the shareholder in conflict should abstain from proceedings and deliberations on said topic. If he/she do not do so, then they are liable for damages for the loss suffered by the company but only if the majority needed was reached through his/her vote. This provision applies to contractual representation, including voting trust if the case may be, when the representative is in a conflictual situation. It is worth noting that the courts found that the payment of damages is not always sufficient to remedy a breach of this kind and challenges and requests for annulment of decisions of the GSM could be admitted (*Supreme Court of Cassation and Justice Decision no. 2177/2011*).

This provision will work as a double-edged sword. If the shareholders' agreement generates conflict of interest, its execution may result in damages and challenges of the resolution. However, a violation of a shareholders' agreement could also (potentially) generate a conflict of interest resulting in the same legal consequences as mentioned above.

Moreover art. 136[1] of Law no. 31/1990 provides that shareholders must exercise their rights in good faith, respecting the rights and legitimate interests of the company and other shareholders. Generally, this provision is the legal basis for majority and minority abuse claims. If a shareholder violates a shareholders' agreement, depending on the type of agreement and the level of holdings of the shareholder, and if the criteria above is met, said shareholder could be faced with a claim of abuse of majority/minority. Usually the application of the provisions results in the annulment of GSM decisions as they most frequently are the fruit of discord among shareholders.

Exclusion (forced exit) from the company is the most severe sanction for a violation of a shareholders' agreement. Art. 222 of the Company Law states that exclusion from the company can take place when: i) the shareholder, after a request has been made, has not legally paid for their share quota; ii) the associate with unlimited liability has become insolvent or legally incapable; iii) the associate with unlimited liability interfere with the management and assets of the company within certain parameters and iv) the shareholder who is a director commits fraud against the company or usurps the capital or the social signature in his or another's interest. The provision applies only to certain general partnerships as well as to limited liability companies (and so not to stock companies). So, if the breach of the agreement generates the application of the provisions above, the shareholder could be excluded from the company. A Supreme Court of Cassation and Justice ruling clarified that the provisions are exhaustive from a legal perspective however, through the articles of incorporation, shareholders could extend the provisions to cover their situation (*Decision no. 3840/2011*).

Partial limitation of membership status can result from application of the conflict of interest provision mentioned above (art. 127 of the Company Law) since the shareholder in conflict must refrain from voting (essentially a suspension of voting rights).

## E. Enforcement of Shareholders' Agreements

The Timisoara Court of Appeal was tasked with answering a dispute over enforcement of obligations of shareholders' agreements in its *Decision no. 158/*

*26.10.2009.* The case followed a dispute between two shareholders, each holding 50 % of the company. Through a GSM-decisions both parties had decided to initiate a possible procedure of division of the company into two separate entities. The claimant, as director, drafted the division project but later the other shareholder changed his mind and decided against the division, refusing to honor its obligation. And so, the claimant came before the court to request the defendant be forced the other party to honor his obligation. To provide further clarification, it should be noted that, under Romanian law, the division procedure has two stages: a drafting of a project of division and then an approval of division by shareholders.

The court found that the initial GSM decisions had not generated any legally binding obligations since the shareholders had only agreed of a possible initiation of division procedure but without an actual project of division they could not have agreed on the division itself. More importantly the court did mention, as *obiter dictum*, that the parties have entered a contractual obligation but since the legal procedure had not been completed, the decision could not be executed. However, this did confirm that, within the parameters of the law, a shareholder could request the execution of a shareholders' agreement against another signing party if the document is binding.

If we expressly consider extra-statutory shareholders' agreements (and exclude agreements within articles of incorporation), the Romanian Civil Code (art. 1516) stipulates that the creditor is entitled to achieving full, accurate and timely fulfilment obligation by debtor. Where, without justification, the debtor fails to fulfil its obligation and the debtor notified as such, the creditor may, at its discretion and without losing the right to damages if he is so entitled: 1. to request or, where appropriate, to require forcible enforcement of the obligation; 2. to obtain, if the obligation is contractual, rescission or termination of the contract or, where appropriate, reducing of his own reciprocal obligations; 3. to use, where appropriate, any other means provided by law to carry out his right.

Furthermore art. 1527 of the Civil Code states that the creditor can always request that the debtor be required to perform the obligation in kind, unless such performance is impossible. The right to performance in kind shall, if necessary, include the right to repair or replace property and other means to remedy a defective performance.

Regarding obligation to not perform (e.g., agreement not to participate in a GSM), art. 1529 of the Code stipulates that in case of default, the creditor can ask the court permission to remove or alter the thing which the debtor made in breach, at the expense of the debtor, within the limit set by court.

However, these rights should be understood through the lens of art. $136^1$ of Law no. 31/1990 which states that shareholders must exercise their rights in good faith, respecting the rights and legitimate interests of the company and other shareholders. This provision is indeed a double-edged sword. While it can protect shareholders (especially minority shareholders), implying an obligation to perform in accordance with the articles of incorporation and tackles abuse in any form (majority and minority abuse), it also can affect private shareholder agreements in that if said agreement affect the genuine interests of the company, it would result in the invalidation of said acts taken and an obligation to pay damages. Usually the application of the provisions results in the annulment of GSM decisions as they most frequently are the fruit of discord among shareholders.

Through a pact of shareholders one may provide means for a rapid resolution of conflictual situations considering that ADR offers the advantage that are commonly accepted in a time when associations are still able to agree and not driven by private interests while dispensing the arduous path of court litigation and avoiding all the inconveniences that may arise from such a court decision (negative publicity, high legal fees, long procedures, overly technical topics that require expert knowledge etc.).[14]

The sample analyzed helped revel that ADR shareholders' agreements are quite frequent although their scope seems to vary. More frequently the agreements refer to arbitration although some have mentioned (as a not binding option) mediation or other forms of ADR. Some clauses expressly excluded court proceedings and identified the arbitration courts where disputes would be resolved. Other agreements offered an alternative mechanism (arbitration or court) to be chosen either by the claimant at his discretion or depending on the topic o litigation (e.g. issues between the company and the shareholders will go through court proceedings while shareholder disagreement would be heard before the arbitrator).

The Civil Code of Procedure validates a flexible approach to ADR. Art. 541 states that, under Romanian law, arbitration is a permitted alternative jurisdiction within the limitation of private relations in which parties can determine and customize rules different from those of the courts with the condition that the rules do not contradict public order or imperative rules.

Art. 542 of the Civil Procedure Code does offer some rules as to who could participate in arbitration. Under said rules, any shareholder of full legal capacity

14 *Sandru* Pacte societare – clauze, pacte, intelegeri intre asociatii societatilor comerciale, Editura Universitara, Bucharest, 2010, pp. 215–223.

can opt for arbitration. However, it does state that a public authority can opt for arbitration only if they are allowed to do so by law or by international conventions. State-owned entities can opt for ADR if they have a economic purpose and they are not restricted to do so by law, articles of incorporation or their administration. This view was validated by the courts. The Timisoara Court of Appeals was tasked with answering a dispute alternative dispute resolution and arbitration of shareholders' agreements in its *Decision no. 25/10.11.2009.* The issue related to an initial joint venture started between a state-owned entity and a private individual. Although they had opted for arbitration in the agreement, the issue under arbitration was of public interest and so the court found that such an issue could not be resolved view this dispute resolution mechanism. So, shareholders' agreements which include state-owned shareholder should consider the purpose of the agreement and the scope in order to determine application of ADR clauses and its legal consequences.

In regard to the scope, the Civil Procedure Code offers more flexibility. Art. 542 § 1 states that arbitration cannot resolve issues relating to civil status, legal capacity, some issues of inheritance, family relations as well as rights over which parties cannot dispose. As it is difficult to associate the above with shareholders' agreements (perhaps issues of inheritance of shares or restriction of shares – we found no relevant jurisprudence on this), the scope of ADR is quite opened to the creativity of shareholders.

A relevant debate was brought before the court regarding the workings of the actual arbitration clause included in the articles of incorporation of a company. The Alba Iulia Court of Appeals *(Decision no. 2/2013)* heard a case in which the claimant had asked for an appeal against the decision of an arbitration court. The claimant was a shareholder which had tried to annul a contract of sale of assets of the company to a third party, contract which had been validated by the majority shareholders. The articles of incorporation held that disputes between shareholders would be handled by the arbitration courts, while legal courts were expressly excluded. The claimant sought action against the contract and the shareholders (partially for majority abuse) in the legal courts where each party initially presented their respective cases. Later, the claimant sought action directly against the shareholders in an arbitration court. The arbiter dismissed the case since the legal courts where already reviewing the claimant's plea. The claimant considered that the arbitration court had erred since the arbitration clause was inserted in the articles of incorporation and so it regarded only disputes between shareholders or between shareholders and the company. Since the contract was signed with a third party, the recovery of assets should be decided by the court while the rest could, presumably, be dealt with the arbitration tribunal.

The court rejected the claimants' request. In doing so, it expressly stated that the arbitration clause had been valid however the claimant had opted to no use it by going before the legal courts. Moreover, since the defendants did not object to the proceedings before the court and presented their case accordingly, the Court of Appeals held that, through the tacit agreements of the parties, the arbitration clause had been *de facto* removed from the contract. Considering this, the claimant could not, later on, invoke the clause since it could not produce any legal effects as per the agreement of the parties.

Through the above decision, it can be determined conclusively that ADR can be used in shareholders' agreements. However, the wording and the behavior of the shareholders can be used to determine an actual effectiveness of the clause and its capability to produce legal effects.

Žofia Mrázová

# Slovakia

## Table of Content



# A. Introduction

The Slovak company law is contained mainly in the second part of the Act No. 513/1991 Coll. Commercial Code (hereinafter referred to as "Commercial

---

**JUDr. Žofia Mrázová,** PhD., MCL (Cantab), née Šuleková, Pavol Jozef Šafárik University in Košice, Slovakia. The report was funded by the Slovak Agency to support research and development APVV-0809-12.

https://doi.org/10.1515/9783110517026-022

Code" or "CC"), and some other relevant individual Acts (e.g. the Act No. 566/2001 Coll. on the securities and investment services). An amendment to the Commercial Code (the Act No. 389/2015 Coll. effective as from 1 January 2017), introduced specific rules for shareholders' agreements (Section 66c Commercial Code). Beside the new statutory rules explicitly regulating shareholders' agreements, a new corporate form – a simple joint-stock company ("*jednoduchá spoločnosť na akcie*") was introduced (Section 220h – 220zl Commercial Code effective as from 1 January 2017),[1] for the purposes of which three new contractual concepts were adopted, namely, the right to accede to the transfer of shares (tag-along right), the right to request the transfer of shares (drag-along right) and the right to request the acquisition of shares (shoot-out clause). The Slovak law now offers an inspiring regulation of not only shareholders' agreements, but also the exit mechanisms which, along with sanctions for a breach of these rights also include the rules for their enforcement, if they are registered by the relevant central securities depository in the respective special registers of rights.

## B. Nature of corporate law rules

When it comes to the nature of the corporate law itself, the Commercial Code does not contain any general provisions concerning the mandatory or dispositive nature of corporate rules. The principle is therefore applied of so called legal license, i.e. all that is not prohibited is allowed. Since the Commercial Code does not contain a general rule or criteria to determine which rules are to be mandatory and which default, as *lex generalis* to identify the nature of a corporation standard, the rule contained in Section 2 subsection 3 of the Civil Code is to be used which lays down that the parties may deviate from a particular provision unless it is explicitly forbidden by the law, or unless the nature of the provision itself implies that it cannot be deviated from. A legal provision is mandatory if any deviation therefrom is explicitly forbidden by the statute, or if a prohibition to deviate from it is implied directly by the nature thereof. In this respect the Slovak doctrine tends to be rather strict in concluding that regarding the nature of

1 A new corporate vehicle is to offer a complex solution for risk investment into companies with innovative potential (start-ups), whose access to the bank funding is quite impossible. New statutory rules are aimed to increase the motivation of investors to provide capital to start-ups, also in the light of the flexibility in determining their mutual relations. See the Resolution of the Government of the Slovak Republic No. 307/2015 of 10 June 2015 "*Concept to support start-ups and development of start-up eco-system in the Slovak Republic*". Also see *Šuleková* Jednoduchá spoločnosť na akcie – nová forma obchodnej spoločnosti. in Súkromné právo, No. 6, 2016, pp. 2–10.

the rules regulating corporations, their mandatory character is to prevail.[2] The question of the nature of the rules should be examined specifically in respect of internal relations among shareholders and specifically in respect of the structure of a corporation, corporate governance and protection of third persons, i.e. so called external world of corporations.[3] Whereas the external world of corporations is more or less mandatory, legal relations among shareholders operate on a default basis.[4] The autonomy of will is restricted by such general principles as protection of public order, legal certainty and protection of a (more vulnerable) party in legal relations. Although, the Commercial Code also contains several explicit formulations of default rules ("unless otherwise provided by the articles of association"), an explicit permission to be contained in the statute, similar to the concept of *Satzungsstrenge* in the German law, is not required to deviate from a statutory rule, since in the area of private law the permission is given implicitly by the law.[5] Nevertheless, there is still a lot of doubt as to the nature of many corporate rules.[6]

## C. Regulation of Shareholders' Agreements

The corporate documents – articles of association ("*spoločenská zmluva*" or "*stanovy*") – are published in the collection of instruments and are available to third persons. Although shareholders' agreements were not regulated by statutory law until recently (with the exception of some of the provisions which will be pointed out later), referring to the principle of contractual freedom and absence of statutory provisions prohibiting such agreements, even until 31 December 2016 shareholders were not precluded from determining their rights and duties in other than corporate documents. Shareholders' agreements were, and still are,

2 *Koláriková* in Žitňanská, L., Ovečková, O. Obchodné právo. Obchodné spoločnosti. 2nd issue. Bratislava: Iuris Libri, 2013, p. 123, *Patakyová* in Patakyová, M. et al. Obchodný zákonník. Komentár. 5th issue. Bratislava: C. H. Beck, 2016, pp. 4–5.

3 *Mamojka* Ekvivalencia práv a povinností spoločníka v spoločnosti s ručením obmedzeným. Bratislava: Veda, 2008, p. 15.

4 The Constitutional Court of the Slovak Republic, case ref. III. ÚS 292/07 of 25 October 2007.

5 *Patakyová* in Patakyová, M. et al. Obchodný zákonník. Komentár. 5th issue, Bratislava: C. H. Beck, 2016, p. 5.

6 *Csach* Miesto dispozitívnych a kogentných právnych noriem (nielen) v obchodnom práve, I. časť – Všeobecné otázky a rozbor kogentných noriem. in Právny obzor, No. 2, 2007, pp. 102–121. *Csach* Miesto dispozitívnych a kogentných právnych noriem (nielen) v obchodnom práve, II. časť – rozbor dispozitívnych noriem a vybraných problémov (nielen) Obchodného zákonníka. in Právny obzor, No. 3, 2007, pp. 247–259.

a common element of the Slovak corporate - practice. With reference to the private law principle of contractual freedom, such agreements were executed as innominate contracts falling under corporate regime (Section 269 subsection 2 in conjunction with Section 261 subsection 6 of the Commercial Code). Nevertheless, the lack of explicit regulation raised doubt about the validity of such agreements that often became a tool to avoid the strict corporate rules.[7] Despite of the fact that statutory rules did not contain any explicit prohibition of the conclusion or enforcement of agreements among shareholders in other forms than the corporate ones, such agreements were not always accepted by domestic courts.[8]

Currently, shareholders' agreements are explicitly provided for in Section 66c of the Commercial Code as follows:

*§ 66c Shareholders' agreements*

*(1) Shareholders may agree their mutual rights and duties related to their shares in a corporation by a written agreement, in particular*

*a) a mode and conditions of the exercise of their rights related to the shares in a corporation,*

*b) a mode of the exercise of their rights related to the corporate governance,*

*c) conditions and extent of their shares in the changes of the registered capital, and*

*d) ancillary covenants related to the transfer of shares in a corporation.*

*(2) A conflict between a decision of corporate bodies and a shareholders' agreement shall not void such a decision.*

The above provisions define shareholders' agreements as agreements on the mutual rights and duties of shareholders concerning their shares in a corporation. Shareholders' agreements are admissible for all types of corporations. The said provision even demonstratively determines the content of such agreements which may, for example, include an agreement on the shareholders' course of procedure in the exercising their right of profit-sharing [(Section 66c subsection 1 para. a) CC], agreement on the right of appointment, or on the procedure when electing members of corporate bodies [(Section 66c subsection 1 para. b) CC], a shareholders' agreement on the extent of their participation in the increase of registered capital [(Section 66c subsection 1 para. c) CC] and last, but not least, agreements related to the transfer of shares, agreements on the pre-emp-

7 *Kubinec* in Mamojka, M. et al. Obchodný zákonník. Veľký komentár. vol. 1, Bratislava: Eurokódex, 2016, p. 246.

8 Explanatory report in respect of the Act No. 389/2015 Coll. of 12 November 2015 amending the Act No. 513/1991 Coll. Commercial Code.

tion rights, or other restrictions on transfer of shares [66c subs. 1 para. d) CC]. Although Section 66c CC defines the agreement only as an agreement among shareholders, the statute does not prohibit a third person to become a party to such an agreement (for example, a corporation, members of corporate bodies, creditors). Shareholders' agreements must be in compliance with the mandatory provisions. The limits of the content of shareholders' agreements may be identified, in particular, in relation to the general principles of private law, for example, the principle of fair trade or ban on the abuse of rights.

The relationship between a corporate decision and a contractual agreement among shareholders is specified in Section 66c subsection 2 CC and states that if a decision of the general meeting or another corporate body has been passed contrary to the shareholders' agreement, this will not void such a decision. A failure to perform contractual obligations among shareholders should therefore be reasonably foreseen and sanction should be formulated in the shareholders' agreement itself through contractual concepts, since in the case of its violation statutory corporate sanctions will not be applied.

The Commercial Code also contains other provisions concerning shareholders' agreements, for example, Section 220w CC regulating ancillary arrangements concerning shareholders' agreements to be applicable only to a simple joint-stock company, Section 186 CC regulating voting agreements which are explicitly prohibited, as well as Section 205 CC relating to the shareholders' agreements in joint-stock companies concerning the extent of their participation in the full increase of the registered capital, which will be dealt with in the respective parts of this report.

## I. Formal requirements for Shareholders' Agreements

The Commercial Code lays down the requirement of a written form for shareholders' agreements. However, if shareholders fail to reduce to writing their agreement on the mutual determination of rights, it will not necessarily render it void. Such an agreement could be treated, for example, as an agreement on the association (Section 829 of the Civil Code) or as a contract of mandate (Section 566 CC). The 66c CC does not prevent shareholders to enter into other agreements, even the oral ones.[9] The doctrine, however, is not quite uniform in this

9 *Csach/Havel* Dohody medzi spoločníkmi (akcionárske dohody) in Csach, K., Havel, B. et al. Akcionářske dohody. Praha: Wolters Kluwer, 2017, p. 6.

respect.[10] In the case of shareholders' agreement of a simple joint-stock company an even stricter rule applies requiring, beside a written form, also an official authentication of the signatures of the parties, whereas the signature authentication is the major condition for such a shareholders' agreement to become effective.[11] If ancillary covenants (right to accede to the transfer of shares and right to request the transfer of shares) are to be established as registered rights, a shareholders' agreement must be drawn up in form of a notarial deed (Section 220w subs. 3 CC). The above stricter requirements apply only to agreements concluded among shareholders of a simple joint-stock company and not need to be applied to shareholders' agreements made by shareholders of other forms of corporations.[12] The Slovak law does not lay down any time limits to shareholders' agreements. Shareholders' agreements may be effective even for an indefinite period of time.

## II. Specific regulation within different types of corporations and cross-border legal relations

As it has been already mentioned, the specific provision of Section 220w and subseq. CC lays down conditions only for shareholders' agreements made among shareholders of a simple joint-stock company the subject-matter of which is the right to accede to the transfer of shares (tag-along right), the right to request the transfer of shares (drag-along right) and the right to request the acquisition of shares (shoot-out clause). Such a provision, however, does not prevent similar rights being provided for in shareholders' agreements in the case of other forms of corporations without a duty to observe the conditions laid down in Section 220w and subseq. CC. This rule provides that only shareholders' agreements of a simple joint-stock company may contain tag-along rights and drag-along rights agreed as rights established by registration whereby they acquire quasi property-right status.

Shareholders' agreements may be associated with various consequences depending on whether they are executed in closely-held or public corporations, i. e. corporations whose shares were admitted for trading on a regulated market. For

10 *Husár* in Suchoža, J. et al. Obchodný zákonník a súvisiace predpisy. Komentár. 4th issue. Bratislava: Eurounion, 2016, p. 243.

11 Official authentication of a signature may include, for example, legalization by a notary public, circuit authorities or municipal office, or authentication by a foreign office.

12 *Pálka* in Patakyová, M. et al. Obchodný zákonník. Komentár. 5th issue. Bratislava: C. H. Beck, 2016, p. 980.

example, shareholders' agreements on the exercise of voting rights may be treated as acting in concert. Legal consequences of acting in concert apply to public joint-stock companies and they are provided for in a separate Act No. 566/2001 Coll. on the securities and investment services (hereinafter also referred to as "SIS"), or in the Act No. 429/2002 Coll. on the stock exchange regulating the capital market.

The Slovak law does not contain a separate regulation of shareholders' agreements with a cross-border element. The Slovak law does not prevent shareholders from choosing the governing law for their shareholders' agreement other than the Slovak law even in the case where the agreement applies to a corporation whose legal entity status is governed by the Slovak law.[13] Since shareholders' agreements mostly have a contractual character, covenants agreed among shareholders should not be excluded from the application of Rome I Regulation.[14] Shareholders should therefore be allowed to opt for the governing law for these agreements within the meaning of Article 3 of the Rome I Regulation.[15] In the absence of a choice made by the parties, the governing law for shareholders' agreements shall presumably be the law which governs the internal affairs of a corporation.

## III. Slovak case law regarding Shareholders' Agreements

Due to informality of shareholders' agreements, the Slovak case law is more or less absent in this area. In one of its rulings the Supreme Court indirectly mentioned a possibility of piercing articles of association via a unanimous shareholders' agreement. In the said matter the court dealt with the validity of a transfer of shares to a third person which was not allowed by the articles, but the transfer was effectuated with the consent of all shareholders. According to the ruling of the Supreme Court, case ref. Obdo V 79/2003 an "*articles of association is manifestation of common will of shareholders and all shareholders together have the right to change it even to the effect that they will act in deviation from its wording in a particular matter.*" However, in this case the Supreme Court did not settle

13 *Pala/Frindrich/Komarník/Mihálikov* in Ovečková, O. et al. Obchodný zákonník. Veľký komentár, Bratislava: Wolters Kluwer, 2017, p. 1552.

14 Regulation of the European Parliament and of the Council (EC) No. 593/2008 of 17 June 2008 on the governing law applicable to contractual obligations (Rome I). (O.J. EU L 177/6, 4/7/2008).

15 *Bříza* Akcionářské dohody a smlouvy o převodu podílu z pohledu mezinárodního práva soukromého. in Csach, K., Havel, B. et al. Akcionářské dohody, Praha: Wolters Kluwer, 2017, p. 108.

a question if a shareholders' agreement has been pierced with effect also for future cases, or if it has only been a temporary ad hoc solution. The case law also partly dealt with agreements made in favour of a third person however the Supreme Court did not take a uniform position. On the one hand, it stated that an innominate agreement on the ground of which a shareholder undertakes to transfer its shares to another shareholder or a third person appointed by the shareholder without a more detailed specification is a valid arrangement (the ruling of the Supreme Court, case ref. 1 Obdo 10/2008 of 30 July 2009), however, in another case the Supreme Court found void such an agreement which the senate deciding the case considered as an agreement to enter into a future contract (ruling of the Supreme Court, case ref. 6 Obdo 37/2008 of 21 May 2009).

# D. Forms of Shareholders' Agreements

## I. Shareholders' Agreements on shareholders' rights

### 1. Shareholders' Agreements regarding voting rights

As follows from Section 66c of the Commercial Code, in the shareholders' agreement shareholders may also determine the manner of exercise of their rights related to the corporate governance. Shareholders may thereby agree on a joint voting procedure (voting agreements). However, in a special regulation for joint-stock companies, the lawmaker explicitly prohibits, in Section 186a CC, voting agreements whereby a shareholder undertakes, toward a corporation or its bodies, or members of its bodies, to vote according to the instructions of a corporation or instructions of some of its bodies, to vote for proposals made by a corporation, or undertakes to exercise (active agreement) or not to exercise (passive agreement) its voting rights in a certain manner for consideration provided by a corporation.[16] Such agreements are void due to their conflict with statutory law (Section 39 of the Civil Code). Hence, not all voting agreements are void, but exclusively those whereby shareholders of a joint-stock company would restrict the exercise of their voting rights in a manner defined in Section 186a subs. 1 of

16 What is interesting is that the former Section 186a CC in force until 31 December 2001 provided that "*Agreements whereby a shareholder undertakes to exercise its voting rights at the general meeting in an agreed manner shall be void.*" According to this provision, any such agreements on the manner of exercise of voting rights were prohibited. The said provision, however, applied only to corporations whose shares were publicly traded.

the Commercial Code.[17] The said explicit prohibition is aimed to protect the voting rights of shareholders and is meant at defence against the self-regulation by the executive bodies of a corporation which would interfere with effective corporate governance.[18]

In general, the law does not provide for any special requirements concerning agreements on the exercise of voting rights. Voting agreements contravening good morals and statutory law would be void. Despite of the fact that the provision of Section 66c CC requires a written form for shareholders' agreements, in our opinion, an agreement concerning the mode of exercise of voting rights made orally would be valid as well. It is disputable whether voting agreements may also be executed as agreements involving a consideration. However some authors conclude that agreements involving consideration should be void on the ground of a prohibition to split the share,[19] or due to a breach of loyalty by a shareholder toward a corporation.[20] Voting agreements may be concluded among all or some of the shareholders, or among the shareholders and third persons. The subject of such an agreement may also be a one time exercise of the voting rights, long-term method of exercising voting rights,[21] or rules to exercise the voting rights in relation to the subject-matter of a decision to be adopted by the shareholders (i.e. distinct rules for the number of voting rights in the matters of articles amendment, appointment of members of corporate bodies, etc.). Agreements on the separation of the voting rights from the ownership rights of shareholders (so called voting trust) are not regulated in Slovakia.

In relation to the agreed exercise of the voting rights it remains disputable whether it is possible that the court substitutes the manifestation of shareholder's will if a shareholder has breached its obligation under the voting agreement to vote in a certain way. Since the voting agreement is not considered as an agreement on the future voting, it should not be possible to achieve the substi-

---

**17** *Baňacká* Dohody o výkone hlasovacieho práva in Právo a obchodovanie, Košice: UPJŠ, 2008, p. 1 and subseq.

**18** It would qualify as a self-regulation as in the case of the acquisition of its own shares. *Patakyová* in Patakyová, M. et al. Obchodný zákonník. Komentár, 5th issue, Bratislava: C. H. Beck, 2016, p. 757.

**19** *Baňacká* Dohody o výkone hlasovacieho práva in Právo a obchodovanie, Košice: UPJŠ, 2008, p. 4.

**20** *Csach* in Ovečková, O. et al. Obchodný zákonník. Veľký Komentár, Bratislava: Wolters Kluwer, 2017, p. 479.

**21** *Baňacká* Dohody o výkone hlasovacieho práva in Právo a obchodovanie. Košice: UPJŠ, 2008, p. 4.

tution of the manifestation of a shareholders' will during the voting of the general meeting.[22]

## 2. Shareholders' Agreements on the financing of a corporation

Within the list provided in the Section 66c of the Commercial Code, shareholders may also agree on methods, conditions and extent in which they will participate in the changes of registered capital. The subject-matter of such agreements is a consensus to increase registered capital from the corporation's own resources or by undertaking an obligation to invest a new contribution in order to prevent the threatening insolvency of a corporation. Agreements related to the financing of a corporation may also include loans to be granted to a corporation or additional contributions to be invested into corporation's funds. The agreement could be formulated as an agreement in favour of a third person – corporation.

A specific provision of Section 205 of the Commercial Code related exclusively to joint-stock companies explicitly provides for a possibility to conclude a shareholders' agreement on the extent of the shareholders' participation in the full increase of registered capital of a joint-stock company. Shareholders may also agree on other extent of participation in the increase of registered capital than the one resulting from their pre-emptive rights to subscribe to the shares. If such an agreement is made by all the shareholders, it is deemed to replace a subscribers' deed. An agreement within the meaning of Section 205 CC determining the extent of participation of individual shareholders in the increase of registered capital must be made in writing. Beside the obligatory written form, the law also prescribes the minimum content requirements which include determination of the number, kind, form, and nominal value of shares subscribed to by each of the shareholders, the amount of issue rate and a term of time to pay up the shares. In the case where the registered capital is to be increased by non-pecuniary contributions, a shareholders' agreement must also contain, inter alia, specification of the object of a non-pecuniary contribution and monetary amount in which the non-pecuniary contribution will be settled in respect of the issue rate of the subscribed shares (Section 205 subsection 2 CC). The agreement will not replace a decision on the increase of registered capital which the general meeting is authorized for. An agreement may be concluded before or after the resolution of the general meeting on the increase of registered capital is passed.

---

**22** *Csach* in Ovečková, O. et al. Obchodný zákonník. Veľký Komentár, Bratislava: Wolters Kluwer, 2017, p. 481.

Where the shareholders do not take part in the full increase of registered capital and new shares are also subscribed to by a third person, the procedure pursuant to Section 205 CC will not be used.

### 3. Shareholders' Agreements and the law of corporate groups

Since a complex legal regulation of the law of corporate groups is absent in Slovakia,[23] shareholders' agreements are important mainly in defining the concept of controlling person. Within the meaning of Section 66a subsection 1 of the Commercial Code, regardless of whether a voting agreement is valid or void (Section 186a of the Commercial Code), if a certain person acquires, on the ground of such an agreement, a majority of voting rights, such a person will be treated as a controlling person. This implies that although a certain person is not a majority shareholder, i.e. does not have a majority of voting rights in a corporation, it may be considered as a controlling person, within the meaning of statutory provisions, if it is empowered to exercise majority of voting rights under a shareholders' agreement. The Commercial Code does not specify the percentage of shares which may be considered as a majority. For a particular person not having a majority of voting rights to be considered as a controlling person there must exist, inter alia, an agreement with another person, i.e. another shareholder of the same corporation or a person exercising the voting rights on behalf of a shareholder. Such an agreement may be an agreement within the meaning of Section 186a CC (i.e. explicitly prohibited by the law), as well as a shareholders' agreement pursuant to Section 66c CC.

## II. Shareholders' agreements on the (limitation for the) transfer of shares

Shareholders' agreements may contain covenants related to various limitations or conditions for the transfer of shares (e.g. pre-emptive rights, options, time limitations for transfers, etc.). In general, such covenants contained in shareholders' agreements have a purely contractual effect and they do not bind third parties. The Slovak law has a certain specific feature in this respect and that is an explicit regulation of ancillary arrangements concerning shareholders' agreements con-

23 *Csach* in Ovečková, O. et al., Obchodný zákonník. Veľký komentár, Bratislava: Wolters Kluwer, 2017, p. 469.

cluded among shareholders of a new form of company – a simple joint-stock company. Pursuant to Section 220w CC such ancillary covenants might include the right to accede to the transfer of shares (tag-along right), the right to request the transfer of shares (drag-along right) and the right to request the acquisition of shares (shoot-out clause[24] reminding most of a contractual arrangement known as Russian roulette). These ancillary covenants may not be assigned to another person without simultaneously transferring the shares to which such a right is bound (Section 220w subs. 5 CC). Despite of the fact that these provisions are applicable only to the shareholders' agreements within a simple joint-stock company, it is possible to agree those rights variously and in another extent than the one determined in Section 220w and subseq. CC. The following part of the report is therefore discussing the legal rules for the above rights related to shareholders' agreements agreed by shareholders of simple joint-stock companies.

Tag-along rights and drag-along rights may be agreed as (i) non-registered rights, or (ii) registered rights established by their registration in the relevant register of rights. The basic distinction rests in the fact that non-registered rights are exclusively of a contractual nature while registered rights are of quasi property rights nature.[25] A registered form of tag-along rights and drag-along rights is available only to the shareholders of simple joint-stock companies. Conditions and procedure for their registration is laid down in the special regulation (Section 107e – Section 107n SIS) and the rules of operation of a particular central securities depository. Tag-along and drag- along rights may be registered in separate registers – in the register of the rights to accede to the transfer of shares (Section 107 f SIS) and in the register of the rights to request the transfer of shares (Section 107j SIS), based upon a request to register which may be filed in both cases by a beneficiary shareholder or an obligated shareholder. In contrast with non-registered rights that are not subject to a duty of mandatory publication and their content remains anonymised toward the public, the existence of a registered right must be published on the website of the central securities depository, and it is available to third persons.[26] Upon a request, the central secur-

24 *Lysina/Zelenáková* in Mamojka, M. et al. Obchodný zákonník. Veľký komentár. Vol. 1, Bratislava: Eurokódex, 2016, p. 948.

25 Registered tag along right and drag along right is largely similar to the concept of tenures provided for in the third chapter of the second part of the Civil Code.

26 https://www.ncdcp.sk/.

ities depository issues extracts from a particular register or a certificate proving that a particular right is not registered in the register.[27]

If an agreement includes non-registered rights, for such an agreement to become effective it suffices that shareholders' signatures are officially authenticated. If shareholders' agreements shall encompass registered tag-along rights and drag-along rights, they must be drawn up in form of a notarial deed, since such an agreement has consequences also for third persons that are not parties to it (Section 220w subs. 3 CC). The law lays down the methods of termination of registered rights [Section 220w subs. 9 paras. a) through i) CC]. They may terminate by discharge, i.e. by their exercise itself, or by termination of shares to which such rights are bound, by the expiry of time for which they were established, by registration of a waiver of such rights, by a change of legal form of a corporation, and also for other reasons set in the agreement. Legal consequences of registered rights are different from the non-registered ones. In the case of a transfer of shares, registered rights operate also toward legal successors of shareholders to which the obligation is bound corresponding to these rights. In the case the beneficiary under the registered right fails to exercise it, such a right will remain effective toward the obliged shareholder as well as toward a legal successor of that shareholder– the acquirer (Section 220 subsection 4 CC).

### 1. Right to accede to the transfer of shares (tag-along right)

The tag-along right is defined in Section 220x of the Commercial Code. Within the meaning of this contractual concept, the beneficiary shareholder of a simple joint-stock company is entitled, under the conditions agreed in the shareholders' agreement, to transfer its own shares simultaneously with the shares of another shareholder to a third person. A tag-along right agreement must contain the details defined in Section 220x subsection 3 CC, in particular, specification of conditions of the exercise, specification of the extent or method of specification of the extent in which the right may be exercised, and a period of time or a method of specification of a period of time during which such a right may be exercised. In order to ensure legal certainty, it is recommended that such an agreement should also contain other specification of conditions for the exercise of a partic-

27 As of 31 August 2017, i.e. eight months after the law became effective, the National Central Depository of Securities has not taken record of any registration of tag-along rights or drag-along rights in their respective registers.

ular right. If the right to accede to the transfer of shares is to be registered, as was mentioned above, a shareholders' agreement must be written in a form of notarial deed. A shareholder bound in relation to the tag-along right must inform a third person of the existence and conditions of such a right prior to the transfer of shares (Section 220x subs. 4 CC). The law distinguishes legal consequences resulting from a breach of tag-along rights by the fact if a particular right was registered or not. If a registered tag-along right was breached, a beneficiary shareholder may claim that a third person (the acquirer of the shares) who has acquired the shares of the obligated person should also acquire the shares of the beneficiary shareholder, under the same conditions, or that the said shares should be acquired by the obligated (original) shareholder under the conditions under which the shares have been transferred to a third person. As from the transfer of the shares by the obligated person to a third person a one-year preclusive period will start running for the beneficiary shareholders after the lapse of which their entitlements toward the third person or the obligated shareholders will extinguish. However, the tag-along right will remain with the beneficiary shareholder, which means that the third person to whom the said shares were transferred, will act as an obligated person in the subsequent transfer of the said shares. In the case of a breach of non-registered tag-along right, the beneficiary shareholder may claim exclusively the acquisition of the shares by the obligated shareholder under the conditions under which such shareholder transferred their shares to the third person. Even this entitlement of the beneficiary shareholder is subject to a one-year preclusive period.

One of the main aspects of the relevant law concerning tag-along rights is the equality of conditions for shares acquisition under which the beneficiary may claim that the obligated person or the third person should acquire the beneficiary's shares within the meaning of Section 220x subs. 5 and subs. 6 CC. The lawmaker does not specify, in more detail, what should be understood by the term *equal conditions*, i.e. whether it will only be identity of substantial terms of an agreement, or if full identity of conditions is to be required. An opinion prevails that the identity of conditions need not be absolute, but equivalence is required of at least substantial terms.[28] It is assumed that the same purchase price will not be sufficient, but there will have to be met some other conditions too, for example, the same method of payment of the purchase price, or the same maturity date. The requirement of the same conditions should apply to the shares of the same kind and the shares of the same nominal value, the conditions will

28 *Pálka* in Patakyová, M. et al. Obchodný zákonník. Komentár. Bratislava: C. H. Beck, 2016, pp. 983–4.

therefore probably be different with various types of shares (ordinary versus preference shares).

## 2. Right to request the transfer of shares (drag-along right)

Another explicitly regulated right is the right to request the transfer of shares that enables the beneficiary shareholder to request from another shareholder (the obligated shareholder) to transfer its shares, simultaneously with the beneficiary shareholder to a third person, under the same conditions under which the beneficiary shareholder is transferring its shares to such a third person (Section 220y CC).[29] Similarly as with tag-along rights, the law lays down the particulars of the content of such an agreement. Drag-along rights may exist in two forms, as registered or as non-registered rights. In the case a breach of a non-registered drag-along right occurs, a third person (shares acquirer) is entitled to claim that the obligated shareholder should transfer the said shares to him under the same conditions under which the acquirer has acquired the shares from the beneficiary shareholder [Section 220y subs. 5 para. c) CC]. Despite of the fact that the acquirer was not/is not a party to the shareholders' agreement, the law admits certain entitlements to such a person and it strengthens its position significantly. No action is required from the beneficiary, nor any agreement between the beneficiary and the acquirer concerning the assignment of a drag-along right. The right to claim the performance of a drag-along right pertains to the party intending to purchase only based on the fact of the acquisition of shares from the beneficiary shareholder. The acquirer is bound to exercise such a right within a one-year preclusive period. The requirement of observing the same conditions works as a statutory form of protection of the obligated shareholder who should not fall into a more disadvantageous position. The same as with tag-along rights, what is problematic here is the statutory requirement of equal conditions for the transfer of shares. The obligated shareholder need not have all the necessary information related to a corporation, and the requirement of equal conditions (for example, rendering equal representations and

---

**29** There is a lack of certainty persisting in practice in relation to the exercise of drag-along rights, in particular, in the case where a drag-along beneficiary shareholder transfer the shares of the obligated shareholder to a third person as a proxy acting on the ground of a power of attorney, since a particular power of attorney could have been cancelled by the shareholder any time (Section 33b subs. 1 para. B) of the Civil Code).

warranties) might be unfavourable for them, eventually.[30] In the case where the acquirer decides not to exercise its right, the drag-along right will be maintained whereby the acquirer will become a beneficiary under that right and in the future will be entitled to request, as the beneficiary, the obligated shareholder to transfer their shares under the same conditions to the third person [Section 220y subs. 5 para. b) CC].

When it comes to a registered drag-along right, if conditions for its exercise have been met: the purchase price for the obligated person is deposited in notarial custody or an irrevocable letter of credit is established in favour of the obligated person, and the meeting of these conditions is acknowledged by a notary public, the beneficiary shareholder may sell the said shares of the obligated person to a third person. During the sale the beneficiary shareholder will act in the name and on the account of the obligated person. The third person will thereby acquire the shares of the obligated person as if acquiring them from the obligated person directly. The exercise of a drag-along right without a necessity of assistance of the obligated shareholder is expected to be a quite effective instrument to enforce the rights from shareholders' agreements.

## 3. Right to request the acquisition of shares (shoot-out clause)

The third explicitly regulated arrangement is the right to request the acquisition of shares which entitles shareholders to determine the price of one share and to request from the obligated shareholder to transfer to them his shares at such a price (Section 220z CC). Several shareholders may become beneficiaries under such a right. The shareholder who will be the first to deliver a specification of the proposed price per share is to be considered as the beneficiary shareholder. The law does not impose any limitation relating to such an arrangement. It is up to the parties to the agreement how they will agree the conditions of the exercise of such a right. The law motivates the shareholder to determine a reasonable price per share because if a proposal is rejected within a period and in a manner laid down in the agreement, the obligated shareholder will be able to acquire the beneficiary's shares under the same conditions as those proposed by the beneficiary. In contrast to tag-along rights and drag-along rights, a shoot-out clause may not be agreed as a registered right, it will therefore not be effective also toward the acquirer of the said shares. In the case where the obligated shareholder

---

**30** *Janáč* Právo požadovať prevod akcií (drag-along právo) in Súkromné právo, No. 10 – 11, 2015, pp. 21 – 29.

does not enter into an agreement on the acquisition of the beneficiary's shares, the law provides for the beneficiary's right to seek a substitute manifestation of will of the obligated shareholder in court, within a period of one year (Section 220z subs. 4 CC).

## III. Shareholders' Agreements on other corporate issues

Shareholders may also make an agreement to provide for the management and control of corporate affairs within a corporation by entering into an agreement on the composition of corporate bodies [Section 66c para. b) CC]. Such agreements may include, inter alia, specification of the number of persons to be nominated or appointed as members of corporate boards. These agreements may contain general rules concerning the mode of submission or negotiation of internal issues. The contractual structure established on the ground of shareholders' agreements, however, may not interfere with the statutory rules of corporate governance. The appointee is not in a third-party position, and therefore these agreements will not be subject to the rules governing agreements in favour of a third person.[31] The elected member of a corporate body must not prefer interests of the shareholder that has appointed him/her to the office.

If a corporation is in an economically unfavourable situation and is threatened by insolvency, the board of directors, along with shareholders and creditors, is to take effort to settle the situation promptly. In this period shareholders' agreements are being modified and supplemented by other covenants and their parties are extended to include major creditors.[32]

# E. Legal effects of Shareholders' Agreements

## I. Legal effects on the corporation and the shareholders

Shareholders' agreements and articles do not operate as independent and isolated agreements. The contractual content of articles may be detailed and elaborated in a shareholders' agreement. The rule is that a shareholders' agreement which is made later among all shareholders does not effectively amend articles.

---

**31** *Csach/Havel* in Csach, K, Havel, B. et al. Akcionářské dohody. Praha: Wolters Kluwer, 2017, p. 37.

**32** *Csach/Havel* in Csach, K, Havel, B. et al. Akcionářské dohody. Praha: Wolters Kluwer, 2017, p. 24.

It remains questionable if a shareholders' agreement is perceived merely as an agreement on a different distribution of relations among shareholders than those envisaged in articles, or if such an agreement may *de facto* change the articles. Slovak courts have not paid much attention to an ad hoc piercing of the articles, yet, but this assumption seems to be quite feasible.[33]

The acquirer of shares does not usually become a party to a shareholders' agreement automatically. The acquirer may become a party to a shareholders' agreement under the conditions resulting from the rules of the law of contract, especially on the ground of a consent of the remaining parties to the agreement. The claims ensuing from a shareholders' agreement may be assigned to the assignee if they are assignable. As for the transfer of other rights, an agreement with other concerned parties to a shareholders' agreement will also be required. As has been mentioned above, specific rules of the transfer of the rights will apply to the registered ancillary covenants in respect of the agreements among shareholders of a simple joint-stock company. In the case of drag-along rights, the acquirer of shares as a single legal successor of the beneficiary shareholder will maintain its drag-along right, if he did not request the share transfer from the obligated shareholder [Section 220y subs. 5 para. b) CC].

Shareholders' agreements concluded among shareholders of a joint-stock company whose shares were admitted for trading on a regulated market are associated with other consequences contained in the special Acts. Where one or more shareholders acting in concert achieves or exceeds the controlling share which represents 33 % of the voting rights related to the shares of a target corporation, such a shareholder is bound to make a public offer toward the rest of the shareholders (so called mandatory offer to acquisition Section 118 g SIS). Where the achievement or exceeding of the controlling share occurs on the ground of a shareholders' agreement, all the persons acting in concert[34] must make a man-

---

**33** Ruling of the Supreme Court of the Slovak Republic, case ref. V 79/2003 (ZSP 28/2006) "*A shareholder may transfer its business share to another person, if it is permitted by the articles. If articles of association have not provided for a possibility of transfer of a business share to a third person, but the transfer has occurred with a consent of all shareholders, such a transfer may not be void only by reason that this is not permitted by the articles. The articles of association are manifestation of the common will of shareholders and all shareholders are jointly entitled to change it also by acting a particular matter in deviated from its provisions.*"

**34** Section 114 subsection 6 SIS defines persons acting in concert as follows: "*For purposes of an offer a person acting in concert means a natural person or legal entity that cooperates with the offeree or with a target corporation based on an oral or written agreement, whether explicit or concluded in another way not raising any doubt about what the parties intended to manifest, while such cooperation is aimed at the acquisition of a control share in a target corporation or to frustrate a successful result of the offer to acquire. Persons controlled by another person pursuant to*

datory offer and purchase the shares from all other shareholders. In order to fulfil the statutory duty, it will suffice to place a public offer by any of these persons (Section 118 g subsection 3 SIS). Persons acting in concert will be bound, jointly and severally. Moreover, shareholders who have become entitled to purchase the shares from other shareholders are restricted in their voting rights in a corporation, and persons acting in concert are entitled to exercise only the voting rights not exceeding a 33% controlling share (Section 118 g subs. 9 SIS).

Regulation of the capital market is also associated with the rules for a notification duty concerning the changes in the voting rights of the issuer. Shareholders of public joint stock company are bound to inform the joint-stock company and the National Bank of Slovakia if their shares while trading in the stock exchange achieved, exceeded or dropped below the limits imposed by the law (5%, 10%, 15%, 20%, 25%, 30%, 50% and 75%).[35] A voting agreement may therefore represent acting in concert which binds these shareholders to inform of the amount of their voting rights.[36] This rule ensures that the issuer should be informed of any changes of the ownership structure that might result in a takeover.[37]

## II. Consequences of a breach of Shareholders' Agreements

Since the Commercial Code does not contain any provisions regulating the consequences of a breach of shareholders' agreements, general contractual remedies are applied, such as contractual fines, withdrawal from a contract or liabil-

---

*Section 8 paragraph h) are considered as persons acting in concert with that person or among each other."*

35 Provision of Section 41 subsection 1 of the Act No. 429/2002 Coll. on the stock exchange *"If a shareholder has acquired or transferred the shares of issuing entity whose shares have been admitted for trading on a regulated stock exchange and which are associated with voting rights, to another person, such a person shall notify the issuing entity the share in the voting rights of the issuer which is owned by such a person as a result of the acquisition or transfer to another person, if such a share has achieved, exceeded or dropped below the limits 5%, 10%, 15%, 20%, 25%, 30%, 50% and 75%. The voting rights are calculated on the ground of all shares with which the voting rights are associated, even in the case where their exercise has been suspended."*

36 Provision of Section 41 subsection 9 para. a) of the Act No. 429/2002 on the stock exchange *"Unless otherwise provided by this Act, notification duties pursuant to subsections 1 and 2 shall also apply to a person in the extent in which such a person is entitled to acquire, transfer or exercise the voting rights: held by a third person with whom this person has concluded a written agreement binding them to take a joint procedure in relation to the management of a particular issuing entity, by acting in concert in relation to the voting rights held by them."*

37 *Janáč* Anonymita akcionárov in Právny obzor, No. 6, 2013, pp. 597–613.

ity for delay. Legal consequences of the breach of shareholders' agreement become manifest only in the sphere of the law of contract. Particular rights and duties resulting from a shareholders' agreement are not of a corporate nature in contrast to the rules contained in articles, the breach of which is associated with corporate sanctions foreseen by the statutory corporate law. For example, a failure to fulfil an obligation to pay an extra contribution assumed by a shareholder of a private limited company may even result in an exclusion of a shareholder from a corporation (Section 113 CC). A breach of an obligation to pay an extra contribution agreed in the shareholders' agreement does not result in a possibility of exclusion of such a shareholder.[38]

In its Section 66c subs. 2, the Commercial Code explicitly provides that if a decision of a corporate body, e.g. a resolution of the general meeting or decision of the board of directors, has been passed contrary to the shareholders' agreement, it shall not void such a resolution. As follows from the above, a breach of a shareholders' agreement will not be accepted by courts as grounds for finding a resolution of the general meeting void in the proceedings pursuant to Sections 131 and 183 of the Commercial Code regarding limited liability company and joint stock company, respectively.

## F. Enforcement of Shareholders' Agreements

Legal consequences of a breach of shareholders' agreements remain in the area of the law of contract. Disputes arise especially in respect of a breach of the obligation to transfer the shares under certain conditions or also the obligation to vote in a certain way. Actions available in such cases include an action to enforce the performance of an obligation by a shareholder, or in some case, also an action to substitute the manifestation of will of a party that has breached its obligation arising out a shareholders' agreement (for example, an obligation to transfer its shares).[39] It should not be allowed to enforce, by a civil action, the substitution of the manifestation of will of shareholders in consequence of violation of a voting agreement.[40] However, a claimant may seek the performance of

---

**38** *Šuleková* Vedľajšie dojednania spoločníkov in Akademické akcenty 2013, Žilina: Eurokódex, 2014, p. 210.

**39** *Lysina / Zelenáková* M. In Mamojka, M. et al. Obchodný zákonník. Veľký komentár. Bratislava: Eurokódex, 2016, p. 947. *Gyarfáš* Riešenie sporov a korporátna arbitráž in Csach, K., Havel, B. et al. Akcionářske dohody, Praha: Wolters Kluwer, 2017, p.125.

**40** *Csach* in Ovečková, O., et al. Obchodný zákonník. Veľký komentár, Bratislava, Wolters Kluwer, 2017, p. 479.

an obligation to vote in a particular way. Where a shareholder votes contrary to the shareholders' agreement such a contravention will not void the resolution of the general meeting (Section 66c subs. 2 Commercial Code).

When it comes to restrictions or conditions for the transfer of shares, a breach of its duties by the selling shareholder will not void the transfer of shares, but it will entitle the beneficiary shareholder to damages and/or payment of a contractual fine, if agreed in a shareholders' agreement. Hence, it would amount only to a breach of a contractual obligation contained in a shareholders' agreement rather than to a defective transfer of shares.

As has been mentioned above, the lawmaker regulates entitlements ensuing from registered and non-registered tag-along and drag-along rights and specific conditions for the execution of ancillary covenants in respect of shareholders' agreements of a simple joint-stock company, so called self-executing mechanisms. If a beneficiary shareholder meets the obligations imposed by the Act on the registered drag-along rights (registration, purchase price deposited in notarial custody/documentary letters of credit, notarial certification of meeting the conditions to exercise the right), such a shareholder may execute a drag-along right on its own based on a statutory power of representation.

Most of disputes arising in the corporate context are arbitrable.[41] The doctrine admits a possibility to enforce a shareholder's obligation to vote in a particular way at the general meeting under a voting agreement not only in court proceedings, but also by arbitration ruling.[42]

## G. Annexes

**Relevant provisions of the Act No. 513/1991 Coll. the Commercial Code, related to the regulation of Shareholders' Agreements:**

**§ 66c Shareholders' Agreements**

(1) Shareholders may agree their mutual rights and duties related to their shares in a corporation by a written agreement, in particular

a) the manner and conditions of the exercise of rights related to their shares in a corporation,

---

41 *Csach/Gyarfáš* Arbitrabilita korporátnych sporov. Terra nova terra incognita in Justičná revue, p. 3, 2015, pp. 316–342. The amended Act No. 244/2002 Coll. on the arbitration proceedings became effective on 1 January 2015 and it provides, inter alia, an arbitration clause in internal regulations of legal entities (Section 4 subsection 5).

42 *Gyarfáš* Riešenie sporov a korporátna arbitráž in Csach, K., Havel, B. et al. Akcionářske dohody, Bratislava, Wolters Kluwer, 2017, p. 124.

b) the manner of the exercise of rights related to the corporate governance,

c) the conditions and extent of shares in the changes of registered capital, and

d) the ancillary covenants related to the transfer of shares in a corporation.

(2) The conflict between a decision of a corporate body and a shareholders' agreement shall not void such a decision.

**Section 186a Voting rights agreements**

(1) Agreements binding a shareholder toward a corporation or any of its bodies, or a member of its bodies

a) to follow, during the voting, instructions of a corporation or any of its bodies concerning the manner of its voting,

b) to vote for proposals submitted by corporate bodies, or

c) to exercise their voting right in a particular manner or to abscond in consideration of advantages rendered by a corporation,

shall be prohibited.

(2) Provisions of articles of association binding a shareholder to act as defined in subsection 1 shall be void.

**Section 205 Agreements on the extent of participation in the full increase of registered capital**

(1) If all shareholders agree, in writing, on the extent of their participation in the full increase of registered capital, such an agreement shall substitute a subscribers' deed. The provision of Section 202 shall not be affected thereby, provisions of Sections 203 and 204 shall apply similarly.

(2) A shareholders' agreement pursuant to subsection 1 shall contain a specification of number, kind, form, manner and nominal value of shares subscribed to by each shareholder, amount of issue rate and period of time for the payment. If registered capital is to be increased by non-pecuniary contributions, an agreement shall also contain a specification of the subject of non-pecuniary contribution and specification of the amount in which such a non-pecuniary contribution is to be counted as the payment of the issue rate of the subscribed shares.

**Ancillary covenants in respect of Shareholders' Agreements**

**Section 220w**

(1) In the shareholders' agreement pursuant to Section 66c (hereinafter referred to as "shareholders' agreement"), shareholders of a simple joint-stock company may agree on the right

a) to accede to the transfer of shares (tag-long right),

b) to request the transfer of shares (drag-along right),

c) to request the acquisition of shares (shoot-out clause).

(2) Signatures on a shareholders' agreement must be officially authenticated. A shareholders' agreement may not take effect prior the day of official authentication of the signatures of the parties.

(3) Tag-along rights and drag-along rights may also be agreed as rights established by registration pursuant to a special regulation. In such a case they shall be established by a notarial deed.

(4) Tag-along rights and drag-along rights that were registered pursuant to a special registration shall not be subject to limitation and shall be effective in the extent laid down in this Act, in the case of transfer of shares on the ground of an agreement, toward legal successors of the owner of the shares that are associated with a duty corresponding to such rights; if they are not exercised by the beneficiary shareholder, they shall be maintained also toward the legal successor of the owner of the shares associated with a duty corresponding to such rights.

(5) The rights defined in subsection 1 may be disposed with only simultaneously with the shares concerned.

(6) One share may be associated with only one pre-emptive right, one tag-along right, one drag-along right and one shoot-out clause. Several persons may become entitled under one pre-emptive right, one tag-along right, one drag-along right and one shoot-out clause. Those parts of a shareholders' agreement which establish another right in contravention with the restrictions pursuant to this subsection shall be void.

(7) If the shares associated with a duty corresponding to the tag-along right or drag-along right registered pursuant to a special regulation have been pledged under a contract or if such shares have become an object of a security transfer of the right with a written consent of a beneficiary shareholder, a creditor may exercise such securing rights regardless of the existence of the obligation corresponding to such rights. Such rights shall extinguish upon their transfer to the acquirer on the ground of the exercise of the pledge or securing transfer of the right.

(8) Provisions of Sections 289 through 292 shall not apply to those provisions of a shareholders' agreement which regulate the rights pursuant to subsection 1.

(9) Tag-along rights and drag-along rights that were registered pursuant to a special regulation shall extinguish

a) by discharge,

b) by termination of shares associated with them,

c) by expiry of time for which they were established,

d) by registration of waiver,

e) by registration of an agreement between the beneficiary shareholder and obligated shareholder,

f) by change of a legal form of a corporation,

g) by merger of a corporation if a legal successor is not a simple joint-stock company,

h) by acquisition of shares from a bankrupt's estate or in distraint proceedings,

i) otherwise as specified in the Act or as agreed in a shareholders' agreement.

**220x Tag-along right**

(1) Tag-along rights shall entitle the shareholder (the beneficiary shareholder) to transfer their shares simultaneously with the shares of another shareholder (the obligated shareholder).

(2) The tag-along right shall be associated with a corresponding duty of the obligated shareholder who has undertaken to enable, with the transfer of their shares, a simultaneous transfer of the shares of the beneficiary shareholder to a third person under the same conditions.

(3) A covenant concerning the tag-along right must contain the following:

a) a specification of the conditions of its exercise,

b) a specification of the extent or a mode of specification of the extent in which the beneficiary shareholder may exercise such a right,

c) a term of time or a mode of specification of a term of time during which such a right may be exercised upon meeting the conditions defined in the paragraph a).

(4) Prior the transfer of their shares under an agreement, the obligated shareholder shall inform the third person of the existence and conditions of a tag-along right.

(5) Where a tag-along right registered pursuant to a special regulation has been breached,

a) the beneficiary shareholders may claim that the third person, that acquired the shares of the obligate shareholder, should also acquire the said shares of the beneficiary shareholder under the same conditions as those applicable to the acquisition of the shares from the obligated person,

b) the beneficiary shareholder may claim that the obligated shareholder should acquire the said shares from the beneficiary shareholder under the same conditions as those under which the obligated shareholder has transferred their shares to the third person,

c) the beneficiary shareholder shall retain their tag-along right if the beneficiary shareholder fails to exercise their rights defined in paragraphs a) and b).

(6) In the case of a tag-along right that has not been registered pursuant to a special regulation, the beneficiary shareholder shall have the right as defined in subsection 5 paragraph b).

(7) The rights defined in subsection 5 paragraphs a) and b) and subsection 6 shall extinguish if not exercised by the beneficiary shareholder within 1 year after the transfer of the shares by the obligated shareholder to a third person.

**Section 220y Drag-along right**

(1) Drag-along rights shall entitle the shareholder (the beneficiary shareholder) to request from another shareholder (the obligated shareholder) that the obligated shareholder should transfer their own shares to a third person simultaneously with the transfer of the shares of the beneficiary shareholder.

(2) The drag-along right shall be associated with a corresponding duty of the obligated shareholder who has undertaken to transfer their shares to a third person simultaneously with the transfer of the shares of the beneficiary shareholder on the ground of an agreement and under the same conditions.

(3) A covenant concerning the drag-along right must contain the following:

a) a specification of conditions of its exercise,

b) a specification of the extent or a mode of specification of the extent in which the beneficiary shareholder may exercise such a right.

(4) Where conditions for the exercise of the drag-along right that has been registered pursuant to a special regulation have been met and the purchase price for the obligated shareholder has been deposited in a notarial custody or an irrevocable letter of credit has been opened in favour of the obligated shareholder, and the meeting of these conditions has been acknowledged by a notary public, the beneficiary shareholder may transfer the said shares to a third person, acting in the name and on the account of the obligated shareholder.

(5) Where a drag-along right that was not registered pursuant to a special regulation has been breached,

a) the acquirer of the shares may claim that the obligated shareholder should transfer to the acquirer the said shares in compliance with the drag-along right under the same conditions as those under which the acquirer has acquired the shares from the beneficiary shareholder, or

b) the acquirer of the shares shall retain the drag-along right.

(6) The right defined in subsection 5 para. a) shall extinguish if not exercised by the acquirer of the shares within one year after the transfer of the shares of the beneficiary shareholder.

**Section 220z Shoot-out clause**

(1) The shoot-out clause shall entitle the shareholder (the beneficiary shareholder) to determine the price per share and to request from another shareholder (the obligated shareholder) to transfer the shares to the beneficiary shareholder for the price determined under a shoot-out clause. The shareholder that is the first to deliver their proposal with a price specification per share to another shareholder shall be considered as the beneficiary shareholder.

(2) Where the obligated shareholder fails to accept the beneficiary's proposal within the term of time and in a mode agreed in a shareholders' agreement, the obligated shareholder shall be bound to acquire the shares from the beneficiary under the same conditions.

(3) A covenant concerning the shoot-out clause must contain a specification of conditions for its exercise.

(4) Where the obligated shareholder fails to enter into an agreement on the acquisition of the beneficiary shareholder's shares in accordance with the conditions of the shoot-out clause, the manifestation of will of the obligated shareholder may be sought in court to be substituted by a judicial decision within one year.

**Particular provisions of the Act No. 566/2001 Coll. on the securities and investment services related to the individual registers of rights:**

**Register of the rights of shareholders of simple joint-stock company**

**Section 107e**

The tag-along rights and the drag-along rights may be registered only in relation to the shares of a simple joint-stock company.

**Register of tag-along rights**

**Section 107f**

(1) A tag-along right shall originate by the registration of such a right in a special register of shares to which the tag-along right pertains (hereinafter referred to as "register of tag-along rights").

(2) A register of tag-along rights shall be maintained by the central securities depository administering the issuer's register.

(3) Registration of a tag-along right shall mean the execution of a particular entry in the register of tag-along rights.

(4) A tag-along right shall change by registering the change of a tag-along right in the register of tag-along rights.

(5) A tag-along right shall extinguish in compliance with the provisions of the Commercial Code.

**Section 107 g**

(1) A register of tag-along rights shall contain the following particulars:

a) business name, registered office and identification number of issuer,

b) details of the obligated and beneficiary shareholders under the tag-along right in the extent entered in the register of shareholders, ISIN designation, kind, nominal value, number of shares of a particular issue and dates of issue of the shares of the obligated and beneficiary shareholders to which the tag-along right pertains,

c) period of time for which the tag-along right is established, or information that it is established for an indefinite period of time,

d) date of registration of the tag-along right in the register of tag-along rights.

(2) Particulars recorded in the register of tag-along rights shall be published by the central securities depository on its website, except for the shareholder's birth registration number and date of birth.

(3) The central securities depository shall be bound, upon a written request of

a) a legal entity or a natural person, to issue its current extract from the register of tag-along rights containing the data published pursuant to Section 107 g subs. 2, or a certificate acknowledging the fact that in relation to the shares of the issuer no tag-along rights have been registered,

b) a simple joint-stock company to which the extract shall apply, or a shareholder of a simple joint-stock company to which the extract shall apply in the part that shall apply to such a shareholder, to issue a current extract from the register of tag-along rights containing the data pursuant to Section 107 g subs. 1.

**Register of drag-along rights**

**Section 107j**

(1) A drag-along right shall originate by the registration of such a right in a special register of shares to which the drag-along right pertains (hereinafter referred to as "register of drag-along rights").

(2) A register of drag-along rights shall be maintained by the central securities depository administering the issuer's register.

(3) Registration of a drag-along right shall mean the execution of a particular entry in the register of drag-along rights.

(4) A drag-along right shall change by registering the change of a particular drag-along right in the register of drag-along rights.

(5) A drag-along right shall extinguish in compliance with the provisions of the Commercial Code.

**Section 107k**

(1) A register of drag-along rights shall contain the following particulars:

a) business name, registered office and identification number of issuer,

b) details of the obligated and beneficiary shareholders under the drag-along right in the extent entered in the register of shareholders, ISIN designation, kind, nominal value, number of shares of a particular issue and dates of issue of the shares of the obligated and beneficiary shareholders to which the drag-along right pertains,

c) period of time for which the drag-along right is established, or information that it is established for an indefinite period of time,

d) date of registration of the drag-along right in the register of drag-along rights.

(2) Particulars recorded in the register of drag-along rights shall be published by the central securities depository on its website, except for the shareholder's birth registration number and date of birth.

(3) The central securities depository shall be bound, upon a written request of

a) a legal entity or a natural person, to issue its current extract from the register of drag-along rights containing the data published pursuant to Section 107 g subs. 2, or a certificate acknowledging the fact that in relation to the shares of the issuer no drag-along rights have been registered,

b) a simple joint-stock company to which the extract shall apply, or a shareholder of a simple joint-stock company to which the extract shall apply in the part that shall apply to such a shareholder, to issue a current extract from the register of drag-along rights containing the data pursuant to Section 107 g subs. 1.

David Pérez Millán

# Spain

## Table of Content



## I. Nature of Corporate Law Regulation

According to Spanish law, rules on corporations in addition to statutory regulation must be provided in the corporate charter (arts. 3, 22, 23, 28 LSC)[1]. Any change of such rules requires an amendment to the bylaws to be filed with the Mercantile Register (art. 290 LSC). One reason among many for this is because the corporate charter is considered to be a special type of contract created for an entity of long duration with future shareholders bound by provisions they did not help to draft[2].

1 Real Decreto Legislativo 1/2010, de 2 de julio, por el que se aprueba el texto refundido de la Ley de Sociedades de Capital (LSC).
2 See *Girón* Derecho de sociedades, Madrid, 1976, 135–137, 278. Cf. also *Duque* La fundación de sociedades anónimas en la LSA, in Derecho de sociedades anónimas, I, Madrid, 1991, 52, 71 ff.

**Prof. David Pérez Millán,** Universidad Complutense de Madrid - Facultad de Derecho

https://doi.org/10.1515/9783110517026-023

As far as the bylaws are concerned, Spanish corporate law recognises the principle of contractual freedom for both close and open corporations. The corporate charter and the bylaws may include any agreements or terms that the founding partners or shareholders deem suitable, provided they are neither unlawful nor breach the principles governing the type of company involved (art. 28 LSC). How to actually specify these principles is still an open question[3].

However, shareholders' agreements play an important role when it comes to the regulation of the relationships among the shareholders themselves and those between them and the company. In this respect shareholders' agreements are usually referred to as "*parasocial* agreements", defined as agreements between some or all of the shareholders of a company regulating their relationships as shareholders outside of the corporate charter[4].

*Parasocial* means in this context both *formally autonomous* yet *functionally dependent* with regard to the corporate charter[5]. As will be shown, shareholders' agreements can particularly affect the company when *all* shareholders are party to the agreement. Hence, recent studies suggest that such agreements amend the corporate charter between the parties[6].

## II. Regulation of Shareholders' Agreements

In Spanish law there is no special legislation on shareholder's agreements, which are instead subject to general contract law. The same can be said about international or cross border agreements.

When a corporation is involved, such agreements are simply implicitly referred to, as when corporate law states that in general, agreements kept private among shareholders will not be effective with respect to the corporation (art. 29 LSC). Other provisions deal with the legal consequences of some share-

3 See *Miquel Rodríguez* in Comentarios a la Ley de Sociedades Anónimas, I, Madrid, 2nd ed., 152–154; *Vaquerizo* in Comentario de la Ley de Sociedades de Capital, I, Madrid, 2011, 394–396.

4 With few variations, for example, *Girón* Derecho de sociedades, 54; *Fernández de la Gándara* Pacto parasocial, EJB, III, Madrid, 1995, p. 4712; *Paz-Ares* El enforcement de los pactos parasociales, Actualidad Jurídica Uría & Menéndez 5/2003, 19; *Alonso Ledesma* Pactos parasociales, Diccionario de Derecho de Sociedades, Madrid, 2006, 853. The terminology and the notion of these agreements are after *Oppo* Contratti parasociali, Milano, 1942, 1 ff.

5 See *Fernández de la Gándara* EJB, 4712–4713; *Alonso Ledesma* Diccionario de Derecho de Sociedades, 853–854; after *Oppo* Contratti parasociali, 2–3.

6 *Sáez Lacave* Los pactos parasociales de todos los socios en Derecho español. Una materia en manos de los jueces, InDret 3/2009, 4, 9, 24–26; *Noval Pato* Los pactos omnilaterales: su oponibilidad a la sociedad, Cizur Menor, 2012, 73 ff., 147–150.

holders' agreements, in as far as they affect the control of a company, by triggering an obligation to draw up consolidated accounts for the corporate group formed in that way (arts. 42.1 CCom)[7], or by establishing specific measures in case the agreements allow the shareholders to gain control of a listed corporation or prevent others from doing so (arts. 128, 135 LMV; RD 1066/2007)[8]. Finally, certain shareholder's agreements are mentioned with respect to mandatory public disclosure obligations (arts. 530 – 535 LSC) or voluntary registration (RD 171/2007)[9].

However, rules on shareholder's agreements themselves, in terms of their definition, validity, duration, forms, content or enforcement, are not found in Spanish corporate legislation thereby giving even more importance to case law and academic literature, the latter greatly influenced by Italian and German scholarship.

Consequently, there is no legal distinction between partnerships or corporations regarding shareholder's agreements. However, agreements in relation to corporations are more interesting because of compatibility problems in coordinating contractual provisions with the mandatory rules on corporations and with the principles governing the type of company involved[10].

There is no legal distinction either, with regard to shareholders' agreements, between open and close corporations, although special rules apply to some agreements in listed companies and particular issues arise in the case of close corporations. With respect to listed companies, shareholders' agreements are held to be possible instruments to either gain or preserve control thus preventing others from acquiring it[11]. With regard to close corporations, the most relevant questions have to do with the enforceability of shareholders' agreements and their possible effects for the company[12]. In this sense, case law deals mostly

---

7 Real Decreto de 22 de agosto de 1885, por el que se publica el Código de Comercio (CCom).

8 Real Decreto Legislativo 4/2015, de 23 de octubre, por el que se aprueba el texto refundido de la Ley del Mercado de Valores (LMV); Real Decreto 1066/2007, de 27 de julio, sobre el régimen de las ofertas públicas de adquisición de valores (RD 1066/2007).

9 Real Decreto 171/2007, de 9 de febrero, por el que se regula la publicidad de los protocolos familiares (RD 171/2007).

10 *Pérez Millán* El contrato de sociedad: los pactos entre socios, in Contratos civiles, mercantiles, públicos, laborales e internacionales, con sus implicaciones tributarias, VI, Cizur Menor, 2014, 149.

11 *Robles Martín-Laborda* Sindicación de acciones y mercado de control societario, Cizur Menor, 2006, 13 – 15, 21 – 29.

12 Hence, the focus of recent books on shareholders' agreements such as *Feliu Rey* Los pactos parasociales en las sociedades de capital no cotizadas, Madrid, 2012; or *Noval Pato* Los pactos omnilaterales.

with the legal consequences of an infringement of shareholders' agreements between all shareholders in relation to close corporations, as will be seen.

In any case, shareholders' agreements do not need to be acknowledged in the corporate charter, in the bylaws or by the shareholders' meeting. In fact, the Spanish Supreme Court has generally admitted the validity of such agreements following the principle of freedom of contract and within the limits of the law, ethics and public order (art. 1255 CC)[13].

Nevertheless, when it comes to corporate law, scholars disagree on what exactly those limits are. Traditionally, it had been said that shareholders' agreements are valid unless they breach mandatory rules or principles governing the type of corporation involved[14]. In recent times, it has been argued instead that substantive mandatory rules need to be distinguished from typological mandatory rules, so that only the former would limit parties' free will, while any shareholders' agreement that diverges from typological mandatory rules should not be criticised from a legal perspective[15].

It seems hard to offer a universal response to the matter of limits, being more appropriate to examine the content of each shareholders' agreement in particular, along with the mandatory rules or principles it may conflict with[16]. Furthermore, the answer to this question will be probably shaped by differing conceptions on mandatory rules and corporate law[17].

In any case, it appears reasonable to consider the particular rule the agreement conflicts with, and additionally to take into account the parties to the agreement with respect to the shareholders as a whole. We can be reasonably sure that a shareholder's agreement would be void when it breaches a mandatory rule aimed at the protection of creditors. Therefore, a shareholder's agree-

---

13 SSTS 24/9/1987 (RJ 1987/6194); 26/2/1991 (RJ 1991/1600); 10/2/1992 (RJ 1992/1204); 18/3/2002 (RJ 2002/2850); 19/12/2007 (RJ 2007/9043); 10/12/2008 (RJ 2009/17); 6/3/2009 (RJ 2009/2793); 6/3/2009 (RJ 2009/2794)].

14 *Girón* Derecho de sociedades, 54; *Fernández de la Gándara* EJB, 4714–4715; *Alonso Ledesma* Diccionario de Derecho de Sociedades, 856.

15 *Paz-Ares* Actualidad Jurídica Uría & Menéndez 5/2003, 21, note 3; *Id.* La validez de los pactos parasociales, La Ley 7714 (2011), 12ff.; *Id.* La cuestión de la validez de los pactos parasociales, Actualidad Jurídica Uría & Menéndez Extraordinario-2011, 252ff., where ius cogens and ius imperativum rules are opposed. See also *Fernández del Pozo* El "enforcement" societario y registral de los pactos parasociales. La oponibilidad de lo pactado en protocolo familiar publicado, RdS 29 (2008), 170.

16 This kind of approach can be found in Italian academic literature: *Torino* Contratti parasociali, 45–46; *Semino* Il problema della validità dei sindicati di voto, Milano, 2003, 373, 387, 388.

17 As can be seen in *Sáez Lacave* Los pactos parasociales de todos los socios en Derecho español. Una materia en manos de los jueces, InDret 3/2009, 8ff., 22ff.

ment which would prevent the parties from winding up the corporation or adopting any other measures in order to recover from losses of equity (*ex* art. 363.1 LSC) must be considered invalid[18]. Similarly, any agreement that allows a shareholder to vote at the general meeting contrary to a legal prohibition or against the interest of the company would also be void[19]. All things considered, a shareholders' agreement would have no effect if it pursued the adoption of a corporate decision that could later be subject to challenge (*ex* art. 204 LSC)[20].

On the other hand, not all shareholders' agreements diverging from the respective mandatory rules applicable to a particular legal type of corporation would be void[21]. However, in this situation, it has to be considered whether all shareholders are bound by the agreement so that the agreement would affect the corporation in a similar manner to the corporate charter and the bylaws. It might be thought that such agreement represents an evasion of rules imposed on the shareholders even if they were not directly seeking to protect the creditors of the corporation[22].

One particular problem regarding the validity of shareholders' agreements relates to their potential duration. In Spanish law there are no specific restrictions on the duration of such agreements, but general contract law applies. Since the parties usually have a common purpose, most shareholders' agreements will be treated as a partnership without legal personality (art. 1669 CC)[23]. Therefore, agreements for a definite period of time will terminate on the expiry of the fixed term (art. 1700.I.1º CC) so that until that time, a party cannot terminate the contract unless there is fair cause (art. 1707 CC); whereas agreements of indefinite duration could be terminated at any time by each party in

---

**18** *Vicent Chuliá* Licitud, eficacia y organización de los sindicatos de voto, in Estudios en homenaje a José Girón Tena, Madrid, 1991, 1237. For Italian Law, *Jaeger* Il problema delle convenzioni di voto, Giur. comm., 1989, I, 240.

**19** *Paz-Ares* Actualidad Jurídica Uría & Menéndez 5/2003, 25. See also *Oppo* I patti parasociali: ancora una svolta legislativa, Riv. dir. civ., 1998, II, 222; *Rodemann* Stimmbindungsvereinbarungen in den Aktien-und GmbH-Rechten Deutschlands, Englands, Frankreichs und Belgiens, Köln-Berlin-Bonn-München, 1998, 59–61; *Schmidt* in Scholz GmbHG, 11. Aufl., Köln, 2014, § 47 Rn. 47; *Zöllner/Noack* in Baumbach/Hueck, GmbH-Gesetz, 21. Aufl., München, 2017, § 47 Rn. 114.

**20** *Vicent Chuliá* in Estudios homenaje Girón, 1235. See also for German law *Schmidt* in Scholz GmbHG, § 47 Rn. 50; *Rodemann* Stimmbindungsvereinbarungen, 59.

**21** See on this subject *Oppo*, Riv. dir. civ., 1987, I, p. 527; *Lutter* in Kölner Kommentar zum AktG, 2. Aufl., Köln-Berlin-Bonn-München, 1988, § 54 Rn. 22.

**22** *Rodemann* Stimmbindungsvereinbarungen, 95.

**23** See *Fernández de la Gândara* EJB, 4714; *Paz-Ares* Art. 1678 CC, in Comentario CC, II, Madrid, 1991, 1399; *Id.* Actualidad Jurídica Uría & Menéndez 5/2003, 28–29; *Alonso Ledesma* Diccionario de Derecho de Sociedades, 855–856.

good faith (arts. 1700.I.4º, 1705, 1706 CC)[24]. Similar provisions would apply even if the shareholders' agreement itself did not qualify as a partnership, for they derive from the general rules of Spanish contract law and the principle that contracts must not bind the parties eternally or excessively[25].

Nevertheless, doubts arise when the agreement does not expressly foresee its duration. When not expressly stated, the duration of a shareholders' agreement can sometimes be inferred from the duration of the company it refers to, at least in the sense that the agreement should not be assumed to last longer than the company itself. Hence, in situations where the company exists only for a fixed term, that same term could be presumed for the agreement[26]. If the company was set up for a single project, so would be the agreement[27].

However, the agreement does not necessarily have to last as long as the company does, particularly when the corporation is understood to have been formed for an indefinite period because of the absence of any provision in the bylaws (art. 25 LSC). Sometimes the duration of the agreement could be inferred from the period for which the parties assume certain obligations[28]. In other cases, there is no option but to conclude that the agreement is for an indefinite period. That being the case, some legal scholars suggest that the agreement could be terminated at any time in good faith[29]. Others think that this solution would normally be against the will of the parties and argue that the agreement binds each party for as long as they are still shareholders of the company[30]. The question would then be to decide whether the parties to the agreement have to remain shareholders for a certain period and how long that would be. General contract law can sometimes offer possibilities to determine the possible duration of

---

**24** For the extension of those rules to shareholders' agreements: *Paz-Ares* Actualidad Jurídica Uría & Menéndez 5/2003, 29.

**25** *Paz-Ares* La denuncia ad nutum de los contratos de duración indeterminada: entre el derecho dispositivo y el derecho imperativo, in Liber amicorum Prof. Iglesias, Cizur Menor, 2014, 843–845, 848 ff.

**26** See *Mambrilla* RDM 181–182 (1986), 321–322, following *Oppo* Contratti parasociali, 74–75.

**27** See *Paz-Ares* in Liber amicorum Prof. Iglesias, 846.

**28** STS 19/12/2007 (RJ 2007/9043), where the duration of the agreement was fixed by the court for the same period as that of the granting of an usufruct right over a mineral spring by one of the two parties in exchange of the obligations assumed by the other.

**29** *Fernández del Pozo* RdS 29 (2008), 162.

**30** *Paz-Ares* Actualidad Jurídica Uría & Menéndez 5/2003, 29; *Id.* in Liber amicorum Prof. Iglesias, 852 ff.

the agreement[31]. Corporate law should also be considered when the agreement diverges from the legal regulation on rights and obligations of the shareholders of a corporation[32]. Moreover, it seems questionable why the parties would have to be forced to leave the company in order to end an agreement concluded for an indefinite period[33].

Given these points, an indefinite or excessive duration does not void the agreement for that reason, but the parties would be able to ask a court to fix a term for the agreement (art. 1128 CC) or terminate it at any time in good faith (arts. 1705, 1506 CC)[34], meaning it would have to last as long as considered reasonable for the parties to recover their investment[35].

# III. Forms of Shareholders' Agreements

## 1. Shareholders' Agreements on Shareholder Rights

Different kinds of voting agreements are principally distinguished by what is agreed and who are the parties to the agreement. Shareholders' agreements in relation to voting rights can specify exactly the way to vote regarding certain corporate resolutions or establish the procedure to determine the way to vote[36]. In terms of the parties to the agreement, on one side there are agreements exclusively among shareholders; on the other side, agreements between shareholders and non-shareholders, the directors, or the company itself[37].

As far as agreements signed only by shareholders are concerned, the parties can pool together the majority of the voting rights and agree to act as a unit to gain corporate control, or they can just be minority shareholders trying to protect

---

**31** In the STS 19/12/2007 (RJ 2007/9043) the duration of 50 years for the obligations assumed by each party from a shareholders' agreement was not considered excessive according to general contract law.

**32** See *Pérez Millán* Sobre los pactos parasociales, RdS 31 (2008), 391; *Feliu Rey* Los pactos parasociales, 198.

**33** See *Pérez Moriones* Los sindicatos de voto, Valencia, 1996, 399–400.

**34** See *Pérez Moriones* Los sindicatos de voto, 400; *Pérez Millán* RdS 31 (2008), 391. However, SAP Ávila (First Section) 5/6/2003, held as void an agreement on voting rights concerning a private corporation because its duration was indefinite.

**35** *Paz-Ares* Art. 1678 CC, in Comentario *CC*, 1510.

**36** *Alonso Ledesma* Sindicato de voto, Diccionario de Derecho de Sociedades, 1032, following Italian scholarship.

**37** *Vicent Chuliá* in Estudios homenaje Girón, 1205; *Pérez Moriones* Los sindicatos de voto, 68. See also in general on shareholders' agreements, *Pérez Millán* in Contratos, 154 ff.

their interests[38]. Since the concept of trust in general is not recognised in Spanish law, there are no such things as voting trusts. Nevertheless, similar effects can be achieved through other mechanisms. Shareholders could coordinate to vote as a unit at the general meeting by utilising different procedures.

To begin with, they could delegate their votes by giving a proxy to a common representative[39]. The proxy could be revoked only by the parties to the agreement as a whole and not simply by any one of them attending the shareholders' meeting. Nevertheless, other legal limits on voting proxies would still apply (arts. 183 – 187 LSC), so that a special proxy would usually be required for each shareholders' meeting[40]. Furthermore, the shareholders could transfer the possession or even the property of their shares to one person who would accordingly exercise the voting rights as previously decided by the parties to the agreement. The risk of this formula is obviously when the person who possesses or formally owns the shares does not respect the instructions of the parties to the agreement[41].

Similarly, the shareholders can jointly own their shares and appoint one person to vote (art. 126 LSC), as well as being able to create an usufruct or a pledge over their shares, amending the bylaws to include that the voting rights are assigned to the usufructuary (art. 127.1 LSC) or to the pledgee (art. 132.1 LSC)[42].

Finally, the parties to the agreement can set up a holding company to hold their shares and vote at the shareholders' meeting of the corporation[43]. In fact, it is common for the parties to a voting agreement concerning a listed company to transfer their shares to a private limited company, which will exercise control of the listed company[44]. Hence, this kind of agreement can generate a corporate group.

---

**38** *Menénez Menéndez* Los pactos de sindicación para el órgano administrativo de la sociedad anónima, in Estudios de Derecho mercantil en homenaje a Rodrigo Uría, Madrid, 1978, 358; *Vicent Chuliá* in Estudios homenaje Girón, 1239; *Pérez Moriones* Los sindicatos de voto, 69 ff.; *Alonso Ledesma* Sindicato de voto, Diccionario de Derecho de sociedades, 1031.

**39** *Vicent Chuliá* in Estudios homenaje Girón, 1240 – 1243; *Pérez Moriones* Los sindicatos de voto, 511 ff.

**40** *Paz-Ares* Actualidad Jurídica Uría & Menéndez 5/2003, 29.

**41** See *Pérez Moriones* Los sindicatos de voto, 503, 510.

**42** See *Vicent Chuliá* in Estudios homenaje Girón, 1240, 1244 – 1246; *Pérez Moriones* Los sindicatos de voto, 533 ff.; *Paz-Ares* Actualidad Jurídica Uría & Menéndez 5/2003, 30.

**43** *Vicent Chuliá* in Estudios homenaje Girón, 1240; *Pérez Moriones* Los sindicatos de voto, 523 ff.

**44** On these kinds of holding companies and disclosure of shareholders' agreements regarding listed companies, *Recalde/De Dios Martínez* Los pactos parasociales en la Ley de Transparencia: una cuestión polémica, Revista jurídica La Ley, 9/1/2004, 4 – 5; *Robles Martín-Laborda* Sindicación de acciones, 69 – 70.

There is no specific regulation on company groups in Spanish corporate law yet a definition of a group can still be found in respect of the obligation to draw up consolidated accounts[45]. In this context, a group is said to exist when a company holds or can hold, directly or indirectly, the control over one or more companies, and control is presumed when a company has at its disposal the majority of the voting rights by virtue of agreements entered into with third parties (art. 42.1.c CC). To the voting rights that a controlling company directly holds are added those it holds through subsidiaries or through persons acting in the interest of the controlling company or it subsidiaries, and those voting rights the controlling company jointly has at its disposal with any other person (art. 42.1 *in fine* LC).

Therefore, shareholders' agreements can create a corporate group, both when the parties to the agreement set up a holding company to hold the majority of the voting rights at a corporation, and when a company jointly holds such a majority with the other parties to a voting agreement. In any case, this notion of a corporate group is based on the idea of control and consequently is focused on hierarchical groups, whereas any allusion to a "unitary direction" (that may include as well horizontal or parity-based groups) appears only in the regulation on cooperatives (art. 137 LCoop)[46].

In addition to agreements among majority or minority shareholders, voting agreements with non-shareholders are commonly acknowledged in Spanish law, providing that shareholders who are parties to the agreement respect their duty of loyalty towards others shareholders[47]. As will be seen, the main question then, is the influence that outside lenders can exert on the management of the corporation.

With regard to an agreement signed by the company itself, the obligations arising from the agreement for shareholders or directors are the real problem[48]. A voting agreement does not create obligations for any current or future shareholders who are not party to the agreement due to the principle of relativity or privity of contracts (art. 1257.I CC). For this reason, the company cannot be bound by an agreement whenever there are shareholders *other than* the parties to the agreement.

**45** See *Girgado* Legislative Situation of Corporate Groups in Spanish Law, ECFR 4/2006, 363 ff.
**46** Ley 12/2015, de 9 de julio, de cooperativas (LCoop). For the same situation in relation to previous regulation on consolidated accounts and cooperatives, *Girgado* ECFR 4/2006, 365–366, 377.
**47** *See Pérez Millán* in Contratos, 165–169, with similar conclusions to those in *Rodemann* Stimmbindungsvereinbarungen, 27 ff.
**48** *Pérez Millán* in Contratos, 157.

On the other hand, shareholders' agreements can in general confer rights on the corporation against the parties as with any contractual provision made for the benefit of third parties (art. 1257.II CC)[49]. In the case of voting agreements, the shareholders can agree to vote as the company or the directors decide, but are limited by the same duty of loyalty they have to respect in agreements with third parties[50]. More dubious seems, conversely, whether the directors can sign an agreement to vote at the board according to the instructions given by the parties to the agreement.

In this respect, the shareholders' meeting can give binding instructions to the directors (art. 161 LSC). In contrast, agreements between shareholders and directors regarding the management of the corporation and the vote at the board of directors are generally held void[51]. However, it has been suggested that those agreements would still be valid if they do not conflict with the interest of the company and the fiduciary duties of the directors[52]. In particular, directors would be bound by agreements between all the shareholders[53]. Moreover, it has been proposed that the validity of agreements between only some shareholders and the directors could be preserved by understanding that they refer instead to how the shareholders will give instructions to the directors at the shareholders' meeting (art. 161 LSC)[54].

Irrespective of whether the agreement is valid or void, when it results in actually giving instructions to the directors outside the shareholders' meeting, the parties to the agreement could be considered shadow directors. To that end, it is not necessary that the agreement transfers the powers of directors to the shareholders who are party to it[55]. On the contrary, merely making suggestions or recommendations and exercising in general control or supervision are not sufficient

**49** *Fernández de la Gándara* EJB, 4715; *Paz-Ares* Actualidad Jurídica Uría & Menéndez 5/2003, 20; *Alonso Ledesma* Pactos parasociales, Diccionario de sociedades, 856.

**50** *Pérez Millán* in Contratos, 157–158. In Spanish law there is no rule similar to German § 136 Abs. 2 AktG.

**51** *Menénez Menéndez* in Estudios homenaje Uría, 351 ff.; *Vicent Chuliá* in Estudios homenaje Girón, 1235–1236; *Pérez Moriones* Los sindicatos de voto, 58; *Paz-Ares* Fundamento de la prohibición de pactos de voto para el consejo, InDret 4/2010, 6 ff.; *Feliu Rey* Los pactos parasociales, 162, 172.

**52** *Alonso Ledesma* Sindicato de voto, Diccionario de sociedades, 1033.

**53** *Pérez Millán* in Contratos, 163–164, in terms corresponding to § 146 CBCA in Canada or § 732 MBCA in USA.

**54** *Fernández del Pozo* Acerca de la licitud de los pactos parasociales para el Consejo. La mala regulación de la cuestión en el proyectado Código Mercantil, La Ley Mercantil 3 (2014), 18 ff.

**55** However, see *Echegaray* El administrador de hecho, Cizur Menor, 2002, 101–103; *Ferré Falcón* Los créditos subordinados, Cizur Menor, 2006, 492–493.

for a person to be held to be a shadow director. The key is the independent power to determine management policy or decide on the commercial and financial future of the corporation[56].

Given these points, the parties to a shareholders' agreement would have to be consider *de facto* directors when they cooperate with the *de jure* directors on an equal level in deciding the future of the corporation[57]. Non-shareholders as well can be involved in the management when they enter into an agreement aimed at financing the company.

Shareholders' agreements regarding the financing of the corporation can consist of: additional capital or equity contributions to be paid in cash or otherwise; providing guarantees or securities; granting loans or in general credit to the company[58]. Equity financing in the future could be agreed along with a "pay-to-play clause", where shareholders not participating in new rounds of funding will lose their right of pre-emption in successive capital increases[59].

Although there is hardly any case law and literature on the matter, it is worth noting that agreements between shareholders' and third parties on financing the corporation could result in outside lenders being considered shadow directors of the company, for example through financial covenants. Nevertheless, a restrictive approach to the matter has been suggested, so that only pathological or extreme cases will be concerned[60].

The key here would be to distinguish legitimate control from undue interference on the management of the corporation[61]. One option is to consider that creditors will only be held to be *de facto* directors when they either give orders to the *de jure* directors or completely replace them[62]. Moreover, creditors could be

---

56 *Latorre* El administrador de hecho, Granada, 2003, 68–72. In similar terms, *Embid* La responsabilidad de los administradores de la sociedad anónima tras la ley de transparencia, RDCI 685 (2004), 2398–2399.

57 See *Pérez Millán* La subordinación de créditos y los pactos de socios, RCP 18 (2013), 153–156, developing ideas that can be found above all in *Abriani* Gli amministratori di fatto, Milano, 1998, 228 ff., for Italian law, and in *Fleischer* Zur aktienrechtlichen Verantwortlichkeit faktischer Organe, AG 10/2004, 525, for German law.

58 See *Paz-Ares* Actualidad Jurídica Uría & Menéndez 5/2003, 20; *Pérez Millán* in Contratos, 170.

59 *Feliu Rey* Los pactos parasociales, 219–220, 233.

60 *Díaz Echegaray* El administrador de hecho, 114. See also *Garrido* "Art. 93", en *Rojo/Beltrán* Comentario de la Ley Concursal, I, Madrid, 2004, 1678; *Ferré Falcón* Los créditos subordinados, 499–500.

61 *Alonso Ledesma* El automatismo en la subordinación de los créditos y la posición de las entidades de crédito, in Implicaciones financieras de la Ley Concursal, Madrid, 2009, 203.

62 *Latorre* El administrador de hecho, 68–69. See also *Alonso Ureba* La aplicación del concepto de administrador de hecho en supuestos de concurso de sociedades integradas en un grupo y de refinanciación", in Implicaciones financieras de la LC, 167–168.

considered shadow directors when they not only appoint different members to the board of directors, give advice or control some decisions, but also assume typical managerial functions from inside the corporate structure[63].

## 2. Shareholders' Agreements on the (Limitation for the) Transfer of Shares

In order to preserve control over the corporation, retain some parties as shareholders, or simply to prevent unknown people from becoming shareholders, the parties to a shareholders' agreement can restrict the free transferability of their shares. Restrictions on transferability basically consist of either prohibiting any transfer without the consent of the others parties to the agreement or incorporating pre-emption rights for the non-selling parties.

Share transfers can be prohibited for a stated period of time. If the prohibition is included in the bylaws of the corporation, it cannot last more than five years for limited liability companies (art. 108 LCS) or two years for joint stock companies (art. 123 RRM)[64]. When the prohibition is provided in a shareholders' agreement through so-called "lock-up clauses", the same time limits are normally respected[65].

Pre-emption rights will commonly be configured as a right of first offer, so that the party wishing to transfer shares is first required to offer those shares to others parties to the agreement and, if there is no agreement on the price, the potential transferor can sell the shares to outsiders for a certain period of time but at a price not less than that offered to the parties[66].

Drag-along and tag-along clauses are commonly acknowledged although no explicit legal mention of such provisions can be found in Spanish law. Such clauses can even be included in the bylaws of the corporation (arts. 144.2.d, 175.2.d, and 188.3 RRM)[67]. In which case, drag-along clauses, for example, will

---

**63** See *Pérez Millán* RCP 18 (2013), 156–159, with special reference to the Dumbrunn case decided by the Swiss Federal Supreme Court (14/9/1981), and to the opinion of *Fleischer* AG 10/2004, 523–527.

**64** Real Decreto 1784/1996, de 19 de julio, por el que se aprueba el Reglamento del Registro Mercantil (RRM).

**65** *Feliu Rey* Los pactos parasociales, 198.

**66** *Feliu Rey* Los pactos parasociales, 218.

**67** For a tag-along clause, Resolution of the General Direction of Registries and Notaries (RDGRN) from 20/5/2016. See also *Sáez Lacave/ Bermejo Gutiérrez* Inversiones específicas, oportunismo y contrato de sociedad (A vueltas con los pactos de tag- y de drag-along, Indret 1/2007,

then make the transfer of shares by a majority shareholder conditional on approval by the company, to be given only when the prospective acquirer also buys the shares of the minority (art. 123.3 LSC). However, some studies recommend leaving tag-along clauses outside the bylaws because third parties are not legally bound to buying more shares than they intended, being more advisable instead to grant the minority shareholders a put option requiring the seller to purchase their shares[68]. Others think the put option can be incorporated into the bylaws as an ancillary commitment to be extended to third parties with the transfer of shares by the majority shareholders[69].

Shoot-out clauses of different kinds are also permitted in shareholders' agreements (despite the silence of corporate law), including Russian roulette or shot-gun, Texas or Mexican shoot-out and Dutch auction[70].

## 3. Shareholders' Agreements on the Constitution of the Corporation

Shareholders' agreements usually regulate the constitution and the organization of the company, in particular, where joint ventures are involved. The parties must decide which provisions of the agreement are to be included in the bylaws and how this has to be done, taking into account that the Spanish Supreme Court tends to give preference to what is agreed in the bylaws over what is only provided in the agreement[71].

The agreement can set out the management structure for the corporation and allow the parties to nominate a certain number of directors. How these provisions are reflected in the bylaws of the corporation is important, for rules in the bylaws can be understood as a specification of the will of the parties to the existing agreement[72]. In any case, directors appointed in accordance with a shareholders' agreement are required to manage the corporation subject to the bylaws and they are bound by fiduciary duties to all shareholders. As has been mentioned, only agreements signed by all shareholders bind the directors;

25–26; *Fernández del Pozo* RdS 29 (2008), 176–177 (note 95); *Feliu Rey* Los pactos parasociales, 226, 228.

**68** *Sáez Lacave/ Bermejo Gutiérrez* Indret 1/2007, 26–27.

**69** *Fernández del Pozo* RdS 29 (2008), 177 (note 95).

**70** A Russian roulette clause can be seen in STS 2/3/1998 (RJ 1998/1126). See also *Feliu Rey* Los pactos parasociales, 246–248.

**71** For example STS 5/7/1994 (RJ 1994/6431).

**72** As in the case considered in STS 6/3/2009 (RJ 2009/2794).

otherwise, binding instructions to the directors can only be given at the shareholders meeting (art. 161 LSC).

Also future variations of company capital can be regulated in a shareholders' agreement. Further equity financing can be agreed along with pay-to-play clauses or rules on pre-emption rights as previously explained. The agreement can also protect some parties to the agreement in successive capital increases by forcing other parties to grant them a fixed shareholding[73].

Finally, the corporation can remain in existence despite the termination of the shareholders' agreement, but some agreements can include specific provisions to end the company at a given point in time or on the occurrence of certain events. Those provisions can consist of including causes for winding up the company in the bylaws (art. 361 LSC) or binding the parties in such circumstances to vote to approve its voluntary liquidation (art. 368 LSC)[74].

## 4. Shareholders' Agreements in pre-insolvency situation

According to Spanish law, the decision on whether a corporation initiates insolvency proceedings is reserved for the directors (art. 3.1 *in fine* LC)[75]. Moreover, the directors must file a request for the opening of proceedings by two months after the date they knew or should have known the corporation was insolvent (art. 5 LC).

Therefore, shareholders do not have to be consulted in the decision-making process on the initiation of such proceedings once the company has become insolvent (although it is possible that the directors must convene the general meeting in any case *ex* art. 365.1 LSC)[76]. Consequently, no shareholder's agreement can prevent the initiation of these proceedings when the corporation is insolvent, unless the agreement provides an alternative mechanism to deal with financial distress, such as a capital increase.

According to a number of studies, the decision on whether to reach any kind of extrajudicial refinancing agreements (including restructuring plans that call for changing the corporation's capital structure) with the creditors (*ex* arts. 71

73 See STS STS 19/12/2007 (RJ 2007/9043), where according to a shareholders' agreement the majority shareholders guarantee the minority a shareholding of 40 % in the company irrespective of capital increases for as long as the agreement lasts.

74 On this two possibilities, *Feliu Rey* Los pactos parasociales, 249.

75 Ley 22/2003, de 9 de julio, Concursal (LC).

76 See *Rojo* Art. 3 LC, Comentario LC, I, Madrid, 2004, 202–204; *Roncero* Art. 3 LC, in Comentarios a la legislación concursal, I, Madrid, 2004, 175 ff.

bis, 231 ff. or DA 4ª LC) also resides with the directors[77]. On the contrary, others suggest the consent of the shareholders is required for the conclusion of a debt-equity swap involving a capital increase[78].

Be that as it may, either to sign or implement the agreement with the creditors needs the approval of a majority at the shareholders' meeting to authorize any capital increase (arts. 296 LSC and DA 4ª.3 LC). In this scenario, shareholders' will be held responsible if they refuse without a reasonable cause a debt-for-equity swap or an issue of convertible bonds thereby frustrating a possible refinancing agreement (arts. 165.2, 172.2.1º and 172 bis LC)[79].

Of course, shareholders can also enter into agreements with the creditors of the company and be parties to refinancing or restructuring plans. In this regard, it is worth noting that Spanish insolvency law subordinates, on one side, all loans or similar credit granted by shareholders with a shareholding of at least 5% (in listed companies) or 10% (in non-listed companies); and on the other side, all claims of any *de jure* or *de facto* directors in the two-year period prior to the opening of insolvency proceedings (arts. 92.5º and 93.2 LC).

As previously described, shareholders' agreements regarding the management of the corporation can in certain circumstances lead to their parties being held to be shadow directors[80]. The shareholding percentages mentioned above would also be reached jointly by adding together the shares held by each of the parties to the agreement. Voting agreements, agreements on dividend distribution and even agreements regarding the financing of the corporation can have an effect in this regard[81].

However, subordination is based on considering those shareholders and directors as "people specially related to the debtor" (art. 93.2 LC). In this respect,

---

77 *Pulgar* Reestructuraciones societarias: incumplimiento de acuerdos homologados de refinanciación, RDBB 141 (2016), 65 ff.

78 *Gallego Córcoles* La capitalización de créditos (Debt-Equity Swap) desde una perspectiva concursal y preconcursal, RCP 24 (2006), 363 ff.

79 See *Recalde* Los acuerdos de refinanciación mediante la conversión de deudas en capital, ADCo 33 (2014), 105–106; *García-Cruces* Los efectos de los acuerdos de refinanciación en el concurso consecutivo: la calificación, ADCo 33 (2014), 198–199; *Marín de la Bárcena* Obstaculización de acuerdos de refinanciación y calificación culpable del concurso, Análisis GA&P, April 2014, 1–5.

80 In particular, on subordination in that case, *Pérez Millán* RCP (2013), 153–158.

81 See *Pérez Millán* RCP (2013), 158–165, with similar conclusions to the ones that can be found for German law, above all in *Pentz* Die Änderungen und Ergänzungen der Kapitalersatzregeln im GmbH-Gesetz", GmbHR 9/1999, 444, 446; *Id.* Zurechnungsprobleme um das Zwerganteilsprivileg des § 32a Abs. 3 S. 2 GmbHG, GmbHR 9/2004, 533–534; and *Krolop* Zur Anwendung der MoMiG-Regelungen zu Gesellschafterdarlehen auf gesellschaftsfremde Dritte, GmHR 8/2009, 400–404.

creditors who exchange debt for equity according to a restructuring plan will not be considered as people specially related to the debtor in relation to other debts originating in the same agreement, even when they become directors for that very reason. Similarly, creditors who signed a refinancing agreement will not be held to be *de facto* directors in relation to the debts assumed by the corporation according to the viability plan, unless further circumstances are demonstrated in order to justify awarding that status (art. 93.2 *in fine* LC)[82].

# IV. Legal Effects of Shareholders' Agreements

## 1. Legal Effects on the Corporation

Shareholders' agreements do not usually effect the interpretation of the corporate charter and the bylaws. Bylaws must be interpreted by not simply considering the will of those shareholders who cooperated in drafting them, but also taking into account other shareholders and third parties[83]. For similar reasons, when all shareholders are parties to the agreement, a subjective interpretation of the bylaws in accordance with the agreement would be possible with regard to the internal relationships among the shareholders, as long as interests of non-shareholders are not involved[84].

## 2. Legal Effects on the Shareholders

Shareholders' agreements do not create obligations or rights apart from those for their parties as a consequence of the general principle on the relativity or privity of contracts (art. 1257.I CC). Whoever purchases shares from the parties to the agreement would have to sign the contract first in order to become a party.

Several studies suggest using the bylaws to extend the obligations or rights arising from the shareholders' agreements to potential purchasers of shares. Ac-

---

**82** See *Recalde* ADCo 33 (2014), 93–94; *García-Cruces* ADCo 33 (2014), 183–185; *Conde Tejón* La capitalización quasi forzosa por compensación de créditos como contenido de acuerdos de refinanciación tras la Ley 17/2014, RdS 43 (2014), 397.

**83** See *Girón* Derecho de sociedades anónimas, Valladolid, 1952, 99; *Duque* in Derecho de sociedades anónimas, 79–83.

**84** See *Pérez Millán* in Contratos, 182. In similar terms, see also *Paz-Ares* Actualidad Jurídica Uría & Menéndez 5/2003, 40 (note 78); *Fernández del Pozo* RdS 29 (2008), 168; NOVAL PATO, Los pactos omnilaterales, 125.

cordingly, it has been recommended to introduce an ancillary commitment in the bylaws, which would consist of accepting and performing the shareholders' agreement[85]. This would be completed by also stipulating in the bylaws a specific cause for exclusion of shareholders' who fail to honour the ancillary commitment. This provision would even be unnecessary for limited liability companies, since the voluntary failure to comply with an ancillary commitment represents a legal cause for exclusion in any case (art. 350 LSC)[86].

However, such a mechanism raises some doubts. In reality, an ancillary commitment to sign or perform the shareholders' agreement could work in two different ways, depending on whether it either conditions the purchase of shares or is to be transferred with them[87]. In the first case, the transfer of shares would have to be authorised by the company (art. 88 LSC), in the sense that consent would only be given once the purchaser had signed the agreement. More difficulties arise regarding the transfer of the ancillary commitment with the shares, for it is not clear what exactly would be transferred: the obligation to sign the shareholders' agreement or the rights and obligations directly arising from the agreement[88]. On the other hand, this kind of ancillary commitment must respect the mandatory rules on the transfer of shares in joint stock companies when securities are issued (arts. 113.1, 114.1, 120.2.II LSC)[89].

In any case, aside from those obligations arising from the contract, shareholders' agreements can trigger capital market obligations for the parties if the control structure of a public corporation is affected. From 2007 onwards, whoever gains control of a listed company is required to make a bid to all holders of securities when that control is acquired through shareholders' agreements, regardless of the acquisition of securities (arts. 128.I.b LMV, 3.1.b RD 1066/2007)[90].

---

**85** In general, *Paz-Ares* Actualidad Jurídica Uría & Menéndez 5/2003, 41. With regard to family agreements, *Vicent Chuliá* Organización jurídica de la empresa familiar, Revista de Derecho Patrimonial 5 (2000), 36; *Fernández del Pozo* RdS 29 (2008), 173, 179–183.

**86** *Paz-Ares* Actualidad Jurídica Uría & Menéndez 5/2003, 42; *Fernández del Pozo* RdS 29 (2008), 181. This kind of sanction would logically also affect the actual parties to the agreement.

**87** On these two possibilities, *Fernández del Pozo* RdS 29 (2008), 173, 180–181.

**88** Apparently in favour of the second option, *Fernández del Pozo* RdS 29 (2008), 173.

**89** See *Pérez Millán* RdS 31 (2008), 395.

**90** After the Spanish reform in 2007 there is no doubt that the obligation to make a bid would be triggered without any acquisition of securities: *Léon Sanz* La reforma de la regulación de OPAs y el régimen de los pactos parasociales de las sociedades cotizadas, Not. UE 285 (2008), 127–128; *De Dios/Recalde* Función y âmbito de la OPA obligatoria, Not. UE 285 (2008), 65, 67, 69; *Muñoz Perez* El concepto amplio de concierto como presupuesto de la OPA imperativa en Derecho español, RdS 30 (2008), 65; *García de Enterría* in La regulación de las OPAs, 2009, 170–175; *Zurita* in La regulación de las OPAs, 2009, pp. 109–111, 123.

Having control of a listed company means either: holding alone or with other persons acting in concert, directly or indirectly, 30 % or more of the voting rights; or, with a lower percentage of voting rights, appointing more than half of the board of directors (arts. 131.1 LMV; 4.1 RD 1066/2007). One person will be assigned the total percentage of voting rights of those who act according to their instructions or in concert with them (art. 5.1 RD 1066/2007).

To that end, acting in concert is *defined* as the cooperation of two or more persons on the basis of an agreement (either express or tacit; either oral or written), aimed at acquiring control of the company; whereas acting in concert is *presumed* in the case of certain shareholders' agreements regarding the company's management (art. 5.1.b RD 1066/2007).

As has been noted, in contrast to European model (art. 5.1 Directive 2004/25/CE) but similar to French or German law, Spanish regulation does not necessarily presuppose the acquisition of securities by persons acting in concert in order to trigger a mandatory bid[91]. Therefore, making a bid would be required, not only in the case of cooperation to acquire securities or acquiring securities by persons cooperating for other purposes, but also by merely acting in concert without acquiring any securities[92].

Spanish regulation combines a definition and several presumptions of acting in concert in relation to certain agreements. What is decisive is not the *nature* of the agreement, but the *cooperation* to gain control of the company[93]. For example, the agreement could be void, yet the parties could still collaborate on its basis[94]. The same could be said about gentlemen's agreements, although they are not legally binding[95]. However, the agreement must be aimed at acquiring control of the company, which entails three conditions: it must be focused on shareholders' voting rights, it must lead to an essential and stable modification in the control structure of the corporation, and the parties must have the intention of acquiring the control of the company that way[96].

The presumptions of acting in concert have different elements. On one side, there has to be an agreement that either regulates the exercise of voting rights at general meetings, the board of directors or the executive committee; or that re-

---

**91** On the differences among European regulations, see *Pérez Millán* Pactos parasociales, actuación en concierto y OPA obligatoria, in Derecho de OPAs, Valencia, 2010, 118 – 121.

**92** *García de Enterría* in La regulación de las OPAs, 2009, 166 ff.

**93** *Pérez Millán* in Derecho de OPAs, 131.

**94** *Sánchez Calero* 2009, 153 – 154; *Léon Sanz* Not. UE 285 (2008), 129.

**95** See *Muñoz Perez* RdS 30 (2008), 51, 68, who thinks they are also shareholders' agreements.

**96** For more details, *Pérez Millán* La noción de actuación en concierto a efectos de OPA obligatoria, DNeg 236 (2010), 5 ff.

stricts or conditions the free transferability of shares. On the other side, any one of those agreements has to be aimed at establishing a common policy or having a relevant influence on the company's management. In order to avoid the obligation to make a bid, it is possible to prove that such an agreement is not objectively able to give control of the company or that it is not subjectively intended for that purpose[97].

Due to their importance for capital markets, only certain shareholders' agreements concerning listed companies are legally subject to public notice, according to rules modelled on the Italian TUF of 1998[98]. There are three means of mandatory disclosure. First, the adoption, extension or amendment of shareholders' agreements on voting rights in shareholders' meetings and agreements that restrict or condition the free transferability of shares (or convertible or exchangeable bonds) must be reported to the company itself and to the National Securities Market Commission (a copy of the relevant clauses must be attached to such a notice) (531.1 LSC). Second, after the notice is served, the agreement must be filed with the Mercantile Registry where the company is registered (531.2 LSC). Third, the shareholders' agreement must be made public in the same way as any other relevant information for investors (531.3 LSC). Any of the parties to the agreement can serve the notices and submit the agreement (532 LSC). Until all these three forms of disclosure are satisfied, shareholders' agreements will have no effect whatsoever on the matters to which they refer (art. 533 LSC). Additionally, the violation of any of those obligations will incur penalties (art. 296 LMV).

It is worth noting that the submission of such shareholders' agreements in the Mercantile Registry is merely informative and does not affect the rights of third parties which the publication of other facts, acts or contracts would (arts. 20, 21 CCom)[99]. As for undisclosed shareholders' agreements, they are not void but simply not binding for the parties[100]. It is uncertain whether a resolution of the shareholders' meeting could be challenged after it was passed as a result of the parties to an undisclosed agreement voting as the agreement stat-

---

97 *Léon Sanz* Not. UE (2008), 128 – 129; *Pérez Millán* in Derecho de OPAs, 143 – 144.

98 *Mambrilla* Los pactos parasociales y la transparencia de las sociedades anónimas cotizadas, RdS 22 (2004), 239; *Léon Sanz* La publicación de los pactos parasociales por las sociedades cotizadas, in Derecho de sociedades anónimas cotizadas, II, Madrid, 2006, 1169.

99 *Léon Sanz* in Derecho de sociedades anónimas cotizadas, 2006, 1179.

100 *Léon Sanz*, in Derecho de sociedades anónimas cotizadas, 1181, after *Oppo* in Commentario al testo unico delle disposizioni in materia di intermediazione finanziaria, II, Padova, 1998, 1134 – 1135.

ed[101]. In any case, it is important to realize that Spanish regulation does not expressly consider challenging decisions of the general meeting or suspending the voting rights of the parties to an undisclosed agreement on such grounds, contrary to what happens in Italy (art. 122, comma 4 TUF)[102].

On the other hand, the disclosure of family agreements regarding unlisted companies is voluntary. Family agreements are legally defined as agreements between shareholders belonging to the same family, and also with non-shareholding relatives, in respect of the connections between family, property and business that affect the company (art. 2.1 RD 171/2007). Directors are given the responsibility to decide whether to make public the agreements in view of the interests of the company (art. 3 RD 171/2007). They can choose between publishing the agreement on the company's website, declaring its existence in the file opened for the company at the Mercantile Registry, or submitting a copy together with the annual accounts to the Registry (arts. 4–6 RD 171/2007). When resolutions of the company have to be registered, it must be declared if they were passed as a result of a published agreement (art. 7 RD 171/2007).

In general, the disclosure of family agreements in unlisted companies is also purely informative[103]. That the agreement has been made public does not mean that it would affect the rights or obligations of whoever acquires shares from parties to the agreement. The situation might be different when the bylaws of the company foresee the signing and performance of the agreement as an ancillary commitment. A number of studies suggest, to that end it would be enough if the bylaws simply mentioned the agreement with its content published elsewhere[104]. Others argue it would be necessary for the agreement to have been filed with the Mercantile Registry[105].

## 3. Consequences of a Breach of the Shareholders' Agreements

Being contracts, shareholders' agreements are legally enforceable and the normal rules of contract law would be applicable in the event of breach. Therefore, a failure by one party to perform a contract entitles the others to a remedy. Basically, an innocent party can choose between either seeking the performance or

101 In favour of that possibility, *Léon Sanz* in Derecho de sociedades anónimas cotizadas, 1184.
102 Underlining the difference with the Italian TUF, *Mambrilla* RdS 22 (2004), 246–247.
103 See *Feliu Rey* Los pactos parasociales, 107–108.
104 *Paz-Ares* Actualidad Jurídica Uría & Menéndez 5/2003, 41.
105 *Fernández del Pozo* RdS 29 (2008), 182–183; *Feliu Rey* Los pactos parasociales, 430–432.

the termination of the agreement, along with the recovery of any eventual damages.

Damages may be recoverable by the innocent party in respect of any loss suffered as a result of the breach (art. 1101 CC). Since damages will only be awarded where the breach is found to have caused a loss, proving and quantifying the loss remains difficult, in particular when a resolution of the shareholders' meeting has been passed in violation of the agreement. For that reason, it is both usual and advisable that the agreement itself includes liquidated damages or penalty clauses[106].

Additionally, an innocent party may elect to terminate the agreement (art. 1124 CC)[107]. However, if shareholders' agreements set up a partnership between the parties, legal provisions on the termination of partnerships by breach of contract must be observed (art. 1707 CC)[108]. As with any partnership, the innocent party has to comply with the agreement irrespective of a breach by others, since the obligations of the parties are not dependent on each other[109].

As an alternative, it has commonly been assumed by most scholars that specific performance would be awarded, even in the case of a breach of voting agreements, although there is no special regulation or case law on the matter[110]. Shareholders' agreements are still thought to be specifically performed according to different legal provisions, depending on whether the contractual promise consists in giving something (arts. 1096 and 1097 CC; 701 LEC), doing something (arts. 1098.I CC; 706, 708 and 709 LEC), or not doing something (arts. 1099 CC; 710 LEC)[111]. In particular, the order or decree for specific performance of voting agreements will differ according to the provisions of the agreement. It has been suggested that the court itself could replace the party in breach by voting at the

**106** *Pérez Moriones* Los sindicatos de voto, 436–438; *Paz-Ares* Actualidad Jurídica Uría & Menéndez 5/2003, 21–22.

**107** For example, in STS 28/09/1965 (RJ 4056/1965).

**108** *Paz-Ares* Actualidad Jurídica Uría & Menéndez 5/2003, 28–29.

**109** See *Feliu Rey* Los pactos parasociales, 336.

**110** In Spanish law there are no rules on specific performance of shareholders' agreements such as § 7.31 (b) MBCA; § 706 (a) California Corporations Code; §. 33–716 (b) General Statutes of Connecticut (Chapter 601); § 7.70 (b) Illinois Compiled Statutes (Chapter 805, Act 5). Nor is there case law on prohibitive injunctions as in Greenwell v. Porter [1902] 1 Ch. 530; and Russel v. Northern Bank Development Corp. Ltd. [1992] 1 W. L. R. 588; or on mandatory injunctions as in Puddelphatt v. Leith [1916] 1 Ch. 200. Not even a decision similar to BGH 29/5/1967 for German law.

**111** See *Vicent Chuliá* in Estudios homenaje Girón, 1212; *Pérez Moriones* Los sindicatos de voto, 468–474; and above all, with references to actual civil procedure rules, *Paz-Ares* Actualidad Jurídica Uría & Menéndez 5/2003, 22–26.

shareholders' meeting in situations where the agreement states exactly what has to be voted for (art. 708 LSC). If the agreement only provides the procedure in order to reach a decision on how to vote, the court could compel the party in breach to honour the agreement or otherwise incur penalties (art. 709 LEC). Breach of a negative stipulation in an agreement, including the prohibition to vote or to vote in a particular way, could be similarly restrained (art. 710 LEC)[112]. The innocent parties could also seek an interim injunction in order to prevent a threatened breach or even seek precautionary measures to get the agreement specifically performed before a definitive decision by the court (art. 726.2 LEC)[113].

Specific performance can also mean removing the consequences caused by the breach of a contract (1098.II CC). As far as voting agreements are concerned, a resolution of the shareholders' meeting might have been passed because parties to the agreement voted contrary to their agreed contractual obligations. The innocent parties could then seek the court to compel the party in breach to collaborate in passing a new resolution of the shareholders' meeting aimed at withdrawing or superseding the previous one (art. 204.2 LSC), on the condition that the rights of third parties would not be affected, particularly with respect to shareholders not party to the agreement[114]. In the case of all shareholders being bound by the agreement, the question becomes whether the original resolution of the shareholders' meeting could be directly challenged and if any of those claims should be brought within the same period of time[115].

Whether a violation of a shareholders' agreement provides for the right to challenge the resolutions of shareholders' meetings is a disputed question. Due to the principle of relativity or privity of contracts (art. 1257.I CC), the agreement should not affect the rights or obligations of third parties such as the company and shareholders who are not parties to the agreement. Nevertheless, when all shareholders have signed the agreement, neither they nor the company can be held to be third parties. However, the problem remains that the grounds for challenging a resolution of the shareholders' meeting are legally restricted

**112** *Paz-Ares* Actualidad Jurídica Uría & Menéndez 5/2003, 22–26, following the solution proposed for German law by *Zutt* Einstwilliger Rechtsschutz bei Stimmbindungen, ZHR 155 (1991), 196–198.

**113** *Pérez Moriones* Los sindicatos de voto, 478–483; and especially *Paz-Ares* Actualidad Jurídica Uría & Menéndez 5/2003, 26–27, again similar to *Zutt* ZHR 155 (1991), 199–203.

**114** *Paz-Ares* Actualidad Jurídica Uría & Menéndez 5/2003, 28, such as the *Naturalrestitution* suggested by *K. Schmidt* in GmbHG, § 47 Rn. 60.

**115** See *Pérez Millán* in Contratos, 176–177.

with no reference at all to any breach of shareholders' agreements (art. 204 LSC)[116].

In the late 80's and early 90's, the Supreme Court acknowledged challenges to resolutions of shareholders' meetings adopted in contravention of shareholders' agreements between all shareholders using two arguments. In the first of two cases, a resolution was considered contrary to the bylaws through lifting the corporate veil with respect to a voting agreement[117]. In the second case, an agreement between all shareholders was held to be a unanimous resolution passed at an informal shareholders' meeting and a later resolution was deemed abusive and detrimental to the interest of the company[118].

Although the reasoning of the Supreme Court is open to criticism, those decisions have been widely held as acknowledging the right to challenge a resolution of shareholders' meeting on the basis of a breach of a shareholders' agreement signed by all shareholders[119]. Subsequently, research has focused on the possible effects on the company of such agreements, usually referred to as *omnilateral* agreements[120].

Almost two decades later, the Supreme Court rejected a challenge to several resolutions of shareholders' meetings alleged to have been passed due to breach of agreements between all the shareholders[121]. Some commentators took this to mean that resolutions of the shareholders' meeting could not be challenged on that basis[122]. Others criticised the decisions precisely for that same reason[123].

---

**116** See *Pérez Millán* in Contratos, 177 ff.

**117** STS 24/9/1987 (RJ 1987/6194).

**118** SSTS 26/2/1991 (RJ 1991/1600); 10/2/1992 (RJ 1992/1204).

**119** *Pérez Moriones* Los sindicatos de voto, 483–485; *Paz-Ares* Actualidad Jurídica Uría & Menéndez 5/2003, 33–35; *Alonso Ledesma* Diccionario de Derecho de Sociedades, 857; *Fernández del Pozo* RdS 29 (2008), 175; *Pérez Millán* RdS 31 (2008), 393. Spanish scholars usually refer to German case law (BGH 20/1/1983; 27/10/1986) or Austrian (OGH 5/12/1995; 11/3/1996; 26/8/1999) for a similar approach.

**120** For example *Sáez Lacave* InDret 3/2009, 1 ff.; *Noval Pato* Los pactos omnilaterales, *passim*. The expression has a German origin: *Noack* Gesellschaftervereinbarungen bei Kapitalgesellschaften, Tübingen, 1994, 33.

**121** SSTS 10/12/2008 (RJ 2009, 17); 5/3/2009 (RJ 2009, 1633); 6/3/2009 (RJ 2009, 2793); 6/3/2009 (RJ 2009, 2794).

**122** *Madridejos Fernández* La inoponibilidad de los pactos parasociales frente a la sociedad, CDC 53 (2010), 295–302; *Sánchez Álvarez* Sentencia de 5 de marzo de 2009: Pactos parasociales, CCJC 81 (2009), 1631, 1638.

**123** *Sáez Lacave* InDret 3/2009, 20. See also *Ruíz/Cámara/Torregrosa* Nuevamente a vueltas con la eficacia societaria de los pacos parasociales, Actualidad Jurídica Uría & Menéndez 24/2009, 68.

However, the Supreme Court had merely pointed out that the infraction of a shareholders' agreement is *not enough on its own* to challenge a resolution passed at the shareholders' meeting, it further being necessary for the resolution to be contrary to the law, the bylaws or the interests of the company as legally stated (art. 204 LSC)[124]. Indeed, it has been suggested that resolutions of the shareholders' meeting in violation of a shareholders' agreement between all shareholders would be detrimental to the interest of the company if that interest has been previously defined in the agreement[125].

It should come as no surprise that in recent times the Supreme Court has conceded the challenge to a resolution approving the annual accounts with regard to a shareholders' agreement subscribed to by all shareholders[126]. The resolution was deemed contrary to the law since the accounts did not show the right arising from the agreement for one shareholder to receive certain properties from the company. At least this decision shows that the Supreme Court is far from ignoring any relevance to the breach of shareholders' agreements in relation to the challenge of resolutions passed by the shareholders' meeting.

Further evidence of the importance of shareholders' agreements for corporate decisions can be found where the Supreme Court has lately denied a party to a shareholders' agreement between all shareholders, the right to challenge a resolution of the shareholders' meeting passed against what the bylaws stated but in accordance with the shareholders' agreement[127]. Challenging a resolution of the shareholders' meeting in that case has been held abusive or contrary to good faith according to the legal doctrine of estoppel[128].

---

**124** *Redondo Trigo* Los pactos parasociales y la impugnación de acuerdos sociales por su infracción tras la reciente jurisprudencia del Tribunal Supremo, RCDI 715 (2009), 2678–2685, 2689; *Pérez Moriones* Presupuestos y fundamento jurídico de la impugnación de acuerdos sociales por incumplimiento de pactos parasociales, RDBB 117 (2010), 241 (nota 1), 251–252; *Pérez Moriones* La necesaria revisión de los pactos parasociales omnilaterales o de todos los socios, Estudios Deusto 61/2 (2013), 18–22.

**125** *Paz-Ares* Actualidad Jurídica Uría & Menéndez 5/2003, 41; *Sáez Lacave* InDret 3/2009, 21–22; *Pérez Millán* RDBB 117 (2010), 254–256; *Noval Pato* Los pactos omnilaterales, 98–100, 138–139; *Pérez Moriones* Estudios Deusto 61/2 (2013), 290–292. A similar argument can be found in *Ehricke* Schuldvertragliche Nebenabreden, Heidelberg, 2004, 29–34, for German law; and in *Vavroski* Stimmbindungsverträge, Wien, 2000, 124–125, for Austrian law.

**126** STS 3/11/2014 (RJ 2014/5870).

**127** STS 25/2/2016 (RJ 2016/635). See also SAP Madrid (28th Section) 16/11/2012; RDGRN 26/10/1989.

**128** *Pérez Moriones* Una vez más sobre la eficacia de los pactos parasociales tras la STS de 25 de febrero de 2016, Revista Doctrinal Aranzadi Civil-Mercantil 5/2016, 167 ff.

In any case, other remedies of company law can hardly be extended to the breach of a shareholders' agreement. The violation of a shareholders' agreement does not generally affect the infractors' membership of the company[129]. As discussed earlier, to that end the bylaws could have included the performance of the agreement as an ancillary commitment (arts. 86, 89.2 and 350–351 LSC). More questionable seems whether it would be possible for the bylaws to simply provide for the exclusion of the shareholder who fails to honour the agreement even where the agreement was filed with the Mercantile Registry[130].

## V. Enforcement of Shareholders' Agreements

Apart from legal remedies, the enforcement of obligations or rights arising from shareholders' agreements could be provided by contractual clauses in the agreement. Different mechanisms are then available for the parties.

As an alternative to legal compensation for damages, shareholders' agreements may include liquidated damages or penalty clauses. According to Spanish law, both remedies are feasible. It is even possible that a clause could allow innocent parties to enforce a penalty and at the same time to claim damages (art. 1152 CC). A clause could permit as well, innocent parties to seek the specific performance of the contract along with the enforcement of the penalty (art. 1153)[131]. In addition to contractual penalties in the agreement, other penalties could be provided in the bylaws of the company, especially when they concern obligations arising from a family agreement filed with the Mercantile Registry (arts. 114.2.a and 175.2.a RRM)[132].

In any case, the performance of the penalty could be guaranteed with a pledge over the shares of the company held by each party to the agreement, but it is doubtful whether the penalty could allow for a transfer of the shares from the party in breach or if the pledge would be able to give innocent parties the right to acquire those shares[133]. In reality, other mechanisms exist that would produce similar effects.

---

**129** *Paz-Ares* Actualidad Jurídica Uría & Menéndez 5/2003, 37. For a different opinion, *Sáez Lacave* InDret 3/2009, 15–16; *Noval Pato* Los pactos omnilaterales, 120.

**130** In favour of that possibility, *Feliu Rey* Los pactos parasociales, 436–437.

**131** For penalties in shareholders' agreements, STS 27/9/1961 (RJ 1961/3029). See also *Paz-Ares* Actualidad Jurídica Uría & Menéndez 5/2003, 21–22; *Pérez Moriones* Los sindicatos de voto, 438–447; *Feliu Rey* Los pactos parasociales, 367 ff.

**132** *Fernández del Pozo* RdS 29 (2008), 165, 179–180.

**133** *Feliu Rey* Los pactos parasociales, 382–384, 387, 394, 398–399.

In that sense, and instead of including a clause allowing the innocent party to leave the company or for the party in breach to be expelled from the company, the breach of shareholders' agreements could trigger put or call options. The non-defaulting parties would usually be entitled to sell their shares (a put) or to buy the shares of the parties in default (a call) at a rate respectively above (in the case of a put) or below (in the case of a call) their market price or fair value[134].

Actual enforcement of shareholders' agreements in respect of tag-along or drag-along clauses may also be possible through put (tag-along) or call (drag-along) options with similar terms[135]. As discussed earlier, voting agreements are enforceable using different methods.

Since most legal or contractual remedies require any breach of a shareholders' agreement to be clearly and quickly stated, making use of ADR mechanisms in shareholders' agreements is the norm. In particular, according to Spanish law there is no problem admitting arbitration for the resolution of disputes on the interpretation or performance of shareholders' agreements, including agreements regarding the voting rights of the parties, since those are held to be rights they are free to dispose of[136]. Arbitration could be voluntarily agreed after the disputes have arisen or provided by the agreement through an arbitration clause (art. 9 LARB)[137]. The same could be said about mediation (art. 6 Ley 5/2012)[138].

## VI. Annexes

*Ley de Sociedades de Capital* **(LSC)**[139]

Article 29 *Reserved agreements*

Inter-partner or inter-shareholder agreements not included in the by-laws shall not be effective in respect of the company.

Article 530 *Shareholders' agreements in listed companies*

---

**134** *Paz-Ares* Actualidad Jurídica Uría & Menéndez 5/2003, 29. See also *Feliu Rey* Los pactos parasociales, 401.

**135** *Sáez Lacave/Bermejo Gutiérrez* Indret 1/2007, 9 – 10, 13. See also *Feliu Rey* Los pactos parasociales, 401 – 402.

**136** See *Pérez Moriones* Los sindicatos de voto, 450 – 451, commenting on the difference to the problems faced by Italian law.

**137** Ley 60/2003, de 23 de diciembre, de Arbitraje (LARB).

**138** Ley 5/2012, de 6 de julio, de mediación en asuntos civiles y mercantiles (Ley 5/2012).

**139** Translation by the Spanish Ministry of Justice.

1. For the present intents and purposes, shareholders' agreements are understood to be agreements that regulate the exercise of voting rights at general meetings or restrict or condition the free transferability of shares in listed joint stock companies.

2. The provisions hereunder shall also be applicable to agreements with the same aims referring to convertible or exchangeable bonds issued by listed joint stock companies.

Article 531 *Public record and disclosure of shareholders' agreements*

1. The adoption, extension and disclosure of shareholders' agreements on voting rights in general meetings or that restrict or condition the free transferability of shares or convertible or exchangeable bonds in listed joint stock companies must be immediately reported to the company itself and to the National Securities Market Commission.

Attached to such notice shall be a copy of the clauses of the document containing the provisions that affect the right to vote or restrict or condition the free transferability of shares or convertible or exchangeable bonds.

2. After the notice is served, the document containing the shareholders' agreement must be field with the Mercantile Registry where the company is registered.

3. The shareholders' agreement must be made public as relevant information.

Article 532 *Legal capacity to publicly disclose shareholders' agreements*

1. Any of the signatories of the shareholders' agreements shall be capacitated to serve the aforementioned notices and deposit the agreement, even where the agreement itself specifically appoints one of them or a third party to take such measures.

2. In shares held in usufruct or pledged, whoever holds the right to vote shall also be capacitated to publicly disclose the foregoing in respect thereof.

Article 533 *Consequences of failure to publicly disclose shareholders' agreements*

Until the respective notices are served, entry in the Registry effected and the announcement as relevant information published, shareholders' agreements shall no have no effect whatsoever on the matters to which they refer.

Article 534 *Inter-shareholder agreements in companies controlling a listed company*

The provisions of the preceding articles shall apply to agreements between partners or shareholders of a company that controls a listed company.

Article 535 *Temporary exemption from public disclosure obligations*

Where public disclosure may be severely detrimental to a company, the National Securities Market Commission, at the behest of the parties concerned, may adopt a substantiated decision to refrain from disclosing all or part of a shareholders' agreement of which it has been notified. Such ruling shall exempt the company itself from the obligation to disclose the agreement, deposit the respective document in the Mercantile Registry and publish it as a relevant information. The Commission shall also establish the time during which the information may be kept secret by the parties concerned.

Rolf Dotevall

# Sweden

**Table of Content**



## A. Nature of Corporate Regulation

Shareholders' agreements are common in Swedish companies. The purpose is to achieve a protection of interests, to regulate decision-making activities on the shareholders meeting in the first place and to regulate transfer of shares.

There are no specific provisions in the Swedish Companies Act[1] or other legislation concerning shareholders' agreements. This doesn't mean that there is no statutory law applicable on this kind of agreements.

Shareholders' agreements are focused on company matters. As a main rule, the provisions in the Swedish Companies Act are mandatory. It is possible to deviate from a provision in the act only when it is explicitly provided.

Swedish Companies Act has a doctrinal concept of the possibility for shareholders to amend the provisions in the articles of association. An alteration of the articles in a private as well as in a public company needs, according to

1 Aktiebolagslag (2005:551).

**Prof. Dr. Rolf Dotevall,** University of Gothenburg

https://doi.org/10.1515/9783110517026-024

Ch. 7 sec. 42–43 Companies Act, a support from shareholders holding not less than two-thirds of both the votes cast and the shares represented at the general meeting. If an alteration of the articles entails a reduction of shareholders' rights to the company's profits, restrictions on the right to transfer or acquire shares in the company or changes in the relationship between shares it must be supported by all of the shareholders who are present at the general meeting. The present shareholders must together represent not less than nine-tenths of all shares in the company.

## B. Regulation of Shareholders' Agreements

The general contract law is applicable on shareholders' agreements. There are few cases from the Swedish Supreme court concerning shareholders' agreements as such. However, the case law concerning contracts is extensive and relevant for shareholders' agreements.

Shareholders' agreements are permitted in Swedish law. This kind of agreements does not have to be admitted by the shareholders meeting or expressly allowed in the articles of association to be valid.

A shareholders' agreement is a contract between two or more shareholders with no formal requirements; it can be written or oral. Shareholders' agreements are, as other contracts were the contractual parties have an obligation to promote a specific common purpose, typically classified as simple partnerships, *enkla bolag* (Gesellschaft bürgerlichen Rechts, société civil). A simple partnership is regulated in Chapter 4 of the Partnership Act from 1980.[2]

A simple partnership is formed as soon as two or more natural persons have agreed to cooperate for a common purpose. The provisions in this regulation are optional. A simple partnership is a contractual relationship between two or more partners and do not have to be registered in a trade register. In general, there are no restrictions on the duration of a shareholders' agreement. It exists for the time period which is stipulated in the agreement. An agreement of this kind can be concluded for an indefinite period of time. In this situation, each partner has the right to terminate the agreement any time without any specific reason. The agreement should then terminate within six month.[3]

If the shareholders' agreement is concluded for a fixed time period, each party has the right to terminate the agreement when a party has essentially ne-

2 Lag (1980:1102) om handelsbolag och enkla bolag.
3 See Ch. 2 sec. 24 lag om handelsbolag och enkla bolag.

glected his or her obligations under the agreement or if there is any other important ground for termination of the agreement.[4] It should be added that a shareholders' agreement may have been entered into for a specific temporary purpose, but without any specific date being given in the agreement. In this case, the contract is concluded for a fixed period.

A shareholders' agreement is for a limited company. In a partnership, the contract between all the partners is the fundament for this type of organization. According to the Swedish Partnership Act, the regulation concerning decision making, profit voluntary with the exception that each partner has a right to supervise the company's affairs.[5] In theory, it is possible for some of the partners in a partnership to make an agreement how to govern the company's affairs if they are for example in a minority position. There is no distinction between public or private companies regarding shareholders' agreements.

It is likely that these kind of agreements are common in companies with a limited number of shareholders. For companies with two shareholders owning half of the shares each, a shareholders' agreement is essential. The Swedish Companies Act does not have specific rules for this situation. The risk for a dead-lock is obvious if there is no shareholders' agreement with focus on the governance of the company.

## C. International or cross border Shareholders' Agreements

Most cooperation agreements of commercial character, such as shareholders' agreements, with an international dimension do normally have a choice of law clause. Article 3 in Rome I-Regulation[6] prescribes that the choice of law the contracting parties has done should be respected. This regulation is applicable also on shareholders' agreements.

According to art. 1(1) the Rome I-Regulation shall apply to contractual obligations. Art. 1(2)(f) of the regulation excludes questions governed by the laws of companies such as the internal organization. A simple partnership – *enkelt bolag*

4 See Ch. 2 sec. 25 lag om handelsbolag och enkla bolag.

5 See Ch. 2 sec. 1–4 and sec. 6–16 lag om handelsbolag och enkla bolag.

6 The Rome Convention on the Law Applicable to Contractual Obligations, concluded on June 19 1980 [1980] O.J. L266/1.

– is not a company in this context. This means that the Rome I-Regulation is applicable on shareholders' agreements.[7]

As I mentioned above, according to art. 3 in the Rome I-Regulation the main rule is that a contract shall be governed by the law chosen by the parties. A limitation of the freedom to choose applicable law shall occur, according to art. 3(3) of the Regulation, when all other elements relevant to the situation at the time of the choice are located in another country than the country which law has been chosen; the choice of the parties shall not prejudice the application of provisions of the law of that other country which cannot be derogated from by agreement.

# D. Forms of Shareholders' Agreements

## I. Shareholders' Agreements on Shareholders' Rights

Agreements between shareholders regarding voting rights do not have any limitation concerning contractual aspects. However, there are some restraints in the company law. A clear and undisputed rule in Swedish law is that a shareholders' agreement doesn't have any effect on the company. This is called the principle of separation.[8] This means that a decision on the general meeting cannot be declared void based on the reason that it violates a shareholders' agreement.

A Swedish private and public companies have a hierarchic organization. The board of directors and other company bodies are obliged to comply with instructions from the general meeting. An instruction is void, according to Ch. 8 sec. 41 Companies Act, if it is in violation of the Companies Act, the applicable annual reports legislation, or expressly allowed in the articles of association. If an instruction does not compel to a shareholders' agreement, it is irrelevant.

When it comes to a voting trust, it can be concluded that according to Swedish company law the rule is that the right to vote cannot be split from the ownership of the share, with an exception in family law. It is however possible for the owner of a share to have a proxy.

The minority protection rules in the Swedish Companies Act require in general that at least ten percent of the shareholders are supporting, for example, a derivative suit with a purpose to make a member of the board liable. The ten per-

7 Se *Dotevall* Samarbete i bolag, 3 uppl., 2015, s. 152.

8 See *Arvidsson* Aktieägaravtal. Särskilt om besluts- och överlåtelsebindningar, 2010, pp. 239 and *Dotevall* Samarbete i bolag, 3 uppl. 2015, pp. 126.

cent limit applies on both private and public companies. If a single shareholder does not own ten percent of the share, it is possible for him to make an agreement with other shareholders to achieve the ten percent threshold.

The concepts of parent company, subsidiary and groups are found in 1 Ch. 11 Companies Act. The definition in the Companies Act 2005 and the annual reports legislation is based on the seventh company law directive from June 15th, 1983.[9] A Swedish limited company, as a main rule, is a parent company and another, domestic or foreign, legal person is a subsidiary where the company holds more than one-half of the voting rights of all shares or interests.

According to 1 Ch. 11 § 1 p. Companies Act a Swedish company is also a parent company if the company owns shares or interests in a legal person, and, as a consequence of an agreement with other owners of such legal persons, controls more than half of the voting rights of all shares or interests in the legal person. A certain threshold for the number of shares or interests the company must own is not stipulated. It is enough to own a single share in the company.

If a Swedish company owns shares or interests in a legal person, foreign or domestic, and is according to a shareholders' agreement entitled to appoint or remove more than one-half of the members of its board of directors or equivalent management body, it will be regarded as a parent company according to Swedish company law.

## II. Shareholders' Agreements and the Transfer of Shares

The main rule for both private and public companies is found in Ch. 4 sec. 7 Companies Act. It stipulates that shares may be freely transferable, unless otherwise provided in the articles of association.

It is possible to include a clause in the articles of association of a company which is not a CSD[10] company pursuant to which, one or more shares may be transferred to a new owner only subject to the company's consent (consent clause).

According to Ch. 4 sec. 9 Companies Act a consent clause shall state whether the general meeting or the board of director shall consider a request for consent. If the general meeting shall consider a request for consent, this shall be an issue which requires a consent of a simple majority of the votes cast. In the event of a

9 The Councils seventh directive 83/349/EEG.
10 Central Securities Depository.

tied vote, the chairman shall have the casting vote. No other alternatives are possible if the consent should be made by the general meeting.

Another possibility to limit the transfer of shares in the articles of association is, according to Ch. 4 sec. 18 Companies Act, a right of first refusal clause. This kind of clause is possible for a company which is not a CSD company. This is a kind of clause pursuant to which a shareholder or other party shall be invited to purchase a share before it is transferred to a new owner.

The basic principle in Swedish company law of free transferability of shares had, until about ten years ago, only one exception. For a long period of time the only possibility to include in the articles of association a clause pursuant to which a shareholder or other person shall be entitled to purchase a share which has been transferred. Then it was important to have a shareholders' agreement to limit the transfer of shares.

Even if the Companies Act now also allows consent clauses and rights of first refusal, it is still common to have restrictions of the free transferability of shares in shareholders' agreements. It is possible to modify the rules in the companies act restricting the free transferability of share as long as this is not unfair for a shareholder. This means that drag along clauses are valid according to Swedish company law. This kind of a clause makes it possible for those who consider buying a majority of the shares in a company to also have the possibility to also buy the shares from minority shareholders to the same conditions. A drag along clause has the purpose to protect interest of a majority shareholder.

A tag along provision has the opposite effect to the drag along provision and is also valid in Swedish law. If the majority shareholders wants to sell shares to a third party, and does not provide notice to the other shareholders, the tag along provisions will enable the minority shareholder to tag along with the majority shareholder and sell its shares on the same terms and conditions.

## III. Shareholders' Agreements in pre-insolvency situation

When a company's financial situation is weak and declining, shareholders have a possibility to make a contribution of assets or cash. This contribution can be stipulated with the condition that the company should pay back the same amount of cash when the financial situation is good enough. The shareholders agree to vote for a dividend to the shareholder who has done the contribution.

This kind of agreement is applicable in bankruptcy averting. This is often done in practice to avoid the effects of the Swedish rules in 25 Ch. 13–20 Companies Act which state that the directors have an obligation to prepare a balance sheet for liquidation purpose when there are reason to believe that the company's shareholders' equity is less than one half of the registered share capital. The minimum share capital for private company is 50 000 Swedish kronor (around 5500 €).

If the balance sheet for liquidation purposes shows that the company's equity has reached this threshold, it is necessary for the board of directors to issue a notice as soon as possible to attend a general meeting. At this meeting, it is possible for the shareholders to decide to continue the company's business even if the economic situation has not improved.

A second general meeting for liquidation purpose must be held within six months of the initial meeting. If the company's shareholders' equity is not equal to the registered share capital at this time, the members of the board of directors shall be jointly and severally liable for such obligations as incurred if the company continues to do business.

To avoid personal liability or the obligation to liquidate the company a common practice is to contribute with cash or other assets to improve the company's shareholders' equity to the level of the registered share capital. If they give a loan, the balance sheet will still show the same relation between the registered share capital and the company's shareholders equity and if the economic situation has not improved as stated in the Companies Act.

# E. Legal Effects of Shareholders' Agreement

## I. Legal Effect on the Corporation

As I mentioned before, Swedish law applies a separation principle which means that a shareholders' agreement does not have any influence on company law. This rule cannot be circumvented if the company itself becomes a party in a shareholders' agreement. It is regarded as an infringement of the Companies Act if the company is a party in a shareholders' agreement.

The function of the board of directors and other company bodies according to the company statute, cannot be changed in that kind of agreements. Another consequence of the principle of separation is that it is not admissible to stipulate that shareholders, according to a shareholders' agreement, should agree on the appointment of directors or managing director (*verkställande direktör*) or to other changes in the capital or organizational structure in general.

Another consequence of this separation is that the shareholders' agreement does not have any impact on the interpretation of the articles of association. The interpretation of the articles should be done in the same way as the interpretation of the companies act. The interpretation of a shareholders' agreement follows the rule in contract law to decide what the agreement means for the contracting parties.

Shareholders' agreements are according to Swedish law only relevant for limited companies (*aktiebolag*) but not for partnerships. A characteristic for a partnership is that the foundation for the cooperation among two or more persons is a contract. The rules regulating the company's internal affairs are non-mandatory, with one exception. This is the right for each partner to supervise the company's activities. In comparison, there are no differences between private and public companies concerning shareholders' agreements. However, these kind of agreements are more common in private companies.

## II. Shareholders' Agreements on the Constitution of the Company

A violation of a shareholders' agreement does not affect the membership of the company for the shareholder who violated the agreement. In this situation only the remedies in contract law could be used.

According to Ch. 7 sec. 50 – 52 Companies Act a shareholder may bring proceedings against the company before a court to set aside or amend a resolution of a general meeting, if it has not been adopted in due order or otherwise contravenes this Act, the applicable annual reports legislation or the articles of association. Such proceedings are not possible if a clause in a shareholders' agreement is violated. This means that if a decision at the general meeting is in violation of a shareholders' agreement it cannot be set aside or amended by a court.

This limitation of the influence of a shareholders' agreement has the effect that a provision in the agreement regarding how to appoint or remove the members of the board could be violated without any possibility to bring proceedings against the company for the court to set aside the election of a board member. Ch. 8 sec. 8 Swedish Companies Act allows that one or two members of the board of directors may be appointed in another manner then by the general meeting. The articles of association may stipulate, that one or more members of the board shall be appointed by, for example, a shareholder or a person outside the company.

The interpretation of a clause in the articles of association is different from the interpretation of contracts in general. The article of association should be interpreted in the same way as the rules in the Companies Act. As a consequence of the fact that the shareholders' agreement does not have any implications on the company law, it is not recommendable to interpret the articles of association in the light of a shareholders' agreement.[11] This is a consequence of the principle of separation.[12] If the shareholders' agreement makes a reference to a clause in the articles of association, it should be interpreted in the same way as the shareholders' agreement because it is a part of the agreement.[13]

## III. Legal Effects on the Shareholders

In Swedish law, a person who acquires shares from someone who is bound by a shareholders' agreement will be a contracting party if he or she is aware of the shareholders' agreement.[14] It is not necessary to register shareholders' agreements or make them public. There are no formal requirements for this type of contracts. Even an oral agreement is binding. The consequences of a breach of a shareholders' agreement are the same as breaking any other contract. The sanctions are: invalidity of the contract, damage and, if it is a contract term, a penalty.

**11** See *Arvidsson* Aktieägaravtal. Särskilt om besluts- och överlåtelsebindningar, 2010, pp. 264.
**12** See *Arvidsson* Aktieägaravtal. Särskilt om besluts- och överlåtelsebindningar, 2010, pp.
**13** See the Supreme Court case NJA 1964 s. 422 and *Arvidsson* Aktieägaravtal. Särskilt om besluts- och överlåtelsebindningar, pp. 266.
**14** See *Dotevall* Samarbete i bolag, 3 uppl. 2015, p. 128.

Michael A. Meer

# Switzerland

**Table of Content**



## I. Nature of Corporate Law Regulation

As per its liberal foundations, Swiss corporate law is, in principle, of **dispositive** nature.[1] Statutory corporate law[2] does provide for default rules, from which a corporation may deviate, unless a statutory rule has mandatory character. Of mandatory character are the rules on the fundamental organization of the corporation, on capital protection, on fundamental shareholders' rights (including mechanisms for minority protection) and on accounting and statutory audits.[3] Therefore, a Swiss corporation has a certain discretion regarding its own organization and governance. Members of Swiss corporations can thus draft their corporate charter (articles of association, *Statuten*) and enter into shareholders'

1 *Christoph Bühler* Zwingendes Aktienrecht: Rechtfertigungsgründe und Alternativen, in: Zeitschrift für Gesellschafts- und Kapitalmarktrecht GesKR 2013, p. 541 et seq.
2 Swiss corporate law is part of the Swiss Code of Obligations, CO.
3 For a recent concise analysis, see *Bühler* op. cit.

**Dr. Michael A. Meer,** LL.M. (NYU), Sirius Legal, Bern

https://doi.org/10.1515/9783110517026-025

agreements according to their needs within the boundaries of mandatory law. This means that a company's articles of association may deviate from statutory corporate law, or complement the legal framework in matters for which corporate law does not provide a default solution. Since per mandatory law a member of a share corporation (*Aktiengesellschaft*) may not be required, not even under the articles of association, to contribute more than the subscription price set on issue[4], shareholders' agreements are of particular importance when it comes to arranging for additional duties and obligations of shareholders.[5]

On the other hand, corporations listed on a Swiss stock exchange[6] have far less discretion in their own organization and governance, with Federal law[7] and self-regulation with mandatory character (such as the Listing Rules issued by SIX Swiss Exchange) imposing a comprehensive set of additional rules.

With regard to shareholders' agreements, Swiss law strictly **distinguishes** between the **corporate** and the **contractual levels.** A shareholders' agreement will always have solely contractual effects among the parties, and does not create any membership rights vis-à-vis the company[8]. Consequently, a company is and cannot be bound by the shareholders' agreement[9], votes cast in a shareholders' meeting in breach of a shareholders' agreement are still valid as cast, and the dissolution of a company does not automatically terminate the shareholders' agreement.[10]

---

**4** Art. 680 para. 1 CO; *von Büren/Hintz* Die Aktiengesellschaft als Partei eines Aktionärbindungsvertrags?, in: Zeitschrift des bernischen Juristenvereins ZBJV 136 (2000), p. 802 et seq. Notably (and other than the quotaholder in a limited liability company), the shareholder has no duty of loyalty with regard to the company.

**5** *Baudenbacher* Basler Kommentar Obligationenrecht, 5th ed., Basel 2016, Art. 620 N 36.

**6** I.e. SIX Swiss Stock Exchange (Zurich) or BX Berne eXchange (Berne).

**7** E.g. the Federal Ordinance against Excessive Compensation of November 20, 2013 (commonly dubbed "Minder Rules", after the member of the national parliament who launched the constitutional initiative and public vote on these new rules). The Ordinance does not only give the shareholders of a listed company a right to vote on compensation matters for the board of directors and the executive management, but also imposes certain rules on corporate governance (e.g. annual re-election of board members).

**8** *Baudenbacher.* cit., Art 620 N 37; *Forstmoser/Küchler* Aktionärbindungsverträge, Zürich 2015, N 113 et seq.

**9** See below, sub III.1.

**10** *Forstmoser/Küchler* op. cit., N 116.

# II. Regulation of Shareholders' Agreements

Switzerland does not have any special **legislation** for shareholders' agreements, and no specific regulation on international or cross-border shareholders' agreements. For issues around applicable law, place of jurisdiction and enforcement of foreign judgements, the general rules on international private law are applicable, in particular the 2007 Convention on jurisdiction and the recognition and enforcement of judgments in civil and commercial matters (Lugano Convention) and the Federal Act on International Private Law of 18 December 1987. Also, published case law on shareholders' agreements is quite scarce. The Swiss Federal Supreme Court has, so far, handled only very few **leading cases** with issues specific to shareholders' agreements. It held that, as a principle, shareholders' agreements regarding voting rights (including a blocking clause) were permissible within the general principles of contract law.[11] Not permissible are, therefore, however agreements which aim at circumventing rules which are set forth in the articles of association (*in casu* transfer restrictions).[12]

Consequently, the rules of **contract law** are applicable. Typically, shareholders' agreements qualify either as a **simple partnership** (*einfache Gesellschaft*)[13], or as a **contract *sui generis***, combining elements of different types of contracts. If the shareholders aim at joint concerted actions (e.g. regarding voting rights or share transfers), the agreement qualifies as a simple partnership. Where the parties to a shareholders' agreement have opposing (instead of parallel) interests and no *animus societatis*, the shareholders' agreement qualifies as a two- or multiparty relationship of (synallagmatic) contractual nature.[14] Given that securing joint concerted actions among shareholders is the primary motive for shareholders to enter into an agreement, the vast majority of shareholders' agreements will qualify as a simple partnership.[15]

If the shareholders' agreement qualifies as a simple partnership, and unless agreed otherwise in the shareholders' agreement, the default statutory rules of Art. 530 et seq. CO apply to the parties. These rules comprise the relationship be-

---

**11** Swiss Federal Supreme Court, BGE 88 II 172 (1962).

**12** Swiss Federal Supreme Court, BGE 109 II 43 (1983).

**13** Art. 530 et seq. CO

**14** *Forstmoser/Küchler* op. cit., N 174.

**15** Interestingly, the Swiss Federal Supreme Court has held that in a Private Equity environment, there is usually no joint concerted action (but rather primarily a financing of the counterpart by investors for remuneration), and a typical Private Equity shareholders' agreement would, therefore, not qualify as a simple partnership, Swiss Supreme Court Decision No. 4C.214/2003 of 21 November 2003.

tween the partners (contributions, profit and loss sharing, partnership resolutions, management of the partnership business, liability between partners, etc.), the relationship between partners and third parties (representation and liability), and the dissolution of the partnership. Consequently, shareholders' agreements need to be drafted carefully and in knowledge of the statutory rules. Otherwise the parties risk facing default legal solutions which may not be in line with their actual interests.

Shareholders' agreements are generally permitted. An **authorization** of the agreement in the articles of association or by the shareholders' meeting is neither required nor even possible under Swiss law.

There are no specific statutory restrictions on the **duration** of shareholders' agreements. Therefore, shareholders' agreements may be entered into for a definite term (e. g. for the duration of the corporation) or an indefinite term (usually with a right to terminate with a defined notice period[16]).

While a shareholders' agreement, in a strict sense, designates a contract by and among the owners of shares (*Aktien*) in a share corporation (*Aktiengesellschaft, AG*) according to art. 620 et seq. CO (the most common form of a corporation in Switzerland), members of legal entities in other forms may enter into agreements to the same effect. For example, quota holders in a limited liability company (*Gesellschaft mit beschränkter Haftung, GmbH*) can adhere to a quota holders' agreement similar to a shareholders' agreement. Partnerships such a general partnership (*Kollektivgesellschaft*, Art. 552 et seq. CO) or a limited partnership (*Kommanditgesellschaft*, art. 594 et seq. CO) on the other hand are *per se* contractual in nature (with a set of default statutory rules), and consequently there is no need for an additional layer of rules in the form of a separate agreement.

Shareholders' agreements are, in general, not subject to any specific requirements regarding **formality.** While they can validly be entered into as oral agreements, shareholders' agreements are usually put in writing for obvious evidence purposes, and also contain a clause requiring any amendments to be made in writing in order to be valid. If the shareholders' agreement contains clauses which according to Swiss law require a special form such as notarisation, the pertinent parts of the shareholders' agreement need to be entered into observing

16 If the shareholders' agreement is entered into for an indefinite term and does not contain a specific termination clause, Swiss law allows terminating the Agreement ordinarily with a six months' notice period, *Forstmoser/Küchler* op cit., N 1844 et seq.

this special form. This concerns, in particular, stipulations involving real estate, marriage and inheritance law.[17]

# III. Forms of Shareholders' Agreements

## 1. Shareholders' Agreements on Shareholder Rights

Within the general boundaries of mandatory law, the parties to a shareholders' agreement are free to tailor agreements regarding **voting rights** according to their own needs[18]. In its simplest form, the voting agreement would require the parties to cast their vote in a shareholders' meeting of the company according to the agreements in the shareholders' agreement and to instruct their representatives accordingly. Alternatively, the shareholders' agreement could also provide for e.g. a voting according to specific instructions by a third party, or a voting according to a resolution taken by the parties of the shareholders' agreement prior to a specific shareholders' meeting.

Shareholders exercise their voting rights at general meetings of shareholders in proportion to the total nominal value of the shares belonging to them[19], but the articles of association may contain restrictions on the voting rights of shareholders and their rights to appoint representatives[20]. Stipulations in shareholders' agreements which circumvent these restrictions are void[21].

Given the strict separation of the corporate and contractual levels (see above, sub I.), a vote in a (valid) shareholders' meeting will be valid as it was cast, even if by doing so the shareholder violates a valid shareholders' agreement. The other shareholders have no recourse under corporate law; they can only claim damages (if any) from the violating shareholder (see below, sub V.).

Arguably, a company may not be part of a shareholders' agreement if that agreement contains obligations which relate to the rights of the other parties as shareholders of that company – which a Shareholders' Agreement typically does[22]. The company should not have any legal ground to control the formation

**17** Stipulations involving marriage and inheritance law (and thus requiring notarization) are quite common in the form of clauses regarding the transfer of shares upon death or divorce of one of the parties.

**18** *Länzliger* Basler Kommentar Obligationenrecht, 5th ed., Basel 2016, Art. 692 N 10.

**19** Art. 692 para.1

**20** Art. 692 para 2, Art. 627 no. 10 CO.

**21** *Länzliger* op. cit., Art. 692 N 12; *Forstmoser/Küchler* op. cit., N 795.

**22** See *von Büren/Hintz* op. cit., p. 802 et seq., for a concise analysis.

of its own corporate will, as this is an unalienable competence of the shareholders[23]. Consequently, while the shareholders may bind themselves in a shareholders' agreement, they may **not bind the company** with regard to any corporate matters.

With regard to the **financing** of the company, shareholders' agreements entered into prior to the incorporation of the company usually contain the obligation of the parties to subscribe for a certain number of shares at a defined subscription price, and to pay the aggregate subscription amount into the specific capital contribution account of the company-in-formation. Moreover, a shareholders' agreement may contain clauses with additional (*pro-rata*) payment liabilities for the parties in pre-defined cases (e. g. upon achievement of certain milestones in the business), or the obligation to participate (*pro-rata*) in financial restructuring measures in case of an overindebtedness of the company (see below, sub. 4). Such additional financial covenants may pertain to equity (in a capital increase, or a non-repayable contributions *à fonds perdu*) or debt (in the form of a shareholder loan).

Swiss law does not have a specific codified corporate **law of groups** ("*Konzernrecht*"), and regulates groups of companies specifically only with regard to accounting: If a legal entity that is required to file financial reports controls one or more undertakings that are required to file financial reports, the entity must prepare consolidated annual accounts in the annual report for all the undertakings controlled[24]. A legal entity controls another undertaking if it

- directly or indirectly holds a majority of votes in the highest management body;
- directly or indirectly has the right to appoint or remove a majority of the members of the supreme management or administrative body; or
- it is able to exercise a controlling influence based on the articles of association, the foundation deed, a contract or comparable instruments[25].

While it is thus possible to create a group of companies ("*Konzern*") contractually by way of a shareholders' agreement with covenants on voting rights, it is not a very common form[26].

---

23 *von Büren/Hintz* op. cit., p. 807; *Böckli* Schweizer Aktienrecht, 4th ed., Zurich 2009, N 578 et seq.

24 Art. 963 para. 1 CO.

25 Art. 963 para. 2 CO.

26 *Forstmoser/Küchler* op. cit., N 58 with references.

Swiss law does not provide for **voting trusts** in the Anglo-Saxon form[27]. However, shareholders may agree to transfer their shares to a third party on a fiduciary basis[28]. The fiduciary becomes the legal owner of these shares, and as such may be recognized as the shareholder vis-à-vis the company[29]. The fiduciary can be, and usually is, obliged to exercise the voting rights of the shares in accordance with stipulations of the shareholders' agreement. This allows the parties of the shareholders' agreement to enforce agreements on voting rights with an effect similar to an Anglo-Saxon voting trust.

## 2. Shareholders' Agreements on the (Limitation for the) Transfer of Shares

Restrictions on the transferability of **registered shares** (*Namenaktien*) by corporate law (*Vinkulierung*) are limited. Swiss law recognizes only one statutory restriction, and only certain specific further restrictions may be included in the articles of association:

- **Statutory restrictions.** Registered shares that have not yet been fully paid up may be transferred only with the consent of the company, unless they are acquired by inheritance, division of estate, matrimonial property law or compulsory execution[30].
- **Restrictions in the articles of association.** The articles of association may stipulate that the transfer of registered shares requires the consent of the company[31]. The law differentiates between transfer restrictions for private and public companies:
  - *Private Companies:* The company may refuse to give such consent providing it states good cause cited in the articles of association or offers to acquire the shares from the party alienating them for the company's

27 Switzerland has ratified, though, the Hague Convention of 1 July 1985 on the Law Applicable to Trusts and on their Recognition, based on which foreign voting trusts may be recognized in Switzerland.

28 *Forstmoser/Küchler* op. cit., N 1657 et seq.

29 If the shares are bearer shares, the fiduciary solely has to show possession of the shares, art. 689a para. 2 CO. If the shares are registered shares, the fiduciary has to request entry into the share register for which the company may request evidence on the assignment of the shares (including the endorsement of the share certificates), Art. 684 para. 2 CO.

30 Art. 685 para. 1 CO. The company may, however, withhold consent only if the solvency of the acquirer is in doubt and the security requested by the company is not furnished, Art. 685 para. 2 CO.

31 Art. 685a CO. Consenting to a share transfer is a competence of the board of directors.

own account, for the account of other shareholders or for the account of third parties at their real value at the time the request was made. Provisions governing the composition of the shareholder group which are designed to safeguard the pursuit of the company's objects or its economic independence are deemed to constitute good cause. Further, the company may refuse entry in the share register where the acquirer fails to declare expressly that he has acquired the shares in his own name and for his own account[32]. Where the consent required for transfer of shares is not given, the ownership of the shares and all attendant rights remain with the alienator.[33]
- *Companies listed on a stock exchange:* In the case of listed registered shares, the company may refuse to accept the acquirer as a shareholder only where the articles of association envisage a percentage limit on the registered shares for which an acquirer must be recognised as shareholder and such limit is exceeded. Further, the company may refuse entry in the share register where at the company's request the acquirer fails to declare expressly that he has acquired the shares in his own name and for his own account[34]. Where listed registered shares are acquired on a stock exchange, the attendant rights pass to the acquirer on transfer. Where listed registered shares are acquired off-exchange, the attendant rights pass to the acquirer as soon as he has submitted a request for recognition as shareholder to the company. Until such recognition of the acquirer by the company, he may not exercise the voting right conferred by the shares or any other rights associated with such voting right. The acquirer is not restricted in his exercise of any other shareholder rights, in particular subscription rights. Acquirers not yet recognised by the company are entered as shareholders without voting rights in the share register once the rights have been transferred. The corresponding shares are deemed to be unrepresented at the general meeting[35].

As these provisions do not adequately cover the needs of shareholders to effectively control the composition of a company's shareholder base, the stipulation

---

**32** Art. 685b CO.
**33** Art. 685c CO. Special rules apply for transfers by inheritance, division of estate, matrimonial property law or compulsory execution, Art. 685b para. 4 and Art. 685c para. 2 CO.
**34** Art. 685d CO. Special rules apply for transfers by inheritance, division of estate, matrimonial property law or compulsory execution, Art. 685d para. 3 CO.
**35** Art. 685f CO.

of further restrictions on the transferability of registered shares in a shareholders' agreement is of particular importance.

Even more important is the inclusion of contractual transfer restrictions with regard to **bearer shares** (*Inhaberaktien*). By law, ownership in bearer shares is transferred by the handing over the physical share certificate to the acquirer (or by signing of a deed of assignment if the shares are not issued on paper)[36]. As a consequence, the statutory transfer restrictions as explained above do not extend to bearer shares. Therefore, shareholders in a company with bearer shares who wish to restrict the transfer of the shares need to include any and all such restrictions in the shareholders' agreement. Moreover, the establishment of a share escrow for the duration of the shareholders' agreement is imperative if adherence to the transfer restrictions is to be secured effectively.

What regards the **forms of contractual transfer restrictions**, all forms commonly seen in shareholders agreements are permissible under Swiss law, i.e. pre-emptive rights, rights of first refusal, call and put options, as well as drag along and tag along clauses. Unlike statutory restrictions, or restrictions contained in the articles of association, these contractual transfer restrictions have effect only among the parties of the shareholders' agreement and do notably not extent to third parties (e.g. a new acquirer of shares). Absent any default statutory rules, the parties should define the mechanisms for the determination of the transfer price as well as for the exercise of these rights (timeframe, payment terms etc.).

## 3. Shareholders' Agreements on the Constitution of the Corporation

The ability of shareholders to change the company's **organizational structure** is limited. Corporate law arranges for the fundamental structure of a share corporation with a clear allocation of competences to the general shareholders' meeting (*Generalversammlung*) on the one hand and the board of directors (*Verwaltungsrat*) on the other hand. The general shareholders' meeting is the supreme governing body of a corporation[37]. The board of directors, elected by the shareholders' meeting, may pass resolutions on all matters not reserved to the general meeting by law or the articles of association and manages the business of the

36 Art. 978 CO.

37 Art. 698 para. 1 CO.

company, unless responsibility for such management has been delegated to an executive team[38].

The following items are **inalienable powers of the shareholders' meeting** as the company's supreme body and may not be transferred to the board of directors[39]:

- to determine and amend the articles of association;
- to elect the members of the board of directors and the external auditors;
- to approve the management report and the consolidated accounts;
- to approve the annual accounts and resolutions on the allocation of the disposable profit, and in particular to set the dividend and the shares of profits paid to board members;
- to discharge the members of the board of directors;
- to pass resolutions concerning the matters reserved to the general meeting by law (e. g. changes in capital) or the articles of association.

Inversely, the **board of directors** has a number of **non-transferable and inalienable duties** which may not be assumed by the shareholders[40]. These duties comprise:

- the overall management of the company and the issuing of all necessary directives;
- determination of the company's organisation;
- the organisation of the accounting, financial control and financial planning systems as required for management of the company;
- the appointment and dismissal of persons entrusted with managing and representing the company;
- overall supervision of the persons entrusted with managing the company, in particular with regard to compliance with the law, articles of association, operational regulations and directives;
- compilation of the annual report, preparation for the general meeting and implementation of its resolutions;
- notification of the court in the event that the company is overindebted[41].

---

**38** Art. 716 CO.

**39** Art. 698 para. 2 CO.

**40** As pointed out, the articles of association may, however, authorize the board of directors to delegate the management of all or part of the company's business to individual members or third parties in accordance with its (internal) organizational regulations, Art. 716/716b CO.

**41** Art. 716a para. 1CO. For listed companies, the composition of the compensation report is an additional non-transferable and inalienable duty, Art. 5 Federal Ordinance against Excessive Compensation.

A shareholders' agreement which disregards this fundamental allocation of powers is void[42].

Consequently, agreements on the **appointment of members of the board of directors** (*Verwaltungsräte*) are permissible, but only as obligations to cast a vote accordingly in the shareholders' meeting. The same applies to agreements on **capital changes**, as decisions on a capital change are also an inalienable power of the shareholders' meeting. Shareholders have a statutory pre-emptive right (*Bezugsrecht*) in proportion to their existing participation with regard to any new shares issued by the company[43]. The shareholders' agreement may contain a clause that obliges the parties to participate fully in any future capital increase by exercising all of their pre-emptive rights. Otherwise it is advisable to include in the shareholders' agreement a clause defining the fate of unused pre-emptive rights, e.g. by applying the transfer clauses of the shareholders' agreement analogously.

## 4. Shareholders 'Agreements in pre-insolvency situation

If a company faces the threat of bankruptcy, incumbent shareholders may enter into a specific agreement to re-finance the company with (subordinated) loans, non-repayable contributions or an equity round, among themselves or with a new investor. Such an agreement may, in effect, avert bankruptcy. However, if the last annual balance sheet shows that one-half of the share capital and the legal reserves are no longer covered, the board of directors must convene a general shareholders' meeting without delay and propose financial restructuring measures[44], even if certain financial restructuring measures (such as a shareholders' agreement on re-financing) have already been taken[45]. Shareholders' agreements which are not entered into in the context of an imminent bankruptcy quite typically contain abstract clauses stipulating the obligation for each shareholder to participate pro-rata in restructuring measures, should these become necessary.

**42** Art. 20 para. 1 CO.
**43** Art. 652b CO.
**44** Art. 725 CO.
**45** *Hanspeter Wüstiner* Basler Kommentar Obligationenrecht, 5th ed., Basel 2016, Art. 725 N 23.

# IV. Legal Effects of Shareholders' Agreements

## 1. Legal Effects on the Corporation

As already pointed out, the strict separation of corporate and contractual levels means that the company cannot be a party to a typical Shareholders Agreement[46]. Moreover, the effect of a shareholders' agreement on the interpretation of the articles of incorporation are very limited, since the articles of incorporation (*Statuten*) of a company are a document not aimed only at the shareholders but also at third parties such as future shareholders, creditors, business partners etc. Therefore, according to legal commentators, a shareholders' agreement may only be taken into consideration for the **interpretation of the articles of incorporation** if all shareholders are party to the agreement and the clause(s) to be interpreted pertain solely to internal matters[47].

## 2. Legal Effects on the Shareholders

If the shareholders' agreement qualifies as a simple partnership, the **transfer of the rights and obligations from a shareholders' agreement to another person or entity** requires the consent of all other parties to the shareholders' agreement, or a corresponding clause in the shareholders' agreement[48]. If the shareholders' agreement qualifies as a contractual agreement under the law of obligations, a change of a party to a shareholders' agreement is done by an assignment of contract which also requires the consent of all other parties. Consequently, a transfer of the shares does not mean a transfer of the shareholders' agreement to the new acquirer[49].

In Switzerland, shareholders' agreements need **not be published or registered** in a public register. To the contrary, such agreements would typically include a strict non disclosure clause keeping the existence and the content of the agreement confidential.

Regarding companies that are listed on a Swiss stock exchange, however, entering into a shareholders' agreement may trigger further obligations for the parties and a material disclosure of the existence and (at least partially) the content

---

46 See above, sub III.1.
47 *Forstmoser/Küchler* op. cit., N 212 with references.
48 Art. 542 CO.
49 *Forstmoser/Küchler* op. cit., N 123.

of a shareholders' agreement. If the shareholders' agreement contains covenants on voting rights, the parties to the Agreement qualify as a **group in the sense of capital market regulations** and are obliged to disclose their group and the group's aggregate shareholding to the public if and when certain thresholds are exceeded (control of 3%, 5%, 10%, 15%, 20%, 25%, 33⅓%, 50% or 66⅔% of the voting rights, whether exercisable or not)[50]. If the group is formed in order to gain control over the target company and controls more than 33⅓% of the voting rights, whether exercisable or not, the group must make an offer to acquire all listed equity securities of the company (public tender offer)[51].

Moreover, concluding a shareholders' agreements to acquire direct or indirect control of one or more previously independent undertakings or parts thereof may qualify as a **concentration of undertakings** under Swiss antitrust law[52], in particular if the shareholders' agreement confers a decisive influence on the composition, deliberations, or decisions of the organs of an undertaking[53]. Also, the establishment of a **joint venture company** by way of a shareholders' agreement qualifies as a concentration of undertakings if the joint venture performs all the functions of an autonomous economic entity on a lasting basis and if business activities from at least one of the controlling undertakings are transferred to the joint venture[54]. Concentrations of undertakings are subject to merger control, triggering the obligation to notify the planned concentration of undertakings to the Competition Commission before their implementation if in the financial year preceding the concentration (i) the undertakings concerned together reported a turnover of at least 2 billion Swiss francs, or a turnover in Switzerland of at least 500 million Swiss francs, and (cumulatively) (ii) at least two of the undertakings concerned each reported a turnover in Switzerland of at least 100 million Swiss francs[55].

---

**50** Art. 120 Financial Market Infrastructure Act, FMIA.

**51** Art. 135 FMIA. A company may, however, increase the threshold for a public tender offer or completely opt out by adding a pertinent clause in its articles of association.

**52** Art. 4 para. 3 lit. b Federal Act on Cartels, CartA.

**53** Art. 1 lit. b Merger Control Ordinance, MCO.

**54** Art. 2 MCO.

**55** Art. 9 para. 1 CartA.

### 3. Consequences of a Breach of the Shareholders' Agreements

The strict separation of corporate and contractual levels and the purely obligatory nature of shareholders' agreements (see above, sub I.) leave the parties with (only) contractual instruments to react to a violation of the Agreement. Absent any other specific instruments implemented in the Agreement itself, the consequences of a breach of a shareholders' agreement are limited, in principle, to claims for (actual) **damages.** In most cases, the right to a **specific performance**, which could be enforced based on general contractual principles, is not helpful since the pertinent act (e.g. the casting of a vote in shareholders' meeting) is already in the past (see below, sec. V). Consequently, the violation of a valid shareholders' agreement does not provide the right to challenge the resolutions of the shareholders' meeting[56]. The violation of a shareholders' agreement does not provide a cause for an expulsion of the violating shareholder either, unless the shareholders' agreement expressly states so[57].

## V. Enforcement of Shareholders' Agreements

As in any contractual relationship, parties to an agreement have the right to a **specific performance** *in natura*. However, in particular concerning agreements regarding voting rights, such a right is usually obsolete since the pertinent act is in the past (e.g. the vote has already been cast in a shareholders' meeting). If the parties to a shareholders' agreement are aware of an imminent breach of a shareholders' agreement (e.g. in an upcoming shareholders' meeting), they can enforce the specific performance by requesting a preliminary injunction (under the penalty of law) from the competent court.

Therefore, in most cases the other parties to a shareholders' agreement are left only with a claim for **damages** against the violating party. Under Swiss law, only actual damages can be claimed, and the claimant has the burden of proof regarding the damage, the breach of the shareholders' agreement and the causal connection between the breach and the damage (loss) sustained by the claimant[58].

**56** *Forstmoser/Küchler* op. cit., N 867 with further references.

**57** *Handschin/Vonzun* Zürcher Kommentar zum Schweizerischen Zivilrecht, Art. 530 – 551 OR, Die einfache Gesellschaft, 4th ed. Zurich 2009, Art. 545 – 547 N 183.

**58** Cf. Art. 97 et seq. CO.

In order to mitigate the pertinent risks, shareholders' agreements usually provide for **contractual penalties.** Contractual penalty clauses need to be drafted carefully, as by default the creditor may only compel performance or claim the penalty (not both)[59], and where the damage suffered exceeds the penalty amount, the creditor may claim further compensation only if he can prove that the debtor was at fault[60] or if the agreement provides otherwise. While the parties are, in principle, free to determine the amount of the contractual penalty, a court may reduce penalties that it considers excessive[61]. Another instrument for effectively securing the performance of a shareholders' agreement is the **fiduciary deposition** of the shares with a third party[62].

If the shareholders' agreement qualifies as a simple partnership (see above, sub. II), a claim against a party requires the consent of the other parties which under applicable civil procedure rules form a **mandatory joinder**[63]**.** In case of a purely contractual shareholders' agreement, consent by all other parties to sue one party is generally not required, unless the Agreement contains a clause to the contrary. Shareholders' agreements usually also contain a clause on the place of jurisdiction and applicable law[64].

Under applicable Swiss civil procedure law[65], the parties of a shareholders' agreement may opt for **arbitration** instead of civil proceedings in state courts for the resolution of any disputes arising out of or in connection with the shareholders' agreement.

---

**59** Art. 160 para. 1 CO.

**60** Art. 161 para. 2 CO.

**61** Art. 163 CO.

**62** See above, III./1 in fine.

**63** *"If two or more persons are in a legal relationship that calls for one single decision with effect for all of them, they must jointly appear as plaintiffs or be sued as joint defendants";* Art. 70 Federal Civil Procedure Code, CPC.

**64** Otherwise, the place of jurisdiction and applicable law need to be determined based on the applicable rules of national and/or international civil procedure.

**65** *"Any claim over which the parties may freely dispose may be the object of an arbitration agreement"*, art. 354 CPC.

Anna Babych

# Ukraine

## Table of Content



## I. Nature of Corporate Law Regulation

### 1. General Overview

Ukraine's legal system belongs to the Romano-Germanic legal family (the continental law system). The main source of legal information is codified law. Customary law and case law are not as common, though the latter is often used in support of the written law, as in many other legal systems. Historically, the Ukrainian legal system is primarily influenced by the French civil code, Roman law, and traditional Ukrainian customary law.

**Anna Babych**, AEQUO, Kiev

https://doi.org/10.1515/9783110517026-026

The primary law-making body is the Ukrainian Parliament (*Verkhovna Rada*)[1], also referred to as the legislature. The power to make laws can be delegated to lower governments or specific state bodies, but only for a prescribed purpose.

The Constitution *"shall be regarded superior law"*, with other laws and legal acts being *"adopted on the basis of the Constitution of Ukraine"* and bound to *"conform to it."*[2]

Together with the laws adopted, the international treaties in force, ratified by the Parliament, *"shall be an integral part of the national legislation of Ukraine"*.[3] As a rule, Ukraine may only enter into international agreements not contravening its Constitution; otherwise, relevant amendments to the basic law shall be implemented to permit such treaties.[4]

Secondary legislation adopted by the government bodies, *e.g.* decrees (*ukazy*) of the President of Ukraine, resolutions (*postanovy*) of the Cabinet of Ministers of Ukraine, the Board of the National Bank of Ukraine, the National Securities and Stock Market Commission etc., then pass specific regulations and guidelines as to the laws implementation.

Lastly, the courts are exclusively administering justice in Ukraine, and the judicial proceedings are carried out by the Constitutional Court of Ukraine and the courts of general jurisdiction.[5]

While the Constitutional Court of Ukraine is in charge of resolving on the issues of conformity of the laws with the Constitution and officially interpreting the Constitution[6], the courts of general jurisdiction are resolving all legal disputes arising in the state.[7]

Judicial decisions are not generally regarded as precedents in Ukraine, but the highest specialized courts, as well as the Supreme Court of Ukraine, issue recommendations on certain dispute resolution matters and, thus, have significant influence on the interpretation of the laws and approach of the local courts.

1 Article 75 of the Constitution of *Ukraine*, adopted on 28 June 1996 (the "**Constitution**").

2 Article 8 of the Constitution.

3 Article 9 of the Constitution.

4 Ibid.

5 Article 124 of the Constitution.

6 Article 147 of the Constitution.

7 Supra note 5.

## 2. Current Corporate Law Regulation

Adhering to the continental law system's approach, Ukraine set out the fundamentals of its civil and commercial legislation in the two major codifications – the Civil Code of Ukraine No. 435-IV as of 16 January 2003 (the "**Civil Code**"), and the Commercial Code of Ukraine No. 436-IV as of 16 January 2003 (the "**Commercial Code**").

The Civil Code, *inter alia*, sets out the basics of the legal entities' regulation, such as the legal capacity of legal entities, general requirements as to the statutory documents and state registration thereof, the management etc., as well as provides for certain specific requirements to the various types of legal entities (limited liability companies, general partnerships etc.). The Commercial Code, in turn, covers mainly similar issues in the light of business relations.

However, the regulations provided by the Civil and Commercial Codes are framework provisions. The main types of business entities in Ukraine are the limited liability companies (*tovarystva z ombezhenoyu vidovidalnistyu*) (551 620 making up approx. 46 % of the total number of legal entities)[8], and the joint stock companies (*akcionerni tovarystva*) (14 957 making up approx. 1.2% of the total number of legal entities[9]). These legal forms are governed by the two main laws – the Law of Ukraine "On Business Companies" No. 1576-XII as of 19 September 1991 (the "**Business Companies Law**"), and the Law of Ukraine on "Joint Stock Companies" No. 514-VI as of 17 September 2008 (the "**JSC Law**").

**Business Companies Law** of 1991 used to be the key specific law regulating the corporate law matters for the entities other than the joint stock companies. It still establishes (i) general requirements to the business entities, including their statutory documents, rights and liabilities of the participants, requirements to their state registration, certain rules of profits distribution, bookkeeping and accounting, as well as (ii) specific regulation of the following types of the business entities: limited liability companies, additional liability companies, limited partnership and general partnership.

However, the Business Companies Law seems to be outdated even after the numerous changes. The reason for that is that the concept of the said law and the types of companies introduced were driven by the after-Soviet transitory environment.

---

**8** As of 1 July 2017, according to the State Statistics Service of Ukraine available at: http://www.ukrstat.gov.ua/.

**9** Ibid.

Now many law experts believe that the business law concept needs to be materially revised. There is an ongoing discussion as to the overall concept of private and public companies in Ukraine, eventually resulting in one of the aspects of the corporate law reform, discussed in more detail in section 3 of Part II.

**JSC Law** of 2008 sets out the detailed rules for operation of the joint stock companies in Ukraine. It regulates incorporation, formation, increase / decrease of the share capital of the JSCs, some issues of securities circulation, rights and liabilities of the shareholders, distribution of dividends, shares buy-out procedures etc. It also contains rules for the protection of minority shareholders, voting, pre-emptory rights, corporate governance etc.

The provisions of the JSC Law also cover certain take-over rules – acquisition of controlling stake, the related buy-out procedures for minority shareholders, interested party and material transactions regulation.

Both the Business Companies Law and the JSC Law provide for strict imperative rules. They allow the shareholders (participants) to enjoy discretion only when and to the extent explicitly set out by the law, which is similar to German corporate law concept of *Satzungsstrenge.*

The said approach is supported and tested by the Supreme Court of Ukraine, which provides the following clarifications to the lower courts: "*Relations between the founders (participants) of a business entity regarding formation of its bodies, setting their competence, procedures for calling the general meetings and adopting the decisions are governed by the provisions of the Civil Code and the Business Companies Law. The said rules are imperative by nature, and violation thereof violates the public order.*"[10]

In addition to the Business Companies Law and the JSC Law, there is a number of other laws and subordinate acts regulating certain issues of corporate law in Ukraine. However, those acts set out only some aspects thereof and do not establish general rules of the shareholders' agreements' regime. As an example, there are specific acts regulating the state registration of legal entities, depository system, securities circulation, investments, privatization, corporate governance with state enterprises etc. They are not covered in this Report because of their irrelevance to the matter discussed.

---

**10** Paragraph 9 of the Resolution of the Plenum of the Supreme Court of Ukraine "On the practice of consideration of corporate disputes by the courts" No. 13 as of 24 October 2008.

# II. Regulation of Shareholders' Agreements

In Ukraine the regulation of the shareholders' agreements evolved in stages. Until 2008 there was no specific law covering this matter and general rules of common law applied. The concept of the shareholders' agreement was first-ever introduced in Ukrainian legislation only in 2008 by the JSC Law. Since then the discussion about this type of agreements indeed made some progress, but the then existing jurisprudence still put limits on execution of the shareholders' agreements under Ukrainian law. Finally, in 2017 a law introducing specific amendments to the Business Companies Law and JSC Law regarding the shareholders' agreements has been passed by the Parliament.[11] The concept used in the said law is yet to be tested in Ukrainian courts.

## 1. The Shareholders' Agreements prior to the JSC Law

The shareholders' agreements under Ukrainian law have been rarely executed.

The vacuum existed until 2008 and was driven mainly by the following factors: (i) mandatory corporate law which did not allow reasonable discretion of corporate governance matters to be agreed upon by the company shareholders in the company's charter or a separate agreement, (ii) court jurisprudence fully supporting the strict imperative rules in corporate governance, and (iii) the multilevel corporate structures of Ukrainian businesses where the shareholders' agreements are executed in other jurisdictions, for example under Cyprus law.

To illustrate the courts approach to the concept of shareholders' agreements below are the key clarifications issued by Ukrainian high courts regarding this matter:

- **Recommendations of the Plenum[12] of the High Commercial Court of Ukraine "On the practice of application of legislation while considering the cases arising from the corporate relations" No. 04 – 5/14 as of 28 December 2007[13]** (the **"Commercial Court Recommendations"**)

11 As of the date of this Report the draft it is yet to be signed by the President of Ukraine.

12 A collective body comprising all members of the high specialized court.

13 Ceased to be in force in February 2016 due to the new version of the recommendations issued by the High Commercial Court of Ukraine.

Section 6 of the Commercial Court Recommendations was specifically devoted to the agreements between the participants / shareholders of business entities. In fact, the High Commercial Court's approach substantially limited the scope of application of the shareholders' agreements.

First of all, it was stressed that the corporate governance matters can be regulated by an agreement between the shareholders only in the circumstances expressly allowed by the laws of Ukraine. In practice, it means that the shareholders cannot step aside from the mandatory law rules of the JSC Law. If the shareholders' agreement nevertheless exists and co-vers such matters in a way other than the law allows, such agreement are voidable in court.[14]

Further on, the Commercial Court Recommendations set out the non-exclusive list of issues which may not be covered in the shareholders' agreement, namely[15]:

- a duty of a shareholder to attend and vote at the shareholders' meetings;
- special voting rules for the shareholders, i. e. a duty of a shareholder to vote in a certain manner;
- special rules of formation of the board and the supervisory board; and
- special voting procedures for other corporate bodies (board, supervisory board etc.);
- a duty of a shareholder to ensure the presence and voting of the members of other corporate bodies.

Finally, the Commercial Court Recommendations banned to govern the shareholders' agreements by foreign law, even if they are made between non-Ukrainian parties only. The explanation for that was that the shareholders' agreements used to be seen as regulating the management of Ukrainian company, but not the relations between its shareholders. Given that the company's management shall be regulated by *lex personalis* of the company, *i. e.* the law of the states of incorporation[16], the shareholders' agreements with respect to Ukrainian companies are bound to comply with Ukrainian law.

**14** Paragraph 6.4 of the Commercial Court Recommendations.

**15** Ibid.

**16** Article 25 of the Law of Ukraine "On Private International Law" No. 2709-IV as of 23 June 2005.

- **Resolution of the Plenum[17] of the Supreme Court of Ukraine "On the practice of consideration of corporate disputes by the courts" No. 13 as of 24 October 2008** (the **"Supreme Court Recommendations"**)

The Plenum of the Supreme Court of Ukraine also addressed the corporate relations issues.

The Supreme Court Recommendations follow the approach of the Commercial Court explained above. It was reinstated that all matters relating to the corporate governance are to be regulated by the laws of Ukraine and the company's charter. It went on to clarify the situation when the shareholders' agreement is supposed to be governed by the foreign law, stating that choosing other law to regulate the relations between shareholders and / or the company amounts to the evasion of law, rather than the choice of law.

Finally, these Recommendations expressly banned the right to choose international commercial arbitration courts as a forum for resolution of any corporate disputes concerning the Ukrainian company, regardless of whether the shareholders are Ukrainian or foreign-based.

The Commercial Court Recommendations and the Supreme Court Recommendations used to be widely referred to by the lower courts when dealing with the shareholders' agreements.

The Commercial Court Recommendations of 2007 were replaced by the new version in February 2016. The new version does not cover the shareholders' agreements, and, as a result, does not contain the above restrictions. However, the said limitations are still present in the recommendations of the Supreme Court of Ukraine.

## 2. The Shareholders' Agreements and the JSC Law

In 2008 the new JSC Law specifically mentioned the shareholders' agreements in the joint stock companies in Ukraine. Article 29 of the JSC Law set out that: "*The company's charter may provide for the possibility of execution of an agreement between the shareholders, which imposes additional duties thereon, including a duty to participate in the shareholders' meeting and establish the liability for the failure*

17 According to Article 46 of the Law of Ukraine "On Judicial System and the Status of Judges" No. 2453-VI as of 7 July 2010, a collective body comprising all members of the Supreme Court of Ukraine.

*to do that"*. The JSC Law does not put any difference in this respect for closed (private) or open (public) JSCs.

However, since then neither the law, nor the subordinate legislation developed the rules regarding how a shareholders' agreement should be used. The law did not provide for a possibility to execute similar agreements for the limited liability companies either.

Thus, even after the concept of a shareholders' agreement was specifically introduced into the Ukrainian corporate law for joint stock companies, it still has been rarely used. The key reasons for that were that (i) the Ukrainian corporate law still remained mostly imperative – JSC Law didn't introduce the discretion of corporate governance being enough to apply the shareholders' agreements in practice, and (ii) the court jurisprudence still supported the idea that the scope of the shareholders' agreement should be very limited and governed by Ukrainian law only.

As a result, it was still common to execute shareholders' agreements regarding Ukrainian businesses under foreign law. To do that, the shareholders' agreement was made at the level of non-Ukrainian shareholder of a Ukrainian subsidiary. The content of such agreement used to be standard and covered voting duties, corporate governance, transfer and exit rights etc.

## 3. Corporate Law Reform

In 2016 the business and legal community pushed for the changes in legislation facilitating the foreign investments to Ukraine and lifting up Ukraine's doing business ranking overall. Material improvement of corporate and business law of Ukraine was among the top priorities of the reform. As a result, the corporate legislation has undergone massive changes.

The suggested changes aimed at (i) corporate governance reform allowing huge discretion for business corporates, (ii) legal instruments required for foreign investors, including the shareholders' agreements, (iii) modern regulation of the most popular legal form – limited liability companies, and (iv) elimination of historical drawbacks of Ukrainian privatization of the 90s.

In particular, two draft laws directly targeted to upgrade of the institute of shareholders' agreements in Ukraine.

- **The Draft Law of Ukraine "On Amending Certain Legislative Acts of Ukraine Regarding Corporate Agreements" No. 4470 as of 19 April 2016** (the "**Corporate Agreements Law**")

The Corporate Agreements Law is passed by the Parliament on 23 March 2017[18] and introduced the concept of shareholders' agreements. The template concept is mainly taken from the latest changes to the Russian corporate law, by which certain English law notions have been introduced thereto.

The Corporate Agreements Law has amended the JSC Law and Business Companies Law and made the shareholders' agreements specifically available for the joint stock companies and the limited liability companies. Fairly to mention, such approach has been criticized by some legal experts who believed it is misleading: since the shareholders' agreements have never been banned in Ukrainian law, such specific 'permission' was named a poor legislative technique that may allow ambiguous interpretation of this and other contract law issues.

Pursuant to the Corporate Agreements Law such agreements may provide for a voting at a general meeting in a specific way, terms and conditions of sale of shares at pre-agreed price or prohibition to dispose of shares for a certain period (lock-up), as well as other issues relating to the management, operation or liquidation of a company.

The shareholders' agreements cannot impose duties on the shareholders to vote under the instructions of the member of the company's management, except for the cases where the shareholder is also a member of the management.

The shareholders' agreements shall be executed in writing for any period. Their provisions are confidential, but either party shall notify the respective company about the fact of execution of the shareholders' agreement within three business days. Additionally, the public JSCs shall notify the National Securities and Stock Market Commission on the existence of the shareholders' agreement, its duration and the parties thereto.

Moreover, the state and state-owned companies may also execute the shareholders' agreements regarding their subsidiaries, though the special permission from the respective state property regulator is required.

Finally, the Corporate Agreements Law specifically allows executing shareholders' agreements with the creditors of the target company in order to secure creditors' rights. Under the shareholders' agreement executed with the creditors the shareholders may agree to exercise their rights, vote at the general meeting, carry out actions related to the management of the company, to acquire and sell participatory interest as prescribed by the shareholders' agreement. It is expected that this instrument will substantially increase the liquidity of the participa-

**18** As of the date of this Report the Corporate Agreements Law is yet to be signed by the President of Ukraine, meaning that technically it is still a draft law.

tory interest as a security and enable easy and smooth enforcement over participatory interest by the creditors.

- **The Draft Law of Ukraine "On Limited Liability Companies and Additional Liability Companies" No. 4666 as of 13 May 2016** (the "**LLC Draft**")

Another law, which is relevant to the development of the shareholders' agreements in Ukraine, is the LLC Draft. It was voted by the Parliament in the first reading on 20 December 2016 and its final reading is expected in 2018. If passed, it will substitute the Business Companies Law in all matters, regulating the limited liability companies.

The LLC Draft also addresses the agreements between participants of the limited liability companies similarly to the Corporate Agreements Law. In particular, the agreements shall be executed in writing for any period. Same as the Corporate Agreements Law, the LLC Draft provides for the possibility to pre-agree the terms of the sale and purchase of the share in the company. Similarly, it prohibits imposing the shareholder's duties to vote under the instructions of the member of the company's management.

The LLC Draft guarantees confidentiality of the shareholders' agreements, but unlike the Corporate Agreements Law, does not require any notice to be made on the company about the fact of its execution.

On top, the LLC Draft suggests to give huge discretion to the participants to decide on the company's management issues. It means they will be able to regulate many corporate governance matters in the agreement between LLC participants.

## III. Forms of Shareholders' Agreements

Shareholders' agreement shall be made in writing.

It is impossible to comment on specific forms of shareholders' agreements governed by Ukrainian law due to rare execution of them. The practice is yet to be formed once the above laws are finally enacted.

Since the shareholders' agreements under foreign law are quite popular in Ukraine, the Ukrainian law analogous, most likely, will try following the same structure and content to the extent they are in compliance with local law. Namely, the shareholders' agreements regarding both the joint stock companies and limited liability companies may cover, *inter alia*, (i) voting arrangements regarding distribution of profits, appointment of management, (ii) share transfer and exit rules, (iii) deadlock resolutions etc.

We would not rule out the use of shareholders' agreements with respect to the financing of the company or the bankruptcy averting.

# IV. Legal Effects of Shareholders' Agreements

## 1. Legal Effects on the Corporation

Since now it is common to execute shareholders' agreements with respect to Ukrainian companies at the level of its holding company, formally there is no competition between the charter of Ukrainian company and the shareholders' agreement. However, in practice the parties to the shareholders' agreements try to broaden the competence of the shareholders' meeting of the Ukrainian company to the extent possible. This allows taking many decisions with respect to Ukrainian subsidiary by the shareholders' representative pursuant to the rules established by the shareholders' agreement.

The normal privacy of contract rules applies to the legal effect of the shareholders' agreements. The agreement shall be binding upon its parties only. Under the general rule, the terms of shareholders' agreement do not prevail over the charter of the company.

## 2. Legal Effects on the Shareholders

Similarly, the normal privacy of contract rules applies to the legal effect of the shareholders' agreements. The shareholders' agreement shall be binding upon its parties only.

Neither the existing law, nor the expected corporate law reform contains specific rules regarding the transfer the obligations and/or rights arising from the shareholders' agreements to another person. Such transfer is possible in case of transfer of title to shares of the company provided that the new shareholder adheres to the shareholders' agreement. No automatic transfer is available by virtue of law.

The applicable law is silent whether the shareholders' agreement may create further rights of the shareholders. On the contrary, Corporate Agreements Law does not exclude this option.

According to the Corporate Agreements Law, either party to the shareholders' agreement shall inform the company on execution of shareholders' agreement within three business days. The public JSC, when it becomes aware of it, in its turn shall disclose this fact at the stock market. The specific rules of such disclosure are yet to be established by subordinate regulations.

### 3. Consequences of a Breach of the Shareholders' Agreements

Under the applicable law, in case of breach of a shareholders' agreement standard rules of contract law shall apply.

The Corporate Agreements Law specifically provides for the following remedies: compensation for the damage caused by the violation of the shareholders agreement (i.e. damages) and penalties (either in fixed amount or in the amount to be determined in order provided by the agreement).[19] However, these remedies are the standard contract remedies available under Ukrainian contract law either way. For that reason, the said clause of the new law has been highly criticised as well as the content of it is not clear.

The existing law is silent whether the company's corporate decisions made in violation of the shareholders' agreement are voidable or void. Based on general principle, the decisions of the company are valid.

Pursuant to the Corporate Agreements Law, any transaction made in breach of shareholders' agreement is voidable only if the other party knew or should have known about the limitations set by the shareholders' agreement.

Finally, the breach of the shareholders' agreement does not affect the title of the defaulting shareholder to the shares in the company.

## V. Enforcement of Shareholders' Agreements

Any dispute arising out of relations between (i) the company and its shareholders, or (ii) the shareholders of the company related to the management of such company or the rights and duties of its shareholders shall be settled by the Ukrainian commercial courts.[20]

Until the existing jurisprudence changes, neither the national, nor international arbitration forum is competent to settle corporate disputes arising from shareholders' agreements and related to the management of Ukrainian legal entity.

---

**19** Part 7 of the Corporate Agreements Law.

**20** Article 12(4) of the Economic Procedure Code of Ukraine No. 1798-XI as of 6 November 1991.

All matters related to the relationships between the shareholders and with the company are expected to be regulated exclusively by Ukrainian law.[21] This approach is upheld by the current court jurisprudence.

The Ukrainian law does not provide for specific mechanism of enforcement of shareholder rights under the shareholders' agreement governed by Ukrainian law. The general rules of enforcement shall apply.

# VI. Annexes

| JSC Law | |
|---|---|
| **Стаття 29. (1) Обов'язки акціонерів** | **Article 29. (1) Shareholders obligations** |
| Статутом товариства може бути передбачена можливість укладення договору між акціонерами, за яким на акціонерів покладаються додаткові обов'язки, у тому числі обов'язок участі у загальних зборах, і передбачається відповідальність за його недотримання. | The company's charter may provide for the possibility to conclude a shareholders' agreement, under which additional obligations are assigned to the shareholders, including the obligation to participate in the general meeting, and also provide for liability for non-compliance. |

| Corporate Agreements Law (Draft) | |
|---|---|
| **Стаття 26[1]. Договір між акціонерами товариства** | **Article 26[1]. Shareholders' agreement of the company** |
| 1. Договір між акціонерами товариства – це договір, предметом якого є реалізація акціонерами – власниками простих та привілейованих акцій прав на акції та/або прав за акціями, передбачених законодавством, статутом та іншими внутрішніми документами товариства (далі – договір між акціонерами). За договором між акціонерами його сторони зобов'язуються реалізувати у спосіб, передбачений таким договором, свої права та/або утримуватися від реалізації зазначених прав. Договором між акціонерами може бути передбачено обов'язок його сторін голосувати у спосіб, передбачений таким договором, на загальних зборах акціоне- | 1. A shareholders' agreement of the company is an agreement, the subject of which is the exercise by shareholders – owners of ordinary and preferred shares of rights to shares and/or rights under the shares as provided by the law, charter and other internal documents of the company (hereinafter referred to as the shareholders' agreement). Under the shareholders' agreement, its parties undertake obligation to exercise their rights and/or refrain from the exercise of the rights subject to such agreement. Under shareholders' agreement the parties may be obliged to vote in the manner prescribed by such agreement, at the general meeting of shareholders of the company, and to approve the acquisition or disposal of shares at a pre-determined price and/or |

21 Commercial Court Recommendations.

*Continued*

| Corporate Agreements Law (Draft) | |
|---|---|
| рів товариства, погоджувати придбання або відчуження акцій за заздалегідь визначеною ціною та/або у разі настання визначених у договорі обставин, утримуватися від відчуження акцій до настання визначених у договорі обставин, а також вчиняти інші дії, пов'язані з управлінням товариством, його припиненням або виділом з нього нового товариства. Договір між акціонерами може передбачати умови або порядок визначення умов, на яких акціонер – сторона договору вправі або зобов'язаний придбати або продати акції товариства, та визначати випадки (які можуть залежати чи не залежати від дій сторін), коли таке право або обов'язок виникає. | in the event of the circumstances specified in the agreement, to refrain from disposal of shares until occurrence of the circumstances specified in the agreement, as well as undertake other actions related to the management of the company, its liquidation or spin off from it of a new company. The shareholders' agreement may stipulate conditions or a procedure for determining the conditions subject to which the shareholder – party to the agreement is entitled or obliged to purchase or sell company's shares and to determine instances (which may or may not depend from the actions of the parties) when such right or obligation arises. |
| Договір між акціонерами укладається в письмовій формі. Справжність підписів учасників (засновників) товариства з обмеженою відповідальністю – фізичних осіб у такому договорі засвідчується у встановленому порядку. Дата набрання чинності договором між акціонерами визначається цим договором. Договір між акціонерами укладається на визначений строк або безстроково. | The shareholders' agreement shall be made in writing. The authenticity of the signatures of the participants (founders) of the limited liability company – natural persons in such agreement shall be certified in accordance with the established procedure. The effective date of the shareholders' agreement is determined by this agreement. The shareholders' agreement is concluded for a fixed term or for an indefinite term. |
| 2. Предметом договору між акціонерами не може бути зобов'язання сторони цього договору голосувати згідно з вказівками органів управління товариства, щодо акцій якого укладений цей договір, крім випадків, якщо стороною договору є особа, яка одночасно входить до складу органу управління такого товариства. | 2. The subject of the shareholders' agreement shall not be the obligation of the party to this agreement to vote in accordance with the instructions of the governing bodies of the company in relation to which shares this agreement is concluded, unless the party to the agreement is a person, who is simultaneously is a member of the governing body of such company. |
| Умови договору між акціонерами, які суперечать вимогам цієї частини, є нікчемними. | The terms of the shareholders' agreement that are in conflict with the provisions of this part are null and void. |
| 3. Договір між акціонерами є обов'язковим лише для його сторін. | 3. The shareholders' agreement is mandatory only for its parties. |

*Continued*

| Corporate Agreements Law (Draft) | |
|---|---|
| Договір щодо прав на акції та/або прав за акціями, укладений стороною договору між акціонерами на порушення цього договору, може бути визнаний судом недійсним за позовом заінтересованої сторони договору між акціонерами лише у разі, якщо буде доведено, що інша сторона договору знала або мала знати про обмеження, передбачені договором між акціонерами. | An agreement on the rights to shares and/or rights under shares concluded by a party to the shareholders' agreement in violation of this agreement may be declared null and void by the court with respect to the claim of the interested party to the shareholders' agreement only if it is proved that the other party to the agreement knew or ought to know about the restrictions stipulated by the shareholders' agreement. |
| Інформація про укладення договору між акціонерами повідомляється товариству однією з сторін договору протягом трьох робочих днів з дати його укладення. Публічне акціонерне товариство розкриває інформацію про наявність договору між акціонерами у порядку, встановленому Законом України "Про цінні папери та фондовий ринок" для розкриття особливої інформації про емітента. | The company shall be notified regarding the conclusion of the shareholders' agreement by one of the parties to the agreement within three working days from the date of its conclusion. A public joint stock company discloses information about the existence of the shareholders' agreement in the manner prescribed by the Law of Ukraine "On Securities and the Stock Market" for the disclosure of the specific information about the issuer. |
| Якщо інше не встановлено законом або договором між акціонерами, інформація про зміст договору між акціонерами не підлягає розкриттю та є конфіденційною. | Unless otherwise provided by the law or shareholders' agreement, information on the content of the shareholders' agreement shall not be disclosed and is confidential. |
| Порушення договору між акціонерами не може бути підставою для визнання недійсними рішень органів товариства. | Violation of the shareholders' agreement shall not be the basis for the invalidation of decisions of the governing bodies of the company. |
| 4. Особа, яка відповідно до договору між акціонерами набула право визначати варіант голосування на загальних зборах акціонерів за акціями товариства, зобов'язана повідомити товариству про набуття такого права, якщо в результаті такого набуття ця особа самостійно або разом з своєю афілійованою особою (особами) прямо або опосередковано отримує можливість розпоряджатися більше ніж 10, 25, 50 або 75 відсотками голосів за розміщеними простими акціями товариства. У такому повідомленні мають міститися відомості про: | 4. A person who, in accordance with the shareholders' agreement, acquired the right to determine the option of voting at the general meeting of shareholders in accordance with the shares of the company, shall notify the company regarding the acquisition of such right if, as a result of such acquisition, this person independently or with its affiliate(s) directly or indirectly receives an opportunity to dispose of more than 10, 25, 50 or 75 percent of the votes cast for the company's ordinary shares. This notification should contain information about: |

*Continued*

| Corporate Agreements Law (Draft) | |
|---|---|
| повне найменування товариства; | Full name of the company; |
| прізвище, ім'я, по батькові фізичної особи або найменування юридичної особи; | Surname, name, patronymic of the natural person or the name of the legal entity; |
| дату укладення та дату набрання чинності договором між акціонерами, дату прийняття рішення про внесення змін до договору між акціонерами та дату набрання чинності відповідними змінами, дату припинення дії договору між акціонерами; | The date of the conclusion and the effective date of the shareholders' agreement, the date of adoption of a decision on amendments to the shareholders' agreement and the effective date of the relevant changes, the date of termination of the shareholders' agreement; |
| строк дії договору між акціонерами; | Term of duration of shareholders' agreement; |
| кількість акцій, що належать особам, які уклали договір між акціонерами, на дату його укладення; | The number of shares owned by the persons who entered the shareholders' agreement on the date of its conclusion; |
| кількість простих акцій товариства, яка надає цій особі можливість розпоряджатися голосами на загальних зборах акціонерів, на дату виникнення обов'язку надіслати таке повідомлення; | The number of ordinary shares of the company that entitles this person to dispose of votes at the general meeting of shareholders, on the date of the obligation to send such notice; |
| дату виникнення обов'язку надіслати таке повідомлення. | Date of obligation to send such notice. |
| Таке повідомлення надсилається в письмовій формі протягом п'яти робочих днів з дня набуття права, зазначеного в абзаці першому цієї частини, але не пізніше дня, що передує дню проведення найближчих загальних зборів акціонерів. | Such notice shall be sent in writing within five working days since the day of the acquisition of the right specified in the first paragraph of this part, but not later than the day preceding the day of the next general meeting of shareholders. |
| 5. Особа, яка зобов'язана надіслати повідомлення відповідно до частини четвертої цієї статті, до дати надіслання такого повідомлення має право визначати варіант голосування лише за акціями, кількість яких не перевищує кількості акцій, що належали цій особі до надсилання такого повідомлення. При цьому всі акції, що належать цій особі, враховуються під час визначення кворуму загальних зборів акціонерів. | 5. A person who is obliged to send a notice in accordance with part four of this article, until the date of sending such notice, is entitled to determine the voting option limited to shares the number of which does not exceed the number of shares owned by that person prior to the sending of such notice. In addition, all shares owned by this person are taken into account when determining the quorum of the general meeting of shareholders. |

*Continued*

| Corporate Agreements Law (Draft) | |
|---|---|
| 6. Договором між акціонерами можуть передбачатися способи забезпечення виконання зобов'язань, що випливають з такого договору, та заходи цивільно-правової відповідальності за невиконання або неналежне виконання таких зобов'язань. | 6. The shareholders' agreement may provide for ways of ensuring the fulfilment of obligations arising from such an agreement and measures of civil liability for failure or improper performance of such obligations. |
| 7. Права сторін договору між акціонерами, засновані на такому договорі, у тому числі право вимагати відшкодування завданих внаслідок порушення договору збитків, стягнення неустойки (штрафу, пені), виплати компенсації (фіксованої грошової суми або суми, що підлягає визначенню в порядку, передбаченому договором між акціонерами), застосування інших заходів відповідальності у зв'язку з порушенням договору між акціонерами, підлягають судовому захисту. | 7. The rights of the parties to the shareholders' agreement under such an agreement, including the right to claim compensation for losses incurred as a result of violation of the agreement, of damages, the imposition of a fine (fine, interest), payment of compensation (a fixed amount of money or the amount to be determined in accordance with the procedure provided by the shareholders' agreement), the application of other measures of liability in connection with violation of the shareholders' agreement , subject to judicial protection. |
| 8. Кредитори акціонерного товариства можуть укласти договір з акціонерами товариства, за яким акціонери з метою забезпечення охоронюваного законом інтересу таких третіх осіб зобов'язуються реалізувати свої корпоративні права у спосіб, передбачений таким договором, або утримуватися (відмовитися) від їх реалізації, у тому числі голосувати у спосіб, передбачений таким договором, на загальних зборах акціонерів товариства, узгоджено вчиняти інші дії, пов'язані з управлінням товариством, придбавати або відчужувати акції за певною ціною чи за умови настання визначених у договорі обставин або утримуватися від відчуження акцій до настання визначених у договорі обставин. До зазначеного договору застосовуються загальні положення про договір між акціонерами, якщо інше не встановлено законом або не випливає із суті відносин сторін. | 8. Lenders of a joint stock company may enter into an agreement with the shareholders of the company in which shareholders, in order to ensure the protection of the interests protected by the law of such third parties, undertake obligation to exercise their corporate rights in the manner prescribed by such agreement, or to refrain from their exercise, including the right to vote subject to such agreement, at the general meeting of the shareholders of the company, to coordinate with others actions related to the management of the company, to acquire or dispose of shares at a certain price or in case of occurrence of circumstances specified in the agreement or to refrain from disposal of shares until the occurrence of circumstances specified in the agreement. The general provisions of the shareholders' agreement apply to the said agreement, unless otherwise specified by law or does not derive from the essence of the parties' relations. |

*Continued*

| Corporate Agreements Law (Draft) | |
|---|---|
| Інформація про укладення договору акціонерами публічного акціонерного товариства з кредитором або іншою третьою особою повідомляється товариству однією з сторін договору, яка визначена цим договором як уповноважена здійснити відповідне повідомлення. Таке повідомлення повинно містити відомості та надсилається у строк, передбачені частиною четвертою цієї статті. | Information on the conclusion of an agreement by shareholders of a public joint stock company with a lender or another third person shall be communicated to the company by one of the parties to the agreement, which is defined by this agreement as one, who is authorized to make the corresponding notification. Such notice must contain information and shall be sent within the time period provided for in part four of this article. |

| | |
|---|---|
| **Стаття 51**[1]. Договір про реалізацію прав учасників (засновників) товариства з обмеженою відповідальністю | **Article 51**[1]. An agreement on realization of rights of participants (founders) of limited liability company |
| Договором про реалізацію прав учасників (засновників) товариства з обмеженою відповідальністю визнається договір про особливості реалізації прав учасників (засновників) товариства з обмеженою відповідальністю. За договором про реалізацію прав учасників (засновників) товариства з обмеженою відповідальністю його сторони зобов'язуються реалізовувати у спосіб, передбачений таким договором, права, що надаються учасникам (засновникам) товариства з обмеженою відповідальністю, та/або утримуватися від реалізації зазначених прав. Договором про реалізацію прав учасників (засновників) товариства з обмеженою відповідальністю може бути передбачено обов'язок його сторін голосувати у спосіб, визначений таким договором, на загальних зборах учасників (засновників) товариства з обмеженою відповідальністю, погоджувати придбання або відчуження частки за заздалегідь визначеною ціною та/або у разі настання визначених у договорі обставин утримуватися від відчуження часток до настання визначених у договорі обставин, а також вчиняти інші дії, пов'язані з управлінням товариством з | An agreement on realization of rights of participants (founders) of limited liability company is an agreement on the peculiarities of exercise of rights of participants (founders) of the limited liability company. Under the agreement on exercise of rights of participants (founders) of the limited liability company, its parties undertake obligation to exercise their rights and/or refrain from the exercise of the rights subject to such agreement. Under the agreement on exercise of rights of participants (founders) of the limited liability company the parties may be obliged to vote in the manner prescribed by such agreement, at the general meeting of participants (founders) of the limited liability company, and to approve the acquisition or disposal of shares at a pre-determined price and/or in the event of the circumstances specified in the agreement, to refrain from disposal of participatory interest until occurrence of the circumstances specified in the agreement, as well as undertake other actions related to the management of the company, its liquidation or spin off from it of a new company. The agreement on exercise of rights of participants (founders) of the limited liability company may stipulate conditions or a procedure for determining the conditions subject to which the participant of the company – party to the agree- |

*Continued*

| Corporate Agreements Law (Draft) | |
|---|---|
| обмеженою відповідальністю, його припиненням або виділом з нього нової юридичної особи. Договір про реалізацію прав учасників (засновників) товариства з обмеженою відповідальністю може передбачати умови або порядок визначення умов, на яких учасник товариства – сторона договору вправі або зобов'язаний придбати або продати частки у статутному капіталі товариства, та визначати випадки (які можуть залежати чи не залежати від дій сторін), коли таке право або обов'язок виникає. | ment is entitled or obliged to purchase or sell participatory interest in the company and to determine instances (which may or may not depend from the actions of the parties) when such right or obligation arises. |
| Договір про реалізацію прав учасників (засновників) товариства з обмеженою відповідальністю укладається в письмовій формі. Справжність підписів учасників (засновників) товариства з обмеженою відповідальністю – фізичних осіб у такому договорі засвідчується у встановленому порядку. Дата набрання чинності договором про реалізацію прав учасників (засновників) товариства з обмеженою відповідальністю визначається цим договором. Договір про реалізацію прав учасників (засновників) товариства з обмеженою відповідальністю укладається на визначений строк або безстроково. | The agreement on exercise of rights of participants (founders) of the limited liability company shall be made in writing. The authenticity of the signatures of the participants (founders) of the limited liability company – natural persons in such agreement shall be certified in accordance with the established procedure. The effective date of the agreement on exercise of rights of participants (founders) of the limited liability company is determined by this agreement. The agreement on exercise of rights of participants (founders) of the limited liability company is concluded for a fixed term or for an indefinite term. |
| Предметом договору про реалізацію прав учасників (засновників) товариства з обмеженою відповідальністю не може бути зобов'язання сторони цього договору голосувати згідно з вказівками органів управління товариства з обмеженою відповідальністю, щодо часток якого укладений цей договір, крім випадків, якщо стороною договору є особа, яка одночасно входить до складу органу управління такого товариства. | The subject of the agreement on exercise of rights of participants (founders) of the limited liability company shall not be the obligation of the party to this agreement to vote in accordance with the instructions of the governing bodies of the company in relation to which participatory interest this agreement is concluded, unless the party to the agreement is a person, who is simultaneously is a member of the governing body of such company. |
| Умови договору про реалізацію прав учасників (засновників) товариства з обмеженою відповідальністю, які супере- | The terms of the agreement on exercise of rights of participants (founders) of the limited liability |

*Continued*

| Corporate Agreements Law (Draft) | |
|---|---|
| чать вимогам частини третьої цієї статті, є нікчемними. | company that are in conflict with the provisions of this part are null and void. |
| Договір про реалізацію прав учасників (засновників) товариства з обмеженою відповідальністю є обов'язковим лише для його сторін. | The agreement on exercise of rights of participants (founders) of the limited liability company is mandatory only for its parties. |
| Договір, укладений стороною договору про реалізацію прав учасників (засновників) товариства з обмеженою відповідальністю на порушення цього договору, може бути визнаний судом недійсним за позовом заінтересованої сторони договору про реалізацію прав учасників (засновників) товариства з обмеженою відповідальністю лише у разі, якщо буде доведено, що інша сторона договору знала або мала знати про обмеження, передбачені договором про реалізацію прав учасників (засновників) товариства з обмеженою відповідальністю. | An agreement concluded by a party to the agreement on exercise of rights of participants (founders) of the limited liability company in violation of this agreement may be declared null and void by the court with respect to the claim of the interested party to the agreement on exercise of rights of participants (founders) of the limited liability company only if it is proved that the other party to the agreement knew or ought to know about the restrictions stipulated by the agreement on exercise of rights of participants (founders) of the limited liability company. |
| Інформація про укладення договору про реалізацію прав учасників (засновників) товариства з обмеженою відповідальністю повідомляється такому товариству однією з сторін договору протягом трьох робочих днів з дати його укладення. У такому повідомленні обов'язково зазначаються строк дії та сторони такого договору, а також може зазначатися інша інформація за бажанням сторін договору. | The company shall be notified regarding the conclusion of the agreement on exercise of rights of participants (founders) of the limited liability company by one of the parties to the agreement within three working days from the date of its conclusion. Such notice shall specify the term of duration of the agreement and the parties to such agreement, other information may be indicated should the parties to the agreement wish to do so. |
| Якщо інше не встановлено законом або договором про реалізацію прав учасників (засновників) товариства з обмеженою відповідальністю, інформація про зміст договору про реалізацію прав учасників (засновників) товариства з обмеженою відповідальністю не підлягає розкриттю та є конфіденційною. | Unless otherwise provided by the law or the agreement on exercise of rights of participants (founders) of the limited liability company, information on the content of the agreement on exercise of rights of participants (founders) of the limited liability company shall not be disclosed and is confidential. |
| Порушення договору про реалізацію прав учасників (засновників) товариства з | Violation of the agreement on exercise of rights of participants (founders) of the limited liability |

*Continued*

| Corporate Agreements Law (Draft) | |
|---|---|
| обмеженою відповідальністю не може бути підставою для визнання недійсними рішень органів товариства з обмеженою відповідальністю. | company shall not be the basis for the invalidation of decisions of the governing bodies of the limited liability company. |
| У разі порушення договору про реалізацію прав учасників (засновників) товариства з обмеженою відповідальністю, яким передбачено обов'язок сторони цього договору придбати або продати частку у статутному капіталі цього товариства за заздалегідь визначеною ціною та/або у разі настання визначених у договорі обставин, заінтересована сторона договору може подати до суду позов про примусове виконання цього обов'язку шляхом зобов'язання сторони договору про реалізацію прав учасників (засновників) товариства з обмеженою відповідальністю придбати (продати) частку на умовах, визначених цим договором. | In the event of violation of the agreement on the exercise of the rights of the participants (founders) of the limited liability company, which provides for the obligation of the parties to this agreement to purchase or sell a stake in the authorized charter capital of this company at a predetermined price and/or in the event of the occurrence of the conditions specified in the agreement, the interested party to the agreement may file a claim to the court for the enforcement of this obligation by obliging the party to the agreement to exercise of the rights of the participants (founders) of the limited liability company to purchase (sell) a share on the terms specified by this agreement. |
| Договором про реалізацію прав учасників (засновників) товариства з обмеженою відповідальністю можуть передбачатися способи забезпечення виконання зобов'язань, що випливають з цього договору, і заходи цивільно-правової відповідальності за невиконання або неналежне виконання таких зобов'язань. | The agreement on realization of rights of participants (founders) of limited liability companies may provide for options to ensure the fulfilment of obligations arising from this agreement and measures of civil liability for non-fulfilment or improper fulfilment of such obligations. |
| Кредитори товариства можуть укласти договір з учасниками товариства з обмеженою відповідальністю, за яким учасники товариства з метою забезпечення охоронюваного законом інтересу таких третіх осіб зобов'язуються реалізувати свої корпоративні права у спосіб, передбачений таким договором, або утримуватися (відмовитися) від їх реалізації, у тому числі голосувати у спосіб, передбачений таким договором, на загальних зборах учасників товариства з обмеженою відповідальністю, узгоджено вчиняти інші дії, | The lenders of the company may conclude an agreement with the participants of the limited liability company whereby the participants of the company, in order to ensure the protection of the interests protected by the law of such third parties, undertake obligations to exercise their corporate rights in the manner prescribed by such agreement, or to refrain to exercise them, including the right to vote at the general meeting of the participants of the limited liability company subject to the agreement, to undertake other coordinated actions related to the management of such company, purchase or sell participatory interest in |

*Continued*

| Corporate Agreements Law (Draft) | |
|---|---|
| пов'язані з управлінням таким товариством, придбавати або продавати частки у його статутному капіталі за певною ціною чи за умови настання визначених у договорі обставин або утримуватися від відчуження часток до настання визначених у договорі обставин. До зазначеного договору застосовуються загальні положення про договір про реалізацію прав учасників (засновників) товариства з обмеженою відповідальністю, якщо інше не встановлено законом або не випливає із суті відносин сторін. | its authorized charter capital at a certain price, with respect to the occurrence of the circumstances specified in the agreement or to refrain from disposal of participatory interest prior to occurrence of the circumstances specified in the agreement. The general provisions of the agreement on the exercise of the rights of the participants (founders) of a limited liability company apply to the said agreement, unless otherwise provided by law or does not derive from the substance of the parties' relations. |

| Draft LLC Law | |
|---|---|
| **Стаття 7. Корпоративний договір** | **Article 7. Corporate agreement** |
| 1. Договір, за яким учасники товариства зобов'язуються реалізовувати свої права та повноваження певним чином або утримуватися від їх реалізації (далі – корпоративний договір), є безвідплатним і вчиняється в письмовій формі. Корпоративний договір, який не відповідає цим вимогам, є нікчемним. | 1. An agreement by which the participants of the company undertake obligation to exercise their rights and powers in a certain way or refrain from their exercise (hereinafter referred to as the corporate agreement) shall be unpaid and shall be made in writing. The corporate agreement that does not comply with these requirements is null and void. |
| 2. Дата укладення та строк дії корпоративного договору визначаються в договорі. | 2. The date of conclusion and duration term of the corporate agreement shall be specified in the agreement. |
| 3. Корпоративний договір може передбачати умови або порядок визначення умов, на яких учасник має право або зобов'язаний купити або продати частку у статутному капіталі (її частину), а також визначати випадки, коли таке право або обов'язок виникає. | 3. The corporate agreement may stipulate conditions or the procedure for determining the conditions on which the participant has the right or obligation to purchase or sell a participatory interest in the authorized charter capital (or part thereof), as well as to stipulate instances, when such right or obligation may arise. |
| 4. Корпоративний договір, яким встановлюється обов'язок учасників забезпечити голосування згідно з вказівками органів управління товариства, є нікчемним. | 4. The corporate agreement, which establishes the obligation of the participants to ensure voting in accordance with the instructions of the governing bodies of the company, is null and void. |

*Continued*

| Draft LLC Law | |
|---|---|
| 5. Зміст корпоративного договору не підлягає розкриттю і є конфіденційним, якщо інше не встановлено законом або договором. | 5. The content of the corporate agreement shall not be disclosed and is confidential unless otherwise provided by law or the agreement. |
| 6. Договір, укладений стороною корпоративного договору на порушення такого корпоративного договору, є нікчемним, якщо інша сторона за договором знала або мала знати про таке порушення. | 6. An agreement concluded by a party to the corporate agreement resulting in violation of such corporate agreement is null and void if the other party to the agreement knew or ought to have known about such violation. |

Wulf A. Kaal

# United States of America

## Table of Content



## I. Nature of Corporate Law Regulation

Since Section 7.32 of the Model Business Corporation Act (MBCA) was passed in 1991, most US states have authorized shareholder control agreements in an effort to support the validity of such agreements. The Official Comment to that section states: *"Heretofore, however, the Model Act has never expressly validated shareholder agreements. Rather than relying on further uncertain and sporadic development of the law in the courts Section 7.32 rejects the older line of cases."*[1] Many US states, including the State of Delaware, have amended their statutes in the aftermath of the passing of Section 7.32 MBCA to indicate that the corporate powers

1 Changes in the Revised Model Business Corporation Act—Amendments Pertaining to Closely Held Corporations, 46 Bus. Law 297, 302 (1990).

**Prof. Wulf A. Kaal**, University of St. Thomas, United States of America.

https://doi.org/10.1515/9783110517026-027

rest within the board of directors, and variations from this norm are permitted if set forth in the corporation's charter.[2]

US law does not typically limit who may draft a corporate charter. While corporate codes are viewed as "enabling" statutes—providing flexibility for different enterprises—mandatory provisions cannot be changed.[3] For example, DGCL Sect. 102(a)(4) mandates a description of the corporation's stock (exception for non-stock corporation); however, it leaves considerable flexibility with regard to the types of classes, powers, preferences, rights, qualifications, limitations or restrictions on the shares issued.

## II. Regulation of Shareholders' Agreements

Special legislation exists that governs shareholders' agreements. Most US states have adopted provisions in corporation codes that address the main types of shareholder agreements. Principle types of shareholders' agreements include: vote pooling agreements, irrevocable proxies, voting trusts and shareholder control agreements.[4] Specific Delaware sections are discussed below. While the agreements are governed by legislation, general rules applicable to contract interpretation govern the construction of shareholders' agreements.[5]

Generally, when a control and voting agreement among shareholders "*aims to secure control without fraud on the corporation or others and does not sever stock ownership from stock control, it is not illegal.*"[6]

Shareholder agreements are generally permitted. Typical provisions in shareholder agreements specify the officers' salaries, require arbitration to resolve disputes, determine the identity of directors and officers of the corporation, set dividend amounts, and provide for share transfer restrictions.[7] Some provisions, such as specifying who the officers are, their compensation, and other financial issues, determine matters that are within the directors' statutory author-

---

**2** See *O'Neal/Thompson* Close Corporations and LLCs: Law and Practice § 4:5 (citing DGCL 141 (a)).

**3** *O'Neal/Thompson* Close Corporations and LLCs: Law and Practice § 3:6.

**4** 5 Fletcher Cyc. Corp. § 2064.

**5** See Salamone v. Gorman, 106 A.3d 354, 367 (Del. 2014).

**6** 5 Fletcher Cyc. Corp. § 2064 (citing Ringling v. Ringling Bros.-Barnum & Bailey Combined Shows, 29 Del Ch 318, 49 A2d 603, mod 29 Del Ch 610, 53 A2d 441).

**7** *Steven N. Bulloch* Shareholder Agreements in Closely Held Corporations: Is Sterilization an Issue? 59 Temp. L.Q. 61 (1986).

ity to "manage the business and affairs" of the corporation.[8] These provisions may be subject to invalidation because they encroach on the statutory authority of the directors.[9] Courts offer varying rationales for nullifying terms of shareholder agreements that limit the board's authority, but most often, courts worry the agreements *"tie the hands of the directors,"* making it impossible for them to exercise their discretion concerning matters decided in the agreement.[10]

Courts consider a variety of factors when determining the validity of a shareholders' agreement. The treatise on corporate law by *James Cox* and *Thomas Hazen* outlines the factors courts considered in judging their validity:

> *"Before such agreements received based approval in most state statutes, a variety of factors were considered in judging their validity: (1) the purpose or object of the agreement, (2) the statutes in force in the particular jurisdiction in which the agreement is made, (3) the conceptions of public policy prevailing in the courts of the jurisdiction regarding the separation of voting power from the beneficial ownership of shares, (4) the situation of the corporation and the shareholders at the time the agreement was made, (5) whether or not all of the shareholders in the corporation are parties to the agreement, (6) whether the contracting shareholders are also directors or expect to be at the time of the performance of the contract, (7) the length of time during which the agreement will control the shareholders' right to vote their shares, (8) whether the person challenging the validity of the agreement is a party to it or is a creditor or shareholder not party to the agreement, (9) whether the person challenging the agreement is simply trying to "welch" on his undertaking, (10) whether or not there is consideration, other than the mutual promises of the parties to support the undertakings, to vote in accordance with the terms of the agreement, (11) how long the contract has been in operation and the extent to which action has been taken or positions have changed in reliance on it, and (12) the kind of corporation whose stock is subject to the voting arrangement."*[11]

Statutes authorizing different types of shareholder agreements sometimes address the maximum length permitted for the agreements.[12] Section 7.32 provides for a maximum limit of 10 years but permits the parties to specify another term.[13] Most voting trust agreements provide for a period of 10 years and often permit a

**8** Id. (citing 15 PA. CONS. STAT. ANN. § 1401 (Purdon Supp. 1985) (board of directors shall manage business of corporation); TEX. BUS. CORP. ACT ANN. ART. 2.31 (Vernon 1980) (board of directors shall manage business and affairs of corporation).

**9** See id.

**10** Id. at 61–62; see also id. at notes 20–37 for discussion on court decisions related to shareholder agreement provisions limiting director discretion.

**11** 3 Treatise on the Law of Corporations § 14:7 (3d).

**12** *O'Neal/Thompson* Close Corporations and LLCs: Law and Practice § 4:37.

**13** Id.

renewal so that the agreement has a reach of 20 years.[14] Duration limitations in the voting trust statutes do not apply to other types of shareholders' agreements.[15] Numerous decisions have sustained shareholders' agreements which were to remain in effect indefinitely.[16]

Delaware voting trusts and other voting agreements allow stockholders to designate the right to vote "for any period of time determined by the agreement." (DGCL § 218(a)). Proxy agreements are limited to three years, unless the proxy provides for a longer period (DGCL § 212(b)).[17]

With the permission of shareholders' agreements modifying the traditional pattern of corporate control show that in most jurisdictions individuals in a closely held enterprise can *"in practical effect be partners among themselves, or nearly so, but a corporation to the rest of the world."*[18] As the Second Circuit stated: *"There is little logical reason why individuals cannot be 'partners inter sese and a corporation as to the rest of the world,' so long as the rights of third parties such as creditors are not involved."*[19]

DGCL 350 specifically regulates close corporation agreements to restrict the discretion of directors of the company. Courts and academics have acknowledged there is a significant difference between shareholders of public and close corpo-

---

**14** Id.

**15** Id.

**16** Id. (collecting cases with the string-citation provided here in full). *See, e.g., Glazer v. Glazer*, 374 F.2d 390 (5th Cir. 1967); *Weil v. Beresth*, 154 Conn. 12, 220 A.2d 456 (1966) (statute limiting shareholders' voting agreement to ten years, enacted after agreement was entered into, held inapplicable); *Compton v. Paul K. Harding Realty Co.*, 6 Ill. App. 3d 488, 285 N.E.2d 574, 579 (5th Dist. 1972); *Galler v. Galler*, 32 Ill. 2d 16, 203 N.E.2d 577 (1964) (shareholders' agreement enforced as long as one of the contracting parties was alive); *Leventhal v. Atlantic Finance Corp.*, 316 Mass. 194, 55 N.E.2d 20, 154 A.L.R. 260 (1944); *E.K. Buck Retail Stores v. Harkert*, 157 Neb. 867, 62 N.W.2d 288, 45 A.L.R.2d 774 (1954) (1954 *("It is also contended that the control agreement is void because it was to remain in effect so long as Buck retained any stock in the corporation. We think not. The purpose of the agreement was to give Buck such protection against mismanagement as to induce him to bring needed money into the corporation. It is reasonable that such protection should be afforded so long as he is a stockholder. It is not a contract which binds the parties in perpetuity), as defendants allege. It is definite as to the term of its existence.")*; *Clark v. Dodge*, 269 N.Y. 410, 199 N.E. 641 (1936); 721 *Corp. v. Morgan Guaranty Trust Co. of New York*, 40 Misc. 2d 395, 397, 243 N.Y.S.2d 198, 200 (Sup 1963) (*"The fact that the agreement [to vote shares of stock in the corporation in a particular manner] does not contain a termination date does not make it any less valid.")*

**17** See also, e.g., Minn Stat § 302 A.453 subd. 1 (voting trust can be created for a period not exceeding 15 years unless connected with a debt of the corporation).

**18** *O'Neal/Thompson* Close Corporations and LLCs: Law and Practice § 4:4.

**19** Id. quoting *Arditi v. Dubitzky*, 354 F.2d 483, 486 (2d Cir. 1965).

rations, specifically in regards to bargaining power, such that close corporation shareholders should have greater flexibility to align their affairs as they see fit.[20] Likewise, shareholders' agreements authorized under MBCA 7.32 are void if the corporation becomes a public corporation.

Advance planning can avoid many of these problems that arise in closely held businesses.[21] Planning may take many forms, ranging from the formal election to be treated as a close corporation to a more customized shareholder agreement such as is permitted under MBCA § 7.32.[22] To be specific, MBCA § 7.32(a) permits a shareholders' agreement that:

(a) eliminates the board of directors or restricts the discretion or powers of the board of directors,
(b) governs the authorization or making of distributions whether or not in proportion to ownership of shares, subject to the limitations in section 6.40,
(c) establishes who shall be directors or officers of the corporation, or their terms of office or manner of selection or removal,
(d) governs, in general or in regard to specific matters, the exercise or division of voting power by or between the shareholders and directors or by or among any of them, including use of weighted voting rights or director proxies,
(e) establishes the terms and conditions of any agreement for the transfer or use of property or the provision of services between the corporation and any shareholder, director, officer or employee of the corporation or among any of them,
(f) transfers to one or more shareholders or other persons all or part of the authority to exercise the corporate powers or to manage the business and affairs of the corporation, including the resolution of any issue about which there exists a deadlock among directors or shareholders,
(g) requires dissolution of the corporation at the request of one or more of the shareholders or upon the occurrence of a specified event or contingency, or
(h) otherwise governs the exercise of the corporate powers or the management of the business and affairs of the corporation or the relationship among the shareholders, the directors and the corporation, or among any of them, and is not contrary to public policy.[23]

**20** See *O'Neal/Thompson* Close Corporations and LLCs: Law and Practice § 4:4.
**21** Financing the Corporation § 5:33.
**22** Id.
**23** Model Bus. Corp. Act § 7.32(a).

Although the stockholders of any corporation may enter into an agreement under Model Business Corporation Act (MBCA) § 7.32, the agreement ceases to be effective when the stock of the corporation is listed on a national securities exchange or regularly traded in a market maintained by one or more members of a national or affiliated securities association.[24]

One of the most profound changes in state regulation of corporations over the past twenty years has been the passage of statutes specifically governing the operation of closely held corporations.[25] Almost all statutes regulating closely held corporations include provisions limiting the common law restrictions on shareholder agreements concerned with impinging on the powers of the board of directors.[26]

Section 7.32 contains several requirements. Most importantly the agreement must be unanimous, so that agreements that do not involve all shareholders, such as agreements designed to keep control within a block, must look elsewhere for their authorization.[27] The agreement must be in writing, but unlike some earlier statutes, the written agreement does not have to be in the articles or bylaws—stand-alone written agreements are specifically allowed.[28] The section specifies a 10 year limit, a similar period to voting trusts, but unlike voting trusts, this period is just a default rule, so that if the parties specify a longer period it is permitted.[29] Finally, the Model Act language requires that a legend appear on the stock certificates flagging the agreement for purchasers who buy shares covered by such an agreement.[30]

*Galler v. Galler* was the first case that a court acknowledged the unique characteristics of a closely held corporation in determining the validity of a share-

---

**24** Model Bus. Corp. Act § 7.32(d).

**25** *Steven N. Bulloch* Shareholder Agreements in Closely Held Corporations: Is Sterilization an Issue? 59 Temp. L.Q. 61 (1986).

**26** Id. (collecting statutes with the string-citation provided here in full). See, e.g., FLA. STAT. ANN. § 607.107(2) (West 1977) (no qualifying shareholder agreement invalid on ground that it attempts to restrict discretion of board of directors in its management of business of corporation); OHIO REV. CODE ANN. § 1701.59.1(F)(3) (Page 1985) (no qualifying agreement invalid on ground that it interferes with discretion of directors). Many statutes permit the total abandonment of the typical corporate structure by allowing the shareholders to dispense with a board of directors and to manage the business of the corporation themselves. *See, e.g.*, ALA. CODE § 10 – 2 A-308 (1980); DEL. CODE ANN. tit. 8, § 351 (1983); KAN. STAT. ANN. § 17 – 7211 (1981).

**27** *O'Neal/Thompson* Close Corporations and LLCs: Law and Practice § 4:6.

**28** Id.

**29** Id.

**30** Id.

holder agreement.[31] In upholding the agreement, the *Galler* court explained that a shareholder agreement is of particular importance in a closely held corporation.[32] Minority shareholders in a closely held corporation are likely to have invested substantial time or capital in the enterprise, but those dissatisfied with the corporation's operation cannot sell their shares easily because the shares are not readily marketable.[33] The *Galler* court viewed the "shareholder agreement as a helpful tool in a closely held corporation," rather than "with suspicion and disfavour."[34] The court concluded:

> Where (..) no complaining minority interest appears, no fraud or apparent injury to the public or creditors is present, and no clearly prohibitory statutory language is violated, we can see no valid reason for precluding the parties from reaching any arrangements concerning the management of the corporation which are agreeable to all.[35]

# III. Forms of Shareholders' Agreements

## 1. Shareholders' Agreements on Shareholder Rights

Agreements regarding voting rights include voting trusts, pooling agreements, and proxy agreements. Under Delaware law, each of these types are governed by DGCL §§ 212 and 218. A voting trust is set up when an individual transfers stock and the associated voting rights to a trustee. Pooling agreements do not require a transfer to a trustee, but rather individuals agree to vote their shares according to their agreement or procedure provided within. Proxy agreements allow shareholders to confer their voting rights upon another person subject to the procedural requirements in DGCL § 212. In addition, MBCA 7.30 regulates voting trusts, and MBCA 7.31 regulates voting agreements. MBCA 7.32 likewise governs shareholder agreements that govern the exercise or division of voting rights.

Voting arrangements may take a variety of forms, including voting trusts; voting agreements or pooling agreements; and irrevocable proxies.[36] For example, a shareholders' agreement could provide that actions of the board and

31 *Steven N. Bulloch* Shareholder Agreements in Closely Held Corporations: Is Sterilization an Issue? 59 Temp. L.Q. 61, 69 (1986) (citing *Galler v. Galler*, 32 Ill. 2d 16, 203 N.E.2d 577 (1964)).
32 Id.
33 Id. (citing *Galler*, 32 Ill. 2d at 27–28, 203 N.E.2d at 583).
34 Id. at 70.
35 *Galler v. Galler*, 32 Ill. 2d at 30, 203 N.E.2d at 585.
36 Business Transactions Solutions § 35:4.

shareholders will not be effective unless they are approved by one of the shareholders designated as the managing shareholder.[37] Voting arrangements may be used as a method for allocating control in the corporation.[38] For example, different shareholder groups may be provided with the ability to elect directors by issuing various classes of stock.[39] Voting arrangements are not self-executing, and the mere existence of a voting arrangement does not mean that the corporation should dispense with the legal formalities of director and shareholder actions.[40]

All US states now have statutes which expressly authorize the creation of voting trusts.[41] The MBCA, followed by a majority of states, provides that one or more shareholders may create a voting trust by signing an agreement and transferring their shares to the trustee.[42] Most voting trust statutes place a maximum on the duration of such a trust—usually 10 years—and also permit renewals or extensions for the maximum period of time.[43] Most of the states placing a maximum on the duration of a voting trust also permit extension or renewal of the trust for varying periods of time.[44] Statutes typically require that the trustee file the agreement at the corporation's office and be subject to inspection by shareholders.[45]

Additionally, if all shareholders of a corporation are parties to a valid agreement, courts have held the corporation bound by the agreement even if it is not formally a party to it.[46] Other courts have not found the corporation to be bound.[47]

---

**37** Id.

**38** Id.

**39** Id.

**40** See id.

**41** *O'Neal/Thompson* Close Corporations and LLCs: Law and Practice § 4:17.

**42** Id. (citing MBCA 7.30).

**43** See id. e.g., Del. Code Ann. tit. 8, § 218(a); NY Bus Corp Law § 621(a); Ohio Rev Code Ann § 1701.49(B) (maximum length of an "irrevocable" voting trust agreement is ten years *"unless the voting or consenting rights granted thereby are coupled with an interest in the shares to which such rights relate"*).

**44** Id. (collecting statute examples with the string-citation provided here in full). *See, e.g.*, Cal Corp Code § 706 (voting trust limited to a 10-year term; may be renewed for additional 10-year terms by written agreement of the beneficiaries and with written consent of the voting trustees; the renewal is limited to the shares of those beneficiaries agreeing to the renewal); Me Rev Stat Ann tit 13-C, § 741 (period not to exceed 21 years, may be extended for an additional 21 years); *Smith v. Wembley Industries, Inc.*, 441 So. 2d 392 (La. Ct. App. 4th Cir. 1983) (court held that a 10-year extension of a 10-year voting trust entered into the same day that the trust was created did not violate the statutory limitation of voting trusts to ten years).

**45** See id.

**46** See *O'Neal/Thompson* Close Corporations and LLCs: Law and Practice § 4:33.

Typically, shareholder claims are enforced through derivative actions, whereby the shareholders pursue claims in a representative capacity on a cause of action that derives from the corporation. However, individuals may sue in their individual capacity as a party to a shareholder agreement for breaches under the agreement by other contracting parties. Enforcement is usually through litigation which can be expensive.[48] When the corporation is harmed, it is the corporation that has the claim, but directors are often unwilling to pursue claims, especially when they are the wrongdoers.[49] Shareholders will often enforce these claims via a derivative action, where the corporation is the real party in interest as the entity injured and recovery belongs to the corporation.[50] The shareholders are simply suing on the corporation's behalf and cannot maintain actions on their own behalf to redress an injury to the corporation even if the value of their stock is impaired as a result of the injury.[51]

To avoid some of the procedural hurdles of derivative litigation and enable direct recovery, shareholders must convince the court that individuals abusing control of the corporation were directly harming the shareholders.[52] These direct suits usually involve contractual or statutory rights of the shareholders, the shares themselves, or rights relating to the ownership of shares.[53] Examples include actions to recover dividends and to examine corporate records.[54] Delaware courts inquire as to who suffered the harm and who would receive the recovery to decide whether the action should be a direct or derivative action.[55]

Many state statutes provide for the specific enforcement of shareholders' agreements,[56] as does the MBCA, which expressly states that voting agreements

---

**47** Id. (collecting case examples with the string-citation provided here in full). See *Nordin v. Kaldenbaugh*, 7 Ariz. App. 9, 435 P.2d 740 (1967) (where stockholders who agreed to issuance of stock were also directors, managers, and officers of the corporation, their agreements were binding on the corporation); *Merlino v. West Coast Macaroni Mfg. Co.*, 90 Cal. App. 2d 106, 111, 202 P.2d 748, 751 (1st Dist. 1949) ("There can be no question but that an agreement between stockholders who own substantially all of the stock of a corporation is enforceable against the contracting parties and the corporation."); *Moss v. Waytz*, 4 Ill. App. 2d 296, 124 N.E.2d 91 (1st Dist. 1955).

**48** *Arthur R. Pinto* Protection of Close Corporation Minority Shareholders in the United States, 62 Am. J. Comp. L. 361, 377 (2014).

**49** See id.

**50** Id.

**51** See id.

**52** See id.

**53** Id. at 378.

**54** See id.

**55** See id. at n. 98 (citing *Tooley v. Donaldson, Lufkin & Jenrette, Inc.*, 845 A.2d 1031 (Del. 2004)).

**56** 5 Fletcher Cyc. Corp. § 2067 (citing Ariz Rev Stat § 10–731; Cal Corp Code § 706; 805 ILCS 5/7.70; Ind Code Ann § 23–1–31–2).

are specifically enforceable.[57] In general, a court may specifically enforce any of the substantive terms of a shareholders' agreement, which may require the buy-out of a shareholder or compelled arbitration.[58] Under the MBCA, rescission may also be available to a purchaser of shares who did not have knowledge of the existence of a shareholder control agreement at the time of purchase.[59]

Shareholder agreements regarding financing of the corporation are regulated under the MBCA§ 6.27 and DGCL § 202. These statutes expressly authorize the most common types of agreements: option agreements permitting the corporation or other shareholders to purchase and binding the selling shareholder; mandatory buyout agreements, in which the corporation or other purchasers are obligated to purchase; and consent agreements that require the corporation or other persons to approve the transfer, or prohibit the transfer to designated persons.[60]

Shareholder agreements routinely cover matters in addition to buy-sell provisions, including loans by shareholders, methods of making and using capital contributions, shareholder salaries for employment, and matters involving control of corporate affairs.[61] For example, minority shareholders may refuse to provide capital contributions unless they are granted veto powers over major corporate decisions such as asset sales, mergers, liquidation, or distributions to shareholders.[62] This is often done by requiring that these decisions obtain approval of shareholders holding considerably more than a majority of the stock.[63]

The distinct needs of close corporations are also shown as courts have recognized an enhanced fiduciary duty among participants in closely held corporations.[64] Courts have held that majority shareholders have a fiduciary duty not only to the corporation but also to minority shareholders as a class[65]:

---

**57** Id. (citing MBCA 7.31(b)).

**58** See id.

**59** Model Bus Corp Act § 7.32(c). However, this section also provides that a purchasing shareholder will be deemed as having received notice of the shareholder agreement should the stock certificate note the existence of such agreement or an information statement is provided at or before the time of purchase that indicates the shares are subject to a shareholder agreement.

**60** See Model Bus Corp Act § 6.27(d)(1)-(4); and DGCL § 202(2)(1)-(4) respectively.

**61** See *William R. Christian et al* 33.07 Other types of provisions for shareholders' agreements, Subchapter S Taxation, 1999 WL 630786, 1.

**62** See id.

**63** See id.

**64** *O'Neal/Thompson* Close Corporations and LLCs: Law and Practice § 1:29. Statutes also govern duties among close corporation shareholders. See *O'Neal/Thompson* Close Corporations and LLCs: Law and Practice § 9.42 (citing Minn. Stat. § 302 A.751(3)(a) as an example statute that au-

- The majority has the right to control; but when it does so, it occupies a fiduciary relation toward the minority, as much so as the corporation itself or its officers and directors. *Southern Pacific Co. v. Bogert*, 250 U.S. 483, 39 S.Ct 533, 63 L. Ed. 1099 (1919).
- The Seventh Circuit certified to the Delaware Supreme Court the question of *"whether majority shareholders in a Delaware Corporation have a fiduciary duty of loyalty to a minority shareholder, who is also an employee under a written contract, with respect to issues affecting that employment." Nagy v. Riblet Products Corp.*, 79 F.3d 572 (7th Cir.), *certified question answered*, 683 A.2d 37 (Del. 1996). The court determined that because there was an employment contract, it governed the relationship in the shareholder's capacity as an employee. The shareholder is still owed the fiduciary duty in his capacity as a shareholder.
- Under California law, a majority shareholder breaches a fiduciary duty if the ability to control the corporation is used to the majority shareholder's own benefit and to the detriment of the minority shareholders. *Eagle v. American Tel. & Tel. Co.*, 769 F2d 541 (9th Cir. 1985).
- Controlling shareholders of national bank were in fiduciary capacity with respect to minority shareholders as well as to the bank. *Garrett v. United States*, 396 F2d 489 (5th Cir. 1968).
- The majority owe to the minority the duty to act in good faith, neither to cause the corporation to act *ultra vires* or to breach valid shareholder agreements to the detriment of the minority shareholders. *Blanchard v. Commonwealth Oil Co.*, 294 F2d 834 (5th Cir. 1961).
- Director and dominant shareholder stood in a fiduciary relationship to the corporation and to the minority shareholders as beneficiaries. *Perlman v. Feldmann*, 219 F2d 173 (2d Cir 1955).[66]

Likewise, shareholders who dominate the company, although not officers, are viewed as fiduciaries to other shareholders as would a director or other officer.[67] If a shareholder *"exercises absolute de facto control over a corporation, such actual dominion carries with it fiduciary responsibility regardless of the presence or*

---

thorizes courts *"to consider the duty that shareholders in a close corporation owe to one another to act in an honest, fair, and reasonable manner in the operation of the corporation"*).

**65** 12B Fletcher Cyc. Corp. § 5811.

**66** Id. at n. 3.

**67** See id. (collecting cases).

*absence of de jure titles.*"[68] Majority shareholders occupying the role of president or chief officer of the corporation will also generally be considered a fiduciary.[69]

The importance of the fiduciary relationship between majority and minority shareholders was shown in *Coleman v. Taub*, 638 F.2d 628 (3d Cir. 1981), where a minority shareholder sued a corporation and its majority shareholders based on his discharge as an employee.[70] The district court had concluded that a merger into a newly-created parent corporation was designed to eliminate the minority shareholder.[71] The merger agreement allowed the company to give the minority shareholder cash in exchange for shares, but the Third Circuit determined that even if a minority shareholder agrees to a cash-out, he may still object to the merger on grounds of a breach of fiduciary duty.[72] The court made clear that the fiduciary duty among shareholders in close corporations goes beyond simply protecting shareholders' financial interests.

## 2. Shareholders' Agreements on the (Limitation for the) Transfer of Shares

US law gives considerable latitude to corporate participants when imposing share transfer restrictions, as restrictions will usually be sustained unless the terms are unreasonable under the circumstances.[73] Restrictions may be imposed by the articles of incorporation, the bylaws, or a shareholders' agreement.[74] However, authorities are split as to whether a transfer restriction imposed by an amendment to the articles or bylaws is binding on all the shares or only on those shares that were voted in favour of the amendment.[75] Important discussion on this issue is found in *Tu-Vu Drive-In Corporation v. Ashkins*, 391 P.2d 828 (Cal. 1964), where the California Supreme Court held a transfer restriction applied to all the shares.[76] California corporate code has since been amended to prohibit the application of any transfer restriction to previously issued shares

68 Id. (collecting cases).
69 See id. (collecting cases).
70 *Julian J.* Garza Rethinking Corporate Governance: The Role of Minority Shareholders-A Comparative Study, 31 St. Mary's L.J. 613, 634 (2000).
71 See id.
72 See id. (citing 638 F.2d at 638).
73 3 Treatise on the Law of Corporations § 14:9 (3d).
74 Id.
75 See id.
76 See id.

unless the shares were voted in favor of the restriction.[77] Likewise, Delaware does not allow transfer restrictions *"unless the holders of the securities are parties to an agreement or voted in favour of the restriction."*[78] Courts have also refused to allow transfer restrictions to be applied retroactively to non-consenting shares.[79]

Minority shareholders make seek tag-along rights to protect them against the possibility that majority owners decide to sell their interests.[80] Tag-along rights allow minority shareholders to sell their interest at the same price and terms that the majority shareholders receive. Drag-along rights protect majority shareholders who plan to sell their interests by requiring that all other shareholders sell their interests in the same transaction.[81] Drag-along rights allow majority shareholders to maximize the chance of receiving full value for their shares because the prospect of having to work with the remaining minority shareholders may lead an interested party to offer a discounted price for the majority stake.[82] Because these govern the transfer of ownership interests, buy-sell agreements are a logical place to provide for tag-along and drag-along rights.[83]

It is unclear, however, how courts will handle drag-along rights if dissenting shareholders believe they are being forced out and are entitled to other statutory remedies, such as appraisal rights. Absent issues of fraud or duress, it seems likely drag-along rights will be enforced for Delaware corporations.[84] Because Delaware does not follow the practical merger doctrine, statutory formalities such as appraisal rights are not implicated.[85] Additionally, in *Shields v. Shields*, a Delaware Chancery court noted that Delaware's statutes permitting shareholder agreements may include agreements on a "forced sale."[86]

Tag-along rights—also referred to as take-me-along provisions or rights of co-sale—also right belong in shareholder agreements and are implicated when a third party attempts to purchase control of the company.[87] If a group of shareholders together hold enough shares for a controlling position, a purchaser

---

**77** Id. (citing Cal. Corp. Code § 204(b) (West 1990)).

**78** See DGCL § 202(b) (2016).

**79** See 3 Treatise on the Law of Corporations § 14:9 (3d) (*B & H Warehouse, Inc. v. Atlas Van Lines, Inc.*, 490 F.2d 818 (5th Cir. 1974); *Sandor Petroleum Corp. v. Williams*, 321 S.W.2d 614 (Tex. Civ. App. 1959)).

**80** See 2 Advising Small Businesses § 21:52 (2017).

**81** See id.

**82** See id.

**83** Id.

**84** EQFIN § 10.15.

**85** See id.

**86** Id. (citing *Shields v. Shields*, 498 A.2d 161, 168 (Del. Ch. 1985)).

**87** See EQFIN § 10.12.

may be inclined to only offer to purchase a block of shares sufficient to take a majority of the board.[88] Not only would minority shareholders be left out of the transaction, the current majority may not receive as high of a price for their shares. As such, tag-along rights are commonly included in shareholder agreements and provide that when the majority sells their shares, a term of the sale must be that the offer is extended to all other shareholders.[89]

## 3. Shareholders' Agreements on the Constitution of the Corporation

The Official Comment to the MBCA underscores the broad reach of the statute: "Section 7.32(a) validates virtually all types of shareholder agreements that in practice, normally concern shareholders and their advisors." The statute provides that an agreement among shareholders that complies with the section will be effective even though it may be inconsistent with one or more other provisions of the act.[90] It specifically lays out seven substantive categories that rightly fit in shareholder agreements:

- eliminating the board or restricting the board's power;
- making distributions;
- naming directors or officers or providing rules relating to their status;
- dividing voting power among directors and shareholders or among either group;
- governing conflict transactions;
- permitting transfer of corporate power to a person to resolve deadlock or in a broader context;
- requiring dissolution of the corporation.[91]

The section further expands the breadth of permission with a catch-all category that permits other provisions governing corporate affairs that "not contrary to public policy."[92] While the DGCL does not list topics for shareholders' agreement, DGCL 141 provides all corporate power to be conferred upon the board, subject to limitations set forth in the articles.

**88** See id.

**89** See id.

**90** Model Bus. Corp. Act § 7.32(a).

**91** *O'Neal/Thompson* Close Corporations and LLCs: Law and Practice § 4:6.

**92** See id.

Shareholders agreements often not only designate who will be directors or how directors must be selected, but they even decide corporate policies that would normally be decided by the board of directors.[93] For example, shareholder agreements may designate officers, fix salaries, and specify the circumstances for when dividends will be declared.[94]

## 4. Shareholders 'Agreements in pre-insolvency situation

Under US Law, bankruptcy trustees may void any agreement that is "executory," so to the extent a buy-sell agreement requires shareholders and the entity to buy and sell, it is more likely to survive bankruptcy.[95] To determine whether to enforce a buy-sell agreement, a bankruptcy court will consider whether: (1) the buy-sell agreement constitutes and executory contract, and (2) the bankruptcy trustee accepts or rejects the agreement.[96]

The case *Portnoy v. Cryo-Cell Int'l, Inc.* addresses such agreements as part of standstill agreements.[97] Additionally, the court in *Schreiber v. Carney* held that vote selling is illegal when it defrauds or disenfranchises other shareholders.[98] Voting restrictions in standstill agreements effectively disenfranchise shareholders not party to the agreement.[99] According to the *Schreiber* court's definition of fraud, standstill agreements defraud shareholders not privy to the agreement in two ways: (1) by violating a shareholder's right to the best available merger or transaction, and (2) by discouraging unsolicited tender offers where a significant control premium can be realized.[100] These agreements tend to entrench management and can lead to stagnation for the company, so they sometimes "operate prejudicially upon" shareholders' property rights.[101]

---

**93** See id.
**94** Id.
**95** ACTEC® Shareholders Agreements for closely-held corporations outline, SY010 ALI-CLE 1367.
**96** See id.
**97** See *Portnoy v. Cryo-Cell Int'l, Inc.*, 940 A.2d 43, 66 (Del. Ch. 2008) (Chancellor Strine examining *Schreiber v. Carney* on vote-buying measures).
**98** *Schreiber v. Carney*, 447 A.2d 17 (Del. Ch. 1982).
**99** *Steven A. Baronoff* The Standstill Agreement: A Case of Illegal Vote Selling and A Breach of Fiduciary Duty, 93 Yale L.J. 1093, 1098 (1984).
**100** See id. at 1098–99 (citing *Schreiber*, 447 A.2d at 24).
**101** See id.

# IV. Legal Effects of Shareholders' Agreements

## 1. Legal Effects on the Corporation

Many shareholder agreements are drafted simultaneously alongside the charter. The articles of a corporation act as a constitution, setting out the basic governance structure of the enterprise.[102] Changing the articles is intentionally made difficult and amendments generally require actions by both the directors and shareholders, unlike most other corporate decisions.[103] Shareholder agreements are often drafted simultaneously alongside the charter, and many states, including Delaware, require shareholder agreements respecting director control to be included in the charter.

Because shareholder agreements are products of negotiation, courts find that they should be construed and enforced like any other contract so as to give effect to the intent of the parties as expressed in the agreement.[104] This is provided that they do not violate a statute or charter provision; contemplate an illegal objective; or involve fraud, oppression, or wrong against other shareholders.[105] Shareholders' agreements may be "free-standing" or they may be incorporated into a corporation's charter or bylaws.[106] When a shareholder agreement is included in the corporate charter or bylaws, it becomes subject to amendment as provided therein or by statute.[107] Because shareholder agreements are often designed to avoid corporate formalities such as majority rule, "it is not unreasonable to require that the degree of deviation intended be explicitly set out."[108]

It is possible to transfer the obligations and/or rights arising from the shareholder agreements to another person. However, the shareholder agreement should describe the limitations on one's ability to do so. Often the rights and obligations can transfer automatically under the agreement, but it is not always the case. Shareholder agreements should specifically provide that the agreement will apply to all transferees, successors, or assigns of shares held by a party to the agreement.[109] Under the MBCA, a purchaser of shares that has no actual

**102** *O'Neal/Thompson* Close Corporations and LLCs: Law and Practice § 3:2.
**103** See id.
**104** See 6 N.C. Index 4th Corporations § 137.
**105** See id.
**106** *O'Neal/Thompson* Close Corporations and LLCs: Law and Practice § 4:33.
**107** See 6 N.C. Index 4th Corporations § 137.
**108** See id. (quoting *Blount v. Taft*, 295 N.C. 472, 487, 246 S.E.2d 763, 773 (1978)).
**109** 1–5 Corporate Attorney's Practice Guide § 5.02 (2016).

or constructive knowledge of the shareholder agreement is entitled to rescission of the purchase.[110]

One of the most common shareholder agreements in a close corporation is a Buy-Sell or Share Transfer Agreement. The first governs exit from an enterprise that otherwise might provide no way out for many investors. The second protects the intimate relationship in a closely held enterprise by regulating who can become members. These agreements create further rights either to receive a specific price for their shares or limiting their right to whom they may sell to.

Shareholders' agreements can also be used as devices to assure certain patterns of control.[111] For example, incorporators may find it useful to have a written documentation on matters such as capital contribution obligations, election of directors and officers, and compensation for stockholder-employees.[112] Ultimately, of course, these issues should be addressed in carefully drafted bylaws, corporate decisions and employment agreements.[113]

Securities regulation also comes into play on shareholder agreements. Aggregation applies when two or more persons agree to act in concert to sell an issuer's securities.[114] A shareholder voting agreement is not necessarily an agreement to "act in concert" to sell the stock, and it is a factual question whether aggregation applies for acting in concert when a shareholder agreement is designed to restrict or manage the amount of stock sold.[115]

Most states have statutes, such as Section 7.32 of the MBCA, authorizing shareholder control agreements; separate statutes authorizing pooling agreements, voting trusts or irrevocable proxies are almost universal among the states.[116] As discussed above, Section 7.32(a) provides seven broad categories and an eighth catch-all provision that covers most types of agreements participants in a close corporation would desire.[117] While not explicitly identified, veto provisions are covered under the category relating to the exercise of voting power among shareholders or among directors.[118]

---

**110** See id.

**111** 1–3 MA Corporations and Other Business Entities § 3–2 (2016).

**112** See id.

**113** Id. Employment agreements are especially useful in addressing intellectual property concerns, non-competition, duties, and fringe benefits. See id.

**114** NOV-02 Koren Est. & Pers. Fin. Plan. Update art.

**115** See id. (citing AMP Incorporated, SEC No-action letter (June 22, 1981); Carnation Company, SEC No-action letter (October 3, 1979)).

**116** *O'Neal/Thompson* Close Corporations and LLCs: Law and Practice § 4:33.

**117** See id.; see supra Section III (3).

**118** See *O'Neal/Thompson* Close Corporations and LLCs: Law and Practice § 4:33.

States that do not specifically authorize shareholder control agreements usually contain a statute allowing parties to make exceptions from the default rule of director control by making providing for it in the corporation's charter or bylaws.[119] Shareholder control agreements in those states should be implemented by charter or bylaw amendments, especially if there is minimal case law governing their interpretation and legality. Alternatively, if all shareholders are not parties to the agreement, as required under Section 7.32, the agreement should be included in the charter.[120]

State statutes also contain specific provisions permitting changes to voting rules to create a veto provision.[121] Such statutes usually authorize a veto arrangement to be placed in the charter, and sometimes in the bylaws.[122] For example, New York permits high voting or quorum thresholds for shareholders' or directors' meetings only when they are in the corporate charter.[123]

Still, shareholders often fail to include their shareholder agreements in the charter or bylaws—whether by ignorance or inadvertence.[124] Sometimes this is intentional because charters are public records, and shareholders may not want their agreements open to outsiders.[125] Without explicit statutory authorization, many courts have refused to enforce veto provisions in shareholders' agreements.[126] Taking New York as an example, despite the clear statutory directive to include agreements on voting requirements in the corporate charter, New York court decisions suggest that shareholders' agreements calling for high voting requirements will probably be specifically enforceable.[127] In *Adler v. Svingos*, 80 A.D.2d 764, 436 N.Y.S.2d 719 (1981), the court upheld a shareholder agreement requiring unanimous approval from all three shareholders before corporate ac-

**119** See id. (citing statute examples).
**120** See id. (citing NY Bus Corp Law §§ 614, 616, 707, 709).
**121** See id.
**122** See id.
**123** See id.
**124** See id.
**125** See id. (collecting cases) (e.g., *Roach v. Bynum*, 403 So. 2d 187 (Ala. 1981) (under the Alabama corporation code a provision mandating a greater than majority shareholder vote may be included in a corporation's certificate of incorporation but not in its bylaws); *Waggoner v. Laster*, 581 A.2d 1127 (Del. 1990) (in absence of authority in corporation's certificate of incorporation to issue convertible preferred shares with supermajority voting rights, those voting rights, used to oust other directors, were null and void); Jones v. Wallace, 291 Or. 11, 628 P.2d 388 (1981) (court held that a bylaw defining a shareholder quorum as all outstanding shares entitled to vote was invalid where Oregon corporation law required super quorum provisions to be placed in the corporate charter).
**126** Id.
**127** See id.

tion could be taken even though it was not in contained in the corporate charter. The court held that the veto provision was valid and did not violate the New York statute, since the court could simply order the corporation's certificate of incorporation be amended to include the veto provision.[128] While shareholders of New York close corporations may be able to set up veto provisions without amending the corporation's charter, the better practice is to amend the charter to insert such arrangements.[129]

## 2. Consequences of a Breach of the Shareholders' Agreements

Because shareholders' agreements are recognized by statutes and case law courts may hold that these agreements should be enforced like any other agreement.[130] However, shareholder agreement cases may not be typical of general contract cases when it comes to remedies.[131] Shareholder agreement suits are more likely to result in specific performance rather than awarding damages.[132] Damages for breaches of provisions of valid shareholder agreements are often too speculative to provide an adequate remedy, even though the individual has a direct cause of action.[133]

Remedies include[134]:

- Voiding corporate actions taken in violation of an agreement;[135]

---

**128** See id.

**129** See id.

**130** *O'Neal/Thompson* Close Corporations and LLCs: Law and Practice § 4:42 (citing *e.g.*, *Blount v. Taft*, 295 N.C. 472, 246 S.E.2d 763, 771 (1978), noted 15 Wake Forest L. Rev 531 (1979), 68 Ky. L.J. 520 to 523 (1980) *("Since consensual arrangements among shareholders are agreements—the products of negotiation—they should be construed and enforced like any other contract so as to give effect to the intent of the parties as expressed in their agreements, unless they 'violate the express charter or statutory provision, contemplate an illegal object, involve ... fraud, oppression or wrong against other stockholders, or are made in consideration of a private benefit to the promisor")*; *Hughes v. Sego Intern. Ltd.*, 192 N.J. Super. 60, 469 A.2d 74 (App. Div. 1983) (court stated that shareholders' agreements are generally enforceable)).

**131** See id.

**132** See id.

**133** Id.

**134** The following list and corresponding footnotes were reproduced in their original form from O'Neal and Thompson's treatise.

**135** *Zion v. Kurtz*, 50 N.Y.2d 92, 428 N.Y.S.2d 199, 405 N.E.2d 681, 15 A.L.R.4th 1061 (1980), noted 33 Syracuse L. Rev 15 to 17 (1982) (court issued an injunction declaring valid a shareholders' agreement providing that no business or activities of a closely held corporation could be con-

- Reforming the agreement, the charter or bylaws to reflect the agreement;[136]
- Having shares transferred;[137]
- Awarding a constructive trust over assets improperly sold;[138]
- Ordering an accounting;[139]
- Providing for compensatory and punitive damages.[140]

A court may specific enforce substantive terms of an agreement or remedies provided for in the agreement.[141] In *Ramos v. Estrada*, a California court ordered the buyout of a breaching shareholder as was a specified remedy in the agreement.[142] The agreement required the members to vote as a single block, and when one member broke off from the voting block, the group responded by replacing him as a director.[143] The court held the dissidents' repudiation of the agreement was a breach and constituted an election to sell their shares according to the buy/sell provisions.[144]

ducted without the consent of the minority shareholder; certain corporate actions taken without the consent of the minority shareholder were void).

**136** In *re Farm Industries, Inc.*, 41 Del. Ch. 379, 196 A.2d 582 (1963) (court reformed a voting trust agreement to include voting rights inadvertently omitted by an attorney, and ordering specific enforcement of the agreement as reformed if that would not harm anyone not a party).

**137** *Scheurer v. Scheurer*, 311 Minn. 546, 249 N.W.2d 181 (1976) (founder of corporation transferred his controlling block of shares to his sons, reserving by agreement the power to vote the shares during his lifetime; following a dispute with his sons the founder attempted to exercise his voting rights to elect new directors; the court enforced the agreement by rescinding the original share transfer transaction).

**138** *Butler v. Attwood*, 369 F.2d 811 (6th Cir. 1966) (the court, applying the equitable doctrine of constructive trust, compelled a third party with notice of an equal ownership agreement between two shareholders to sell to plaintiff shareholder one-half of the shares he had purchased from one of the contracting shareholders).

**139** For a case in which a minority shareholder in a close corporation who was a party to a shareholders' agreement brought suit against his two fellow shareholders and the corporation seeking an accounting and corporate dissolution as a result of a breach of his rights under the agreement, see *Wasserman v. Rosengarden*, 84 Ill. App. 3d 713, 40 Ill. Dec. 430, 406 N.E.2d 131 (1st Dist. 1980).

**140** *Sankin v. 5410 Connecticut Ave. Corp.*, 281 F. Supp. 524 (D. D.C. 1968), judgment aff'd, 410 F.2d 1060 (D.C. Cir. 1969) (punitive and injunctive relief, as well as compensatory damages awarded against the breaching shareholder and the corporation).

**141** *O'Neal/Thompson* Close Corporations and LLCs: Law and Practice § 4:42.

**142** Id. (citing *Ramos v. Estrada*, 8 Cal. App. 4th 1070, 10 Cal. Rptr. 2d 833 (2d Dist. 1992), reh'g denied and opinion modified (Sept. 11, 1992).

**143** *See Ramos*,8 Cal. App. 4th at 1072–74, 10 Cal. Rptr. 2d at 834–36.

**144** O'Neal and Thompson's Close Corporations and LLCs: Law and Practice § 4:42.

## V. Enforcement of Shareholders' Agreements

Typically, shareholder claims are enforced through derivative actions, whereby the shareholders pursue claims in a representative capacity on a cause of action that derives from the corporation. However, individuals may sue in their individual capacity as a party to a shareholder agreement for breaches under the agreement by other contracting parties. Enforcement is usually through litigation which can be expensive.[145] When the corporation is harmed, it is the corporation that has the claim, but directors are often unwilling to pursue claims, especially when they are the wrongdoers.[146] Shareholders will often enforce these claims via a derivative action, where the corporation is the real party in interest as the entity injured and recovery belongs to the corporation.[147] The shareholders are simply suing on the corporation's behalf and cannot maintain actions on their own behalf to redress an injury to the corporation even if the value of their stock is impaired as a result of the injury.[148]

Many state statutes provide for the specific enforcement of shareholders' agreements,[149] as does the MBCA, which expressly states that voting agreements are specifically enforceable.[150] In general, a court may specifically enforce any of the substantive terms of a shareholders' agreement, which may require the buy-out of a shareholder or compelled arbitration.[151] Under the MBCA, rescission may also be available to a purchaser of shares who did not have knowledge of the existence of a shareholder control agreement at the time of purchase.[152]

Shareholders voting agreements adjudicated under actions for declaratory judgment or specific performance.[153] This trend has supplanted more restrictive opinions as earlier courts had a general dislike and distrust for voting agree-

**145** *Arthur R. Pinto* Protection of Close Corporation Minority Shareholders in the United States, 62 Am. J. Comp. L. 361, 377 (2014).

**146** See id.

**147** Id.

**148** See id.

**149** 5 Fletcher Cyc. Corp. § 2067 (citing Ariz Rev Stat § 10 – 731; Cal Corp Code § 706; 805 ILCS 5/ 7.70; Ind Code Ann § 23 – 1 – 31 – 2).

**150** Id. (citing MBCA 7.31(b)).

**151** See id.

**152** Model Bus Corp Act § 7.32(c). However, this section also provides that a purchasing shareholder will be deemed as having received notice of the shareholder agreement should the stock certificate note the existence of such agreement or an information statement is provided at or before the time of purchase that indicates the shares are subject to a shareholder agreement.

**153** See *O'Neal/Thompson* Close Corporations and LLCs: Law and Practice § 4:42.

ments.[154] Most often a suit for damages does not provide an adequate remedy for a breach of a shareholder agreement, so the denial of specific enforcement essentially declares the agreement invalid.[155] It is likely that for this reason, recent court decisions have recognize that shareholders' voting agreements are enforceable by an injunction or through specific performance.[156]

Shareholder agreements also allow shareholders to contract how they will settle disputes that arise under the relationship, such as providing for arbitration or specific remedies such as dissolution or buyout.[157] Provisions for the arbitration of disputes are especially common in shareholders' agreements. Pooling agreements, where shareholders agree to vote as a block on all or certain corporate matters, sometimes contain clauses where shareholders agree to vote according the decision of an arbitrator should they disagree on how to vote on a matter.[158] Shareholder agreements may even provide for management decisions to be made by arbitrators.[159]

# VI. Annexes

- MBCA Sect. 7.30 on Voting Trusts
- MBCA Sect. 7.31 on Voting Agreements
- MBCA Sect. 7.32 on Shareholder Agreements
- MBCA Sect. 6.27 on Financing Agreements
- DGCL 212 on Voting Proxies
- DGCL 218 on Voting Trusts
- DGCL 202 on Financial Agreements.

List of Controlling Delaware case law on Shareholder Agreements by subject area (cases in red are leading cases):

**154** See id. (citing *Haldeman v. Haldeman*, 176 Ky. 635, 651 197 S.W. 376 (1917); *Sullivan v. Parkes*, 69 A.D. 221, 74 N.Y.S. 787 (1st Dep't 1902); *Gage v. Fisher*, 5 N.D. 297, 304, 65 N.W. 809, 811 (1895); *Gleason v. Earles*, 78 Wash. 491, 139 P. 213 (1914); *Kennedy v. Monarch Mfg. Co.*, 123 Iowa 344, 98 N.W. 796 (1904)).

**155** See id.

**156** See id.; see also infra section IV(2) for discussion on remedies.

**157** See Close Corp and LLCs: Law and Practice § 4:10.

**158** See id.

**159** See id.

### Shareholders' Agreements

*Genger v. TR Investors, LLC,* July 18, 2011 26 A.3d 180 Acceptance by investor group of vote to enter into funding agreement with investor group by stockholder of corporation, made on behalf of trust to which stockholder had, through company he controlled, made transfer of shares that was unauthorized under his shareholder agreement did not constitute investor group's acquiescence to, and ratification of stockholder's unauthorized transfer of shares to trust; investor group agreed to enter into funding agreement because stockholder represented that he would rectify his unauthorized transfer of shares violation, the investor group never received any benefit from the funding agreement, in that, the parties never executed or performed the funding agreement because stockholder subsequently repudiated it, and the language of the agreement contemplated that the transfer of shares to trust may subsequently be determined to be void.

### Enforcement of Shareholders' Agreements

*Julian v. Eastern States Const. Service, Inc.*, 2008 WL 2673300 (2008) Plain language of shareholder agreements entered into by shareholders in closely held S corporations established that shareholder and officer of such corporations was "employee" thereof, for purposes of provisions of shareholder agreements requiring sale of shares upon termination of employment; plain language of agreements established that all signatories considered themselves to be "employed by" corporations covered by such agreements in the ordinary, colloquial sense of working for corporations in some gainful capacity, irrespective of whether their status as shareholders and officers qualified them as employees in legal sense of such term for purposes of employment law.

### Agreements as to Voting

*Ringling Bros.-Barnum & Bailey Combined Shows v. Ringling,* May 3, 1947 29 Del.Ch. 610 Under agreement between two stockholders that they should act jointly in exercising voting rights, and that in case of disagreement a named arbitrator's decision should be binding, each party agreed to comply with arbitrator's decision but arbitrator was without power to enforce his decisions, and in case of refusal to abide by arbitrator's decision neither party was empowered to exercise voting rights of the other. Stockholders may lawfully contract with one another to vote as they, or a majority of their group from time to time determine, and reasonable provisions for cases of failure of the group to reach a determination because of an even division in their ranks are unobjectionable.

*Salamone v. Gorman*, 106 A.3d 354 (2014) Voting agreement provision for selecting to corporation's board of directors "Two persons elected by the Key Holders," majority shareholder and two others, created per capita, rather than per share, scheme for designating nominees, and, thus, did not allow majority shareholder to remove "Key Holder," corporate officer, from board, even though agreement contemplated removal of directors by per share vote; agreement also permitted removal upon request of any party entitled to designate director, the "Key Holders" were three persons who were not required to own stock, and employee investors, including officer and their families, together invested same amount as majority shareholder's friend with right to designate board member and more than other "Key Holders."

*Brady v. Mexican Gulf Sulphur Co., 1952, 88 A.2d 300* The powers of voting trustees within legal and public policy limits are to be found in the voting trust agreement, and by such agreement the stockholders constitute the trustees their irrevocable proxies for the period of the agreement.

*Kurz v. Holbrook* February 9, 2010 989 A.2d 140 A vote-buying arrangement in a shareholder vote must not be the product of fraud.

*Crown EMAK Partners, LLC v. Kurz,* April 21, 2010 992 A.2d 377, Stockholder's purchase of other stockholder's shares, which included restricted shares subject to restricted stock grant agreement, for the purpose of giving purchasing stockholder a majority of **votes** necessary to remove certain directors violated restricted stock grant agreement, which prohibited the sale, transfer, or assignment of restricted shares, and thus, the purchase agreement did not operate as a legally valid sale of the shares and purchasing stockholder was not entitled to **vote** those shares.

*Schreiber v. Carney* May 11, 1982 447 A.2d 17 An agreement involving transfer of stock voting rights without the transfer of ownership is not necessarily illegal and each arrangement must be examined in light of its object or purpose.

*Abercrombie v. Davies,* March 19, 1957 36 Del.Ch. 371 Not all stock pooling agreements of stockholders are lawful.

*Most Worshipful Prince Hall Grand Lodge of Free and Accepted Masons of Del. v. Hiram Grand Lodge Masonic Temple,* April 19, 1951 32 Del.Ch. 85 Where agreement, executed about same time that common stock in defendant corporation was issued to plaintiff corporation, made invalid attempt to suspend voting rights of stock issued to plaintiff and plaintiff abstained from voting stock for long period of time and treated agreement as valid, plaintiff was not barred by laches or acquiescence from voting its stock, since right to vote is continuing one.

*Omnicare, Inc. v. NCS Healthcare, Inc.*, 818 A.2d 914 (2003) Deal protection devices adopted by target corporation's board of directors coerced the consummation of proposed merger and precluded consideration of any superior transaction, and thus, the deal protection devices were invalid; requirement in merger agreement that proposed merger be placed before target corporation's shareholders for a vote even if board no longer recommended it, shareholder voting agreements requiring two directors, whose stock represented majority ownership of target, to vote their shares in favor of merger, and absence of effective fiduciary-out clause in merger agreement, made it mathematically impossible and realistically unattainable for any competing proposal to succeed.

*Hirschwald v. Erlebacher, Inc.* July 23, 1943 27 Del.Ch. 180 Failure of voting trustees for more than two years after execution of voting trust agreement to comply with statutory provisions concerning filing of copy of agreement and issuance of stock certificates in names of voting trustees did not evidence an "abandonment" of agreement, where conduct of voting trustees evidenced exercise of their powers as such.

*Shields v. Shields,* July 22, 1985 498 A.2d 161 Whether merger which has effect of eliminating restrictions of shareholder agreement from stock is valid is to be tested by provisions of corporation law governing mergers, and in appropriate cases by fiduciary standards imposed upon directors and controlling shareholders, not by provisions of shareholder agreements.

## Voting Trusts

*Tracey v. Franklin,* May 23, 1949 31 Del.Ch. 477 Provision in voting trust agreement whereby two stockholders, owning a majority of one class of stock in corporation, conveyed stock to themselves as trustees for purpose of voting such stock jointly in order to secure competent management of corporation and put into effect beneficial policies, and agreed not to sell or transfer stock for about ten years without consent of both parties, was invalid as an unreasonable restraint on alienability.

*Oceanic Exploration Co. v. Grynberg,* February 26, 1981 428 A.2d 1 In determining applicability of statute relating to creation of voting trust of stock of Delaware corporation, test is whether substance and purpose of stock arrangement is sufficiently close to substance and purpose of the statute to warrant its being subject to the restrictions and conditions imposed by that statute.

*Smith v. Biggs Boiler Works Co.*, 1951, 82 A.2d 372 Agreement by which the two owners of all the outstanding stock in a Delaware corporation then in escrow attempted to form a voting trust of such stock was not enforceable as a "pooling agreement", where party named as third voting trustee owned none of the stock in question, since in a pooling agreement the owners of shares combine and vote them in accordance with agreement.

*Lehrman v. Cohen,* July 8, 1966 43 Del.Ch. 222 Voting trust statute regulates trusts and pooling agreements amounting to trusts, not other and different types of arrangements and undertakings possible among stockholders. Voting trust statute does not require that all stock of a Delaware corporation must have both voting rights and proprietary interests. Main purpose of voting trust statute is to avoid secret, uncontrolled combinations of stockholders formed to acquire voting control of corporation to possible detriment of nonparticipating stockholders.

*Aldridge v. Franco Wyoming Oil Co.,* July 18, 1939 24 Del.Ch. 126 Whether a particular agreement constitutes a "voting trust" within intendment of statute must ordinarily be ascertained from the provisions of the agreement, when read as a whole, and the rights and powers given thereby.

*Foye v. New York University,* May 20, 1970 269 A.2d 63 "Beneficiary" of voting trust is stockholder concerned with, and relieved of, vote and control of corporation for purposes which seemed good and sufficient to him when he entered into voting trust agreement.

*Belle Isle Corp. v. Corcoran,* September 26, 1946 29 Del.Ch. 554 A voting trust agreement which by its terms recited that it extended the original voting trust agreement was an extension of the original agreement and not a new agreement.

*Grynberg v. Burke*, 1979, 410 A.2d 169 Statute, which governs voting trusts of corporate stock of a Delaware corporation, governed voting trust agreements entered into by corporation shareholders, who thereby surrendered their voting control of corporation to voting trustees for specified period of time.

*Winitz v. Kline,* 1971, 288 A.2d 456 Parties to voting trust may contract for terms as to both substance and mechanics of trust.

*Clarke Memorial College v. Monaghan Land Co.,* 1969, 257 A.2d 234 Apart from limitations imposed by statute or public policy, parties to a voting trust agreement may adopt any provisions they want as to substance or mechanics.

### Buy-Sell Agreements

*Lawson v. Household Finance Corp.,* February 27, 1930 17 Del.Ch. 343 "Reasonable restrictions on transfer of corporate stock" as are necessary and convenient to attainment of objects for which company was incorporated are valid.

*Dolese Bros. Co. v. Brown,* January 27, 1960 39 Del.Ch. 1 Agreement of stockholders, not to sell to anyone not a stockholder without first offering **shares** to other stockholders and to corporation, gave corporation some sort of expectancy in purchase of stock, and exact scope of that expectancy would not be important in determining liability of president and dominating director if, as alleged, he had recognized existence of such expectancy and had undertaken (in effect) by unilateral action to waive corporate rights for his own benefit.

### Tag-Along, Drag-Along, Shoot-Out

*Hollinger Int'l, Inc. v. Black,* 844 A.2d 1022, 1031 (Del. Ch. 2004) The public disclosures create the impression that this was a substantial tag-along right, because the certificate provision (the "Tag–Along Provision") seems designed to make sure that Inc. would share any control premium ratably with the other International shareholders. The Tag–Along Provision does so by stripping the Class B shares of their super-voting power if they are sold, transferred or disposed of in a non-Permitted Transaction.

### Stand-still

*Ivanhoe Partners v. Newmont Min. Corp.*, October 15, 1987 533 A.2d 585 Given that dividend to shareholders to induce largest shareholder to agree to a **stand-still** agreement did not violate either Delaware general corporation law or corporation's certificate of incorporation or bylaws, court could interfere with corporation's board of directors' decision to pay dividend only if dividend was product of self-dealing and directors failed to prove that dividend was entirely fair, or if no self-dealing was present and corporation seeking to acquire target corporation was able to prove that dividend could not be grounded on any reasonable business objective.

# Subject Index



https://doi.org/10.1515/9783110517026-028

www.ingramcontent.com/pod-product-compliance
Lightning Source LLC
Chambersburg PA
CBHW051356240926
51852CB00001B/44
*9783110501568*